# SECTION V  CORRECTIONS  349

# CONTENTS

Bassim Hamadeh, CEO and Publisher
Carrie Montoya, Manager, Revisions and Author Care
Kaela Martin, Project Editor
Jess Estrella, Senior Graphic Designer
Alexa Lucido, Licensing Manager
Natalie Piccotti, Director of Marketing
Kassie Graves, Vice President of Editorial
Jamie Giganti, Director of Academic Publishing

Cover:
Copyright © 2011 Depositphotos/Nomadsoul1.
Copyright © 2014 Depositphotos/AndreyPopov.
Copyright © 2013 Depositphotos/Enigmangels.

Printed in the United States of America.

cognella® | ACADEMIC PUBLISHING
3970 Sorrento Valley Blvd., Ste. 500, San Diego, CA 92121

# Crime, Law, and Justice

STUART HENRY, DESIRÉ J.M. ANASTASIA,
SANNA KING, AND NICOLE L. BRACY

*Second Edition*

cognella®

SAN DIEGO

# Crime, Law, and Justice

# Introduction

DESIRÉ J. M. ANASTASIA, NICOLE L. BRACY, AND STUART HENRY

*Crime, Law, and Justice* provides criminology and criminal justice students with an essential understanding of the criminal justice system in the United States based on criminological research and theoretical analysis. This book is designed to introduce students to the complete field of criminology and criminal justice, including: definitions, types, and extent of crime; the role of criminal and constitutional law in the context of due process justice; law enforcement at local, state, and federal levels; the functions of federal law enforcement agencies, such as the Federal Bureau of Investigation (FBI), the Drug Enforcement Administration (DEA), the Bureau of Alcohol, Tobacco, Firearms, and Explosives (ATF), and U.S. Immigration and Customs Enforcement (ICE); and corrections, probation, parole, and alternatives to these formal methods of social control. This book will lay the foundation for more in-depth examinations of each of these areas of study, and it does so by asking critical questions about why the system is the way it is and how it could be different. The overall approach this book takes is that we can make a difference to improve the system and develop policies that reduce crime and the forces that the justice system tries to combat.

Section One, "What Is Crime and Who Are Its Victims?" begins by defining crime as the intentional or avoidable violation of criminal law subject to specified penalties imposed by a politically authorized state (government). It is assumed that crime is behavior harmful to individuals, communities, organizations, or societies. It is also assumed that criminal law is designed to protect people from harm. However, it soon becomes clear that some people's harm creating counts as crime and is included in the legal definitions of crimes, whereas others' harm creation is not. Central issues in answering the question of "What is crime?" become "How is behavior defined as crime? Who defines it, and with what interests?" Criminologists study different ways societies define crime that expand the simplistic legal definition to include those that are based in harm creation that are not always criminally defined, such as white-collar crime, corporate crime, environmental crime, and state or government crime. Indeed, this has led to some criminologists calling for a harm-based definition of crime and has spawned a whole field of study called "zemiology," which is the study of social harms (Boukli & Kotzé, 2018). The chapter by Joycelyn M. Pollock goes into more detailed description about crime in American society. She examines the role of legislators, victims, police, and prosecutors in defining crime. She delves into the data available to inform us about the types and patterns of crime, and she looks at the crimes that appear most frequently in the arrest statistics. It is important to note that arrest rates vary enormously for different crimes, and while they are high for homicide and auto theft, they are low for burglary and white-collar crimes such as embezzlement. The rate of arrest for particular crimes relative to the number of crimes reported is known as the clear-up rate. Moreover, not all crimes committed are known to the police because, like arrest rates, crime reporting varies depending on the crime. The estimated gap between crimes known to the police from victim reports and the crimes reported through surveys of victims is known as the "dark figure" of unknown crime. Research suggests that as much as two-thirds of crimes are unknown to police. Pollack focuses on homicide, the most reported crime, as an illustrative case study. She then turns to the historical pattern for crime and shows how, in spite of media coverage that leads people to perceive crime is increasing, it actually has consistently declined since the early 1990s in spite of episodic crime waves.

The centrality of victims of crime and harm lead us to the study of victims, which is known as "victimology." Indeed, victimology is "the scientific study of the physical, emotional, and financial harm people suffer because of illegal activities" as well as "the study of who becomes a victim, how victims are victimized, how much harm they suffer, and their role in the criminal act" (Karmen, 2013, p. 2; Lanier & Henry, 2010, p. 19). Thus, we include an article by William G. Doerner and Steven P. Lab that discusses the scope of victimology and another by Marilyn D. McShane and Traqina Q. Emeka on the politics of victimization. This builds on Robert Elias's classic work *The Politics of Victimization: Victims, Victimology and Human Rights*, in which Elias argues that the study of victimology requires going beyond criminal justice. He argues that victimization is linked to the wider social, political, and economic system. He argues that victimology should include the victims of both crime and repression and sees crime as a response to various forms of social oppression and violations of human rights. This takes us right back to what harms should be described in concepts of crime and questions again whether crime is too limited a concept.

Section Two, "Introduction to Criminology," focuses on defining and outlining the scope of criminology as well as reviewing the process of criminological research. Criminology is the systematic study of the nature of crime, types of crime, and causes of crime and systems societies use to control it. It is an applied social science that draws on multiple disciplines to inform its study and analysis. Indeed, criminology is informed by biology, psychology, social psychology, social constructionism, geography, sociology, political science, anthropology, cultural studies, Marxism, feminism, and postmodernism. An illustration of this is found in school violence, which involves micro-level examination of the biological, psychological, and interactive causes that predispose certain students to become shooters; meso-level analyses involving families, peer groups, neighborhoods, and the institution of the school; and macro-level analysis that includes geographical and spatial factors affecting communities, societal-level causes (including socioeconomics and the role of violence in the media as well as political decisions resulting in policies such as zero tolerance and access to guns), and cultural contexts that shape the school learning environment. "Drawing from different fields, including sociology, psychology, and law, criminology provides an interdisciplinary approach in order to better understand crime" (Klutz & Lanier, 2012, p. 55). Criminology is "an applied social science in which criminologists work to establish knowledge about crime and its control based on empirical research. This research forms the basis for understanding, explanation, prediction, prevention, and criminal justice policy" (Lanier & Henry, 2010, p. 78). After an overview of the scope of criminology by Mark M. Lanier and Stuart Henry, we include an article by Joycelyn M. Pollock that reviews the major theories that explain why people commit crime. She reviews three types of criminological theory—biological, psychological, and sociological—and then briefly considers other theories. The next two articles, one by Timothy Newburn on the process of criminological research and the other by Belinda R. McCarthy, Robin J. King, and Jennifer A. Pealer on the ethics of criminological research, round out this section. Criminological and criminal justice research is also considered scientific inquiry, "a method of inquiry—a way of learning and knowing things about the world around us" (Maxfield & Babbie, 2011, p. 1) that has particular characteristics that make it systematic and controlled. These characteristics distinguish scientific research from commonsense everyday research. In addition, scientific research has to be ethical. That means it should not harm the subjects of the research (human subject protection) and the subjects have to voluntarily participate; they cannot be coerced or forced to participate. Voluntary participation is protected by a process known as "informed consent" in which researchers intending to study a particular population of human subjects have to provide their research protocol to a review board (known as an Institutional Review Board, or IRB) explaining the purpose of the research and the intended use of any findings or results, and subjects have to be informed that their identity will remain anonymous and that the information they provide will be kept confidential. Only after the "informed consent form" is signed by the potential research subject can the research begin. Several groups of subjects are in protected categories, as they are seen as vulnerable to exploitation or coercion, and that includes children, the mentally ill, and prisoners.

Generally, there are two broad areas of research in criminology and criminal justice. The first is research on the nature, extent, and causes of crime (i.e., criminal behavior). The second is research on the effectiveness of policies and practices that deal with crime—in particular, the effectiveness of the police, courts, corrections, and alternative programs within the criminal justice system. In conducting criminal justice research, a researcher can explore all aspects of crime: who becomes a criminal, what crimes are committed and why, who becomes a victim, why and how these individuals experience victimization, who is employed in crime control, why and how these individuals decided on criminal justice careers, and myriad other questions. These are narrowed down to specific research questions, such as "Are disgruntled employees more likely to steal from their employers than happy or respectful employees?" and "Are victims of child abuse more likely to themselves become violent offenders as adults?"

Research methodology is the process by which the researcher conducts the study. Put simply, there are two broad types of methods: quantitative and qualitative research. Quantitative research uses large sets of data gathered anonymously and using a random selection process, through surveys of victims or offenders, or data compiled by criminal justice personnel, such as the police or corrections officers. When using the qualitative method, a researcher interviews subjects face to face, either in institutions or in their neighborhoods. Qualitative research can also involve studying the subjects in the act of crime, such as selling drugs in a neighborhood bar or committing acts of shoplifting or embezzlement. This type of "participant observation" is similar to the ethnographical research methods used by anthropologists when they live in the societies they are studying to obtain a deeper understanding of the cultures' customs and practices. This kind of research methodology also raises important and challenging ethical issues, particularly when the researcher is involved in the scene of crime. In addition to the possible legal ramifications of associating with subjects involved in illegal activities, the researcher must also consider the threat of violence often associated with this type of behavior. The choice of method depends upon the kind of questions the researchers are trying to answer (Tewksbury, 2009). Some researchers combine qualitative and quantitative methods, which is called "mixed method." Others may use case studies of one or two offenders, and yet others may conduct experimental research measuring, for example, whether the rate of rearrest of offenders charged with substance abuse (called recidivism) is lower if they are sentenced by drug courts rather than regular criminal courts.

While there are many reasons to conduct research exploring why crimes occur, a major reason is to find ways to develop policies, programs, or practices that prevent, reduce, or control crime. Crime control policies explicitly refer to laws, regulations, and other governmental actions that are designed to reduce criminal acts. Data and results from criminal justice research may also drive the creation of crime control policies, as do specific criminal events, such as those leading to the passage of Megan's Law and Chelsea's Law (both dealing with sex offenders) or the Polly Klaas murder, which led to California's Three Strikes Law in 1994. Of course, whether research influences policy development as much as criminal justice researchers hope it does is an open question (see Garrison, 2009). Criminal justice research also uses evaluation methods to determine the effectiveness of policies, programs, or criminal justice practices, such as those used by the police and the courts or in corrections.

Section Three, "Policing and Law Enforcement," presents an overview of formal social control in the United States, with a specific focus on both community and ethical policing. Law enforcement is the general description of formal social control that operates at federal, state, and local levels through a variety of policing agencies. These agencies maintain public order and enforce the law and are charged with the powers of crime prevention, detection, investigation and apprehension of suspected offenders using techniques of surveillance, tracking, investigating, and monitoring and the latest in crime analysis involving GIS mapping (Bureau of Justice Statistics, 2013; Manning, 2008). Current trends in law enforcement as well as the use of force by police officers are also discussed in this section. The article by Lanier and Klutz provides a general overview of policing in the United States. The article by Alpert and Dunham looks at the historical development of policing, starting with the British roots of policing that emerged from what began as a private system and transformed into "night watchmen" until population growth and social changes led to a more formalized system of policing. This was exemplified by the formation of the London Metropolitan Police through an act of Parliament in 1829, which became the model for the modern police department. Alpert and Dunham discuss aspects of contemporary policing in America, outlining the recruitment and selection of officers as well as the content of police academy training, field training, and in-service training. They then turn to discuss police operations and their primary crime control functions: preventative patrol, problem identification and solving, service call response, and criminal investigation. These authors move to discuss the uniqueness of police culture—the military-style bureaucracy—before highlighting some critical issues in policing, including the hiring of more women and minorities and the police use of force, particularly deadly force and police pursuits. They conclude with a review of contemporary policing, the role of new technology and crime analysis, and the importance of community and problem-solving approaches to policing.

These overviews of policing are followed by a more focused examination of certain key themes within policing. The article by Kappeler and Gaines provides a comprehensive review of community policing, which they describe as the "first substantive reform in American police" in a century, as it shifts the relationship between the police and the public and addresses crime from a preventative approach through problem solving at the community level. They also distinguish problem-oriented policing from community policing. The authors describe community policing's philosophy of community empowerment, community engagement, and community partnerships. They evaluate and compare traditional policing with community policing and debunk some of the myths that surround community policing. The final contribution, by Snook et al., takes a critical look at the issue of criminal profiling as a strategy in crime prediction and prevention based on crime scene evidence. Criminal profiling is not the same as police racial profiling, which is illegal under the United States Constitution (i.e., the 14th Amendment's Equal Protection Clause) because it is based on the use of race, ethnicity, national origin, or religion, among other protected characteristics. In contrast, criminal or offender profiling is legal and based on behavioral and crime pattern characteristics. The article's authors define criminal profiling as a process of "predicting a criminal's personality, behavioral, and demographic characteristics based on crime scene evidence." They argue that the "belief that profilers can accurately and consistently predict a criminal's characteristics based on crime scene evidence" has no scientific support and that criminal profiling is ineffective. Moreover, they say that criminal profiling "has the potential to mislead criminal investigators, and thereby either hinder the apprehension of guilty criminals or lead to wrongful convictions." They seek to explain why, in spite of this, people believe profiling works. They argue that this is because of a mythology around criminal profiling that is "heavily influenced by anecdotes, repetition of the message that profiling works, the expert profiler label, and a disproportionate emphasis on correct predictions." Their article makes sobering reading for those who see offender profiling as the future direction of policing.

Section Four, "Law, Courts, and Judicial Process," examines the court system in the United States and the judicial process within it. Our court system consists of two types of courts: trial courts and appellate courts. Travis distinguishes between trial courts, which "are fact-finding bodies whose job it is to determine the facts of a case" and appellate courts, which "are law-interpreting bodies whose job it is to determine if the laws were correctly applied and followed" (Travis III, 2012, p. 207). In other words, trial courts deal with the substance of the law and whether it has been violated, whereas appellate courts deal with whether the correct principles and due process procedures were followed by the trial courts.

For the purpose of this text, courts are concerned with criminal law that "specifies the acts or omissions that constitute crime" (Lanier & Henry, 2010 [in Klutz & Lanier, 2012, p. 8]). Due process provides protection for the individual against state power and was derived from the 13th-century English Magna Carta (1215), which states, "No free man shall be seized or imprisoned, or stripped of his rights or possessions, or outlawed or exiled, or deprived of his standing in any other way, nor will we proceed with force against him, or send others to do so, except by the lawful judgment of his equals or by the law of the land." In contemporary America, due process includes the following four elements: a) equality between the parties (i.e., prosecution and defense); b) rules protecting the defendant against error; c) restraint of arbitrary power; and d) presumption of innocence. In contrast to this "due process" model is the model of "crime control," which: a) presumes guilt; b) disregards legal controls; and c) seeks efficiency at the expense of protecting rights (Packer, 1968). Our examination of the courts also includes a discussion of how our court system *really* operates versus what is typically portrayed on television and in movies.

The article by Jocelyn M. Pollock focuses on the purpose and practice of criminal courts as the forum for criminal prosecution in the criminal justice system. She distinguishes different levels of courts: U.S. federal courts, which include district courts, circuit courts of appeal, and the U.S. Supreme Court, and state courts, which include state trial courts, intermediate courts of appeal, and state supreme courts. She also considers the purpose and effectiveness of specialized courts (of which there are many), such as drug courts, mental health courts, domestic violence courts, sex offender courts, prostitution courts, and community courts, among others. Pollack then looks at the function of prosecutors and how they decide upon charges against an accused offender. Similarly, she considers the roles of the defense attorney, the judge, and the judicial process as well as the scope of federal courts. This is followed by an overview of the value of due process protection in our criminal justice system. She concludes with an examination of the steps in the trial process.

The article by Altschuler, Sgroi, and Ryniker looks in more depth at the system of due process, including its limits. The authors start out by defining due process as a system to protect people against the arbitrary or unfair use of government power. However, this protection is limited to "life, liberty or property." It does not include other perceived losses. Nor does due process protect a person from private harms—only those by public entities, such as government agencies—although the authors point out that because of the interconnectedness of the public and private in modern society, these distinctions are not easy to make. The authors draw distinctions between procedural and substantive due process. Procedural due process refers to the process that requires various elements to be in place before a government agency, such as the police, can proceed with any coercive action against you. This includes being notified of the charge and being given the opportunity for a fair hearing before a neutral party, such as a judge. Substantive due process means that the laws themselves should be reasonable and clearly articulated attempts to achieve a government objective but not excessively burdensome on people's rights. So, under this dimension of due process, laws are subject to scrutiny by the courts to ensure they, too, are fair. The authors then provide a series of case readings to illustrate the way due process works and some of the challenges of applying it.

The articles by Toggia and Langer focus on different components of the criminal justice system that affect the perceived fairness of the system, since they can override its protections. Pietro Toggia tackles the question of bail, which occurs before a trial and is the restriction placed on the temporary pretrial release of a charged suspect being held in jail awaiting trial to ensure he or she appears in court. It sometimes involves money paid in the U.S., either privately or by a bail bondsman. In the U.S. system, criticism has been made of the amounts set for bail in spite of constitutional protections to make it reasonable or appropriate for an office. Bail is also criticized because it disproportionally impacts lower-income people and minorities, such that some states—such as California, New Jersey, and Alaska—have moved to abolish all or part of it. Máximo Langer's article reviews plea bargaining. Plea bargaining is how over 94% of criminal cases are settled; they do not go to trial. Plea bargains involve negotiated settlements between prosecutors and defense attorneys, typically to settle cases for lesser charges to which defendants agree to plead guilty. The problem with this system is that while it makes courts more efficient, it potentially deprives the accused of justice and due process because they are sometimes pressured to accept plea bargains for fear of worse consequences if they are found guilty of more serious charges; this can and does happen in some cases in which defendants are innocent.

In the final article in this section, Rosemary Sarri provides an overview of the juvenile justice system in the United States, which handles cases of youths accused of violating the criminal law. This system was designed both to be separate from the criminal justice system for adults and to focus on rehabilitating adolescent offenders to maximize their possibilities of desisting from offending.

Section Six, "Corrections," centers on the United States corrections system. This section focuses on "the variety of programs, services, facilities, and organizations responsible for the management of individuals who have been accused or convicted of criminal offenses" (Klutz & Lanier, 2012, p. 8). In this final section of the book, the authors explore the history and diverse forms of correctional styles and institutions, including institutional corrections and community corrections. "Institutional corrections" refers to those people either convicted or charged with an offense. Institutional corrections consists of three basic types. First are local jails operated by counties or cities designed to hold people convicted of misdemeanors or awaiting trial who could not meet or who were denied bail. These people are typically held for periods of up to a year. Second are prisons, consisting of facilities designed for long-term incarceration of convicted offenders who have committed felonies, and these are operated by states or by the federal government. Some states, such as California, have recently blurred this distinction through a process called "realignment," which means the courts can send various categories of offenders who normally would have been sent to prison to jails for sentences longer than a year. This is to reduce the state's overcrowded prison situation, which was mandated for reduction under a federal court order. Third, there also increasingly exist private prisons run by different companies, such as The Corrections Corporation of America, which operate under contracts to house convicted offenders. Beyond these three types of prison are a variety of correctional facilities operated under special jurisdiction (Bureau of Justice Statistics, 2013b).

The first article, by Peter Wood, looks at the history of prisons in the United States from the 20th to the 21st century. He covers the growth of the prison industrial complex and the era of mass incarceration with the world's highest imprisonment rate. He also looks at the politics of prison building and locating prisons in communities, the impact of prison on the communities from which prisoners originate, and the movement of urban populations of prisoners into rural communities. He also reviews issues related to reentry, such as housing, employment, health, substance abuse, communities, public safety, and supervision in the community. He then turns to the barriers to reentry and the relationship between race and prison in the 21st century. The article by Franklin Zimring directly addresses the growth in the prison population as well as the magnitude of the prison population, its impact on society, and how it affects different states.

In contrast to prisons, "community corrections" refers to various practices used for supervising offenders in the community. Probation is one example that is familiar to most criminal justice students and involves close monitoring and supervision by probation officers to whom offenders have to report once a week. Another type is parole, in which a person is given an early release date from a correctional facility in order to finish out the rest of his or her sentence under supervision in the community. More recently, community corrections has also included restorative justice possibilities, by which offenders are brought to account for their actions and share solutions in collaborative discussions with the victims and the community to compensate for the harm they have caused. These community restorative practices have the potential to prevent future crimes occurring by demonstrating the skills necessary to resolve minor conflicts before they manifest into serious conflicts. The article by Lawrence F. Travis III and Bradley D. Edwards reviews these various alternatives to prison.

Finally, this book assumes the viewpoint of social constructionism (Henry, 2009; Sutton, 2011). This is the theoretical approach that sees social institutions such as the law, the courts, policing, and corrections as the product of human interaction, negotiation, and settlement. Social constructionism also argues that just because things are the way they are, they do not have to be this way. They can be un-made and re-made. The challenge is to engage criminal justice critically, always suggesting ways it could improve, while not becoming bogged down in the minute detail of its daily operations, which clouds any ability to move forward.

In summary, this book introduces students to the critical cornerstones of the study of criminal justice—deviance, crime, law, research methods, criminal behavior, and criminal justice operations—and the interplay among them. The aim is to give students a fundamental understanding of how crime is defined to include certain behaviors and exclude others; how the law works to control the behavior of citizens and justice system professionals; why some people violate the law and others do not; the mechanisms employed to control crime and deal with criminal offenders; and the research techniques we use to discover what works, what does not, and what needs to change.

## References

Boukli, A., & Kotzé, J. (2018). *Zemiology: Reconnecting crime and social harm.* London: Palgrave Macmillan.

Bureau of Justice Statistics. (2013a). *Law enforcement.* Retrieved from http://www.bjs.gov/index.cfm?ty=tpandtid=7

Bureau of Justice Statistics. (2013b). *Corrections.* Retrieved from http://www.bjs.gov/index.cfm?ty=tpandtid=1

Einstadter, W. J., & S. Henry. (2006). *Criminological theory: An analysis of its underlying assumptions* (2nd ed.). Boulder, CO: Rowman and Littlefield.

Elias, R. (1986). *The politics of victimization: Victims, victimology and human rights.* New York, NY: Oxford University Press.

Garrison, A. H. (2009). The influence of research on criminal justice policy making." *Professional Issues in Criminal Justice, 4*(1): 9–21.

Karmen, A. (2013). *Crime victims: An introduction to victimology* (8th ed.). Belmont, CA: Wadsworth.

Klutz, D., & Lanier, M. M. (2012). *From the crime to the courts: An overview of criminology and criminal justice.* San Diego, CA: Cognella.

Henry, S. (2009). Social construction of crime. In J. Mitchell Miller (Ed.). *21st century criminology: A reference handbook, vol 1* (pp. 296–304). Thousand Oaks, CA: Sage Publications.

Manning, P. K. (2008). *The technology of policing: Crime mapping, information technology, and the rationality of crime control.* New York, NY: New York University Press.

Maxfield, M. G., & Babbie, E. R. (2011). *Research methods for criminal justice and criminology* (6th ed.). Belmont, CA: Wadsworth Cengage.

Lanier, M. M., & Henry, S. (2010). *Essential criminology* (3rd ed.). Boulder, CO: Westview Press.

*Magna Carta.* (1215). Retrieved from https://www.bl.uk/learning/timeline/item95692.html

Packer, H. (1968). *The limits of the criminal sanction.* Stanford, CA: Stanford University Press.

Remington, F. J. (1960). Criminal justice research. *Journal of Criminal Law, Criminology and Police Science, 51:* 7–18.

Sutton, L. P. (2011). *Social construction of justice: A new approach to understanding crime, criminality and criminal justice.* San Diego, CA: Cognella.

Tewksbury, R. (2009). Qualitative versus quantitative methods: Understanding why qualitative methods are superior for criminology and criminal justice. *Journal of Theoretical and Philosophical Criminology, 1*(1): 38–58.

Travis III, L. F. (2012). *Introduction to criminal justice* (7th ed.). Burlington, VT: Anderson Publishing.

# What is Crime and Who are its Victims?

# Crime

STUART HENRY

## Definition

Crime is conventionally defined as an intentional or avoidable violation of criminal law subject to specified penalties imposed by a politically authorized state. Since law is socially constructed by the political processes of law makers who classify behaviour deemed offensive, crime is not unitary concept. Its constitution is diverse, because its historical, cultural and situational definitions are relative, and as a result it is continually contested. Thus, an answer to the question 'what is crime?' depends upon which of its multiple constitutive elements is emphasized and on the theoretical position taken by those defining crime (Henry and Lanier, 2001; Law Commission of Canada, 2004). Because of its variability and relativity, some criminologists have argued for an 'absolute' definition of crime, independent of the legislative process and based on essential characteristics of the offensive behavior (Sellin, 1938) that are tied to the power over others it expresses (Milovanovic and Henry, 2001) and to the harm and loss it produces for its victims (Lynch, Stretesky and Long, 2015; Hillyard and Tombs, 2007; Sullivan and Tifft, 2001).

## Distinctive Features

Key constitutive elements in determining whether an act is a crime are: (1) harm; (2) social agreement or consensus; and (3) official societal response. 'Harm' includes the nature, severity and extent of harm or injury caused and the kind of victim harmed. 'Consensus' refers to the extent of social agreement about whether victims have been harmed. 'Official societal response' refers to the existence of criminal laws specifying under what conditions (such as intent and knowledge of the consequences) that an act resulting in harm can be called crime, and the enforcement of such laws against those committing acts that harm (Hagan, 1985). Other important factors that affect these three constitutive elements are (a) power and economic interests that influence law makers in the law creation process, (b) the policy and practice of law enforcement that affects whose actual behavior is policed into the criminal justice system and (c) traditional and social media that shape and impact public perceptions of crime seriousness, nature and extent. These dimensions have emerged from, and been differently emphasized, by six basic theoretical traditions: legal, moral consensus, sociological positivism, social constructionism, political conflict, and power-harm (Henry and Lanier, 2001).

In early formulations, a simple relationship was assumed between each of the three key constitutive dimensions, such that if an action caused harm, people would be outraged and lobby legislators or political authorities to enact laws that the state would enforce to penalize and thereby control the perpetrator(s). Thus, emerged what became known as the moral or consensus position on crime that states that crimes are acts, which shock the common or collective morality, producing intense moral outrage among people. In founding this view Durkheim stated that, 'an act is criminal when it offends the strong, well-defined states of the collective consciousness' (1984 [1893], p. 39). Specifically, crime was a term used, 'to designate any act, which, regardless of degree, provokes against the perpetrator the characteristic reaction known as punishment' (1984 [1893], p. 31). As a result, the basic definition of crime became behaviour defined and sanctioned by criminal law. Thus, there is no crime without law, and law is based on the 'injury' or 'harm done'. In a seminal statement reflecting the Durkheimian consensus view, Michael and Adler (1933, p. 5) asserted that 'criminal law gives behaviour its quality of criminality' and that 'the character of the behaviour content of criminal law will be determined by the capacity of behaviour to arouse our indignation' (1933, p. 23).

## Evaluation

Several flaws in the legal consensus view of crime led to various critical challenges that stemmed from those holding different theoretical positions. The first problematic is the issue of what harm has been caused and what counts as harm. Even classical thinkers of the eighteenth century disagreed about this. The concept of 'harm' according to eighteenth century Enlightenment theorist Cesare Beccaria refers to restrictions on the freedom of individuals to accumulate wealth. Beccaria identified three categories of crime based upon the seriousness of their harm to society. The most serious of these crimes were those against the state, followed by crimes that injure the security and property of individuals; last in importance, were crimes disruptive to the public peace. But for eighteenth century philosopher Jeremy Bentham, harms were behaviours that caused 'pain' rather than restrictions of freedom to accumulate wealth. Bentham discusses twelve categories of pain whose measurement was necessary in to give legislators a basis on which to decide whether to prohibit an act. He believed that no act ought to be an offence unless it was detrimental to the community. An act is detrimental if it harms one or more members of the community. Bentham elaborated a list of offence categories that he considered to be of five classes: public offences, semi-public offences, self-regarding offences (offences detrimental only to the offender), offences against the state, and multiform or anomalous offences. Each should carry a punishment determined by the circumstances.

Bentham declared that only harms to others should be criminal offences; cases of public morality and transactional crimes, where 'consent has been given,' should not be subject to the criminal law. In considering crime as defined in law therefore, the concern is not with those who commit crime, only with those acts that harm others.

Social constructionists, also called rule-relativists, further argued that the meaning of what is defined in law, or in moral consensus as 'harm,' is not fixed but varies. They argued that what is defined as crime in law is historically, temporally and culturally relative. Their insight highlights the role of changing, rather than absolute, values about crime. Their challenge to the strict legal view of crime has been developed further by social constructionist arguments that show how, what is harm depends on social context and situational meaning, itself shaped by the interaction between interest groups, such as offender, victim, community organizations, police agencies in the local setting. The emergence of an act as a harmful 'offence' depends how these groups negotiate and honour claims that harm has been created (Schnorr, 2001).

A related issue is who should determine whether a consensus of outrage exists on whether harm has been committed. Those who have been termed 'sociological positivists' argue that the measure of such consensus or outrage is the purview of social scientists. Thorsten Sellin (1938), for example, advocated a science of criminal behaviour free from the politics of criminal law, legislators and law-yers. Instead scientists should employ their own value-neutral techniques to measure independently whether harm had been caused and to establish whether outrage existed and through these means establish scientific definitions of crime (1938, pp. 20–1). Sellin proposed to do this based on studying naturally existing 'conduct norms' rather than using legally constructed laws. Such study 'would involve the isolation and classification of norms into universal categories, transcending political and other boundaries, a necessity imposed by the logic of science' (Sellin, 1938, p. 30).

A similar critique of the definition of crime by political process has been offered more recently by radical criminologists. Thus Lynch, Stretesky and Long (2015, p.2) argue that 'Limiting the definition of crime to a violation of the criminal law rules out the legitimate criminological study of certain kinds of harmful behaviors that have the same characteristics and effects as behaviors defined as crime by the criminal law.' They argue that since 'power impacts the definition of crime presented in the political construction of the criminal law,' the definition of crime relied on by crim-inologists is biased and renders their analysis of crime trends, and crime causation, invalid. Instead, and somewhat paradoxically, and echoing Sellin's critique, Lynch, Stretesky and Long (2015, p.8) propose an absolutist scientifically objective (positivist) definition of crime that is 'independent, well-reasoned, and widely applicable' (2015, p. 58) based on identifying the 'inherent character-istics that define acts as crime as opposed to those political forces that define acts as crime' (2015, p. 8). By failing to do this, they argue, criminologist have 'given their scientific responsibility for deriving a conceptual definition crime to politicians' (2015, p. 15) and held back progress of the discipline (2015, p. 72). The problem here is the assumption that science, and the scientific process itself, is any freer of political influence than law in identifying the behaviors that count as harmful (Schwendinger and Schwendinger, 1970).

The legal consensus position is also criticized because it ignores the politics of law-making. Radical conflict theorists claim that what gets defined as crime depends on having the power to define and the power to resist criminalizing definitions. Indeed, if economic and political interests influence the law creation process, then not all acts causing indignation or outrage will be legislated against.

Only those harms that powerful interests deem worthy will be subject to criminalization. As Edwin Sutherland (1940) first stated, this would mean that many harms, particularly those perpetrated by powerful corporations, remain outside the criminal law, even though they may be subject to civil regulation. For Sutherland, an adequate definition of crime should be based on an expanded definition of harm that includes 'social injury'. Similarly, Quinney (1977) wanted to expand the definition of crime to include not only the legal harms resulting from economic domination in a capitalist society, but also the crimes of government and of their agencies of social control. However, legalists such as Paul Tappan (1947) vigorously disagreed with expanding the legal definition arguing that without adhering strictly to law, the concept of crime was open-ended and meaningless.

Building on this tradition Lynch, Stretesky and Long (2015) critique not only the legal definition, but also the relativist position saying that like the legal definition, it is as variable. Instead of being grounded in objective science it is the outcome of local political struggles between interest groups, each with their own definitions of crime and interests. In contrast, 'The construction of an absolute definition of crime' creates one based on a notion of harmful behavior that 'does not vary across time and place' (2015, p. 122). Their definition of crime comprises three universal dimensions of harmful behavior, independently of whether these have been defined in law as crime. First, crimes are harmful behaviours 'that disadvantage others by preventing others from maintaining their physical health and well-being.' This includes behaviors that cause physical and emotional harm to others and 'limits their well-being.' (2015, p. 122). Second, crimes are harmful behaviors that 'use of deception, trickery, expropriation, and force … to take possession of the property, monetary, or financial holdings or property rights held by others' (2015, p. 123). Third, are harms 'by the state, crimes between states, or their agencies that violate human rights' (2015, p. 124) that 'impact the rights of citizens of states as recognized by the United Nations Declaration of Human Rights' (2015, p. 9).

Indeed, for critical criminologists an adequate definition of crime must be based on a definition of harm tied neither to law nor consensus but to an independent notion of 'human rights'. Without such independent anchoring of the definition of crime, those victimized are subject to the tyranny of moral majorities or the bias of powerful interests who determine the law. Because of this the harms that result from racism, sexism, ageism, or from 'insidious injuries' perpetrated by corporations through harmful work conditions, or harmful products, or polluted toxic environments, were for years neither acknowledged in society nor in law (Schwendinger and Schwendinger, 1970; Hillyard and Tombs 2007; Stretesky, Long, and Lynch 2013).

Postmodernist criminologists have also developed the idea that harm must be related to a concept of humanity and they argue for a dynamic conception of the different ways that humanity can be harmed. The constitutive postmodernist approach to defining crime goes beyond powerful groups and classes to the total context of powerful relations in situational and global contexts. For example, Henry and Milovanovic (1996, p. 104) state that 'crimes are nothing less than moments in the expression of power such that those who are subjected to these expressions are denied their own contribution to the encounter and often to future encounters.' They argue that crime 'is the power to deny others … in which those subject to the power of another, suffer the pain of being denied their own humanity, the power to make a difference.' Henry and Milovanovic (1996, p. 103) distinguish between 'harms of reduction' and 'harms of repression.' Harms of reduction occur when an offended party experiences a loss of some quality relative to their present standing that results from another's action. Harms of repression (or oppression) result from the actions of another that limit or restrict a person from achieving a future desired position or standing, though one achieved without harming others. Harms of repression have also been described as crimes against human dignity: acts and conditions that obstruct the spontaneous unfolding of human potential (Sullivan and Tifft, 2001).

The idea of criminalizing the use of power to reduce or suppress another is particularly important in order to expose the previously hidden crimes of gender oppression, sexual harassment, hate crime and racism that critical theorists have long complained are neglected in the legal and consensus definitions. It is also central to the unveiling of white collar, corporate and state crimes. Indeed, the analysis of power relations in the creation of crime highlights the intersecting forces of class, race and gender relations which coalesce in law and social institutions to legitimize harm and thereby render legalized relations, relations of harm. It follows, therefore, that law itself can create crime, not merely by definition but by its use of power over others and its concealment of the harms of others within the protection of law (Sullivan and Tifft, 2001).

Finally, there has been an increased recognition of the need to integrate each of the different dimensions of crime. This began explicitly with John Hagan's (1985) notion of the pyramid of crime which was further developed by Henry and Lanier (1998; 2001) in their notion of the 'prism of crime'. The aim of these approaches is to capture the multiple dimensions of crime simultaneously, rather than emphasizing any one element as pre-dominant. Henry and Lanier's prism, for example, affords a way of incorporating individual and social harm; crimes of the powerful and those of the powerless; crimes that are invisible as well as those that are highly visible; and crimes that are selectively enforced as well as those more consistently enforced. Embedded in this analysis is the important role played by both traditional and social media in manufacturing crime news, and crime talk, and in denying and legitimizing crimes of the powerful (Surette and Otto, 2001). In this way they aim for a more comprehensive definition that transcends the politics of the law-making process.

**Associated Concepts:** conflict theory, constitutive criminology, corporate crime, crimes against humanity, hate crime, hidden crime, integrative criminology, labelling, organized crime, political crime, social harm, state crime, transnational crime, transnational organized crime, war crimes

# Key Readings

Durkheim, E. (1984) [1893] *The Division of Labor in Society*. New York, The Free Press.

Hagan, J. (1985) *Modern Criminology*. New York, McGraw-Hill.

Henry, S. and Lanier, M. (1998) 'The prism of crime: arguments for an integrated definition of crime', *Justice Quarterly*, 15 (4), pp. 609–27.

Henry, S. and Lanier, M. (2001). *What is Crime? Controversies over the Nature of Crime and What to Do About it*. Boulder, CO: Rowman and Littlefield.

Henry, S. and Milovanovic, D. (1996) *Constitutive Criminology: Beyond Postmodernism*. London, Sage.

Hillyard, P. and Tombs, S. (2007) 'From 'crime' to social harm?' *Crime, Law and Social Change* 48 (1–2), pp. 9–25.

Law Commission of Canada (2004) *What Is a Crime? Defining Criminal Conduct in Contemporary Society* (Legal Dimensions). Vancouver, University of British Columbia Press.

Michael, J. and Adler, M.J. (1933). *Crime, Law and Social Science*. New York, Harcourt Brace and Jovanovich.

Milovanovic, D. and Henry, S. (2001). 'Constitutive definition of crime: Power as harm,' in Henry, S. and Lanier, M. eds. *What is Crime?* Boulder, CO: Rowman and Littlefield, pp. 165–178.

Lynch, M. J. Long, M. A. and Stretesky, P. B. (2013): 'Add parsimony and stir ... exploring the explanation of state crime.' *American Journal of Criminal Justice* 38, (1), pp. 99–118.

Lynch, M. J. Stretesky, P.B. and Long, M.A. (2015). *Defining Crime: A Critique of the Concept and its Implications*. Basingstoke, Palgrave-Macmillan.

Quinney, R. (1977) *Class, State, and Crime*. New York, David McKay.

Schwendinger, H. and Schwendinger, J. (1970) 'Defenders of order or guardians of human rights?', *Issues in Criminology*, 5, pp. 123–57.

Sellin, T. (1938) *Culture, Conflict and Crime*. New York, Social Science Research Council.

Schnorr P. (2001) 'Defining crime in a community setting negotiation and legitimation of community claims,' in Henry, S. and Lanier, M. eds. *What is Crime?* Boulder, CO: Rowman and Littlefield, pp. 115–38.

Surette R. and Otto C. (2001) 'The media's role in the definition of crime' in Henry, S. and Lanier, M. eds. *What is Crime?* Boulder, CO: Rowman and Littlefield, pp. 139–154.

Sutherland, E.H. (1940) 'White-collar criminality', *American Sociological Review*, 5, pp. 1–12.

Tappan, P.R. (1947) 'Who is the criminal?', *American Sociological Review*, 12, pp. 96–102.

Tifft L. and Sullivan D. C. (2001) 'A needs-based social harms definition of crime' in Henry, S. and Lanier, M. eds. *What is Crime?* Boulder, CO: Rowman and Littlefield, pp. 177–202.

# Crime in Society

## JOYCELYN M. POLLOCK

## What is Crime?

What is crime? This seems like an easy question, and it is, in a way. However, the answer is not necessarily murder, robbery, or rape. Those may be examples of crime, but the definition of **crime** is simply "an action that is prohibited by law." For instance, the definition of simple **assault** in one state is as follows:

1. Intentionally, knowingly, or recklessly causes bodily injury to another, including the person's spouse.
2. Intentionally or knowingly threatens another with imminent bodily injury, including the person's spouse.
3. Intentionally or knowingly causes physical contact with another when the person knows or should reasonably believe that the other will regard the contact as offensive or provocative.[1]

So, if you pushed or even hugged someone who you knew would consider it to be provocative or offensive, you have committed simple assault. This is a Class A misdemeanor unless some other conditions are met; therefore, it is not a very "serious" crime. Most simple assaults are not brought to the attention of the criminal justice system. However, many other, more serious crimes are also never reported. This creates what is known as the **dark figure of crime**, which is crime that does not find its way into official numbers. Crimes such as domestic violence, acquaintance rape, and even theft, are more likely than other crimes to be part of this dark figure of crime.

Because the dark figure of crime is so high, it makes theorizing about who commits crime difficult. We do not know if the offenders who never come to the attention of authorities are similar to those who do. We do not know if these unknown offenders have similar motivations and patterns of criminal offending.

### Chapter Preview

Studies that are based only on known offenders may be faulty in that they are not able to present findings on all offenders—only those we know about. It is important to ask relevant questions about crime, e.g. has homicide increased or not; but, it is also important to note the weaknesses of our data sources when trying to understand crime patterns.

## What is the Role of Legislators, Victims, Police, and Prosecutors in Defining Crime?

Crime is called a "constructed reality" because it is created by the definitions and perceptions of the legislators, perpetrators, observers, victims, and formal system actors (such as police and prosecutors). Take for instance, the following scenario: Person A shoves Person B. Is it a crime? It might be simple assault if Person A did it intentionally, believing it to be offensive to Person B. Is it prosecutable? It might be, only if Person B reports it to police or perhaps if a police officer happened to be close enough to see it and chose to arrest. Will it be prosecuted? A variety of factors affect the decision to prosecute, including the wishes of the victim, the resources of the prosecutor's office, the nature of the evidence and, some would say, perhaps the race and ethnicity of the offender and/or victim.

Before we can punish any act as a crime, a law has to be created by legislation. As we learned [...], most of our laws come from common law; however, state and federal legislators are constantly fine-tuning our criminal codes and adding new laws or changing existing laws. Recent changes in some states have legalized possession of small amounts of marijuana, and the carrying of guns on college campuses. Other changes in some states' laws have criminalized talking on your cellphone while driving, and posting nude pictures of someone on social media sites without their permission. [...] States are free to create new crimes as long as they do not violate individuals' federal constitutional rights. It is not at all unusual to have one state legislature pass a new law that criminalizes behavior that is still legal in other states or vice versa.

Before a crime can be counted by officials, it must be reported by the victim. Why might someone *not* report a crime to authorities? The most common reason is that they believe police can't do anything about it, but they might also interpret the event as a private matter and not a crime. Domestic violence victims sometimes do not want the involvement of the police, even though they are obviously victims of assault. Rape victims also may not report their own victimization, sometimes because they do not want formal intervention, but sometimes because they do not interpret the event as a crime. Studies have shown that female victims who are raped in "date-rape" scenarios by someone they know in circumstances where the lack of consent may be somewhat ambiguous sometimes do not define what occurred as a crime. If the victim does not perceive the event as a crime, or does not want formal system intervention, then the event is never reported to police and does not appear in our crime statistics.[2] In 2007, only 40 percent of all criminal victimizations were

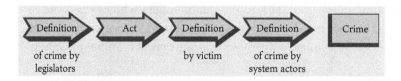

FIGURE 2-1 Crime: A "Constructed Reality."

reported to police. Robberies with injury and auto theft were reported by 85 percent of victims, but only a quarter of some other types of crimes were reported to police.[3] In Figure 2.2, we display 2013 figures, but also show those for 2004. We see that the percentage of individuals who report their victimization to the police has decreased in many crime categories since 2004, but has increased in some crime categories.

Even if the victim calls police, there may not be an arrest. Police do not arrest in a large percentage of cases where an arrest is legally justified; perhaps in as many as half of all cases. Although arrests are usually made in serious felony cases, or in situations in which victims demand an arrest, even assaults may be dealt with informally rather than by initiating a formal report or arrest.[4] Obviously, arrest statistics represent only the cases in which police officers receive a report and decide to make an arrest. These numbers represent only a small portion of the total number of criminal incidents.

Before we can ask [...] "Why do people commit crime?" we need to become familiar with the patterns and characteristics of crime. We use a number of sources that provide crime data. These are not perfect and each has inherent weaknesses, but they are the source of everything we think we know about crime in this country.

To find the most current statistics regarding victim reporting, go to the website of the Bureau of Justice Statistics. The 2014 report can be found at: http://www.bjs.gov/content/pub/pdf/cv14.pdf.

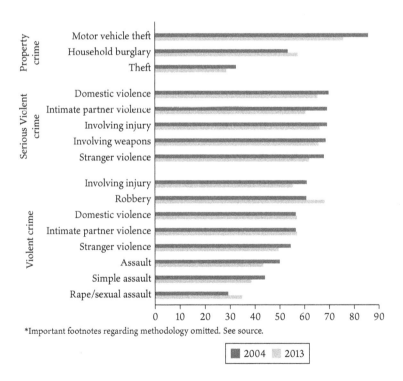

*Important footnotes regarding methodology omitted. See source.

2004    2013

**FIGURE 2.2** Percent of victimizations reported to police, by type of crime, 2004 and 2013*

*Source*: J. Truman and L. Langton, 2014. *Criminal Victimization, 2013*. Washington, DC: Bureau of Justice Statistics, DOJ. Retrieved from: http://www.bjs.gov/content/pub/pdf/cv13.pdf

# What Sources Do We Use to Find Out About the Patterns of Crime?

The two most common sources of crime data are the Uniform Crime Reports (which includes both reports to police and arrests) and the National Crime Victimization Survey. It is important to note that everything that we think we know about crime is derived primarily from these sources; thus, if there is some bias (inaccuracy) in the way these sources present the patterns of crime, then what we think we know is not necessarily accurate. It is important to know when you are looking at crime statistics whether the numbers reflect "reports to police," "arrests," or respondents reporting in a victimization survey. Each reflects slightly different realities of crime.

## The Uniform Crime Reports

The most well-known and used source of crime statistics in this country is the **Uniform Crime Reports**. This collection of local crime reports and arrest data began in 1929 and is now produced by the Federal Bureau of Investigation. The numbers come either directly from local law enforcement agencies or from a state agency that collects the data from local agencies and delivers it in a centralized format. About 98 percent of law enforcement agencies submit crime data to the FBI.[5]

You can find the UCR at https://www.fbi.gov/about-us/cjis/ucr/ucr

The Uniform Crime Reports present crime reports in terms of rates as well as raw numbers. The rates you will see in the Uniform Crime Reports are the number of crimes divided by the population and then multiplied to display by a standard number. You can compute a rate (per 100,000) using the following mathematical formula. The rate tells you how many crimes took place for each 100,000 people.

$$\textbf{Rate} = (\textbf{Number of Crimes} \div \textbf{Population}) \times \textbf{100,000}$$

The advantage of a rate is that it allows us to compare patterns of crime in very different populations. For instance, with rates, we can compare the same city in two different periods, even if the city's population has dramatically changed. We can also compare two different cities, even if one is very large and the other very small. Knowing, for instance, the raw number of burglaries in New York City; Portland, Oregon; Austin, Texas; and Los Angeles, California, tells us something,

| City | Population | Number of Burglaries | Rate |
|------|-----------|---------------------|------|
| New York City | 8,396,126 | 16,606 | 197 |
| Portland | 609,136 | 4,128 | 678 |
| Austin | 859,180 | 6,550 | 752 |
| Los Angeles | 3,878,725 | 15,728 | 405 |

but it doesn't tell us the relative risk of victimization in these cities because they do not have similar populations. The only way to compare the crime of two different populations is to compute the rate of each city, then compare the rates. In 2013, the *numbers* of reported burglaries and the *rates* for these cities looked like this:[6]

Who would have thought that there were more burglaries per 100,000 people in Portland, Austin, and Los Angeles than in New York City? Compare other big cities which also show quite different rates for burglary.

| City | Population | Number of Burglaries | Rate |
| --- | --- | --- | --- |
| Houston | 2,180,606 | 23,733 | 1088 |
| Chicago | 2,720,554 | 17,775 | 653 |

The FBI cautions against anyone using these numbers to compare the crime risk between cities because there are so many variables that go into them, including police departments' recording practices, urban density, victim reporting practices, and so on. If city limits extend out into the suburbs, the crime rate will be lower because crime occurs less often in suburban than in urban areas. Any or all of these factors may help to explain why New York's burglary rates are so much lower than other cities. New York City also may have a low rate of burglaries because of a higher percentage of buildings with security, a lower percentage of occupied dwellings than other metropolitan areas, or a number of other factors that affects the number of burglaries in that geographic area. Even though we want to be cautious when comparing rates across cities, an examination of these rates do tell us that just because New Yorkers report over 16,000 burglaries and citizens of Austin report only about 6,500 does not mean necessarily that an individual has a greater risk of being burgled in New York City.

It is very important to have an accurate population base for rates to mean anything. If the population base is inaccurate, then so too will be the rate. If, for instance, the population base is out of date and the actual population has grown considerably, then the crimes (which inevitably would increase with a larger population) will be divided by an artificially small population indicating that the rate of crime in that locale (the amount of crime per person) is higher than what it actually is. In contrast, if the population used is inaccurate in the other direction and shows a much larger population than what actually exists (perhaps because people have been moving away from that area), and the crime rate is computed using this inaccurately high population, then the crime rate will appear to be lower than it actually is. Usually, the FBI uses the most recent census numbers for the area, but these numbers may be vulnerable to rapid fluctuations in population/migration.

Crime reports are gathered from law enforcement agencies via a standard reporting form so that, for instance, larceny means the same thing in all states whether or not state laws differ in defining the dollar amount that would change larceny from a misdemeanor to a felony. Because these are standard definitions, they may or may not conform to the state's definition for that particular crime.

The UCR provides the total number of reported crimes for the eight **index crimes**: murder and non-negligent manslaughter, forcible rape, robbery, aggravated assault, burglary, larceny-theft, motor vehicle theft, and arson. Violent crimes include the first four crimes and property crimes include the last four crimes. These index crimes are also presented as rates per 100,000. In Figure 2.3a and b, we see the UCR rates for violent and property crimes across several decades. Note that all crime categories show dramatic declines in the crimes reported to the police.

One of the most oft-cited criticisms of the UCR is that it represents only reported crimes. If someone does not report a criminal victimization to the police, it does not get counted as a crime. Consequently, there is a "dark" figure of crime that never appears in the UCR. The amount of unreported crime varies by the type of crime. We saw in Figure 2.2 that less than half of violent crime victimizations and a little over a third of property crime victimizations are reported to police and, thus, are represented in the UCR. This presents a distinct problem if one uses the UCR as a measure of crime. In fact, it is not a measure of crime, but only a measure of *reported* crime. Another problem is that crimes such as identity theft, cybercrimes, and domestic violence are not easily identified in the traditional UCR because the reporting system is not set up to identify them.

One more potential problem is that some police departments have been exposed as "cooking" their numbers, meaning that they systematically downgrade citizens' reports of crimes in official reports. Scandals in New York City,[7] Chicago, and other cities[8] are troubling reminders that what we think we know about crime is dependent on accurate crime counts. When police departments categorize deaths as "undetermined" despite clear indications of homicide, they are not counted; when they record a robbery as theft instead of robbery, the true nature of the crime is hidden. These troubling incidents potentially make it unwise to utilize the UCR as the only source of understanding crime patterns—at least in specific cities.

The FBI also presents statistics on arrests. Arrest data is presented for 21 crime categories. In addition to the eight index crimes, arrests are also reported for other assaults, forgery, fraud, prostitution, and even curfew violations. The numbers of arrests are by no means a measure of crime, because they capture only the crimes in which a suspect was identified and a decision to arrest was made. Arrest data are presented for 21 crime categories in Figure 2.4, arranged in order of frequency. The graph shows that arrests for most crimes decreased. For some crimes, such as prostitution, changes over time are likely due to changes in decisions to arrest; for other crimes, such as homicide, arrest decisions are less likely to change because of discretionary enforcement. We must always remember that fluctuations in arrest rates may be real differences in such behavior, differences in perception and/or enforcement of the behavior, or differences in counting crimes. In this graph, the last several crimes are displayed separately since they show up as almost non-existent when in the same display as more frequent crimes.

To see clearance rates, go to http://www.fbi.gov/ucr/cius_04/offenses_cleared/index.html

Many crimes go unsolved or are not cleared. Crimes are considered cleared when an arrest is made for an offense. The FBI reports on the number of crimes cleared by arrest with a statistic called the **clearance rate**. The clearance rates vary greatly by crime. In 2004, murder and non-negligent homicide had the highest clearance rate (62.6 percent), while burglary had the lowest clearance

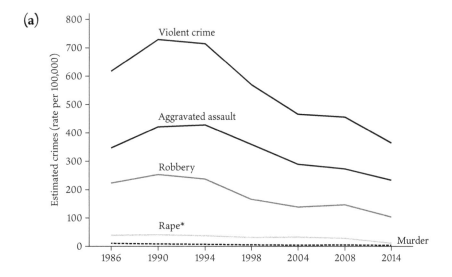

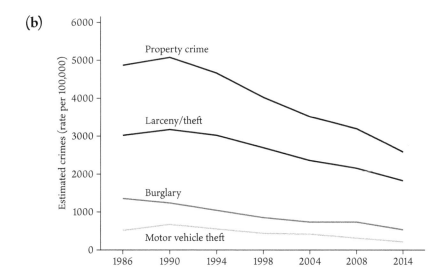

**FIGURE 2.3a** and **2.3b** Uniform crime reports—violent crime and property crime, 1986–2014

*The definition of rape changed for reporting purposes and the 2014 report included both the "legacy" rape rates (with the word forcible included) as shown here, but also a rate of 36.6 for the new definition: The revised UCR definition of rape is: "penetration, no matter how slight, of the vagina or anus with any body part or object, or oral penetration by a sex organ of another person, without the consent of the victim."

*Source:* UCR, Table 1, Crime in the United States, Table 1. By Volume and Rate, 1986–2005. Retrieved from www.fbi.gov/ucr/05cius/ data/table/_01/html. Crime in the United States, 2008, Table 1. By Volume and Rate, 1989–2008. Retrieved from www.fbi.gov/ucr/ cius2008/data/table_01.html. Crime in the United States, 2014. Table 1. By Volume and Rate. Retrieved from https://www.fbi.gov/ about-us/cjis/ucr/crime-in-the-u.s/2014/crime-in-the-u.s.-2014/tables/table-1.

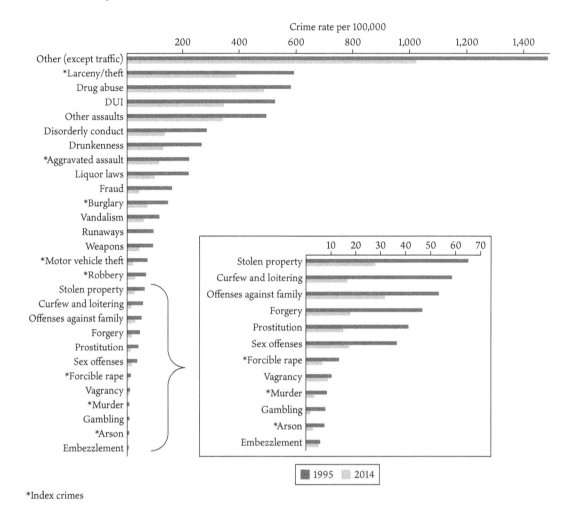

**FIGURE 2.4** Uniform crime report arrests, 2014.

*Source*: FBI, *Crimes in the United States, 2014, Arrest Rates.* https://www.fbi.gov/about-us/cjis/ucr/crime-in-the-u.s/2014/crime-in-the-u.s.-2014/tables/table-30

*Note*: Murder includes murder and non-negligent manslaughter.

rate (12.9 percent).[9] In 2009, the clearance rate for murder and non-negligent homicide increased to 66.6 percent, while motor vehicle theft and burglary declined to 12.4 percent and 12.5 percent, respectively.[10] In 2014, the clearance rate for murder and non-negligent manslaughter slipped to 64.5 percent. The clearance rate for motor vehicle theft and burglary was 12.8 percent and 13.6 percent, respectively.[11]

The FBI has also been collecting crime statistics in a different format to address other recognized problems. The National Incident-Based Reporting System (**NIBRS**) gathers much more detailed information about each criminal incident. While the UCR reporting format is hierarchical, meaning that only the most serious crime is counted, NIBRS requires information to be submitted on each crime within a criminal transaction. Instead of reporting crimes via the eight index offenses, NIBRS will display information on Group A offense categories (22 different crimes) and Group B offenses (11 different crimes). More information is obtained about each offense, including information about the victim and offender. For 22 offense categories, the following information is being collected and will be reported in NIBRS reports, also available on the FBI website:

- Victim, offender, and arrestee data
- Location and time of day of incidents
- Weapon data for select offenses
- Drug, alcohol, and gang involvement in offenses
- Attempted versus completed offenses
- Clearances by incidents
- Relationship of victims to offenders.

NIBRS reports are not comparable to the UCR because the way crimes are counted is different. For instance, a robbery, rape, and murder would only be reported as a murder in the UCR, but as three separate crimes under NIBRS. Law enforcement agencies have been slow to adopt the NIBRS reporting procedures, probably because it is much more detailed, requiring more effort to enter the data. There is also the concern that NIBRS will make it appear that there is an increase in crime because it would report each separate criminal incident instead of the hierarchical reporting system of the UCR. In 2012, about 30 percent of the nation's population was represented by crime statistics reported under NIBRS.[12] Currently only fifteen U.S. states have complete NIBRS agency participation, with an additional 18 states that submit both summary UCR and NIBRS data.[13]

## Victimization Studies

Another source of crime statistics comes from victimization surveys. The Bureau of Justice Statistics presents findings from the **National Crime Victimization Survey** (NCVS). Begun in 1973 as the National Crime Survey, the U.S. Bureau of the Census has been interviewing household members in a nationally representative sample. In 1992–93, the survey was redesigned and relabeled as the National Crime Victimization Survey. The redesign effort was intended to obtain more information and include less serious crimes. The items in the survey capture more information than what is available through the UCR. For instance, one question asks the respondent whether the crime was reported to the police. This is the source for our information in Figure 2.2, about how much crime goes unreported. Findings from the National Crime Victimization Survey can be accessed most easily through the Bureau of Justice Statistics, an agency that also presents other statistics about corrections, police, and specific crimes.

For more information, go to http://bjs.gov/

These two sources of crime data may be compared, but it is important to note their differences. The NCVS excludes homicide, arson, commercial crimes, and crimes against children under age twelve (the UCR includes these crimes). The NCVS also does not include any information on victimless crimes such as drug crimes, gambling, or prostitution. The UCR only collects arrest data on simple assault and sexual assaults other than rape, not reported crimes. Further, the NCVS calculates rates on the basis of 1000 *households,* while the UCR calculates rates based on 100,000 *persons.* Thus, it would be a mistake to treat findings from the two sources as comparable statistically. In general, the UCR gives us a broad picture of crime patterns (as reported to police) in the United States, while the NCVS gives us more information about the characteristics of victimizations in certain selected crime categories and reporting trends by victims.

Because the NCVS is based on a random sample of the population and does not collect reports of all victimizations, it is subject to all the potential problems of sampling and survey weaknesses. If any principles of **random sampling** are violated, then the applicability to the general population is in doubt. The sample size of the NCVS has been decreasing over the years, and some observers have begun to worry that the smaller sample size has begun to affect the representativeness of the sample.[14]

The advantage of having both the UCR (reports to police) and the NCVS (survey respondents' reports of victimization) is that, even if not completely comparable, we can note whether the general crime patterns are similar, thus being more confident in the accuracy of either source. Recall that the UCR shows a dramatic decline in crime reports across the last several decades. We can be more confident that the UCR is accurately representing a crime decline because the NCVS also shows dramatic declines in the number of people reporting victimization (whether or not they reported the victimization to the police). We will explore these patterns more closely when we answer the question about crime patterns below.

## Self-Report Studies

Another source of crime data is simply to ask the offender. Self-report studies ask individuals to report the crimes they have committed. Obviously, there are problems inherent in such an approach, such as whether the individual is answering honestly or not. Self-reports are generally only obtained from targeted groups, specifically juveniles (who are still in school) and offenders (who are incarcerated). We do not administer self-report surveys door-to-door to samples of citizens. Self-report studies provide interesting information, but the findings must be considered in light of the characteristics of the sample. For instance, self-report studies of juveniles often use measures of behavior that stretch the definition of "crime" to the breaking point by including minor deviances, such as truancy and other forms of juvenile misbehavior. The definitions of wrongdoing are expanded in such studies because the vast majority of students have not committed any criminal acts. Therefore, in order to get sufficient numbers for statistical analysis, the definition of "offender" is expanded. It should be kept in mind when reading these studies that these "offenders" are not necessarily who we think of as criminals.

Part of the reason that student self-report studies have difficulty obtaining sufficient numbers of offenders for statistical analysis when testing crime theories is that by the time they are administered in junior or senior years, many high-risk juveniles have already dropped out or are not in school the day the study is administered. Therefore, the young people most likely to have committed crimes are likely to be absent from the study, and the reports of criminal activity are likely to under-represent the true nature of juvenile crime.

Like school samples, prisoner samples are relatively easy to obtain, but non-representative. Prisoners do not represent all offenders (only those who are caught and sentenced to prison). They also may not admit or may exaggerate their criminal activities. In addition, these surveys are subject to the potential inaccuracies of all surveys in that respondents may forget or misremember when events occurred. Self-report studies are typically used to understand behavior differences between offenders; for instance, the finding that a small percentage of offenders are responsible for a disproportional number of crimes came from offender self-report studies.

## Cohort Studies

One other source of crime data is the **cohort study**, which follows a group of subjects over a long period. For instance, one cohort study followed all males born in Philadelphia in 1948.[15] Another longitudinal study conducted by the Harvard Program on Human Development and Criminal Behavior collected data on a cohort sample.[16] Typically, the follow-up period extends throughout childhood and into adulthood. A large number of factors have been identified as influencing criminality, including family factors, genetic factors, school and neighborhood factors, and peer factors. Proponents of longitudinal research argue that this method of data collection can illuminate how causal factors work at various times in one's life.

# What Crimes are People Most Frequently Arrested For?

When people think of crime, they probably think of robbery, murder, or violent assault. These crimes fill our newspapers and prime-time television, either as drama or reality television. It is important to note, however, that the most common crimes are fairly mundane. Looking again at Figure 2.4, we see that, in reality, the picture of crime is much different than what is reflected in the popular media. Murder, rape, and even robbery arrests are extremely rare. In contrast, the most common arrests are for a wide variety of minor misbehavior ("other"), drug violations (possession and distribution combined), and theft.

Since one of the most frequent types of arrest is for a drug offense, this category bears further scrutiny. In Figure 2.5, we see that over 80 percent of all drug arrests are for possession, and the most common drug for those arrests is marijuana. In fact, about 40 percent of all drug violation arrests are for marijuana possession.[17]

As we noted before, it is important to remember that arrests are not a true reflection of crimes committed; they only represent who is arrested. Reports to police would provide more information about frequency of crimes, but the UCR only offers information on the eight index crimes. Figure 2.6 below presents these reports for 2014. We see that the most frequent crime reports are of larceny/theft, and following far behind are reports of burglaries. Recall, however, that most people report only a fraction of all crimes to police, thus, this picture of crime is also an inaccurate representation of crime.

Victimization surveys are closer to approximating the true prevalence of crime, but they are not comparable to the crime categories of the UCR or arrest tables. Recall that the most frequent arrests are for drug violations, but that crime category is not represented at all in the victimization reports. In the latest NCVS report, the most frequently reported victimization was theft (at 6.41 reports per 1,000), followed by burglary (at 1.67 reports per 1,000). Thus, these two crimes appear as the most

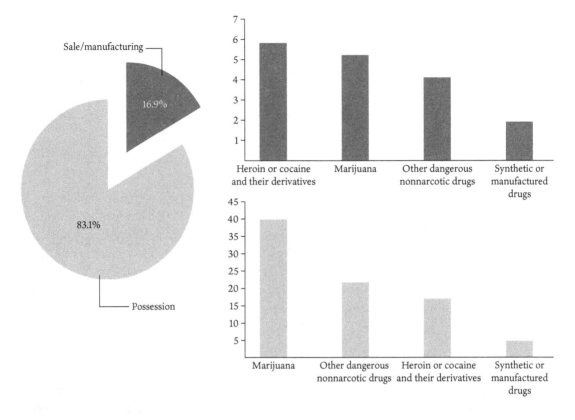

**FIGURE 2.5** Arrests for drug abuse violations

*Source*: FBI, *Crimes in the United States, 2014. Arrests*, main page. Retrieved 12/9/2015 from https://www.fbi.gov/about-us/cjis/ucr/crime-in-the-u.s/2014/crime-in-the-u.s.-2014/persons-arrested/main

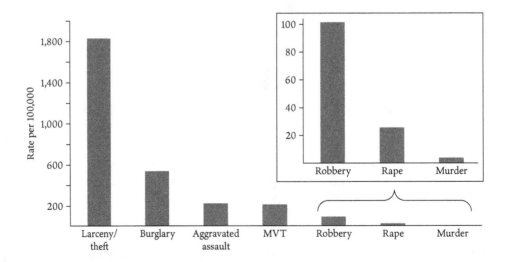

**FIGURE 2.6** Crime reports rate, 2014

*Source*: FBI, *Crime in the United States, 2014.* https://www.fbi.gov/about-us/cjis/ucr/crime-in-the-u.s/2014/crime-in-the-u.s.-2014/tables/table-1

frequent crimes in both reports to the police (UCR) and reports in the NCVS. In contrast, the least frequently reported victimization was serious intimate partner violence (at 0.05 reports per 1,000), which does not have a crime category parallel in the UCR, and rape/sexual assault (at 0.06 reports per 1,000).[18]

To summarize, our crime sources give us fragmented information about the true prevalence of crime. The most frequent arrests in 2014 were for drug offenses, and the most frequent victim-harming crimes seem to be larceny/theft and burglary, as reported to police and in victimization reports. The constant media focus on violent crimes is highly disproportionate to the true prevalence of crime categories.

## What do We Know about Homicide?

Even though homicide is a very rare occurrence, people are quite rightly more fearful of homicide, rape, aggravated assault, and robbery than property crimes. The rate of homicide has been declining for decades—the murder rate fell by more than half nationally from its peak in 1980, as seen in Figure 2.7. It is also true, however, that some cities have experienced increases in some years.

We can obtain more detailed information about homicides from the supplemental homicide reports of the FBI. Figure 2.8 shows that the most recent report indicates that homicides are most likely to be single victim and single offender.

Figure 2.9 displays information from the FBI's supplemental information on homicides. We see that, in 2012, information was known about the relationship between victim and offender in only slightly more than half of all cases. Of those cases, the most common relationship between victim and offender was

You can explore the statistics on homicide by going to a data analysis tool offered by the Office of Juvenile Justice and Delinquency: http://www.ojjdp.gov/ojstatbb/ezashr/asp/off_selection.asp

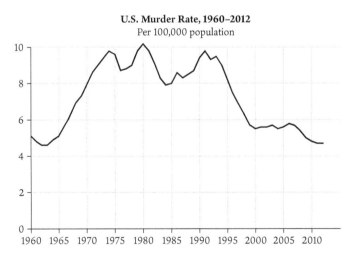

**FIGURE 2.7** Homicide rates over time

*Source*: C. Bialik, "Scare headlines exaggerated the US crime wave." Fivethirtyeight.com. Retrieved 12/12/2015 from https://fivethirtyeight.com/features/scare-headlines-exaggerated-the-u-s-crime-wave/

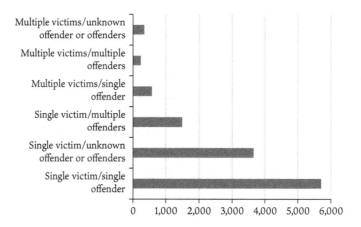

**FIGURE 2.8**  Murder: victim/offender situation

*Source: Crime in the U.S.*, 2014, Table 4.

acquaintance. The family members most likely to be killed by another family member were wives. Only 12 percent of the victims where the relationship between victim and offender was known were killed by strangers. However, because that information seems to be missing from almost half of all homicides, we must be cautious about assuming anything about the relationship between victim and offender from those cases where we do have the information.

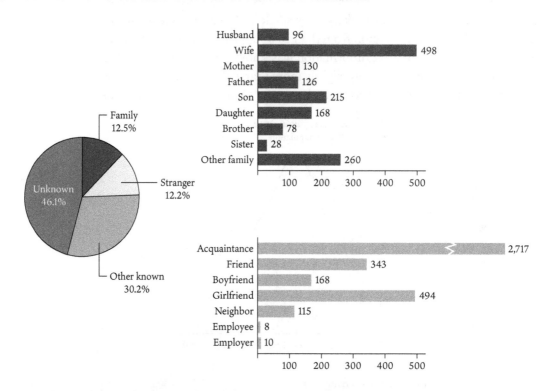

**FIGURE 2.9**  Relationship between homicide victims and offenders

*Source:* FBI. Retrieved 1/4/2016 from https://www.fbi.gov/about-us/cjis/ucr/crime-in-the-u.s/2012/crime-in-the-u.s.-2012/offenses-known-to-law-enforcement/expanded-homicide/expandhomicidemain

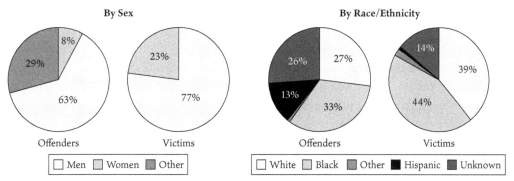

**FIGURE 2.10**  Homicide offenders/victims

*Source: Crime in the United States, 2014, Table 3; 4; Table 6*

Using 2013 data, it is clear that homicide offenders *and* victims are likely to be male and disproportionately African American (Figure 2.10).

It is important to note that these percentages are of total homicide numbers. Rates (per 100,000) would look much different since African Americans comprise only about 13 percent of the total population; thus, the fact that 44 percent of all murder victims are African American is a truly astounding figure. Data analysis from the time period of the most dramatic decline in homicide illustrated the fact that between the mid-1990s and late 2000s, the most dramatic declines in homicide also took place with African American men (see Figure 2.11).[19]

It is important to note that when there are changes in the number of homicides, not all racial/ethnic and gender groups are equally at risk. Homicides have increased in some urban areas, but, similar to past patterns, not everyone is equally vulnerable.

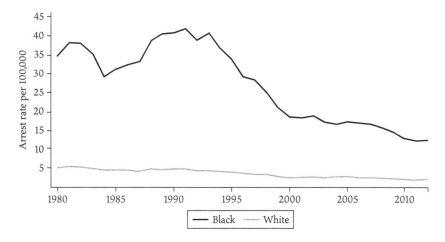

**FIGURE 2.11**  Homicide declines by race, 1985–2012

*Source: Crime in the United States, 2014, Table 3; 4; Table 6*

# What has been the Pattern of Crime Over the Years? Has it Declined?

Recall from the above discussion that the UCR has recorded dramatic declines in all crime categories in the last twenty years. This could be due to a true decrease in criminal activity, or it could be due to less people reporting their victimization. The way to know for sure is to compare victimization reports to crime reports. [...] Triangulating data utilizes different sources to compare facts. We can be more confident that we have truly experienced a decline in crime because the UCR, the National Crime Victimization Survey, and arrest tables all show a steady overall decline since the early 1990s. Figure 2.12 illustrates this consensus. Although there was a bit of an increase in 2012, the decline continued afterwards.

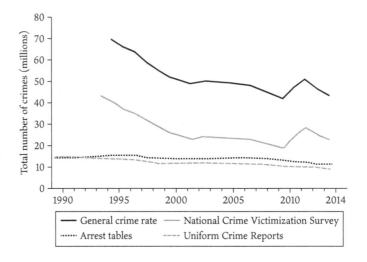

**FIGURE 2.12** Composite view of decline in crime, 1990–2014

*Source*: Bureau of Justice Statistics, *Criminal Victimization Survey*, 1994–2014. Online Sourcebook of Criminal Justice Statistics, Table 3, Estimated number and rate of offenses known to police, 1990–2014. UCR, Crime in the United States, 1995–2014.

# Does the Public have An Accurate Perception about the Prevalence of Crime?

There is no doubt that our crime rates are about as low as they have been since the 1970s, but does the public know that? The short answer is no. A Gallup poll indicates that about 70 percent of Americans think there is more crime in the U.S. now than there was a year ago. In fact, in most years, the majority of Americans think crime was higher than the year before, but they have been wrong. The only year the minority of citizens (41 percent) thought crime had declined was in 2001.

It is also interesting to note that women are more likely to think crime has risen. Conservatives (80 percent) are more likely than liberals (57 percent), and those in rural towns are more likely than urban residents to think crime has risen. Figure 2.13 shows these differences. In 2015, nearly six in

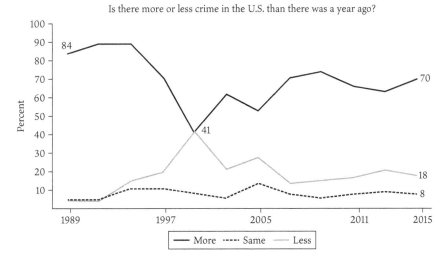

Is there more or less crime in the U.S. than there was a year ago?

FIGURE 2.13  Public perceptions of crime in the U.S., 1989–2015

*Source*: Gallup Poll. Retrieved 1/4/2015 from http://www.gallup.com/poll/186308/americans-say-crime-rising.aspx?utm_source=alert&utm_medium=email&utm_content=morelink&utm_campaign=syndication

ten Americans (59 percent) said U.S. crime is an "extremely" or "very" serious problem—up slightly from 55 percent in 2014.[20]

# How Do the Crime Rates of the United States Compare to Other Countries?

There is a widespread perception that one of the reasons the United States leads the world in incarceration rates is because there is more crime here than in similar Western countries such as the United Kingdom, France, or Canada. This is true only for homicide. Property crime rates in the United States are roughly comparable to those of other countries. It should be pointed out that comparing crimes cross-culturally is difficult because definitions and reporting practices that affect crime statistics vary. The United Nations Office of Drugs and Crime, however, has collected and makes available crime rates as reported by member nations in order to make some tentative comparisons. In the latest report available, about 138 countries are represented. In Figure 2.14 below, certain selected countries and crimes are displayed.

Homicide is perhaps the most consistently reported crime and offers the most reliable comparison. The homicide rate per 100,000 of the United States is about 3.8. That is down from previous years, but still higher than many European countries, Canada, and Australia. On the other hand, the rate of homicide in the U.S. is much lower than Mexico's or other countries in South America and Africa. Mexico's robbery rate is extremely high compared to other countries. France has a higher robbery rate than the U.S. and Australia has a higher burglary rate.

To explore for yourself some of these statistics, go to https://data.unodc.org/#state:14

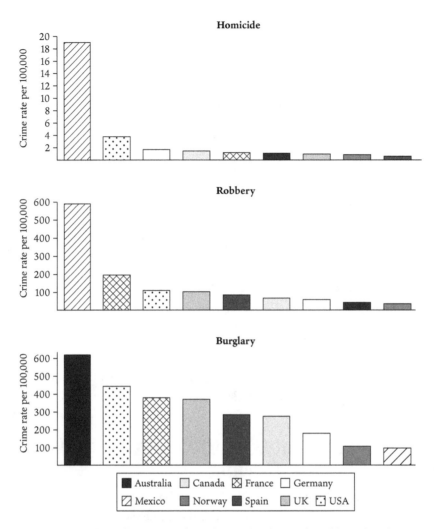

**FIGURE 2.14** Selected crimes in selected countries: homicide, robbery, burglary

*Source*: United Nations Office of Drugs and Crimes, Crime Data tool, retrieved 12/9/2015 from https://data.unodc.org/#state:14

While we must be careful with these statistics because it is unknown how accurate or consistent reporting is across all the countries, it does indicate that the crime rate in the U.S. is not wildly disproportionate to other Western, industrialized countries, except for the homicide rate.

Before we leave this chapter on crime statistics, we will offer a discussion that illustrates how important accurate data and reasonable data interpretation can be when discussing current events. A current controversy playing out in newspapers and other public arenas today is whether there has been a "**Ferguson Effect**" on American policing that has resulted in "**de-policing**" which, in turn, has led to a spike in homicides and violent crimes in major cities. The Focus on Data section below examines this question.

# Focus on Data: Is there a Ferguson Effect? Is there a Current Crime Wave?

In the summer and fall of 2014, the shooting of young Black men by police officers led to a number of violent protests in several American cities, most notably in Ferguson, Missouri and Baltimore, Maryland. Some argued that the public scrutiny and criticism of police led to a change in police behavior, dubbed the "Ferguson Effect," which referred to police officers choosing not to engage with citizens for fear of being labeled racist or violent. This "de-policing," as it was also called, then, arguably, led to a spike in homicide.

Beginning in 2015, major news outlets began reporting on big-city crime spikes. Eventually the *Washington Post*, *New York Times*, NPR, CNN, BBC, *USA Today*, Reuters, *Time*, and other major news outlets had "crime spike" stories. In August of 2015, the Major Cities Chiefs Association (MCCA) reported increased homicides as a problem. In contrast, others (*New York Daily News*, Brennan Center, Marshall Project) argued that there was no evidence yet to indicate alarm was warranted. Let's look at the facts.

Heather MacDonald's much publicized article in the *Wall Street Journal* reported that gun violence was up 60 percent in Baltimore with May 2015 as the most violent month the city had seen in fifteen years. A list of cities with percentage increases were offered, including Milwaukee (180 percent by May 17 over the same period the previous year), St. Louis (25 percent), Atlanta (32 percent), Chicago (17 percent), and New York (13 percent). Then she argued that city-wide statistics masked much larger neighborhood increases such as 500 percent in one East Harlem neighborhood. Because the first six months of 2014 continued a twenty-year pattern of decline, her argument was that the increases in the first six months of 2015 were due to a surge of lawlessness because of people's agitation against police departments and media focus on the events. MacDonald noted the "Ferguson Effect" (a term evidently coined by St. Louis police chief Sam Dotson) was the phenomenon of police officers disengaging from discretionary enforcement activity, with a resulting feeling of empowerment by criminals. She pointed to the fact that arrests in St. Louis city and county had dropped a third since the shooting of Michael Brown in August, while homicides surged 47 percent and robberies were up 82 percent through November 2014. Other cities also showed a decline in arrests; for instance, she reported that Baltimore had 56 percent fewer arrests by May 2015 compared to 2014. In New York City, stop-and-frisk policies led to a lawsuit and intense media scrutiny; consequently, stops dropped 95 percent from the 2011 high according to MacDonald. She further argued that aggressive policing has led to urban reclamation and saved thousands of Black lives and warned that continued criticism of police would lead to losing the gains in crime reduction that had been achieved in the last twenty years.[21] There are four arguments to this position:

1. Homicides and other crimes in American cities are increasing.
2. Police officers are not policing in the way they have in previous years, meaning they are less likely to engage in "pro-active" policing such as stop-and-frisks and arrests for minor crimes due to the public and media scrutiny and criticism that has arisen since the summer of 2014.
3. The reduction in pro-active policing, if it exists, caused the increase in homicides and other crime, if the increase exists.

## Are Homicides and Other Crimes in American Cities Increasing?

Unfortunately, the UCR and the FBIs Supplemental Homicide Report are not as current as we would need to answer this question. It usually takes six months to a year before crime reports are available for public consumption. The latest FBI data (UCR) for 2014 indicate that there was a 2 percent decrease in homicide rates per 100,000 nationwide, however, the pattern was different between cities and suburban and rural areas. In the largest cities (over 1 million), there was a 2.2 percent *increase* in homicides per 100,000, but a 16 percent *decrease* in non-metropolitan counties. Thus, contrary to MacDonald's proposition that the first months of 2015 were an aberration due to changing circumstances after the Michael Brown shooting, homicides had already begun to increase in cities (as opposed to suburban and rural areas) in 2014.

Recent analyses of 2015 homicides for the largest American cities showed that there was probably about a 17 percent increase in homicides in the first six months of 2015 compared to the first six months of 2014—a dramatic increase, but this increase seems to be confined to only some cities.[22] In fact, the pattern is highly skewed: ten cities account for two-thirds of the increase. These cities are characterized by: higher poverty, a falling population, and high unemployment.[23] The National Institute of Justice published an analysis of the increase (using data collected by the *New York Times* and *Washington Post*) and showed that from 2014 to 2015, 127 more people were killed in Baltimore (a 59 percent increase); 61 more people were killed in Milwaukee from the year before (a 73 percent increase); 57 more people killed in Cleveland (a 91 percent increase) and 34 more people killed in Nashville (an 83 percent increase).[24]

Note that, even with over 200 murders in 2015, that number is dramatically lower than the high in 1993 when New York City recorded 1,946 murders.[25] UCR trend data shows that homicide and violent crime has been declining for the last twenty years.

News headlines that refer to large percentage increases in murder rates in specific cities usually neglect to mention that large percentage increases happen more easily with small base numbers. A 50 percent increase in murders sounds ominous, but a 50 percent increase of twelve is six additional homicides. Homicide numbers, because they have been quite small in the last decade, can be influenced by such things as an intra-familial multiple murder, or police recording practices, such as reclassifying cases from undetermined to homicide, or other reporting changes. In fact, several journalists, in articles analyzing crime increases in certain cities such as Chicago, New York, and Los Angeles, have suggested that at least part of the increase might be due to changes in reporting practices after major scandals that exposed police departments as not recording crime reports accurately. For instance, Domanick reported that violent crime in Los Angeles rose more than 20 percent during the first half of 2015, with felony assaults up 26 percent and robberies up 19 percent and suggested that the increase might be due, in part, to a *Los Angeles Times* investigation of the department's crime numbers for the first half of 2014, which discovered the misclassification of 1,200 violent felony assaults as misdemeanors, thus making it appear that serious violent crime was going down when, in fact, it went up by 14 percent.[26] A similar article describing Chicago's crime reporting described how, by categorizing a death as "undetermined," despite clear indices of murder, the number of homicides were artificially reduced.[27] While some amount of misrepresenting the seriousness of crimes probably would not significantly influence percentage increase numbers of burglary because the base numbers are so large, such practices could definitely result in significant increases or decreases in crime categories that involve smaller numbers such as homicide and robbery.

| City | Absolute Increase | % Increase | Cumulative % of Total Increase |
|------|------|------|------|
| Baltimore | 127 | 58.5 | 15.5 |
| Chicago | 61 | 15.0 | 22.9 |
| Houston | 61 | 25.2 | 30.3 |
| Milwaukee | 61 | 72.6 | 37.8 |
| Cleveland | 57 | 90.5 | 44.7 |
| Washington DC | 57 | 54.3 | 51.6 |
| Nashville | 34 | 82.9 | 55.8 |
| Philadelphia | 32 | 12.9 | 59.7 |
| Kansas City | 29 | 37.2 | 63.2 |
| St. Louis | 29 | 18.2 | 66.7 |

FIGURE 2.15  Rising murder rates in big cities, 2014–2015

*Source*: City police departments, reported in M. Davey and M. Smith. "Murder Rates Rising Sharply in Many Cities." *New York Times* (September 1, 2015), p. A1.

While the MacDonald article presented data from cities that had increased homicides, others have noted that the pattern is not uniform across American cities. An analysis by FiveThirtyEight.com utilized city data, news reports, and other sources to construct a table with 60 cities and homicide numbers for 2015 compared to the same time period in 2014.[28] In 26 cities, homicides were up by 20 percent or more from a year ago, but the number of homicides was down in nineteen other cities.

More generally, crime analysts will warn against year to year comparisons of homicide, or any crime, because year-to-year rates fluctuate. The better way to understand data is by looking at longer periods of time. When we examine murder trends we see that, although there may be year-to-year increases, the general trend has been downward, in this set of tables from a report produced by the Brennan Center.[29]

Moving from homicide to all violent crime, the UCR reported that nationwide violent crime reports to police were down by 0.2 percent and property crime declined by 4.3 percent in 2014.[30] The latest National Crime Victimization Survey, released in August 2015, reported no significant change in violent crime victimization, and property crime victimization fell from 131.4 per 1,000 to 118.1 per 1,000 in 2014.[31]

In summary, many American cities, but not all, have seen recent increases in homicides. Further, it may be that the increases are occurring in large cities, not in smaller towns and suburban areas. The FBI had reported a small increase in large metropolitan areas in 2014 so this increase began at least as early as 2014. Further, analysts point to trend data to show that year-to-year fluctuations have occurred continuously even throughout the twenty-year decline in homicide and other violent crimes.

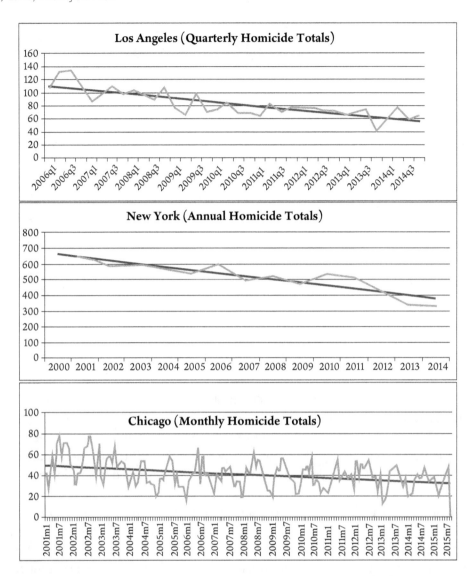

**FIGURE 2.16** Homicide patterns in selected cities: Los Angeles, New York, Chicago

*Source*: M. Friedman. "Just facts: America's non-existent 'spike in crime.'" Brennan Center for Justice (August 10, 2015). Retrieved 12/12/2015 from https://www.brennancenter.org/blog/americas-non-existent-spike-crime.

## Are Police Officers Not Policing in the Way They Have in Previous Years? If So, Is This Due to the Public and Media Scrutiny and Criticism That Have Arisen Since the Summer of 2014?

MacDonald reported fairly dramatic declines in arrests in some cities, arguing this was evidence of "de-policing." Interestingly, fewer arrests can be presented as a decline in crime or a decline in policing, depending on one's perspective. While MacDonald reported dramatic declines, criminologists have pointed to other cities that have not shown declines in arrests.[32] Misdemeanor arrests, traffic tickets, and investigative stops are subject to more discretionary decision making by officers than felony arrests, therefore, all three should be considered to determine if "de-policing" is occurring.

New York City has definitely seen a dramatic drop in the number of stop-and-frisks undertaken by New York City police officers, but the decline had begun earlier than the summer and fall of 2014 when the protests in Ferguson, Missouri and Baltimore, Maryland occurred. A report by the John Jay College of Criminal Justice indicated that between 2011 and 2014 the total number of arrests for felonies and misdemeanors, criminal summonses, and stop-and-frisks fell by more than 800,000, or 31 percent. Street stops declined from a high of 685,000 in 2011 to under 46,000 in 2014, a 93 percent decline in only three years. The declines were mostly in poorer and minority neighborhoods where they had grown the fastest over the previous decade. The decline in stops occurred because of a court ruling in 2013 that found such stops unconstitutional as well as a growing public outcry that the stops were unfairly targeting minority and poor residents who had the misfortune to live in certain areas of the city. Despite the multi-year decline in such stops, crime reports continued to decline as well. In 2014, rates of both violent and nonviolent crime in New York City were lower than the year before, and were almost 90 percent lower than they were in 1980.[33]

Another city that saw arrests and investigative stops decline was Seattle. In May of 2014 it was reported that police enforcement of lower-level crimes, traffic offenses and infractions dropped dramatically, including a 49 percent decline in misdemeanor criminal arrests between 2005 and 2013. While service calls had increased by 9 percent between the first quarter of 2010 and first quarter of 2014, independent officer-initiated activity had dropped by 44 percent, from 15 percent of their time in 2011 to only 8 percent of their time in the same quarter in 2014. Officer checks of suspicious people and suspicious vehicles dropped by 80 percent. Bookings into the jail fell by 51 percent between 2006 and 2013. Between 2007 and 2013, infractions filed in Seattle Municipal Court fell 71 percent, covering unlawful activity such as liquor violations, public urination, and noise problems. Because the Seattle Police Department was investigated by the Department of Justice and entered into a consent decree that required substantial changes in policies and practices to address alleged racism and use of force abuses, the dramatic decline was attributed to "de-policing."[34] Others pointed to alternative explanations such as programs of diversion. Recall, also, that Washington legalized small amounts of marijuana effective December 2012, which must have had a significant effect on the number of police investigative stops and misdemeanor arrests. More importantly, however, there has not yet been a connection shown between decreased police actions and UCR index crimes or victimization reports. Unfortunately, the time lag that occurs in our ability to access this information will prevent any immediate analysis.

We can count arrests, stops, and traffic tickets, and we can document whether or not totals are higher, lower, or the same as the year before, but we can't say for certain why such police actions have declined because we have no way of knowing whether or not the number of underlying acts have changed, other factors have affected the decision (e.g. charging practices of the prosecutor's office or changes in the law), or the officers have changed their policing practices (e.g. less likely to arrest or stop-and-frisk). As noted above, court orders requiring the NYPD to change their stop-and-frisk practices and Washington's legalization of marijuana possession have probably more to do with the observed changes than police officers changing their decision-making practices on patrol in these cities than "de-policing."

Anecdotal evidence has been offered (e.g., quotes from individual officers or police administrators) that police officers felt scrutinized and unfairly criticized after the public protests in 2014 and 2015 and reacted by "de-policing." One small study that surveyed officers in a small police department found that officers reported a decline in motivation to do their job and work with the community because of public criticism, but that they did not change their decisions. Further the decline in motivation evidently was also influenced by administrative and managerial practices of the police department, not simply the "Ferguson Effect."[35]

## Is the Reduction in Pro-Active Policing (If It Exists), the Cause of the Increase in Homicides and Other Crime (If There is Significant Increase)?

Proposed explanations for the increase in violent crime, including homicides, in some cities have included (in addition to the Ferguson Effect) a rise in heroin use; increased gang violence; entrenched poverty and hopelessness; release of career criminals from prison (who have served their 25–30-year sentences from the high-crime years of the 1980s); more guns, especially automatic weapons like the AK-47; and, as noted before, simply yearly fluctuations in a two-decade decline. What we do know about these homicides is that they are often gang-related and occur most often in poverty-stricken areas of the city. The only academic study thus far that has addressed this question specifically looked at violent crimes in 81 cities in the year before and the year after the Michael Brown shooting in Ferguson and concluded that the only crime that showed a significant change in direction (from decease to increase) in the second time period was robbery. The study's authors cautioned that even documenting the increase could not "prove" that the increase was due to de-policing because there might be many other factors that affect the increase in robbery.[36] Also, as noted earlier, there have been previous upticks in homicide and violent crime in some cities periodically in the last several decades, even within a general trend of decreasing homicide rates over those years.

A recent study paper from the National Institute of Justice also offered the hypotheses of the growth of heroin markets, an increase in the number of parolees in the community, and a loss of "legitimacy" in Black communities as explanations for the increase in homicide in some American cities.[37] There is no doubt that heroin/opiate deaths have increased, but part of the well-known heroin epidemic is legally obtained opiates through prescriptions so there is no data as yet to prove that illegal heroin markets are fueling the homicide increase. Also, there has been no increase in the number of drug arrests. An increase in the number of parolees contributing to the homicide increase would require a knowledge of whether or not perpetrators were on parole—data we do not have yet for 2015, even for those arrested (and recall that a certain portion of homicides are not ever solved). As for the hypothesis that a legitimacy crisis in the minority community toward the police is causing an increase in homicide, Rosenfeld, in the NIJ analysis referred to above, pointed out that the cities with the largest homicide increases also had higher percentages of Blacks, and public opinion polls show that Blacks have historically low confidence in policing today. He argued that it is a difficult methodolgical problem to determine to what extent a rise is homicides is due to a loss of legitimacy of police and the justice system and suggested ethnographic research.[38] Another possibility is to look at the motivations for killings since part of the loss of legitimacy argument is that people who do not trust the justice system engage in retaliatory behavior. A good question to ask might be: what portion of homicides in these cities are due to retaliation? Also, is the proportion of retaliatory homicides correlated with a decrease in trust in police? We don't have motivation data yet for 2015 (although it will eventually be available in Suppmental Homicide Reports from the FBI).

To conclude, there is no evidence of a trend of increasing homicides at this point. We don't know if the recent increase in some cities will continue nor do we know whether it will spread to more cities. An increase in 2006 spurred similar concern, which proved to be unnecessary since the increase evaporated and the decline in homicides and other violent crimes continued their multi-decade decline after a couple of years.[39] As for "de-policing," there is some quantitative evidence that police discretionary actions (investigative detentions, traffic tickets, and misdemeanor arrests) have declined in some cities, but not the cities that have experienced the most dramatic increase in homicides.

The proposed explanations for the increase in homicides in some American cities offered instead of a "Ferguson Effect" include: growing heroin markets, an increase in parolees returning from prison, and a loss of legitimacy of police and the justice system in the Black community leading to retaliatory and vigilante justice. Absence of current data make any study of these hypotheses difficult.

# Summary

## What is Crime? What is the Role of Legislators, Victims, Police, and Prosecutors in Defining Crimes?

Crime is a "constructed reality" created by legislators who define acts as crimes, acts of the perpetrator, the perceptions of the victim and decision to report to authorities, and decisions by system actors (e.g., the decision to arrest). Only a portion of all crimes find their way into official statistics.

## What Sources Do We Use to Find Out About the Patterns of Crime?

The Uniform Crime Reports present data on eight index crimes that are reported to police. They can be accessed from the FBI's website, which also has data on arrests on a larger number of crime categories. Problems with the UCR include the fact that many people do not report crimes to the police and arrests are not necessarily an accurate representation of crimes committed. We also have the National Crime Victimization Survey, which is a random survey of the population to discover the number of people who have been victimized and some characteristics of their victimization. We also use self-report studies and cohort studies in our study of crime.

## What Crimes are People Most Frequently Arrested for?

The largest category of arrests in 2014 was for drug crimes and possession was the most frequent of these arrests. Larceny/theft is the next most frequent arrest category, along with DUI and non-aggravated assault. The crimes the media focuses on (murder, rape, robbery) are extremely rare.

## What Do We Know About Homicide?

Homicide, as most crime, has been on the decline since the mid-1990s. It is important to remember that the relative risk of being a homicide offender or a homicide victim is dramatically dependent on population group. Young Black males are much more likely than other population groups to be both homicide victim and offender.

## What Has Been the Pattern of Crime Over the Years? Has It Declined?

All measures of crime (UCR, arrests, and victimization reports) show dramatic declines over the last two decades so that today's crime rates—for both violent and property crimes—are about the same as they were in the 1970s.

## Does the Public Have an Accurate Perception About the Prevalence of Crime?

The public seems incredibly unaware of the dramatic declines in crime that have taken place in the last decades. A majority of the public thinks that crime is increasing despite all measures showing declines. It is possible that recent upticks in homicides and violent crimes in cities may be a sign that crime rates may be poised to begin an upward trend.

## How Do the Crime Rates of the United States Compare to Other Countries?

While the U.S. has higher murder rates than European countries, other crimes do not show any consistent pattern. In general, property crimes in the U.S. are not higher than many other countries.

## CRITICAL THINKING EXERCISES

1. Go to the FBI website for the UCR which is reported in *Crime in the United States*. The 2015 crime statistics have just recently been released at: **https://ucr.fbi.gov/crime-in-the-u.s/2015/crime-in-the-u.s.-2015**. See if homicide and/or violent crime rates are higher than they were in 2014. Write an update to the Focus on Crime section—is there more information available regarding any of the questions raised in the section?

2. Go to the United Nations Office of Drugs and Crime website: **https://data.unodc.org/#state:4**. Look up the crime rates (not raw numbers) for other crimes to see how the United States compares to other countries. Why do you suppose the homicide rates are so much higher here? How would you test your hypothesis?

## Notes

1. Texas Penal Code. Retrieved 4/10/2007 from http://tlo2.tlc.state.tx.us/statutes/docs/PE/content/htm/pe.005.00.000022.00.htm#22.01.00.

2. See H. Cleveland, M. Koss and J. Lyons, "Rape tactics from the survivor's perspective." *Journal of Interpersonal Violence* 14 (5) (1999): 532–548.

3. *Sourcebook of Criminal Justice Statistics 2010*. Retrieved 9/9/2010 from http://www.albany.edu/sourcebook/pdf/13332007.pdf.

4. See C. Mendias and E. Kobe, "Engagement of policing ideals and the relationship to the exercise of discretionary powers." *Criminal Justice and Behavior* 33 (2006): 70–77.

5. N. James, *How Crime in the United States Is Measured*. Washington, DC: Congressional Research Service (CRS), 2008.

6. Federal Bureau of Investigation, *Crime in the United States, 2013*, Table 6, Crime in the United States by State, by City, 2013. Retrieved 9/12/2007 from https://www.fbi.gov/about-us/cjis/ucr/crime-in-the-u.s/2013/crime-in-the-u.s.-2013/tables/6tabledatadecpdf/table-6.

7. J. Eterno and E. Silverman, "The trouble with Compstat: Pressure on NYPD commanders endangered the integrity of crime stats." *New York Daily News*, February 15, 2010. Retrieved 9/15/2010 from http://www.nydailynews.com/opinions/2010/02/15/2010-02-15_the_trouble_with_compstat.html; J. Eterno, A. Verma, E. Silverman, "Police manipulations of crime reporting: Insiders' revelations." *Justice Quarterly*, 2014. Accessed from: doi.org/10.1080/07418825.2014.980838.

8. D. Bernstein and N. Isackson, "The truth about Chicago's crime rates, Part I and II." *Chicago Magazine* (May, June, 2014) Retrieved 12/9/2015 from http://www.chicagomag.com/Chicago-Magazine/June-2014/Chicago-crime-statistics/.

9. Federal Bureau of Investigation, *Crime in the United States, 2004*. Retrieved 8/1/2006 from http://www.fbi.gov/ucr/cius_04/offenses_cleared/index.html.

10. Federal Bureau of Investigation, *Crime in the United States, 2009*. Retrieved 9/15/2010 from http://www.fbi.gov/ucr/cius2009/offenses/data/table_25.html.

11. Federal Bureau of Investigation, *Crime in the United States, 2014*. Retrieved 12/5/2015 from https://www.fbi.gov/about-us/cjis/ucr/crime-in-the-u.s/2014/crime-in-the-u.s.-2014/tables/table-25.

12. Bureau of Justice Statistics, NIBRS. Retrieved 12/5/2015 from BJS website, note on methodology on NIBRS. http://www.bjs.gov/index.cfm?ty=dcdetail&iid=301#_ftnref3.

13. D. Roberts, "Why participating in NIBRS is a good idea." *Police Chief Magazine*, December 2015. Retrieved 12/5/2015 from http://www.policechiefmagazine.org/magazine/index.cfm?fuseaction=display&issue_id=92014&category_ID=4.

14. S. Ansari and N. He, "Convergence revisited: A multi-definition, multi-method analysis of the UCR and the NCVS crime series." *Justice Quarterly*, 32 (2012): 1–31.

15. M. Wolfgang, R. Figlio and T. Sellin, *Delinquency in a Birth Cohort*. Chicago: University of Chicago Press, 1978.

16. M. Tonry, L. Ohlin and D. Farrington, *Human Development and Criminal Behavior: New Ways of Advancing Knowledge*. New York: Springer-Verlag, 1991.

17. Federal Bureau of Investigation, *Crime in the United States, 2014*. Retrieved from https://www.fbi.gov/about-us/cjis/ucr/crime-in-the-u.s/2014/crime-in-the-u.s.-2014/persons-arrested/main.

18. J. Truman and L. Langton, *Criminal Victimization, 2014*. Table 4. Retrieved from http://www.bjs.gov/content/pub/pdf/cv14.pdf.

19. See, for instance, J. Cancino and J. Pollock, "Gender, race, and ethnicity: An analysis of homicide rates and trends in San Antonio, 1990–2004." Paper presented at the American Society of Criminology Meeting, Los Angeles, CA (2006, November).

20. Gallup poll. Retrieved from: http://www.gallup.com/poll/186308/americans-say-crime-rising.aspx?utm_source=alert&utm_medium=email&utm_content=morelink&utm_campaign=syndication.

21. H. MacDonald, "The new nationwide crime wave." *The Wall Street Journal*, May 29, 2015. Retrieved 12/12/2015 from http://www.wsj.com/articles/the-new-nationwide-crime-wave-1432938425.

22. R. Rosenfeld, *Documenting and Explaining the 2015 Homicide Rise: Research Directions*. Washington, DC: NIJ, OJP, June 2016, p. 6.

23. J. Gravwert and J. Cullen, *Crime in 2015: A Final Analysis*. Washington, DC: Brennan Center, April 2016.

24. R. Rosenfeld, *Documenting and Explaining the 2015 Homicide Rise: Research Directions*. Washington, DC: NIJ, OJP, June 2016, p. 8.

25. D. Hamill, "Keeping a running score of New York's homicide rate seems a bit ridiculous." *New York Daily News*, June 28, 2015. Retrieved 12/15/2015 from http://www.nydailynews.com/new-york/murder-statistics-don-show-return-bad-old-days-article-1.2273859.

26. J. Domanick, "Why L.A.'s crime rise is no surprise." *Los Angeles Times* (August 27, 2015). Retrieved 12/12/2015 from http://www.latimes.com/opinion/op-ed/la-oe-domanick-los-angeles-rising-crime-20150827-story.html.

27. D. Bernstein and N. Isackson, "The truth about Chicago's crime rates, Part I and II." *Chicago Magazine* (May, June) Retrieved 12/9/2015 from http://www.chicagomag.com/Chicago-Magazine/June-2014/Chicago-crime-statistics/.

28. C. Bialik, "Scare headlines exaggerated the US crime wave." Fivethirtyeight.com. Retrieved 12/12/2015 from https://fivethirtyeight.com/features/scare-headlines-exaggerated-the-u-s-crime-wave/.

29. M. Friedman, "Just facts: America's non-existent 'spike in crime'." Brennan Center for Justice (August 10, 2015). Retrieved 12/12/2015 from https://www.brennancenter.org/blog/americas-non-existent-spike-crime.

30. Federal Bureau of Investigation, *Crime in the United States, 2014*. Tables 12. Retrieved 12/12/2015 from https://www.fbi.gov/about-us/cjis/ucr/crime-in-the-u.s/2014/crime-in-the-u.s.-2014.

31. Bureau of Justice Statistics, *Criminal Victimization, 2014*. Office of Justice Programs. Retrieved 12/12/2015 from http://www.bjs.gov/content/pub/pdf/cv14.pdf.

32. L. Bui, A. Phillip and W. Lowery, "Around St. Louis, bloodshed rises in year since Michael Brown was killed." *Washington Post*, August 11, 2015. Retrieved from http://www.washingtonpost.com/national/around-st-louis-bloodshed-rises-in-year-since-michael-brown-was-killed/2015/08/11/b0ea430c-405c-11e5-bfe3-ff1d8549bfd2_story.html?hpid=z7

33. New York Times Editorial Board, "New York policing, by the numbers." *New York Times*, December 28, 2015, p. A18.

34. S. Miletich, "Report cites plunge in SPD enforcement of low-level crime." *Seattle Times*, May 24, 2014. Retrieved 1/3/2016 from http://www.seattletimes.com/seattle-news/report-cites-plunge-in-spd-enforcement-of-low-level-crime/.

35. Scott E. Wolfe and Justin Nix, "The alleged 'Ferguson Effect' and police willingness to engage in community partnership." *Law and Human Behavior*, 2015; DOI: 10.1037/lhb0000164.

36. D. Pyrooz, S. Decker, S. Wolfe and J. Shjarback, "Was there a Ferguson Effect on crime rates in large US cities?" *Journal of Criminal Justice* 46 (2016): 1–16.

37. R. Rosenfeld, *Documenting and Explaining the 2015 Homicide Rise: Research Directions*. Washington, DC: NIJ, OJP, June 2016.

38. R. Rosenfeld, *Documenting and Explaining the 2015 Homicide Rise: Research Directions*. Washington, DC: NIJ, OJP, June 2016.

39. R. Rosenfeld, *Documenting and Explaining the 2015 Homicide Rise: Research Directions*. Washington, DC: NIJ, OJP, June 2016.

# The Scope of Victimology

## WILLIAM G. DOERNER AND STEVEN P. LAB

## Introduction

Something not very funny happened on the way to a formal system of justice. The victim was left out. As strange as it may sound, the bulk of history has seen crime victims become further removed from being an integral part of dealing with criminals. Fortunately, this trend is beginning to reverse itself. Recent years have seen an increased interest in the plight of crime victims and a movement toward reintegrating the victim into the criminal justice system. This chapter will look at the role of the victim throughout history and will trace the elimination of the victim from the social processing of criminal acts. We will see how victimology emerged and we will investigate the resurgence of interest in the victim.

## The Victim Throughout History

Most people take the existence of the formal criminal justice system for granted. They do not realize that this method of handling deviant activity has not been the norm throughout history. Indeed, the modern version of criminal justice is a relatively new phenomenon. In days gone by, responsibility for dealing with offenders fell to the victim and the victim's kin. There were no "authorities" to turn to for help in "enforcing the law." Victims were expected to fend for themselves, and society acceded to this arrangement.

This state of affairs was not outlined in any set of laws or legal code. With rare exceptions, written laws did not exist. Codes of behavior reflected prevailing social norms. Society recognized murder and other serious affronts as *mala in se* (totally unacceptable behavior). However, it was up to victims or their survivors to decide what action to take against the offender. Victims who wished to respond

LEARNING OBJECTIVES

After reading Chapter 3, you should be able to:

- Discuss the change from a victim justice system to a criminal justice system.

- Outline the early interest in victim typologies.

- Account for the attention paid to victim precipitation, some findings, and some shortcomings.

- List the areas that fall under "general victimology."

- Provide an overview of the broad topics which victimologists study.

- Talk about the victim movement and how it has increased public interest in crime victims.

to offenses could not turn to judges for assistance or to jails for punishment. These institutions did not yet exist. Instead, victims had to take matters into their own hands.

This depiction does not imply that there were no provisions for victims to follow. Society recognized a basic system of retribution and restitution for offenders. In simplest terms, *retribution* meant the offender would suffer in proportion to the degree of harm caused by his or her actions. Oftentimes, retribution took the form of *restitution*, or making payment in an amount sufficient to render the victim whole again. If the offender was unable to make restitution, his or her kin were forced to assume the liability.

This response system emphasized the principle known as *lex talionis*—an eye for an eye, a tooth for a tooth. Punishment was commensurate with the harm inflicted upon the victim. Perhaps the most important feature of this system was that victims and their relatives handled the problem and were the beneficiaries of any payments. This arrangement was truly a "victim justice system."

This basic system of dealing with offensive behavior found its way into early codified laws. The Law of Moses, the Code of Hammurabi (2200 B.C.E.), and Roman law all entailed strong elements of individual responsibility for harms committed against others. Restitution and retribution were specific ingredients in many of these early codes. Part of the rationale behind this response was to deter such behavior in the future.

The major goal of *deterrence* is to prevent future transgressions. The thinking is that the lack of any enrichment or gain from criminal activity would make transgressive acts unattractive. Retribution and restitution attempt to re-establish the status quo that existed before the initial action of the offender. Thus, removing financial incentives would make it unprofitable to commit crimes.

This basic system of dealing with offensive behavior remained intact throughout the Middle Ages. Eventually, though, it fell into disuse. Two factors signaled the end of this victim justice system. The first change was the move by feudal barons to lay a claim to any compensation offenders paid to their victims (Schafer, 1968). These rulers saw this money as a lucrative way to increase their own wealth. The barons accomplished this goal by redefining criminal acts as violations against the state instead of against the victim. This strategy recast the state (the barons being the heads of the state) as the aggrieved party. The victim diminished in stature and was relegated to the status of witness for the state. Now the state could step in and reap the benefits of restitution.

A second factor which reduced the victim's position was the enormous upheaval that was transforming society. Up until this time, society was predominantly rural and agrarian. People lived in small groups, eking out an existence from daily labor in the fields. Life was a rustic struggle to meet day-to-day needs.

People, for the most part, were self-sufficient and relied heavily upon their families for assistance. Families often lived in relative isolation from other people. Whenever a crime took place, it brought physical and economic harm not only to the individual victim but also to the entire family network. This simple *gemeinschaft* society (Toennies, 1957) could rely on the individual to handle his or her own problems.

As the Middle Ages drew to a close, the Industrial Revolution created a demand for larger urbanized communities. People took jobs in the new industries, leaving the rural areas and relocating to the cities. They settled into cramped quarters, surrounded by strangers. Neighbors no longer knew the people living next door. As faces blended into crowds, relationships grew more depersonalized. The interpersonal ties that once bound people together had vanished.

As this *gesellschaft* type of society continued to grow, the old victim justice practices crumbled even further. Crime began to threaten the delicate social fabric that now linked people together. At the same time, concern shifted away from making the victim whole to dealing with the criminal. Gradually, the *victim* justice system withered and the *criminal* justice system became its replacement. In fact, some observers would contend that the victim *injustice* system would be a more apt description.

Today, crime victims remain nothing more than witnesses for the state. Victims no longer take matters into their own hands to extract retribution and restitution from their offenders. The victim must call upon society to act. The development of formal law enforcement, courts, and correctional systems in the past few centuries has reflected an interest in protecting the state. For the most part, the criminal justice system simply forgot about victims and their best interests. Instead, the focus shifted to protecting the rights of the accused.

# The Re-Emergence of the Victim

The criminal justice system spends the bulk of its time and energy trying to control criminals. It was within this preoccupation of understanding criminal activity and identifying the causes of criminal behavior that the victim was "rediscovered" in the 1940s. Interestingly, the victim emerged not as an individual worthy of sympathy or compassion but as a possible partner or contributor to his or her own demise. Students of criminal behavior began to look at the relationship between the victim and the offender in the hopes of better understanding the genesis of the criminal act.

As interest in victims began to sprout and attract more scholarly attention, writers began to grapple with a very basic issue. What exactly was victimology? Some people believed that victimology was a specialty area or a subfield within criminology. After all, every criminal event had to include a criminal and a victim, by definition. Others countered that because victimology was so broad and encompassing, it deserved to stand as a separate field or discipline in its own right. They foresaw the day when college catalogs would list victimology as a major area of study along with such pursuits as biology, criminology, psychology, mathematics, and political science.

Early scholarly work in victimology focused considerable energy upon creating victim typologies. A *typology* is an effort to categorize observations into logical groupings to reach a better understanding of our social world (McKinney, 1950, 1969). As we shall see in the following sections, these early theoretical reflections pushed the field in a direction that eventually created an explosive and haunting reaction, nearly crippling this fledgling enterprise.

**WEB ACTIVITY**

The concept of *victim* and the growth of interest in victims may be examined through a range of materials available through the Office for Victims of Crime (**http://www.ojp. gov/ovc**) and the documents in the OVC archive (**http:// ovc.gov/archive/index. html**).

## The Work of Hans von Hentig: *The Criminal and His Victim*

An early pioneer in victimology was a German scholar, Hans von Hentig. As a criminologist, von Hentig spent a great deal of time trying to discover what made a criminal predisposed to being a criminal. As he focused on crime victims, von Hentig began to wonder what it was that made the victim a victim. The key ingredient, according to von Hentig, was the *criminal–victim dyad*.

In an early publication, von Hentig (1941) claimed that the victim was often a contributing cause to the criminal act. One example would be an incident in which the ultimate victim began as the aggressor. However, for some reason, this person wound up becoming the loser in the confrontation. Von Hentig's message was clear. Simply examining the outcome of a criminal event sometimes presents a distorted image of who the real victim is and who the real offender is. A closer inspection of the dynamics underlying the situation might reveal that the victim was a major contributor to his or her own victimization.

Von Hentig expanded upon the notion of the victim as an *agent provocateur* in a later book called *The Criminal and His Victim*. He explained that "increased attention should be paid to the crime-provocative function of the victim. ... With a thorough knowledge of the interrelations between doer and sufferer new approaches to the detection of crime will be opened" (1948: 450).

Von Hentig was not naive enough to believe that all victim contribution to crime was active. Much victim contribution results from characteristics or social positions beyond the control of the individual. As a result, von Hentig classified victims into 13 categories depending on their propensity for victimization (see Table 3.1).

**TABLE 3.1    Hans von Hentig's Victim Typology**

| Type | Example |
|------|---------|
| 1. The Young | Children and infants |
| 2. The Female | All women |
| 3. The Old | Elderly persons |
| 4. The Mentally Defective and Deranged | The feeble-minded, the insane, drug addicts, alcoholics |
| 5. Immigrants | Foreigners unfamiliar with the culture |
| 6. Minorities | Racially disadvantaged persons |
| 7. Dull Normals | Simple-minded persons |
| 8. The Depressed | Persons with various psychological maladies |
| 9. The Acquisitive | The greedy, those looking for quick gains |
| 10. The Wanton | Promiscuous persons |
| 11. The Lonesome and the Heartbroken | Widows, widowers, and those in mourning |
| 12. The Tormentor | An abusive parent |
| 13. The Blocked, Exempted, or Fighting | Victims of blackmail, extortion, confidence games |

*Source*: Adapted from von Hentig (1948: 404–438).

Many of von Hentig's victim types reflect the inability to resist a perpetrator due to physical, social, or psychological disadvantages. For example, very young people, females, and elderly persons are more likely to lack the physical power to resist offenders. Immigrants and minorities, due to cultural differences, may feel they are outside the mainstream of society. This lack of familiarity may lead them into situations in which criminals prey upon them. Individuals who are mentally defective or deranged, "dull normal," depressed, lonely, or blocked may not understand what is occurring around them or may be unable to resist. The acquisitive person and the tormentor are individuals who, due to their own desires, are either directly involved in the criminal act or place themselves in situations in which there is a clear potential for victimization.

The typology von Hentig created does not imply that the victim is always the primary cause of the criminal act. What he does suggest is that victim characteristics may contribute to the victimization episode. According to von Hentig (1948: iii), we must realize that "the victim is taken as one of the determinants, and that a nefarious symbiosis is often established between doer and sufferer."

## The Work of Beniamin Mendelsohn: Further Reflections

Some observers credit Beniamin Mendelsohn, a practicing attorney, with being the "father" of victimology. Indeed, he coined the term *victimology*. Mendelsohn, like von Hentig, was intrigued by the dynamics that take place between victims and offenders. Before preparing a case he would ask victims, witnesses, and bystanders in the situation to complete a detailed and probing questionnaire. After examining these responses, Mendelsohn discovered that there was usually a strong interpersonal relationship between victims and offenders. Using these data, Mendelsohn (1956) outlined a six-step classification of victims based on legal considerations of the degree of the victim's blame (see Table 3.2).

Mendelsohn's types range from the *completely innocent victim*, who exhibited no provocative or facilitating behavior prior to the offender's attack, to the victim who is *more guilty than the offender*, because the victim instigates or provokes the criminal act. The person who comes out on the losing end of a punch after making an abusive remark or goading the other party would fit this description. The *most guilty victim* is one who entered the situation as the offender and, owing to circumstances beyond his or her control, ended up as the victim. Mendelsohn's classification is useful primarily for identifying the relative culpability of the victim in the criminal act.

**TABLE 3.2   Mendelsohn's Victim Types**

| | |
|---|---|
| Completely Innocent Victim | No provocation or facilitating behavior |
| Victim with Minor Guilt | Victim inadvertently places him- or herself in a compromising situation |
| Victim as Guilty as Offender | Victim was engaging in vice crimes and was hurt; suicide victim |
| Victim More Guilty than Offender | Victim provokes or instigates the causal act |
| Most Guilty Victim | Started off as the offender and was hurt in turn |
| Imaginary Victim | Those who pretend to be a victim |

*Source*: Mendelsohn (1956).

## The Work of Stephen Schafer: *The Victim and His Criminal*

Scholarly interest in victims and the role they played in their own demise evoked little interest throughout the 1950s and 1960s. Stephen Schafer, in a playful twist on Hans von Hentig's seminal work, revisited the victim's role in his book *The Victim and His Criminal*. The key concept that undergirded Schafer's thinking was what he termed *functional responsibility*. Once again, the victim–offender relationship came under scrutiny.

As Table 3.3 shows, Schafer (1968) provided a typology that builds upon victim responsibility for the crime. In many respects, Schafer's groupings are a variation of those proposed by von Hentig (1948). The difference between the two schemes is primarily one of emphasis on the culpability of the victim. Where von Hentig's listing identifies varying risk factors, Schafer explicitly sets forth the responsibility of different victims.

## Other Scholarly Efforts

Von Hentig, Mendelsohn, and Schafer were not the only persons to produce significant analyses regarding victims during this time. Most assuredly, some other scholars began recognizing the importance of a victim-based orientation. These early attempts to probe the victim–offender relationship signaled the beginning of a renewed academic interest in the victim.

**TABLE 3.3   Schafer's Victim Precipitation Typology**

| | |
|---|---|
| 1. Unrelated Victims (no victim responsibility) | Instances in which the victim is simply the unfortunate target of the offender |
| 2. Provocative Victims (victim shares responsibility) | The offender is reacting to some action or behavior of the victim |
| 3. Precipitative Victims (some degree of victim responsibility) | Victims leave themselves open for victimization by placing themselves in dangerous places or times, dressing inappropriately, acting, or saying the wrong things, etc. |
| 4. Biologically Weak Victims (no victim responsibility) | The aged, young, infirm, and others who, due to their physical conditions, are appealing targets for offenders |
| 5. Socially Weak Victims (no victim responsibility) | Immigrants, minorities, and others who are not adequately integrated into society and are seen as easy targets by offenders |
| 6. Self-Victimizing (total victim responsibility) | Individuals involved in such crimes as drug use, prostitution, gambling, and other activities in which the victim and the criminal act in concert with one another |
| 7. Political Victims (no victim responsibility) | Individuals who are victimized because they oppose those in power or are made victims in order to be kept in a subservient social position |

*Source*: Adapted from Schafer (1968).

This concern, however, was lopsided. The early victimologists generally failed to look at the damage which offenders inflicted upon their victims, ignored victim recuperative or rehabilitative efforts, and bypassed a host of other concerns. In an attempt to understand the causes of crime, they concentrated on how the victim contributed to his or her demise. Eventually, the idea of victim precipitation emerged from this preoccupation with "blaming the victim." As we shall see later in this chapter, the assumption that somehow the victim shared responsibility for or instigated the criminal episode would spark a major ideological confrontation and would temporarily paralyze the field.

# Empirical Studies of Victim Precipitation

*Victim precipitation* deals with the degree to which the victim is responsible for his or her own victimization. That involvement may be either passive (as much of von Hentig's typology suggests) or active (as seen in Mendelsohn's classification). Each typology presented in this chapter implicates victim contribution as a causative factor in the commission of a crime. However, the first systematic attempt to provide empirical support of this argument was Wolfgang's (1958) analysis of police homicide records. A few years later, one of Wolfgang's students, Menachem Amir, applied this framework to forcible rape cases. His formulation and interpretation quickly met with a barrage of stinging criticism.

## The Work of Marvin E. Wolfgang: *Patterns in Criminal Homicide*

Using homicide data from the city of Philadelphia, Wolfgang reported that 26 percent of the homicides that occurred from 1948 through 1952 resulted from victim precipitation. Wolfgang (1958: 252) defined victim-precipitated homicide as those instances in which the ultimate victim was:

> the first in the homicide drama to use physical force directed against his subsequent slayer. The victim-precipitated cases are those in which the victim was the first to show and use a deadly weapon, to strike a blow in an altercation—in short, the first to commence the interplay of resort to physical violence.

Wolfgang identified several factors as typical of victim-precipitated homicides. First, the victim and the offender usually had some prior interpersonal relationship. Typical examples include relationships of spouses, boyfriends, girlfriends, family members, and close friends or acquaintances. In other words, victims were more likely to die at the hands of someone they knew rather than from the actions of a complete stranger.

Second, the homicide act is often the product of a small disagreement that escalates until the situation bursts out of control. That change in degree could be either short-term or the result of a longer, drawn-out confrontation. For instance:

> A husband had beaten his wife on several previous occasions. In the present instance, she insisted that he take her to the hospital. He refused, and a violent quarrel followed, during which he slapped her several times, and she concluded by stabbing him.

> (Wolfgang, 1958: 253)

Third, alcohol consumption by the victim is a common ingredient in many victim-precipitated homicides. Several possibilities surface here. It may be that as intoxicated persons lose their inhibitions, they vocalize their feelings more readily. Eventually, these inebriated parties grow more obnoxious and belligerent and unwittingly provoke their assailants into a deadly confrontation. Another alternative is that alcohol consumption renders these people so impaired that they lose the physical ability to defend themselves in a skirmish. In any event, Wolfgang (1958: 265) points out that "connotations of a victim as a weak and passive individual, seeking to withdraw from an assaultive situation, and of an offender as a brutal, strong, and overly aggressive person seeking out his victim, are not always correct."

## The Work of Menachem Amir: *Patterns in Forcible Rape*

Several years later, Menachem Amir undertook what perhaps became the most controversial empirical analysis of rape. Amir (1971) gathered information from police records on rape incidents that took place in Philadelphia between 1958 and 1960. Based on details contained in the files, he claimed that 19 percent of all forcible rapes were victim precipitated.

According to Amir (1971: 266), victim-precipitated rape referred to those situations in which:

the victim actually, or so it was deemed, agreed to sexual relations but retracted before the actual act or did not react strongly enough when the suggestion was made by the offender. The term applies also to cases in risky situations marred with sexuality, especially when she uses what could be interpreted as indecency in language and gestures, or constitutes what could be taken as an invitation to sexual relations.

Amir proceeded to list a variety of factors that helped precipitate the criminal act. Similar to Wolfgang's homicide findings, alcohol use—particularly by the victim—was a major factor in a precipitated rape. The risk of sexual victimization intensified if both parties had been drinking.

Other important factors include seductive actions by the victim, wearing revealing clothing, using risqué language, having a "bad" reputation, and being in the wrong place at the wrong time. According to Amir, such behaviors could tantalize the offender to the point that he simply "misreads" the victim's overtures. At one point, Amir (1971) even suggested that some victims may have an unconscious need to be sexually controlled through rape.

In the concluding remarks of the section on victim precipitation, Amir (1971: 275–276) commented:

These results point to the fact that the offender should not be viewed as the sole "cause" and reason for the offense, and that the "virtuous" victim is not always the innocent and passive party. Thus, the role played by the victim and its contribution to the perpetration of the offense becomes one of the main interests of the emerging discipline of victimology.

## Criticisms and Reactions

The notion of victim precipitation, particularly regarding Amir's claims about rape, came under swift attack. Weis and Borges (1973; Weis, 1976), for example, attributed Amir's conclusions to faults implicit in relying on police accounts, to a host of procedural errors, and to ill-conceived theoretical notions. For example, Amir suggested that victims may *psychologically* prompt or desire the rape as a means of rebelling against accepted standards of behavior. In contrast, though, the male is simply responding to *social* cues from the female. Interestingly, Amir does not provide any justification for why female behavior stems from psychological factors while male actions derive from social variables. Amir's study attracted blistering rebuttals from academic quarters along with enraged reactions from women's groups and victim advocates. This reception made many victimologists very uncomfortable with the precipitation argument as it had developed to that point.

Cooler heads soon prevailed. Rather than abandoning the idea of victim precipitation, some scholars began a more sensitive probing. Curtis (1974), for one, suggested that what was needed was a more accurate definition of victim precipitation. For example, one set of researchers might define hitchhiking as a precipitating factor. Other studies may not make such a blanket assumption or may view hitchhiking as substantively different from other precipitating actions.

A more productive approach came from a critical examination of the underpinnings of the victim-precipitation argument. Franklin and Franklin (1976) exposed four major assumptions behind this victimological approach (see Box 3.1). First, victim precipitation assumes that the behavior of the victim can explain the criminal act. However, some factors often identified as precipitous also appear in instances where no criminal act takes place. For example, many people go to bars at night. Sometimes they drink excessively and then stagger home alone without becoming victimized. Thus, supposedly precipitating acts are not enough, in and of themselves, to cause criminal behavior.

Second, victim precipitation assumes that the offender becomes activated only when the victim emits certain signals. This belief ignores the fact that many offenders plan their offenses ahead of time and do not simply react to another person's behavior. For these criminals, crime is a rational, planned enterprise.

Third, Franklin and Franklin (1976) disagree with the assumption that a victim's behavior is necessary and sufficient to trigger the commission of a criminal act. In fact, the opposite is probably closer to the truth. Many offenders commit crimes despite any specific action by the victim. Others will not seize the opportunity to commit a crime, for whatever reason, although a potential victim presents him- or herself.

Finally, victim precipitation arguments assume that the intent of the victim can be gauged by the victimization incident. Unfortunately, if intent is equivalent to action, there would be no need for criminal court proceedings beyond the infallible identification of the person who perpetrated the crime. Our criminal justice system, however, explicitly assumes possible variation in intent, regardless of the action.

Although each of these assumptions shows how the victim precipitation argument falters, there is a much larger issue requiring attention. Studies of victim involvement tend to be myopic; that is, they do not address the offender. Instead, they imply that all offenders are equal in their drive and

---

## BOX 3.1 Problematic Assumptions of Victim Precipitation

- The behavior of the victim may explain the criminal act.
- The offender becomes activated only when a victim emits certain signals.
- A victim's behavior is necessary and sufficient to cause a criminal act.
- The intent of the victim may be gauged by the victimization incident.

*Source*: Compiled by the authors, from Franklin & Franklin (1976).

desire to engage in deviant activity. This assumption, however, is untenable. Some offenders may actively hunt for the right situation, while others display little or no prior intent. What was needed was an integrated approach that would take both the victim and the offender into account.

Curtis (1974) attempted to do just this when he outlined a simple grid that allows the degree of victim precipitation to vary. As Table 3.4 shows, Curtis merged victim provocation with offender intent. This strategy results in recognizing five degrees of precipitation, ranging from pure victim precipitation to total offender responsibility. This presentation shows that even in the position of clear outright provocation by the victim, the offender may still be an equally responsible partner in the final outcome. What is important to remember here is that, at best, one should conceive of victim precipitation as a contributing factor and, certainly, not as the predominant force.

# A New Approach: General Victimology

The preoccupation with victim precipitation, along with its divisiveness and ensuing fragmentation, threatened to stagnate this fledgling area of interest. The lack of theoretical advances brought genuine worries from some quarters that victimology was becoming bogged down in an academic quagmire (Bruinsma & Fiselier, 1982; Levine, 1978). In response to this situation, Beniamin Mendelsohn called for victimology to move out of the provincial backwaters of criminology and into its own rightful domain. Mendelsohn attempted to assure victimology of its independence from criminology by devising the term *general victimology*.

According to Mendelsohn (1982: 59), victimologists aim to "investigate the causes of victimization in search of effective remedies." Because human beings suffer from many causal factors, focusing on criminal victimization is too narrow a perspective. A more global term, like *general victimology*, is needed to convey the true meaning of the field.

According to Mendelsohn (1976), *general victimology* subsumes five types of victims. They include victims of:

- a criminal;
- one's self;
- the social environment;

---

**TABLE 3.4    The Precipitation Grid Outlining the Relative Responsibility of Both Victim and Offender**

| Degree of Offender Intent | Degree of Victim Involvement | | |
| --- | --- | --- | --- |
| | Clear Provocation | Some Involvement | Little or No Involvement |
| Deliberate premeditation | Equal | More offender | Total offender responsibility |
| Some intent | More victim | Equal | More offender |
| Little or no intent | Pure victim precipitation | More victim | Equal |

*Source*: Adapted from Curtis (1974: 35).

- technology;
- the natural environment.

The first category (crime victims) is self-explanatory. It refers to the traditional subject matter that victimologists have grown accustomed to studying. Self-victimization would include suicide as well as any other suffering induced by the victims themselves. The term *victims of the social environment* incorporates individual, class, or group oppression. Some common examples would include racial discrimination, caste relations, genocide, and war atrocities. Technological victims are people who fall prey to society's reliance on scientific innovations. Nuclear accidents, improperly tested medicines, industrial pollution, and transportation mishaps provide fodder for this category. Finally, victims of the natural environment would embrace those persons affected by such events as floods, earthquakes, hurricanes, and famine.

In line with Mendelsohn's formulations, Smith and Weis (1976) proposed a broad overview of the areas encompassed by general victimology. As Figure 3.1 illustrates, there are four major areas

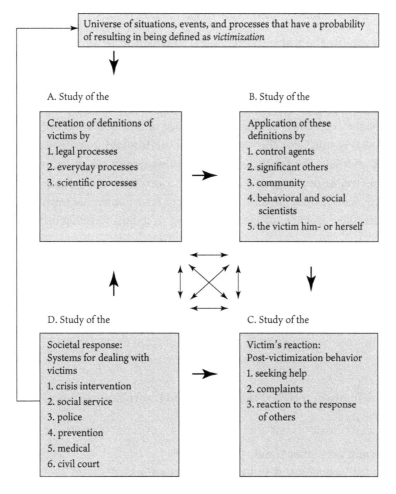

**FIGURE 3.1** General model of the areas of research and application in the field of victimology

*Source*: Smith & Weis (1976: 45).

of concern. They include the creation of definitions of victims, the application of these definitions, victim reactions during the post-victimization period, and societal reactions to victims.

When viewed in this context, general victimology becomes a very broad enterprise with extensive implications. As Mendelsohn (1976: 21) explains:

> Just as medicine treats all patients and all diseases, just as criminology concerns itself with all criminals and all forms of crime, so victimology must concern itself with all victims and all aspects of victimity in which society takes an interest.

# Critical Victimology

One trend in victimology since the 1990s is the call to shift focus from the more general approach outlined in the preceding section to what some people call *critical victimology*. Proponents of this move maintain that victimology fails to question the basic foundations of what crime is, overlooks the question of why certain acts are sanctioned, and, consequently, has developed in the wrong direction. Mawby and Walklate (1994: 21) define *critical victimology* as:

> an attempt to examine the wider social context in which some versions of victimology have become more dominant than others and also to understand how those versions of victimology are interwoven with questions of policy response and service delivery to victims of crime.

Central to critical victimology, therefore, is the issue of how and why certain actions are defined as criminal and, as a result, how the entire field of victimology becomes focused on one set of actions instead of another. The result, according to this line of thinking, is a set of blinders that causes victimologists to neglect important issues, restricts their interests, and takes an overly conservative approach. Rather than curtailing attention to traditional concerns, critical victimologists would be more interested in expanding the field so as to include, among other things, some of the following topics:

- genocide;
- war crimes;
- bribery of government officials and political campaign law violations;
- clandestine arms sales and weapons of mass destruction;
- corporate involvement in ecocide and environmental degradation;
- smuggling;
- piracy;
- trading human organs on the black market and transplant tourism;
- human slave trade;
- deportation;
- investment and consumer fraud;
- the market for archeological and antiquities treasures;
- human rights violations.

Under critical victimology, most victim-oriented initiatives tend to perpetuate the existing definitions of crime by failing to question the supportive social factors that give rise to the action and the response (Elias, 1990). The reason for this failure is multifaceted. One contributing factor is the reliance on official definitions and data in most analyses of victim issues. This inevitably leads to solutions that do not question the underlying social setting. Another factor is the ability of existing agencies to co-opt and incorporate emerging movements (such as children's rights) into existing social control systems. A more radical argument posits that the control of criminal justice and victimology rests in the hands of a powerful few who would view a critical approach as a threat to the status quo.

While critical victimology offers an interesting viewpoint and carries great potential for the field, debating its merits is beyond the scope of this text. Instead, we have elected to develop a unique orientation, which we will unveil at the end of this chapter, and which provides a distinct prism with which to view the field. Various points throughout this book, however, will raise issues that are relevant to a critical approach. Examples include sociocultural discussions of why violence occurs and investigations of impediments to victim programs. A deeper and more intense examination of critical victimology will be left for other forums.

# The Victim Movement

While academicians were debating the victim-precipitation argument, practitioners had pinpointed the victim as someone who deserved assistance from society and the criminal justice system. To some extent, this grassroots concern for the victim's well-being was a reaction to the charges of victim complicity in the offense. Several different movements occurred simultaneously and contributed to the renewed interest in the plight of the victim. Among them were: (1) the women's movement; (2) efforts to establish children's rights; (3) concerns over the growing crime problem; (4) the advocacy of victim compensation; (5) legal reforms; and (6) some other factors. While we will devote greater attention to these areas in Part 3 of this book, what follows is an abridged rendition of some of these developments.

## The Women's Movement

The women's movement, especially in the mid- to late 1960s, included a large component dealing with victims. Victim-blaming arguments often dealt with rape and sexual assault. The female victim found herself and her lifestyle on trial whenever an offender was apprehended. Reformers complained that the system dealt with sexual assault victims as if they themselves were the offenders. Advocates pushed for equal treatment. They found the actions of the criminal justice system to be strong ammunition for their arguments. Beyond simply calling for changes in the formal system of justice, the women's movement made many gains. A short list would include the development of rape crisis centers, shelters for battered women, counseling for abused women and their children, and other forms of assistance. As women demanded an equal place in society, they worked to overcome the disadvantages of the criminal justice system.

## Children's Rights

A growing concern over the needs and rights of youths blossomed during the 1960s. Many writers point to the mid-1960s as the time when child abuse was "discovered." It was around this time that society decided to define abuse against children as a social problem. However, that does not mean that child abuse was a new phenomenon. Child abuse is an age-old practice and, by many accounts, may have been much worse in the past than today. The difference in the 1960s, however, was that many physical and psychological actions used with children began to be questioned and labeled as abuse. States enacted legislation outlining the limits to which a child could be physically "disciplined." Specific children's bureaus within criminal justice agencies were either established or expanded to deal with the growing recognition of child maltreatment. Shelters were created to house children from abusive situations.

Runaways also gained publicity as a serious problem in the late 1960s. The general rebellion of youths in the U.S.A. enticed many juveniles to seek freedom from authority. Consequently, runaway shelters appeared in most large cities for the purpose of assisting the youths rather than returning them to their homes. Children were emerging as a new class of victims—both of abuse at home and of society in general.

## The Growing Crime Problem

The level of crime in the U.S.A. began to register giant strides in the 1960s and throughout the 1970s. According to Uniform Crime Reports (UCR) data, crime in the U.S.A. more than doubled from 1960 to 1980. Along with concern over the Vietnam War, crime was the most important issue of the day. Presidential and local elections targeted the problem of law and order as a major concern. In an attempt to identify the causes of the growing problem and possible solutions, President Johnson appointed a commission to examine crime and the criminal justice system. Victim issues were a major focus of the 1967 President's Commission on Law Enforcement and the Administration of Justice. Among the victim components of the commission report (1967) were the beginnings of systematic victimization surveys, suggestions for the means of alleviating the pain and loss of victims, ideas for community programs aimed at providing victim services, and calls for involving victims further in the criminal justice system.

Some 15 years after this report was aired, another national task force concluded that victims still had substantial needs that were going unfulfilled. Many of the identified problems were similar to those noted by the earlier commission.

## Victim Compensation

One suggestion made by the President's Commission (1967) was the establishment of methods for reimbursing crime victims for their losses. Among these techniques were restitution and *victim compensation*. Neither of these ideas, however, originated with the Commission. As was mentioned earlier in this chapter, restitution was the common method for dealing with crime throughout most of history. Victim compensation (state payments made to crime victims) was first introduced in Great Britain by Margery Fry in 1957. Although that early attempt failed, victim compensation quickly became a major issue around the world.

New Zealand passed the first compensation legislation in 1963, closely followed by England in 1964. In the U.S.A., California established victim compensation in 1965, New York in 1966, Hawaii in 1967, and Massachusetts in 1968. The federal government enacted legislation in 1984 that outlined compensation in instances where federal crimes were committed. The statute also provided for monetary assistance to states with compensation programs. By 1989, 45 states had enacted compensation statutes. Other countries, such as Australia and Finland, have also established compensation programs. While each program may differ in its particulars, the basic premise of assisting crime victims remains the same.

## Legal Reforms

In addition to the establishment of compensation legislation, a variety of legal reforms aimed at protecting and helping crime victims began to appear during the 1960s. Among the changes that emerged were statutes that protected the rape victim's background and character in court proceedings. New laws were designed to help battered spouses and their children. Legislation mandating that doctors and teachers report suspected cases of child abuse represented a bold initiative. Guidelines for informing victims about court proceedings and the legal system, as well as provisions that allowed victim impact statements in sentencing and parole decisions, began to surface. In some instances, states passed a "Victims' Bill of Rights." These provisions outlined the rights of the victim in a manner similar to those appearing in the U.S. Bill of Rights, which focuses on protections for the accused (see Table 3.5 for more recent developments).

## Other Factors

Other factors have played either a direct or an indirect role in emphasizing victim issues. One such source of influence has been the mass media. Rarely a week goes by in which a "crime of the week" does not appear in a special movie or as part of an ongoing series. Shows such as *America's Most Wanted* portray not only the offender but also the harm to the victim, often relying on interviews with the victim or the victim's family. Such media attention and interest in the victim naturally influence viewers in the audience.

Another aspect not to be overlooked is the increasing interest in victims among academics. Five decades ago there were virtually no books focusing specifically on victims. The publication of Schafer's (1968) *The Victim and His Criminal* signaled an era of increasing interest in victimology. Many texts have appeared since then. They range from general victim topics to specific discussions of compensation, intimate partner violence, child abuse, victim services, and other areas of interest. The first International Symposium on Victimology was held in Jerusalem in 1973. Since then, there have been dozens more worldwide gatherings and an uncounted number of national, state, and local meetings of academics and professionals working with crime victims. These efforts culminated in the

**WEB ACTIVITY**

While we will examine victim compensation in depth later in the book, you can take a look at this approach and investigate its impact on victimology at the National Association of Crime Victim Compensation Boards (**http://www.nacvcb.org**); the Office for Victims of Crime (**http://ovc.ncjrs.gov/topic.aspx?topicid=58**).

**TABLE 3.5  Examples of Landmark Federal Victims' Rights Legislation Enacted from 2006 through 2015**

| | |
|---|---|
| 2001 | *Air Transportation Safety and System Stabilization Act* |
| | Created a new federal victim compensation program specifically for the victims of September 11. The program includes many types of damages normally available only through civil actions, such as payment for pain and suffering, lifetime lost earnings, and loss of enjoyment of life. |
| 2003 | *PROTECT Act ("Amber Alert" Law)* |
| | Created a national AMBER network to facilitate rapid law enforcement and community response to kidnapped or abducted children. |
| 2003 | *Fair and Accurate Credit Transactions Act* |
| | Provided new protections against identity theft and helped victims of identity theft recover their financial losses. |
| 2004 | *Justice for All Act* |
| | Provided mechanisms at the federal level to enforce the rights of crime victims, giving victims and prosecutors legal standing to assert victims' rights, authorizing the filing of writs of mandamus to assert a victim's right, and requiring the Attorney General to establish a victims' rights compliance program within the Department of Justice. |
| 2006 | *Adam Walsh Child Protection and Safety Act* |
| | Increased supervision of sex offenders; also extended the federal Crime Victims' Rights Act to federal habeas corpus proceedings arising out of state convictions, eliminated the statute of limitations for federal prosecution of sexual offenses or child abduction, and extended the civil remedy for child sex crime victims to persons victimized as children, even if their injuries did not surface until the person became an adult. |
| 2008 | *Protect Our Children Act* |
| | Improved the ability of law enforcement to prosecute child predators. |
| 2008 | *Identity Theft Enhancement and Restitution Act* |
| | Permits courts to order restitution to cybercrime victims. |
| 2009 | *Matthew Shepard and James Byrd, Jr. Hate Crimes Prevention Act* |
| | Changes the federal definition of hate crimes to include crimes based on sexual orientation, gender identity, or disability. |
| 2012 | *Uniform Crime Reports Changes Definition of Rape* |
| | Victim or perpetrator can be any gender, and defines instances in which the victim is incapable of giving consent because of temporary or permanent mental or physical incapacity. |
| 2013 | *Violence Against Women Reauthorization Act* |
| | Expands protections for lesbian, gay, bisexual, and transgender survivors; provides funding for developing responses to violence against women. Requires jurisdictions to provide examinations to sexual assault victims free of charge. |
| 2013 | *SAFER Act* |
| | Provides grants to analyze backlogged sexual assault kits. |

| 2013 | *Trafficking Victims Protection Act Reauthorization* |
|------|------|
| | It is a crime to destroy, conceal, or confiscate someone's passport for more than 48 hours for the purpose of smuggling or controlling that person. |
| 2014 | *National Defense Authorization Act* |
| | Addresses sexual assault reforms in the military. |
| 2014 | *White House Task Force to Protect Students from Sexual Assault* |
| | Establishes a task force to prevent violence and support victims of sexual assault on college campuses. |
| 2014 | *Victims of Child Abuse Reauthorization Act* |
| | Funds children's advocacy centers and the development of multidisciplinary child abuse investigation and prosecution programs. |
| 2015 | *Preventing Sex Trafficking and Strengthening Families Act* |
| | Requires states to develop policies and procedures to identify, document, screen, and determine appropriate services for children in foster care who are victims of sex trafficking. |
| 2015 | *White House Conference on Aging Convened* |
| | Reflects on issues affecting America's seniors. |
| 2015 | *The Center for Changing Our Campus Culture* |
| | Launches a clearing house of resources related to sexual assault, domestic violence, dating violence, and stalking on campus. |

*Source*: Compiled by the authors, from the U.S. Department of Justice (2016b) and Fisher & Lab (2010).

establishment of the American Society of Victimology in 2003. The spurt in college courses devoted to victimology or topical victim issues is encouraging. Some campuses (e.g., California State University–Fresno, Sam Houston State University, University of New Haven) now offer specialized programs in victim services. Box 3.2 lists a variety of specialty journals devoted to victim issues that now exist. In short, the victim movement has made strides over a relatively short period and continues to gain momentum.

## BOX 3.2 Selected Journals Devoted to Victim Issues

*Child Abuse & Neglect*
*Child Maltreatment*
*Homicide Studies*
*International Review of Victimology*
*Journal of Child Sexual Abuse*
*Journal of Elder Abuse & Neglect*
*Journal of Family Violence*

*Journal of Interpersonal Violence*
*Trauma, Violence, & Abuse*
*Victims & Offenders*
*Violence Against Women*
*Violence & Abuse Abstracts*
*Violence and Victims*

**WEB ACTIVITY**

John Dussich offers a good discussion and overview of the development of victimology and key concepts in the field. Look over his comments at **www.unafei.or.jp/ english/pdf/RS_No70/ No70_12VE_Dussich.pdf.**

# An Overview of This Book

As you have read, Mendelsohn (1976) saw general victimology as addressing five distinct types of victims. In addition to crime victims, he listed self-victimization, social victims, technological victims, and victims of the natural environment as legitimate focal concerns. All these victims suffer some degree of social or physical pain or loss. Each deserves assistance to offset the devastating effects of the victimization episode.

While Mendelsohn's vision of general victimology is quite impressive, it does cover a huge territory. Because Mendelsohn's approach is such a large undertaking, we will confine ourselves to a more manageable task. For that reason, this text must restrict itself to only the first category: crime victims. By the time you finish this book, we think you will agree with us. Victimology is so broad and complex that it makes sense to look at it in slices.

A glimpse of what lies ahead in the upcoming pages will reveal a unique and very different orientation compared to what most readers might expect to encounter. The overarching theme this book pursues is the idea that the American approach to the pursuit of justice is currently in the midst of a dramatic transition. It is moving away from a "criminal's justice system" and embracing more of a "victim's justice system." This distinction is not just one of semantics. It is intended to stimulate critical thinking and to impart a deeper appreciation of how the search for justice continues to evolve. A few key points emerge here that will hopefully whet the reader's appetite until we are able to establish a solid foundation.

First, take note of the intentional, and not so subtle, switch in the terms used here. Instead of relying mindlessly on the default phrase "the criminal justice system," we prefer the more vivid possessive format to capture the reader's attention. The harsh reality is that the halls of justice actually reflect the dominion of the "criminal's justice system." For more than two centuries now, the pursuit of justice in this country has highlighted offender rights and neglected victim interests. This justice apparatus has been contoured to safeguard and protect the rights of the accused. Your authors absolutely understand the importance of the federal Constitution to this endeavor. That document was purposively designed to insulate citizens from the unbridled power of government. Our reliance on the term "the criminal's justice system" does not deviate from this viewpoint. Instead, it brings that preoccupation squarely to the forefront.

Second, we are all indebted to the guiding principles that undergird the Constitution. Jurists have toiled long and hard to reach a number of interpretations detailing just what those words actually mean. However, your authors sincerely question whether the Framers intended for these protections to come at the expense of one group over another. In other words, the "criminal's justice system" effectively disenfranchises law-abiding citizens who are unfortunate enough to have sustained damages as a result of criminal deeds.

Third, the term "criminal's justice system" inevitably spawns the notion of a "victim's injustice system." A true justice system does not champion the rights of any one particular party. It does not devalue the plight or suffering of victims. Instead, an actual justice system seeks an equitable balance for all the involved parties.

These considerations make sense if one thinks about the system as a pendulum. The task of protecting the rights of the accused lies at one extreme. Advocating on behalf of crime victims occupies the other side. As the pendulum swings away from a preoccupation with offender rights, it begins to gravitate toward victim rights. The real task is to locate that delicate balance which lies somewhere between these two extremes.

What your authors strive to do in this book is to introduce the reader to this transition from the "criminal's justice system" to the "victim's justice system." Victimology was in its infancy when we wrote the first edition of this book some two decades ago. The field has matured immensely since then. Our task is to provide readers with a backdrop they can use to view these changes.

This book is divided into three sections. That strategy will allow us to pursue these themes in greater detail. This first chapter has already laid the foundation for a host of issues and ideas that we will take up in greater detail in later chapters. Many topics will appear in the context of more than one discussion. Chapter 2 examines methods for measuring victimization, particularly the development of victimization surveys. Victim surveys have become a key measure of crime and contribute a great deal of information to the study of victimization. However, you will notice that the first victimization survey took place in 1967. What this means is that victimization surveys are still in a youthful stage. Adjustments became necessary, and it took a number of years to refine this technique. So when we ask a question along the lines of "Do victims of child abuse and neglect grow up to mistreat their children?," we have to realize that the field is not yet old enough to have tracked two generations of people and offer clues as to how to answer this query.

Part 2 of the book addresses the impact of victimization. The theme we cultivate here is that victims sustain two distinct sets of losses. First, they suffer as a direct result of their criminal victimization. Then, when victims turn to the justice system for redress, they continue to absorb more losses. Eventually, victims come to realize that the quest for justice merely compounds their losses. At that point, a sizable proportion of participants resolve not to relive those same experiences in the event of a future victimization. Instead, they will avoid any prolonged contact with the "criminal's justice system." System representatives came to the realization that the focus on the "criminal's justice system" was depleting the ranks of cooperative citizens. As a result, they began to introduce reforms intended to offset this burden.

In order to show how these experiences unfold, Chapter 3 looks at the costs associated with being a crime victim and the additional burdens that result from becoming involved with the criminal justice system. As you will see, many people wrongly assume that victims do not cooperate with the authorities because of apathy. This chapter will demonstrate that the real reason reflects a very sensible cost–benefit analysis. Sometimes it is just too costly and too painful to be a "model citizen." Chapter 4 examines financial remedies for victimization intended to help lure victims back into the "criminal's justice system." Included here are discussions of restitution, civil court, and victim compensation. Chapter 5 focuses on addressing the non-financial impact of victimization. The chapter addresses the emergence of restorative justice as well as the development of victim-witness projects within the criminal's justice system. Chapter 6 traces the development of victims' rights and discusses the growth of legislation that mandates a role for victims in the system that is not limited to them being just a witness for the state.

The third and final section of the book continues to rely on the notion that we are seeing a transition from the "criminal's justice system" to the "victim's justice system." After showing how each specific type of victimization has become formally recognized, the chapters go on to explain the extent of these kinds of victimizations, present theoretical notions that help us reach a fuller understanding of the phenomenon, and discuss how the justice system has crafted various policies to help remedy past shortcomings. After examining traditional crimes handled by the criminal justice system, the book moves on to topics that include sexual battery, intimate partner violence, child maltreatment, elderly abuse, and hate crimes. Victimization that takes place on school campuses and in the workplace is discussed in the final two chapters.

In short, we hope to convince readers that, while the system has not completed the transformation from a "criminal's justice system" to a "victim's justice system," it has made and continues to make a substantial number of inroads intended to ease the plight of victims.

## KEY TERMS

| | |
|---|---|
| agent provocateur | lex talionis |
| criminal–victim dyad | mala in se |
| critical victimology | restitution |
| deterrence | retribution |
| gemeinschaft | typology |
| general victimology | victim compensation |
| gesellschaft | victim precipitation |

## CRITICAL THINKING EXERCISES

1. A common occurrence of criminal behavior that takes place on college campuses everywhere is the problem of theft. Do the typologies outlined in this chapter help you reach a better understanding of this behavior? Why or why not?

2. Suppose that you are going to conduct a research project about the problem of theft on campus. You have decided to mirror the approaches taken by Wolfgang (*Patterns in Criminal Homicide*) and Amir (*Patterns in Forcible Rape*) and have titled your forthcoming report "Patterns of Campus Theft." What types of things would you look at and why? What types of things would you avoid?

# Bibliography

Amir, M. (1971). *Patterns in forcible rape*. Chicago, IL: University of Chicago Press.

Bruinsma, G. J. N., & Fiselier, J. P. S. (1982). The poverty of victimology. In H. J. Schneider (ed.), *The victim in international perspective*. New York: Walter de Gruyter & Company.

Chilton, R. (2010). Uniform Crime Reporting (UCR) program. In B. S. Fisher & S. P. Lab (eds), *Encyclopedia of victimology and crime prevention*. Los Angeles, CA: Sage.

Curtis, L. A. (1974). *Criminal violence: National patterns and behavior*. Lexington, MA: D.C. Heath and Company.

Elias, R. (1990). Which victim movement? The politics of victim policy. In A. J. Lurigio, W. G. Skogan, & R. C. Davis (eds), *Victims of crime: Problems, policies and programs*. Newbury Park, CA: Sage.

Fisher, B. S., & Lab, S. P. (2010). *Encyclopedia of victimology and crime prevention*. Los Angeles, CA: Sage.

Franklin, C. W., II, & Franklin, A. P. (1976). Victimology revisited: A critique and suggestions for future direction. *Criminology, 14*, 177–214.

Levine, K. (1978). Empiricism in victimological research: A critique. *Victimology, 3*, 77–90.

Mawby, R. I., & Walklate, S. (1994). *Critical victimology*. Thousand Oaks, CA: Sage.

McKinney, J. C. (1950). The role of constructive typology in scientific sociological analysis. *Social Forces, 28*, 235–240.

McKinney, J. C. (1969). Typification, typologies, and sociological theory. *Social Forces, 48*, 1–12.

Mendelsohn, B. (1956). The victimology. *Etudes Internationale de Psycho-sociologie Criminelle*, July, 23–26.

Mendelsohn, B. (1976). Victimology and contemporary society's trends. *Victimology, 1*, 8–28.

Mendelsohn, B. (1982). Socio-analytic introduction to research in a general victimological and criminological perspective. In H. J. Schneider (ed.), *The victim in international perspective*. New York: Walter de Gruyter & Company.

President's Commission on Law Enforcement and Administration of Justice (1967). *Task Force report: Crime and its impact—An assessment*. Washington, DC: U.S. Government Printing Office.

Schafer, J. (1996). Measuring spousal violence with the conflict tactics scale: Notes on reliability and validity issues. *Journal of Interpersonal Violence, 11*, 572–585.

Schafer, S. (1968). *The victim and his criminal: A study in functional responsibility*. New York: Random House.

Smith, D. L., & Weis, K. (1976). Toward an open-system approach to studies in the field of victimology. In E. C. Viano (ed.), *Victims & society*. Washington, DC: Visage Press.

Toennies, F. (1957). *Community and society* (trans. C. P. Loomis). East Lansing: Michigan State University.

U.S. Department of Justice (2016b). *National crime victims' rights week resource guide: Landmarks in victims' rights and services*. Washington, DC: National Center for Victims of Crime. Retrieved on May 18, 2016, from http://ovc.ncjrs.gov/ncvrw2016/pdf/2016NCVRW_5_Landmarks_FINAL-508.pdf.

von Hentig, H. (1941). Remarks on the interaction of perpetrator and victim. *Journal of Criminal Law, Criminology and Police Science, 31*, 303–309.

von Hentig, H. (1948). *The criminal and his victim: Studies in the sociobiology of crime*. New Haven, CT: Yale University Press.

Weis, K. (1976). Rape as a crime without victims and offenders? A methodological critique. In E. C. Viano (ed.), *Victims & society.* Washington, DC: Visage Press.

Weis, K., & Borges, S. S. (1973). Victimology and rape: The case of the legitimate victim. *Issues in Criminology, 8,* 71–115.

Wolfgang, M. E. (1958). *Patterns in criminal homicide.* Montclair, NJ: Patterson Smith.

# The Politics of Victimization

## MARILYN D. MCSHANE AND TRAQINA Q. EMEKA

## Introduction

In this chapter we explore some examples of how politics comes into play when victims' needs are considered in our complex and very diverse society. As we will see, the enactment of legislation related to crime and victimization is often the way the public demonstrates its commitment to those who have been adversely affected by crime. We will examine how specific social problems, such as certain types of crime and criminals, come to attain a priority position on political agendas. This usually occurs through the experiences of famous or celebrity cases, or through relatively unknown individuals who somehow capture the public's attention and create a national media frenzy. One might argue that there is a "right time" and "right place" for the recognition of certain issues such as stalking or domestic violence and that the creation of laws is just a natural product of our government in action. Others might argue that high-profile cases such as those involving O. J. Simpson or Columbine High School will stir up public and political energy to the point where laws are passed to address the needs of victims, as well as groups and agencies that champion their causes. Either way, a new law generates a complex array of programs and policies that at the time seem essential to the well-being of our society. Certainly the creation of new laws dictates the way our criminal justice system responds. Police, courts and corrections agencies must adjust appropriately every time changes are made to criminal law. It is also our duty to systematically assess the effects of those changes through meaningful research and analysis.

## Little Words Mean A Lot

State laws vary tremendously across the country and thus courts are overwhelmed with trying to interpret and evaluate their constitutionality and enforceability. For example, victim compensation may involve criminal or civil remedies depending on statutes in any jurisdiction. In some areas, restitution is considered a "debt" which may allow collectors more power in extracting that payment while such terminology may also qualify the debt for discharge under federal bankruptcy law. This was the opinion of the U. S. Supreme Court in *Pennsylvania v. Rutherford* (1990) when they cited a 1984 decision that "restitution is intended to promote the rehabilitation of the offender, not compensate the victim" (*In re Pellegrino*, 1984). In other discussions, it has been argued that because there is no right to victim restitution, it cannot be considered a "claim" and thus, a debt. This would preclude it from being negated in a bankruptcy judgment.

While many people may equate restitution with some type of repayment to victims, the concept of victim compensation is more accurately applied to that process. It is likely that offenders would be confused by supervised release orders to pay victim compensation and/or restitution and it is as likely that the public would be confused as well.

Victim assistance is also a vague concept that many take on many functions and services. In a critique of the way this popular concept has been abused by prosecutors and other agents of the criminal justice system, McShane and Williams (1992) outline the specific provisions of most victim assistance programs. Many components of such programs appear to focus on improving prosecutorial conviction rates and perhaps enhance their political reputation for "getting tough." Examples of these components are:

*Victim notification*: notifying victims of the status of court proceedings involving the offender, such as plea negotiations, sentencing and parole decisions;

*Victim impact statements*: informing the judge of the physical, financial and emotional impact of the crime on the victim, or the victim's survivors, to be used in consideration of the offender's sentence;

*Court orientation*: providing information on the operation of the criminal justice system and emphasizing the victim's or witness' responsibilities in court to assist in the prosecution of the defendant;

*Transportation*: transporting the victim or witness to and from court, so that their presence may be used in the trial to help convict the defendant;

*Escorting*: accompanying victims or witnesses to the courtroom and sitting with them during proceedings against the defendant (McShane & Williams, 1992, p. 264).

While these activities may benefit the political careers of aspiring district attorneys, they only seem to address the needs of a subset of victims who are specifically interested in being involved in the punishment of the guilty.

Many victims have personal reasons for not becoming involved in the criminal-justice processing of their offenders. For example, Caroline Seawell was one of thirteen victims shot by Washington, DC, area snipers over a three-week period in 2002. Although ten others died in the highly publicized attacks, she never even told her younger son, now almost a teenager, about the case. She says she has relocated, moved on, and become a stronger person, but one with no interest in attending the convicted murderer's execution (Potter, 2009). On the other hand, the father of one of the Columbine High School victims, Brian Rohrbough, used the memorial created near the campus to vent his feelings about government lies and cover ups, abortion, and moral decline in general. He argues that his inflammatory inscriptions as a permanent part of the stone panel in the "ring of remembrance" was the way he wanted to remember his son (Banda, 2007).

## Legislation: The Process and the Products

The legislative process is a complex system of governance that uses the checks and balances of three different branches of government: the legislative branch made up of the Senate and the House of Representatives, the Executive branch anchored by the Presidency and the Judicial branch that reviews laws and makes rulings on their constitutionality.

A piece of legislation, or a Bill, may have a number of different titles that come together under it and each title may have sections or subtitles that address various areas of concern. Even these subtitles may be divided into chapters that are more specific in the types of activities and services called for. In many cases a piece of legislation will have funding attached to it in order to carry out the required mission, such as providing the training, research, data collection or equipment necessary to be in compliance with the law. These monies are usually distributed in the form of grants that states, counties, agencies, private entities, and other jurisdictions may apply for. Unfortunately, however, the funding is often limited and expires after a set period of time unless new funds are allocated and approved in subsequent years. One of the consequences of bipartisan government is that what was popular and well-funded under one administration is often abandoned in the next. This makes it difficult to determine which law enforcement or treatment efforts really are successful and it is often frustrating for the criminal justice system to be continually redirected to new initiatives and new priorities.

Since the 1980s, it has been common for each Presidential Administration to introduce a crime bill that brings together issues to be prioritized during the forthcoming term. Victims, as a popular political topic, have figured prominently in these crime bills and several victim-related issues have had significant staying power or longevity. However, the type of victims and the range of responses or services, funding and programming receiving attention will change with society's values and attitudes.

# Law As A Response to A Perceived Social Problem

Experts who study social problems argue that there is a set life-span to an issue; that is, the problem will only be controversial and engaging for a limited period of time. We often call this the "lifespan" of a social problem, which follows a fairly predictable chronology. During that time period, proponents of various positions on the issue will debate the merits of particular approaches to addressing the social problem and compete for resources to be spent on one solution or another. Experts will claim control over the definition, measurement and evaluation of that social problem. Laws will be passed and agencies will be designated to provide certain programs or services. Monies will be allocated for research, training, treatment or enforcement of the strategies most successfully competing in the political arena. Over time, the problem will be eclipsed by some new crisis and the "fifteen minutes of fame," so to speak, will be over for the social problem.

There is much evidence to support the cycle, or "rise and fall," of phenomena such as drunken-driving, cyber-bullying, missing children, and terrorism. In this chapter we will focus on a number of specific laws that have been passed dealing with victims and how certain high profile cases or causes may have generated interest and effort toward these various issues. We will also compare various types of legislation and examine their short- and, possibly, long-term effects.

One important aspect of the politics of legislation that will be noted is the name of the legislation. While Romeo may not have felt that names mattered in that famous Shakespearean play, for the study of victimology, the name is often the most obvious indication of the politicization of the process. For example, California voters passed a referendum in 1990 called the *Crime Victims Justice Reform Initiative*. This complicated piece of law was a collection of bills that had all been previously rejected by lawmakers and offered little if anything to victims. The thrust of the act was a series of shortcuts in the judicial process which seemed oriented toward improving the "get tough" records of judges and prosecutors at a time when the public was high on expectations and short on patience with the courts. Legislators who supported the initiative were attempting to ride the wave of law and order embraced by the voting public. Faced with spending caps on their own election campaigns, political candidates backed this referendum with their excess campaign funds. Thus, they were able to successfully run for office on a single popular issue while avoiding legal limitations on campaign spending. Both the candidates and the initiative benefited from their association with "pro-victim" rhetoric. Meanwhile, the primary message that caught people's attention was that their chances of becoming a victim were greater than ever before and that something needed to be done about it (as suggested by the summary of the proposition on the ballot).

Legislation related to victim needs seems to be generated in two distinct patterns. One is a broader and slower progression of efforts in recognition of human rights and social responsibilities, [...], while the other is a quick and sporadic knee-jerk change in response to some high-profile criminal event that appears to need an immediate and showcase response. We will look at examples of both types of legislation and evaluate the impact these laws have had on victims and victim services.

## Legislation and Politically-Popular Causes

Hate crime laws are a good example of this first type of implementation process. The emergence of hate crime as a social problem is consistent with forces that generated progress in the overall victims' rights movement. While there were significant events and notable cases, they were combined with energetic grassroots efforts, powerful leadership, and lobbying efforts to make it the right time in history for broad-based support for a range of hate crime laws to be consistently enacted across the country. People at this time were generally amenable to not only enhanced penalties for violent offenders but also official recognition of the social harms caused by bias and hate perpetrated against vulnerable populations. Popular media and literature on hate crime developed its own hate crime vocabulary with terms such as "bashing" for assault, "heterosexism" and "ethnoviolence" for what had previously been termed "racial incidents."

Still, there are many weaknesses in existing hate crime laws that make them difficult to use in the legal system, often resulting in frustrating and painful experiences for victims. Technically, a hate crime is not a separate offense, but an enhancement to an existing crime such as assault, attempted murder, arson, or criminal threats. Theoretically, an affirmative finding of a hate crime allows for longer sentences to be imposed, as well as more stringent restrictions on possible probation or parole and the recording of such a finding in one's criminal history. In the case of a 17-year-old Hispanic student in Texas who was seriously beaten and sodomized with a piece of pipe, one of the perpetrator's affiliation with supremacist groups, their use of racial slurs, and their attempt to carve a swastika on his chest were enough to raise a vehement public outcry to have the attackers charged with a hate crime. However, the fact that the crime took place in a private citizen's backyard resulted in the authorities' inability to use the federal law's enhancement under a hate-crime statute. Critics have also complained that discrepancies in the sentencing structures of the state and federal courts mean that hate crimes are pursued more often as regular crimes in the state judicial system where the penalties are already more severe than federal law permits (George, 2007).

## Violence Against Women Act

*The Violence Against Women Act* is another good example of legislation that was part of a greater social movement of awareness of victims and the need for services and programs. *The Violent Crime Control and Law Enforcement Act of 1994* was a crime bill signed into law by President Bill Clinton. Its Title IV contained the *Violence Against Women Act* (VAWA), which was a comprehensive law aimed at reducing bias against women, offering legal protections for women victims of crime, and clarifying the incorporation of gender as a distinct and protected status. The VAWA produced seven separate subtitles related to gender-based violence.

Subtitle A was called "Safe Streets for Women." This section introduced lengthier sentences for repeat offenders whose crimes were committed against women. Through this initiative, $800 million was dedicated to the program STOP (Services Training Officers Prosecutors) which was to strengthen law enforcement and prosecution strategies to reduce violence against women with special emphasis on safety in public parks and on public transit. Probation and parole officers also received $2 million over two years to work with sex offenders upon release. Another important feature of this section was the barring, under most circumstances, of evidence in criminal court about a victim's other sexual conduct as had been used in the past to erode the testimony of rape victims. Subtitle II, "Safe Homes for Women" focused on domestic violence and, in particular, brought full faith and credit to the restraining orders of one state so that they might be honored and enforced in another state. Subtitle III, "Civil Rights for Women" created the first civil-rights remedies for gender-based violence, although the right of these victims to sue in federal court was later struck down by the Supreme Court (2000). Subtitle IV, "Safe Campuses," specifically allocated funds to research problems facing women on college campuses. Subtitle V, "Equal Justice for Women in the Courts," provided training for judges so that they might be better equipped to solve some of the problems of gender bias in the legal system.

All of the efforts sponsored under the VOWA have helped to launch programs and research specifically designed to use gender equality as a means for reducing the level of victimization of women in society. Similar measures have been undertaken in legislation to protect children from abuse and exploitation.

## Child Victims of Pornography and Sexual Abuse

In 1982, California legislators lined up to be associated with the *Roberti-Imbrecht-Rains-Goggin Child Sexual Abuse Prevention Act*. After careful examination of this legislation, one could argue that it had been mislabeled. While discussing this act, an assistant in the California Attorney General's Office told a meeting of the Association of Criminal Justice Researchers-California in Pomona, California, that mislabeling was a misleading, but common, ploy to gain voter's support. In reality, this popular bill was not directed at preventing child sexual abuse nor offered assistance to victims, *per se*; it simply instituted harsher punishments for those caught molesting children, extended the statute of limitations for filing charges, and provided funds for police and prosecutors to be trained in handling cases. A more appropriate and, perhaps just as popular a title, may have been, "The Child Sexual Abuse Prosecution Enhancement Act." Likewise, the *California Child Protection Act of 1984* was similarly misnamed. The act did nothing to directly protect children, rather it allowed the state to confiscate property derived from the profits of child pornography and the cameras, film and lights used in such a criminal enterprise. Another interesting feature of this law was that it eliminated the need to prove intent in the prosecution of child pornography, a change that made it easier for prosecutors to obtain convictions. While it can be argued that putting child pornographers in prison is a way to protect children from future victimization, one can't help but wonder if there are other ways to address the prevention of child pornography than indirectly through prosecutorial enhancements, with a secondary purpose of enhancing prosecutors' political careers.

The impetus to make broad and sweeping claims beyond the direct or practical scope of a piece of legislation is perhaps one way to appear to be serving and addressing the needs of victims. Otherwise, it may be more controversial to say, "We need more resources to go to police and prosecutors" when many taxpayers may believe that these agencies have sufficient resources, and that the funds may just need to be re-prioritized. In a sense, law enforcement agencies are willing participants in this manipulation as they can claim that they cannot possibly address this deserving victim group without additional funds. In hindsight it is often the case that such appropriations were used for personnel overtime, additional hires and equipment that is only tangentially related to the task at hand. Still, it is a rare agency that will reject an opportunity for more funding.

## Cybersafety and Cybersecurity

Another area that is popular with politicians is preventing victimization on the internet. Whether it is children being stalked by predators or elderly couples being bilked of their savings, fears about vulnerability and exposure have led many citizens to demand more be done about network protection. Still, legislative initiatives in the realm of cyberspace have been extremely controversial and, thus, limited in their scope and impact. When the Rockefeller-Snowe bill was proposed there was a outpouring of criticism from all areas of the technology industry over provisions that would allow the government to shut down or take over the internet and other computer networks in order to address a crisis or threat. In such a vast business empire, it is understandable that any measures, regardless how noble the intent, will be difficult to reach consensus on. A more indirect and low-level plan to shore up cybersecurity was recently passed by the House in the form of the *Cybersecurity Enhancement Act of 2009*. This measure, with far less invasive features, provides funding to train technology students and allows them to offset their expenses with national service. It funds academic consortium arrangements that would coordinate with agencies like the National Science Foundation and the Department of Commerce to advance security in cyberspace.

# Legislation on Significant Victims and Events

Anti-Stalking laws are a good example of legislation that researchers and analysts frequently tie to a significant victim, this time via the murder of a popular young actress in 1989. When an obsessed fan showed up at the door of television star Rebecca Schaffer and shot her, the media seemed to rally around the cause, gathering up any related cases that could be used to identify this phenomenon as a fear-inducing social problem. As Kinkade et al. (2005, p. 4) explain,

> To add to the furor, statistical estimates related to stalking began to emerge and suggested that its occurrence was at an epidemic level. ... Legislative action directed toward stalking behavior became a 'hot issue' agenda item for state legislators and subsequently resulted in the creation of many new laws that criminalized such activity ... to stem a perceived increase in stalkers victimizing the American citizenry. ...

The idea of crime victims providing a powerful media image and creating a political force to be reckoned with is controversial and often a psychological dilemma. In the more notorious cases, lobbying and legislative efforts often become directed at whatever measures are believed to be relevant to a crime. Table 4.1 illustrates a number of well-known cases and the laws resulting from them. As the chronology indicates, more punitive and restrictive sanctions seem to be evolving over time as older laws and policies appear ineffective in preventing new cases.

For others, however, there is great reluctance to allow politicians to use their personal victimization experiences to further their careers. In California, the use of a highly-publicized case of a murdered child to dramatize issues in a heated political race backfired when relatives challenged the politicization of their little girl. A newspaper article (Bailey & Reza, 1994) summarized the situation this way:

> Atty. Gen. Dan Lungren and other Republican candidates are "dancing a jig" on the grave of Polly Klaas to push their own agenda on crime, the murdered girl's grandfather charged Tuesday at a campaign event for Democratic challenger Tom Umberg. Joe Klaas lashed out at Lungren, Gov. Pete Wilson and GOP senatorial candidate Mike Huffington and is appearing in an Umberg television commercial that blames Lungren for contributing to 12-year-old Polly's death. Lungren, Wilson, and Huffington—who is co-chairman of Proposition 184, the so-called "three strikes" initiative—have all used Polly's death to push for stricter sentencing laws. ... Umberg joined Klaas in charging that the girl's death might have been prevented if Lungren had maintained funding for a statewide computer database designed to give officers quick access to criminal records. Umberg and Klass contend that if the system had been operational, Polly's alleged killer, Richard Allen Davis, could have been apprehended before she died.

Still, as we all know, the "Three Strikes" legislation passed.

**TABLE 4.1   Examples of Popular Legislation Related to High Profile Crimes**

| Law | Victim & State | Crime | Terms of Law | Date | Comment |
|---|---|---|---|---|---|
| Megan's Law | Megan Kanka, 7 years old, New Jersey | rape/murder by neighbor sex offender | States must notify public of addresses of known sex offenders, Electronic list to be posted | 1996 | Amended Jacob Wetterling Act |
| Jessica's Law | Jessica Lunsford, 9 years old, Florida | Rape/murder | Various terms depending on state: Bans predators from living near where children gather, longer mandatory sentences & electronic monitors | FLA law passed 2005 | Controversial, 42 states have similar laws but no federal law resulted |
| Amber Alert | Amber Hagerman, 9 years old, Arlington, TX | Kidnapped & murdered | Emergency notification via coordinated effort of law enforcement, media & transportation | 1996 | Not a law, but government program, service, DOJ tasked w/assisting states w/setup |
| Jacob's Law | Jacob Wetterling, 11 year old, St. Joseph, MN | Abducted, never found | State sex offender websites required by federal, must post residence though jobs & schools suggested | 1994 | Set national standards for sex offender registration |
| J. Clery Act | Jeanne Clery, 19 years old, student in Pennsylvania | rape/murder in college dorm room by another student | Broader mandatory campus crime reporting & public dissemination w/sanctions for non-compliance | 2000 | Parents pressured for change; revised previous legislation |

| | | | | | |
|---|---|---|---|---|---|
| Chelsea's Law | 17-year-old, San Diego, CA | rape/murder by paroled sex offender | Proposes life electronic monitoring for all sex offenders, life w/out parole for force sex crime against child | Not passed | Being proposed around the U. S., controversial sentencing |
| Matthew Shepard & James Byrd Hate Crimes Prevention Act | Shepard, Wyoming; Byrd, Texas | Shepard: gay college student tortured & murdered Byrd: African-American dragged to death by young men w/ties to Supremacist groups | Adds gender, sexual orientation, gender identity & disability to categories considered bias-motivated, funds for training CJ system personnel & monies to aid in investigation & prosecutions | 10/28/09 | endorsed by over 300 law enforcement, civil rights, civic & religious groups |
| Adam Walsh Act | Adam Walsh | Abducted & murdered | Increased penalty for failure to register, adds DNA, photo & fingerprints, allow fed prosecution if fail to register—involves travel between jurisdictions, establishes three tiers of registrants | 2006 | Amended Jacob Wetterling Act, launched TV career of father, John Walsh |
| Pam Lyncher Act | Pam Lyncher, Houston founder of Justice for All | Pam Lyncher victim of attempted sex assault, became activist, killed in plane crash | Requires lifetime registration for certain sex offenders, FBI to maintain national sex offender registry | 1996 | Amended Jacob Wetterling Act |

As mentioned earlier, politicians also can claim support for a popular victim group based on the title of a proposed law, knowing that most citizens will never read the actual content of the bill. At campaign events they can boast in short sound bites what they have done to reduce or prevent crime simply based on the title of the legislation. Often, the images projected by the memory of a particularly heinous crime or offender are enough to popularize a proposed law regardless of the merits of its content. The Son of Sam Laws are a goodexample of the dramatic impact that legislators can obtain simply by choosing a high-profile name with which to associate policy changes.

## Son of Sam Laws

The infamous serial killer, David Berkowitz, is the namesake of the Son of Sam laws that swept through most jurisdictions in the 1990s. However, efforts to control profits generated by the stories of convicted felons actually dates back a little further to another case that, though no less notorious, would not have had the same dramatic effect because they would have been called "Henry Hill laws." In 1985, Nicholas Pileggi wrote a book called *Wiseguy* based on the life of mobster Henry Hill which later became the basis of Martin Scorsese's Oscar-nominated film, *Goodfellas.* Under existing New York laws, the state had empowered the Victim Compensation Board to seize profits from depictions of crimes and use them as payments to any victims who successfully sued an offender for compensatory damages. It was this law that became the basis of a suit filed by the publisher, Simon and Schuster, who claimed that the law was written in a way that was overly broad and thus in violation of the First Amendment.

In *Simon and Schuster v. Members of the New York State Crime Victims Board,* the U. S. Supreme court analyzed two important questions in order to determine whether to uphold the law. The first question was whether the state had a compelling interest in the process New York had adopted that would outweigh the possible infringement of First Amendment rights. The Court determined that it did not. While it might be a function of justice to keep offenders from profiting from their crimes, it was not part of that obligation to then transfer garnished earnings into victim-based accounts. This is important because later versions of these laws that have been found to be constitutional simply prohibited those convicted from being paid or compensated through the sale of accounts of the crime. Secondly, the court wanted to be sure that laws specifically focused on controlling the exploitation of the crime, its details, and its effects on the victim—not on other subject matter that might involve the offender but not that particular offense (Vaughn, 1996). This means that the writing of prisoner narratives, their life stories, and their experiences in the justice system were protected so long as the basis of the work was not the perpetrating of the crime for which victims had suffered.

Clarification of what profits are and what parts of the criminal's history are permissible in the writing of a book, play or movie has continued since these laws were adopted. Jean Harris, the elite private school headmistress who shot and killed her former lover (famous Scarsdale diet author Herman Tarnower), also ran into a publishing prohibition for her work *Stranger in Two Worlds* and *They Always Call Us Ladies.*

There are several important facts to remember about these high profile cases. First, David Berkowitz (Son of Sam) never tried to profit from his crimes. He never sought money or opportunities to produce media versions of his story. Harris had planned to donate all of the proceeds from her publication to a non-profit charity that sponsored visits for the children of inmates. The rush to pass legislation barring offenders from profiting from the sale of their "stories" was generated by perceptions that publishers, media outlets, film writers, and popular culture agents would generate interest in products that were believed to be offensive to victims, their survivors, and society in general (and that the offender was going to profit from the crime). Today the concerns of victim advocacy groups, legislators, and policymakers have expanded beyond the concept of a book or personal accounts of a crime to the internet marketing of items associated with serial killers and other high-profile criminals. The term "murderabilia" connotes the promotion of any items or artifacts tied to the crime itself, or the offender charged with the crime.

Murderabilia, a concept that appears unsavory and morally reprehensible to many victims' advocates and citizens, seems to have been distinguished to some degree from memorabilia which has been used to raise money to make awards to victims and survivors. After winning $8.5 million in compensatory damages and half of $25 million in punitive damages against O. J. Simpson in wrongful death litigation, Fred Goldman, father of the deceased victim Ron Goldman, sought to recover the football legend's memorabilia as part of that judgment. The collectable items included Simpson's Hall of Fame certificate, autographed footballs, a gold watch, and the suit he wore during his criminal trial that ended in an acquittal (Marquez, 2007). Had he been convicted, would this material be murderabilia? Is the civil verdict enough to change the category from memorabilia to murderabilia? Obviously, the issues are not as simple as some would have us believe.

Since the earliest court cases, laws have had to be revised to best meet First Amendment standards. Some states have attempted to force offenders who are entering into contracts for some type of potentially-profitable product to first have that contract reviewed and approved by the state's attorney general. In what might be their most constitutionally viable form, these laws would allow offenders to write and to engage in free expression in areas that do not specifically address the particular victimization for which the offenders are currently serving time. There is much we can learn about childhood abuse, and abandonment, as well as juvenile and mental health system shortcomings, in these biographical works. However, attempting to control access to murderabilia may be more difficult. Language that relies on a somewhat vague assessment of the value of items that increases because of the notoriety of the offender may be legally problematic (Hurley, 2009).

Still other forms of legislation appear to have elements of both evolving social movements and celebrated cases, which become the faces and the forces behind their passage. Another crucial element of the issues resulting in many of the widespread legal changes is the organized lobbying efforts of victims' families and support groups. Campus Crime legislation illustrates these concepts well. As we will see, it took a number of pieces of legislation, revised and implemented using various strategies over a period of years, to come up with the comprehensive campus-crime-reporting system that we have today.

## The Clery Act and Campus Crime

Early research on campus crime seemed to indicate that only about 60 percent of victims reported offenses to campus police. Victims as well as authorities seemed to be confused about jurisdiction and many students indicated that they did not report crimes because they did not have confidence in campus police or believed that the officers would not be able to do anything. Those who were younger and more economically disadvantaged were also less likely to report. Still, studies reflected that women were more worried about crime on campus regardless of the time of day or the location (parking lots, gyms, auditoriums, library, etc.). Ironically, the crimes most likely to be experienced, larceny/theft, harassment, vandalism, and threats, were not even those that would be tracked by the early reporting systems (Fisher, 1995).

During the 1980s there was considerable pressure on the government to employ more accountability measures, particularly in the reporting of crime, spending, and any information that might affect the health, safety and well-being of all citizens. Inefficient and underperforming government agencies were phased out or reorganized. New management and budgeting processes were experimented with and more computerized data-systems set up to track and report social statistics.

The *Student Right-To-Know and Campus Security Act* of 1990 reflected all of these trends. Parents were concerned about graduation rates, not only for student-athletes but across higher education. Making choices about where to send their children and invest their college savings meant being well-informed as higher percentages of high-school graduates sought degrees. More assertive and protective baby-boomer parents wanted trustworthy information about campus crime rates, something both they and legislators had reason to be suspicious about. Attempting to enhance recruitment efforts, universities were often less than honest about the risk of victimization on campus and in the surrounding areas. These concerns were the focus of the campaign waged by Jean Clery's parents.

After 19-year-old Jeanne Clery was raped and murdered in her Lehigh University dorm room, her parents pressed for changes in Pennsylvania law that would require reporting campus crime. They, like many other parents, were unaware that their daughter's school had recorded 38 violent campus crimes in the three years prior to Jeanne's murder. On this issue, the efforts of parents, victims and security organizations, as well as policymakers, all combined to develop a meaningful reporting system for campus crime. As a result of the various federal and state laws passed, schools receiving government funds and federal financial aid were required to annually and publicly report their traditional index-crime statistics in a Uniform Crime Report format, much like cities and towns across America. In addition, schools were required to track the number of arrests on campus for alcohol and drug violations, as well as any weapons offenses.

The passage of the *Campus Security Act of 1990* began a long and slow process of developing a culture of accountability in colleges and universities which they had no history of, and little support for, accomplishing. The Act was unfunded and colleges often stumbled along unclear about how to designate reporting authorities and train, staff, and manage a sophisticated reporting system. It was also unclear just how the information had to be disseminated and how validity and reliability could be enforced. The 2000 *Jeanne Clery Disclosure of Campus Security Policy and Campus Crime Statistics Act* added crimes committed in areas bordering campuses, as well as the reporting of hate crimes and manslaughter. To provide some incentive for compliance, punishments have been put in place for not meeting reporting mandates.

The political activity of Connie and Howard Clery later became channeled into the founding of "Security on Campus Inc." Their website pledges to insure that Jeanne's death would continue to have a purpose. Today, one of the organization's interests is supporting the use of unified campus alert systems. These private-vendor-supplied, emergency web-based notification systems are used on most campuses in one form or another. However, effective implementation of such mechanisms in an actual emergency has yet to be fully realized, as has been noted in several high-profile events, including a shooting episode at Virginia Tech.

## Transparency in the Interest of Victims

Popular political trends (like transparency in government, accountability, and more public access to information on how government agencies operate) that have arisen in this past decade have influenced a number of victims' issues. In 2010, a law went into effect in Texas requiring Child Protective Services, a state agency, to publically release information and reports on any child who dies from abuse. In a newspaper article, Langford (2010), reports on some of the law's requirements:

> … within five days of a child abuse death, the agency will have to provide the child's gender, age, date of death, and whether the child was in a foster home or living with a parent or guardian or someone else at the time of death … . CPS will now have 10 days to produce a report to the public after the agency completes its own investigation into how the child died.

Other indications of the move toward more openness in reporting have been the Senate Judiciary Committee hearings on the possibility of closing Guantanamo Bay (used for incarcerating persons suspected of crimes against the United States), political refugees, and persons held indefinitely under the *Patriot Act*. Ironically, it was not until the media exposed prisoner abuses by U. S. military forces in Afghanistan and in Iraq that the public became aware that these same procedures had long been practiced at Guantanamo. Various forms of torture were used, such as water boarding, short-shackling detainees to the floor in awkward positions, using duct tape over their mouths, and threatening to kill them and their families. Also, tactics that degraded prisoners and violated their religious beliefs were particularly reviled by the public and the greater global community. Reports indicated that U. S. military personnel forced prisoners to appear nude in front of female soldiers, put women's under-wear on their heads, and sexually humiliated them. According to a report in the *Washington Post*,

> One was attached to a leash and made to walk around the room and "perform a series of dog tricks." The report also notes the use of "gender coercion," in which women straddle a detainee or get too close to them, violating prohibitions for devout Muslim men on contact with women. Interrogators also threatened to tell other detainees that an individual is gay, according to the report. Detainees were posed in mock homosexual positions and photo-graphed (White, 2005).

The outpouring of condemnation over these accounts threatened to redefine the enemy com-batants as victims, which would have been an uncomfortable image for the war on terrorism to reconcile. Many believe that moving the prisoners back to the United States would provide more oversight of their treatment than the remote Cuban facility. These examples demonstrate that it is not always more law that is needed, but sometimes simply better agency regulation and supervision.

# Planning for the Unknown

According to Yu (2009), there is evidence that crime concentrates in time as well as in space. This means that government and civic initiatives seeking to address crime in specific locations such as campuses, hot spots or other crime-prone areas (like socially disorganized neighborhoods), would need to be aware of the temporal aspects of crime and their implications. Daily, seasonal, or even long-term changes in patterns of activity may increase or decrease the need for law enforcement or other crime prevention strategies. Urban renewal, changing land use patterns, resident mobility, and the economy of neighborhoods all hold the potential to alter the urban landscape and its potential for victimization. It is possible then, that strategies appearing to be practical or necessary at one point in time are no longer feasible in another time, yet may still be mandated under policy or law. Unfortunately, laws are often passed in haste and the consequences of committing resources on a relatively permanent basis may make communities less responsive to new needs that arise.

Victims groups are a powerful political lobby. Organizations such as MADD, Parents of Murdered Children, and those representing other activist causes are able to evoke strong emotional responses to issues during elections and other significant government milestones. The demands made by these various interests consume disproportionate amounts of criminal justice research, training, and prosecutorial monies. The more politically-popular one victim is over another, the more poised that group will be to divert funds toward their causes. Still, there are some issues like campus crime and child sexual abuse, arising at just the right time in history, that seem to result in the passage of laws that are supported by a majority of victims, policymakers, and citizen groups alike.

## DISCUSSION QUESTIONS

1.  Is the politicizing of victims' issues unavoidable? How can victims be insulated or protected from the negative effects of the political processing of their needs?

2.  Discuss the factors that seem to make some issues move to legislation faster than others. Also what factors seem to make some pieces of legislation more effective than others?

3.  How can more transparency in government work to the advantage of victims?

4.  Look at your campus' crime data, what trends if any are apparent? How would you characterize crime on your campus? When was the last time you received notice of a crime on your campus and how did you receive it?

## References

Bailey, E., & Reza, H. G. (1994, October 26). Grandfather of slain girl lashes out at Lungren. *Los Angles Times*. Retrieved from *http://articles.latimes.com/keyword/tom-umberg*

Banda, P. S. (2007, September 22). A site "about remembrance." *Houston Chronicle*, A7.

Bronk, C. (2010, February 11). In new federal legislation, a victory for cybersecurity. *Houston Chronicle*, B11.

Fisher, B. (1995). Crime and fear on campus. *Annals of American Academy of Political & Social Sciences, 539*, 85–101.

George, C. (2007, October 13). Feds often yield to states in hate-crime cases. *Houston Chronicle*, B4.

Hurley, E. (2009). Overkill: An exaggerated response to the sale of murderabilia. *Indiana Law Review, 42*, 411–440.

*In re Pellegrino* 42 B. R. 129 (1984).

Kinkade, P., Burns, R., & Ilarraza Fuentes, A. (2005). Criminalizing attractions: Perceptions of stalking and the stalker. *Crime & Delinquency, 51*, 3–25.

Langford, T. (2009, September 26). CPS now must give details on victims. *Houston Chronicle*, B1.

Marquez, J. (2007, September 18). Goldmans to seek Simpson memorabilia. Associated Press. Retrieved from http://news.yahoo.com.

McShane, M., & Williams, F. P., III (1992). Radical victimology: A critique of the concept of victim in traditional criminology. *Crime & Delinquency, 38*, 258–271.

*Pennsylvania Department of Public Welfare et al. v. Davenport et ux*, 495 U. S. 552, 110 S.Ct. 2126, 109 L. Ed. 2D 588 (1990).

Potter, D. (Associated Press) (2009, November 8). Victims, relatives await sniper's execution. *Houston Chronicle*, A25.

Vaughn, M., & del Carmen, R. (1996). Legal issues: V. Constitutional issues in prison operations In M. McShane & F. P. Williams, III (Eds), *Encyclopedia of American prisons* (pp. 289–298). New York: Garland Publishing.

White, J. (2005, July 14). Abu Ghraib tactics were first used at Guantanamo. *Washington Post*, A1.

## Books You May Want to Read

Pierce-Baker, C. (2000). *Surviving the silence: Black women's stories of rape*. New York: Norton.

Krakauer, J. (2003). *Under the banner of heaven: A story of violent faith*. New York: Doubleday.

Wilson, B. (1991). *Wouldn't it be nice: My own story*. New York: HarperCollins.

## Movies You May Want to See

*The Burning Bed* (1984)

*A Mighty Heart* (2007)

*Shake Hands with the Devil* (2005)

## Web Links

http://www.securityoncampus.org/

http://www.e2campus.com/

Sex offender registry laws: http://www.ojp.usdoj.gov/smart/pdfs/so_registry_laws.pdf

National Center for Missing and Exploited Children: http://www.ncmec.org/missingkids/servlet/PublicHomeServlet?LanguageCountry=en_US

# Introduction to Criminology and Criminological Research

CHAPTER

# What is Criminology?

## THE STUDY OF CRIME, CRIMINALS, AND VICTIMS IN A GLOBAL CONTEXT

MARK M. LANIER AND STUART HENRY

The horrendous events of September 11, 2001, in which the World Trade Center in New York was totally destroyed, and the Pentagon in Washington substantially damaged, by hijacked commercial airliners that were flown into them, killing 2,982 people, have proved to be the defining point of this decade. The United States was horrified, unified, motivated, and eager to apply its superior military might immediately and unequivocally against the aggressors. However, unlike the Japanese attack on Pearl Harbor on December 7, 1941, this time it was not clear who to strike or what effect a strike would have. For the first time in its history the United States did not have a well-defined nation-state enemy. Clearly, the nature of war, the American way of life, what counts as "crime," and how a society responds to harms, internal or external, changed on that day. This act of terrorism was undoubtedly aimed at the American people. The terrorist organization al-Qaeda claimed responsibility. From a geopolitical perspective, the major consequence of 9/11 was that an explicitly hostile Islamic state, Iraq, was soon invaded/liberated/occupied on the rationale that it was storing weapons of mass destruction that could be targeted at Western interests. (We purposefully say "invaded/liberated/occupied," as one's worldview, political beliefs, and context determine which word is most appropriate.) The logic was that a preemptive attack was necessary to prevent a catastrophe worse than 9/11 (a concept known as the Bush Doctrine). Yet the 9/11 attackers were predominantly from Saudi Arabia, and al-Qaeda was substantially based in Afghanistan; seven years later the 2008 presidential debate was dominated by discussions about whether Iraq or Afghanistan was the best place to fight against those who perpetrated this and other acts of terrorism. The purpose of this introductory chapter is to show how the changing geopolitical landscape and other factors shape our renewed discussion of crime and its causes, as well as possible policy responses.

Six fundamental changes can be identified that demonstrate the changed nature of our world. These changes all move toward increasing interconnection and inter-dependence. They are: (1) globalization; (2) the communications revolution, particularly the Internet; (3) privatization and individualization; (4) the global spread of disease; (5) changing perceptions of conflict and national security; and (6) the inter-nationalization of terrorism.

## Globalization

Globalization is the process whereby people react to issues in terms of reference points that transcend their own locality, society, or region. These reference points include material, political, social, and cultural concerns that affect the planet, such as environmental challenges (e.g., global warming or overpopulation) and commercial matters (e.g., fast food, in particular so-called McDonaldization, which describes the spread of McDonald's restaurants throughout the world's economies). Globalization is a process of unification in which differences in economic, technological, political, and social institutions are transformed from a local or national network into a single system. Globalization also relates to an international universalism, whereby events happening in one part of the world affect those in another, none more dramatic than the collapse of world financial markets (Stiglitz 2002, 2006), which went global in September 2008. Indeed, the emergence of worldwide financial markets and under- or unregulated foreign exchange and speculative markets resulted in the vulnerability of national economies. In short, "'Globalization' refers to all those processes by which peoples of the world are incorporated into a single world society, global society" (Albrow 1990, 9). Conversely, while globalization relates to the way people in different societies identify with values that cut across nations and cultures, it also relates to the recognition of different cultures' diversity of experience and the formation of new identities. As globalization integrates us, these new identities and our sense of belonging to differentiated cultures are also driving many of us apart (Croucher 2004, 3).

The greatest effect of the global society is the global economy as it relates to the increasing multi-nationalization of corporations that produce on the "global assembly line" (Ehrenreich and Fuentes 1994). The result is that "economic goods, services, and personnel flow back and forth across national, hemispheric and continental boundaries" such that "economic, social, political and environmental events in one part of the world have significant impacts in other parts of the world ... beyond the ability of any one society to control" (Soroka and Bryjak 1999, 176). Indeed, both advocates and critics of globalization agree that it has resulted in the circumvention of both national boundaries and state controls over economic trade and production processes. Further, ethnic identities and religious affiliations transcend both political and geographic boundaries. As Frank Schmalleger says:

> On a global scale, there appears to be a shared agreement that society is experiencing a period of unprecedented change. Both the substance and the pace of change are fundamentally different from what has occurred in past decades and centuries. No longer are sequences of events occurring in relative isolation over longer patterns of time. No longer are discrete groups of people affected by each change; rather, there is a greater

simultaneity of occurrence, swifter interpenetration, and increased feedback of one set of changes upon another. ([1999] 2002, 480)

A classic example of the interconnection and inability of individual societies to influence and control the crime and harm created by globalization is the case of one of the worst industrial accidents in the world: In 1984, in Bhopal, India, Union Carbide's insecticide plant leaked toxic gas, resulting in between 4,000 and 15,000 deaths and injuries to as many as 600,000 people (Beirne and Messerschmidt 2000, 494–495).

> What is most frightening about Bhopal is … the way people are routinely treated by corporations. … Cancer-causing pesticides banned in the West are freely sold to farmers in Latin America, Eastern Europe and Asia. Native American Nations are bribed to accept nuclear waste. … Malaysian hill people are killed or run off their land so Japanese companies can cut down their forests to make chopsticks. Leaded gasoline, banned in the West because of its devastating health effects on children, is sold to Thailand, Mexico and India. This kind of corporate violence is repeated in every corner of the Earth. (Cohen 1998, 3, cited in Beirne and Messerschmidt 2000, 494–495)

Some critics of globalization, known as the antiglobalization movement, such as Nikos Passas (2000), have argued that the process of globalization, including the spread of capital, labor, management, news, and information across national borders, is itself "criminogenic," because it provides motivation and opportunities for corporate deviance at the same time that it leads to less effective control systems (M. Robinson 2004). Other critics, such as Noam Chomsky, argue that it is not so much the existence of global integration they oppose but the way in which it occurs, in that it benefits the rich nations at the expense of the poor and polarizes and accentuates inequality within societies.

## The Globalization of Communications

Prior to 1985 global communication was largely restricted to the affluent. The advent of the personal computer and the development of the Internet transformed the way we communicate. Now people connect daily with others all over the world at little or no expense. They exchange ideas, performances, propaganda, ideologies, and technical information; through Internet search engines they can draw on knowledge from any part of the globe. Members of any society can read newspapers and opinions, engage in chat-room discussions, and take university courses via the Internet. They can also share the most intimate details of their daily lives through Web blogs and social-networking sites such as YouTube, Facebook, and MySpace, communication mechanisms that have become global. No longer are people limited to what their own government's or society's ideology and culture feed them, which paradoxically can lead to expanded knowledge and perspectives or reinforcement for any idea or view, however strange or outrageous it may seem. This means that we are increasingly interconnected with the world in both positive and negative ways. What affects people in one part of the globe can affect others in another.

At the same time, the development in global communications has led to a massive shift of jobs from manufacturing into service, communications, and information (called the postindustrial society), and because the latter jobs require higher education and training, increasing numbers of people the world over are underemployed or unemployed. The result has been to increase worker anxiety and job stress among those who have "not yet been 'bumped,' 'deselected,' 'surplussed,' 'vocationally relocated,' 'de-hired,' 'decruited' or otherwise done away with" (Soroka and Bryjak 1999, 180). Work-related stress leads to increased competition, "backstabbing," isolation, detachment, and alienation as well as increased family and workplace violence.

Increased global communication has also brought a rush of new crimes that are perpetrated on and via the Internet, such as fraud and identity theft, drug smuggling, and bomb making. The growing dependence on global communications has also made national infrastructures and governments vulnerable to Internet terrorism through hacking and computer viruses.

## Privatization and Individualization

Related to globalization and global unemployment are two trends that, in spite of our being connected to ever-greater numbers of people, have produced a reduction in our concern for others. We have already mentioned the increased competition in the workplace, the attitude of everyone looking out for themselves. This is in contrast to the shared movement around trades and professions that culminated in unionization and collective action during the middle of the twentieth century, when people banded together for strength and solidarity.

More and more we are seeing the "death of society," that is, the decline in collective action and social policy requiring some to give up part of their wealth to help the less fortunate or to increase the public good. Instead, partly because of government fiscal crises and partly because of conservative ideology, the twenty-first century has witnessed a growing privatization of government, particularly in the areas of welfare and social programs. Privatization reinforces the individualization of human actions, as well as allowing major policy decisions to be made not in terms of a society's public or social interests but in terms of what maximizes profit for corporate shareholders. Thus, the 1980s and 1990s saw massive deregulation and privatization, from transportation, communications, and energy to finance, welfare, and even law enforcement.

We have also seen the increasing tendency for family members to stay at home, not as families but as appendages to technology, such as televisions, computers, and video games. The result is an impersonal society, one where we are living in isolation from other real people, "bowling alone" (Putnam 1995), where media images and game characters become interspersed with real people who are seen as superficial, objectlike caricatures.

Moreover, because of the impact of globalization on the economic structures of societies, there has been a polarization of rich and poor, with numerous groups excluded from opportunities (J. Young 1999). In their relatively impoverished state, they are vulnerable to violence, both in their homes and in their neighborhoods.

## Globalization of Disease

Although the black death, or plague, smallpox, and polio have demonstrated that throughout human history, disease can be a global phenomenon, the systemic use of hygienic practices, including clean water and effective sanitation and sewerage, and the discovery and use of antibiotics, vaccines, and other drugs meant that for much of the twentieth century the global spread of disease was seen as a thing of the past, or at least occurring only in underdeveloped countries. But by the end of the twentieth century, through the advent of increased global travel, the terror of disease on a global scale was given new meaning, first with HIV/AIDS, then with mad cow disease, West Nile virus, SARS (severe acute respiratory syndrome), and resistant strains of tuberculosis. Worse was the fact that, unlike times past, groups could potentially introduce disease, such as smallpox or anthrax, on a global scale as part of a terrorist operation against individuals or governments. Like the previous developments, the dual effect was, on the one hand, to render people increasingly fearful of contact, especially intimate contact with strangers, tending to undermine interpersonal relations, while, on the other, demonstrating just how interconnected we have become.

This area of change has led to the development of an emerging semiparadigm in criminology. Timothy Akers and Mark Lanier (2009) founded the Virtual Center for Epidemiological Criminology (VCEC) to address the correlates and causes of crime and health issues. Public health and criminal justice issues are closely related and often inseparable. Many diverse entities are now acknowledging the connections between crime and health variables. For example, recent data sets released by the Centers for Disease Control and Prevention (CDC) include crime statistics. On January 8, 2008, the CDC made the following announcement: "The CDC Behavioral Surveillance Branch (BSB) is pleased to announce the release of a county-level data set [that] will allow users to compare health behaviors with ... core health outcomes and risk factors such as cardiovascular disease (CVD), diabetes, asthma, physical activity, obesity, and smoking. ... These variables include health care delivery information, health and vital statistics indicators, environmental measures, *crime statistics*, business indicators, and poverty/income figures" (emphasis added).

Moving beyond what the CDC and others have accomplished, VCEC seeks to theoretically and empirically link and examine the two disciplines of crime and public health. VCEC's primary function is to research specific strategies that integrate long-tested public health and criminological theories to produce practical interventions that will improve the well-being of communities. The objective is to isolate interventions that simultaneously impact the co-occurrence of crime and public health problems. VCEC and the related online journal *Epidemiological Criminology* clearly suggest the linkages between the issues.

## The Changing Nature of Global Conflict

During the twentieth century, until the end of the cold war, each generation faced a significant war or warlike threats to its survival. Examples include the two world wars, Korean War, Vietnam War, and cold war. In these twentieth-century global conflicts it was possible to clearly identify the enemy posing the threat, and to come together as nations to wage war to defeat that threat. In contrast, in the twenty-first century it is becoming ever more apparent that for many nations, "the enemy" is multiple, diffuse, and interwoven into the very fabric of society.

*Globalization* is not simply an economic process but, rather, the term for the technological movement away from the dyadic analysis of "independent events" toward complex, interdependent "systems analysis." The most fundamental questions for peace researchers at the present time include: "What is the general quality of peace and is it improving, stagnating, or deteriorating?" "Where, and under what conditions, is organized violence most likely to occur?" "How do we understand the quality of peace in its many systemic variations, both successes and failures?" (CSP 2009).

Nations in the continent of Africa, for example, face very serious threats on several fronts, including starvation, the spread of HIV/AIDS, and numerous civil wars. For example, civil wars in Sierra Leone, Rwanda, Ethiopia, and Mozambique have resulted in the deaths of millions of

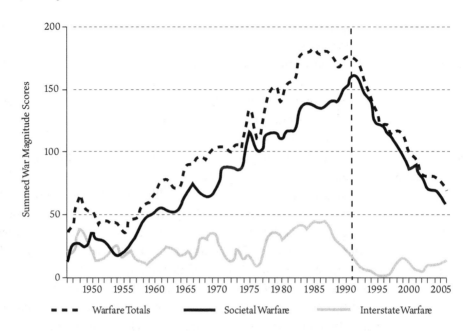

**FIGURE 5.1** Global trends in armed conflict

*Source*: Center for Systemic Peace. http://www.systemicpeace.org.

innocent people over the past two decades. But as the Center for Systemic Peace (CSP) indicates, although "the level of societal warfare increased dramatically and continuously through the Cold War period," it was a result of "the protractedness of societal wars during this period and not from a substantial increase in the numbers of new wars" (ibid.). In the twentieth century former colonial powers would step in during such times of civil conflict, while multinational peacekeeping forces, such as the United Nations, NATO, and the "Coalition of the Willing," appeared, at least on the surface, to provide both clarity and stability. Since the 1990s, however, these bodies seem reluctant to intervene everywhere that violence occurs. Part of the explanation may be that the "international community is increasingly reluctant to provide peacekeeping forces for difficult, expensive and politically unrewarding operations" (Brayton 2002, 304).

Another part of the explanation is the changing nature of war and conflict. The two superpowers of the cold war, the United States and the Soviet Union, no longer square off since the latter's breakup in 1991, and so far Russia has presented a limited challenge to America. The United States has emerged as the world's dominant military power, and as a result, "America has reduced the military role of its European allies in NATO to that of its strategic reserve, to be used where the job is relatively easy, requires less capable forces, and where such tasks require long-term commitment of troops and peace building rather than fighting duties" (Cilliers 2003, 112). The role of allies and multinational organizations, such as NATO and the United Nations, is changing. Consequently, the nature of war is also changing. Today, "to an extent unprecedented in modern times, entities other than nation-states wage war across multiple physical and ideological boundaries. The Cold War's clear dichotomies and array of proxy wars have devolved into myriad intrastate conflicts and cross-border wars of uncertain and shifting ideological foundation" (Brayton 2002, 305).

The incidence of both societal and interstate warfare has declined dramatically since the 1990s, and this trend continues in the early 2000s, falling more than 60 percent from its peak level. For example, there were twenty-five major armed conflicts (societal warfare) in 2000, yet only two were between nation-states (interstate warfare), according to a 2001 report by the Stockholm International Peace Research Institute (cited in Brayton 2002). If nation-states are not waging war with each other, and if major powers are not intervening in conflict resolution or conflict promotion (except, of course, when oil is involved), how are the conflicts that do occur resolved, and why are their numbers declining? Part of the answer is the withdrawal of superpowers supporting civil unrest, particularly since the end of the cold war.

In the poorest of countries and regions, conflicts do continue, albeit at a lesser rate. According to the CSP:

> In late 2007, there are 24 states directly affected by ongoing wars (28 wars total, up from 26 at the end of 2006). Of these 24 states, half (12) are affected by protracted wars, that is, armed conflicts persisting for more than ten years. These protracted societal conflicts include Afghanistan (30 years), Colombia (24), D. R. Congo (16), India (56), Iraq (28), Israel (43), Myanmar (60), Nigeria (11), Philippines (36), Somalia (20), Sri Lanka (25), Sudan (25), Turkey (24), and Uganda (37). These wars continue to defy concerted efforts to gain settlement or resolution. (CSP 2009)

Moreover, the end of the cold war saw the rise of numerous ethnic wars: "Ethnic wars, which had previously paralleled the trend of revolutionary war, continue to rise through the late 1980s and early 1990s as separatists and other political entrepreneurs attempt to take advantage of the vast changes in political arrangements that accompanied the transformation of the post–Cold War world system" (ibid.).

One way the conflicts that do occur are being resolved is through the use of armies for hire, that is, mercenaries who fight for pay. Increasingly, small countries, and some large ones, are finding themselves unable to "protect the political, military, economic social and cultural life of their citizens" (Brayton 2002, 303). Papua New Guinea provides an illustrative example. In 1997, the Bougainville Revolutionary Army was seriously threatening the regime of Prime Minister Julius Chan. As a result of this conflict the Panguan copper mine was closed—the source of 30 percent of the country's export income. Chan hired the mercenary force Sandline International for $36 million. Sandline recognized the economic advantages of opening and protecting the mine, and Chan was able to obtain the military assistance he needed.

What's wrong with using private security firms? Some argue that "in proffering security to collapsing, mineral-rich states ... multinational corporations accentuate the international exploitation and marginalization of the states in question" (ibid., 310). The proliferation of these large, well-organized private armies also alarms the United Nations, which views them as a threat to "sovereign equality, political independence and territorial integrity" (ibid., 304). There are dozens of these huge corporate armies for hire around the world. Their "peacekeeping" role is based solely on profit and armed conflict.

Large, well-funded nation-states, such as the United States, are also increasingly using mercenaries. In fact, the best-known example of a private army served primarily at the discretion of the second Bush administration. Founded in 1997, Black water Worldwide is an American company that provides military private-sector solutions to both government and nongovernment clients. A former Navy Seal, Erik Prince, started the company as a basic-training operation to help support the needs of local and regional law enforcement. Its main headquarters is in Moyock, North Carolina,

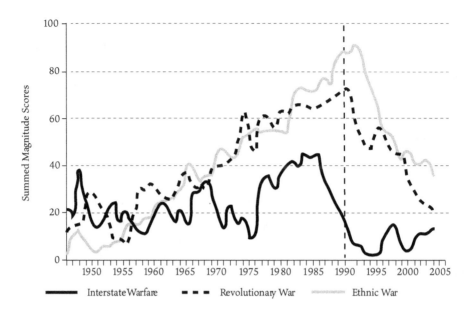

**FIGURE 5.2** Trends by armed conflict type

*Source*: Center for Systemic Peace. http://www.systemicpeace.org.

where its 7,000-acre training facility is the largest private training center in the United States. The company claims to be the world's most successful security-service corporation, having designed and manufactured remotely piloted airships, IED safe-armored personnel carriers, and training support systems. It operates in nine countries, delivering critical assistance to clients focused on postconflict and postdisaster stabilization efforts (Blackwater, USA 2008).

Through its contract with the U.S. Defense Department, Blackwater Worldwide and two other security companies had an estimated 137,000 employees working in Iraq as of 2007. The U.S. government pays these private firms to supply armed guards to protect people and buildings and furnish transportation in hostile areas. The security contractors also provide protective services for diplomats and for companies working on reconstruction projects, including escorting people to and from meetings and job sites.

On September 16, 2007, Blackwater employees were on a mission to evacuate senior American officials after a nearby explosion. (Some question the need for the evacuation because the officials were already in a secure compound.) After the explosion at 11:50 A.M., the diplomats were escorted via a Blackwater convoy to a Green (safe) Zone. To get to the Green Zone they had to go through Nisour Square, in Baghdad. Another convoy went to Nisour first to block off traffic so the convoy could get through without delay. At least four SUVs blocked lanes entering the square, and some guards got out of their vehicles and took positions on the street. At 12:08 P.M. at least one guard began to fire in the direction of a car, killing its driver. The same guard walked toward the car, firing more shots, killing a woman and an infant.

There are several different versions explaining how the shooting began. The Blackwater guards said they believed they were fired upon first. An Iraqi preliminary investigation concluded that there was no enemy fire, but some Iraqi witnesses said that Iraqi commandos in nearby guard towers could have been shooting. Ultimately, eight civilians were killed and fourteen others injured.

Whereas national conflicts have become decentralized, global conflicts have become dispersed. Rather than nations facing off, we now have terrorist tactics, once limited to anarchists and fringe radical groups, becoming a method of war for a variety of causes, from antiabortionists to Muslim extremists.

## Global Terrorism

The single most feared event, and according to surveys of public opinion the "crime" considered most serious, is a terrorist attack. Events such as the September 11, 2001, suicide airliner bombings and the Mumbai hotel takeover in December 2008 illustrate that the threat of terrorism on a global scale has become part of the daily fear of populations around the world, not least because of the ways these events are instantly communicated to everyone, everywhere, as they happen. No longer restricted to the tactics of a few extreme radical or fringe groups in certain nations, terrorism has become the method of war for any ethnic or religious group that does not have the power to succeed politically. It has been facilitated by developments in communication, transportation, and technology that have enabled explosives and other weapons to become smaller and more lethal. Whether there is an interconnected web of terrorism around fundamentalist Muslim religious extremism (such as that claimed by followers of Osama Bin Laden and al-Qaeda), an Arab-led terrorist movement opposed to Western culture, more specific actions such as those in Northern Ireland by the IRA and splinter groups against Protestants and the British government, or in Indonesia or Bali against supporters of the West, it is clear that terrorism has become a global threat. Data assembled by the Center for Systemic Peace show that since 2001, both the number and the severity of terrorist incidents have increased.

What is significant about the way terrorist tactics are used is that they exploit the very systems of interconnection that globalization has spawned, whether these are via transportation, communication, energy, or immigration and democracy. Theories based on particular assumptions of biology, or psychology, or those based on the sociology of particular societies are inadequate to deal with the global dimensions of twenty-first-century crime.

So how do societies reconfigure their vision of crime to deal with its global dimensions? Should acts of terrorism and acts of war be considered crimes? What about the actions of states that abuse human rights? Are there new criminologies that are able to confront these more integrated global-level forms of harm creation?

In part due to these changes, in the early twenty-first century we have witnessed some surprising and shocking changes in the study of crime. Theoretically, the most significant change is the increased attention given to defining crime [...], not least because global terrorism has caused us to question the connection among politics, harm creation, and what kinds of actions should count as crime. There is also greater attention being focused on crimes of the powerful, from governments to corporations, more generally known as white-collar crime. In practical terms the increase in severity and frequency of terrorism has altered our belief in the amount of freedom that individuals are prepared to sacrifice to the government in exchange for state protection. Instead of security in the home to protect our private property, we are now more interested in "homeland security," to protect our energy resources, health network, water supply, communications system, and mass transportation facilities, including ports, airports, and trains. We are also strengthening public safety services: police, firefighting, emergency medical services, and

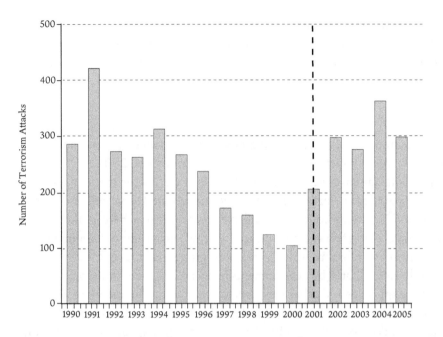

**FIGURE 5.3** Annual number of international terrorist attacks

*Source*: Center for Systemic Peace. http://www.systemicpeace.org.

the National Guard. We are moving from decentralized and fragmented protective services to an integrated national system of security designed to protect "the homeland" of America. Fear in the minds of Western populations has shifted from burglars in the night to low-flying aircraft and bombs at movie theaters and sporting events. The perceived vulnerability of Western civilizations stemming from the combination of openness and large concentrations of population has reached a national crisis.

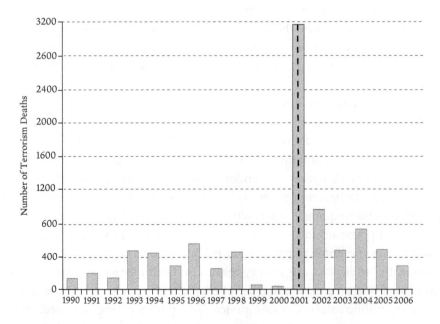

**FIGURE 5.4** Annual number of deaths from international terrorism

*Source*: Center for Systemic Peace. http://www.systemicpeace.org.

As a result of these changes, criminology is itself undergoing major changes. What historically has been a discipline focused on explaining individual criminal motivations in relation to domestic institutions and social processes has become a multifaceted examination that links genetic disposition to political and global forces. What is this discipline, this study of crime? To contemporary criminologists, the scope of crime is much broader than media portrayals of inner-city gang violence, child abductions, carjackings, drive-by shootings, serial murders, workplace homicides, and drug wars. Crime also includes a variety of misdeeds by governments, political corruption, corporate fraud, employee theft, and offenses committed by "ordinary" Americans.

Ever since the watershed of Watergate in the early 1970s when it was reluctantly realized that even a president could be a "crook," there has been accelerating media coverage of crimes by those in positions of power. Former president Bill Clinton reinforced this realization. The incredibly bad intelligence—or, worse, outright lies—that led to the hunt for weapons of mass destruction in Iraq provides yet another presidential example of abuse of power. Also consider the harm caused by U.S. government radiation experiments on unknowing citizens who subsequently developed cancer. Consider also the 1930s syphilis experiments that were conducted on African American men in Tuskegee, Alabama. These infected men were diagnosed with syphilis but deliberately not treated, even when penicillin was discovered as a cure, in order for government doctors to study the long-term effects of syphilis. False advertising and price-fixing by corporate giants like the Archer Daniels Midland Company (forcing consumers to pay more than the market price by undermining competition) are just some of the crimes committed by corporations. Other crimes of the powerful involve corporate executives deceiving investors, as in the Enron, WorldCom, and Arthur Andersen scandals; even Martha Stewart has made *insider trading* a household phrase. Corporate crime can also include manufacturers and hazardous-waste companies that pollute the environment; the knowing manufacture of defective products, as in the case of the Ford Pinto gas tank that exploded on low-speed rear-end impact or the use of dangerous Firestone tires on Ford Motor Company automobiles, particularly its SUVs; and unsafe food-handling practices by meat-processing companies resulting in E. coli contamination.

Also falling within the scope of criminology are the unsafe production practices that result in death and injury in the workplace, such as the case of the Imperial chicken plant in Hamlet, North Carolina, where twenty-five deaths occurred when the factory caught fire. Imperial's owners had padlocked the plant's fire exits to stop petty pilfering of chicken; each of the owners received a ten-year prison sentence for nonnegligent manslaughter. Contemporary criminologists also study employees who steal from their bosses, bosses who employ workers "off the books" to evade taxes, and professionals such as doctors who defraud the government and rob the public purse through Medicare and Medicaid fraud.

Finally, and most glaring, the United States has become the target of terrorist groups, as evidenced by the 9/11 suicide hijackings and the attacks on American interests abroad, including the USS *Cole* and the U.S. Embassy in Nairobi. What light can criminology shed on the political movements that lead humans to commit suicide bombings in furtherance of their cause? What global forces congeal to produce such widespread human suffering, and what can we learn about the forces that prevent these devastating consequences?

Criminologists study not only the nature of this harmful behavior but also its causes and the systemic practices that produce patterns of harms in a variety of social contexts. Take something as seemingly innocent as a recreational activity like surfing. This may seem to be a crime-free activity, and generally it is. But in September 1995 at Laguna Beach, California, two surfers were videotaped beating another surfer who had ventured into their designated contest area. The two surfers were arrested and charged with felony assault. In court on December 20, 1995, the two surfers had their charges reduced through a plea bargain, and each was released on three years' probation. The videotape played a vital role in the case. Media coverage was vast, and the case was featured on *Court TV.* Since we first provided this example, there has been a flurry of similar cases involving surfers and violence. A September 2, 2002, *People* article on the problem may have further influenced the prosecution of these territorial violent surfers, or it may have increased the violence. Indeed, the media play a significant role in shaping our conception of what crime is, especially through such infamous cases as the police beating in Inglewood, California, of a young teen, the Clarence Thomas–Anita Hill sexual harassment hearings, and the murder and kidnapping trials of O. J. Simpson and Michael Skakel (Barak 1994, 1996). The movie *Point Break* (1991) with Keanu Reeves even focused on territorially violent surfers.

What do these various crimes have in common? What kinds of cases grab media attention? Which do people consider more criminal? Which elicit the most concern? How does the social context affect the kind of crime and the harms suffered by its victims? How are technology and the media changing the face of crime? What do these events have to do with criminology? After reading this book, you should have a better understanding of these issues, if not clear answers.

## What is Criminology?

At its simplest, criminology can be defined as the systematic study of the nature, extent, cause, and control of lawbreaking behavior. Criminology is an applied social science in which criminologists work to establish knowledge about crime and its control based on empirical research. This research forms the basis for understanding, explanation, prediction, prevention, and criminal justice policy.

Ever since the term *criminology* was coined in 1885 by Raffaele Garofalo (1914), the content and scope of the field have been controversial. Critics and commentators have raised several questions about its academic standing. Some of the more common questions include the following: Is criminology truly a science? Does its applied approach, driven predominantly by the desire to control crime, inherently undermine the value-neutral stance generally considered essential for scientific inquiry? Is criminology an autonomous discipline, or does it rely on the insights, theory, and research of other natural and social science disciplines, and increasingly the media and public opinion? Which of the several theories of criminology offers the best explanation for crime? Answers to these questions are complex, and they are further complicated by criminology's multidisciplinary nature, its relative failure to recommend policy that reduces crime, and its heavy reliance on government funding for research. The complexity of these issues has been further compounded by increasing globalization, which has spawned crimes across national boundaries, and the failure of national enforcement agencies to prevent crime's global effects.

Criminology's subject matter is elastic. Unquestionable core components include: (1) the definition and nature of crime as harm-causing behavior; (2) different types of criminal activity, ranging from individual spontaneous offending to collective organized criminal enterprises; (3) profiles of typical offenders and victims, including organizational and corporate law violators; (4) statistical analysis of the extent, incidence, patterning, and cost of crimes, including estimates of the "dark figure" of hidden or unreported crime, based on surveys of victims and self-report studies of offenders;

BOX 5.1 **Crime, Risk, and the Changing World Order.**
           **Christiaan Bezuidenhout, University Of Pretoria**

As perceived risks increase, spurred on by the global spread of crime, particularly terrorism, many countries around the world are having to pay excessive prices for freedom, liberty, and equality. The global terrorist attacks on innocent people to convey a specific message in an attempt to achieve political and ideological objectives illustrate the extent of the problem. Following the 9/11 attacks on the United States, the United Kingdom and Spain were also targeted. The attacks in Spain (2004) and in the UK (2005) highlighted the change in global risk and challenged our conception of crime. India has also been the target of several terrorist attacks on hotels in which many innocent people were killed, most recently in December 2008. These criminal attacks have impacted the global community on several levels. For the members of any specific country, death, destruction, financial loss, as well as psychological and physical suffering are some of the direct, blatant aftereffects of such an attack. However, the impact on confidence and security in the global community is more indirect but perhaps more pervasive in its long-term implications. Consider how global air travel has changed in the past few years. Travelers face security delays and invasive screening, are required to remove shoes and clothing at the security and customs areas at airports, and are not allowed to carry any liquids or knives on board the airplane. The risks and resultant security measures have become very apparent and present challenges for newly formed, struggling democracies.

Consider South Africa as an example. The changes within the "new" South Africa as well as the adoption of a Bill of Human Rights and Constitution have resulted in drastic changes being made to the way in which accused offenders are being processed and treated in this country. More restorative justice programs and less incarceration are being utilized. In addition, the freedoms that have come with South African democracy have been accompanied by extraordinarily high crime and homicide rates. Serious crimes in any country cause fear and insecurity, and dramatic increases in crime rates intensify the perceived personal risk of victimization. Risk is part of any society and does not discriminate with regard to social class, level of development, or the size of law enforcement or defense budgets. Risk is real and very relevant to the study of criminology. In this context it could be assumed that many governments have lost their monopoly on crime control, and this predicament has forced them to adapt to the changing landscape of crime, order, and control. Increasingly, law enforcement is being contracted out to private security organizations.

Taking this argument to the next level, some criminologists (e.g., Garland 2001) have proposed that because crime and risk have become part of everyday life, and because governments in general have lost their ability to control crime over the past thirty years, societal adjustments, particularly in the manner of governance, have become obligatory for survival. The new global hum in governance is "risk," "actuarial thinking," and "early intervention"—also known as proactive prevention. The logic of risk is inherently political, stimulates action, and triggers communication (Loader and Sparks 2002). The term *risk society* is used to describe a society that is organized in response to risk. According to sociologist Anthony Giddens, a risk society is "a society increasingly preoccupied with the future (and also with safety), which generates the notion of risk" (1999, 3). Risk here can be defined as a systematic way of dealing with hazards and insecurities induced and introduced by modernization itself. Risk becomes a way of thinking in all spheres of day-to-day life. We live in a world of manufactured uncertainty (crime, terrorist attacks, school and hotel shootings) and external risks (hurricanes, tsunamis, earthquakes). Risk management—in other words, how to identify and manage risk—has become the focus of the new actuarial criminology (Beck 1992; Giddens 1999).

Garland refers to the changing landscape of the global crime canvas in his theory on social control and governance through crime as the "new predicament" (2001, 110). In his view, the government's capacity to deliver security is being questioned. Globally, police and criminal justice officials are finding it more and more difficult to control crime. A managerial or value-for-money approach in crime prevention is becoming increasingly evident in a global context. Local-level crime-prevention partnerships between the police and the citizens are being formed, and citizens are increasingly expected to take responsibility for their own safety. They should install safety mechanisms such as alarms in their homes and electric fences around their properties, or consider moving to a gated community. In addition, policing and security have become commodities for the so-called haves. The middle and upper classes can afford private security, armed-response protection, and closed-circuit television monitoring. Security companies categorize citizens as high or low risk and adapt their policies and payouts based on age, gender, and level of risk. This commodity (security) and the false belief in safety do not take the lower classes and the poorest of the poor into consideration (e.g., the majority of citizens in South Africa). Think too of a country like Zimbabwe, where daily survival is a huge challenge. It is probably the country with the poorest citizens in the world; food is its most valuable commodity. Thus, the safety commodity is of little value to them (although they really are in need of safety and protection), as they have to struggle on a daily basis to get food to see the next day.

The changing world order and the crime phenomenon have changed significantly in the new millennium. Criminology as a science is therefore challenged in many new ways to provide answers to these changes. It is becoming apparent that criminology not only offers theoretical insights but also serves a practical function in society.

**Christiaan Bezuidenhout** is Associate Professor in the Department of Social Work and Criminology at the University of Pretoria in Pretoria, South Africa.

## References

Beck, Ulrick. 1992. *Risk Society: Towards a New Modernity.* London: Sage.

Garland, David. 2001. *The Culture of Control: Crime and Social Order in Contemporary Society.* Oxford: Oxford University Press.

Giddens, Anthony. 1999. "Risk and Responsibility." *Modern Law Review* 62, no. 1: 1–10.

Loader, Ian, and Richard Sparks. 2002. "Contemporary Landscapes of Crime, Order, and Control: Governance, Risk, and Globalization." In *The Oxford Handbook of Criminology,* edited by M. Maguire, R. Morgan, and R. Reiner, 83–111. 3d ed. Oxford: Oxford University Press.

and (5) analysis of crime causation. Less agreement exists about whether the scope of criminology should be broadened to include society's response to crime, the formulation of criminal laws, the role of victims in these processes, and the extent to which criminology needs to adopt a comparative global perspective.

In the United States, the inclusive term *criminal justice* generally refers to crime-control practices, philosophies, and policies used by the police, courts, and system of corrections (in Europe it is called penology). Those who study such matters are as likely to identify themselves, or be identified by others, as criminologists, however, as are those who study criminal behavior and its causes. Criminology, by contrast, concerns itself with the theoretical and empirical study of the causes of crime. The two areas are obviously closely related, but a distinction is necessary.

## Is Criminology Scientific?

Criminology requires that criminologists strictly adhere to the scientific method. What distinguishes science from nonscience is the insistence on testable hypotheses whose support or refutation through empirical research forms the basis of what is accepted among scientific criminologists as valid knowledge. Science, then, requires criminologists to build criminological knowledge from logically interrelated, theoretically grounded, and empirically tested hypotheses that are subject to retesting. These theoretical statements hold true as long as they are not falsified by further research (Popper 1959).

Theory testing can be done using either qualitative or quantitative methods. Qualitative methods (Berg [1989] 2000) may involve systematic ethnographic techniques, such as participant observation and in-depth interviews. These methods are designed to enable the researcher to understand the meaning of criminal activity to the participants. In participant observation, the researcher takes a role in the crime scene or in the justice system and describes what goes on between the participants. Criminologists using this technique study crime and its social context as an anthropologist would study a nonindustrial society. These methods have produced some of criminology's richest studies, such as Laud Humphries's study of homosexuality in public restrooms, *Tearoom Trade* (1970), and Howard Becker's study of jazz musicians and marijuana smoking in his book *Outsiders* ([1963] 1973).

Quantitative methods involve numbers, counts, and measures that are arrived at via a variety of research techniques. These include survey research based on representative random samples and the analysis of secondary data gathered for other purposes, such as homicide rates or corporate convictions for health and safety violations. Criminologists using quantitative techniques make up the mainstream of academic criminology. Perhaps one of the most illustrative examples of quantitative research is the series of longitudinal studies of a cohort of 10,000 boys born in Philadelphia in 1945 and followed through age eighteen with respect to their arrests for criminal offenses (Wolfgang, Figlio, and Sellin 1972) and a second cohort of 27,000 boys and girls born in 1958 (Tracy, Wolfgang, and Figlio 1990). Each study seemed to indicate that a small proportion of offenders (6 percent), called "chronic offenders," accounted for more than half of all offenses. Other quantitative research methods include the use of historical records, comparative analysis, and experimental research. Unfortunately, most quantitative research is not theory driven; in other words, it does not involve theory testing. A survey conducted in 1992 revealed that only 27 percent of the articles published over a period of twenty-eight years in the journal *Criminology* tested theory (Stitt and Giacopassi 1992). Thus, apparently, theoretically grounded research is lacking. This begs the question: Is criminology scientific?

## Disciplinary Diversity

Although strongly influenced by sociology, criminology also has roots in a number of other disciplines, including anthropology, biology, economics, geography, history, philosophy, political science, psychiatry, psychology, and sociology (Einstadter and Henry 2006). Each of these disciplines contributes its own assumptions about human nature and society, its own definitions of crime and the role of law, its own preference of methods for the study of crime, and its own analysis of crime causation with differing policy implications. This diversity presents a major challenge to criminology's disciplinary integrity. Do these diverse theoretical perspectives, taken together when applied to crime, constitute an independent academic discipline? Are these contributing fields of knowledge merely subfields, or special applications of established disciplines? Alternatively, is criminology interdisciplinary? If criminology is to be considered interdisciplinary, what does that mean? Is interdisciplinarity understood as the integration of knowledge into a distinct whole? If so, then criminology is not yet interdisciplinary. Only a few criminologists have attempted such integration (see Messner, Krohn, and Liska 1989; Barak 1998; and M. Robinson 2004). There is sufficient independence of the subject from its constituent disciplines and an acceptance of their diversity, however, to prevent criminology from being subsumed under any one of them. For this reason, criminology is best defined as multidisciplinary. Put simply, crime can be viewed though many lenses. This is well illustrated through an overview of its component theories, [...]. There is, however, a caveat that suggests a question: Because globalization makes us interdependent, is integrated theory more necessary in the future to capture this complexity?

## Comparative and Global Criminology

Comparative criminology has been defined as the systematic study of crime, law, and social control of two or more cultures (Beirne and Hill 1991). As Winslow has argued, "The global approach to the study of crimes recognizes its growing international nature and, in time, may become the primary focus of criminology in a world rapidly being unified by technological improvements in transportation and communication" (1998, 6). Winslow and Zhang's *Criminology: A Global Perspective* (2007) includes a Web site that provides a window on global crime (http://www-rohan.sdsu.edu/faculty/rwinslow/index.html). Beirne and Messerschmidt have argued that comparative analysis of crime enables criminologists to overcome their ethnocentric tendencies and sharpen their understanding of key questions: "Indeed, one reason why the United States has experienced such relatively high crime rates is that policy makers have relied on limited parochial theories regarding the causes of crime" (2000, 478). They show the value of looking at cross-national data on crime and victimization and countries and cities with low crime rates. Increasingly important also is the ability of corporations to evade the regulatory policies of one country by moving their operations to other countries. Clearly, this applies to regulatory attempts to control environmental pollution. However, it also applies to the ways that deliberately contaminated food, such as the Chinese production of milk products containing melamine that injured many babies, can be distributed globally.

# What is Victimology?

The scientific study of victimology is a relatively recent field, founded by Hans von Hentig (1948) and Benjamin Mendelsohn (1963), who claims to have coined the term in 1947. It is almost the mirror image or "reverse of criminology" (Schafer 1977, 35). Criminology is concerned mainly with criminals and criminal acts and the criminal justice system's response to them. Victimology is the study of who becomes a victim, how victims are victimized, how much harm they suffer, and their role in the criminal act. It also looks at victims' rights and their role in the criminal justice system.

Victimology has been defined as "the scientific study of the physical, emotional, and financial harm people suffer because of criminal activities" (Karmen 2001, 9). This interrelationship has a long history. Prior to the development of formal social control mechanisms, society relied on individualized informal justice. Individuals, families, and clans sought justice for harms caused by others.

Endless feuding and persistent physical confrontation led to what has been called the "Golden Age" (Karmen 2001), when restitution became the focus of crime control [...]. With the advent of the social contract, individuals gave up the right to retaliation, and crimes became crimes against the state—not the individual. The classicist social contract, simply put, says that individuals must give up some personal liberties in exchange for a greater social good. Thus, individuals forfeited the right to individualized justice, revenge, and vigilantism. This creed is still practiced today. For that reason, O. J. Simpson's first criminal trial for murder was *The State of California v. Orenthal J. Simpson*, not *Goldman and Brown-Simpson v. Orenthal J. Simpson*, which was the realm of the civil trial. Advanced societies relying on systems of justice based on the social contract increasingly, though inadvertently, neglected the victims of crime. In the United States, "Public prosecutors ... took over powers and responsibilities formerly assumed by victims. ... Attorneys decided whether or not to press charges, what indictments to file, and what sanctions to ask judges to invoke. ... When the overwhelming majority of cases came to be resolved through confessions of guilt elicited in negotiated settlements, most victims lost their last opportunity to actively participate" (Karmen 1990, 17).

Since the founding of victimology, there has been controversy between the broad view (Mendelsohn 1963) that victimology should be the study of all victims and the narrow view that it should include only crime victims. Clearly, if a broad definition is taken of crime as a violation of human rights (Schwendinger and Schwendinger 1970; S. Cohen 1993; Tifft and Sullivan 2001), this is more consistent with the broad view of victimology.

It is only since the early 1970s that victimization has been included in mainstream criminology. This followed studies by Stephen Schafer (1968, 1977) and a flurry of victimization studies culminating in the U.S. Department of Justice's annual National Crime Victimization Survey, begun in 1972. There are numerous texts on the field (see Elias 1986; Walklate 1989; and Karmen [2001] 2006).

Victimology has also been criticized for the missionary zeal of its reform policy (Fattah 1992; Weed 1995) and for its focus on victims of individual crimes rather than socially harmful crimes, although there are rare exceptions to this in French victimology studies (Joutsen 1994). The more recent comprehensive approach considers the victim in the total societal context of crime in the life domains of family, work, and leisure as these realms are shaped by the media, lawmakers, and interest groups (Sacco and Kennedy 1996).

## Summary

We began this chapter by showing how the "world" has changed and how criminology has had to change with it. We looked at six major changes that have impacted the ways that we see crime and the way that we think about its causes: (1) globalization and its impact on economic, social, and political institutions; (2) the globalization of communications, particularly the advent of the Internet; (3) privatization and individualization and the decline of group and class solidarity; (4) the global spread of disease and the development of epidemiological criminology; (5) changing perceptions of conflict and national security since the end of the cold war; and (6) the internationalization of terrorism. Criminology has evolved and will continue to expand to provide improved methods of study and more comprehensive explanatory theories for understanding crime. The current direction is moving toward a more inclusive and expansive criminology that considers crime as deprivation and harm—regardless of legislated law. It also is beginning, through comparative and global criminology, to move toward recognizing the interconnectedness of people across countries and cultures, and so needs to be both integrated and comparative in its approach.

We have also seen that criminology has a much broader scope than simply studying criminals. If nothing else, the reader should have developed a sense that there are few definitive "truths" in the study of crime. Controversy and diverse views abound. This is not without good reason. Criminology is perhaps the most widely examined (by the public, media, and policy makers) of the social sciences. As a result of the nightly news, talk shows, newsmagazine programs, and popular television dramas, such as *Law and Order*, *CSI*, and *Criminal Minds*, crime and its control are topics in which everyone's interest is engaged and everyone has an opinion.

Criminology is clearly also policy oriented. The criminal justice system that implements the law and policy of governments itself is a significant source of employment and expenditure. Considering only corrections, twenty years ago the combined states spent $10.6 billion from their general funds on corrections. In 2007, they spent more than $49 billion—a 362 percent increase. By comparison, inflation-adjusted prison spending increased 127 percent, while the budget for higher education increased only 21 percent nationwide (Pew Charitable Trusts 2008). In 2008 the states spent a record $51.7 billion on corrections, 6.7 percent of state budgets, which rises to $68 billion when local, federal, and other funding is included. Moreover, in 2008, 7.3 million, or 1 in 31, Americans were under some supervision by the U.S. corrections system, including people on probation and parole (Pew Charitable Trusts 2009). The long-term implications of this decreased emphasis on education and increased focus on punishment and incarceration are disturbing and the subject of much debate. Several states have taken steps to reduce prison expenses. California has taken the lead, reducing its prison population by 4,068 in 2007 (Pew Charitable Trusts 2008). However, thirty-six states and the Federal Bureau of Prisons experienced increases in 2007. Similar debate was lacking, however, following the terrorist attacks against the United States. Government powers were increased dramatically following the events of September 11, 2001, with little or no debate.

Regardless of one's theoretical inclinations, preferred research tools, or policy preferences, dissension demands a clear articulation of one's position. Such articulation requires considerable thought in order to make convincing arguments and the insight to appreciate other positions. The end result is that criminology as a whole is strengthened.

[...]

# What are the Major Criminological Theories of Crime?

JOYCELYN M. POLLOCK

The earliest criminogical theories are usually described as the **classical school** and marked by the contributions of Cesare Beccaria (1738–94) and Jeremy Bentham (1748–1832).[1] Both theorists, writing in the 1700s, operated under a fundamental assumption that men were rational and operated with free will. Therefore, the elimination of crime could be achieved by the threat of punishment for offenses, which would act as a deterrent to crime. Bentham's "**hedonistic calculus**," for instance, was the idea of carefully weighing punishment to slightly outweigh the potential pleasure or profit that might be obtained, in order to deter. Philosophers during this period did not view women in the same manner as men and viewed their mental abilities to be more akin to children; therefore, their discussions applied specifically to men. The focus of these thinkers was on the legal system; the assumption was that everyone would respond to the legal system in a similar, rational manner.

The field of criminology is generally said to have begun with the "Positivists" in the 1800s. **Positivism** can be described simply as "scientific method" or the search for causes using scientific method. It is typically associated with Cesare Lombroso (1835–1909),[2] who is often referred to as the "grandfather of criminology." Lombroso believed the cause of crime lies in the individual. He developed a typology of criminals, including those he believed were "born criminal" with genetic defects that made them commit criminal acts. Other types included criminals influenced by opportunity, influence, and passion. Later positivists in the early 1900s also looked at individual causes, and both biological and psychological factors were examined. According to positivists, criminals were different from non-criminals and criminologists merely needed to understand those differences. We can say that the field of criminology really began with the positivists because they initiated the search for differences between criminal men and women and law-abiding men and women. Their findings do not hold up over the passage of time and their scientific method was primitive, but their approach is still the basic approach of most criminologists today—that is, to seek out differences that motivate some people to choose crime. Although we will not cover any theories in depth, the sections below briefly introduce you to three different categories of theories in criminology: biological, psychological, and sociological theories.

## What do Biological Theories of Crime Say about Who Commits Crime and Why?

Recall that the three strongest predictors of crime—sex, age, and race—are biological constructs. Of the three, only race shows strongly different patterns cross-culturally. Also, race is mediated by inter-racial mixing so that most people do not represent pure racial **phenotypes**. Further, biologists themselves argue about whether it makes sense to discuss race as a biological construct at all since the genetic difference between the races is minuscule. However, the other two correlates are age and sex and these do show strong cross-cultural patterns. Thus, it would seem that biology should be at least explored as a factor in crime causation. However, research on biological factors has been given little attention in most criminology textbooks. Part of the reason biological approaches in criminology have been so completely rejected is that there are serious policy implications for such theories. It is argued that such theories lead to **eugenics,** which is the idea of improving the human race through controlled procreation, and other forms of control repugnant to our democratic ideals.

Biological factors may be a) inherited genetic traits, or b) biological factors that are not genetic. For instance, a brain tumor that puts pressure on an area of the brain that is instrumental in aggressive impulses and results in irrational violence is obviously a biological cause of crime, but tumors are not thought to be inherited. Chemicals or other environmental toxins, such as lead, can also affect the brain and are non-genetic biological factors that may influence criminal choice. Some researchers are convinced that the reduction in lead-based paint has contributed to some extent to the dramatic decline of violent criminality. There is no question that lead is tremendously detrimental to brain development affecting the pre-frontal lobe and impulse control; and, the percentage of lead in children's blood was alarmingly high as late as the 1970s because of lead-based paints and lead in gasoline. In the United States, blood lead levels in children dropped by 79 percent between 1976 and 1991, the period over which leaded fuel was phased out. The same data showed that blood lead levels, although lower, remained higher among minorities and those with lower socio-economic status.[3] Some research shows a correlation between levels of lead and rates of violent crime, arguing that the greatest spike in crime (early 1990s) corresponded to when cohorts exposed to lead entered their crime-prone age years and, subsequently, the decline of crime occurred when childhood cohorts not exposed to as high levels of lead as past generations grew into the crime-prone age years.[4]

Other researchers have shown that the rise and fall of violent crime was not limited to birth cohorts who were exposed to lead but, rather, all birth cohorts increased their criminality in the 1990s and decreased crime rates could be seen consistently across all birth cohorts in the 2000s.[5] This area of research has become extremely important after it was revealed in the fall and winter of 2015–16 that lead levels in the city water supply in Flint, Michigan, vastly exceeded safe levels because the city did not add a non-corrosive agent to the water when it switched from Detroit to the Flint River as a water source. Testing of children has found blood lead levels to be in the range that developmental and behavioral effects might result. To the great misfortune of its residents, Flint may become a natural laboratory in the study of lead and its effects.

More controversial than toxic agents or tumors is the idea that criminality is inherited. Is there a criminal gene? Of course not, but the argument of biological criminologists is that there are some inherited characteristics that predispose individuals to criminal choices.[6] The methodological problem has always been trying to isolate genetic influences from socialization influences. If you are like your mother or father, is it because you have inherited traits from them or because they raised you (nature versus nurture)? Trying to separate these influences is very difficult, even with the use of twin studies which have looked at the **concordance** between the criminality of children and their adoptive parents and biological parents.[7] Statistical and methodological criticisms of twin studies continue to call into question their findings.[8] Opposing arguments strongly refute the methodological criticisms leveled against twin studies, but the two opposing camps agree more than they disagree since both sides accept the importance of both genetics and environment on observable behaviors, including criminal behavior.[9]

Some criminologists estimate that genetics can explain about half of criminality.[10] When a personality trait is believed to be inherited, scientists look for the actual physical components of the trait. These origins lie in the neural structures of the brain, brain chemistry, and hormones. For instance, although such research has been subject to criticism, a fairly impressive body of knowledge has developed on the correlation between testosterone and aggression.[11] If it exists, this biological reality could help to explain the gender differential in violent crime.

Brain chemicals affect personality traits. Monoamine oxidase (MAO) is a chemical found in the brain and low levels have been linked to psychopathy, alcoholism, sensation-seeking, impulsivity, extroversion, schizophrenia, and criminal behavior.[12] Men, on average, have about 20 percent less MAO than women, and this difference exists at all ages. Boys with low MAO levels were found to be more impulsive and sensation-seeking than other boys and were more likely to have drug and alcohol problems.[13] Associations are consistently found between low MAO activity and various correlates of criminal behavior, such as impulsiveness, childhood hyperactivity, learning disabilities, sensation-seeking, substance abuse, and extraversion. MAO activity seems to be correlated with age, sex, and race. Testosterone evidently depresses MAO levels. In fact, testosterone levels are at their highest and MAO levels are at their lowest during the second decade of life (ten to twenty years of age).[14] Thus, these findings provide intriguing possibilities that MAO is perhaps part of the explanation for age and sex differences in crime.

Other research shows interesting connections between serotonin levels and negative emotionality and impulsivity.[15] Serotonin also seems to be linked with norepinephrine levels and, together, they may play a role in conditionability or the ability to learn.[16] Some individuals might be predisposed toward antisocial behaviors because these behaviors are exciting and produce the level of cortical arousal that extraverts seek.[17]

Sex differences exist in cortical arousal levels, and men, in general, are more likely to have low cortical arousal.[18] Hyperactivity and attention deficit disorder (ADD) are more common in boys than girls.[19] These learning issues are also correlated with delinquency. It has been reported that those diagnosed with hyperactivity as children were 25 times more likely to exhibit later delinquency.[20]

Denno[21] reports that chronic delinquency is linked to overactivity, perceptual-motor impairments, impulsivity, emotional lability, attention deficits, minor disturbances of speech, intellectual defects (learning disabilities), clumsiness, neurodevelopmental lag, psychogenic factors, and minor physical anomalies. These features may be the result of genetic transmission, poor living environment, prenatal or birth trauma, or a combination of the above. It is also important to note that critics argue that observed differences in brain chemicals may be due to environmental conditions that also affect the potential for criminality. For instance, studies have found that exposure to abusive, unpredictable, or harsh childhood conditions is associated with changes in the **amygdala** and **prefrontal cortex,** both instrumental in emotional regulation. Severe adversity affects the oxytocin receptor gene which is associated with empathy/callousness so it is possible that the brain molds itself to adapt to the environment.[22] Other researchers have begun to identify how environmental conditions such as violence, emotional abuse, discrimination, and poverty can result in long-term stress creating elevated levels of cortisol that eventually changes brain chemistry, which, in turn, affects the potential to react with aggression to perceived threat.[23] What percent of behavior is "nature" (inherited) versus "nurture" (influenced by the environment) is impossible to determine because the brain itself changes in reaction to the environment.

To summarize: there are sex differences in the relative levels of brain chemicals and hormones associated with delinquency. Furthermore, these chemicals and hormones fluctuate over the life course, and help to explain why younger people are more impulsive and thrill-seeking than older individuals. Biological predispositions don't always result in delinquency and the relationship between these factors is much more complex than what has been sketched here. Critics argue that biological factors can't explain the crime decline of the last two decades because biological factors would be presumed to be fairly stable (the same percentage of the population experience low MAO levels or low cortical arousal). However, we could hypothesize that because situational factors interact with biological factors, something might have changed which affected the relationship between biological factors and criminal behavior. For example, advances in education, earlier intervention in environmental stressors, or other changes, may have taken place and affected particular birth cohorts who did not then grow up to engage in criminality as frequently as prior cohorts. Arrest patterns, however, do not lend strong support to this hypothesis since arrest rates declined across all age groups.

Many criminologists reject biological explanations of criminal choices. This rejection is somewhat understandable given the sordid history of eugenics; however, it is not consistent with the critical approach we are modeling in this text to reject a school of theories without objectively considering the evidence. The field of **epigenetics** is the study of cellular and physiological phenotypic trait differences that result from external or environmental factors that, in effect, switch genes on and off and affect how cells express genes. Great strides are being made in the fields of medicine and nutrition once people accept that the biology is not destiny. Genetic inheritance can only ever explain some portion of health and behavior.

# What do Psychological Theories of Crime Say About Who Commits Crime and Why?

Criminologists have largely ignored psychological theories of deviance and crime.[24] This is largely because criminology has emerged as a discipline from the field of sociology, not psychology. To say that psychology is ignored in criminology textbooks is perhaps a misstatement because many of the major theories of criminology could be described as socio-psychological in that they focus on how the individual reacts to his or her environment.

The most obvious contribution of psychological theory to an understanding of criminality is the concept of **sociopathy** or **psychopathy**. The psychopath has been differentiated from the sociopath in the following way: "[the psychopath is] an individual in whom the normal processes of socialization have failed to produce the mechanisms of conscience and habits of law-abidingness that normally constrain antisocial impulses" and the sociopath as "a person whose unsocialized character is due primarily to parental failures rather than to inherent peculiarities of temperament."[25] The *Diagnostic and Statistical Manual* (**DSM-IV**), a type of dictionary for mental health workers to diagnose and categorize all mental health problems, has replaced the terms "psychopathy" and "sociopathy" with the term "**antisocial personality disorder.**" Regardless, these definitions describe an individual who is without a conscience and unable to form sincere, affectionate bonds with others. This describes many, but not all, of those who engage in criminal behavior.

Psychological explanations for behavior generally identify agreed-upon personality trait models (i.e., neuroticism, extroversion, openness to experience, agreeableness, conscientiousness), and then identify certain traits as associated with criminal propensity.[26] The traits of sensation-seeking, overactivity, low self-control, emotionality, and callousness, as well as "negative emotionality," which includes aggression, alienation, and anger/irritability as a stress reaction, are associated with persistent criminality.[27] While researchers note that the traits seem to equally predict male and female offending, it is also true that there are fewer female offenders; therefore, there are either fewer young women who possess the predisposing traits, at least to the degree that young men do, or alternatively, there are environmental mediators that operate differently between the sexes so that young men and women with similar personality traits experience life differently and, therefore, take different behavioral paths.

Psychology focuses on the individual and, thus, psychological theories of criminality focus on developmental reasons for criminal choices. A variety of developmental theories propose that delinquent and criminal offenders are "stuck" at lower levels of development and have not reached emotional maturity which includes developing empathy (e.g. caring about others). Delinquents and criminals are immature, either in their response to the world, their interactions with others around them, and/or in their putting self above others.[28]

**Learning theory** proposes that individuals act and believe the way they do because they have learned to do so. Learning takes place through modeling or reinforcement. **Modeling** stems from the desire to be like others, especially those whom one admires; therefore, children will act as they see their parents or peers act. The other form of learning is through **reinforcement**. That is, one will continue behaviors and beliefs for which one has been rewarded, and eliminate behaviors and beliefs that have been punished or not rewarded. Albert Bandura,[29] for instance, argues that individuals are not necessarily inherently aggressive, but rather learn aggression. He and others also point out that learning is mediated by intelligence and temperament. Personality traits such as impulsivity, aggressiveness, and emotionality affect one's ability to absorb learning.

One of the most enduring explanations of why women commit less crime, by both laypeople and criminologists, is the idea that they learn to be law-abiding and that the social sanctions against deviance for women and girls are much stronger than those boys or men would experience. If true, learning theory is perfectly consistent with the lower crime rates observed for women.

Psychological theories identify individual factors as affecting criminal choice. More sophisticated theories also refer to environmental factors. So, for instance, Andrews and Bonta[30] developed a psychological theory of crime that includes the characteristics of the immediate environment and individual characteristics to explain crime choices. They point to the attitudes, values, beliefs, and rationalizations held by the person with regard to antisocial behavior, social support for antisocial behavior (perceived support from others), a history of having engaged in antisocial behavior, self-management and problem-solving skills, and other stable personality characteristics conducive to antisocial conduct. Then, they relate these to a behavioral explanation of criminality where rewards and costs of crime are mediated by these individual differences. By including environmental factors (e.g. social support) this type of psychological theory overlaps with sociological theories that focus on the environment and situational factors that lead to criminal choices.

Some of the theories above may at least partially help us understand the gender differential in crime and even perhaps the fact that crime is committed disproportionally by the young. No psychological theory of crime by itself would help to explain the crime decline unless psychological factors interacted with environmental changes. Any hypothesis that utilized psychological factors in explanations of crime would first have to establish whether or not there had been changes in the relative levels of such factors in the population; we presume that biological and psychological factors in a population do not change over time, thus any perceived change (such as the decline of crime) would have to be explained by an interaction between the factor and some environmental (societal) change.

## What do Sociological Theories of Crime Say About Who Commits Crime and Why?

Adolphe Quetelet (1796–1874) and Émile Durkheim (1858–1917) are credited as early sociologists who established the foundations of sociological criminology. Quetelet discovered that crime occurred in reasonably predictable patterns in society, thus supporting the notion that there was something about society that caused crime rather than crime occurring at random or because of individual causes. Émile Durkheim offered the principle that crime was normal and present in all societies. The absence of deviance or crime, in fact, was evidence of cultural stagnation.

Recall the difference between macro and micro theories of crime. Macro theories look at societal factors that affect the amount of crime. We could also call these social structure theories. Micro theories look at how individuals react to their environment by making criminal choices. We could call these social process theories (and they are very similar to some of the psychological theories described earlier). Both approaches reject the idea of the "criminal as different." In these theories, it is assumed that anyone who happens to be exposed to these factors would become criminal.

The so-called **Chicago school** in the 1930s and 1940s truly began the study of societal influences on criminality when sociologists at the University of Chicago observed that crime occurred more often in **mixed zones** of the city. In these zones, residential, commercial, and industrial activity could be observed. The zones were also characterized by low home ownership, property damage, graffiti, and high rates of alcoholism, domestic violence, and mental health problems. Early sociologists discovered that these mixed zones always had higher crime rates, even though different demographic groups moved in and out of them over the decades. Thus, it seemed that there was something about the zone, rather than the people who lived within it, that generated crime.[31]

Observers from the Chicago school noted that **subcultures** emerged in the mixed zone, and these subcultures promoted values and beliefs that were different from the dominant culture and encouraged criminal behavior (such as prostitution, gambling, and other forms of deviance). **Subculture theory** and **cultural deviance theory**, first developed in the 1950s, observed that there are some groups in society who teach antisocial behaviors (instead of socializing its members to follow the norms of the dominant culture). According to this theory, if one lives in these areas of the city, then one will most likely become delinquent because the subculture defines such behavior as acceptable.[32] Cultural deviance theory identifies cultures that clash when individuals migrate to a new culture. Subcultural theories look at subcultures that exist within the dominant culture but have different values and belief systems. Gangs are an example of a subculture, although this stretches the classic definition of a subculture, because members of any gang also participate and are socialized, to some extent, by the dominant culture as well. Women were largely ignored in early subcultural theories even though they obviously lived in the mixed zones alongside the boys and men who were being socialized to criminality.

Another factor observed in the mixed zones was lack of opportunity. The individuals who lived in these neighborhoods had very little hope of economic success. **Strain/opportunity theory**, popularized in the 1960s, argued that lack of opportunity is the cause of crime. Individuals who are blocked from legitimate means of economic success, such as employment, family, or education, will experience strain because of blocked goals and then choose crime as a way to achieve goals according to this theory.[33] A later application of the theory enlarged it to groups, so that those who were blocked from opportunities would form groups (gangs) distinct from those who had legitimate opportunities.[34] Because everyone is socialized to believe that they can and should achieve material success, those who do not have the means feel particular stress. In static cultures, that is, where the poor have no expectations or hope that they will achieve wealth, there is less pressure or inclination to use illegitimate means to get ahead. However, a line of research going back decades has not produced a definitive link between socio-economics and crime on the macro level, and unemployment doesn't have a strong correlation with crime at the micro level.[35] One caution, however, is that much of this research involves examining the effects of employment that involves transitory and low-paying jobs. It is possible that the jobs offenders might be able to obtain are not sufficiently motivating to counteract the lure of criminal opportunities.

More recently, the ideas of the Chicago school have been revived with **social support theory** and **social disorganization theory**. Basically, both point to the community as a prime factor in crime causation, either because of the lack of supportive elements in a neighborhood, or, alternatively the lack of cohesion and elements of "community" of some neighborhoods.[36] These researchers believe that the community is the primary element in social control and can be undercut by oppressive formal control, such as law enforcement.[37]

**Social process theories** focus on the individual's interaction with the world around him or her and have more in common in this respect with psychological theories. **Differential association**

**theory,** introduced originally by Edwin Sutherland in 1939, is very similar to learning theory.[38] Later, others applied social learning principles to the theory to make it even more similar to learning theory.[39] Researchers have utilized these theories to explain why girls and women are less likely to commit crime—in short, it is because they are socialized to be "nicer" than boys.[40] The increasing participation of women in some crime areas is explained by many as due to changing roles and expectations for women.

   **Labeling theory** assumes that even though almost all of us have engaged in "primary deviance," only certain individuals are labeled as deviant. This results in their accepting and absorbing the deviant role and committing further delinquency because of the label.[41] In contrast, **control theory**, as presented by Travis Hirschi in 1969,[42] presumed that most of us would drift to delinquency, but we don't because of the "bonds" of society that control us—specifically attachment, commitment, involvement, and belief. Delinquency was correlated with the absence of these types of ties. Control theory provides a relatively adequate explanation for the sex differential in crime rates if we can assume that girls have more attachments and other bonds than boys. It is generally found that girls profess stronger ties to friends, family, and school, and they tend to possess more prosocial belief systems than boys. The theory is also consistent with the age correlate because one can assume that "bonds" to society increase as a young man matures and obtains a job, wife, and family. It does not necessarily explain the country's crime decline unless one could identify major changes in schools and other social institutions that created greater attachments that, in turn, led to a decrease in delinquency and subsequent criminality of youth.

   While control theory postulates that various bonds to society (attachment, commitment, belief, and involvement) control the individual and prevent delinquency, Hirschi and Gottfredson's[43] **general theory of crime** proposes that individuals are born with and/or are raised to have different levels of self-control and those with low self-control are more likely to commit crime and a host of other dangerous and impulsive behaviors (such as smoking, drinking, using drugs, gambling, having illegitimate children, and engaging in illicit sex). The major cause of a lack of self-control, according to these authors, is ineffective parenting. They argue that the conditions necessary to teach self-control include monitoring behavior, recognizing deviant behavior, and punishing such behavior.[44] Criticisms of the theory argue that self-control does change over the life course and it does respond to different parenting techniques and can be strengthened.[45] A major weakness of the theory is that it does not adequately explain the sex differential in crime unless one was to assume that women generally have more self-control than men.[46] Some research shows, in fact, that moral norms may be more predictive of delinquency/criminality than low self-control.[47]

   Agnew's **general strain theory**[48] reformulates strain/opportunity theory, which focused on the level of legitimate opportunities in a neighborhood, into a social process theory that examines how individuals deal with various types of strain, including a lack of opportunity. According to this theory, individuals may experience strain from not getting what they want, losing something that was important, or in other ways being in a situation that is experienced as noxious. The strain generates negative emotions, such as disappointment, fear, depression, and anger, and these negative emotions cause delinquency/crime. Individuals commit delinquent acts in order to relieve the strain of the negative emotions. As the theory was refined over the years, theorists also recognized that different people have different coping abilities and react differently to the strains they experience.

An entirely different direction to explaining crime is offered by Tom Tyler. Hirschi's earlier social control or bond theory in the 1960s asked the question, "Why do people obey the law?" and answered they do so because of their bonds to society like school, attachment to parents, and a belief in their future. Tyler also asks the question, "Why do people obey the law?" but his answer is that they do so when they believe in the legitimacy of the law and the legal institutions of society. Tyler also maintains that individuals are more likely to conform their behavior to the law when they believe in its legitimacy (i.e., people who disobey marijuana laws do so because they believe marijuana should be legal) or they distrust and reject the legal institutions of society. There is evidence to indicate, for instance, that those who have more distrust of the police are more likely to commit crime. Tyler also notes that legitimacy is tied to **procedural justice**; when people believe that the justice system is fair and just, there is more adherence to the law itself.[49]

## What are Some Other Theories of Crime?

The premises of the classical school have been revived with **rational choice theory** and **deterrence theories**.[50] Modern deterrence theory is more complicated, however, than the simplistic approach of the classical school and recognizes the influence of individual factors that mediate how deterrent messages are received, such as low self-control or impulsivity, personal experience, belief systems, and perceptions of punishment.[51] **Routine activities theory** ignores criminal motivation, assuming that a motivated offender exists all the time.[52] According to routine activity theorists, for a crime to happen there must be a motivated offender, suitable targets of criminal victimization, and the absence of guardians of persons or property. Any changes in routine activities lead to changing opportunities for crime. **Environmental criminology** is an area of criminology that explores the factors involved in where crime occurs, but does not focus much on the offender. Theories in environmental criminology test physical and spatial factors in how they encourage or discourage crime (e.g., lighting, door and window placement, presence of "shared space," and so on). The important thing to note about routine activity theory and environmental criminology is that there is little focus on the offender or offender's motivation to choose criminality, although generally these approaches are consistent with deterrence theory.

**Integrated theories** combine elements of psychological theories and sociological theories, and even accept some elements of biological criminology in a more complicated and comprehensive approach to explaining criminal choices. The methodology typically associated with integrated theories is the cohort study, also called **longitudinal research** because it involves following a sample of individuals for a long period, beginning in childhood and extending into adulthood, looking for factors that correlate with delinquency and adult criminality. For instance, Farrington et al.[53] identified the following as correlates of delinquency and crime:

> We know that the typical high-rate offender is a young male who began his aggressive or larcenous activities at an early age, well before the typical boy gets into serious trouble. We know that he comes from a troubled, discordant, low-income family in which one or both parents are likely to have criminal records themselves. We know that the boy has had trouble in school—he created problems for his teachers and does not do well in his studies. On leaving school, often by dropping out, he works at regular jobs only intermittently.

Most employers regard him as a poor risk. He experiments with a variety of drugs—alcohol, marijuana, speed, heroin—and becomes a frequent user of whatever drug is most readily available, often switching back and forth among different ones.

Thus, individual differences, family influences, school influences, and peer influences were all identified as potential predictors of the onset of, continuation in, and desistance from crime.

Another finding of the longitudinal research studies is that there seem to be two separate groups of delinquents/criminals. The first group begins committing delinquent acts very early and these individuals are chronic and serious criminal offenders; however, the second "late onset" group drifts into delinquency during their teenage years and matures out fairly quickly. Their delinquency seems to be episodic and peer-influenced. The following traits or characteristics seem to be correlated with the group who begin delinquency very early: low intelligence; high impulsiveness; child abuse victimization; harsh and erratic parental discipline; cold and rejecting parents; poor parental supervision; parental disharmony, separation, and divorce; one-parent female-headed households; convicted parents or siblings; alcoholic or drug-using parents or siblings; non-White race membership, low occupational prestige of parents; low educational level of parents; low family income; large family size; poor housing; low educational attainment of the child; attendance at a high delinquency school; delinquent friends; and high-crime area of residence.[54]

Denno utilized biological and sociological factors in an integrated explanation of criminality and delinquency.[55] She identified predisposing factors (that increase the likelihood of criminality), facilitating variables (that, in combination with predisposing factors, increase the likelihood of delinquency), and inhibiting variables (that counteract predisposing factors and decrease the probability of delinquency). At birth, individuals are already affected by such factors as culture, gender, prenatal maternal conditions, pregnancy and delivery complications, socio-economic status, and family stability. By age seven, other factors, such as cerebral dominance, intelligence, and physical and health development, have influenced their predisposition to delinquency; during the pre-teen and teen years, school behavior, achievement, and learning disabilities are affected by intelligence and influence, in turn, the likelihood of delinquency and, eventually, adult crime.

Robert Sampson and John Laub also present an integrated theory of delinquency, suggesting:

- A set of predisposing factors:
  - low family socio-economic status, family size, family disruption, residential mobility, parent's deviance, household crowding, foreign-born, mother's employment;
- Individual characteristics:
  - difficult temperament, persistent tantrums, early conduct disorder;
- And interactions with social control processes as the child develops:
  - family, lack of supervision, erratic/harsh discipline, parental rejection, school, weak attachment, poor academic performance, delinquent influences, sibling delinquent attachment, and peer attachment that leads to delinquency and incarceration.

These factors, in turn, lead to fewer social bonds, weak labor force attachment, and weak marital attachment that influences the continuation of crime and deviance.[56] The other idea proposed by these researchers is that "turning points" in life lead to desistance or continued criminality; for instance, a job or stable marriage might shift a person to law-abiding behavior. Contrarily, the loss of a job or marriage might kick them back into drug use, alcohol use and/or criminal choices. Others argue the causal direction and suggest that there is a cognitive shift in the offender first before a stable job or successful marriage can occur.[57]

Integrated studies are comprehensive in that they include precursors and facilitators of delinquency. In fact, most of the elements identified by all previous theories are incorporated into these integrated theories. While some may say that is the strength of these theories, others argue that it is a weakness because it makes the theory more complicated, and by using every explanation, in effect, there is no explanation that easily explains crime choice. On the other hand, it is probably unrealistic to assume that there is a simple answer to criminal behavior—or any human behavior, for that matter.

One other category of theories basically challenges all theories discussed thus far in that they challenge the very legitimacy of the definition of criminal. Radical, Marxist or **critical criminology** can be distinguished, but, in general, they contest the assumption of criminal as it is defined by official sources of crime. These theories propose that the powerholders of society define criminality and, thus, our official definitions of criminality do not include the activities of the powerful. The argument would be that the typical criminal is minority and poor only because of official definitions of what is defined as criminal. The victim-harming activities of the powerful (e.g., toxic waste dumping, price gouging on life-saving pharmaceuticals, defective products that pose lethal risks to consumers) are never described as crimes. These theories do remind us that, generally, criminology tends to ignore white-collar crimes; however, it is not true that such activities are ignored completely, or are not defined as crimes. It is important to note and ponder whether a trader on Wall Street who sells junk bonds he or she knows to be extremely high risk or even worthless is, in any way, different from someone who shoplifts or engages in credit card fraud since both are willing to profit from victimizing others. Our arrest figures very well may skew our understanding of criminality in that those who have criminal tendencies and are poor will pursue the opportunities open to them (shoplifting, credit card theft, robbery), while those with more opportunities may pursue other criminal activities (embezzlement, fraud, real estate swindles, insider trading and other SEC crimes). These crimes are less likely to be discovered, more likely to be regulatory or punished by fines, and, perhaps, less likely to find their way into our crime statistics. In this sense the only difference between a robber and a real estate swindler or Ponzi schemer (e.g., Bernie Madoff) is the criminal choices open to him or her.

Courses in criminology cover a multitude of theories that have been created and tested to attempt to answer the question, "Why do people commit crime?" This chapter barely skims the surface of this material, but it provides some general descriptions of the types of theories that have been developed. Any good theory should be able to explain the sex and age differential, as well as why minorities are over-represented in street and violent crimes. Generally, the field of criminology has de-emphasized biological and psychological factors of crime causation and focused solely on sociological causes of crime. More recent theories, such as the general theory of crime and general strain theory, bring the focus back to the individual and, thus, one can argue that the pendulum of scientific/criminological thought has swung from the legal system (classical) to the individual (positivist), to the society and neighborhood (Chicago school), and back to the individual (general strain theory and integrated theories).

New theories continue to be proposed. One new theory proposed by Simons and Burt called **social schematic theory** (SST), proposes that individuals who live in social environments characterized by victimization, poverty, lack of opportunity, and conflict with authority develop a "criminogenic knowledge structure (CKS) that encourages criminality." The specific components of this CKS are: a) hostile views of relationships; b) immediate gratification/discounting the future; and c) disengagement from conventional norms. Expansion of the theory adds that CKS affects routine activities and placing oneself in situations where criminal opportunities are likely to emerge is consistent with CKS.[58] Similar to learning theory and differential organization, this theory proposes that individuals absorb messages from their environment that develop their worldview. It is similar to social disorganization theory in identifying the environment as causal in the development of criminal choice. It is also not inconsistent with some biological theories that propose chronic stress through childhood can affect brain development and the body's reaction to external threats. The CKS of individuals is resistant and helps to explain recidivism presumably. It does not, however, explain white-collar crimes or crimes committed by individuals who are not exposed to criminogenic environments and it presumes that "street crimes" are a true representation of all crimes, a presumption with which critical criminologists would argue.

In Figure 6.1, there are very brief descriptions of the theories discussed in this chapter.

## Biological Theories

*Nongenetic:* idiopathic tumors, brain injuries, toxins
*Genetic:* testosterone, brain chemicals, neural conditionability, other inherited personality traits, such as impulsiveness

## Psychological Theories

*Personality trait:* traits are either conducive to or not conducive to criminal choices
*Developmental:* individual does not progress to mature social-interpersonal levels
*Learning:* individual is rewarded for criminal behavior

## Sociological Theories

*Chicago School:* individual lives in the mixed zone of a city where crime occurs
*Cultural Deviance:* individual is socialized to deviant norms
*Strain:* individual is blocked from achieving societal goals so resorts to illegitimate means
*Social Support:* individual lives in area with low social support
*Social Disorganization:* individual lives in area with indices of social disorganization

## Social Process Theories

*Differential Association:* individual learns to be criminal
*Labeling:* individual is labeled a deviant and so lives up to the label
*Rational Choice (Deterrence):* individual weighs options and chooses crime
*Routine Activities:* crime occurs when there is motivated offender and opportunity
*Control (Bonds):* individual has few bonds to society
*General Theory of Crime:* individual has low self-control
*General Strain Theory:* individual suffers strain, which leads to crime
*Procedural Justice:* individual is more apt to obey the law when they believe in it
*Integrated Theories:* different aspects of the theories above explain crime at different periods in the life course
*Radical, Critical or Marxist Theories:* the power holders in society define crimes which are the actions of the powerless

# Summary

## What are the Explanations for the Decline of Crime?

Researchers have studied all of the following as potential factors in the decline of crime: aging birth cohort of baby boomers, stabilization of drug markets, higher incarceration rates, community policing, "zero tolerance" policing, home health care and pre- and post-natal health services, violence prevention programs in schools, reduction of exposure to lead-based paint, and increased numbers of abortions in the late 1970s and 1980s. Although research is continuing, the factors that may be most influential include decreased alcohol consumption, increased use of incarceration, and increased numbers of police.

## What are Some Methodological Issues in the Question: Why Do People Commit Crime?

It is important to distinguish between macro- and micro-level factors when understanding crime. Macro-level theories explain why crime goes up or down in particular time periods or in certain socities (or parts of society). The field of criminology generally is a study of micro factors, or those factors that influence why one individual over another makes criminal choices. In constructing and testing crime theories, it should be remembered that crime and deviance are not synonomous and not all crimes are deviant. Victim-harming crimes may have different motivations and correlational factors than victimless crimes.

## Who Commits Crime?

Official reports indicate that 73.3 percent of all persons arrested in the nation in 2014 were men. They accounted for 79.8 percent of persons arrested for violent crime and 61.8 percent of persons arrested for property crime. Further, young people 18–30 account for a disproportional amount of crime. Also, although Blacks represent only about 13–14 percent of the population, their rate of arrest for most crimes, especially violent crimes, exceeds this percentage.

## What are the Major Criminological Theories of Crime?

Criminology is the study of crime and criminal motivation. The classical school and the positivist school form the history of criminology and current theories can be categorized, for the most part, into biological, psychological and sociological theories.

## What do Biological Theories of Crime Say about Who Commits Crime and Why?

Biological theories identify biological factors that may affect criminal choices—either genetic or not. Genetic influences have been identified in neurobiology that affect such things as serotonin, oxytocin, and MAO levels which, in turn, have implications for behavior. There is no criminal gene, but there may be genetic influences that predispose individuals to aggression or a lack of control.

## What do Psychological Theories of Crime Say about Who Commits Crime and Why?

Psychological theories explain crime by looking at personality traits that influence criminal choice or developmental difficulties, e.g., the individual has not progressed to a level of emotional maturity marked by empathy that characterizes normal adult development. Another psychological theory is learning theory and proposes that criminals choose crime because of modeling or rewards.

## What do Sociological Theories of Crime Say about Who Commits Crime and Why?

The beginning of criminology in this country occurred with the Chicago school of the 1930s. Sociological theories identify elements of society (social structure theories) or the interaction of the individual with his or her environment (social process theories) as the reason that people commit crimes.

## What are Some Other Theories of Crime?

Modern deterrence theories and environmental criminology are theoretically consistent with the classical school. Integrated studies are comprehensive in that they include most of the elements identified by all previous theories. Radical, Marxist or critical criminology contest the assumption of criminal as it is defined by official sources of crime. These theories propose that the powerholders of society define criminality and, thus, our official definitions of criminality do not include the activities of the powerful.

## CRITICAL THINKING EXERCISES

1.  Find a news story that describes a crime and criminal in detail. What theory of crime best fits the facts of the case? What theories don't fit the facts? What would you want to know (whether or not that information was available in the news reports) in order to see which theory of crime was best able to explain the crime?

2.  Ask ten people why they think some people commit crime. Categorize the answers into biological, psychological, and sociological explanations. Did you discover any explanation that does not fit into one of the theories discussed in this chapter? How would you test the theory to determine how well it fits with what we know about crime patterns?

## Notes

1. J. Bentham, "The rationale of punishment." In R. Beck and J. Orr (Eds.), *Ethical Choices: A Case Study Approach*. New York: Free Press, 1843/1970, pp. 326–340.
2. C. Lombroso and W. Ferrero, *The Criminal Man*. Montclair, NJ: Patterson Smith, 1895/1972; C. Lombroso and W. Ferrero, *The Female Offender*. New York: Philosophical Library, 1894/1958.

3. J. Pirkle, D. Brody, E. Gunter, R. Kramer, D. Paschal, K. Flegal and T. Matte, "The decline in blood lead levels in the United States. The National Health and Nutrition Examination Surveys." *JAMA* 272 (July 27 1994): 284–291.

4. P.B. Stretesky and M.J. Lynch, "The relationship between lead and crime." *Journal of Health and Social Behavior* 45(June 2004): 214–229.

5. P. Cook and J. Laub, "After the epidemic: Recent trends in youth violence in the United States." *Crime and Justice* 29 (2002): 1–37.

6. O. Jones, "Behavioral genetics and crime, in context." *Law and Contemporary Problems* 69 (2006): 81–100.

7. D. Andrews and J. Bonta, *The Psychology of Criminal Conduct*, 4th edn. Newark, NJ: LexisNexis/Matthew Bender, 2006, pp. 128–129.

8. C. Burt and R. Simons, "Pulling back the curtain on heritability studies: Biosocial criminology in the postgenomic era." *Criminology* 52 (2014): 223–262.

9. J. Barnes, J.P. Wright, B. Boutwell, J. Schwartz, E. Connolly, J. Nedelec and K. Beaver, "Demonstrating the validity of twin research in criminology." *Criminology* 52 (2014): 588–626.

10. D. Dick and A. Agrawal, "The genetics of alcohol and other drug dependence." *Alcohol Research and Health* 31 (2008): 111; J. Barnes, J.P. Wright, B. Boutwell, J. Schwartz, E. Connolly, J. Nedelec and K. Beaver, "Demonstrating the validity of twin research in criminology." *Criminology* 52 (2014): 588–626.

11. E. Maccoby and C. Jacklin, *The Psychology of Sex Differences*. Stanford, CA: Stanford University Press, 1994. See also J. Tedeschi and R. Felson, *Violence, Aggression and Coercive Actions*. Washington, DC: American Psychological Association, 1977; S. Mednick and K. Christiansen (Eds.), *Biosocial Bases of Criminal Behavior*. New York, NY: Gardner Press, 1987; S. Mednick, T. Moffitt and S. Stack (Eds.), *The Causes of Crime*, New York, NY: Cambridge University Press, 1991; A. Walsh, *Intellectual Imbalance, Love Deprivation and Violent Delinquency: A Biosocial Perspective*. Springfield, IL: Charles C. Thomas, 1974.

12. H. Eysenck and G. Gudjonsson, *The Causes and Cures of Criminality*. New York, NY: Plenum, 1991, p. 135. See also A. Walsh, *Intellectual Imbalance, Love Deprivation and Violent Delinquency: A Biosocial Perspective*. Springfield, IL: Charles C. Thomas, 1989, p. 140.

13. A. Walsh, *Intellectual Imbalance, Love Deprivation and Violent Delinquency: A Biosocial Perspective*. Springfield, IL: Charles C. Thomas, 1991, p. 127.

14. A. Walsh, *Biosociology: An Emerging Paradigm*. Westport, CT: Praeger, 1995, pp. 50–54. See also L. Ellis, "Monoamine oxidase and criminality: Identifying an apparent biological marker for antisocial behavior." *Journal of Research in Crime and Delinquency* 28 (1991): 227–251.

15. A. Caspi, T. Moffitt, P. Silva, M. Stouthamer-Loeber, R. Krueger and P. Schmutte, "Are some people crime prone? Replications of the personality-crime relationship across countries, genders, races, and methods." *Criminology* 32 (1994): 163–195.

16. A. Raine, *The Psychopathology of Crime: Criminal Behavior as a Clinical Disorder*. San Diego, CA: Academic Press, 1993, p. 93; J. Portnoy, A. Raine, F. Chen, D. Pardini, R. Loeber and J.R. Jennings, "Heart rate and antisocial behavior: The mediating role of impulsive sensation seeking." *Criminology* 52 (2014): 292–311.

17. H. Eysenck and G. Gudjonsson, *The Causes and Cures of Criminality*. New York, NY: Plenum, 1989, p. 55.

18. P. Wood, B. Pfefferbaum and B. Arneklev, "Risk-taking and self-control: Social psychological correlates of delinquency." *Journal of Criminal Justice* 16 (1993): 111–130.

19. D. Denno, *Biology and Violence: From Birth to Adulthood*. New York, NY: Cambridge University Press, 1990, p. 17; T. Moffitt, "The neuropsychology of juvenile delinquency: A critical review." In M. Tonry and N. Morris (Eds.), *Crime and Justice: A Review of Research*, vol. 12. Chicago, IL: University of Chicago Press, 1990, pp. 99–171.

20. H. Sandhu and H. Satterfield, "Childhood diagnostic and neurophysiological predictors of teenage arrest rates." In S. Mednick, T. Moffitt and S. Stack (Eds.), *The Causes of Crime*. New York, NY: Cambridge University Press, 1987, pp. 146–168.

21. D. Denno, *Biology and Violence: From Birth to Adulthood*. New York, NY: Cambridge University Press, 1990, p. 15.

22. C. Burt and R. Simons, "Pulling back the curtain on heritability studies: Biosocial criminology in the postgenomic era." *Criminology* 52, (2014): 223–262.

23. M. Rocque, C. Posick and S. Felix, "The role of the brain in urban violent offending: Integrating biology with structural theories of 'the streets'." *Criminal Justice Studies*, 2015. DOI: 10.1080/1478601X.2014.1000006.

24. D. Andrews and J. Bonta, *The Psychology of Criminal Conduct*, 4th edn. Newark, NJ: LexisNexis/Matthew Bender, 2006.

25. D. Lykken, *The Antisocial Personalities*. Hillsdale, NJ: Lawrence Erlbaum, 1995, pp. 6–7.

26. J. Miller and D. Lyman, "Structural models of personality and their relation to antisocial behavior: A meta-analytic review." *Criminology* 39 (4) (2001): 765–799.

27. T. Moffit, "Males on the life-course-persistent and adolescent-limited antisocial pathways: Follow-up at age 26 years." *Development and Psychopathology* 14 (2002): 179–207.

28. J. Piaget, *The Moral Judgment of a Child*. New York, NY: Free Press, 1965; L. Kohlberg, *The Philosophy of Moral Judgment*. San Francisco, CA: Harper and Row, 1981.

29. A. Bandura, *Social Learning Theory*. Englewood Cliffs, NJ: Prentice-Hall, 1977.

30. D. Andrews and J. Bonta, *The Psychology of Criminal Conduct*, 2nd edn. New Providence, NJ: Anderson, 2010.

31. C. Shaw and H. McKay, *Juvenile Delinquency and Urban Areas*. Chicago, IL: University of Chicago Press, 1942.

32. See, for instance, C. Shaw and H. McKay, *Juvenile Delinquency and Urban Areas*. Chicago, IL: University of Chicago Press, 1934/1972.

33. R. Merton, "Social structure and anomie." *American Sociological Review* 3 (6) (1938): 672–682.

34. A. Cohen, *Delinquency in Boys: The Culture of the Gang*. New York, NY: Free Press, 1960. See also R. Cloward and L. Ohlin, *Delinquency and Opportunity*. New York, NY: Free Press, 1955.

35. Note this study was conducted in Norway and it may be that the social network system of Norway makes it problematic to generalize to what might be found in the U.S. T. Skardhamar and J. Savolainen, "Changes in criminal offending around the time of job entry: A study of employment and desistance." *Criminology* 52 (2014): 263–291.

36. R. Bursik and H. Grasmick, *Neighborhoods and Crime: The Dimensions of Effective Community Control*. New York, NY: Lexington Books, 1994. See also F. Cullen, "Social support as an organizing concept for criminology." *Justice Quarterly* 11 (4) (1993): 528–559; A. Reiss and M. Tonry, *Communities and Crime*. Chicago, IL: University of Chicago Press, 1989. See also R. Sampson and W. Groves,

"Community structure and crime: Testing social disorganization theory." *American Journal of Sociology* 94 (1986): 774–802. See, for instance, R. Sampson, "Local friendship ties and community attachment in mass society: A multilevel systemic model." *American Sociological Review,* 53 (1988): 766–779.

37. M. Carey, "Social learning, social capital, and correctional theories: Seeking an integrated model." In American Correctional Association, *What Works and Why: Effective Approaches to Reentry.* Lanham, MD: American Correctional Association, 2005, p. 9; R. Bursik and H. Grasmick, *Neighborhoods and Crime: The Dimensions of Effective Community Control.* New York, NY: Lexington Books, 1993.

38. E. Sutherland and D. Cressey, *Principles of Criminology.* Philadelphia, PA: Lippincott, 1960/1966.

39. R. Akers, *Deviant Behavior: A Social Learning Approach.* Belmont, CA: Wadsworth, 1966. R. Burgess and R. Akers, "A differential association-reinforcement theory of criminal behavior." *Social Problems* 14 (1973): 128–147.

40. R. Burgess and R. Akers, "A differential association-reinforcement theory of criminal behavior." *Social Problems* 14 (1973): 128–147.

41. See, for instance, E. Lemert, *Social Pathology: A Systematic Approach to the Theory of Sociopathic Behavior.* New York, NY: McGraw-Hill, 1951.

42. T. Hirschi, *Causes of Delinquency.* Berkeley, CA: University of California Press, 1969.

43. M. Gottfredson and T. Hirschi, *A General Theory of Crime.* Stanford, CA: Stanford University Press, 1990.

44. M. Gottfredson and T. Hirschi, *A General Theory of Crime.* Stanford, CA: Stanford University Press, 1990, p. 97.

45. C. Na and R. Paternoster, "Can self-control change substantially over time? Rethinking the relationship between self- and social-control." *Criminology* 50, (2012): 427–462. Also see A. Piquero, W. Jennings and D. Farrington, "On the malleability of self-control: Theoretical and policy implications regarding a general theory of crime." *Justice Quarterly* 27 (2010): 803–834.

46. S. Miller and C. Burack, "A critique of Gottfredson and Hirschi's general theory of crime: Selective (in)attention to gender and power positions." *Women and Criminal Justice* 4 (1993): 115–134.

47. O. Antonaccio and C. Tittle, "Morality, self control and crime." *Criminology* 46 (2008): 479–510.

48. R. Agnew, *Pressured into Crime: An Overview of General Strain Theory.* New York, NY: Oxford University Press, 2007.

49. T. Tyler, *Why People Obey the Law.* Princeton, NJ: Princeton University Press, 2006.

50. D. Cornish and R. Clarke, *The Reasoning Criminal: Rational Choice Perspectives on Offending.* New York, NY: Springer-Verlag, 1986.

51. See, for instance, M. Stafford and M. Warr, "A reconceptualization of general and specific deterrence." *Journal of Research in Crime and Delinquency* 30 (1993): 123–135.

52. L. Cohen and M. Felson, "Social change and crime trends: A routine activities approach." *American Sociological Review* 44 (1979): 588–608.

53. D. Farrington, L. Ohlin and J. Wilson, *Understanding and Controlling Crime: Toward a New Research Strategy.* New York, NY: Springer-Verlag, 1986, p.2.

54. M. Tonry, L. Ohlin and D. Farrington, *Human Development and Criminal Behavior: New Ways of Advancing Knowledge.* New York, NY: Springer-Verlag, 1991, p. 142.

55. D. Denno, *Biology and Violence: From Birth to Adulthood.* New York, NY: Cambridge University Press, 1990.

56. R. Sampson and J. Laub, *Crime in the Making: Pathways and Turning Points through Life*. Cambridge, MA: Harvard University Press, 1993, p. 244.

57. For a review of this argument, see T. Skardhamar and J. Savolainen, "Changes in criminal offending around the time of job entry: A study of employment and desistance." *Criminology* 52 (2014): 263–291.

58. R. Simons, C. Burt, A. Barr, M. Lei and E. Stewart, "Incorporating routine activities, activity spaces, and situational definitions into social schematic theory of crime." *Criminology* 52 (2014): 655–687.

# Understanding Criminological Research

TIMOTHY NEWBURN

## Introduction

The purpose of this [...] chapter is not to provide you with everything you need for the purpose of doing your first piece of criminological research—a long essay or a dissertation. Rather, it is to give you an overview of some of the important things you will probably need to take into consideration; to provide a short overview of a number of things—such as research methods—that you will undoubtedly need to read about in much greater detail in due course; to provide some tips about how to go about the task in front of you and, perhaps, to save you from one or two of the difficulties you might otherwise face. So, what follows is not a *how to* guide. It is not all the nuts and bolts of doing criminological research—that would require another textbook, quite possibly as large as this one. What I want to do here is walk you through some of the main features of research so that you have a general feel for what is involved and know where to go next in search of further information.

## Research Methods

Broadly speaking, we may distinguish between *quantitative* and *qualitative* research. Quantitative research tends to be relatively large-scale and uses numerical data and statistical procedures to analyse such data and reach conclusions. Research strategies that employ quantitative methods tend to be more heavily influenced by models of inquiry derived from the physical sciences than are qualitative methods. They also tend to be *deductive* in approach, with the testing of theories or hypotheses being a favoured approach in such research studies [...]. By contrast, qualitative research is often based on relatively small samples—and is therefore often smaller in scale than quantitative research. It is also more likely to be used in the generation of hypotheses, or an *inductive* approach to the research/theory relationship. In broad terms, where quantitative research focuses its attention on the search for representative samples and generalisable findings, qualitative research tends to be more concerned with understanding the world through the eyes of its human subjects. That said, all such distinctions are tentative rather than definitive, for there is much that quantitative and qualitative methods have in common (see Table 7.1).

Many researchers seem to specialise in one type of research or the other, preferring to use qualitative or quantitative methods. Whilst this is understandable, there is much to be gained from a working knowledge of a range of methods and, indeed, in many cases some of the most useful research will involve a combination of qualitative and quantitative approaches. Sometimes you will see this referred to as *triangulation*. Essentially, this term refers to the idea of looking at a particular phenomenon from a number of different points—as one might do in surveying or navigation—and using these together to produce a more accurate understanding than would be possible with only a single viewpoint.

In effect, this general assumption is also largely true in social research. It is often helpful to be able to look at things from different angles, and using different methods. Not only does this help refine one's position, but it is also very helpful in checking the validity of one data source against another. Though both are quantitative methods, we came across a very good example [...] of how different data sources may complement each other. There we looked at trends in crime and discovered that on the surface police-recorded crime statistics and the British Crime Survey appeared to indicate differing trends in crime in the mid- to late 1990s. However, the BCS enabled us to assess the impact of changes in reporting practices on police-recorded crime trends. Taking these changes into account, together with changes in recording practices, indicated that the underlying trends were rather different from what recorded crime statistics alone suggested.

**TABLE 7.1   Contrasting Quantitative and Qualitative Research**

| Quantitative | Qualitative |
| --- | --- |
| Numbers | Words |
| Point of view of researcher | Point of view of participants |
| Researcher distant | Researcher close |
| Theory testing | Theory emergent |
| Static | Process |
| Structured | Unstructured |
| Generalisation | Contextual understanding |
| Hard, reliable data | Rich, deep data |
| Macro | Micro |
| Behaviour | Meaning |
| Artificial settings | Natural settings |

*Source:* Bryman (2001).

## Surveys

Much large-scale (and, indeed, smaller-scale) quantitative research is undertaken using survey research methods. We are all used to the idea of surveys. Most of us will have been interviewed at one time or another—on the street, at home or elsewhere—as part of a survey. Moreover, terms like 'opinion polls', which are now an everyday part of the political landscape, are just another way of talking about surveys. Surveys are generally fairly large research instruments that obtain data through the use of a standardised questionnaire. In the main, because of their size and the nature of the questions that can be asked effectively in this manner, surveys are used for gathering quantitative data, though this is not exclusively the case, and often researchers will also include a small qualitative component.

Two terms you may come across in connection with surveys (and with other research methods also) are those of the *dependent* and *independent variable*. Put simply, the independent variable is the *cause* in the cause and effect relationship; the dependent variable is the effect. So, as a criminologist, it is highly likely that the dependent variable in your study will be offending or crime; the independent variable might be anything from unemployment to school underachievement. Some other factor that might interfere with the relationship between the independent and the dependent variable is likely to be referred to as an *extraneous* or *confounding variable*.

Surveys can be undertaken in a number of ways. They may be conducted by post, face-to-face interview or, as is now the case with the Crime Survey, through a combination of face-to-face interview and computer-assisted personal interviewing. Computers are used for particularly sensitive questions so that respondents can answer questions directly on to a laptop computer without the interviewer knowing how they have answered [...].

*Postal surveys* have the advantage that they are cheap. It is obviously much simpler and cheaper to send questionnaires out through the post, with a stamped addressed envelope, asking people to complete them and return them to you. Because there is no interviewer present, the instruments used in postal surveys (and in other circumstances where appropriate) are called *self-completion questionnaires* (see Table 7.2). The downside, and it is a major one, is that the *response rate* for postal surveys tends to be very low. Questionnaires arrive and many people, even if they show some interest in responding initially, may simply forget, or forget within the time period that has been set, to complete and return it. The presence of an interviewer for *face-to-face interviews* tends to ensure much greater compliance and can also have the advantage of sorting out any misunderstandings, should they arise.

A further method that can be used that contains more of a personal element than the postal survey, but involves less expense than face-to-face interviews, is to conduct a *telephone survey* (see Table 7.3). Response rates are rarely as good as face-to-face interviews, and there are certain questions that are more difficult to ask over the phone than personally. In addition, there are practical issues such as getting hold of telephone numbers for those in the sample. In earlier times one of the shortcomings of telephone surveys was the limitation placed on sampling by the fact that not everyone had access to a telephone. This is much less of a problem these days, but has been replaced by a number of practical difficulties relating to the growing use of mobile phones: phones being turned off or turned to voice-mail and the problem that some mobile phone networks charge the call recipient for particular types of call. All of these may limit the researcher's ability to make contact with potential respondents.

**TABLE 7.2**   Advantages and Disadvantages of the Self-Completion Questionnaire

| Advantages | Disadvantages |
|---|---|
| • They are relatively cheap to produce and to administer.<br>• The low cost potentially allows large samples to be surveyed.<br>• Large territories can be covered—if the questionnaire is posted or emailed.<br>• The absence of an interviewer potentially means:<br>  • sensitive topics can be addressed;<br>  • the respondent won't be affected by the personal characteristics of an interviewer (interviewer effects);<br>  • there can be no interference in the process of answering the questions (interviewer bias). | • Response rates tend to be poor—without an interviewer present there is no opportunity to build rapport with the respondent. In the absence of some other reminder, questionnaires will often remain uncompleted.<br>• In order to encourage reasonable response rates it is often necessary to ensure that:<br>  • questionnaires are kept short;<br>  • questions are very simple;<br>  • there are few opportunities for 'open' questions: most have to be 'closed'.<br>• The absence of an interviewer may mean:<br>  • any misunderstanding of questions goes uncorrected;<br>  • any misunderstanding of the structure of the questionnaire—the routing of questions, etc.—goes uncorrected;<br>  • there is a response bias, as potential respondents with, say, literacy problems will be less likely to complete the questionnaire. |

Finally, there is the *internet-based survey*. The advantages of this approach are obvious, for it is relatively cheap and, in principle, a great many people can be reached and followed-up fairly easily and quickly. Like telephone surveys, it is necessary to have the contact information (an email address rather than phone number in this case) in order to make the survey possible. The major limitation is the same as the postal survey. My university conducts internet surveys of students. Unfortunately, the response rates are generally so poor that the results are often barely usable. Most people reading this will, like me, no doubt already receive more emails than they feel they can easily deal with. It is easy to understand why extra ones, especially those that require an investment of time, might be discarded or ignored. I certainly don't fill in every email questionnaire I receive—even though as a researcher I feel pangs of guilt whenever I decline to do so. Finally, as with telephone surveys, there is the issue of coverage in such surveys, in that not everybody has access to the internet. Moreover, the fact that it is particular segments of the population that are disproportionately likely to be in the group without access (e.g. the elderly) means that there is a high probability of systematic bias in the survey.

**QUESTIONNAIRE DESIGN**   There are a number of basic features of questionnaires that you should bear in mind when thinking about their construction. First of all, they should be set out clearly and simply. Your aim is to elicit information from respondents. You need to make this as straightforward as possible. Most people are busy, have probably been asked to fill in questionnaires before and will, in all likelihood, be fairly easily put off. You need to think about what will make them, and keep them, interested in your survey. At the outset you need to explain, in plain English, the aims of the study, why you are doing it and what you are hoping to achieve, and outline any confidentiality agreement that there may be.

Second, and linked with this, you need to think through what it is vital to ask and what not. It is all too easy to throw everything in and end up with a questionnaire that is too long. Think about how much time you can reasonably expect an interview to take, and what is the minimum number of questions you need to ask? Keeping things short will almost certainly increase your response rate (i.e. increase the proportion of people you approach who complete a questionnaire).

What sorts of questions will you ask? You will almost certainly need to know some details about the respondent, such as their age, sex, ethnicity and some other demographic details. There are some fairly standard ways of doing this, and one example is shown in Figure 7.1.

Because the questionnaire-based survey is primarily a method of eliciting quantitative data, you need to think carefully about the phrasing of questions and the range of answers that will be necessary or allowed. Most questions will be *closed*. That is to say, they will only offer respondents a limited range of possible answers. You may occasionally include a small number of more *open* questions such as 'What was the most positive/negative aspect of your experience?' There are two main reasons for including such questions: first, in order to gather some more detailed information about particular aspects of what is being studied and, second, to give the respondent some space in which to express themselves. Page after page of closed questions can feel a little constricting. It is important to bear in mind, however, that open questions are both difficult and time-consuming to analyse.

| 22a | Are you | | 1 Male | 2 Female? | |
|-----|---------|---|--------|-----------|---|
| 22b | How old are you? | | | | |
| 22c | Which of the following best describes you? (circle one) | | | | |
| | **White** | | | **Asian or Asian British** | |
| 01 | White British | | 11 | Indian | |
| 02 | White Irish | | 12 | Pakistani | |
| 03 | Any other white | | 13 | Bangladeshi | |
| | background | | 14 | Any other Asian background | |
| | **Mixed** | | | **Black or Black British** | |
| 21 | White and Black Caribbean | | 31 | Black Caribbean | |
| 22 | White and Black African | | 32 | Black African | |
| 23 | White and Asian | | 33 | Any other Black background | |
| 24 | Any other mixed background | | | | |
| | **Chinese or Other ethnic group** | | | | |
| 41 | Chinese | | | | |
| 42 | Any other ethnic group (describe) | | | | |
| 99 | Not stated | | | | |

**FIGURE 7.1** An example of standard demographic questions in a self-completion survey

The majority of questions should generally remain closed. Some of these may be a simple 'yes/no/don't know'. In such cases, you should almost always include a 'don't know' category, for it is important not to force people into answering in ways that might be misleading. Others may involve scales of one sort or another in order to allow respondents to differentiate between, say, the strength of their opinion about something, or the frequency with which they have done or felt something. There are a number of different scales, but one of the most common is that which is called a *Likert scale*. This is mainly used to gather data on attitudes and opinions and will tend to look something like:

*Strongly agree (2) Agree (1) Neither agree nor disagree (0) Disagree (–1) Strongly disagree (–2)*

As you can see there are an equal number of positive and negative statements, as well as a neutral one, and this allows mean (average) scores to be calculated as well as the proportions answering in each category, or positively/negatively, and so on.

The wording of questions is vitally important to the potential success of surveys. The words and phrases one chooses to use in questionnaires will affect, often very profoundly, the answers that one receives. As we saw [...], for example, for some years the CSEW has asked questions about 'fear of crime'. This has generated a vast literature and some interesting debates and findings. However, in recent years some criminologists have come to question the usefulness of the term 'fear of crime' and have argued that by beginning to ask different questions it appears that one of the primary responses to criminal victimisation is not *fear* but *anger*. On a more mundane level, it is important in questionnaire design that careful consideration is given to the meaning of questions and how they are likely to be interpreted by respondents. There are a number of basic rules, including (May, 2001):

- *Don't use leading questions*—'By how much do you think prison numbers will go up next year?' (they may go down).
- *Use simple language wherever possible.*
- *Don't ask two questions in one*—'Are you in favour of the government's recent proposals on youth crime, and do you think they will be successful?'
- *Be very careful about asking personal questions*—especially in a questionnaire.
- *Ask questions that the respondent can answer*—In a survey of police officers there is no point in asking relatively new recruits what they think of the changes in operational policing over the last ten years.
- *Remember that there are limits to what people may be able to remember.*

As we have seen, the style in which questions are asked determines the type of data that are forthcoming. In surveys it is usual to ask 'closed' questions and then produce numerical tallies summarising the results. This is done by *coding* the data—essentially assigning a numerical code to a particular answer (so, in the example above, 'Strongly agree' might be 2, 'Agree' 1 and so on). Answers are usually precoded allowing the results to be entered swiftly and accurately into SPSS or a similar statistical package for analysis. In thinking about the coding of potential answers there are two vital considerations:

- *Answers must be mutually exclusive*—It should not be possible for an answer to fall into more than one of the categories offered. You would be falling into this trap if you asked respondents: 'How often do you go to the pub?' and then offer the following categories as possible answers: Very often; often; occasionally; seldom; never. Although on the surface, the scale looks reasonable, there is no easy way of differentiating 'occasionally' and 'seldom', and no guarantee that respondents with very similar habits will answer the question in the same way.

- Answer categories should be *exhaustive*—In response to the pub question it would be insufficient simply to have 'daily', '3–4 times per week', 'once or twice a week' and 'never' as the categories don't cover the full range of possible answers to the question.

## Interviews

We have already briefly come across interviews in our discussion of survey methods. Interviews may be used in a variety of research settings and have uses well beyond survey research. In general terms, interviews may be divided into three main types: *structured, semi-structured* and *unstructured*. Different types are used depending on whether the research is largely quantitative or largely qualitative in nature.

The ideal type of a *structured* interview is one in which the same questions are asked of all participants, the questions are asked in the same way, and they are generally closed in nature. As such, therefore, it is fairly clear that it is typically the structured interview that is used in large-scale quantitative research. By contrast, within highly qualitative research, or work that borders on ethnography (see below), where the concern is to understand certain things in detail and in depth and to hear how respondents perceive matters, one is much more likely to use *unstructured* interviews. Here the questions are open-ended and there is no set structure for the ordering of questions, no necessary wording for questions, and no necessity that all questions be asked of all respondents. Such interviews are much closer to conversations, though they will be steered by the interviewer who, perhaps by using a *topic guide,* will use their skills and experience to explore various issues with the respondent. Lying in between these two ends of the interviewing spectrum are *semi-structured interviews*, where there may be some form of fairly formal interview schedule, but where there remains sufficient freedom for the interviewer to follow up things that they are especially interested in, and room for the respondent to talk at some length about what concerns them.

By definition, structured interviews are guided by a set of standardised questions. But how are unstructured interviews undertaken? For this approach you will need to construct what is referred to as an 'interview guide' or 'topic guide'. This is the unstructured version of the interview schedule. It will contain the areas you will, in principle, want to cover. It may even contain one or two specific questions. But, in the main, its phrasing and ordering are relatively inconsequential. The nature of the research process here means that it is much more important to form some type of relationship with the respondent, to get them to talk, and to allow them to do so in a way that they are comfortable with. This means following their physical and verbal cues, allowing and enabling a more organic interview to take place.

That said, unstructured interviews are neither 'formless' nor without rigour. You will want to think carefully about what you are trying to investigate. When interviewing you will have to be alive to what is important to the respondent, to how they see and talk about things, and you will have to adapt your approach to the situation you are confronted with. Being adaptable takes skill. There is security in a structured interview that disappears when one is faced with a more free-flowing approach. Thinking about how to phrase questions is important, and being able to use open

## How Leading Questions can Affect the Outcome of a Poll

To my mind, one of the funniest, and most instructive, examples of the use and abuse of 'leading questions' is from an episode of the BBC TV series *Yes, Prime Minister*. The exchange is between the fictional Cabinet Secretary, Sir Humphrey Appleby, and the Prime Minister's Private Secretary, Bernard Woolley.

*Sir Humphrey*: 'You know what happens: nice young lady comes up to you. Obviously you want to create a good impression, you don't want to look a fool, do you? So she starts asking you some questions: Mr. Woolley, are you worried about the number of young people without jobs?'

*Bernard Woolley*: 'Yes'

*Sir Humphrey*: 'Are you worried about the rise in crime among teenagers?'

*Bernard Woolley*: 'Yes'

*Sir Humphrey*: 'Do you think there is a lack of discipline in our Comprehensive schools?'

*Bernard Woolley*: 'Yes'

*Sir Humphrey*: 'Do you think young people welcome some authority and leadership in their lives?'

*Bernard Woolley*: 'Yes'

*Sir Humphrey*: 'Do you think they respond to a challenge?'

*Bernard Woolley*: 'Yes'

*Sir Humphrey*: 'Would you be in favour of reintroducing National Service?'

*Bernard Woolley*: 'Oh ... well, I suppose I might be.'

*Sir Humphrey*: 'Yes or no?'

*Bernard Woolley*: 'Yes'

*Sir Humphrey*: 'Of course you would, Bernard. After all you said you can't say no to that. So they don't mention the first five questions and they publish the last one.'

*Bernard Woolley*: 'Is that really what they do?'

*Sir Humphrey*: 'Well, not the reputable ones no, but there aren't many of those. So alternatively the young lady can get the opposite result.'

*Bernard Woolley*: 'How?'

*Sir Humphrey*: 'Mr. Woolley, are you worried about the danger of war?'

*Bernard Woolley*: 'Yes'

*Sir Humphrey*: 'Are you worried about the growth of armaments?'

*Bernard Woolley*: 'Yes'

*Sir Humphrey*: 'Do you think there is a danger in giving young people guns and teaching them how to kill?'

*Bernard Woolley*: 'Yes'

*Sir Humphrey*: 'Do you think it is wrong to force people to take up arms against their will?'

*Bernard Woolley*: 'Yes'

*Sir Humphrey*: 'Would you oppose the reintroduction of National Service?'

*Bernard Woolley*: 'Yes'

*Sir Humphrey*: 'There you are, you see Bernard. The perfect balanced sample.'

Source: *Yes, Prime Minister* ('The Ministerial Broadcast', first broadcast BBC, January 1986): www.yes-minister.com/ypmseas1a.htm

questions, and clear follow-up questions, is crucial. You will almost certainly need a variety of neutral prompt questions. You must be careful not to push respondents into answering in particular ways because of the nature of the prompts you use. Also, vary what you say—it will get terribly boring for your interviewee if you use the same prompt question the whole time. Irrespective of the nature of your interview, but especially where they are semi- or unstructured, your aim is to build rapport with your respondent—to reach a sufficient level of trust that your interviewee feels that it is safe to share information with you.

How should you capture the data in an unstructured interview? Unless you have mastered shorthand, you are faced with having to try to take notes whilst conducting the interview or, alternatively, recording the interview. If you are going to write notes, then some practice is important. It is not easy to conduct an interview, ask questions, listen to the answers and write notes simultaneously. Without shorthand, you will only be able to capture a proportion of what is said and so you need to think carefully about what it is you are trying to capture and what implications the missing material has for your research.

In many cases recording will be preferable. Again, you will often need to have established a degree of rapport with your interviewee prior to using a tape recorder. If you are going to record an interview, make sure that your recording equipment works, that you have spares (batteries, tapes, mini-disks, etc.) and that you are comfortable working the machinery. Every experienced researcher has at least one horror story of the equipment not working or, worse still, some failure to operate it efficiently themselves. I have a vivid memory of a researcher I worked with coming back from one very important interview. It was important in two senses. The respondent was crucial to the study, but was also an important person. The researcher concerned was pleased to have secured the interview. Having settled into the interview, and secured agreement that it be recorded, about half way through the interview he realised that he hadn't turned on the tape recorder. Showing great presence of mind, he made some excuse to mess with the recorder, turned it on, and carried on with the interview. Knowing that a lot had been missed he decided to try to go over some of the

**TABLE 7.3   Advantages and Disadvantages of Telephone Interviews**

| Advantages | Disadvantages |
| --- | --- |
| • The fact you don't have to travel potentially means:<br>  • they are cheaper than face-to-face interviews;<br>  • samples can be larger;<br>  • geographical spread can be greater.<br>• The 'anonymity' of the telephone potentially means that there are fewer 'interviewer effects' (the respondent being affected by the personal characteristics of the interviewer).<br>• There is no issue of 'interviewer safety' (interviewing in people's homes, for example, raises questions of safety). | • It is more difficult to establish rapport between interviewer and interviewee.<br>• Response rates may be lower—especially now that 'cold-calling' is such a common sales technique.<br>• With closed questions it is difficult to use scales (1 = very much; 2 = quite a lot, etc.) as they are difficult to remember, are time-consuming, and can become very tedious.<br>• Open questions can be a problem as people may not wish to speak at length on the phone, or feel uncomfortable doing so.<br>• Interviewers find it more difficult to judge how 'well' the interview is going when they can't see the respondent.<br>• The growing use of mobile phones makes telephone interviews more difficult. |

questions covered earlier, but to do so in as subtle a manner possible. Again, this worked well, the interview proceeded without further mishap and some considerable time later the interviewer drew the session to a close, packed up the equipment and left, happy about a situation saved. When he got back to the office and checked the tape he realised that for the whole time the microphone had been plugged into the wrong socket and so nothing had recorded anyway! The moral of the tale is, be sufficiently familiar with the equipment so that you can operate it without having to double-check.

The choice between these three basic approaches to interviewing will very much depend upon the aim of the research. To summarise what we've covered so far: where a core objective concerns the testing of a hypothesis, it is the *survey methodology* that tends to be most appropriate. Where the concern is with attitudes, beliefs and perceptions, then *qualitative* or *semi-/unstructured interviews* will tend to fare better. The choice of approach will have a knock-on effect on sample size, and quite probably sampling method—a matter we come to in more detail below. Because of their suitability to quantitative research, structured interviews will demand much larger sample sizes than qualitative interviews. The nature of data collected via unstructured or in-depth interviews is such that it is generally only possible to make use of a relatively limited number of cases. Often researchers will argue that 40–70 interviews is the optimum number using this type of method (though often there will be fewer). Any more and it is difficult to deal with the data.

As suggested, where large samples are concerned, it will generally be *structured interviewing* that is required. However, there are still choices to be made. Which will be best: the telephone interview, the face-to-face interview, or a self-completion questionnaire? Self-completion questionnaires and telephone interviews are significantly cheaper than face-to-face interviews, with postal surveys being cheapest of all. However, postal questionnaires tend to have significantly poorer response rates. A comparison of the characteristics of structured interviews and self-completion questionnaires can be found in Table 7.4.

## Focus Groups

A focus group is, in effect, a form of group interview, or a 'group discussion exploring a specific set of issues' (Kitzinger and Barbour, 1999). Rather than simply interviewing a single person, the focus group involves several people. The group is asked a series of questions and the data gathered are a combination of the answers individuals give to these questions as well as any discussions the group has collectively. It is this interactional element that distinguishes focus groups from group interviews more generally. Like one-to-one interviews, focus groups may vary considerably in the extent to which they are structured. They are a relatively efficient and rich way of getting information from a number of people. There are obviously limits to what can be discussed in focus groups and personal matters are rarely likely to be best explored in this type of context, though there are circumstances where focus groups have been used in researching sensitive topics such as sexual health (Farquhar and Das, 1999).

According to Kitzinger and Barbour (1999: 5) focus groups are best used in the exploration of people's 'experiences, opinions, wishes and concerns'. More particularly, they are useful 'for allowing participants to generate their own questions, frames and concepts and to pursue their own priorities on their own terms, in their own vocabulary'. The term 'vocabulary' is key here, for it points to an important quality of focus groups. This method is especially good when one's interest is in understanding the terminology and language people use in describing and evaluating particular

TABLE 7.4    Comparing Qualitative Interviews with Self-Administered Questionnaires

| Characteristics | Qualitative Interviews | Self-Administered Questionnaires |
|---|---|---|
| Provide information about ... | As questionnaires, but in greater depth | Attitudes, motivation, opinions, events |
| Best at ... | Exploring informants' stories and perspectives | Checking whether sample shares research hypothesis |
| Also useful for ... | Surveys: closed questions can be asked, as in opinion polls | Open-ended questions allow researcher to investigate informants' stories/views |
| Richness of response ... | Dialogue between researcher and informant allows nuances to be captured and questions to be clarified. Long interviews quite common | Questions cannot be modified once printed, nor can nuances of respondents' views be easily detected |
| Sensitive to ... | Informants. Good for finding out about the individual, specific and particular | The research literature and the range of responses amongst groups |
| Anonymity ... | Some things can be difficult to say face to face | Sensitive questions may be more acceptable |
| Ethics ... | Although interviewers know who they have spoken to, transcripts can be anonymised | Anonymous questionnaire responses easily ensured |
| Sample size ... | With exception of telephone interviews, less suitable for wide coverage | Can be very large, and as generalisation is often the aim, samples may need to be big |
| Time costs ... | Devising interview guide, piloting, arranging interviews, establishing rapport, transcription and data analysis | Devising and distributing questionnaire, checking data, analysing data |
| Money costs ... | Travel, transcription, equipment, phone bills | Printing, distributing and retrieving questionnaires, especially where response rates are low |

*Source*: Arksey and Knight (1999).

phenomena. Thus, if the aim of a piece of research is to gauge how popular a particular politician is, then the most suitable method is almost certainly a survey. However, if you want to explore how people think about, and the ways in which they talk about, that politician, then the focus group may well be the appropriate way forward. Similarly, if you want to explore group norms, values and attitudes, then group interviews/focus groups may be particularly useful.

What size should focus groups be? To some extent this depends on the subject being investigated. Often it is assumed that the standard group will contain somewhere between 6 and 12 people, but in social research—as opposed to market research—the group may be smaller, more usually between 4 and 8. Any more than 8 to 12 people and the group can easily become unmanageable. The make-up of the group, again, will depend on what is being investigated. Sampling is generally purposive (see below), and groups will tend either to be made up of people from a range of backgrounds—in order to stimulate discussion and possibly disagreement—or from largely the same background, in which any comparisons tend to arise *between* rather than *within* focus groups. The great skill in focus groups lies in *facilitation* (sometimes called *moderation*)—stimulating and managing interaction between the members of the group. The other great challenges concern data analysis. Here, as with all qualitative research, a computer package, such as *NUD*IST* or *Ethnograph*, is likely to be helpful in the process of identifying themes, and manipulating and summarising data.

There are a number of limitations to focus groups that need to be borne in mind:

- As indicated above, they are not necessarily an appropriate setting for dealing with sensitive topics.
- They are time-consuming and sometimes tricky to organise.
- One or two members of the group may dominate or, alternatively, the group may veer toward consensus with the more unusual views in the group being partly suppressed.
- They can be difficult to 'control' and may be more resistant to management by the interviewer/moderator than individual interviewees.
- The data can be difficult to analyse, both in terms of the quantity of material that is collected, and because of the interaction between members of the group.

## Ethnography

When discussing ethnography, we move about as far from large-scale quantitative methods as it is possible to go. Interpretive sociologists from Max Weber onwards have noted that the very fact that humans are reflexive beings, capable of giving meaning to their actions, requires us to consider this in our attempts to understand the social world. We cannot simply rely upon observation, but need to consider the meaningfulness of the behaviour to human actors. One way in which this can be done is via interviews or indeed through questionnaire-based surveys. However, there are clear limitations to such approaches. Let's say we wish to study the interaction between prison officers and prisoners. We could conduct interviews and ask both sets of actors their impression of how they interact with each other, and we could use survey techniques to gather information on officers' and inmates' attitudes and perceptions of conduct within the prison. Though potentially of great value, however, neither approach would necessarily tell us all that much about the ways in which interaction unfolds, and how different circumstances affect what occurs. For this, we really need to be able to observe what happens, and this is where ethnography comes in.

Ethnography, certainly as I shall use the term here, is closely associated with the types of fieldwork undertaken by cultural anthropologists such as Margaret Mead whose studies were often based on lengthy periods of time spent living among particular tribal peoples. Through observation and close social relationships, Mead, and other anthropologists, including Malinowski and Radcliffe-Brown, sought to understand the cultural and interior life of the communities in which they temporarily lived. Though criminologists may rarely immerse themselves to quite this extent, the underlying principles are the same. Willis and Trondman (2000: 5) describe ethnography as 'a family of methods involving direct and sustained social contact with agents, and of richly writing up the encounter, respecting, recording, representing at least partly *in its own terms*, the irreducibility of human experience. Ethnography is the disciplined and deliberate witness-cum-recording of human experience.'

At the heart of much ethnographic research, therefore, is some form of observational data gathering. This activity is generally broken down into two major categories (Gold 1969)—*participant observation* or *non-participant observation*—or a continuum in which there are four main categories:

*complete participant—participant-as-observer—observer-as-participant—complete observer*

The complete participant role occurs where the researcher effectively lives or functions as part of a particular community. This is sometimes referred to as 'covert participation' because it is usually undertaken without the knowledge of the other members of the community. The greatest danger—methodologically—in such research is of completely losing critical distance, or 'going native' as it is sometimes called. Covert research also raises a number of tricky ethical issues [...].

The participant-as-observer role is very similar, except that it is not undertaken covertly. Here, the researcher is known to be just that but, nevertheless, joins the group they are studying and participates in many of their activities. Close to this, the observer-as-participant role is where there is more limited interaction with those being studied—they are observed, but there is relatively little participatory activity. The final role is the complete observer, where there is no participation as a member of the group, although there is interaction with the group. Again, this may be overt or covert.

There are undoubtedly occasions when research has to be conducted covertly. Nigel Fielding's (1981) study of the National Front is a case in point. Equally, however, there are others where the necessity to hide the fact that research is being undertaken is more open to question, and where some awkward moral dilemmas must be considered. In addition to whether the ethnographer's role is overt or covert, such studies may also be distinguished by the nature of the setting in which the research takes place—in particular, whether the situations are 'open' or 'closed' (or 'public'/'private'). Table 7.5 gives examples of ethnographies carried out under these different conditions.

**TABLE 7.5    Ethnographic Research**

|  | Open/Public Setting | Closed Setting |
|---|---|---|
| Overt role | Taylor's (1993) study of intravenous drug users; Maher's (1997) study of drug use and sex work | Punch's (1979) study of police corruption in Amsterdam |
|  | Willis' (1977) study of working-class 'lads' | Smith and Gray's (1983) study of police and people in London |
|  | Hobbs's (1988, 1993) research on the East End; Matthew Desmond's (2016) study of eviction | Pilfering in a bakery (strictly speaking Ditton was 'partially open' about his research) |
|  | Whyte's (1955) classic study of street-corner life in Boston | Colosi's (2012) study of lap-dancing |
| Covert role | Patrick's (1973) study of a violent Glasgow gang (though he was 'known' by one of the gang members) | Holdaway's (1982, 1983) study of a police force in which he worked |
|  | Parker's (1974) study of the Roundhouse boys in Liverpool | Fielding's (1981) study of the National Front |
|  |  | Winlow's (2001) study of bouncers |

*Source*: Adapted from Bryman (2004).

One obvious question is what sort of data does ethnography generate? The answer, often, is *field notes*. These are reflections written at the time, or shortly after, by the researcher, who records what they have witnessed and heard, together with some thoughts or observations about what this might mean and how it fits with other observations. How to take field notes can sometimes be a problem for the covert researcher. Williams *et al.*'s (1989) study of football hooliganism, for example, required frequent visits to the toilet to scribble down memorable snippets of conversation and a similar technique was used by Jason Ditton in his wonderful study of petty pilfering (see box below).

In practice field notes may take many different forms. They may be highly formal, full notes written whilst under little or no pressure after a period of observation has been completed. By contrast, they may be some scribbled or jotted notes written, as in Ditton's and Williams's experiences—whenever there is a 'convenient' moment.

In practice, qualitative studies using ethnography often combine a range of approaches—most probably interviews of various sorts—including some observational fieldwork, possibly some documentary analysis (see below) of the local press and other materials, and also even bits and pieces of quantitative fieldwork. Winlow and Hall's recent study of urban leisure is a good example of just such an approach. As they described it (2006: 13):

> Drawing upon our sympathies for ethnographic method in depicting social and cultural life in all its richness, we set out to develop a range of key contacts, whom we hoped would become portals to contemporary youth culture. Our aim was to observe and engage with young people in a natural everyday setting, and, to the researchers' eternal gratitude, this occasionally involved going out drinking. Our primary method of data collection was, however, semi-structured and unstructured interviews, the majority of which we recorded. We also conducted quite lengthy observational work, primarily to add depth and insight into how young people's night-life tends to be organized and performed.

## Documentary Analysis

Many research projects will involve some analysis of documentary records alongside other approaches such as interviews, surveys and the like. For students writing dissertations or long essays, the limited resources available often mean that primary research involving interviews is extremely difficult, and documentary analysis is an attractive option. The focus of such analysis may be very varied, but might include:

- Official documents such as parliamentary debates, policy documents, political speeches, statistical series, official inquiries, etc.
- Media output, such as newspaper reports, magazine articles, television or radio programmes.
- Internet-based resources.
- Personal documents such as diaries, autobiographies, letters, etc.

In thinking about how to assess the quality of documents, Scott (1990) suggests that four criteria be considered:

- *Authenticity*—Do the documents appear to be genuine and of unquestionable origin?

- *Credibility*—Is the evidence free from error and distortion?
- *Representativeness*—Is the evidence typical of its kind and, if not, is the extent of the untypicality known?
- *Meaning*—Is the evidence clear and comprehensible?

How are such materials to be analysed? The most usual systematic method is known as *content analysis*. This means applying some set categories to particular texts in order to count the number of occasions particular things appear or occur. These could be particular words or, more often, they will be particular themes that you are looking for. These themes may be known from the start or, more probably, will in part be generated as the analysis proceeds. The effectiveness of such analysis depends partly on the thoroughness of the process, but also on the authenticity, credibility and reliability of the sources. Other less quantitatively oriented approaches to analysis may involve a similar process of identifying themes, but will be less concerned with assessing the frequency with which particular things appear, and more focused upon the way in which things are said/written and the messages that are conveyed.

## An Ethnography of Fiddling and Pilferage

Right from the start, I found it impossible to keep everything that I wanted to remember in my head until the end of the working day (some of the shifts were over twelve hours long) and so had to take rough notes as I was going along. But I was stuck 'on the line', and had nowhere to retire to privately to jot things down. Eventually, the wheeze of using innocently provided lavatory cubicles occurred to me. Looking back, all my notes for that third summer were on Bronco toilet paper! Apart from the awkward tendency for pencilled notes to be self-erasing from hard toilet paper (sometimes before I could even get home), my frequent requests for 'time out' after interesting happenings or conversations in the bakehouse and the amount of time that I was spending in the lavatory began to get noticed. I had to pacify some genuinely concerned work-mates, give up totally undercover operations and 'come out' as an observer, albeit in a limited way. I eventually began to scribble notes more openly, but still not in front of people when they were talking. When questioned about this, as I was occasionally, I coyly said that I was writing things down that occurred to me about 'my studies'.

*Source*: Ditton (1977: 5).

## Case Studies

This approach can be used in quantitative or qualitative research, but is most usually associated with the latter. It rests on a single case or a small number of cases and is characterised by intensive investigation of the setting (Bryman, 2004). These cases may be an individual person, a particular group of people, a neighbourhood or community, an event, an area or even a country. As such, therefore, the choice being made is not actually a methodological one, but a design one—something akin to sampling. It is a choice about the object of research, and is usually undertaken for one or more of the following reasons:

- The phenomena being studied involve relationships and links that would be unlikely to be understood using experimental or survey approaches.
- There is little or no concern with generalisation from the results.
- Understanding the social context of the matters being studied is vital.
- It is the only practical way of undertaking research in the area concerned—e.g. in relation to community responses to drug use, or in the day-to-day operation of police authorities.

A number of famous examples within criminology illustrate the potential of the case study approach:

- Clifford Shaw's (1930) study, *The Jack Roller,* of a single 'delinquent boy'.
- Edwin Sutherland's (1937) *The Professional Thief* is a case study of a single individual: 'Chic Conwell'.
- Stan Cohen's (1972/2002) study of moral panics was based around a case study of reactions to the mods and rockers during the 1960s.
- Bill Chambliss's (1978) study of organised crime was based on a case study of a single city: Seattle.
- Matthew Desmond's (2016) study, *Evicted,* focuses on the lives of eight people.

## REVIEW QUESTIONS

1. For what types of research might you select primarily quantitative methods?
2. For what types of research might you select primarily qualitative methods?
3. What are the differences between 'open' and 'closed' questions?
4. What is a leading question? Why are leading questions problematic in the context of research?
5. What are the main differences between structured, semi-structured and unstructured interviews?

## Sampling

Having spent a little time outlining the basic parameters of some of the major research methods used by criminologists, we need briefly to consider one or two more technical issues. Once again, the intention is not to provide the nuts and bolts, rather to sketch out elements of the general territory so that you have a sense of some of the key issues and can make some educated decisions about where to go next with your reading and your studies.

When conducting research, you will almost always have to give some thought to sampling. Who will you be researching? Is it possible for you to include the whole *population*? If so, then you don't need to worry about sampling. However, if you are only able to, say, survey or interview a proportion of the population you are interested in, then you will need to think about sampling. Thus, you might decide that you want to do some research on the drinking habits of undergraduate students at your university. However, there are almost certainly several thousand undergraduates and you haven't the time or the means to speak with them all. Consequently, you need to choose a more limited group to interview or send questionnaires to. The process by which you make this selection is *sampling*. Your *sampling frame* is provided by a list of the population from which you will select your respondents. There are then a number of sampling techniques you can use, depending on the nature of your study and what you are trying to achieve.

## Random (or Probability) Sampling

This approach selects people randomly for inclusion in the research and is used to eliminate systematic bias so that the eventual sample is as representative as possible of the overall population. There are various types of probability sampling. The most straightforward is a *simple random sample*, where everyone in a particular population has an equal chance of being selected for inclusion in the sample. If you wish to interview a random sample of adults in a particular neighbourhood, then so long as you have the names of all adults in that neighbourhood, you can create a random sample. You allocate numbers to all the adults and then using a table of random numbers, you can select the number of adults according to the sample size you have decided upon.

## Stratified Sampling

However, things are usually more complex than this. Let's say that you are still conducting your survey in the same neighbourhood, but it is a fairly mixed neighbourhood and you are concerned to ensure that particular groups are included. You may be worried that because you are doing most of the interviews during the daytime, you will over-sample those not going out to work and under-sample those with full-time jobs. Moreover, because of the nature of your survey you may want to hear from people who are owner-occupiers, people living in rented accommodation and those who are in local authority-owned housing. Immediately, you can see that the application of random numbers to your sampling frame may not produce a sample that will necessarily have all the features you need. You are going to need to rework it a little. In which case, what you may well need to do is construct a *stratified sample*.

You can do this so long as you have the information that would allow you to stratify the sample according to the characteristics you are interested in—home ownership or by other demographic characteristics. In order to ensure that your sample is selected in proportion to the overall totals of adults falling into each of the home ownership categories in the population, you randomly sample within each of the strata. Within criminology, the best-known example of this type of sampling is the Crime Survey. The intention behind the CSEW is to be representative of two linked populations:

- Households in England and Wales living in private, residential accommodation.
- Adults aged 16 and over living in such accommodation (with the addition, since 2009, of 12–15-year-olds—[...]).

The sample size is now approximately 35,000 and the sampling frame is provided by the Postal Address File (PAF), which is the most comprehensive database of private residential accommodation in the country. Because a certain number of interviews in each police force area in England and Wales is required and this cannot be achieved naturally in the smaller police force areas, some over-sampling (increasing the numbers in other areas) is undertaken to meet this requirement.

The CSEW also employs a process called *clustering*. A random sample—even one as large as 35,000—of the whole population would inevitably be geographically very dispersed and, consequently, very expensive to interview. To manage this process, cluster sampling produces what is called *primary sampling units* which are effectively subgroups of the population, from which the eventual sample is constructed. In the CSEW the primary sampling units are postcode areas. Within the eventually selected postcode areas (selected according to complex criteria), households are ranked and then randomly selected. Within the selected households an interviewee is randomly selected from all household members aged 16 or over. No substitution is allowed if the person selected is unavailable or refuses. In addition to this procedure, a *booster sample* (an extra sample) of non-white respondents is generally added. This is done by identifying areas with high minority ethnic populations, randomly selecting households, and then screening potential respondents face to face. The booster sample is added in order to ensure that the number of people from ethnic minority groups in the survey is large enough to support meaningful analysis.

The reason for discussing this in some detail is merely to illustrate some of the complexities that can be involved in producing a sample that researchers can be reasonably confident reflects the general make-up of the population. We have briefly discussed probability sampling. However, there are a number of other ways of sampling for research purposes which are not based on random selection, and these are generally referred to as *non-probability sampling*. We begin with *quota sampling*.

## Quota Sampling

Quota sampling is probably the best-known form of non-probability sampling. On the surface it looks very like stratified random sampling. However, it has one major difference. It does not involve any randomisation. If you have ever been interviewed as part of a market research study, or for a political opinion poll, you will almost certainly have been part of a quota sample. Thus, for example, if you have been stopped on the street by someone with a clipboard and asked questions about your shopping habits, you were most likely initially asked questions that screened you for matters like your age or other demographic details. Your answers to such questions are used both for the usual purpose of analysing the eventual data, but also as a means of deciding whether or not to ask you to continue with the interview after the initial questions have been asked. This is because the interviewer will usually be working to a quota sample; they will be trying to interview a specific number of people with certain characteristics, rather than simply approaching anyone who happens to pass them on the street and agrees to be interviewed. Thus, if the questionnaire is about beer sales and preferences, it is highly likely that men in certain age categories will form the bulk of the intended sample. But the main reason is to ensure that the sample approximates to the general population as, for example, with opinion polls.

The great advantage of quota sampling is that it is reasonably efficient and therefore a comparatively cheap method of constructing a varied and *broadly* representative sample. However, the word *broadly* here gives the game away. Often the apparent representativeness of the sample is illusory, and the fact that decisions about who to approach for interview are left to the interviewer leaves considerable room for bias. Moreover, the way in which such surveys are conducted—often, as in the example above, outside shops during the daytime—means that there may be *systematic bias* in the sample—excluding all those not shopping at particular times of day, or days of the week, for example.

## Purposive Sampling

This form of sampling will tend to be used in qualitative studies, particularly when relatively small numbers are being selected for inclusion in a sample. In essence, it is a form of selective sampling designed by the researcher to reflect a range of experiences or attributes. In effect, it is a little like a quota sample in survey research—it enables the researcher to ensure that certain types of people, or people with certain experiences, are included within the sample frame. Thus, you might wish to undertake a qualitative study of defendants' experiences in court. As you are conducting in-depth interviews, you might decide that 40 interviews is the upper limit of what you can reasonably manage. However, you are concerned to ensure that your sample includes both male and female defendants, people of different ages, and defendants who were in court for different reasons, as well as ensuring that you include people found guilty and not guilty. The only way that this can successfully be achieved is through purposive sampling.

## Convenience Sampling

This is what it says: a sample that is accessible or available. You might do a small piece of research using your fellow students as your sample—perhaps those from your tutor group, from your course or from your hall of residence. This is a convenience sample. Its strength lies in the ease of access that you have. It is fairly easy for you to find respondents, and the chances are you'll get a decent response rate. Its limitation is that whilst it should tell you quite a lot about this particular group of students, the findings cannot be generalised to any larger group because it is not representative.

Given this limitation, is it best to avoid convenience sampling? The answer to this question is, no, not necessarily. It may be the only way you can do research in a particular area. Let's say you want to do a small study of people who are sleeping rough. Because of the nature of homelessness there is no obviously available sampling frame (a list of homeless people that you can select from randomly). You may be constrained in other ways also, and find that the only way you can do the research is to interview anyone you happen to be able to find sleeping rough. This is a convenience sample and whilst not necessarily representative of the homeless population generally, it may still tell you quite a lot about the experience of homelessness (see also box on sampling marihuana users).

## Snowball Sampling

Rather like convenience sampling—or perhaps even a form of it—the metaphor is of the snowball gathering size as it is rolled. In snowball sampling one starts with one or more respondents and then, using their recommendations/contacts, gradually increases the size of the sample. Howard Becker's classic study of marijuana users began with interviews with people he knew in the music business and progressed from there. His sample 'snowballed' from his initial contacts.

This is, in effect, a convenience sample, as it is exploiting a situation that presents itself in order successfully to manage a research problem. As such, it has much to commend it. Its shortcoming, as with all convenience sampling, is that it produces a sample that is very far from representative. It is, predictably enough, generally used within qualitative research studies, where the aim is not to make statistical generalisations to a wider population.

### Sampling Marihuana Users

I conducted fifty interviews with marihuana users. I had been a professional dance musician for some years when I conducted this study and my first interviews were with people I had met in the music business. I asked them to put me in contact with other users who would be willing to discuss their experiences with me. Colleagues working on a study of users of opiate drugs made a few interviews available to me which contained, in addition to material on opiate drugs, sufficient material on the marihuana to furnish a test of my hypothesis. Although in the end half of the fifty interviews were conducted with musicians, the other half covered a wide range of people in the professions. The sample is, of course, in no sense 'random'; it would not be possible to draw a random sample, since no one knows the nature of the universe from which it would have to be drawn.

*Source*: Becker (1963: 45–46).

# Statistics

Depending on what sort of student you are, this may be the point at which you stop reading. I would urge you not to do so, however. Unfortunately, there seems to be a mindset within British education that leads some people to recoil from all things statistical. Even if you never plan to do any quantitative research, you should still be able to understand the basics. How can you form a judgement about it otherwise? Now, there is not the space here to do any more than introduce one or two ideas, but these are the basic building blocks that will give you a start. Anyone wishing to take this further—and, again, I would urge you to do so—can follow up the suggested reading at the end of the chapter. All I intend to cover in this short section is the difference between *numerical* and *categorical data,* introduce the idea of a *normal distribution* and the linked term *standard deviation,* and briefly discuss the terms *probability* and *significance*. If you understand this much, then you will be able to make sense of basic quantitative data that you will undoubtedly come across in your studies.

# Descriptive Statistics

As the term suggests, descriptive statistics are used in a general way to describe or outline information about a particular subject. I might be able to tell you a number of things about my university using descriptive statistics such as the number of students, their age range, average qualifications and so forth. You might be able to do the same for your university and then the two could be compared. As I have implied, one of the commonest forms of descriptive statistic is to talk of *averages*. Most people understand what this means. In common terms, it is generally thought of as the figure you get when, say, you add the ages of everyone in a particular class, and then divide the total by the number of people in the class. This will tell you their average age. In fact, there are three types of average, and the one just described is known as the *mean*. The other two ways of calculating averages are called the *mode* and the *median*. The mode tells you which is the most commonly occurring value in any group, and the median tells which value occurs at precisely the mid-point in a group of values (see box).

## Numerical and Categorical Data

Categorical data, as the name implies, divide things into categories. Such data come in two basic forms: *nominal* and *ordinal*. Nominal data are found when the categories do not have any inherent order. There can be any number of categories, but where there are only two, the data are said to be binary. Examples include: male/female, black/white, young/old, etc. Ordinal data refer to situations where the data are organised into categories that can be ranked in some form of order: very satisfied/ quite satisfied/quite dissatisfied, etc. By contrast, numerical data generally refer to scales where the data are in rank order from a zero point and are based on a consistent unit of measurement where the categories are equally spaced. Because of this, differences between categories can be specified numerically—we can say, for example, somebody with a score of 20 has twice as much of something as somebody with a score of 10 but half as much as someone with a score of 40, and so on. Age in years provides a classic example, with the numerical data going 0, 1, 2, 3, 4 ... and so on. These are referred to as *ratio data*. There is a further subset of numerical data, called *interval data*, and these occur where there is no zero point—such as the measurement of temperature—but such scales are extremely rare. Just to complicate matters there is a further subdivision of numerical data: *discrete data* are those expressed on whole numbers only (age in years would, again, be an example); *continuous data* are those where a decimal division is possible (e.g. per capita alcohol consumption in litres).

### Mean, Mode and Median

Take the following list of values, representing the ages of an imagined group of 35 undergraduate students, already ordered so that the mid-point can easily be seen:

> *42, 39, 38, 32, 26, 26, 23, 23, 22, 22, 22, 21, 21, 20, 20, 20, 20, 19, 19, 19, 19, 19, 19, 19, 18, 18, 18, 18, 18, 18, 18, 18, 18, 18, 18*

What is the average age? Well, the mean is 22 (all the figures above added together and divided by 35). The mode is 18 (the most common age) and the median is 19 (the age that appears in the middle of the ordered list). Each of these measures tells you something slightly different about that group of students, but each is an average.

## Normal Distribution

The mathematical calculation of what is called the *normal distribution* is generally associated with Karl Friedrich Gauss and is sometimes referred to as the Gaussian curve (see Figure 7.2). This distribution plays a key role in statistics and the application of quantitative methods and relates to numerical data.

Under these conditions the value of the mean, mode and median will be the same. Where this is not the case and the mean, mode and median have different values (as in the mean, mode and median box), the data are said to be *skewed*. How much variation is there in the data around the mean point? The answer to this question is usually made using the *standard deviation*. Suppose, for example, your survey told you that the average alcohol consumption of a particular group was 20 units per week. Without another measure you cannot know whether, for example, most people

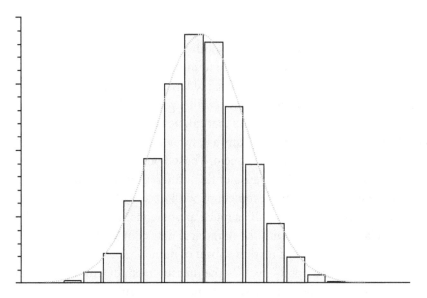

**FIGURE 7.2** Normal distribution

*Source:* www.statsdirect.com/help/default.htm#distributions/normal.htm (2016).

in the group drank between 15–25 units or whether the variation in drinking patterns was much greater. *Standard deviation* is one way of indicating the extent of variation—in this case of drinking patterns—around the average.

The other term you may hear in this connection is *confidence interval*. This is a descriptive statistic that indicates the degree of certainty/uncertainty associated with a particular finding. Thus, survey data may suggest that in a particular local population 20 per cent of people think that the police do a 'very good job'. Because the finding is based on the answers drawn from a sample of the local population, there is a continuing possibility of measurement error. The confidence interval describes the range within which the 'true' value (i.e. that which exists in the population) is likely to lie.

## Correlation

In research, one of the standard things we investigate is the relationship between two variables. We may wish to look at a group of juveniles and their offending patterns and see, for example, to what extent their offending is related to age. We shall probably find that it is—for research tends to do so pretty consistently [...]. What do we mean when we say that these things are *related*? Generally, we mean they are *positively correlated*. That is, if the data were plotted on a graph, for example, the level of offending might increase as age increases. If the reverse were the case—offending decreased as age increased—there would still be a relationship, but this would be described as an inverse relationship and would give rise to a *negative correlation*. The extent or degree of correlation refers to how close this relationship is. In statistics, the strength of a relationship is usually indicated using a *correlation coefficient*—generally presented within a range from—1.0 (which indicates a perfect negative correlation) to 1.0 (which indicates a perfect positive correlation).

## Probability and Significance

If we find a measurable difference between two groups as a result of a survey we have conducted, how do we know whether this is meaningful or not? One of the ways in which we make such assessments is through calculating *probability*. Probability, in the way it is used here, expresses the likelihood that the findings displayed might have arisen as a result of chance. Assuming we have a random sample, probability values or p-values show the probability of finding a relationship at least as strong as the one observed in our data when there is no such relationship in the population:

- The smaller the p-value, the less likely it is that the relationship we have observed could have occurred by chance.
- When the p-value is quite large, say 0.20, we would say that a relationship at least as strong as the one observed could occur quite often when there is no such relationship in the population.
- If the p-value is very small, say less than 0.01, then it is very unlikely that a relationship as strong as the one observed would occur simply by chance.

Statistical convention dictates that a cut-off is chosen for assessing probability values and this is called the *critical value*. Although the choice of cut-off is arbitrary, 0.05 is conventionally used and 0.01 is sometimes used. When the p-value falls below the critical value, the relationship is said to be *statistically significant*, and when it falls above the critical value, it is said to be *not significant*. This simply provides a judgement about whether the relationship we have observed in a sample is likely to exist in the population.

A finding of statistical significance doesn't guarantee that a relationship was not observed by chance, but suggests that this was probably not the case.

There is a wide range of statistical tests that can be used to generate p-values. This is not the place to begin to describe them all, but you may see or read reference to such things as *t-tests*, and the *chi-squared test*. Different tests are appropriate under different circumstances and depend, for example, on the level of measurement of the data (nominal, ordinal or numerical). Each test produces a p-value, however, and the basic interpretation of this value is the same across the various tests. As you begin to manipulate data, you will need to know the difference between the tests and understand why one rather than the other is considered appropriate under certain circumstances. If you use a statistical package such as *SPSS*, it is possible to produce results with such tests of significance without understanding their relevance. This is unwise and either a methods course in your university, or one of the good textbooks listed at the end of this chapter, will guide you through basic statistical tests of significance and how they should be used. Understanding such things is actually quite straightforward and you will quickly discover that you don't need to be Stephen Hawking to make sense of this stuff. Once you have mastered the basics, it will give you considerable confidence in discussing all manner of research findings. Moreover, it may well help to get you a job when you graduate!

## Controversy: Evaluation and Experimentation

I want to close this chapter by looking briefly at an area of methodological debate that is currently causing something of a stir within British criminology. In short, it concerns the value of what is generally referred to as 'experimental methods'. As we will see, experimental methods have rarely been used in British criminological research, but the government has recently shown an increasing interest in their use, particularly in evaluations of interventions with offenders. This has been the cause of some debate. I don't wish to give a blow-by-blow account of this dispute, merely outline some of the basic points of departure between scholars who hold differing views on how to conduct rigorous evaluation research.

## Experimental Methods

Experimental methods are commonly associated with medical research, particularly the evaluation of a new treatment or a new drug. The use of such methods probably dates back to the late nineteenth century, though it was relatively rare at this stage, and only grew in popularity in the early twentieth century (Oakley, 1998). At the heart of experimental research is the process of randomisation, which is used in an effort to eliminate extraneous factors in the search for cause and effect relationships. Under experimental conditions, random sampling is usually achieved by allocating research subjects to two groups: a *treatment* group, which will be receiving whatever intervention is being evaluated (a new drug, for example), and a *control* or *non-treatment* group, which receives no intervention, or just a placebo. Subjects are allocated to the groups randomly in order to ensure that there is no consistent feature (e.g. age, sex, ethnicity, criminal history) that might distinguish the two groups. On the basis that they can, therefore, be assumed to be equivalent in every other respect except for the fact that one receives the treatment and one does not, any measurable differences between the groups at the end of the research can safely be attributed to the effects of the treatment.

The best-known experimental design is known as the *Randomised Controlled Trial (RCT)*. The standard basic design of such trials can be seen in Figure 7.3. The model is generally referred to as the standard 'pre- and post-test' in which measurements are taken before and after the intervention and are then compared in order to assess the impact of that intervention […]. There is also a simpler post-test measurement design in which, as implied, it is only the outcome measurements that are taken. This approach is more usual when there is the possibility that pre-test research—say the use of a questionnaire—will provide information to participants that would affect the 'blindness' of the process.

In some studies, researchers may attempt to reduce any biases through a process called *blinding*. There are two main types. *Single blinding* is where the subjects in the research don't know whether they are in the treatment or the control group. *Double blinding* is where neither the subjects of the research nor those providing treatment—which usually means administering the drug—know

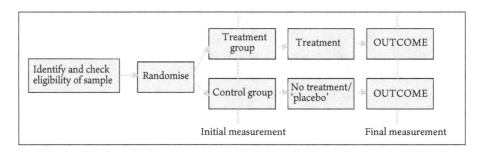

FIGURE 7.3 The classic design of a randomised controlled trial (RCT)

*Source*: Clegg and Kirwan (2006).

which group they are in. There is a further option for RCTs in which those participants who have a preferred treatment option are allocated to that group and the remainder are randomly allocated between the two groups (sometimes referred to as a *preference trial*).

The RCT is often referred to as the 'gold standard' in research methods, implying that it is the ideal to be striven for. This is unfortunate, because it rather glosses over the important point that the appropriateness of any research method depends upon the thing being studied and the questions being asked. Thus, there are clearly areas of inquiry to which the RCT is ideally suited, and where it might reasonably be referred to as the gold standard—the testing of pharmaceuticals, for example. However, there are many other areas where such a methodology would be entirely unsuitable. The study of police culture would be one. Such a study would almost certainly be better undertaken using a range of other approaches, some of which would quite probably be qualitative. The implication that such approaches are not the 'gold standard' devalues their worth.

## Quasi-Experimental Methods

This range of approaches has many but not all of the attributes of the full experimental design outlined above. Generally, it is randomisation that is absent and researchers use a variety of techniques in an attempt to generate a situation that is as close to the effect that randomisation would have as is possible. Thus, in *matched pairs* designs, the sample to be studied is matched into twos along a set of key characteristics—which could involve such things as age, sex, ethnicity, education, occupation, medical history, offending history, and so on—in an attempt to control for the influence of these factors. That is, if people are matched on a whole range of potentially important variables, then any differences between them after 'treatment' are more likely to be as a result of that intervention (and not age, sex, ethnicity, etc.). The major difficulty with such an approach is that it is extremely difficult to match across a sufficient number of factors to be certain that one has 'controlled' for all major extraneous variables.

A second approach is to compare *non-equivalent* groups using a treatment group and a comparison group. In such research there is no randomisation, merely a group of subjects who are subject to an intervention and another group that is not. Often, great efforts are made to try to ensure that the two groups are as similar as possible to each other. However, it is accepted that the groups will inevitably differ. The approach taken thereafter is usually to attempt to control for any major differences between the groups using statistical techniques at the analytical stage. The data are *weighted* to take account of identified disparities between the groups, helping to increase the likelihood that any statistically significant differences between the intervention and non-intervention groups can be attributed to the intervention itself. Weighting refers to a process of adjustment whereby the emphasis that is placed on each case varies according to certain criteria. This process is generally used to take account of bias and to increase accuracy.

## Evaluation Research

Like so many other features of the British social world, much of what we understand by 'evaluation' derives from the United States. Evaluation research has a longer and more privileged history in the USA than it does in the UK, dating back to the post-war Keynesian reconstruction and the major social programmes of the 1950s and 1960s. Initially, at least, evaluation was dominated by experimental and quasi-experimental approaches, with the period from the 1960s to the 1980s sometimes being referred to as the 'golden age' of evaluation (Rossi and Wright, 1984).

A large number of experimental evaluations of major policy initiatives were undertaken during this period covering such areas as welfare, health, education, housing, fiscal and penal policy—and federal spending in this area grew sixfold between 1969 and 1972. A number of factors influenced this development. Public services were widely perceived to be poorly organised and inefficient; there was no dominant model of public policy decision-making that offered an easy solution of how this problem of inefficient public services might be resolved. Into this breach stepped the new 'science' of evaluation (Oakley, 1998). For many in the field, experimental methods were not only dominant at this time but, in Campbell and Stanley's (1963: 3) phrase, were considered to be 'the only available route to cumulative progress'.

Whilst experimental methods have remained important, they have been gradually superseded by evaluations that were tailored more to informing or influencing decision-making processes (Robson, 2000). Weiss (1987) described this as being a shift from knowledge-driven to use-led approaches to evaluation, or towards what Patten called 'utilization-focused' evaluation. One consequence of this was that a diversity of evaluation practice began to emerge, with methodological pluralism becoming increasingly visible.

What then happened to experimental and quasi-experimental methods? In fact, something rather interesting: whereas, as I have suggested, the early days of evaluation were dominated by experimental methods—at least in the USA—this is now much less the case. Or, rather, there are certain fields of inquiry—health and medicine, for example—where such methods continue to enjoy a dominant position, and others—social welfare, for example—where, despite the continued assumption that experimental methods represent the so-called 'gold standard' in evaluation, they are hardly ever used.

Why should this be? Oakley (1998: 94; see also Oakley, 2000) points to five 'reasons' that have often been advanced against the use of experimental methods:

- Prospective experimental designs are often not feasible in social situations (you cannot easily randomly assign serious offenders to prison on the one hand and some other form of intervention on the other).
- They are inappropriate for assessing complex, multilevel interventions, especially those that take place in community settings.
- 'Withholding treatments' from a control group is unethical.
- Such designs are too expensive, take too long and are too remote from the policy-making process.
- Such research tends to be method-driven and atheoretical; it tends to ignore subjective meanings and underemphasises human agency.

It is as much the last point as any other that is, arguably, key. This has been part of a paradigm shift within social sciences over the past few decades. From the 1970s onwards, just as social science generally was gripped by a debate over the limits of positivism (Giddens, 1974—[...]), so experimental methods in evaluation were subjected to a critique from what became known as 'constructivism'. As Pawson and Tilley (1997: 17) summarise it, this approach

urges us to consider again the nature of what it is we are evaluating. The argument goes as follows: that the initiatives and programmes which go under the microscope cannot and should not be treated as 'independent variables', 'things', 'treatments', or as 'dosages'. Rather, all social programmes are constituted in complex processes of human understanding and interaction. [Such programmes] work through a process of reasoning, change, influence, negotiation, battle of wills, persuasion, choice increase (or decrease), arbitration or some such like.

One of the consequences of this critique was to place much greater emphasis on 'process' in evaluation: 'instead of concentrating on questions such as "does the program improve reading standards?" ... research is directed primarily to the internal dynamics of such schemes, by seeking the views of those present on why (if at all) the implicit ideas behind a scheme' have influenced them (Pawson and Tilley, 1997: 17–18). A much greater emphasis was placed on 'stakeholders' in evaluation.

Perhaps the most lasting contribution of the constructivist critique was to point to the absence of theory (understanding of process) in much (quasi-)experimental evaluation. Such evaluation, the critics suggested, even where it was capable of identifying success, which did not appear to be often, could not explain why such success occurred. The paradigm war between experimentalists and constructivists has led to the development of various alternative approaches which seek to deal with both agency and structure in explanation. One of the most recent and best-known of these is what is now referred to as 'realistic evaluation'.

'Realistic evaluation', as outlined in Figure 7.4, focuses on explaining how particular outcomes (O) are produced by interventions (the way in which an intervention produces an outcome they call a 'mechanism' (M)) within particular salient conditions, or the 'context' (C). Crucially, realistic evaluation is theory driven, having at its core both hypotheses about 'mechanisms' and the influence of variations in 'context'.

Just as there was something of a paradigm shift and experimental methods fell out of favour in the evaluation field, so they are now beginning to reemerge. As I have suggested, this has proved controversial in some quarters. A number of semi-official sets of research guidelines have begun to appear which rank evaluation methods in terms of their reliability and rigour. One of the more influential, generally referred to as the 'Scientific Methods Scale' (Sherman *et al.*, 1997), places

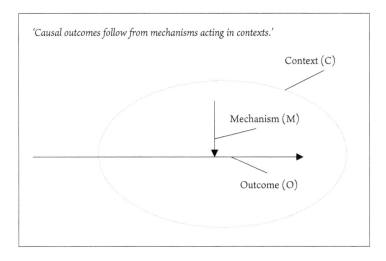

**FIGURE 7.4** Pawson and Tilley's model for 'realistic evaluation'

*Source*: Pawson and Tilley (1997).

experimental methods at the top of a hierarchy of approaches to evaluation and such rank-ordering of approaches to research has drawn considerable criticism (Hope, 2006). The danger both in the promotion of hierarchies in this fashion and in the disputes between the proponents of such a position and scholars who take a different view—the so-called 'paradigm wars'—is that we lose sight of the two important lessons that apply in relation to social scientific—in this case, criminological—research. First, that the choice of method will very often depend upon the nature of the questions being asked, as well as the resources available to the researcher. Second, whatever the method employed, it is the responsibility of the social scientist to ensure that the work is conducted to the highest standards and utmost rigour.

## Evaluation Research—A Hot Topic?

Much academic debate is pretty dry and often fairly tame. However, occasionally, scholars are brave enough to take the gloves off and engage in vigorous debate (though they can sometimes stray beyond reasonable limits). Intriguingly, evaluation research is one of those areas that has occasionally stimulated such debate. Two examples are outlined below, both involving the 'realists' Pawson and Tilley.

The first debate took place in the *British Journal of Criminology* (*BJC*) between Pawson and Tilley and Trevor Bennett, then of the Institute of Criminology, Cambridge. Pawson and Tilley responded critically to an article written by Bennett on a police fear-of-crime reduction strategy. Bennett responded and then Pawson and Tilley replied to Bennett. The relevant articles are:

Bennett, T. (1991) 'The effectiveness of a police-initiated fear-reducing strategy', *BJC*, 31, 1, 1–14 (http://bjc.oxfordjournals.org/cgi/reprint/31/1/1).

Pawson, R. and Tilley, N. (1994) 'What works in evaluation research?', *BJC*, 34, 3, 291–306 (http://bjc.oxfordjournals.org/cgi/reprint/34/3/291).

Bennett, T. (1996) 'What's new in evaluation research?', *BJC*, 36, 4, 567–573 (http://bjc.oxfordjournals.org/cgi/reprint/36/4/567).

Pawson, R. and Tilley, N. (1996) 'What's crucial in evaluation research: A response to Bennett', *BJC*, 36, 4, 574–578 (http://bjc.oxfordjournals.org/cgi/reprint/36/4/574).

The second debate concerns methods for the evaluation of complex, multisite community initiatives. In this case the original article was published by David Farrington. That article, and the ensuing debate, can be found in:

Farrington, D.P. (1997) 'Evaluating a community crime prevention programme', *Evaluation*, 3, 1, 57–73.

Pawson, R. and Tilley, N. (1998) 'Caring communities, paradigm polemics, design debates', *Evaluation*, 4, 1, 73–90.

Farrington, D.P. (1998) 'Evaluating communities that care: Realistic scientific considerations', *Evaluation*, 4, 2, 204–210 (http://evi.sagepub.com/cgi/reprint/4/2/204).

Pawson, R. and Tilley, N. (1998) 'Cook-book methods and disastrous recipes: A rejoinder to Farrington', *Evaluation*, 4, 2, 211–213 (http://evi.sagepub.com/cgi/reprint/4/2/211).

# Summary

As a student of criminology you have to read and analyse criminological research. You may well also need to undertake a small-scale piece of research yourself—for a long essay or dissertation. Both of these tasks require you to develop the ability to assess, in a critical manner, how research is undertaken and what it is (and is not) able to tell us.

In this chapter we:

- take a quick journey through research methods, exploring the differences between 'quantitative' (numerical) and 'qualitative' (non-numerical) methods;
- look at each of the main research methods in turn, exploring the basic techniques and looking at the strengths and limitations of each.

Most research involves some sort of 'sampling'—selecting respondents from a larger population—and we explore the main methods of making such selections.

Although we won't look at statistical techniques in any detail, it is, nevertheless, important to understand the most frequently used terms and we briefly consider some of the most common bits of statistical language—the things you are most likely to come across when reading criminological books and articles.

Research methods can occasionally cause controversy and we finish by looking at one such: the debate over evaluation in criminological research and, more particularly, the place of what is often referred to as 'experimental methods'.

## REVIEW QUESTIONS

1. What are the main differences between probability and non-probability sampling?
2. What is quota sampling and where might it be used?
3. What is the difference between numerical and categorical data?
4. What is the primary difference between experimental and quasi-experimental methods?

## QUESTIONS FOR FURTHER DISCUSSION

1. Do different standards apply to quantitative and qualitative research?
2. What are the pros and cons of interview-based and postal surveys?
3. Why is sampling important?
4. What is the value of qualitative research?
5. Is it appropriate to talk of a 'gold standard' in relation to research methods?

## FURTHER READING

I have said on several occasions during the course of this chapter that it is designed very much as an introduction to some important issues and ideas. Its aim is to help guide you towards further study. There are a huge number of 'methods' books out there, many of them terrific. Arguably, an almost equivalent number are either deadly dull, or just too much like plain hard work without much reward. Learning about how to do research (well) can be fun, but it is important to find the right books. In my opinion, the following are all reliable and interesting:

Bryman, A. (2015) *Social Research Methods,* 5th edn, Oxford: Oxford University Press.

Healey, J.F (2014) *Statistics: A tool for social research,* 10th edn, London: Wadsworth Press.

Pawson, R. (2013) *The Science of Evaluation,* London: Sage.

Pawson, R. and Tilley, N. (1997) *Realistic Evaluation,* London: Sage.

Robson, C. and McCartan, K. (2016) *Real World Research,* 4th edn, Oxford: Blackwell.

There are also some useful articles by criminologists reflecting on the task of research in:

Caulfield, L. and Hill, J. (2014) *Criminological Research for Beginners,* London: Routledge.

Chamberlain, J.M. (2014) *Understanding Criminological Research: A guide to data analysis,* London: Sage.

Davies, P., Francis, P. and Jupp, V. (2010) *Doing Criminological Research,* London: Sage.

Gadd, D., Karstedt, S. and Messner, S. (eds) (2012) *The Sage Handbook of Criminological Research Methods,* London: Sage.

King, R. and Wincup, E. (eds) (2007) *Doing Research on Crime and Justice,* 2nd edn, Oxford: Oxford University Press.

In addition to reading books about how to do research, there's nothing like reading original research using the methods themselves. So, possibly, you might care to try:

*Surveys*

Hough, M. and Mayhew, P. (1983) *The British Crime Survey,* London: Home Office; and

Jones, T. *et al.* (1986) *The Islington Crime Survey,* Aldershot: Gower.

*Interviews and focus groups*

Heidensohn, F. (1995) *Women in Control,* Oxford: Oxford University Press.

Reiner, R. (1991) *Chief Constables,* Oxford: Oxford University Press.

Worrall, A. (1990) *Offending Women,* London: Routledge.

*Ethnography*

Desmond, M. (2016) *Evicted,* London: Penguin.

Hobbs, D. (1988) *Doing the Business,* Oxford: Oxford University Press.

Maher, L. (1997) *Sexed Work,* Oxford: Clarendon Press.

*Documentary analysis*

Reiner, R. *et al.* (2000) 'No more happy endings? The media and popular concern about crime since the Second World War', in Hope, T. and Sparks, R. (eds) *Crime, Risk and Insecurity*, London: Routledge.

*Case studies*

Cohen, S. (1972/2002) *Folk Devils and Moral Panics*, London: Routledge.

## WEBSITES

Apart from doing research yourself, one of the most straightforward ways of learning about research is to read first-hand accounts. The best source is to look at the main journals:

*British Journal of Criminology*—https://bjc.oxfordjournals.org
*Criminology and Criminal Justice*—http://crj.sagepub.com
*Howard Journal of Crime and Justice*—http://onlinelibrary.wiley.com/journal/10.1111/(ISSN)2059–1101;
    jsessionid=F4EF34B60550CDC65422BFBDED4DEEE3.f03t03
*Punishment and Society*—http://pun.sagepub.com
*Theoretical Criminology*—http://tcr.sagepub.com/

There are also some specialist journals worth looking at:
*Ethnography*—http://eth.sagepub.com
*Evaluation*—http://evi.sagepub.com

The Social Research Association maintains a website with information about developments in particular areas: http://the-sra.org.uk

## Bibliography

Arksey, H. and Knight, P. (1999) *Interviewing for Social Scientists*, London: Sage

Becker, H. (1963) *Outsiders: Studies in the sociology of deviance*, London: Macmillan

Bennett, T. (1991) 'The effectiveness of a police-initiated fear-reducing strategy', *British Journal of Criminology*, 31, 1, 1–14

Bennett, T. (1996) 'What's new in evaluation research?', *British Journal of Criminology*, 36, 4, 567–573

Bryman, A. (2001) *Social Research Methods*, Oxford: Oxford University Press

Bryman, A. (2004) *Social Research Methods*, 2nd edn, Oxford: Oxford University Press

Bryman, A. (2015) *Social Research Methods*, 5th edn, Oxford: Oxford University Press

Campbell, D.T. and Stanley, J.C. (1963) *Experimental and Quasi Experimental Designs for Research*, Chicago, IL: Rand McNally

Chambliss, W. (1978) *On the Take: From petty crooks to presidents*, Bloomington, IN: Indiana University Press

Clegg, M. and Kirwan, S. (2006) *Police Service Strength 2006*, HOSB 13/06, London: Home Office

Cohen, J.M. (2002) *Inside Appellate Courts: The impact of court organization on judicial decision making in the United States Courts of Appeals*, Ann Arbor, MI: University of Michigan Press

Cohen, P. (1972) 'Subcultural conflict and working class community', in Hall, S., Hobson, D., Lowe, A. and Willis, P. (eds) *Culture, Media, Language,* London: Hutchinson

Desmond, M. (2016) *Evicted,* London: Penguin

Ditton, J. (1977) *Part-Time Crime,* London: Macmillan

Farquhar, C. with Das, R. (1999) 'Are focus groups suitable for "sensitive" topics?' in Barbour, R. and Kitzinger, J. (eds) *Developing Focus Group Research,* London: Sage

Farrington, D.P. (1997) 'Evaluating a community crime prevention programme', *Evaluation,* 3, 2, 157–173

Farrington, D.P. (1998) 'Evaluating "communities that care": Realistic scientific considerations', *Evaluation,* 4, 2, 204–210

Fielding, N. (1981) *The National Front,* London: Routledge and Kegan Paul

Giddens, A. (ed.) (1974) *Positivism and Sociology,* London: Heinemann

Gold, R. (1969) 'Roles in sociological field observation', in McCall, G. and Simmons, J. (eds) *Issues in Participant Observation,* London: Addison Wesley

Hobbs, D. (1988) *Doing the Business,* Oxford: Oxford University Press

Hobbs, D. (1994) *Interpreting the Field,* Oxford: Oxford University Press

Hope, T. (2006) 'What do crime statistics tell us?', in Hale, C., Hayward, K., Wahidin, A. and Wincup, E. (eds) *Criminology,* Oxford: Oxford University Press

Kitzinger, J. and Barbour, R.S. (1999) 'Introduction: The challenge and promise of focus groups', in Barbour, R. and Kitzinger, J. (eds) *Developing Focus Group Research,* London: Sage

Maher, L. (1997) *Sexed Work,* Oxford: Oxford University Press

May, T. (2001) *Social Research, Issues, Methods and Process,* Buckingham: Open University Press

Oakley, A. (1998) 'Public policy experimentation: Lessons from America', *Policy Studies,* 19, 2, 93–114

Oakley, A. (2000) *Experiments in Knowing: Gender and method in the social sciences,* Cambridge: Polity

Parker, H. (1974) *View from the Boys,* London: David and Charles

Patrick, J. (1973) *A Glasgow Gang Observed,* London: Methuen

Pawson, R. and Tilley, N. (1994) 'What works in evaluation research?', *British Journal of Criminology,* 4, 3, 291–306

Pawson, R. and Tilley, N. (1996) 'What's crucial in evaluation research: A reply to Bennett', *British Journal of Criminology,* 36, 4, 574–578

Pawson, R. and Tilley, N. (1997) *Realistic Evaluation,* London: Sage

Pawson, R. and Tilley, N. (1998a) 'Caring communities, paradigm polemics, design debates, evaluation', *International Journal of Theory, Research and Practice,* 4, 1, 73–90

Pawson, R. and Tilley, N. (1998b) 'Cook-book methods and disastrous recipes: A rejoinder to Farrington's evaluation', *International Journal of Theory, Research and Practice,* 4, 2, 211–213

Robson, C. (2000) *Small-Scale Evaluation,* London: Sage

Rossi, P.H. and Wright, J.D. (1984) 'Evaluation research: An assessment', *Annual Review of Sociology,* 10, 331–352

Scott, J. (1990) *A Matter of Record: Documentary sources in social research,* Cambridge: Polity

Shaw, C.R. (1930) *The Jack-Roller: A delinquent boy's own story,* Chicago, IL: University of Chicago Press

Sherman, D., Iacono, W. and McGue, M. (1997) 'Attention-deficit hyperactivity disorder dimensions: A twin study of inattention and impulsivity-hyperactivity', *Journal of the American Academy of Child & Adolescent Psychiatry,* 36, 6, 745–753

Smith, D.J., Gray, J. and Small, S. (1983) *Police and People in London,* London: Policy Studies Institute

Sutherland, E.H. (1937) *The Professional Thief by a Professional Thief,* Chicago, IL: University of Chicago Press

Weiss, C.H. (1987) 'The circuitry of enlightenment', *Knowledge, Creation, Diffusion, Utilisation,* 8, 274–281

Williams, J., Murphy, P. and Dunning, E. (1989) *Hooligans Abroad,* London: Routledge

Willis, P. (1977) *Learning to Labour: How working class kids get working class jobs,* Farnborough: Saxon House

Willis, P. and Trondman, M. (2000) 'A manifesto for ethnography', *Ethnography,* 1, 1, 5–16

Winlow, S. and Hall, S. (2006) *Violent Night: Urban leisure and contemporary culture,* Oxford: Berg

# Ethics and Criminal Justice Research

BELINDA R. MCCARTHY, ROBIN J. KING, AND JENNIFER A. PEALER

All areas of life contain ethical dilemmas, and the field of research is no exception. A number of concerns related to the professional behavior of academic researchers have made newspaper headlines, stirred government inquiries, and have ultimately raised questions about what is considered appropriate within the research process. Academic researchers have been accused of such acts as falsifying data to obtain additional research funding and fabricating or misrepresenting results in order to get their research published. Even celebrated researchers have been found to have fabricated some or all of the research upon which their scholarship is based (Bhattacharjee, 2013).

One of the most notorious cases in recent times involved Diederik Stapel, a psychologist whose research demonstrated that exposure to litter and graffiti makes people more likely to commit small crimes (Kahn, 2011). Motivated by a desire to continue to produce clear and consistent results that he believed would be more readily published, his efforts at deception were extensive, elaborate, and lasted for many years. His efforts compromised the scholarship of the graduate students he supervised as well as his own integrity.

The issue of research fabrication or misrepresentation in academic publications is an area that merits considerable concern. Published research has the potential to influence criminal justice policy and planning (Garrison, 2009) as well as practice. The strategy of developing guidelines for practice based on research findings, often referred to as "evidence-based practice", is increasingly utilized in the human services professions including corrections. Decisions related to community safety and offender supervision are being made based on research that has identified "a few core principles [that] stand out as proven risk reduction strategies" (National Institute of Corrections, 2013, p. 3).

Issues of plagiarism and theft of data may also arise during the process of publishing research results. Sociology faculty once levied such vitriolic charges and countercharges against their department colleagues that a dispute at Texas A&M University escalated to a degree that required investigation by the university, the National Science Foundation, and the American Sociological Association (Leatherman, 1999).

One might think that scientific endeavors, with their objective and unbiased approach for the world, would create fewer dilemmas than other occupational activities. Although most researchers are not faced with the same kind of corrupting influences confronting street-level criminal justice officials, the pressures of "grantsmanship" and publication provide significant motivations for researchers to engage in unethical behaviors. The dilemmas of working with human participants in a political environment can be equally challenging. In addition, the goal of scientific purity and unbiased objectivity, may be corrupting, because adherence to these perspectives may encourage researchers to put scientific objectives before their concern for the welfare of others; namely, those whom researchers will collect data from or about.

This chapter examines the nature of ethical dilemmas confronting the criminal justice researcher. To a large degree these problems are comparable to the difficulties faced by other social scientists. However, additional problems may arise as a result of the particular research focus on deviance and lawbreaking.

## Ethical Considerations Involving Work with Human Participants

Researchers typically work with other individuals when conducting research. Most notable are the individuals from or about whom they will collect data. These individuals are often referred to as research "subjects." Considering that the study of ethics focuses on how individuals treat one another, one could argue whether it is ethical to apply such a label within the research process. Could referring to an individual as a research "subject" have any influence on how researchers treat those individuals within the process? Could the term "subject" influence how individuals engage with the researcher? Furthermore, could such a term influence an individual's responses? Accordingly, this chapter will utilize the term "participant" rather than "subject" when referring to individuals who provide information to researchers.

Stuart Cook (1976, p. 202) lists the following ethical considerations regarding research with human participants:

1. Involving people in research without their knowledge or consent.
2. Coercing people to participate.
3. Withholding from the participant the true nature of the research.
4. Deceiving the research participant.
5. Leading the research participants to commit acts which diminish their self-respect.
6. Violating the right to self-determination: research on behavior control and character change.
7. Exposing the research participant to physical or mental stress.
8. Invading the privacy of the research participant.
9. Withholding benefits from participants in control groups.

**10.** Failing to treat research participants fairly and to show them consideration and respect.

# Involving People in Research without Their Knowledge or Consent

Ideally for gaining accurate information, the best way to study human behavior is to observe people in a natural setting without their knowledge. Self-reported descriptions of behavior may be unreliable because people forget or are uncertain about their actions. Furthermore, most people might tell you that they would attempt to return a lost wallet, but a hidden camera focused on a wallet lying on the sidewalk might reveal very different behaviors. People who know they are being watched often act differently, especially when unethical, deviant, or criminal behaviors are involved. For these reasons, researchers may prefer to study deviance through direct observation, which involves listening as well as visual examination.

At times, the observer participates to some degree in the activities being studied. For example, Whyte's (1955) study of street-corner society involved just this form of participant observation, as Whyte resided with an Italian family in the community where he was conducting research. Likewise, Humphreys's (1970) examination of homosexual behavior in public restrooms, Short and Strodtbeck's (1965) study of delinquency in Chicago, and Cohen's (1980) observations of female prostitutes in New York all involved the observation of persons who did not consent to becoming research participants.

Research efforts about persons on the other side of the criminal justice process have also been undertaken without their knowledge or consent. Meltzer (1953) studied jury deliberations through the use of hidden microphones as part of a growing research interest regarding the judicial process. The significance of discretion in the criminal justice process and the hidden nature of most decision making provide support for arguments calling for greater use of such techniques. These efforts are generally favored when the desire is to understand how police, prosecutors, correctional personnel, jury members, or other persons involved in the process of criminal justice carry out their duties.

The ethical dilemma, however, is a complicated one: Is the value of the research such that persons should be turned into study "participants" without their permission? The conditions of the research are extremely important to this deliberation. If the behaviors being studied would have occurred without the researcher's intervention, the lack of consent seems less troubling. Such studies involve little personal cost to unknowing subjects. Unobtrusive research that involves only behaviors that occur in public view is also less questionable, because the invasion of personal privacy is not at issue.

What about experiments that create situations to which participants must react, such as those involving a "lost" wallet? Or a study of witness response to crimes that involve an actor or actress screaming and running from an apparent assailant down a crowded street? Observation might be the only method for determining how citizens would truly respond, but the personal cost of being studied could be considerable.

Not only may such research be troubling for the persons involved, but when sensitive activities that are normally considered private or confidential are the subject of study, additional problems can arise. Cook (1976, p. 205) reports that Meltzer encountered such difficulties in his study of jury deliberations:

Members of Congress reacted to the jury recording as a threat to fundamental institutions. When the news of the study came out, a congressional investigation resulted. Following the investigation legislation was passed establishing a fine of a thousand dollars and imprisonment for a year for whoever might attempt to record the proceedings of any jury in the United States while the jury is deliberating or voting.

Although the response might be less severe, one could anticipate similar objections to the taping of discussions involving police personnel, attorneys, judges, correctional officials, and probation and parole authorities.

## Coercing People to Participate

You have probably received a questionnaire in the mail at some time that offered some small incentive for completing the form, perhaps a free pen or a dollar bill. Similarly, college students are often provided a grade incentive for participation in their instructor's research. Dillman, Smyth, and Christian (2009) explain this process from the perspective of social exchange theory—that such incentives are designed to establish trust between researcher and participant. The researcher both demonstrates and encourages trust by providing the incentive before data collection. These practices are common, reflecting the assumption that people who are compensated for their efforts are more likely to participate in research projects than those who receive nothing.

When, though, does compensation become **coercion**? When is the researcher justified to compel participation? The issues here involve not only the nature and quantity of the incentives that can be ethically provided without creating an undue influence, but also the concern of having the freedom not to participate.

The person receiving the questionnaire in the mail is free to keep the compensation and toss away the form. Students may be similarly free not to participate in their instructor's research, but the instructor's power over the grading process might make students feel compelled to participate. Thus, the relationship between students and researcher as teacher can be particularly coercive.

One example of the coercive nature of this relationship can be seen when researchers, acting as teachers, *require* student participation in a research project as part of their course grade (Moreno, 1998). Again, there is a discernible difference in power that could eliminate students' capacity to refuse participation in the research project. This problem becomes especially critical when research participants are vulnerable to coercion. Although students might be considered a captive population, jail and prison inmates are clearly some of the most vulnerable research participants.

In the early 1990s, research on prisoners was allowed under federal regulations. In order to pass federal guidelines, research on prisoners had to take one of four forms: (1) studies of treatment or therapies that were implemented with the goal of helping prisoners; (2) low-risk research examining inmate behavior and inmate criminality; (3) studies of correctional institutions; and (4) research that examines inmates as a class or group (Moreno, 1998). The standards by which prisoner or prison research was determined to be ethical would depend on the degree to which the research would ultimately benefit individual prisoners or prisoners as a class or group.

The history of inmate involvement in research is not a very proud one. For example, prisoners have been used as "guinea pigs" by pharmaceutical companies that set up laboratories at correctional institutions. For minimal compensation, or the possibility that participation might assist in gaining parole, inmates have participated in a variety of medical research projects. In the United States, the first use of inmates for medical experiments took place at the Mississippi state prison in 1914, when researchers attempted to discover the relationship between diet and the disease pellagra. The Governor of Mississippi promised pardons to persons volunteering for the experiment. Another experiment in New York was completed in which eight prisoners were inoculated with a venereal infection in order to test possible cures. In exchange for their voluntary participation, the subjects, in their own words, "got syphilis and a carton of cigarettes" (Geis, 1980, p. 226). Today, prisoners are forbidden to engage in such research efforts, but inmates are still frequently required to participate in efforts to evaluate the impact of correctional treatment, work, or education programs.

It might seem that the easiest way out of this dilemma is to simply rely on volunteers for research participants. However, volunteers are different from others simply by virtue of their **willingness to participate**; at a minimum they are more highly motivated than nonvolunteers. Also, relying on their participation might produce more positive outcomes than the intervention alone would merit. Ideally, the researcher aspires to obtain a group of participants who are representative of the actual persons to whom results of the study will be applied.

Freedom of choice is highly valued in our society, but how much freedom of choice should prisoners have? Before denying a participant the opportunity to refuse participation, it should be clear that the overall value of the research outweighs the harm of coercion. In this consideration, the nature of the participation must be carefully evaluated; coercion to participate in weekly group therapy is quite different from coercion to participate in eight weeks of paramilitary training. One must also assess whether coercion is the only or best means available to obtain research results. Confronting this dilemma requires a balancing of such research matters with a concern for individuals' rights.

## Withholding from the Participant the True Nature of the Research

Ethical codes of conduct require researchers to disclose the nature of their research to potential respondents prior to data collection. Such information is typically communicated within an **informed consent** document. The informed consent document explains the general purpose of the research inquiry, the perceived importance and usefulness of participation, and how the data will be both collected and used. However, even in the most benign circumstances, written notification may deter further action. Furthermore, full and complete disclosure has the added potential of influencing responses. Often more accurate assessments are achieved when the participant believes that one aspect of his or her behavior is the focus when the research interest is actually elsewhere.

Researchers are understandably reluctant to provide too much information in this regard, especially in the early stages of a project, when the need to develop trust and a willingness to cooperate are especially important. From a research perspective, fully disclosing the purpose of the research could severely limit findings of the study. For example, a participant's mindfulness of being observed can seriously alter his or her behaviors. Specifically, research participants are typically less willing and likely to admit to undesirable attitudes or behaviors if they know they are being studied (Singleton & Straits, 1988). This *social desirability effect* can produce error in the data collected from the research

(DeVellis, 2003; Fowler, 2002). Ethically speaking, informed consent should precede involvement in the study, so that individuals are given a meaningful opportunity to decline further participation.

Balancing research interests and respect for human dignity requires that participants are informed about all aspects of the research that might reasonably influence their willingness to participate. Any risks that participants may expect to face should be fully discussed. Geis (1980) recommends that researchers remember the example of Walter Reed, who participated as a subject in his own experiments on yellow fever because he could ask no one to undergo anything that he himself was not willing to experience.

## Deceiving the Research Participant

A key ethical dilemma within social science research is the issue of deception (Warren & Karner, 2005). Perhaps the most flagrant example of deception in criminological research is provided by Humphreys's (1970) study, *Tearoom Trade*. Humphreys assumed the role of lookout in public restrooms so that strangers unaware of his research objective could engage in uninterrupted homosexual activity. After observing the individuals in the restroom, Humphreys copied down the automobile license tags of the individuals he observed and obtained their addresses from police. Later, he went to their homes, explaining that he was conducting a health survey. Humphreys then asked the respondents many personal questions that became part of his research on public homosexual conduct.

### Learn More on the Internet

Go to http://web.missouri.edu/~bondesonw/Laud.html to read a brief description of Laud Humphreys's study (1970), *Tearoom Trade*.

The rationale for deception emphasizes the importance of research and the difficulties of obtaining accurate information through other means. Deception may be considered an affront to individual autonomy and self-respect or an occasionally legitimate means to be used in service of a higher value (Cook, 1976). All deceptive acts are not equal. There are differences between active lying and a conscious failure to provide all available information. The researcher must evaluate the nature of the research and weigh its value against the potential impact the deception may have on the integrity of participants.

The degrees to which privacy is invaded and the sensitivity of the behaviors involved are important considerations. Moreover, the possibility of harming the research participant should be considered before attempting to deceive the participant. If the nature of the research is potentially harmful, the research participant should be able to fully assess whether he or she wishes to risk participating in the study. One alternative to deception is to provide only general information about the research project prior to the experiment and offer full disclosure after the research has been completed. Another technique relies on participants to role-play their behavior after the nature of the research project has been explained. There is mixed evidence, however, on the effectiveness of this technique (Cook. 1976). Contrary to deception, establishing trust with potential research participants may also increase both participation and the truthfulness of the information received.

## Learn More on the Internet

Go to www.experiment-resources.com/deception-and-research.html and consider the following questions: What are the ethical concerns for the studies mentioned on the website? What could the researchers have done to alleviate these concerns?

# Leading the Research Participants to Commit Acts that Diminish Their Self-Respect

Research participants are sometimes experimentally induced into states of extreme passivity or extreme aggression. Efforts provoking participants to lie, cheat, steal, and harm have proven very effective. Cook (1976) describes a study in which students were recruited to participate in a theft of records from a business firm. The inducements described included an opportunity to perform a patriotic service for a department of federal government. A substantial number of students were significantly encouraged to take part in the theft, although ultimately the burglary was never completed.

Research conducted by Haney, Banks, and Zimbardo (1973) involved the simulation of prison conditions, with 21 participants assuming the roles of prisoner or guard. After a very short time, the guards began behaving in an aggressive and physically threatening manner. Their use of power became self-aggrandizing and self-perpetuating. As a result, the prisoners quickly experienced a loss of personal identity, exhibiting flattened affect and dependency; eventually they were emotionally emasculated by the encounters.

Despite planning to observe the simulation for a two-week period, the extreme nature of the participants' responses to the guards' encouraged termination of the project after only six days. The debriefing sessions that followed the research study yielded the following comments:

## Guards

"They (the prisoners) seemed to lose touch with the reality of the experiment—they took me so seriously."

"I didn't interfere with any of the guards' actions. Usually if what they were doing bothered me, I would walk out and take another duty."

"Looking back, I am impressed by how little I felt for them."

"They (the prisoners) didn't see it as an experiment. It was real, and they were fighting to keep their identity. But we were always there to show them just who was boss."

"I was tired of seeing the prisoners in their rags and smelling the strong odors of their bodies that filled the cells. I watched them tear at each other, on orders given by us."

"Acting authoritatively can be fun. Power can be a great pleasure."

"During the inspection, I went to cell 2 to mess up a bed which the prisoner had made and he grabbed me, screaming that he had just made it, and he wasn't going to let me mess it up. He grabbed my throat, and although he was laughing, I was pretty scared. I lashed out with my stick and hit him in the chin (although not very hard), and when I freed myself I became angry."

## Prisoners

"The way we were made to degrade ourselves really brought us down, and that's why we all sat docile towards the end of the experiment."

"I realize now (after it's over) that no matter how together I thought I was inside my head, my prison behavior was often less under my control than I realized. No matter how open, friendly and helpful I was with other prisoners I was still operating as an isolated, self-centered person, being rational rather than compassionate."

"I began to feel I was losing my identity, that the person I call _____, the person who volunteered to get me into this prison (because it was a prison to me, it still is a prison to me, I don't regard it as an experiment or a simulation … ) was distant from me, was remote until finally I wasn't that person; I was 416. I was really my number, and 416 was really going to have to decide what to do."

"I learned that people can easily forget that others are human."

In Milgram's (1974) research, participants showed "blind obedience" to a white-coated "researcher" who ordered them to provide what appeared to be electric shocks of increasing intensity to persons who failed to respond correctly to a series of questions. Although they were emotionally upset, the participants continued to follow their instructions as the "shocked" individuals screamed in agony. Follow-up research revealed that participants in Milgram's study experienced only minor and temporary disturbances (Ring, Wallston, & Corey, 1970). One might argue that some participants benefited from the project as a result of their greater self-awareness, but the fact that the educational experiences occurred without their initial understanding or consent raises ethical concerns.

To what degree should participants be asked to unknowingly engage in activities that may damage their self-esteem? Again, the researcher is required to engage in a balancing act, reconciling research objectives and the availability of alternative methods with a concern for the integrity of research participants. At a minimum, such research efforts should provide means to address any possible harm to those involved, including debriefings at the conclusion of the research and follow-up counseling as needed. See Box 8.1.

## Violating the Right to Self-Determination: Research on Behavior Control and Character Change

The film *A Clockwork Orange* provides an excellent illustration of the dilemmas of behavior-modifying research. In the film, a thoroughly violent and irredeemable individual named Alex is subjected to therapy that requires him to observe violent acts on film while simultaneously ingesting chemicals that make him physically ill. After a while, the violent acts Alex has observed make him sick as well, and he is changed from a violent individual to one who avoids violence at all cost, including

### BOX 8.1  The Lucifer Effect

Philip Zimbardo is most commonly known for his role as researcher in the Stanford Prison Experiment. Zimbardo's more recent research interests focus on *The Lucifer Effect: Understanding How Good People Turn Evil*. How would you design a research project to study this particular topic?

Go to the following link to visit the homepage for Professor Philip G. Zimbardo: http://zimbardo.com/ At the top of the link, click "Enter Here" to enter Dr. Zimbardo's website. Next, click on the link to the right titled "Prison Experiment" to view a slideshow about the experiment. What are your thoughts that required for his own self-defense. At the end of the film, the "powers that be" decide to reverse his treatment for political reasons.

Although there is little possibility of behavior modifications being used to exact such effect in the near future, the question remains: To what extent should experimental efforts be made to alter human behavior against the will of the participant? Remembering the vulnerability of the inmate to coercion (in the film, Alex only participated in the violence control therapy because he thought it would help him gain early release), it becomes clear that the greatest desire to use behavior control strategies will be evident in areas involving those persons most vulnerable to coercion—criminals and persons with problems of substance abuse. Although research on crime prevention and control generally has only the most laudable aims, it should be remembered that it is often well-intentioned actions that pose the greatest threat to individual freedoms and **self-determination**.

## Exposing the Research Participant to Physical or Mental Stress

How would you evaluate the ethics of the following research project: an evaluation of a treatment program in which persons convicted of drunk driving are required to watch and listen to hours of films depicting gory automobile accidents, followed by horrifying emergency room visits and interviews with grieving relatives? Would it matter whether actions of the drunk drivers had contributed to similar accidents? When thinking about your answer, consider whether the viewers deserve the "punishment" of what they are forced to observe on film.

This not-so-hypothetical scenario raises a difficult issue. Is it acceptable for a research project to engage in activities that punish and perhaps harm participants? To test various outcomes, participants in different settings have been exposed to events provoking feelings of horror, shock, threatened sexual identity, personal failure, fear, and emotional shock (Cook, 1976). Some of the participants in Haney, Banks, and Zimbardo's study and Milgram's research were clearly stressed by their experiences. To what extent is it acceptable to engage in these practices for the objective of scientific inquiry?

In most situations, it is impossible to observe human reactions such as those described above in their natural settings, so researchers feel justified in creating experiments that produce these reactions. The extent of possible harm raises ethical dilemmas; however, theoretically there is no limit to what might be contrived for creating "researchable" reactions. Thus, balancing research objectives with a respect for human participants is a delicate undertaking, requiring researchers to scrutinize their objectives and the value of their proposed studies dispassionately.

## Invading the Privacy of the Research Participant and Maintaining Confidentiality

**Privacy** and confidentiality are related concerns. Ethical questions arise from research that invades an individual's privacy without his or her consent. Consider information about participants that has been obtained for reasons other than research (e.g., the development of a criminal history file); there are questions about the extent to which such data should be released to researchers. Some records are more sensitive than others in this regard, depending on how easily the offender's identity can be obtained, as well as the quantity and nature of the information recorded. Even when consent has been given and the information has been gathered expressly for research purposes, maintaining the confidentiality of responses may be a difficult matter when the responses contain information of a sensitive or illegal nature.

Respondents are most likely to participate in research projects when they are allowed to participate anonymously—that is, when it is impossible for the researcher to associate any particular data with the individual that provided that data (Dillman et al., 2009; Neuman, 2004). Anonymity is not always possible; therefore, researchers typically offer research participants the protection of confidentiality.

**Confidentiality** is especially important in the study of crime and deviance. Participants will generally not agree to provide information about criminal and deviant behaviors unless their responses are to remain confidential. This is sometimes a more difficult task than it appears. Sometimes it is important to be able to identify a research participant so that his or her responses can be linked to other sources of data that he or she has provided. For example, institutionalized delinquents might be asked in confidence about their involvement in drug use and other forms of misconduct during confinement. An important part of the research might involve gathering background information from the offender's institutional files to determine what types of offenders are most likely to be involved in institutional misconduct. To do this, the individual's confidential responses need to be identifiable; therefore, complete anonymity is unfeasible and confidentiality becomes increasingly important.

As long as only dispassionate researchers have access to this information, there may be no problems. Difficulties arise when third parties, especially criminal justice authorities, become interested in the research responses. Then the issue becomes one of protecting the data (and the offender) from officials who have the power to invoke the criminal justice process. However, the relationship between researcher and research participant is not privileged; researchers can be called upon to provide information to courts.

One response to this dilemma is to store identifying information in a remote place; some researchers have even recommended sending sensitive information out of the country. Lewis Yablonsky, a criminologist/practitioner, while testifying in defense of Gridley White (one of Yablonsky's main informants in his study about hippies), was asked by the judge nine times if he had witnessed Gridley smoking marijuana. Yablonsky refused to answer because of the rights guaranteed him in the Fifth Amendment of the U.S. Constitution. Although he was not legally sanctioned, he said the incident was humiliating and suggested that researchers should have guarantees of immunity (Wolfgang, 1982).

It is also important that researchers prepare their presentations of research findings in a manner that ensures that particular responses of individuals cannot be discerned. Presentation of only aggregate findings was especially important for Marvin Wolfgang (1982) when he reinterviewed persons in a birth cohort who were included in his earlier study of delinquency. His follow-up consisted of hour-long interviews with approximately 600 youths. The participants were asked many personal questions, including questions about their involvement in delinquency and crime. Four of his respondents admitted committing criminal homicide, and almost 75 admitted to forcible rape. Many other serious crimes were also described, for which none of the participants had been arrested.

At the time of the research, all of the respondents were orally assured that the results of the research would remain confidential, but Wolfgang raises a number of ethical questions regarding this practice. Should written consent forms have been provided to participants, detailing the nature of the research? Wolfgang concludes that such forms would have raised more questions than they answered. Could a court order impound the records? Could persons attempting to protect the data be prosecuted for their actions? Could the data be successfully concealed?

The general willingness to protect participants who admit to serious crimes also requires close ethical scrutiny. Wolfgang (1982) takes the traditional scientific stance on this issue, proposing that such information belongs to science. Since the information would not have been discovered without the research effort, its protection neither helps nor hinders police. The ethical judgment here requires a weighting of interests—the importance of scientific research balanced against society's interest in capturing a particular individual.

It should be noted that if researchers were to inform on their participants routinely, it is likely that all future research relying on self-reports could be jeopardized. The issue at hand is not simply that of the value of a particular study, but the value of all research utilizing personal disclosure. Researchers are generally advised not to undertake such research unless they feel comfortable about protecting their sources. This requires that all research involving the use of confidential information provides for controlled access to the data and protects the information from unauthorized searches, inadvertent access, and the compulsory legal process (Cook, 1976).

# Withholding Benefits to Participants in Control Groups

The necessity of excluding some potential beneficiaries from initial program participation arises whenever a classical experimental design is used to evaluate a program. This research design requires random assignment, or **randomization**, of participants to experimental and control groups. Research participants in the control group are excluded from the program, or receive "standard" treatment rather than "experimental" treatment.

In a program evaluation, it is important that some participants receive the benefits of the program while others do not, to determine whether the outcomes observed are the direct result of the experimental intervention and not something else (e.g., participant enthusiasm or background characteristics). It is important for those who receive the program/treatment (the experimental group) and those who do not (the control group) to be as identical in the aggregate as possible, so that a clear assessment of program impact, untainted by variation in the characteristics of participants, can be obtained. The best way to ensure that experimental and control groups are identical is randomization, which requires that every participant have an equal chance to be assigned to either the experimental or control group.

In many ways, randomization may be more ethical than standard practices based on good intentions. Geis (1980, p. 221) reports:

> For most of us, it would be unthinkable that a sample of armed robbers be divided into two groups on the basis of random assignment—one group to spend 10 years in prison, the second to receive a sentence of 2 years on probation. Nonetheless, at a federal judicial conference, after examining an elaborate presentence report concerning a bank robber, 17 judges said they would have imprisoned the man, while 10 indicated they favored probation. Those voting for imprisonment set sentences ranging from 6 months to 15 years.

Although randomization is inherently fair, it often appears less so to the participants involved. Surveys of prisoners have indicated that need, merit, and "first come, first served" are more acceptable criteria than a method that the offenders equated with gambler's luck (Erez, 1986). Consider Morris's (1966) description of "the burglar's nightmare":

> If eighty burglars alike in all relevant particulars were assigned randomly to experimental and control groups, forty each, with the experimental to be released six months or a year earlier than they ordinarily would be and the control released at their regularly appointed time, how would the burglar assigned to the control group respond? It is unfair, unjust, unethical, he could say, for me to be put into the control group. If people like me, he might complain, are being released early, I too, deserve the same treatment.

> (cited in Erez, 1986, p. 394)

Program personnel are also frequently unhappy with randomization because it fails to utilize their clinical skills in the selection of appropriate candidates for intervention. Extending this line of thought, consider the likely response of judges requested to sentence burglary offenders randomly to prison or probation. While this might be the best method of determining the effectiveness of these sanctions, the judicial response, and perhaps community response as well, would likely be less than enthusiastic. This is because it is assumed, often without any evidence, that standard practices are achieving some reasonable objectives, such as individualizing justice or preventing crime.

Randomization is acceptable under law, because its use is reasonably related to a governmental objective; that is, testing the effectiveness of a program intervention (Erez, 1986). Though randomization is important and appropriate from a methodological perspective, the participants who, by chance, end up in the control group, are often denied treatment, or possibly services, that could be of the utmost importance to their lives. The Minneapolis Domestic Violence Experiment is a classic example of how those persons involved in the control group were denied potential law enforcement interventions that could have benefited them. Box 8.2 is a description of Sherman and Berk's (1984) study which looked at various responses to domestic violence.

Randomization does produce winners and losers. Of critical importance in weighing the consequences of randomization are the differences in treatment experienced by those in experimental and control groups. The Federal Judicial Center (1981, pp. 31–40) highlights six factors that are relevant:

1. *Significance of the interest affected.* Early release is of much greater consequence than a change of institutional diet.
2. *Extent of difference.* Six months' early release is of greater significance than one week's early release.
3. *Comparison of the disparity with standard treatment.* If both experimental and control group treatment is an improvement over standard treatment, then the discrepancy between the experimental and control group is of less concern.
4. *Whether disparity reflects differences in qualifications of participants.* If the disparity is reasonably related to some characteristic of the participants, the denial of benefits to the control group is less significant.
5. *Whether the experimental treatment is harmful or beneficial to participants compared with the treatment they would otherwise receive.* A program that assigns members of the experimental

## BOX 8.2   The Minneapolis Domestic Violence Experiment

Domestic violence was beginning to be recognized as a major public affairs and criminal justice problem. Victim advocates were demanding the automatic arrest for domestic violence offenders. However, there was no empirical research that showed that arresting domestic violence offenders deterred future acts of domestic violence. Thus, Sherman and Berk, sponsored by funding from the National Institute of Justice, designed a randomized experiment that looked at the effects of arrest on domestic violence.

Sherman and Berk enlisted the help of the Minneapolis Police Department. When on misdemeanor domestic violence calls, the police were to respond to the call depending on the random call response they were assigned. There were three responses with which the police could respond to the misdemeanor domestic violence call: arrest, removal of batterer from the premises without an arrest, or counsel the batterer and leave the premises. While the initial findings of this research indicated that arresting domestic violence offenders reduced the incidence of future incidents, the methodology and ethics of this experiment have been heavily scrutinized. The victims of the misdemeanor domestic violence certainly did not consent to the randomized assignment of response to the situation. Thus, not only were potential benefits withheld from certain women, some victims could have been placed at greater risk as a result of the random treatment. While the benevolent intentions behind this research agenda were admirable, the implementation of the experiment and the variable being randomized (i.e., type of response to domestic violence) should have been further considered before implementation of the research.

*Source*: Based on Sherman & Berk (1984).

group to six weeks of "boot camp" may be more demanding of inmates than the standard treatment of six months' incarceration.

6. *Whether participation is mandatory or voluntary.* Voluntary participation mitigates the concern of denial of benefit, while coercion exacerbates the dilemma.

Similar to the management of other ethical dilemmas, a substantial effort is required to balance values of human decency and justice with the need for accurate information about intervention effectiveness. Problems arise not in the extreme cases of disparity but in more routine circumstances. Consider the following example: How do we judge a situation in which a foundation grant permits attorneys to be supplied for all cases being heard by a juvenile court in which attorneys have previously appeared only in rare instances? A fundamental study hypothesis may be that the presence of an attorney tends to result in a more favorable disposition for the client. This idea may be tested by comparing dispositions prior to the beginning of the experiment with those ensuing subsequently, though it would be more satisfactory (from a research perspective) to supply attorneys to a sample of the cases and withhold them from the remainder, in order to calculate in a more experimentally uncontaminated manner the differences between the outcomes in the two situations.

The matter becomes more complex if the researchers should desire to determine what particular attorney role is the most efficacious in the juvenile court. They may suspect that an attorney who acts as a friend of the court, knowingly taking its viewpoint as *parens patriae,* and attempting to interpret the court's interest to his or her client, will produce more desirable results than one who doggedly challenges the courtroom procedure and the judge's interpretation of fact, picks at the probation report, raises constant objections, and fights for his or her client as he would in a criminal court. What results are "more desirable" (Geis, 1980, pp. 222–223)?

It could be contended that little is really known about how attorney roles influence dispositions and that, without the project, no one would have any kind of representation. Over the long term, all juveniles stand to benefit. On the other hand, it could be argued that it is wrong to deprive anyone of the best judgment of his or her attorney by requiring a particular legal approach. What if there are only enough funds to supply one-half of the juveniles with attorneys anyway? Is randomization more or less fair than trying to decide which cases "need" representation the most?

Randomization imposes a special ethical burden because it purposefully counters efforts to determine the best course of action with the element of chance. The practice is justifiable because the pursuit of knowledge is a desirable objective—as long as the overall benefits outweigh the risks. The balancing of risks and benefits is complicated by the fact that judgments are often made in a context of ambiguity, attempting to predict the benefits of an intervention that is being tested precisely because its impact is unknown.

The Federal Judicial Center (1981, p. 7) recommends that program evaluations should be considered only when certain threshold conditions are met:

1. the status quo warrants substantial improvements or is of doubtful effectiveness;
2. there must be significant uncertainty about the value or effectiveness of the innovation;
3. information needed to clarify the uncertainty must be feasibly obtainable by the program experimentation but not readily obtainable by other means; and
4. the information sought must pertain directly to the decision whether to adopt the proposed innovation on a general, nonexperimental basis.

Several conditions lessen the ethical burdens of evaluative research. Random assignment is especially acceptable when resources are scarce and demand for the benefit is high. Additionally, denying benefits to the control group is acceptable when members of the control group can participate in the program at a later date. Finally, discrepancies between the treatment of experimental and control groups are less noteworthy when the groups are geographically separated (Federal Judicial Center, 1981).

Some experimental studies on the effectiveness of "hot spot policing" have been particularly well received because they utilized place-based randomization rather than person-based randomization (Weisburd, 2005). This place-based approach was developed "not because of ethical or practical concerns, but rather as a direct response to the theoretical innovations in criminology and criminal justice (Weisburd, 2005, p. 223). Routine activities theory promoted a situational approach to crime prevention; the goal became reducing opportunities to commit crime in specific areas, as opposed to focusing on the individuals who might commit a crime. In these studies, benefits were not denied to the control group; preventive policing continued to be implemented in the control areas and "higher dosages" of preventive patrol were utilized in the intervention sites.

# Failing to Treat Research Participants Fairly and to Show Them Consideration and Respect

The basic tenets of professionalism require that researchers treat participants with courtesy and fulfill the variety of commitments they make to participants. For example, in an effort to obtain cooperation, participants are often promised a follow-up report on the findings of the research although such reports may be forgotten once the study has been completed. Participants also are often led to believe that they will receive some personal benefit from the research. This may be one of the more difficult obligations to fulfill. For some, the opportunity to be heard and to share their experiences will provide some benefit. More important is the notion that researchers should treat the individuals they collect data from with respect.

Researchers need to treat their human participants with constant recognition of their integrity and their contributions to the research endeavor. This is especially important when participants are powerless and vulnerable. Although such treatment may be a time-consuming chore, it is the only ethical way to practice scientific research. It may also be the best way to acquire the information sought.

# Balancing Scientific and Ethical Concerns

This discussion has emphasized the importance of balancing concerns for research participants against the potential benefits of a research inquiry. Cook (1976, p. 235) identifies the following potential benefits of a research project:

1. Advances in scientific theories that contribute to a general understanding of human behavior.
2. Advances in knowledge of practical value to society.
3. Gains for the research participant, such as increased understanding, satisfaction in making a contribution to science or to the solution of social problems, needed money or special privileges, knowledge of social science or of research methods, and so on.

The potential costs to research participants can be considerable, and it is often difficult for the researcher to be objective in assessing such issues. For these reasons, many professional associations have established guidelines and procedures for ethical research conduct. Because little active monitoring occurs in social science research, the professional is honor-bound to follow these guidelines.

# Institutional Review Boards and Setting Ethical Standards

How are the ethical standards being set within the criminal justice community, and how and to what degree are ethics being taught in criminology and criminal justice academic settings? To ensure that their faculty follow acceptable procedures (and to protect themselves from liability), universities have established Institutional Review Boards (IRBs) to scrutinize each research project that involves human participants. Specifically, a university's IRB reviews each submitted research project prior to implementation. The purpose of these reviews is to ensure the protection of human participants within the research design. IRBs are generally incapable of providing direct monitoring of research

---

### ETHICAL DILEMMA  Ethics and Criminal Justice Research

---

Imagine you are a professor, newly graduated from your doctoral program and recently hired in a tenure-track position as an assistant professor at the university of your choice. Your new position requires you to maintain an active scholarly agenda, meaning you must activate a research agenda to progress toward earning tenure.

You have always been interested in aspects related to policing. Perhaps this is because your father and brother are police officers, and you have more family members who have worked in other areas of the criminal justice system. Regardless, you decide to design a research study that will examine job satisfaction among police officers. Specifically, you are interested in individual-level and organizational-level variables that influence police officer satisfaction.

Individual-level variables may include age, race, gender, level of education, marital status, officer rank, and number of years as a police officer. Organizational-level variables might include the structure and mission of the police department, organizational policies, elements of shift work, amount of training received, and administrative support.

Think about the items discussed in the chapter when answering the following questions:

1.  Are there any personal biases that may affect your research study? If so, how will you control for such biases?

2.  How will you collect data? What will you do if an administrator at your university suggests that you should pick a different topic? Why would some people not want to know about police officer satisfaction?

3.  How will you provide/maintain confidentiality of the data? What will you do if the police chief wants a copy of your data?

4.  What concerns must you address regarding the presentation of research results? What if university officials do not want the data published? What if the police chief or some of the officers do not want the data published?

---

projects, so again the responsibility for ethical conduct falls on the researcher. IRBs serve a valuable function and often are the primary source for ethical guidance and standards for the criminal justice academic researcher (McSkimming, Sever, & King, 2000).

McSkimming, Sever, and King (2000) analyzed 11 research methods textbooks frequently used in criminal justice and criminology courses to determine the types of ethical issues that were covered and the extent to which they were addressed. The authors found there was no collective format being utilized in the major criminal justice texts regarding ethics in criminal justice research methods. Furthermore, the significance and positive functions of institutional review boards were rarely mentioned. Of further concern was the noticeable absence of some important ethical topics related to the dissemination of information into the criminal justice audience, such as "plagiarism, fabrication of data, authorship rank, and ethical considerations in journal editing and grant-writing" (p. 58). It is imperative that graduate students, publishing professors, and other disseminators of information within the criminal justice discipline have some instruction or gauge with which to measure ethical standards.

## Learn More on the Internet

Go to the following links from university websites to review the institutional review board (IRB) process:

www.etsu.edu/irb/
www.iup.edu/page.aspx?id=6637
http://gero.nku.edu/research/rgc/irb/irb.html

What similarities do you see within each of the IRB processes? Are there any differences between the various IRB processes?

## POLICY AND ETHICS **Facebook Study Sparks Controversy**

Given the explosion of social media over the past few years, have you ever stopped to think if these companies are collecting data on your behavior or maybe even conducting experiments on you without your consent? Wanting to test whether emotional states can be transferred to others via emotional contagion, researchers at Facebook, Inc. and Cornell University manipulated the news feed of nearly 700,000 Facebook users (Kramer, Guillory, & Hancock, 2014). They wanted to determine whether exposure to positive content resulted in the user posting positive messages or if negative content caused the user to post negative messages. The results indicated emotional contagion with users whose news feed showed more negative content posting less positive messages and slightly withdrawing from social media.

After the study was published, some in the scientific community cried foul and questioned the ethics of the study (Albergotti & Dwoskin, 2014). The claims center around three important ethical issues—informed consent, no harm to subjects, and the use of Institutional Review Boards. First, there were claims that the Facebook users were not properly notified of the experimental changes in their news feed nor were they informed that their posting patterns would be collected. However, Facebook, Inc. stated that users agree to data collection efforts when they sign up for Facebook as part of the user agreement. Second, the critics of the study blasted Facebook for manipulating the mental state of the users by intentionally posting negative content without first knowing the mental stability of the users. In addition, neither Facebook data collectors nor Cornell University researchers ensured that the negative postings did not cause additional harm for the users. Lastly, Cornell University researchers did not obtain a full review of the study from the IRB because they received de-identified, aggregate, preexisting data. Thus, it appears there was no oversight body that examined the costs and benefits of the research against the costs and benefits to the participants.

1. Do you believe that Facebook, Inc. should be collecting data on its users? Why or why not?

2. If Facebook, Inc. should be allowed to collect data on its users or to conduct experiments such as the one above, do you believe they should independently notify the user instead of having a blanket notification at the beginning of the sign-up process?

3. Should IRBs examine projects using hundreds of thousands of anonymous users in more detail instead of just using an expedited process?

# Ethical/Political Considerations

Applied social research, that is, research that examines the effectiveness of social policies and programs, carries with it additional ethical responsibilities. Such research influences the course of human events in a direct fashion; occupations, education, future opportunities, and deeply held values and beliefs often are affected by the outcomes. Researchers must be prepared to deal with a variety of pressures and demands as they undertake the practice and dissemination of research.

According to MacCoun (1998), some research topics are matters of eternal debate; examples include research about pornography (see Linz & Malamuth, 1993), gun control (see Nisbet, 2001), the death penalty (see Costanzo & White, 1994), and drug prohibition (see MacCoun, 1993; MacCoun & Reuter, 1997). In fact, on several occasions government officials have attempted to condemn or prohibit entire topics of research. One such effort attempted to discredit early studies reporting that some individuals diagnosed as alcoholics are able to engage in sustained drinking at less problematic levels (see Chiauzzi & Liljegren, 1993; Marlatt, Larimer, Baer & Quigley, 1993). Other examples (as cited by MacCoun, 1998) include the cancellation of a National Institutes of Health-funded conference about genetic influences affecting violence (see Johnson, 1993), an effort to ban epidemiological research about gun violence by the Centers for Disease Control and Prevention (see Herbert, 1996), and several attempts to prevent research about adolescent and adult sexual behavior (see Gardner & Wilcox, 1993; Miller, 1995). The private sector also engages in research censorship. Consider the actions of a pharmaceutical company that blocked publication of study results revealing the effectiveness of its drug and less expensive generic alternatives (see Dong, Hauck, Gambertoglio, Gee, & White, 1997; Rennie, 1997).

It is generally acknowledged that organizations asked to measure their own effectiveness often produce biased results. Crime statistics provide a notorious example of data used to show either an effective police department (falling crime figures) or a need for more resources (rising crime figures). Criminal justice researchers are often asked to study matters that are equally sensitive. For instance, a correctional treatment program found to be ineffective may lose its funding, or a study that reveals extensive use of plea bargaining may cost a prosecutor his or her election.

The truth can be complicated. A survey revealing the decline of drug use in the general population may prove troublesome for those lobbying for the establishment of more drug treatment facilities. The survey results may lead the public to believe the problem is diminishing while at the same time there is a substantial need for treatment facilities for indigent persons.

Such research has been known to produce unintended consequences. Consider the publication of selected results of a study on the effectiveness of correctional treatment programs (Martinson, 1974), which was used by many persons to justify limiting funds for education and treatment programs in correctional institutions. The research revealed that there was little evidence that correctional treatment programs were effective means of reducing recidivism (a finding that has been widely challenged). Rather than stimulating the development of more theoretically supported programs and rigorous evaluations of these efforts, the apparent product of the research was a decrease in the humaneness of conditions for confinement.

Research results can sometimes conflict with cherished beliefs. Studies of both preventive police patrol (Kelling, Pate, Dieckman, & Browne, 1974) and detective investigations (Chaiken, Greenwood, & Petersilia, 1977) revealed that these practices were of little value to police; these practices were long assumed to be essential elements of effective law enforcement. Researchers can expect findings such as these to meet considerable resistance.

Researchers may be asked to utilize their skills and their aura of objectivity to provide an organization or agency with what it wants. When the group that pays the bills has a direct interest in the nature of the outcome, the pressures can be considerable. Marvin Wolfgang (1982, p. 395) reports:

> I was once invited to do research by an organization whose views are almost completely antithetical to mine on the issue of gun control. Complete freedom and a considerable amount of money to explore the relationship between gun control legislation and robbery were promised. I would not perform the research under those auspices. But the real clincher in the decision was that if the research produced conclusions opposite from that the organization wanted, the agency would not publish the results nor allow me to publish them. Perhaps their behavior, within their ideological framework, was not unethical. But within my framework, as a scientist who values freedom of publication as well as of scientific inquiry, I would have engaged in an unethical act of prostituting my integrity had I accepted those conditions.

In-house researchers, who are employed by the organization for which the research is being conducted, face special problems in this regard, because they lack the freedom to pick and choose their research topic. These individuals must balance their concern for rigorous scientific inquiry with their need for continued employment.

Generally, the issues confronted are subtle and complex. Although researchers may be directly told to conceal or falsify results, more often they are subtly encouraged to design their research with an eye toward the desired results. The greatest barrier to such pressures is the development of a truly independent professional research unit within the organization. Such independence protects the researcher from political pressures and at the same time promotes the credibility of the research being conducted. Without this protection, the individual is left to his or her own devices and standards of ethical conduct.

# The Purity of Scientific Research

The end of the twenty-first century was wrought with assertions about the perceived legitimacy of science for determining truth (MacCoun, 1998). Keltner and Robinson (1996) offer the concept of *naïve realism* to explain the disjuncture between individuals' perceptions, and, perhaps, an elemental explanation for the erosion of scientific-based thinking. People often assume their own worldviews are objective, based on science or truth, while the views of others (and the reason why others do not agree with their perspective) are subjective, or based on personal ideology as opposed to some objective criteria. Unfortunately, individuals on both sides of such debates tend to function similarly in terms of their one-sided views.

Often, these discussions are centered on the issue of bias. In some instances, biased interpretations are justifiable (MacCoun, 1998). However, the claim that a social science researcher has produced biased results is often perceived by the researcher as not only a scornful criticism about his or her work, but also as a personal attack about his or her credibility, integrity, and honor. In fact, the very decision to study a particular topic can lead some consumers of research to assume the investigator is biased.

The idea of scientific inquiry is the pure, objective examination of the empirical world, untainted by personal prejudice. However, research is carried out by human beings, who typically have a variety of motivations for undertaking their research endeavors. Topics may be selected because of curiosity or from a perceived need to address a specific social problem; the availability of grants in a particular field may also encourage researchers' efforts. This is critical if one is working for a research organization dependent upon "soft" money. In addition, the need for university faculty members to publish and establish a name for themselves in a particular area may encourage them to seek "hot" topics for their research, or to identify an extremely narrow research focus in which they can become identified as experts.

Merton (1973) expressed four *norms of science* that are widely acknowledged by both scientists and nonscientists alike:

1. *Universalism*—scientific accomplishments must be judged by impersonal criteria; the personal attributes of the investigator are irrelevant.
2. *Communism* (as in communalism)—scientific information must be publicly shared.
3. *Disinterestedness*—cautions investigators to proceed objectively; researchers must be aware of and guard against personal biases and prejudices.
4. Finally, *organized skepticism*—new findings must be scrutinized rigorously through peer review, replication of experiments, and the testing of rival hypotheses.

There is some evidence that the nature of one's research findings influences the likelihood of publication (Coughlin, 1989). A curious author submitted almost identical articles to a number of journals. The manuscripts differed only in one respect—the nature of the conclusions. One version of the article showed the experiment had no effect; the other described a positive result. The experiment produced some interesting results—the article with positive outcomes was more likely to be accepted for publication than the other manuscript.

As reported by the *New York Times*, Diederik Stapel did not deny that his deceit was driven by ambition. But it was more complicated than that:

> He insisted that he loved social psychology but had been frustrated by the messiness of experimental data, which rarely led to clear conclusions. His lifelong obsession with elegance and order, he said, led him to concoct sexy results that journals found attractive. "It was a quest for aesthetics, for beauty—instead of the truth," he said. He described his behavior as an addiction that drove him to carry out acts of increasingly daring fraud, like a junkie seeking a bigger and better high.

(Bhattacharjee, 2013)

If research studies concluding that "the experiment didn't work" or that "differences between Groups A and B were insignificant" are indeed less likely to be published, then pressure to revise one's research focus or to rewrite one's hypotheses to match the results produced can be anticipated. These elements of the research process should function to remind us that actions justified in the name of scientific inquiry may be motivated by reasons far less "pure" than the objective they serve.

# Public Policy Pronouncements and Teaching Criminal Justice

When is a researcher speaking from the facts and when is he or she promoting personal ideology? If there were any fully conclusive and definitive studies in the social sciences, this question would not arise. However, research findings are always tentative, and statements describing them invariably require conditional language. On the other hand, researchers have values and beliefs like everyone else, and few of us want to employ the same conditional language required to discuss research when we state our views on matters of public policy and morality. Researchers thus have a special obligation to carefully evaluate their remarks and clearly distinguish between opinion and apparent empirical fact. This is not always an easy task, but it is the only way to safeguard the objectivity that is critically important to scientific inquiry.

Criminal justice researchers acting as teachers and mentors have a responsibility to students, due to the influence their position has concerning the lives of their students (ACJS, 2000). Specifically, a researcher's influence and authority used inappropriately has the potential to mislead and distort the perspectives of their students by disseminating information that was based merely on personal ideology rather than scientific findings.

# Ethical Codes

In order to address ethical considerations related to the research process, associations of academic researchers develop and make known standards or codes of ethics. The Academy of Criminal Justice Sciences (ACJS) has advanced a standard for those persons researching and writing within the discipline of criminal justice. It does an excellent job of addressing the ethical standards of conducting social science research as well as the dissemination of information within the criminal justice discipline. The ACJS code provides criminologists with ethical standards concerning fair treatment; the use of students in research; objectivity and integrity in the conduct of research; confidentiality, disclosure, and respect for research populations; publication and authorship standards; and employment practices (ACJS, 2000). See Box 8.3.

## Learn More on the Internet

View the complete Academy of Criminal Justice Sciences (ACJS) code of ethics at: www.acjs.org and search for "code of ethics" in the search box.

What are your general thoughts about the ACJS code of ethics?

The American Society of Criminology (ASC) is another professional association of academic researchers and practitioners who contribute to further understanding within the criminal justice discipline through research. As well as the ASC's recently adopted code of ethics, its website refers interested persons to various codes of ethics, including the ACJS code.

## BOX 8.3  Members of the Academy as Researchers

**Objectivity and Integrity in the Conduct of Criminal Justice Research**

1.  Members of the Academy should adhere to the highest possible technical standards in their research.

2.  Since individual members of the Academy vary in their research modes, skills, and experience, they should acknowledge the limitations that may affect the validity of their findings.

3.  In presenting their work, members of the Academy are obliged to fully report their findings. They should not misrepresent the findings of their research or omit significant data. Any and all omitted data should be noted and the reason(s) for exclusion stated clearly as part of the methodology. Details of their theories, methods, and research designs that might bear upon interpretations of research findings should be reported.

4.  Members of the Academy should fully report all sources of financial support and other sponsorship of the research.

5.  Members of the Academy should not make any commitments to respondents, individuals, groups or organizations unless there is full intention and ability to honor them.

6.  Consistent with the spirit of full disclosure of method and analysis, members of the Academy, after they have completed their own analyses, should cooperate in efforts to make raw data and pertinent documentation available to other social scientists, at reasonable costs, except in cases where confidentiality, the client's rights to proprietary information and privacy, or the claims of a field worker to the privacy of personal notes necessarily would be violated. The timeliness of this cooperation is especially critical.

7.  Members of the Academy should provide adequate information, documentation, and citations concerning scales and other measures used in their research.

8.  Members of the Academy should not accept grants, contracts or research assignments that appear likely to violate the principles enunciated in this Code, and should disassociate themselves from research when they discover a violation and are unable to correct it.

9.  When financial support for a project has been accepted, members of the Academy should make every reasonable effort to complete the proposed work on schedule.

10. When a member of the Academy is involved in a project with others, including students, there should be mutually accepted explicit agreements at the outset with respect to division of work, compensation, access to data, rights of authorship, and other rights and responsibilities. These agreements should not be exploitative or arrived at through any form of coercion or intimidation. Such agreements may need to be modified as the project evolves and such modifications should be clearly stated among all participants. Students should normally be the principle author of any work that is derived directly from their thesis or dissertation.

11. Members of the Academy have the right to disseminate research findings, except those likely to cause harm to clients, collaborators and participants, those which violate formal or implied promises of confidentiality, or those which are proprietary under a formal or informal agreement.

**Disclosure and Respect of the Rights of Research Populations by Members of the Academy**

12. Members of the Academy should not misuse their positions as professionals for fraudulent purposes or as a pretext for gathering information for any individual, group, organization or government.

13. Human subjects have the right to full disclosure of the purposes of the research as early as it is appropriate to the research process, and they have the right to an opportunity to have their questions answered about the purpose and usage of the research. Members should inform research participants about aspects of the research that might affect their willingness to participate, such as physical risks, discomfort, and/or unpleasant emotional experiences.

14. Subjects of research are entitled to rights of personal confidentiality unless they are waived.

15. Information about subjects obtained from records that are open to public scrutiny cannot be protected by guarantees of privacy or confidentiality.

16. The process of conducting criminal justice research must not expose respondents to more than minimal risk of personal harm, and members of the Academy should make every effort to ensure the safety and security of respondents and project staff. Informed consent should be obtained when the risks of research are greater than the risks of everyday life.

17. Members of the Academy should take culturally appropriate steps to secure informed consent and to avoid invasions of privacy. In addition, special actions will be necessary where the individuals studied are illiterate, under correctional supervision, minors, have low social status, are under judicial supervision, have diminished capacity, are unfamiliar with social research or otherwise occupy a position of unequal power with the researcher.

18. Members of the Academy should seek to anticipate potential threats to confidentiality. Techniques such as the removal of direct identifiers, the use of randomized responses, and other statistical solutions to problems of privacy should be used where appropriate. Care should be taken to ensure secure storage, maintenance, and/or destruction of sensitive records.

19. Confidential information provided by research participants should be treated as such by members of the Academy, even when this information enjoys no legal protection or privilege and legal force is applied. The obligation to respect confidentiality also applies to members of research organizations (interviewers, coders, clerical staff, etc.) who have access to the information. It is the responsibility of administrators and chief investigators to instruct staff members on this point and to make every effort to insure that access to confidential information is restricted.

20. While generally adhering to the norm of acknowledging the contributions of all collaborators, members of the Academy should be sensitive to harm that may arise from disclosure and respect a collaborator's need for anonymity.

21. All research should meet the human subjects requirements imposed by educational institutions and funding sources. Study design and information gathering techniques should conform to regulations protecting the rights of human subjects, regardless of funding.

22. Members of the Academy should comply with appropriate federal and institutional requirements pertaining to the conduct of their research. These requirements might include, but are not necessarily limited to, obtaining proper review and approval for research that involves human subjects and accommodating recommendations made by responsible committees concerning research subjects, materials, and procedures.

*Source*: ACJS (2000).

## Learn More on the Internet

Go to the American Society of Criminology (ASC) website: www.asc41.com/ethicspg.html and click on Code of Ethics for ASC's recently adopted code of ethics. What are your general thoughts about the ASC code of ethics? Compare and contrast the ASC and ACJS code of ethics. What similarities do you see within each of the codes? Are there any differences between the various codes?

# Conclusion

It would be convenient to conclude that the best research is that which is conducted in an ethical fashion, but such a statement would skirt the dilemma. Conducting ethical scientific research in criminal justice and criminology can be a difficult task; it requires constant weighing and balancing of objectives and motivations. This is the exact nature of the problem: Those actions required to meet the demands of scientific rigor sometimes run counter to ethical behavior. However, evaluating rather than avoiding ethical dilemmas does provide a learning experience, the benefits of which can be expected to spill over into all aspects of human endeavor. Thinking and doing in an ethical way requires practice, and conducting research provides considerable opportunities for the evolution of experience.

## KEY CONCEPTS

| | |
|---|---|
| codes of ethics | privacy |
| coercion | randomization |
| confidentiality | self-determination |
| informed consent | willingness to participate |

## DISCUSSION QUESTIONS

1. Discuss the importance of research in criminal justice. Are there any circumstances in which it is acceptable for a research project to involve activities that punish and perhaps harm participants? Where should the researcher draw the line? Can you think of any situations in which the ends justify the means? Support your answer.

2. What are some of the benefits gained by doing a research project? Do the benefits outweigh the costs to participants? Explain. What are some of the pressures that may be placed on researchers that could compromise the integrity of their research results?

3. Go to the following website to take an online tutorial for Human Participants Protection: http://cme.cancer.gov/clinicaltrials/learning/humanparticipantprotections.asp You will be prompted to create a user account (at no charge) and will then be able to navigate through the tutorial and corresponding quiz to determine if you meet the requirements for conducting research with human participants.

4.  Pick one of the following studies: the *Stanford Prison Experiment* (Zimbardo, 1999), *Tearoom Trade* (Humphreys, 1970), *Obedience to Authority* (Milgram, 1974), the *Kansas City Preventive Patrol Experiment* (Kelling et al., 1974), or the *Minneapolis Domestic Violence Experiment* (Sherman & Berk, 1984) and answer the following questions.

   a.  What are the ethical issues that need to be addressed to determine if the study could be regarded as ethical? Which ethical model (e.g., utilitarianism, deontology, or peacemaking) supports your answer? Explain.
   b.  Could the researcher(s) have used alternative methodological strategies to acquire the same information?
   c.  Do you think this study should have been done? Why or why not?

# References

ACJS (2000). *Academy of Criminal Justice Sciences: Code of Ethics.* Greenbelt, MD: ACJS.

Albergotti, R., & Dwoskin, E. (2014). Facebook study sparks soul-searching and ethical questions. *Wall Street Journal*, June 2014. www.wsj.com/articles/facebook-study-sparks-ethical-questions-1404172292

Bhattacharjee, Y. (2013). The mind of a con man. *New York Times*, April 26. www.nytimes.com/2013/04/28/magazine/diederik-stapels-audacious-academic-fraud.html?pagewanted=1&_r=0

Chaiken, J., Greenwood, P., & Petersilia, J. (1977). The criminological investigation process: A summary report. *Policy Analysis, 3*, 187–217.

Chiauzzi, E. J., & Liljegren, S. (1993). Taboo topics in addiction treatment: An empirical review of clinical folklore. *Juvenile Substance Abuse Treatment, 10*, 303–316.

Cohen, B. (1980). *Deviant street networks: Prostitutes in New York City.* Cambridge, MA: Lexington Books.

Cook, S. W. (1976). Ethical issues in the conduct of research in social relations. In C. Sellitz, L. Rightsman, & S. Cook (Eds.), *Research methods in social relations* (3rd ed.). New York: Holt, Rinehart and Winston.

Costanzo, M., & White, L. T. (Eds.). (1994). An overview of the death penalty and capital trials: History, current status, legal proceedings, and cost. *Journal of Social Issues, 50*(2), 1–18.

Coughlin, E. K. (1989). Concerns about fraud, editorial bias prompt scrutiny of journal practices. *Chronicle of Higher Education, 35*(23).

DeVellis, R. F. (2003). *Scale development: Theory and applications* (2nd ed.). Thousand Oaks, CA: Sage.

Dillman, D. A., Smyth, J. D., & Christian, L. M. (2009). *Internet, mail and mixed-mode surveys: The tailored design method* (3rd ed.). Hoboken, NJ: John Wiley.

Dong, B. J., Hauck, W. W., Gambertoglio, J. G, Gee, L., & White, J. R. (1997). Bioequivalence of generic and brand-name levothyroxine products in the treatment of hypothyroidism. *Journal of American Medical Association, 277*, 1205–1213.

Erez, E. (1986). Randomized experiments in correctional context: Legal, ethical and practical concerns. *Journal of Criminal Justice, 14*, 389–400.

Federal Judicial Center. (1981). *Experimentation in the law: Report of the Federal Judicial Center Advisory Committee on experimentation in the law.* Washington, DC: Federal Judicial Center.

Fowler, F. J. (2002). *Survey research methods* (3rd ed.). Thousand Oaks, CA: Sage.

Gardner, W., & Wilcox, B. L. (1993). Political intervention in scientific peer review: Research on adolescent sexual behavior. *American Psychology. 48*, 972–983.

Garrison, A. H. (2009). The influence of research on criminal justice policymaking. *Professional Issues in Criminal Justice, 4*(1), 9–21.

Geis, G. (1980). Ethical and legal issues in experiments with offender populations. In S. Talarico (Ed.), *Criminal justice research: Approaches, problems & policy.* Cincinnati, OH: Anderson.

Haney, C., Banks, C., & Zimbardo, P. (1973). Interpersonal dynamics in a simulated prison. *International Journal of Criminology and Penology, 1,* 69–97.

Herbert, B. (1996). More N.R.A. mischief. *New York Times,* July 5, A15.

Humphreys, L. (1970). *Tearoom trade: Impersonal sex in public places.* Chicago: Aldine.

Johnson, D. (1993). The politics of violence research. *Psychological Science, 4,* 131–133.

Kahn, A. (2011). Dutch scientist accused of falsifying data. *Los Angeles Times,* November 5. http://articles.latimes.com/2011/nov/05/science/la-sci-science-fraud-20111106

Kelling, G. L., Pate, T., Dieckman, D., & Browne, C. E. (1974). *The Kansas City preventive patrol experiment.* Washington, DC: Police Foundation.

Keltner, D., & Robinson, R. J. (1996). Extremism, power, and the imagined basis of social conflict. *Current Directions in Psychological Science, 5,* 101–105.

Kramer, A., Guillory, J., & Hancock, J. (2014). Experimental evidence of massive-scale emotional contagion through social networks. *Proceedings of the National Academy of Sciences, 111,* 8788–8790.

Leatherman, C. (1999). At Texas A&M, conflicting charges of misconduct tear a program apart. *Chronicle of Higher Education, 46*(11).

Linz, D., & Malamuth, N. M. (1993). *Pornography.* Newbury Park, CA: Sage.

MacCoun, R. J. (1993). Drugs and the law: A psychological analysis of drug prohibition. *Psychology Bulletin, 113,* 497–512.

MacCoun, R. J. (1998). Biases in the interpretation and use of research results. *Annual Review of Psychology, 49,* 259–287.

MacCoun, R. J., & Reuter, P. (1997). Interpreting Dutch cannabis policy: Reasoning by analogy in the legalization debate. *Science, 278,* 47–52.

Marlatt, G. A., Larimer, M. E., Baer, J. S., & Quigley, L. A. (1993). Harm reduction for alcohol problems: Moving beyond the controlled drinking controversy. *Behavioral Therapy, 24,* 461–504.

Martinson, R. (1974). What works? Questions and answers about prison reform. *Public Interest, 35,* 25–54.

McSkimming, M. J., Sever, B., & King, R. S. (2000). The coverage of ethics in research methods textbooks. *Journal of Criminal Justice Education, 11,* 51–63.

Meltzer, B. A. (1953). A projected study of the jury as a working institution. *Annals of the American Academy of Political and Social Sciences, 287,* 97–102.

Merton, R. K. (1973). *The sociology of science.* Chicago: University of Chicago Press.

Milgram, S. (1974). *Obedience to authority: An experimental view.* New York: Harper and Row.

Miller, P. V. (1995). They said it couldn't be done: The national health and social life survey. *Public Opinion Quarterly, 59,* 404–419.

Moreno, J. D. (1998). Convenient and captive populations. In J. P. Kahn, A. C. Mastroianni, & J. Sugarman (Eds.), *Beyond consent: Seeking justice in research.* New York: Oxford University Press.

Morris, N. (1966). Impediments to penal reform. *Chicago Law Review, 33,* 646–653.

National Institute of Corrections. (2013). *Evidence-based practices in the criminal justice system*. Washington, DC: U.S. Department of Justice.

Neuman, W. L. (2004). *Basics of social research: Qualitative and quantitative approaches*. Boston: Pearson Education.

Nisbet, L. (Ed.). (2001). *The gun control debate: You decide*. (2nd ed.). Amherst, NY: Prometheus Books.

Rennie, D. (1997). Thyroid storm. *Journal of American Medical Association, 277*, 1238–1242.

Ring, K., Wallston, K., & Corey, M. (1970). Mode of debriefing as a factor affecting subjective reaction to a Milgram type obedience experience: An ethical inquiry. *Representative Research in Social Psychology, 1*, 67–88.

Sherman, L. W., & Berk, R. A. (1984). The specific deterrent effects of arrest for domestic assault. *American Sociological Review, 49*, 261–272.

Short, J. F., Jr., & Strodtbeck, F. (1965). *Group processes and gang delinquency*. Chicago: University of Chicago Press.

Singleton, Jr., R. A., & Straits, B. C. (1988). *Approaches to social research* (3rd ed.). New York: Oxford University Press.

Warren, C. A., & Karner, T. X. (2005). *Discovering qualitative methods: Field research, interviews, and analysis*. Los Angeles: Roxbury.

Weisburd, D. (2005). Hot spots policing experiments and criminal justice research: Lessons from the field. *Annals of the American Academy of Political and Social Science, 599*, 220–245.

Whyte, W. F. (1955). *Streetcorner society*. Chicago: University of Chicago Press.

Wolfgang, M. (1982). Ethics and research. In F. Elliston & N. Bowie (Eds.), *Ethics, public policy and criminal justice*, Cambridge, MA: Oelgeschlager, Gunn and Hain.

Zimbardo, P. G. (1999). *Stanford prison experiment: A simulation study of the psychology of imprisonment conducted at Stanford University*. Retrieved March 11, 2011 from the Stanford Prison Experiment at www.Prisonexp.org

# Policing and Law Enforcement

# Overview of Policing and Law Enforcement in the United States

## DOUGLAS KLUTZ AND MARK M. LANIER

L aw enforcement officers, or as they are more commonly called, "police," are the most visible arm of government. "Government" itself is not something we often observe; as the most visible component of government, the police place an important symbolic role. As the agency vested with the power to take citizens' liberty and life without specific judicial approval, the police function is extremely powerful in the criminal justice system. *Despite* their visibility and power, or perhaps *because* of their visibility and power, law enforcement officials are often unpopular with large segments of society (we suspect CJ majors reading this text will probably have a more positive view of police).

It is easy to criticize the police. They have to make split-second decisions in extremely stressful situations. These decisions are generally correct; however, sometimes they are wrong. We often neglect to applaud the numerous correct choices police make on a daily basis, but society is quick to pounce on the few incorrect decisions. This is perhaps inevitable and may serve to create a positive check on police behavior. One of the best contemporary illustrations of checks on police behavior stems from the evolution of social media technologies in our digital world. YouTube© videos can be uploaded almost instantaneously from the scene of an event and disseminated across social media outlets like Facebook© to the tune of thousands of viewers within minutes. This form of instant news to a mass audience creates new challenges in policing. On one hand, it creates even better checks on police abuse of power and authority. Conversely, these videos might provide just a small segment of the entire event, and in turn distort the true rendition of the situation. Video documentation that is piecemealed together can create a negative bias in public perception to policing efforts even when proper procedures are being followed. The evolution in technology places even greater pressures on the police and coupled with their visibility, makes police the widely studied, critiqued, and displayed (think of the television shows and movies devoted to police) part of American Criminal Justice. This section explores the history of American police, the source of their power, the art and science that underlie police practice, and the inherent problems that exist with policing a free, democratic society.

There are differences in policing between the United States and the rest of the world. Some policing systems are similar (e.g., American policing can trace their roots to the English, as can the Canadians). Even within the U.S. there are significant differences in policing; these variations are based on the level of jurisdiction: local, state, or federal and on the specific mandate (e.g., traffic enforcement, firearms control, drug eradication, tax evasion, etc.).

The widespread discretion of the Progressive Era led to abuses of power and unequal treatment. Members of minority groups in particular were subjected to uneven policing. The Professional-ization era developed in response to these problems. The Professional era was characterized by uniform treatment, higher standards (both for employment and day-to-day practice), and further militarization of the police with specialized units such as vice and SWAT. The number of arrests and things such as response time measured police success. Unfortunately, response time means the crime has already occurred and the police simply "react" or respond. Crime skyrocketed in the U.S. during the professional era. The police solution was proactive or community-oriented policing.

The Community Policing or Proactive Policing era is still occurring. Proponents of community policing argue that the community itself has some responsibility for crime control and the police must work closely within specific neighborhoods to solve problems *prior* to a crime occurring. Perhaps the seminal article that argued for Community Policing ironically did not appear in a peer-reviewed academic journal. Instead James Q. Wilson and George Kelling published "Broken Windows" in the March 1982 edition of *Atlantic Monthly*. Academics, mostly at Harvard University's Kennedy School of Government and the National Center for Community Policing at Michigan State University (the nation's oldest Criminal Justice program), seized on this philosophy and greatly expanded its use. Today virtually every law enforcement agency incorporates some aspect of proactive or com-munity-oriented policing; however, none have reached the full potential suggested by advocates.

True, or pure, community policing has characteristics that are simply not compatible with con-temporary American police. For example, the hierarchical rank-and-file military structure (Chief, Deputy Chiefs, Colonels, Majors, Captains, Lieutenants, Sergeants, Patrol, etc.) under pure commu-nity policing would be a flat structure—one chief and everyone else. Each office would be "chief" or in charge of their specific neighborhood. There are many problems and reasons that this will never happen—although the Aurora, Colorado, Police Department under Chief Jerry Sloan attempted it. First, since police have followed the military model, rank is necessary to convey orders; rank signifies seniority, experience, and higher pay; and police unions would bitterly oppose abolishing rank, as would any officer who had achieved rank. This is but one example of why the idealized version of community policing will not be fully implemented. However, many important aspects are compatible with modern American policing and have already reduced crime and proven successful.

For example, community policing seeks to replace the isolation that officers experience by simply patrolling and the responding—"reacting"—to call for service. Instead it advocates officers walking (or riding bicycles) in the form of foot patrols. Police officers conducting foot patrols informally and conversationally get to know community residents in specific areas, work with the community to solve problems that develop into serious crime, and work to improve the area in ways seemingly unrelated to crime. Both small and large cities with serious crime problems have experienced success when implementing these strategies (e.g., New York, NY, and Flint, MI). Regardless of the style of policing employed by an agency (professional or proactive), there are certain intangibles that will affect police success or failure.

# Intangibles

The first intangible is officer discretion, or lack thereof. The Professional era sought to remove or greatly reduce officer discretion. This was due to abuses, excessive force, and community demand. Laws also aim to limit an officer's discretion. However, proactive policing argues that discretion is needed and will occur regardless of legal mandates. What exactly is police officer discretion? Think about a time you were pulled over for speeding or failure to yield. If a police officer lets you off with just a warning instead of issuing a citation, this is a perfect example of the concept of discretion being employed. The police officer might see it as a better use of their time and resources to focus on apprehending more serious offenders. Discretion is a concept that permeates the entire criminal justice system due to the reality of strained resources.

The second intangible is acknowledgment that the police have the authority to deprive citizens of their liberties in specific circumstances. Police also have the right to use physical, chemical, electronic, and deadly force against citizens. This is area that has caused the most public outcry against police due to abuse of power. It is also the area that causes the most anxiety for police administrators and government officials. Because the police are charged with maintaining order in the community, they are called to oversee any form of public unrest and demonstration. This is where most visible problems occur.

Birmingham, Alabama, police Chief Bull Conner is infamous for his use of police dogs and fire hoses against non-violent African American Civil rights demonstrators in the 1960s. In 1968, the Chicago, Illinois, police department under Mayor Daley violently beat protestors at the Republican National Convention. Police officers were also captured on videotape violently beating Rodney King in Los Angeles, California, and replayed on national news outlets for millions to see. The Rodney King incident sparked the infamous LA Riots and led to an intense standoff between the police and the LA community. After Hurricane Katrina, New Orleans police and National Guard went door to door taking legal firearms from citizens under martial law, then New Orleans Police officers were caught shooting unarmed citizens on a freeway bridge where they sought safety from rising Katrina floodwaters. All of these events were anomalies, rare events that statistically hardly ever occur, yet they are seared into the American consciousness and reflect negatively on police. All involved the police exceeding their legally mandated use of force. They all illustrate the importance of proper police procedure.

The final factor is that crime control and criminal apprehension are considered prime police functions, yet many of the factors that cause, contribute to, or increase crime are beyond the control of the police. For example, the police cannot influence the economy. The police cannot be in every home of drunken and abusive parents. The police cannot, seemingly, even control the flow of illegal drugs into our country. What the police can do is provide a visible, reassuring, and 24-hour available presence.

# Art or Science?

We want to conclude this section, and introduce you to the selected police readings, by asking you to consider and try to answer some fundamental questions. Is good policing the result of *scientifically* verified practices, procedures, and policies? For example, has significant research demonstrated that community policing is effective at reducing crime? Have tasers reduced the use of lethal force by police? Or, have tasers increased the frequency of police use of force? Can you apply scientifically derived policy in every situation? Are all traffic stops the same, for instance?

Or, on the other hand, is the "best" police officer the one who never needs to make an arrest (or use a taser) since s/he addresses *artfully* or creatively addresses crime problems before they escalate into an event requiring arrest? How do you measure this type of officer success? In short, is good policing the result of science or immeasurable, intangible personal skills of individual officers? Which should it be?

We present these as questions rather than as definitive statements because we do not know the answers! We suspect that the best answer is "a little of each." Clearly science and research provide a vital role in all aspects of modern society, policing included. However, individual officer characteristics, traits, beliefs, and practices might ultimately determine what "good" policing is. This is why careful pre-employment screening, experience, and careful monitoring are all important. Consider this analogy. Do you have some professors whose class you really look forward to attending? Do you have others whom you really dislike? They probably all desire to be liked and all wish to convey important useful knowledge, and hope they all present you the necessary information to be successful. So why the difference? As you read this section, bear in mind that policing is much more varied and difficult than teaching.

# The Police

## HISTORICAL AND CONTEMPORARY PERSPECTIVES

GEOFFREY P. ALPERT AND ROGER G. DUNHAM

The police have been a common feature in American society for more than a century. Today, police officers are seen patrolling streets, directing traffic, and serving the public in a multitude of ways. It has not always been so. Historically, the police were political assets for the power elites and had no pretence of treating everyone equally. The purpose of this chapter is to review briefly the history of the police, discuss the modern-day reality of police work, and assess the future of policing.

## British Tradition

A great deal of U.S. policing heritage can be linked directly to its British roots. Policing in the community, crime prevention, and elected sheriffs all have origins in English law enforcement. The history of policing in England includes a variety of stories and scenarios that involve radically conservative interpretations of law enforcement and a liberal view of governmental intervention (Reith, 1938). Originally, all security in England was private. Those who could afford the luxury lived in well-built houses that were guarded by servants who acted as bodyguards. The remainder of the population merely hoped that their neighbors and those chosen as "watchmen" would protect them and chase away the criminal element. This system of shared and informal policing was referred to as "kin" policing (Reith, 1956) and the "frankpledge system." It was established to encourage citizens to act as the "eyes and ears" of the authorities, to protect their family and neighbors, and to deliver to the court any member of the group who committed a crime.

The pledge to protect others created a sense of security based on being protected by one's family and neighbors. Communities were organized into *tythings,* or groups of 100 citizens, which were part of larger units called *shires* (similar to counties today). Shires were headed by *shire reeves* (later called "sheriffs"). Shire reeves were appointed by the king, and were primarily responsible for civil duties, such as collecting taxes and ensuring obedience to the authority of the king. From the frankpledge system came the *parish constable system*. In the 13th century, the position of the constable was formalized, thus permitting the appointment of watchmen to assist in their duties (Bayley, 1999). Watchmen had numerous responsibilities, from guarding the gates of town at night to watching for fires, crimes, and suspicious persons. This system of law enforcement continued without much change until the 18th century.

During the 18th century, there was unprecedented population growth and the population of London more than doubled. Accompanying the growth was a more complex and specialized society, resulting in law enforcement problems that challenged the control systems in existence. Rioting in the cities, which the existing system could not control, is one such example. As a result of the changing social climate, a more formal and organized method of law enforcement became necessary. It was around this time that Henry Fielding (author of *Tom Jones*) and his brother, Sir John Fielding, helped improve policing in London and all over England by suggesting changes to the existing system of control that developed into what is known as the modern police department.

## The First Modern Police: London

It was Sir Robert Peel, the British Home Secretary, who created a 3,000-strong police force. Peel drafted and then guided through Parliament the "Act for Improving the Police in and Near the Metropolis," which is better known as the Metropolitan Police Act of 1829. Under the direction of Peel, the police were organized for crime prevention. By 1829, the entire city was patrolled by men assigned specific territories, or beats, on a 24-hour-a-day basis (Reith, 1956). The officers, or "bobbies," wore blue uniforms so that they could be easily recognizable as public servants whose purpose was to deter crime. The leaders of the London police force provided a central administration, strict discipline, and close supervision of the officers. They eventually decided to introduce a military structure to what had been a rather loose organization. Peel and his bobbies were so successful that requests for help from outside areas were received and assistance was sent. This movement set the stage for modern police departments, which were developed according to the principles of what has become known as "the London model of policing," Thus, the structure and function of current police agencies, as well as their overall mission, are heavily influenced by Sir Robert Peel.

# The Modern Era

In fundamental ways, modern police departments remain slaves to their history. In the 1970s, Jonathan Rubinstein (1973) commented that understanding what police do is difficult because they have such a wide variety of tasks. Thirty-six years later, this statement remains as true as it did then. Citizens are split between viewing the police in positive terms, calling them brave "crime fighters" and heroes, and referring to them negatively, as corrupt, heartless, and brutal. Often, these different views are influenced by a citizen's experiences with the police and whether it was a positive or a negative one. Partly because of severe criticisms of the police by citizens, policing has been forced to change and develop into what it is today.

Although much of policing has changed drastically since its initiation into American government, changes in the selection and training of officers have been among the most important. There were few standards when hiring officers during the early years of policing, and practically no training. In fact, positions on the police force often were viewed as a reward for loyalty to political parties who were in power. Newly elected officials often fired existing officers and hired their political supporters. As a result, citizens thought of the police as nothing more than political "hacks," enforcing the interests of those in power. This corrupt system of hiring officers has developed into the very elaborate and professional civil service hiring systems present in most departments today. Further, the practice of virtually no training of officers that existed earlier has progressed into the long and arduous training programs found in most departments today.

## Recruitment and Selection of Officers

The importance of recruitment and selection cannot be emphasized enough. As police work is labor-intensive, and a large percentage of an agency's budget is devoted to personnel issues, the officer is the most significant investment a police department can make. Police agencies are always looking for innovative ways to attract and retain good officers. Once an individual decides he or she wants to enter police work, the agency must screen the person for characteristics that make a good police officer. This is known as "selecting in," a strategy that identifies those individuals best suited for police work. The agency must also eliminate or "screen out" those applicants who are unfit for police work. Many tests are available to evaluate someone's psychological and physical characteristics to determine if success in police work is likely. There are multiple hurdles for recruits to pass. Unfortunately, there are no clear and accepted criteria to determine which candidates will make the best police officers. One reason for this uncertainty was suggested by Brenner (1989), who noted that an officer must be able to adapt to various situations and use a variety of styles and approaches, depending on the circumstances. He points out that officers must interact with violent criminals and distressed victims, perhaps during the same interaction, and it is unlikely that an officer's behavior will satisfy all of the stakeholders all of the time. As it is extremely difficult to determine an applicant's fitness for duty, officers must pass the many hurdles. Each decade or era has its own problems associated with the recruitment of police officers. The overall economy plays a role, as does the country's involvement in war and the use of the military. In fact, these and other issues also impact trained police officers when they return from a leave or other assignment. There is enormous variance in the selection procedures and training among agencies, so the following discussion illustrate the options agencies have at their disposal to review and assess candidates.

Traditionally, police departments use standardized written tests to assess basic skills and attitudes. The use of traditional pen-and-pencil tests has been criticized for its lack of predictive ability, which has led many agencies to supplement these tests with a more comprehensive assessment procedure. Departments using this method process applicants through a series of assessments, including simulated and role-play activities. The activities are developed to force a person to respond to situations and individuals who "test" the person's character and ability to negotiate in a specific situation. Common examples of simulations used in assessment centers include a domestic altercation, a routine traffic stop, or a bar fight.

In addition, officers are given medical exams and physical agility tests that involve job task simulations, such as lifting weights through windows, carrying heavy objects, and other tasks that might confront a police officer on the job. Officer candidates are often given a polygraph test to determine if they have told the truth about their backgrounds or past experiences on their application forms and in their interviews. One area that is investigated is prior drug use history.

Further, applicants are often interviewed by an individual or a group of commanders. These interviews are designed to determine a candidate's ability to communicate and to respond to difficult questions. Once an applicant has passed these initial hurdles, he or she is sent to training. This training varies from state to state and agency to agency, but all have some common elements, including preservice, field, and in-service training.

## Academy Training

Police academies can be run by the department or by the state, and they can be independent or connected to community colleges or universities. The average length of academy training is approximately 600 hours, but varies from state to state. Regardless of the total number of hours required at the academy, the training and education is an experience that plays a significant role in shaping the officer's attitudes about policing in general, including ways to address specific tasks, and the role of the police in society.

The building blocks of a good law enforcement training program are anchored to two issues: First, the programs should incorporate the proper statement of mission and ethical considerations, which should be taught in the context of what an officer will do on a daily basis. Second, there must be a balance of time spent on "high-frequency" versus "high-risk" activities in the required training. In the 21st century, it is also necessary to prepare police officers to think, make good decisions, and to respond to a variety of difficult situations.

Recruits must pass the requirements of the academy to graduate. Many academies insist that the recruit pass all courses the first time to graduate, while other academies have built-in provisions for remedial training to help marginal students pass. Academies use a variety of methods to evaluate and grade the progress of their recruits, such as multiple-choice tests, role-play exercises, written answer tests, and oral tests. Once graduated, with newly acquired attitudes and skills, the young officer is often required to enroll in departmental training or could be assigned street work with a field training officer. Unfortunately, others are sent directly to the street, with gun, badge, and vehicle, with no further training.

## Field Training

Most departments provide training after completion of the academy through a field training officer (FTO) model. Although recruits should have been exposed to a number of real-life experiences during academy training, those were created for training or role-play scenarios and are conducted in an artificial atmosphere. Field training is meant to bridge the gap between the protected environment of the academy and the isolated, open danger of the street. The new officer, or "rookie," is paired with a more experienced police officer(s) for a period of time, usually several months.

It is the field training officer's job to teach the young rookie how to survive and how to become a good police officer. Field training programs are often divided into several phases. Although agencies vary the length and scope of their field training, all programs should include introductory, training, and evaluation phases. The introductory phase is structured to teach the rookie officer about the agency's policies, procedures, and local laws and ordinances. Departmental customs and practices are also communicated at this time. During the training and evaluation phases, the young officer is gradually introduced to complex tasks that require involved and complicated decisions. The young officer will have to interpret and translate into action what was learned in the academy and the field. The field training officer then evaluates the decisions and actions made by the recruit. Eventually, the successful trainee will be able to handle calls without assistance from the field training officer.

There exists a long-standing concern in policing that each rookie is told by an experienced officer to forget what was learned at the academy and to just watch and learn how things are done right. As Van Maanen (1978) described, "The newcomer is quickly bombarded with 'street wise' patrolmen assuring him that the police academy was simply an experience that all officers endure and has little, if anything, to do with real police work" (p. 300). This unfortunate message is that the formal training received at the academy is irrelevant or unrealistic. It is hoped that field training officers are selected and trained to make sure these types of counterproductive messages do not occur. After an officer has passed the probationary period, he or she may think training is over. However, most states and many departments require refresher courses, training on new issues, and other sorts of in-service training.

## In-Service Training

Many states have now mandated in-service training for police in the same way lawyers and teachers must continue their education. In-service training is designed to provide officers with new skills and changes in laws, policies, or procedures. Also, since many skills learned at the academy or while in field training are perishable, in-service training can restore an officer's skills. Some agencies send officers to lengthy management schools or specialized trainings. It is hard to believe that some agencies still do not train veteran officers aggressively. Police work is constantly changing, and remaining a good police officer is different from the process of becoming one.

If conducted properly, in-service training can provide a critical component to the agency's training scheme. There must be training for supervisors and managers, communication specialists and investigators, as well as street officers. In other words, patrol officers need certain skills and those on specialized assignments need others. Some skills, such as those used in the control of persons, emergency vehicle operations, and other high-risk activities, need more frequent and in-depth training than those engaged in more routine tasks. Officers must not only be provided with proper information, but they must also be given the opportunity to ask "What if" questions of the instructor. Further, officers must pass an examination before it can be assumed that they know the information and are competent to put it into practice in real-world situations.

The Internet is providing a new forum for training police officers. Many departments are creating home pages that provide information about the agency and the community served. There are also many police "chat rooms," which allow officers to share information and have discussions about many topics and issues. Innovative trainers can take advantage of these technological advancements for the improvement of their officers' knowledge and experience.

The expense of training is one of the important issues many departments must consider. Not only is it costly to evaluate needs, to plan and to provide for training, but it is also very expensive to remove officers from the streets to be trained. In the short term, the expenses are great, but in the long term, the training and its related costs will pay off.

Once selected and trained, there are many recruits who enter into police work only to realize that the work, schedule, and rewards are not what they anticipated. In addition, administrators will learn that some of the citizens they recruit and even train are not able to perform the required task appropriately. Other reasons officers do not make careers in policing include family influences, "burn out," and better-paying job offers.

After officers have negotiated successfully their initial training, most are assigned to the patrol function and, as a result, have the most contact with the public. There are multiple methods of patrol, including automobile, foot, horse, motorcycle, bicycle, and boat. Each type serves a different function, promotes different relationships, and creates different problems. In any case, these officers are now prepared to police independently and to interact with citizens on their own.

# Police Operations

## Police Patrol

Patrol has long been considered the "backbone" of policing, as this is where almost every police officer gets his or her "street experience." This experience on the street with citizens is vital in shaping the outlooks and views of the police officer. While many patrol officers will go on to supervisory or investigative positions, this starting point creates shared experiences and facilitates socialization with fellow officers. An important question is, what are the major factors that influence a patrol officer's behavior?

Although officers experience similar situations, their responses may differ due to the complexities and special circumstances of interactions. They soon learn that they cannot enforce all laws, and as Kenneth Culp Davis (1975) observed, the police must use discretion and selective enforcement.

Written guidelines or policies direct police officers' activities, reactions, and behavior. Policies are based on relevant laws and presumably best practices. They are directives that provide members of the organization with sufficient information so that they can successfully perform their day-to-day operations. Some agencies provide their officers with very detailed policies, while others have promulgated more general policies but have supplemented those with detailed in-service training. While officers are allowed discretion with specified boundaries, it is an important research question to determine what factors explain why police officers respond differently to the same conditions.

For example, the process of forming suspicion has been a topic that has received relatively little attention in the research literature. Jonathan Rubinstein (1973) was one of the first scholars to thoroughly discuss the formation of suspicion. He notes the following:

> Many of the things the officer is looking for are a product of prior situations, a consequence of events about which he knows nothing, although he often makes assumptions about some of them. ... While the patrolman is looking for substantive cues indicating flight, fear, concealment, and illegal possession, he is also making judgments based on his perception of the people and places he polices. (pp. 255, 257)

After an exhaustive review of the literature, the National Research Council (2003) concluded that a suspect's social class, gender, as well as other social factors do not explain variance in behavior in police-citizen interactions.

An important area of police behavior to address is the foot pursuit. Similar to vehicular pursuits, these activities were not regulated until the 1990s. Around that time, it became apparent that officers and suspects were unnecessarily injured or put in situations that resulted in unnecessary force and deadly force because they abandoned proper practices and went on foot pursuits alone, or were separated from other officers in an attempt to corner or head off a fleeing suspect. Without proper communication, or a plan, officers put themselves in dangerous situations, which can result in crossfires and unnecessary force.

It appears that officers' beliefs and prior experiences strongly influence their responses to citizens. Perhaps the cognitive theorists are correct in arguing that officers learn by experience, and that the relative power of that learning is influenced by one's degree of familiarity and repeated associations in a fashion similar to the theory of differential association. In other words, these developed schemas form a mental model and illusory correlation that strongly influence a person's responses to people and places in future encounters (Alpert, MacDonald, & Dunham, 2005). This is all extremely important because officers' behavior creates an image for a police department, and supervisors must manage how the officers act and respond to situations. While the patrol function forms what has been called the backbone of policing, perhaps it is the first-line supervisors who form the nervous system of the agency. The patrol officers are the ones closest to the community and know the most about the people and places they police. It is they who are crime fighters, community policing officers, and problem solvers—all at the same time. It is the supervisor who directs and manages their activities.

## The Crime Control Function

What are the major operations by which the police set out to control crime? The crime control function of the police relies on four primary tactics: (1) randomized and directed patrol (preventative patrol), (2) problem identification and solving, (3) response to calls for service by citizens, and (4) criminal investigation.

Preventive patrol is largely based on the assumption that it serves as a deterrent effect on crime. Although this assumption was questioned in the Kansas City Preventive Patrol Experiment, other studies have indicated that citizens' attitudes and beliefs are impacted by seeing officers on motorized and foot patrols. Problem identification involves the identification of specific locations and times wherein crime is most likely to occur or that are otherwise deemed most problematic.

The effectiveness of rapid responses to calls has been examined over the years. The initial rationale behind a speedy response is that it will improve the likelihood that police will apprehend a suspect. Unfortunately, citizens often report crimes after the fact, and a few seconds shaved by the police responding at breakneck speeds to a call for service does not make much difference in the officer's likelihood of affecting an arrest. Interestingly, whether or not the initial officer responding to a scene can identify a suspect may make a difference in whether the case is resolved, but the time differential is measured in minutes, not seconds.

Finally, the work of detectives and the criminal investigation process have been studied in a variety of ways. The RAND Corporation study provides an important benchmark for establishing what is known about the effectiveness of retrospective investigation of crimes (Greenwood & Petersilia, 1975). There are several important findings in this report that merit discussion. First, detectives spend very little of their time (less than 10%) on activities that directly lead to solving crime. A large proportion of the time they do spend on casework is often used on cases after they have been solved (e.g., preparing a case for court). Second, solving crimes has little to do with any special activities performed by investigators. Instead, the most important factor affecting case clearance (e.g., whether a suspect can be identified) is the behavior of the initial responding officer and members of the public. As noted above, clearance rates are related to whether either the initial responding officer (or a victim or witness on the scene) was able to identify a suspect. It is usually a civilian and not the officer who can make an identification, thereby reducing the need for officers to risk the safety of civilians on the streets by driving at high speeds to get to a call.

While patrol is an important aspect of policing, police departments and their officers perform functions other than crime fighting. Order maintenance, rather than law enforcement, may be a better approach in certain places and with certain people. As police officers are available 24/7, they are called on to provide emergency aid, information, and animal control and to make referrals to other human welfare agencies, among other responsibilities. The time spent on these services can be significant and can be seen as taking away from routine crime-fighting activities. Even some terrorist threats that require attention can be seen as taking away resources from immediate community-level crimes and problems.

Several issues that require time and effort are gangs and weapons. Although these concerns are neither new nor novel, the police response must change continually to be effective. Taking guns off the street and reducing gang violence must be goals of every police department, As new strategies are developed, new techniques by gang members are discovered.

## Important Influences on Officers' Behavior

A considerable amount of research has been conducted on the influences on officers' behavior while on the job. Policing is an occupation for which the behavior of the incumbent can have very serious implications for those they police. Few occupations give individuals as much power over others as the police position. In exercising their discretionary power over others, officers may severely injure citizens; end their lives; destroy their reputations; or send them to jail or prison, among many other very severe penalties. Thus, it is important to monitor how officers make such decisions and try to understand which factors influence them.

## The Culture of the Police

The nature of police work is different from that of work performed in most other occupations. As has been noted, the police are among the few professionals that are required to be available 24 hours a day, 7 days a week, 52 weeks a year. Furthermore, the police deal with social problems and societal ills that extend beyond simply fighting crime. The police are also unique in terms of the persons with whom they most routinely interact. While police officers deal with the entire spectrum of humanity, they spend the majority of their time dealing with the seamier side of society. The central features of the police culture may be categorized according to the way officers relate to the unique nature of the job, the special category of persons with whom they come into contact, and the environment in which they work. In other words, the unique aspects of the police role, such as being given tremendous authority, and the corresponding right to use force on citizens; morality issues related to the police being the enforcers of right over wrong; and danger, or the threat of danger, shape the nature of the police and their work.

Research indicates that the environment in which police do their work is shaped by their isolation from citizens, their solidarity within the police subculture, their loyalty to each other, and their desire for autonomy in carrying out policing duties. These conditions all contribute to the character of the police subculture, which has been characterized by extreme loyalty to one's coworkers, particularly one's partner. However, the police operate in a bureaucracy that is based on a paramilitary model with many guidelines or policies, rigid lines of authority, and communication that is authoritative and clear. These also make important contributions to the police culture and have an important impact on how the police do their work.

## Police Bureaucracy

Police departments are organized in a manner similar to the military, using ranks to designate authority (captain, lieutenant, sergeant, etc.). True to the bureaucratic form of organization, the larger police departments are divided into special divisions and units with lines of authority leading from the chief to the line officers. Police department hierarchies of authority vary in respect to how tasks are divided and which divisions report to which supervisors.

The traditional hierarchy is represented by a pyramid-type structure. On the top, to set and enforce policies and to provide overall leadership, is the chief. Other divisions include at least internal affairs, communication, and patrol. Smaller agencies may combine different elements into one division, but all agencies must perform the same basic duties.

For example, internal affairs or professional compliance bureaus investigate all allegations of police misconduct. These concerns can be initiated by civilian complaints or by fellow police officers. This division or section is of paramount importance to the operations of any law enforcement agency and must receive support from the chief administrators. Most Internal Affairs Division managers report directly to the chief of police to avoid any question of prominence or importance.

One of the most critical elements of police work is its system of communication. It is this "heart line" that receives calls for service and forwards information to officers in the field. The communication process forms the link between the community and the police. The information provided to officers is the basis on which they prepare and respond. In other words, if the police department is told about a particular situation, officers and supervisors must recognize how many officers are needed, how quickly they need to respond, and where they need to be sent.

The degree of centralization in the organization is one of the most critical decisions an administrator must make. A centralized structure, with a dominant supervisor, will have strong controls and may be cost effective. A decentralized structure will have flexibility and will be cost efficient as it emphasizes team building as a mode of problem solving. As each structure has positive and negative characteristics, the goals of the organization, with input from the community, should serve to design the structure. Certainly, large departments can centralize administrative and certain investigative functions while they decentralize patrol and other activities. The trend has been to decentralize many police functions and to be more responsive to the unique characteristics of communities. Regardless of the type of organization, there are always going to be critical concerns and high-risk activities performed by the police. The next section looks at these activities and places them in their proper perspective.

# Critical Issues and High-Risk Activities

Given the large number of issues that exist in policing today, this discussion must be limited to the most important ones. The approach here is therefore selective and focuses on a limited number of critical issues: minority hiring and promotion, women in policing, the use of force, and pursuit driving.

## Minorities in Policing

Tremendous strides have been made in hiring minorities in recent years. Since the mid-1990s, police agencies have increased significantly the hiring and promoting of minority officers.

Advocates for the hiring and promoting of minorities argue that if minorities are adequately represented in police departments, departments become representative of the communities they serve. Police departments that reflect the racial and ethnic characteristics of the communities they serve may increase the respect of community residents and thereby increase the flow of information concerning crime and the identification of criminals. Similar to ethnic minorities, females have not played an important role in law enforcement until relatively recently.

Until the early 1980s, the few females who were involved in police work were often assigned to clerical duties or restricted to work with either female or juvenile offenders. The reasons for this exclusion were many: First, male officers did not want to put up with the social inhibitions placed on them by the presence of women; second, they did not want to be overshadowed by or even to take orders from women; finally, most men did not want to be supported by a female in the performance of potentially dangerous work (Caiden, 1977; Martin, 2001). The common belief was that females would not function to the level of their male counterparts—specifically, that they would react improperly and would not be able to apprehend suspects in violent or dangerous situations. Recently, the myths about women in the police world have been debunked, and benefits connected with recruiting more female officers have been stressed. For example, female officers are often better than male officers at avoiding violence and de-escalating potentially violent situations. Moreover, while women currently represent approximately 13% of all sworn personnel, they are responsible for only 5% of citizen complaints, 2% of sustained allegations of excessive use of force, and 6% of the dollars paid out in judgments and settlements for excessive use of force (National Center for Women in Policing, 2002).

The next issue is the use of force by police officers, which often is handled more appropriately by female officers than by their male counterparts. The use of force is a highly controversial issue, and this examination will look at both the problems connected to it and some of the potential solutions that can prevent the abuse of this most necessary of police powers.

## Use of Non-Deadly Force

The use of force, particularly deadly force, has traditionally been one of the most controversial aspects of police work. Clearly, a distinction must be made between appropriate police use of force and excessive force. While some level of force is legitimate and necessary to control suspects and protect innocent citizens, the use of excessive force is unacceptable and is one of the most troubling forms of police misconduct. New technologies, such as the Electronic Control Device or the Conducted Energy Device, provide police officers with alternatives to traditional batons, fists, and fights.

While these technologies can lead to fewer injuries than traditional uses of force, they also create their own issues, such as device malfunctions that have been linked to several deaths. Although a disproportionate amount of media attention is given to the use of force by the police, it is a rare event considering the numerous times police officers have encounters with citizens.

To understand police use of force, it is important to examine the sequence of events as they unfold in police–citizen interactions. The way to accomplish this task is to understand how the levels of force and resistance, and the sequence in which they take place, affect the outcome of the encounter. This effort requires using detailed information on the sequence of actions and reactions to make sense of the interaction process of the encounter (Alpert & Dunham, 2004).

Alpert and Dunham (2004) have formulated an interaction theory to help understand police use of force and the overall interaction processes between officers and citizens that lead to using force. The *authority maintenance theory* depicts the police–citizen encounter as an interaction process that is somewhat unique because authority dominates the process and it is more asymmetrical than in most other interactions. Another aspect of police–citizen interactions, according to the theory, is that the expectations and behaviors of these actors are more likely to violate the principle of reciprocity, an important function of human interactions. Officers are more likely to resort to using force when suspects block the officers from reaching their goals concerning the outcome of the encounter. Likewise, citizens respond to the blockage of their goals with varying degrees of resistance. The resistance/force sequence typically escalates until one party changes the other's expected goals voluntarily or involuntarily.

## Use of Deadly Force

Since police use of force is often measured by its severity, deadly force is often analyzed as a separate category. It is estimated that each year, approximately 400 persons are killed by the police, and the issue becomes particularly problematic due to the widespread perception that minorities are more likely than white subjects to be killed by the police. Regardless of the research evidence that shows the threatening behavior of the suspect is the strongest indicator of police use of deadly force, the perception of racially biased or motivated killings by the police remains.

The authority to use deadly force can be traced to English common law, when police officers had the authority to use deadly force to apprehend any suspected fleeing felon (the "fleeing felon" doctrine). During this time period, the fleeing-felon doctrine was considered reasonable. First, all felonies were punishable by death in England, and second, defendants did not possess the rights or the presumption of innocence that they enjoy today. In 1985, the U.S. Supreme Court modified the fleeing-felon doctrine in the *Tennessee v. Garner* (1985) decision.

The landmark case of *Tennessee v. Garner* (1985) involved the use of deadly force against a fleeing felon: At approximately 10:45 on the night of October 3, 1974, a slightly built eighth grader, Edward Garner, unarmed and alone, broke a window and entered an unoccupied house in suburban Memphis with the intent of stealing money and property. Two police officers, Elton Hymon and Leslie Wright, responded to a call from a neighbor concerning a prowler. While Wright radioed dispatch, Hymon intercepted the youth as he ran from the back of the house to a 6-foot cyclone fence. After shining a flashlight on the youth who was crouched by the fence, Hymon identified himself and yelled at Garner to stop. Hymon observed that the youth was unarmed. As the boy jumped to get over the fence, the officer fired his service revolver at the youth, as he was trained to do. Edward

Gamer was shot because the police officers had been trained under Tennessee law that it was proper to kill a fleeing felon rather than run the risk of allowing him to escape.

A lawsuit filed by the family ended up reaching the U.S. Supreme Court. The underlying issue being decided by the Court was when and under what circumstances police officers can use deadly force. The Court held that the Tennessee statute was "unconstitutional insofar as it authorizes the use of deadly force against ... unarmed, nondangerous suspect[s]" (*Tennessee v. Garner*, 1985, p. 11). The Court cited with approval the Model Penal Code:

> The use of deadly force is not justifiable ... unless (i) the arrest is for a felony; and (ii) the person effecting the arrest is authorized to act as a police officer ... ; and (iii) the actor believes that the force employed creates no substantial risk of injury to innocent persons; and (iv) the actor believes that (1) the crime for which the arrest is made involved conduct including the use or threatened use of deadly force; or (2) there is a substantial risk that a person to be arrested will cause death or serious bodily harm if his apprehension is delayed. (cited in *Tennessee v. Garner*, 1985, pp. 6–7, note 7)

In the final analysis, the Court ruled that "where the suspect poses no immediate threat to the officer and no threat to others, the harm resulting from failing to apprehend him does not justify the use of deadly force to do so" (*Tennessee v. Garner*, 1985, p. 11). The nature of this threat is also clear: "a significant threat of death or serious physical injury" (p. 11). In other words, the *Garner* decision created a modified "defense of life" standard. It is significant that this pronouncement can be reduced to a moral judgment. This was made clear when the Court noted, "It is not better that, all felony suspects die than that they escape" (p. 11).

## Police Pursuits

The use of deadly force by the police, involving the use and abuse of firearms, has been under scrutiny for a long time by police administrators, by the public, as well as by the courts. Another use of potentially deadly force that has only recently attracted significant attention is the police pursuit (see Alpert, Kenney, Dunham, & Smith, 2000). The purpose of a pursuit is to apprehend a suspect following a refusal to stop. When an officer engages in a chase in a high-powered motor vehicle, that vehicle becomes a potentially dangerous weapon. As the training guide for the California Peace Officer Standards and Training (CPOST) explains, firearms and vehicles are instruments of deadly force and the kinetic energy or kill power of a vehicle is far greater than that of a firearm.

Considered in this light, it is not surprising that there is such great concern over police pursuits. Each year, the National Highway Traffic Safety Administration (NHTSA) collects data on police-pursuit-related fatalities. The data are collected as part of the Fatality Analysis Reporting System (FARS); however, they do not capture all of the pursuit-related deaths. For example, many law enforcement officers are not trained to check the "pursuit related" box when a fatality occurs. Similarly, if the police vehicle is not involved in the crash, officers don't always report a death on the form. Nonetheless, the NHTSA data show that at least one person will die every day of the year in a police pursuit, with approximately one third of those deaths being innocent bystanders.

While the costs of pursuits are high, the benefits should not be discounted. On the one hand, it is the mission of the police to protect lives and, clearly, pursuits are inherently dangerous to all involved. On the other hand, there is an ongoing need to immediately apprehend some law violators.

Determining how to balance these two competing goals will shape the future of police pursuits. Depending on the reason for the chase and the risk factor to the public, abandonment or termination of a pursuit may be the best choice in the interests of public safety. The critical question in a pursuit is what benefit will be derived from a chase compared to the risk of a crash, injury, or death, whether to officers, suspects, or the public. In other words, a pursuit must be evaluated by weighing the risk to the public against the need to immediately apprehend a suspect.

There are two myths that are commonly stated by proponents of aggressive pursuit policies. The first myth is that suspects who do not stop for the police "have a dead body in the trunk." The thinking behind this statement is that people who flee from the police are serious criminals who have something to hide. While the empirical truth is that many who flee from the police are "guilty" of offenses other than the known reason for their flight, the offense is most often minor, such as a suspended driver's license (Alpert et at., 2000). The second myth is that if the police restrict their pursuits, crime will increase and a significantly greater number of citizens will flee from the police. While this myth helps justify aggressive pursuit policies, it is not substantiated by empirical data. In fact, agencies that have restricted pursuits do not report any increase in fleeing suspects.

Police pursuits are dangerous activities involving risk to all persons involved, and even to those innocent bystanders who might be in harm's way. Research shows that approximately 40% of pursuits result in a crash, 20% result in an injury, and 1% result in a death (Alpert & Dunham, 2004). It is very difficult to force a vehicle to stop without the use of a deadly force tactic, such as ramming or shooting at a vehicle. As these tactics are also very dangerous, it becomes important to develop technologies to get vehicles to stop without risking lives. These technologies are being developed, and military technology is being declassified and used to assist law enforcement officers in stopping vehicles and avoiding unnecessary high-speed pursuits.

# The Future of Policing

Although this chapter has presented only a snapshot of policing issues and research, a number of areas have had an increasing influence on policing and will guide policing in the future: (a) continued and concerted attempts by the police to be more attentive to the needs of citizens and solving the underlying problems that contribute to crime (e.g., community policing and problem-oriented policing); (b) responses by the police to demands for greater accountability from citizens, policymakers, and police administrators (e.g., Early Warning or Identification Systems, COMPSTAT, and citizen review boards); and (c) the application of new technologies to help officers and administrators accomplish these goals, including face recognition software and other computer applications.

## Community and Problem-Solving Policing

One of the most important factors that moved policing strategies in new directions was the body of research indicating that traditional methods of policing (e.g., rapid response to citizen calls for service, preventive patrol, and the criminal investigation process) were not as efficient as expected in combating crime. The results of this research, and anecdotal information, highlighted the central role that the community played in the detection and prevention of crime. It is clear that without the cooperation of the community, very little crime would be solved at all, and public attitudes concerning the police would be very unfavorable. The argument that traditional policing is reactive rather than preventative, and treats the symptoms of crime rather than broaching the fundamental problems themselves, forced policing specialists to become proactive and to solve problems rather than simply respond to them after the fact. As these techniques improve and sufficient resources are allocated to proactive strategies, there may be a reduction in crime and a corresponding improvement in public perceptions of the police.

## Responding to Demands for Greater Accountability

An integral part of community policing is greater accountability on the part of the police for their actions. In recent years, departments have adopted several strategies to facilitate an increase in officer accountability, both internally to superiors and externally to the citizens they serve. In order to promote accountability within police departments, police organizations across the United States are experimenting with COMPSTAT and other programs that develop, gather, and disseminate information on crime problems and hold police managers accountable to reduce the problems. Another innovation in accountability is the early identification of potentially problem officers. The Early Identification System (EIS) includes three basic elements: identification and selection of officers, intervention, and post-intervention monitoring. Each element selects a variety of performance indicators that capture officers' behavior or compare officers in similar situations. The goal is to identify and intervene with officers whose behavior may be problematic.

## New Technology

The improvement and application of technology is perhaps most likely to influence policing in the future. Implicit in this discussion of the implementation of community- or problem-oriented policing and the concomitant and innovative methods of enhancing police accountability has been the advent of technology. Perhaps the most important technological advancements inside a police department are crime analysis, computerized reports, GPS systems and car locators, and crime mapping. In the community, the use of cameras may result in crime deterrence or displacement and the enhanced ability to solve crimes.

Crime analysis has three primary functions. These include assessing the nature, extent, and distribution of crime for the purpose of allocating resources. The second primary function is to identify suspects to assist in investigations. The final function of crime analysis is to identify the conditions that facilitate crime and incivility and to direct approaches to crime prevention. The ability of law enforcement agencies to engage in crime analysis and fulfill these three primary functions has been greatly enhanced by advancements in information technology (IT). For example, computer-aided dispatch (CAD) systems have had a tremendous impact on the ability of the police to analyze and prioritize calls for service. CAD systems automatically collect and organize certain information from every call including the type of call, the location, the time, and the date. When these data sources are linked to others, crime analysts are capable of identifying "hot spots" of crime, detecting patterns of crime and disorder, and identifying factors or conditions that may be contributing to crime.

Most police officers complete handwritten reports on paper. New technology now permits many functions to be completed on computers in vehicles and automatically uploaded to agency computers as the vehicles drive by radio towers. Computerized reports can also permit key words, names, and specific information to be searched among all reports, and similarities can be flagged for further investigation of people and places.

New technologies installed in vehicles allow officers to access maps and allow managers to see where officers are located, at what speed they are driving, and where they have been. These new systems can assist the police function, protect officers, and serve as an accountability feature at the same time. In addition, experiments with license plate and face recognition software are taking place that allow officers while driving to be notified when a person or vehicle license of interest is observed.

The origin of crime mapping goes back to crude statistical analysis: a series of color-coded "push pins" in maps displayed on precinct station walls. Today, the police are able to use geographic information systems (GIS) technology to create maps that show the type of crime, victim information, location, time, and a variety of other criteria, all of which can be compared to census information or other databases containing what would otherwise be unconnected information. These data can be analyzed over time and space for trends or similarities, which can subsequently assist a department with crime detection, crime prediction, and resource analysis, among other things.

## Conclusion

Increased interaction with the community, greater accountability within the police force and to the public, as well as technological advances will all increase and will ultimately have an effect on the police function and how it is carried out. As officers are provided with more time and resources, allowing them to interact more positively with citizens, the police will likely recognize the constructive results of these contacts. Innovative approaches to community mobilization should be designed to empower citizens and build trust in the government. Clearly, the application of technology will provide unique and innovative means of identifying, creating, and updating blueprints for resolving the many problems faced by the police.

## References and Further Readings

Alpert, G., & Dunham, R. (2004). *Understanding police use of force: Officers, suspects, and reciprocity.* New York: Cambridge University Press.

Alpert, G., Kenney, D., Dunham, R., & Smith, W. (2000). *Police pursuits: What we know.* Washington. DC: Police Executive Research Forum.

Alpert, G., MacDonald, J., & Dunham, R. (2005). Police suspicion and discretionary decision making during citizen stops. *Criminology, 43,* 407–434.

Bayley, D. H. (1998). *Policing in America: Assessments and prospects.* Washington, DC: Police Foundation.

Bayley, D. H. (1999). Policing: The world stage. In R. Mawby (Ed.), *Policing across the world: Issues for the twenty-first century* (pp. 3–22). London: UCL Press.

Brenner, A. (1989). Psychological screening of police applicants. In R. G. Dunham & G. P. Alpert (Eds.), *Critical issues in policing: Contemporary readings* (pp. 72–86). Prospect Heights, IL: Waveland Press.

Caiden, G. (1977). *Police revitalization.* Lexington, MA: Lexington Books.

Davis, K. C. (1975). *Police discretion.* St. Paul, MN: West Publishing.

Greenwood, P. W., & Petersilia, J. (1975). *The criminal investigation process: Summary and policy implications.* Santa Monica, CA: RAND.

Langworthy, R. H., & Travis, L. F. (2002). *Policing in America: A balance of forces* (3rd ed.). Upper Saddle River, NJ: Prentice Hall.

Martin, S. (2001). Female officers on the move? A status report of women in policing. In R. G. Dunham & G. P. Alpert (Eds.), *Critical issues in policing: Contemporary readings* (4th ed., pp. 401–422). Prospect Heights, IL: Waveland Press.

Miller, W. R. (1977). *Cops and bobbies: Police authority in New York and London, 1830–1870.* Chicago; University of Chicago Press.

National Center for Women in Policing. (2002). *Men, women, and police excessive force: A tale of two genders. A content analysis of civil liability cases, sustained allegations, and citizen complaints.* Los Angeles: Author.

National Research Council. (2003). *Fairness and effectiveness in policing: The evidence.* Washington, DC: National Academies Press.

Reith, C. (1938). *The police idea: Its history and evolution in England in the eighteenth century and after.* London: Oxford University Press.

Reith, C. (1956). *A new study of police history.* Edinburgh, Scotland: Oliver & Boyd.

Rubinstein, J. (1973). *City police.* New York: Farrar, Straus & Giroux.

Stead, P. (1985). *The police of Britain.* London: Macmillan.

*Tennessee v. Garner,* 471 U.S. 1 (1985).

Uchida, C. D. (1997). The development of the American police: An historical overview. In R. G. Dunham & G. P. Alpert (Eds.), *Critical issues in policing: Contemporary readings* (3rd ed., pp. 18–35). Prospect Heights, IL: Waveland Press.

Van Maanen, J. (1978). Observations on the making of policemen. In P. K. Manning & J. Van Maanen (Eds.), *Policing: A view from the street* (pp. 292–308). Santa Monica, CA: Goodyear.

Walker, S. (1983). *The police in America: An introduction.* New York: McGraw-Hill.

Wilson, J. Q. (1968). *Varieties of police behavior: The management of law and order in eight communities.* Cambridge, MA: Harvard University Press.

# The Idea of Community Policing

## VICTOR E. KAPPELER AND LARRY K. GAINES

## The Community Policing Revolution

Community policing is the first substantive reform in the American police institution since it embraced the professional model more than a century ago. It is a dramatic change in the philosophy that determines the way police agencies engage the public. It incorporates a philosophy that broadens the police mission from a narrow focus on crime and law enforcement to a mandate encouraging the exploration of creative solutions for a host of community concerns—including crime, fear of crime, perceptions of disorder, quality of life, and neighborhood conditions. Community policing, in its ideal form, not only addresses community concerns, but is a philosophy that turns traditional policing on its head by empowering the community rather than dictating to the community. In this sense, policing derives it role and agenda from the community rather than dictating to the community. Community policing rests on the belief that only by working together with people will the police be able to improve quality of life for all members of a community. This implies that the police must assume new roles and go about their business in a very different way. In addition to being law enforcers, they must also serve as advisors, facilitators, supporters, and leaders of new community-based initiatives. The police must begin to see themselves as part of the community rather than separate from the community. In its ideal form, community policing is a grassroots form of participatory democracy, rather than a representative top-down approach to addressing contemporary community life. In this sense, police become active participants in a process that changes power configurations in communities. It challenges and empowers the police to work with ordinary people to bring their real-life problems to those governmental authorities with the capacity to develop meaningful public policy and provide needed services to communities.

### LEARNING OBJECTIVES

After reading the chapter, you should be able to:

- Discuss the ways in which the community impacts the police mandate when a department has implemented community policing.

- Describe why community policing encourages decentralized police service and changes in patrol.

- Discuss the sources of confusion surrounding the implementation of community policing.

- List and describe the four major facets of community policing.

- Understand why community policing is an overarching philosophy, not a technique or program.

- Discuss how community policing entails the

use of discretion and
working with other
agencies to find other
means of dealing with
problematic situations.

- List and discuss what
community policing
does NOT constitute.

- Discuss how com-
munity policing is
sometimes used as a
cover for aggressive
police tactics.

- Describe how commu-
nity policing affects
officer activity.

**Community policing** consists of two primary components: community partnerships and problem solving. It is a partnership or enhanced relationship between the police and the community they serve. It is a partnership in that the police must assist people with a multitude of problems and social conditions including crime, and it is a partnership because the police must solicit support and active participation in dealing with these problems (Wood & Bradley, 2009). It is an enhanced relationship, since the police must deal with substantive issues. Police must go beyond merely responding to crime and calls for service. They must recognize and treat the causes of these problems so that they are resolved. When problems are resolved, there is a higher level of civility and tranquility in a community. Thus, the two primary components of community policing are community partnerships and problem solving. **Community partnerships** are the engagement by the police with the community to cooperatively resolve social problems. On the other hand, **problem solving** is where community policing officers (CPOs) attempt to deal with the conditions that cause crime and negatively affect the quality of life in a community. Problem solving is an important part of community policing.

Community policing also embodies an **organizational strategy** that allows police departments to decentralize service and reorient patrol (Skogan & Hartnett, 1997). The focus is on the police officer who works closely with people and their problems. This CPO has responsibility for a specific beat or geographical area and works as a generalist who considers making arrests as only one of many viable tools, if only temporarily, to address community problems. As the community's conduit for positive change, the CPO enlists ordinary people in the process of policing and improving the quality of life in a community. The CPO serves as the community's ombudsman to other public and private agencies that can offer help. If police officers are given stable assignments to geographical areas, they are able not only to focus on incidents that are problems, but also to become directly involved in strategies that may forestall long-range problems. Also, by giving people the power to set local police agendas, community policing challenges both police officers and community members to cooperate in finding new and creative ways to accurately identify and solve problems in their communities.

What started as an experiment using foot patrols (Trojanowicz, 1982) and problem solving in a few departments (Goldstein, 1990) exploded into a national mandate. As a result of the Violent Crime Control and Law Enforcement Act of 1994 and its provision to fund 100,000 more CPOs, most police departments in the United States now say they ascribe to community policing. In the 1990s, community policing became an institutionalized and publicly understood form of policing (Morabito, 2010; NIJ, 1997; Gallup, 1996). In 2010, Reaves (2010) reported that 53 percent of police departments have community policing as part of their mission statements. As shown in Figure 11.1, community policing has become an important part of policing in all but the smallest departments.

Even the media presented a limited but very positive depiction of community policing (Mastrof-

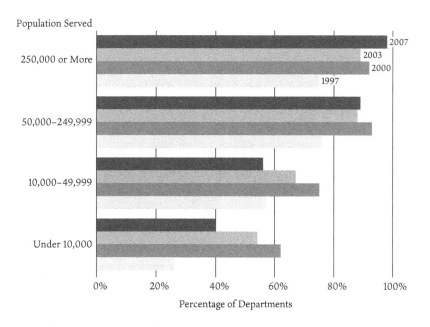

FIGURE 11.1 Local police departments using full-time community policing officers, by size of population served, 1997–2007

*Source*: BJS (2010). *Local Police Departments, 2007*. Washington, DC: U.S. Department of Justice

ski & Ritti, 1999; Chermak & Weiss, 2006). "Community policing, or variations of it, has become the national mantra of American policing. Throughout the United States, the language, symbolism, and programs of community policing have sprung up in urban, suburban, and even rural police departments" (Greene, 2000:301). Additionally, community policing became a standard in many other countries. Police departments all over the world embraced the language of community policing. It has become ingrained throughout departments as managers attempt to develop strategies and tactics to deal with day-to-day issues and community problems.

Despite this impressive progress, many people, both inside and outside police departments, do not know precisely what "community policing" is and what it can do (Chappell, 2009). Although most everyone has heard of community policing, and most police departments say that they have adopted the philosophy, very few actually understand how it works and the possibilities it has for police agencies and communities. Indeed, it is viewed from a number of different perspectives. Is community policing simply a new name for police–community relations? Is it foot patrol? Is it crime prevention? Is it problem solving? Is it a political gimmick, a fad, or a promising trend, or is it a successful new way of policing? Perhaps David Bayley (1988:225) best summarized the confusion about community policing:

> Despite the benefits claimed for community policing, programmatic implementation of it has been very uneven. Although widely, almost universally, said to be important, it means different things to different people—public relations campaigns, shop fronts, and

mini-stations, re-scaled patrol beats, liaisons with ethnic groups, permission for rank-and-file to speak to the press, Neighborhood Watch, foot patrols, patrol-detective teams, and door-to-door visits by police officers. Community policing on the ground often seems less a program than a set of aspirations wrapped in a slogan.

There is substantial confusion surrounding community policing (Colvin & Goh, 2006). It stems from a variety of factors that, if not attended to, can undermine a department's efforts to successfully implement community policing and be responsive to the need of the community. The sources of confusion are:

- Community policing's introduction into American policing has been a long, complicated process. It is rooted in team policing, police–community relations, and crime prevention (Rosenbaum & Lurigio, 1994).
- Some police departments are using community policing as a cover for aggressive law enforcement tactics rather than serving the needs of their communities. When this happens, confusion arises about a police department's real commitment to the community.
- The movement continues to suffer because some police departments claim to have implemented community policing, but they violate the spirit or the letter of what true community policing involves and demands.
- Most police agencies have adopted the language of community policing, but have yet to change their organizational structures and value systems to bring them into line with the community policing philosophy (Kappeler & Kraska, 1998a).
- Community policing threatens the status quo, which always generates resistance and spawns controversy within police organizations (Gaines & Worrall, 2012). This is because community policing challenges basic beliefs in the foundation of traditional policing. It requires substantive changes in the way police officers and commanders think, the organizational structure of departments, and the very definition of police work.
- Community policing may generate public expectations that go unfulfilled, thus creating a backlash against community policing and the department (Klockars, 1988; Manning, 1988).
- Community policing is often confused with problem-oriented policing and community-oriented policing. Community policing is not merely problem-oriented policing or becoming community "oriented." While community policing does use problem-solving approaches, unlike problem-oriented policing, community policing always engages the community in the identification of and solution to problems rather than seeing the police as the sole authority in this process (see Table 11.1).

## The Philosophical and Structural Facets of Community Policing

Although community policing has taken a number of directions, there is a common overarching logic and structure to it. Four major facets occur when community policing is properly implemented: (1) the **philosophical facet**, (2) the **organizational and personnel facet**, (3) the **strategic facet**, and (4) the **programmatic facet** (see Colvin & Goh, 2006). All four facets must exist if a department is indeed implementing community policing. The following section explains the philosophy and structure of community policing.

TABLE 11.1   Selected Comparisons between Problem-Oriented Policing and Community Policing Principles

| Principle | Problem-Oriented Policing | Community Policing |
|---|---|---|
| Primary emphasis | Substantive social problems within police mandate | Engaging the community in the policing process |
| When police and community collaborate | Determined on a problem-by-problem basis | Always or nearly always |
| Emphasis on problem analysis | Highest priority given to thorough analysis | Encouraged, but less important than community collaboration |
| Preference for responses | Strong preference for alternatives to criminal law enforcement be explored | Preference for collaborative responses with community |
| Role for police in organizing and mobilizing community | Advocated only if warranted within the context of the specific problem being addressed | Emphasizes strong role for police |
| Importance of geographic decentralization of police and continuity of officer assignment to community | Preferred, but not essential | Essential |
| Degree to which police share decision-making authority with community | Strongly encourages input from community while preserving ultimate decision-making authority to police | Emphasizes sharing decision-making authority with community |
| Emphasis on officers' skills | Emphasizes intellectual and analytical skills | Emphasizes interpersonal skills |
| View of the role or mandate of police | Encourages broad but not unlimited role for police, stresses limited capacities of police, and guards against creating unrealistic expectations of police | Encourages expansive role for police to achieve ambitious social objectives |

*Source*: Scott, M. (2000). *Problem-Oriented Policing: Reflections on the First 20 Years*, p. 99. Washington, DC: Office of Community-Oriented Policing Services, U.S. Department of Justice

## The Philosophical Facet

Historically, even though there have been sporadic variations in the underpinnings or theme for American law enforcement, it has remained substantively a legal-bureaucratic organization focusing on professional law enforcement (Gaines & Worrall, 2012). Outputs such as numbers of arrests and criminal investigations, reductions and increases in crime rates, volume of recovered property, numbers of citations issued, and a rapid response to calls for service have been more important than the end result of police work. This philosophy translated into a reactive police institution that does little to deal tangibly with social and community problems. A substantial body of research that began in the 1970s questions a number of the basic assumptions associated with the legal-bureaucratic model (Bittner, 1970; Wilson, 1968; Reiss & Bordua, 1967). Consequently, people began to search for a new philosophy and way to envision and conduct police work.

Philosophically, community policing consists of a number of community-based elements that differentiate it from the traditional professional model. Some of community policing's core ideas are: (1) **broad police function and community focus**, (2) **community input** (3) **concern for people**, (4) **developing trust**, (5) **sharing power**, (6) **creativity**, and (7) **neighborhood variation**.

**BROAD POLICE FUNCTION AND COMMUNITY FOCUS** Community policing is a philosophy of policing, based on the concept that police officers and people working together in creative ways can help solve contemporary community problems related to crime, fear of crime, quality of life, and neighborhood conditions. The philosophy is predicated on the belief that achieving these goals requires that police departments develop a new relationship with people by expanding their role in the community, allowing ordinary people the power to set local police priorities, and involving them in efforts to improve the overall quality of life in their neighborhoods. It shifts the focus of police work from responding to random crime calls to proactively addressing community needs and concerns (see Figure 11.2).

Community policing dictates that police departments move from law enforcement or crime fighting as the primary function. The police should have a **broader function** that incorporates fear reduction, reasonable community-based order maintenance, and community health. Indeed, fear reduction, order maintenance, and a community's overall health become the primary goals for the department, supplanting crime reduction and effecting arrests as the central organizing themes of

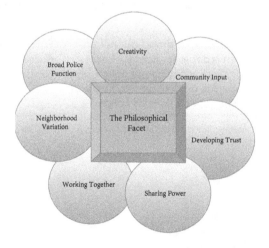

FIGURE 11.2 The philosophical facet of community policing

*Source*: Authors

police work. Research demonstrates that community policing can reduce people's fear of crime and enhance feelings of security and safety (Weisburd & Eck, 2004; Roh & Oliver, 2005).

This change in police philosophy emanates from three general observations. First, research examining police operations and crime statistics shows that police are not effective, nor will they become effective, in controlling crime by law enforcement alone. Crime is largely a product of socio-economic conditions and poor public policy; therefore, it cannot be controlled through police action alone. Crime can be affected only through the control and manipulation of social conditions and enlightened public policy. The police can, at best, only manage, document, and push around most crime. Order maintenance and addressing the health of a community are legitimate police goals in themselves. For the police to have an impact on crime they must first impact the social conditions and public policies that generate crime.

Second, fear has a far greater debilitating effect on a community or individuals than does actual crime or crime rates. In fact, most people don't even know when actual crime rates are rising or falling within their community. They often only see the "signs" of crime that cause fear. The fear of crime results in persons becoming virtual prisoners in their own homes; it inhibits commerce; and it imposes a subtle psychological cost to everyone (Hale, 1996). Fear destroys community because it isolates people and causes apprehension and suspicion. Research shows that oftentimes an individual's fear of crime bears no relationship to the actual amount of crime or victimization (Jackson & Gray, 2010). The traditional approach to fear reduction, however, has been to attack crime and criminals, hoping that reducing crime will ultimately lessen fear. Because traditional policing relies primarily on motor patrol, which is basically reactive, there are obvious structural limitations that make it difficult to provide an effective means of confronting fear of crime separately and directly. The simple fact of the matter is that most crime in American society is not committed or solved on the streets, nor is it committed by strangers in public places (Kappeler & Potter, 2005). The types of crimes the police have historically addressed are only a fraction of the crime problem. Though crime prevention and police–community relations programs have helped broaden the traditional police role in ways that impinge on fear of crime, these peripheral attempts tended to chip away at problems that demand a bulldozer. Police-sponsored fear-reduction programs have the potential to yield positive results in a number of areas: community participation in crime prevention programs, increased crime reporting, and positive relations with people (see Zhao et al., 2002).

Community policing recognizes that fear of crime can be as much of a problem as crime itself. It is fear of crime that can trap the elderly in their homes or can make people afraid to venture out alone. Traditional policing efforts have had little, if any, ability to reduce fear. Until the last few decades, fear of crime was not even a consideration or objective in traditional policing. Periodically the police would make arrests that might have had a short-lived impact on fear, but, for the most part, people sustained a fairly significant level of fear for which the police did little. Adding to the problem, political leaders often used the fear of crime to garner support by pandering to "law and order" or "get tough" approaches to crime that have little real effect on the crime problem. This fear adversely affected people's daily lives. An important ingredient in community policing is active police involvement with people through a wide range of programs designed to reduce fear. Police must get people out of their homes and get actively involved in their communities. This means police must become directly involved in community activities and become the organizers of community. Police must also be careful not to promote unnecessary fear of crime to gain short-lived political and community support. Even more important, the police must address the sources that cause fear of crime—most often the politicization of crime and the media's distortion of crime (Kappeler & Potter, 2005). Historically, political leaders and the media used fear of crime to promote their own interests and agendas. Today, they use terrorism and the fear of terrorism for much the same purposes.

Third, we have long debated the primary role of the police in society (Wilson, 1968; Manning, 1997; Bittner, 1970), and over the past 40 years we have come to the point whereby everyone accepts that the police role has expanded well beyond law enforcement and "crook catching." In fact, reviews of police activities show that the majority of calls and the vast amount of time police spend on the job have little to do with actual crime (see Gaines & Kappeler, 2014). The advent of community policing has resulted in a broader police mission evolving. Today, police should see crime, fear of crime, and the general quality of life all as being important parts of the police mission. Indeed, all of these societal factors are intertwined and interact with one another to determine the health of a community.

**COMMUNITY INPUT** The police have traditionally developed and implemented programs that involved community members. For the most part, however, these programs bordered on public relations schemes with little consideration given to community or human needs. Team policing programs of the 1970s and some of the police–community relations programs of earlier years never seriously involved and considered people; for the most part, the police were concerned with educating the public about their own needs rather than listening to the public about community needs. One of the most difficult aspects of community policing is determining the needs, concerns, and desires of the community. Real community policing requires the police to set aside their own agendas to fairly and accurately measure the needs of the communities they serve. This requires not only listening to people but also acting on their concerns.

Community policing employs methods that cause the police to work more closely with people. To develop a better relationship, police departments have attempted to collect information about people's attitudes toward crime problems and the effectiveness of the police. For example, the police in Baltimore County, Reno, Atlanta, Newport News, St. Louis, and other cities have requested that community members complete surveys. Other departments have attempted to collect information by holding town or neighborhood meetings or by regularly meeting with minority and business groups. Gathering information from people allows the police to accomplish several tasks. Survey information can be used to evaluate the effectiveness of police programs in terms of fear reduction or attitudes toward the police. They also gauge behavior such as victimization or crime prevention efforts. Finally, they can also be used to collect data to assist the police in establishing community goals and priorities (Peak & Glensor, 2007). Community policing gets people involved in developing communities through two-way communication. Only by engaging the people and by collecting information from them can the police begin to understand the real needs and concerns of the community and begin to develop a community-based agenda rather than merely fostering traditional police agendas.

**CONCERN FOR PEOPLE** The professional model of policing was institutionalized in the early 1900s. It dictated that police officers remain aloof and detached from the people they served. Police administrators believed that, if officers were "professional" in their interactions with people, as defined by this aloofness and detachment, then there would be less possibility of police corruption and political intervention into police affairs, which were two significant problems at the time (Bracey, 1992). The professional model resulted in police departments and police officers having little concern or knowledge about community and neighborhood problems. Officers acted more like robots who responded to one call after another, calculated whether laws were violated, and made arrests or filed reports. This detachment resulted in people having little confidence in the police and it negatively affected police departments' ability to serve communities.

Police officers, to be effective, must be genuinely concerned with the welfare of people and the community. The primary role of the police is not to arrest people, write citations, or answer calls. These activities are merely tools by which to accomplish the police's primary objective, ensuring the safety, domestic tranquility, and health of a community. This equates to the police being concerned with people and their problems. It means the police must understand community problems and effectively respond to them.

**DEVELOPING TRUST** Community policing suggests that, to get "the facts," the police must do more than attempt to impose their authority and sense of order on a community, that they must find new ways to promote cooperation between community members and the police. Information is the lifeblood of both traditional and community policing. Without information, police officers cannot solve crimes or social problems. The challenge the police face in getting information is that there must be a high level of trust for people to cooperate with the police. Historically, the affluent and middle-class segments of a community had a great deal of trust for their police, but relationships with most poor and minorities left a great deal to be desired (Kappeler et al., 1998; Carter, 1985; Scaglion & Condon, 1980). In many instances, the police were seen as armed, uniformed strangers who could hurt you, but would not help you. The police were imposing and often intimidating. For far too many in the community and for far too many years, contact with the police could lead to nothing good. Today, officers must continue fostering better relations with all segments of society. They must attempt to gain all community members' trust so that they can also gain their cooperation.

A prime example of the trust problem occurred in New Orleans in the mid-1990s. During that period, the police department was rife with corruption and the police were known for their brutality. The police essentially were out of control. The problem came to a culmination with the shooting of a police officer by another officer who was committing an armed robbery. During the period, people had good reason not to trust the police. Some people stated that, when cases went to court, they would have more faith in the defendants' testimony than that of police officers. Not only was there a lack of trust of the police, but people were afraid of them. After national attention and substantial public outcry, the city began a reform of the police department. History shows that it is a long and arduous process for a police department to reform itself and regain public support and trust once it is lost (Kappeler, Sluder & Alpert, 1998).

In contrast, a central part of community policing is building trust with the entire community. An important strategy is for community officers to directly communicate with as many individuals and groups of people as possible. CPOs not only portray themselves as friends and partners in the community—they must become friends and partners with the community. This philosophy ultimately fosters greater trust and cooperation.

**SHARING POWER** The third dramatic departure from the past is that a community policing agenda is influenced by the community's needs and desires, not just the dictates of the department. Historically, politicians and police administrators have set the agenda for policing, often without any regard or input from the people who were being policed. Policing in this manner is little more than occupation and comes to be a source of resentment by the community. The police, from chief to line police officer, must recognize that people have a legitimate right to make demands on the police and control their agenda. Police departments, in addition to being law enforcement organizations, are service organizations and, as such, they should provide the best level of service possible. This means asking all community members, not just those supportive of the police or those with political or economic power, about the kinds and levels of services they need and want. There is a wide divide in American society between those who have power and those who experience the victimization of crime—power sharing can close this divide.

Empowering a community requires an important adjustment in the line officer's thinking. Traditional officers who believe their authority should be sufficient to demand compliance may find it difficult to make the shift to sharing power as demanded by community policing. A traditional officer might find it difficult or unwieldy to chat with people about seemingly petty concerns, but this is an important part of community policing. It builds a bond between the police and community members, and it allows officers to gather information about what they should be doing to serve their communities (Reisig & Parks, 2004). The best CPOs understand that people are not obstacles that the officer must overcome to do the job, but a tremendous resource that can be tapped to make the community a safer, more harmonious environment. It also takes the sustained presence of a CPO to persuade people that the department now sees them in this new light, and that there is a real commitment to **sharing power**.

The community policing challenge includes involving people directly in efforts to identify and solve problems in the community. Community policing is not just a tactic to make people the eyes and ears of the department, but it solicits their direct participation in identifying and solving problems. In this regard, community policing goes well beyond other programs such as foot patrol, neighborhood watch, crime prevention, or police–community relations. It might mean encouraging volunteers to help staff the local office. It could mean urging groups of parents to volunteer their time to coach summer athletic activities for kids. It often means asking businesses to donate goods, services, or expertise for neighborhood projects. Perhaps more importantly, it means organizing people to bring pressure on policymakers who have ignored community problems. The goal is for the CPO to recruit as many volunteers as possible and to organize them, so that the community has dozens of people working together to make a difference. Generating community involvement is one of the most difficult aspects of community policing (Skogan & Hartnett, 1997) but it is essential.

**CREATIVITY** Community policing can work in any kind of police department, from large municipalities to small towns. Community policing can be successful because it is not a static program. It represents a philosophy whereby problems are identified and the community, not just the police, determines strategies and tactics to address them. As Weisburd and Eck (2004) advise, police officers must possess a variety of tools with which to deal with community problems. Community policing, in its ideal sense, is a form of accountable creativity whereby officers are allowed to experiment with a variety of tactics that directly involve people (Spelman, 2004). Community input and participation can be a rich source of innovation and creativity—it opens up possibilities that the police and political leaders may never consider. Since community members come from all walks of life and have a rich diversity of knowledge and occupational experience, they can be a vital source of innovation. If police view people as "know-nothings" who have little knowledge or nothing to contribute, then innovation and creativity is not really possible. Accountability is interjected into the process because officers are forced not only to successfully address specific problems and community concerns but also to seek community involvement in possible solutions. This is a departure from traditional policing whereby a police department had a limited repertoire of enforcement-based programs, and all problems were essentially addressed using the same strategies and tactics. Also, officers in traditional policing were evaluated on response times, the numbers of arrests they made, the numbers of citations they issued and how many convictions they obtained. These measures have little to do with community policing or the quality of police work (Stephens, 1996). Community policing demands that the people become the judges of the quality of police service, rather than just relying on the crime accounting practices of the past.

**NEIGHBORHOOD VARIATION** Traditional, professional policing mandated that officers disavow the existence of discretion, and police attempted to create the appearance that they handled every situation and neighborhood as if they were the same. That is, the police cultivated the image of full or uniform enforcement of the law. This, however, has never been a reality in policing. There has always existed variation in law enforcement and service delivery across communities and different neighborhoods and among diverse people (Williamson, Ashby & Webber, 2006). Community policing, on the other hand, recognizes that a political jurisdiction is composed of a number of communities or neighborhoods, each with its own set of problems and expectations. Suttles (1972) notes that people develop "cognitive maps" where they designate certain places as theirs, or their neighborhood. Stable neighborhoods have relative homogeneity of activity, people, and values. Because neighborhoods are defined by ethnic, religious, and socioeconomic factors and geographical boundaries, differential expectations evolve within neighborhoods. Particular neighborhoods develop expectations not only about what the police should do, but also about what types of behavior by residents and nonresidents is acceptable or unacceptable—police cannot afford to ignore these variations.

Community policing dictates that the police follow the "will of the community" when dealing with situations and enforcing the law. This means that police must first learn to accurately read the will of the community rather than projecting their will onto the community. This requires the police to get out of their cars, engage the community, collect information, and begin a dialog with the people living in the neighborhoods they serve. It also requires the police to become more open minded and think outside their comfort zone, occupation filters, and their own socialization. For the most part, there is little variation in how the police react to serious crimes or felonies. However, the police must be cognizant of community standards when policing minor infractions of the law and dealing with activities that may be acceptable in one neighborhood, but not another. For example, a person working on his car while parked on the street would not be acceptable in many upper-class neighborhoods, but it is a way of life for many people residing in poor neighborhoods. Police must begin to realize these variations and that the law is a tool that can be used to either build community or to cause conflict. Police officers must rely on community or neighborhood standards when encountering such situations. The police must maintain a balance between neighborhood values and overall legal goals and objectives. A poor person cited by the police for repairing a car on the street is not very likely to be either supportive of the police or to provide much needed information to solve a serious crime. In this situation police have not gained a partner or supporter but rather alienated a member of the community. The overall mission of the police should not be subordinated to the issuance of a traffic ticket or the enforcement of a city ordinance. Police must recognize variation in communities and use the law as a responsive tool rather than a tool of repression.

## The Organizational and Personnel Facet

Community policing requires both a philosophical shift in the way that police think about their mission, as well as a commitment to the structural changes this form of policing demands. Police organizations must decentralize their organizations to be more responsive to the community. Community policing provides a new way for the police to provide decentralized and personalized service that offers every community member an opportunity to become active in the policing process. In this way, people who have been isolated or disenfranchised, either because of economics or the lack of political power, can have both a voice in police activities and an interest in the development and health of their community. Community policing can help mitigate some of the harsh realities of modern life. Community policing is more than involving people in crime control; it is active involvement in enhancing the health of the community (see Figure 11.3).

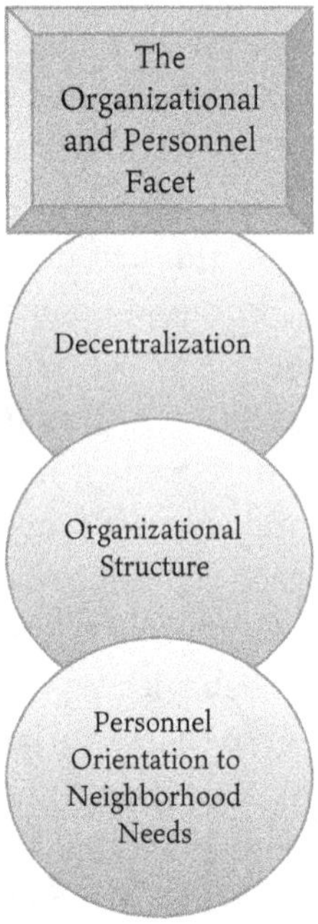

This helps explain why it is crucial to understand that community policing is a philosophy that offers a coherent strategy that departments can use to guide them in making the structural changes that allow the concept to become real. Community policing is not just a tactic that can be applied to solve a particular problem—one that can be abandoned once the goal is achieved. It implies a profound difference in the way the police view their role and their relationship with the community. Just adopting one or more tactics associated with community policing is not enough. Police must change their organizational structures, modify their personnel's orientation, and adjust their value systems to allow for community policing.

A police department's philosophy sets the stage for the development and implementation of strategies and specific tactics. A philosophical change, as required with the implementation of community policing, generally is enumerated in a department's mission statement. Mission statements should endorse the most essential aspect of the community policing philosophy: giving people the power to set the agenda and developing people-based accountability of the police. Also a mission statement must find its expression in coherent strategies. That is, strategies must be employed that will further the overarching philosophy or mission of the department. In fact, Reaves (2010) found that 53 percent of departments have a community policing policy. This means that about half of American police departments have not formally endorsed community policing as an organizational imperative. A philosophy serves as the department's rudder, which helps guide the department as it serves the public.

FIGURE 11.3 The organizational and personnel facet of community policing

*Source*: Authors

Community officers answer calls and make arrests, just like any other police officer, but these activities are done in a knowing and purposive way and actually are only a small part of the job. The community policing officer acts as an innovator, looking beyond individual crime incidents for new ways to solve problems. They are the police department's direct link to the community, providing policing with a human touch as an officer who people know on a first-name basis and as a friend who can help. They act as catalysts, involving people in efforts to police themselves. They are mini-chiefs in beat areas, with the autonomy to do what it takes to solve problems. They are referral specialists, the community's ombudsman who can link people to the public and private services that can help and who can jog reluctant bureaucracies to do the jobs they are supposed to do.

The hallmark of community policing is that policing is tailored to neighborhood needs. In some programs, the officers operate out of offices in schools, public housing, or even in shopping malls. Police service and access are decentralized so that the police are more approachable to community members. When the police are accessible, people are more likely to cooperate with them, to have a reduced fear of crime, and to provide crime-related information.

Some officers walk the beat, while others may ride a horse or a bike; and yes, they may even ride in a patrol car. The mode of transportation is not as important as the commitment to ensuring that the officer has the time and opportunity to talk and be with people formally and informally. The police mode of transportation is merely the vehicle by which officers get into contact with the members of their community.

## SPOTLIGHT ON COMMUNITY POLICING PRACTICE

**Community Policing: Home Sweet Home**

It's been nearly 20 years since the Racine (WI) Police Department embraced the community policing philosophy and changed how the organization delivers police services. Their approach? Where crime was its worst was where the police department wanted to be. Rather than saturating officers to a crime hot spot, they moved in. Literally. "We explored the storefront idea," said Deputy Chief Smetana, "but, we could never get what we wanted." So instead, the police department decided to invest in the community by building its own house and setting an example for the neighborhood. Making this possible was state funding directed towards local initiatives and a partnership with the Racine Community Outpost, a local non-profit organization currently run by three retired Racine officers: Dave Voss, Marty DeFatte, and former Chief Richard Polzin.

The purpose of these Community Oriented Policing (COP) Houses is long-term stabilization by way of building relationships with the community, improving the quality of life, reducing crime, consolidating resources, and providing programming. The COP Houses have become an anchor of their community. Initially, the communities were not enthusiastic. The first House was built in a drug-infested neighborhood and was firebombed. But now they have become a hub of positive activity. "If we asked the community," said Lt. Mark Esch, "we would have ten. Everyone wants one in their neighborhood." Today there are six.

The COP Houses have served as catalysts of change, leading to improved property maintenance and lower crime. In some COP House neighborhoods crime has been reduced up to 70 percent. And, it is crime that is one of the primary driving forces behind where a COP House is located. The criteria for establishing a community policing house is based on factors such as Part I crime, calls for service, and nuisance calls for service. "After being through some years of having 18–19 homicides and shots fired," said Deputy Chief Smetana, "calls for service are now complaints about loud car stereos."

Being assigned to a COP House has become a premier assignment in the department, with only 12 positions available among the 202 sworn personnel. Officers go through a competitive application and interview process. They need to demonstrate their communication and problem-solving skills. "Our agency has emphasized problem-solving throughout the department. It comes from the top down and we promote qualified candidates with an emphasis on the importance of problem-solving," said Deputy Chief Smetana. "What we look for is self-motivated officers and we give them the latitude and freedom to make decisions." Officers realize it's labor intensive work, but rewarding. Their focus is helping people and this is a chance for them to do that in a specific neighborhood and see the fruits of their efforts every day.

The COP Houses also serve as "Positive Alternative Centers," providing a positive and structured environment focused on learning. The police department provides the classroom and a computer lab, while the program provides everything from help with homework to arts and crafts. Every semester students from local Carthage College volunteer their time to the program and the kids. Carthage even offers independent study credits to students who become leaders of the program—that's how much emphasis and value they place on the partnership.

Through the establishment of the COP Houses, "the police department is closer to the community, closer to their neighbors, and cooperation is tremendous," said Deputy Chief Smetana. "The community feels comfortable because they trust us."

Amy Schapiro
Senior Social Science Analyst
The COPS Office

*Source*: The e-newsletter of the COPS Office, Volume 4, Issue 4, April 2011

## The Strategic Facet

The police must develop strategies by which to implement the philosophy of community policing. Strategies provide guidelines for the development of specific programs. Community policing has at least three strategic facets. These facets include: (1) **geographic focus and co-ownership**, (2) direct, daily, **face-to-face contact**, and (3) **prevention focus** (Figure 11.4). These three parameters should guide operational planning when implementing community policing.

**GEOGRAPHIC FOCUS AND CO-OWNERSHIP** Traditional law enforcement focuses on time, function, and place as opposed to geographies within a community. In terms of time, police departments revolve around shift work. Patrol officers, detectives, and other officers are assigned to shifts. Police effectiveness is measured by activities across time, that is, what occurred on a particular shift. In terms of function, police departments are highly specialized with a number of different units—patrol, criminal investigation, traffic, community relations, etc.—responsible for their own unique tasks. Officers assigned to one functional area seldom have the time or inclination to work on or worry about activities that fall into another functional area. In fact, typically only the chief in small and medium departments and precinct commanders in large departments have full responsibility for a given geographical area. Specialization by time and task inhibits the evaluation, or even articulation, of policing at the neighborhood level.

For community policing to be successful, there must be some level of geographical permanence. Officers must work a geographical area on a permanent basis so that they become familiar with residents, activities, and social problems. Geography is not a sole matter of place, territory, or location; it is the product of complex human interactions. Furthermore, if police officers are permanently assigned to an area, they hopefully will come to identify with the area and take greater care in safeguarding it and working to solve its problems. While the **territorial imperative** does not end, police must begin to understand the human geography of the areas in which they work. Command staff must also come to identify with and take responsibility for "geographical" areas. Once there is a level of geographical accountability within police departments, officers and units will respond more effectively to human and neighborhood needs and demands.

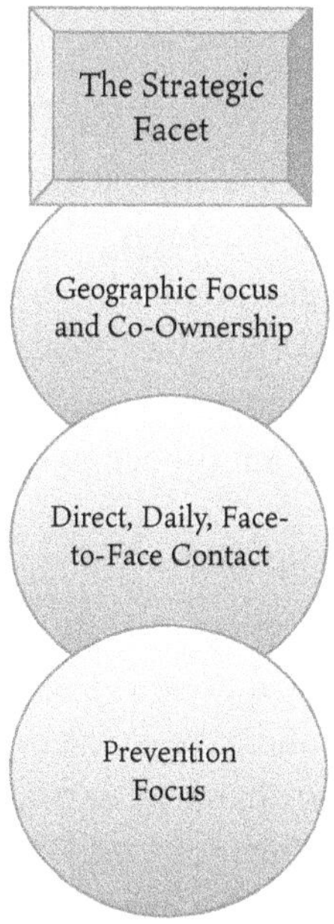

The importance of stationing a CPO permanently in a specific beat rests on allowing the officer to co-own that particular piece of turf and to begin to understand how that space is created and given meaning by human subjects who interact and actually create the contours of a space. The optimal size of each beat can differ dramatically from place to place, but it will always involve people and human interactions. The goal is to keep the geographic area small enough so that the officer can get around the entire beat often enough to maintain direct contact with the people who create it. In high-density areas, an officer might only be able to handle a few blocks at most, while in a relatively tranquil residential area of single-family homes, the officer's ability to cover the physical distance might be the primary limiting factor.

**FIGURE 11.4** The strategic facet of community policing

*Source:* Authors

Another important consideration in setting up beats is for the department to identify areas of community cohesion. Whenever possible, it pays to not divide a distinct neighborhood so that it falls into two or more beats. Along these same lines, it is not a good idea to have more than one distinct neighborhood group in the same beat. The goal is to decentralize police service by dividing the area into natural and manageable units that are derived from human interactions, not maps, so that people can receive quality police service regardless of whether they live in little-town, Texas, or mid-town Manhattan. Beats should be as homo geneous and natural as possible and not based solely on the frequency of crime in a given area. Crime is only one human social interaction that creates geography, not the sole determinate, and, in many cases, not even the most important one.

A major misunderstanding about community policing stems from the misconception that the reward reaped for freeing officers from patrol cars transforms them into visible deterrents to crime. While that may be seen as a useful by-product of freeing officers from the patrol car or even a specific tactic in a high-crime area, the more important purpose is to involve the officer in the life of the community. This allows officers to integrate into the community. Obviously, the size of the beat significantly affects the quality of this integration process.

**DIRECT, DAILY, FACE-TO-FACE CONTACT** Community policing also rests on maintaining the same officers in the same beat every day. The goal is to involve officers so deeply in the life of the community that the officers feel responsible for what happens in their beats, and the people who live there learn to trust them and work with them, and hold them accountable for their successes and failures. Community officers should not be used to back-fill vacancies elsewhere in the department, nor should they be frequently rotated in and out of different beats. The only way that community policing can work is when both the officers and the residents can count on a continued, daily presence. This breeds familiarity on the part of the officers and community members, which is an important ingredient in community policing.

There is considerable debate around the question of whether community officers should be allowed to use cars for at least part of their shifts, simply to get around their beat areas more quickly. The optimal situation allows officers to walk or ride a horse, motor-scooter, or bicycle around the beat area, at least some of the time. These modes of transportation make it easy to stop and chat and to reassure people that the officer is concerned with them and their problems. Freeing officers from patrol cars altogether may be an essential step in reversing the pitfalls of traditional policing. The foot patrol studies in Flint, Michigan, affirmed this important concept (Trojanowicz, 1982).

The danger in the traditional system's over-reliance on the patrol car is that it becomes a barrier to communication with people in the community. Officers trapped inside cars are segregated from the public. They become slaves to the police radio, which serves less as a link to people in the community and more as a means for the department to control the officers' behavior and activities. This is especially true in large cities where officers run from one dispatched call to another. In some cities, officers never have the opportunity to talk with pedestrians or business owners in their beat areas.

**PREVENTION FOCUS** As previously alluded to, community policing dictates that the police be proactive rather than reactive to problems and situations. A crucial part of proactive policing is prevention. Prevention is a much more attractive alternative when dealing with crime as compared to enforcement because it reduces the level of victimization in a community. Prevention subsumes a number of operational possibilities. Prevention refers to ferreting out the problems and conditions that cause crime. In essence, the police must examine the conditions surrounding crime in an effort to develop effective measures of eliminating it. This requires thinking about crime in a very different way. For hundreds of years, police have seen crime as a product of the individual actions of "bad" people who make the decision to engage in crime, rather than viewing crime as convergence of an act of "agency" (the ability to freely choose) that is carried out under "structural" conditions (the social, political, and economic conditions that guide a decision). Patrol, criminal investigation, and other operational units must become actively involved in prevention and seeing the structural and social conditions that contribute to the crime equation. Crime prevention units in police departments must become more involved and broaden their range of activities. Historically, crime prevention in a given police agency has centered on a few activities such as home and business surveys, neighborhood watches, and presentations to the community. Crime prevention units must become more active, and, in addition to regular target-hardening activities, CPOs should assist operational units by serving as a resource when dealing with specific crime problems or **hot spots**, and they should work closely with crime analysis and operational units to identify crime, problems, and solutions.

A part of a police department's crime prevention responsibility includes attacking the conditions that contribute to, or result in, crime. Police departments must take the lead in implementing programs that attack causes of crime. Here, the police can assume a number of social welfare roles. Police departments now have programs to assist and refer people in need to appropriate social welfare agencies; they have initiated educational and recreational programs aimed at providing wholesome life skills experiences for underprivileged youth; and, in some cases, police departments have begun to provide direct services to the needy. Crime prevention also means helping people at risk attain a minimum standard of living.

## The Programmatic Facet

The above philosophy and strategies must be operationalized into specific tactics or programs. For the most part, community policing comes to life through: (1) **reoriented police operations**, (2) **problem solving** and **situational crime prevention**, and (3) **community engagement** (Figure 11.5).

**REORIENTED POLICE OPERATIONS** The traditional police response to crime primarily consisted of random, routine patrols. It was believed that random patrols would deter crime through a consistent, unpredictable police presence. If patrols were unable to prevent crime, then officers, as a result of their distribution across beats, would be in a good position to observe the criminal activity and apprehend criminals. Finally, if this failed, detectives would be dispatched to investigate the crime and make arrests.

Community policing requires going beyond this reactive strategy. It means not waiting to be called, but instead identifying and targeting problems and implementing solutions. Police operational units must use foot patrols, directed patrols, surveys, and alternatives to random patrol to target community problems. In other words, the police must devise and implement police strategies based on the problems at hand. Community policing requires the police to tailor services to community needs. The police must ensure that they have an intensified police presence through larger numbers of positive community contacts.

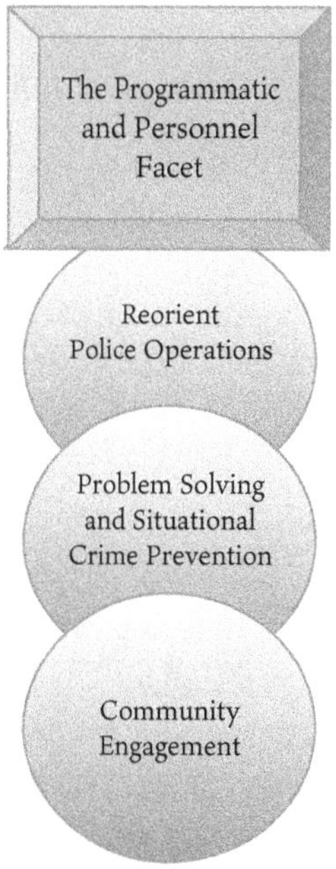

**PROBLEM SOLVING AND SITUATIONAL CRIME PREVENTION** Two primary tactics in community policing include problem solving (Eck & Spelman, 1987) and situational crime prevention (Clarke, 1992). Problem-oriented policing evolved as a result of the writings of Herman Goldstein and work by the Police Executive Research Forum (PERF). Goldstein (1979, 1990) observed that American police had devolved into call-takers. That is, police officers typically responded rapidly to calls for service, attempted to deal with problems or issues as quickly as possible, and then returned to their cars so as to be available to respond

FIGURE 11.5 The programmatic and personnel facet of community policing

*Source:* Authors

to another call. Goldstein noted that the police did little substantively when responding to calls for service and, if the police were to be effective, officers must devote more time and attention to calls. They must attempt to understand the issue at hand and provide some meaningful, not just short-term, solution. In other words, the police should engage in problem solving, rather than focusing solely on responding. Goldstein's idea evolved into problem solving, which now falls under the broader umbrella of community policing.

Problem solving consists of the following four-step process: (1) specific identification of the problem, (2) careful analysis of the problem and its attributes, (3) identification of possible solutions, and (4) implementation of a solution and a subsequent evaluation to measure the effectiveness of the solution. Simple questions, such as "What is the problem?," "What is causing the problem?," and "What can I do to resolve it?," should be asked by officers when attempting to address problems. Effective solutions require comprehensive responses. When effective problem solving occurs, solutions that go beyond traditional police responses become the norm. Such solutions include encouraging the city to demolish an abandoned building being used as a crack house; strictly enforcing alcohol laws in and around bars and taverns that experience high levels of violent crime; addressing the problem of housing for the homeless; or encouraging people to construct fences around residential areas to prevent transients from entering the neighborhood and committing property crimes. Problem-solving ventures beyond responding to and documenting calls. It represents a sincere attempt by the police to eliminate the conditions and problems that result in community problems and calls to the police.

Situational crime prevention, a form of problem solving, comprises

> opportunity-reducing measures that: (1) are directed at highly specific forms of crime, (2) involve the management, design, or manipulation of the immediate environment in as systematic and permanent a way as possible, and (3) reduce the rewards as perceived by a wide range of offenders.

> (Clarke, 1992:4)

Adherents to situational crime prevention believe that crime is a product of "rational choice," where criminals weigh the likelihood of being discovered with the potential benefits of the act (Cornish & Clarke, 1987). They believe increases in difficulty in committing crime or likelihood of apprehension result in reduced levels of crime. This approach, however, does not really get at the social and structural conditions that co-determine crime. Often it only diverts or displaces crime from one location to another and does not involve community development as a crime prevention effort. While situational crime prevention and problem solving play a role in community policing, they are not by themselves community policing. By altering the environment or increasing the probability of detection, this push away from crime may not be as strong as the economic, structural and social conditions that pull one towards crime. And, needless to say, all crimes are not rational or the product of rational choices.

In essence, community policing requires that police officers be creative when devising solutions and attacking community problems. Police must think "outside the box" and beyond the simple deterrence philosophy by considering nontraditional solutions to community problems. Too often, police officers restrict their thinking to the same old responses to problems. Problem solving requires a substantial amount of innovativeness, and police managers must give officers the freedom to innovate.

**COMMUNITY ENGAGEMENT** Community engagement implies that the police must depart from the professional model, and work with individuals and groups. Community policing dictates that the community become involved in protecting itself. People must realize that crime is not the exclusive domain of the police and government. People can become involved in a variety of ways. They can form neighborhood watches or patrols, report criminal or suspicious activities, become involved in sports or educational activities for disadvantaged youth, assist nongovernmental agencies in providing social services to the disadvantaged, or volunteer services. The police must encourage, motivate, or otherwise induce people to become involved in their communities. This is best with police supporting opportunities for involvement. In other words, create a need, and the police and the community will fulfill it with the appropriate amount of effort.

The police must also become involved in community building and empowerment. In some cases, a neighborhood or community will be so disorganized that it does not have the resources to become involved in helping itself. In these instances, the police must engage the community, identify leaders, and begin building the community. The police must work with religious and civic leaders to increase the level of neighborhood self-governance, and they must work to improve governance even when a neighborhood has a strong infrastructure. There should be a reduction in crime concomitant with increases in local governance. In essence, the police must assist in building a neighborhood's ability to ward off crime.

Community engagement is often best accomplished through the establishment of partnerships. Not only must the police partner with community and neighborhood leaders, but the police must also work with other governmental and private agencies. Many governmental agencies have not embraced the concept of community policing. Rather, they still view their roles in the community as bureaucracies whose purpose is to follow bureaucratic rules when serving clients. The police must be leaders in identifying partner agencies and encouraging their involvement in addressing community problems.

The above sections provide a theoretical foundation for community policing. Community policing, as a model, is very complex because it entails implementation throughout a police department, not just selected units or officers. It is complex because it requires that the police department, at a number of levels, be in synchronization with the community it serves. Finally, it is complex because it requires not only that police agencies do different things (i.e. meet with the community, allow the community to decide police operations, or emphasize community health over law enforcement), but it also means that police departments perform many of their old tasks differently.

There is an obvious danger in suggesting that police administrators can consider the elements that make up community policing as a shopping list from which they can pick and choose the things that sound easy to adopt and ignore those that are difficult to implement. [...] Yet, community policing can and must take different forms in different areas, depending on the internal dynamics of the department and the external situations in the community (Gaines & Kappeler, 2014). Ultimately, the sincerity of the commitment to the philosophy probably matters more than the particular strategies or tactics, and some departments may have good reason to phase in aspects of community policing over time.

# What Community Policing Does Not Constitute

The above sections provide a fairly in-depth discussion of the idea of community policing. Community policing is a comprehensive philosophy that affects every person and part of a police department. It is also an overarching philosophy that dictates a department's operational strategies and tactics. To reinforce understanding of what community policing is, it is important to understand what community policing does not constitute. By understanding what does not constitute community policing, we get a better idea of what needs to occur if it is to be implemented correctly.

*Community policing is not a technique.* Many police departments have moved away from the old quasi-military model, but many others are rapidly embracing military tactics under the language of community policing (Kappeler & Kraska, 1998b; Kraska & Kappeler, 1997). Additional movement and redirection by many departments is required if they are to embrace the spirit of community policing successfully. Regardless, community policing is not a technique that departments can apply to a specific problem, but an entirely new way of thinking about the role of the police in the community. It says that the police must focus on addressing community concerns rather than their own agendas.

*Community policing is not public relations.* Improved public relations are a welcome by-product of community policing, though not its sole or even primary goal. Public relations units, however, tended not to attempt to help the community or focus on community needs, but rather they were designed to "sell" the police department. The underlying philosophy was that a substantial amount of dissatisfaction with the police was the result of people not understanding the police and the difficulties facing them as they enforce the law (Wintersmith, 1976). Police–community relations programs were seen as vehicles to educate the public and lessen the strains between the police and community. Community policing, on the other hand, enhances the department's image because it is a sincere change in the way in which the department interacts with people in the community. Police–community relations, by and large, was appearance, while community policing is substantive. It treats people as partners and establishes a new relationship based on mutual trust and shared power. The traditional system often makes people feel that the police do not care about their needs (see, Reisig & Parks, 2000; Sampson & Jeglum-Bartusch, 1998). In traditional departments, officers often see people in the community as "them," those nameless and faceless strangers whose reluctance to cooperate and share what they know makes them indistinguishable from the criminals (see Van Maanen, 2006). Community policing instead treats people in the community as an extension of "us."

*Community policing is not soft on crime.* Critics suggest that community policing's broad mandate, its focus on the community as opposed to crime, and its use of tactics other than arrest to solve problems detract from a proper focus on serious crime. CPOs often face ridicule from fellow officers who call them "lollicops" or the "grin-and-grin" squad. The reality is that CPOs make arrests just like other officers do, but CPOs deal with a broader variety of community problems in addition to crime, not as a substitute for addressing serious crime. In fact, as Scott and Goldstein (2005:2) observe, "There is growing evidence that by addressing the conditions that underlie crime and disorder problems, rather than merely looking to arrest offenders, police can more effectively prevent and control such problems." The major difference is that CPOs ask themselves whether an arrest will solve the problem or make matters worse, and what solutions can prevent this problem from happening again in the future.

TABLE 11.2   Traditional versus Community Policing Models

| Question | Traditional Policing (TPM) | Community Policing (CPM) |
|---|---|---|
| 1. Who are the police? | A *government agency* principally responsible for law enforcement | *Police are the public* and the public are the police; police officers are those who are paid to give full-time attention to the duties of every citizen |
| 2. What is the relationship of the police to other public service departments? | *Priorities often conflict* | The police are *one department among many responsible* for improving the quality of life |
| 3. What is the role of the police? | Focusing on *solving crimes* | A broader *problem-solving* approach |
| 4. How is police efficiency measured? | By detection and *arrest rates* | By the *absence of crime and disorder* |
| 5. What are the highest priorities? | *Crimes* that are high value (e.g., bank robberies) and those involving violence | Whatever *problems* disturb the community most |
| 6. What specifically do police deal with? | *Incidents* | Citizens' *problems* and concerns |
| 7. What determines the effectiveness of police? | *Response* times | *Public cooperation* |
| 8. What view do police take of service calls? | Deal with them only if there is no *real police work* to do | Vital function and great *opportunity* |
| 9. What is police professionalism? | Swift/effective response to *serious crime* | Keeping close to the *community* |
| 10. What kind of intelligence is most important? | *Crime intelligence* (study of particular crimes or series of activities crimes) | Criminal intelligence *(information about* individuals or *groups)* |
| 11. What is the essential nature of police accountability? | *Highly centralized;* governed by rules, regulations, and policy directives; accountable to the *law* | Emphasis on *local accountability* to community needs |
| 12. What is the role of headquarters? | To provide the necessary *rules and policy* directives | To preach organizational *values* |
| 13. What is the role of the press liaison department? | To *keep the "heat"* off operational officers so they can get on with the job | To *coordinate* an essential channel of communication with the community |
| 14. How do the police regard prosecutions? | As an *important goal* | As *one tool* among many |

*Source*: Adapted from M. Sparrow (1988). *Implementing Community Policing. Perspectives on Policing*, pp. 8–9. Washington, DC: National Institute of Justice and Harvard University

Crime analysis routinely shows that the majority of calls for service come from a relatively small number of locations (Braga & Weisburd, 2010; Sherman, 1987). An important ingredient of community policing is to focus on these "hot spots." But merely focusing on hot spots fails to recognize that police behavior and programs influence who will and who will not call the police for assistance. Furthermore, applying location-oriented policing based on traditional notions of what calls are worthy of a police response violates the spirit of community policing. If people call the police, the problem is important to them and CPOs should see this as an opportunity, no matter how trivial the call seems. CPOs must dissect these areas, determine what is occurring in terms of problems, and develop strategies for reducing problems. CPOs must also be mindful that their behaviors, programs, and data collection techniques, at least in part, determine what constitutes a "hot spot," By way of example, one rarely hears police speak of a concentration of drug users as a hot spot for the transmission of HIV, an abandoned part of a city as a hotbed of unemployment, or an area devoid of social activities for youth as a cause of juvenile crime. Community policing dictates that officers consider strategies and tactics, which include, but are not limited to, arrest and suppression. This does not mean that community policing is soft on crime; it means that community policing is smart about crime and open to suggestions on solving broader social problems that generate crime.

*Community policing is not flamboyant.* When a SWAT team successfully disarms or kills a sniper or a barricaded person (a very rare event), their work makes the headlines. When police officers engage in high-speed pursuits, it often makes the nightly news. When a CPO helps organize a summer softball league for idle neighborhood youngsters, the long-term impact may be equally as dramatic, but the effort will not rate a feature on the nightly TV news. It is unlikely to be picked up by the media. An officer may not experience the cultural and occupational satisfaction associated with the crime-fighter image. The media reinforces the image of the macho police officer whose job is glamorous, tough, and often dangerous (Kappeler & Potter, 2005; Kasinsky, 1994). The "hero myth" and "warrior fantasy" (Kraska, 1996; Crank, 2004), which accounts for a substantial degree of resistance to community policing, also appeals to far too many police officers themselves. Community policing recognizes that the job gets done through steady hard work, not warrior images and tactical exercises. CPOs must learn to defer traditional-cultural sources of gratification and notoriety and focus on the job and the long-term benefits of community building.

*Community policing is not paternalistic.* Police departments are organized as a paramilitary hierarchy where those at the top, to some extent, expect to set the department's agenda, based on their experience and expertise. This organizational structure and mentality often extend beyond the police department itself and are manifested in the way officers typically interact with the community (Kappeler et al., 1998). In its most extreme form, the message to the average person is that the police think people do not know enough about police work to do much more than pay taxes and respond to officers when questions are asked. The traditional, paternalistic police attitude suggests that crime is so complex and difficult that it must be left in the hands of skilled professionals specifically trained for the job. How many police officers, however, are trained at creating jobs and social activities for youth? How many police officers know the signs of mental and physical health problems? How many police officers know the relationship between crime, mental health, and the provision of meaningful activities for youth? How many police officers know how to deal with substance abuse? Community policing threatens those who enjoy the traditional system, because it requires that police superiors empower officers and people with the decision-making authority to properly serve communities.

*Community policing is not an independent entity within the department.* Ultimately, the community policing philosophy must inundate the entire department. There are a number of ways of implementing community policing, including doing so gradually. Piecemeal arrangements include the formation of a special unit or concentration on specific geographical areas. In fact, it is virtually impossible to suddenly and comprehensively implement community policing in all but the smallest departments. When community policing is implemented piecemeal, it can generate tremendous pressure on the CPOs, who are the most visible expression of the new commitment. The challenge is in finding ways to demonstrate to noncommitted members of the department how the community policing philosophy works.

Patrol officers in particular must be shown that CPOs not only help them by providing information, but also that they help ease tensions between the police and the community, which can be a particular problem in minority neighborhoods. In the Flint, Michigan, experiment, a foot patrol officer arrived on the scene shortly after patrol officers had responded to a call about a man brandishing a gun. The foot officer was able to tell his motor patrol peers that the man inside was known as a heavy drinker and that his wife routinely visited her sister when he got drunk. A phone call there confirmed that the wife was safe and had her children with her, and that the man was probably asleep in the back bedroom. When the officers entered, they found the man passed out in bed as predicted. By working together, the motor officers and the CPO solved the problem with the least risk to themselves and others and avoided using a SWAT team. This is quite a different approach to the problem when compared to the use of paramilitary teams using force to extract people from their homes. CPOs are able to assist other officers because of the intimate knowledge they amass as a result of close ties with the community—thus, hopefully reducing the need for force-based actions.

*Community policing is not cosmetic.* Unlike crime prevention and police–community relations programs, community policing goes beyond providing information and expressing goodwill. Community policing requires that departments make substantive changes in how the department interacts with the public. Community policing broadens the police mandate to focus on proactive efforts to solve problems. CPOs are simply the patrol officers who serve as community outreach specialists, offering direct, decentralized, and personalized police service as part of a full-spectrum community policing approach that involves the entire department in new community-based efforts to solve problems.

Unlike limited proactive or community-relations efforts of the past, community policing not only broadens the agenda to include the entire spectrum of community concerns, but it offers greater continuity, follow-up, and accountability. It is important to understand that community policing goes beyond handing out brochures, making speeches, talking with community leaders, telling people how to guard against crime, and urging fellow officers to treat people with respect. As line officers directly involved in the community, CPOs have the opportunity to make real, substantive changes.

In Florida, a CPO concerned about the poverty and high unemployment in his beat area actively solicited leads on jobs, which he posted in the neighborhood community policing office. Officers in the Jefferson County, Kentucky, Police Department participated in neighborhood programs in public housing where youths were tutored in reading and mathematics. Community policing's proactive focus goes beyond target hardening, street sweeps of so-called hot spots, and other relatively superficial solutions, to initiating creative efforts that attack the very social fiber of crime problems. Such solutions hold the promise of long-term changes whose full impact may not become fully evident for years.

*Community policing is not just another name for social work.* The broad constellations of problems that plague society, especially in the inner city, defy simple solutions. Yet critics of community policing think that involving officers in efforts that have not traditionally been viewed as part of the police mandate is not only wasteful, but also silly. Traditionalists insist that the police have their hands full trying to battle serious crime, so efforts that detract from that effort not only waste valuable time and money, but they can erode the credibility and authority of the police. Their attitude is that the police should leave social work to the social workers, so that the police can focus all their energies on their real and important job of fighting crime.

Yet, this position ignores the fact that serious crime constitutes only a very small portion of what the police are called upon to do (Greene & Klockars, 1991). Further, Famega (2005) examined police workload studies and found that about 75 percent of officers' time is not devoted to answering crime-related calls for service. Indeed, if the police actually attempted to limit their mandate solely to crime, it would be almost impossible for most departments to justify the bulk of their budgets, especially since crime has been declining for over four decades (Kappeler & Potter, 2005). The fact is police officers are already involved in many nonlaw-enforcement activities that have little, if anything, to do with serious crime. These activities include: crowd control at public events, protecting politicians, issuing traffic tickets, providing people with directions, investigating accidents, and helping stranded motorists. The issue is not whether the police should become involved in efforts that do not directly focus on serious crime, but what other kinds of services the police should provide. Is it more effective to have another police officer issuing traffic citations or to have an officer in public schools speaking to youths about the hazards of drinking and driving or the unsafe operation of motor vehicles?

The police officer must be many things, law enforcer and peacekeeper, armed symbol of authority and part-time social worker. It is this blend of force and compassion that makes the job so potent and unique. No other job in civilian society permits a person to choose from an array of responses that range from flashing a friendly smile to using deadly force.

*Community policing is not elitist.* One of the biggest difficulties that CPOs often face is that they are different kinds of heroes in the community, but also too often the objects of sarcasm and scorn among their peers. Some of the resentment stems from CPOs receiving seemingly preferential treatment or special consideration by the department. Left unchecked, this friction can erupt into outright hostility. Departments that launch new community policing efforts must pay particular attention to educating everyone in the department about the community policing philosophy, the role of the CPO, and how this new way of policing can benefit everyone in the department directly. It takes constant reinforcement from the top to explain that CPOs are not being treated like an elite corps, but as the department's direct link to the community. It is also important to establish CPO standards and allow everyone the opportunity to become involved. If everyone is given an opportunity to participate, it generally reduces some of the hostility.

*Community policing is not designed to favor the rich and powerful.* The dramatic surge in drug-related murders in Washington, DC, prompted more than one commentator to suggest that, if these murders were occurring in an affluent enclave nearby such as Georgetown, the police would be forced to take more action. Likewise, when a white child from the affluent suburb goes missing the media cover the crime in great detail, political leaders pressure the police to take action and police scurry about to address the disappearance. Situations like these speak volumes to politics and policing in America, but they don't tell the whole story.

The damning indictment that the police pay more attention to the problems of the rich and powerful deserves a closer look because it offers more than a kernel of truth. The fact is, of course, that the odds are that an upscale community like Georgetown will never suffer a similar spate of drug-related murders. The mistake is to think that this is because most of the residents of Georgetown obey the law, while the majority of those who live in poor neighborhoods in the District of Columbia do not. But what it does mean is that the high price tag required to afford to live in Georgetown means the community does not suffer from poverty, unemployment, illiteracy, overcrowdedness, substandard education, declining health care, or despair, the myriad of social ills that plague many inner-city neighborhoods. Crime clusters in neighborhoods that already suffer from social and economic problems, and these problems can overwhelm the people forced to live there.

Yet there may well be more than a little truth to the persistent allegations that the police often accede to pressures to pay more attention to the wants and needs of the rich and powerful. Though this can include paying attention to even the most serious crime of murder or kidnapping, any gap in the level of service between rich and poor is likely to grow even wider in the level of response for less important calls for service. In fact, one of the most common complaints from inner-city residents is under-enforcement of the law. Inner-city residents complain that the police do not give their problems the same consideration that they give to problems in more affluent communities.

It is easy to see why the police might hustle faster to investigate an abandoned car, up on blocks with no wheels, if the call comes from a senator in Georgetown rather than someone from a bad section in the District. The first reason is that the police in Georgetown may well be far less busy, because there are fewer emergency calls demanding an immediate response. Second, that abandoned car would be a relative rarity in Georgetown, which makes it seem more suspicious. And the unfortunate and unavoidable third reason is that a senator who is unhappy with the police response can do far more to make problems for the department. The senator may well know the chief personally and would have few qualms about calling at home to complain. Senators also have access to the media, a bully pulpit from which they can denounce the department's inefficiency. Poor people, on the other hand, seldom have any access whatsoever when they feel grieved as a result of government inaction or insufficient action.

Community policing is egalitarian in the sense that it says that regardless of whether you have money and power, and despite whether you do or do not vote or pay taxes, regardless of whether you are black or white, all people deserve direct assistance and support from the police. For example, today some people are outraged over undocumented immigrants residing in their communities and advocate that they should not receive any form of government service. Yet, in order to maintain community tranquility and ensure justice, the police should treat these people no differently than citizens. Community policing requires that every area within a city be evaluated and serviced. Community policing mandates that the police not disregard the needs of the poor, disadvantaged, or least powerful in society (see Bursik, 2000; Taylor, 2001; Velez, 2001). Research shows that officers who value equality are more willing to work with minorities (Zhao et al., 1999) in their communities. In fact, the police can play an important role in leveling many of the disadvantages created by the political and economic system in which we live.

*Community policing is not "safe."* Allowing officers the freedom to attempt creative solutions to problems carries with it the risk of mistakes that can range from the embarrassing to the disastrous. The traditional system instead focuses on routinizing tasks and codifying procedures as a way to eliminate the potential for mistakes that can threaten the department's reputation.

At issue, of course, is whether police officers are educated professionals who can be trusted to do their jobs. Community policing dictates that police departments must learn to suffer the occasional mistakes, so that officers can bring the full impact of their education, training, experience, professional instincts, and imagination to bear on solving community problems. History shows that the traditional approach is far from being error-free, and that treating personnel as if they cannot be trusted cannot eliminate problems.

*Community policing is not a series or bundle of programs.* Although many departments have implemented a number of new programs under the rubric of community policing, they have not yet achieved an operational level whereby they should declare themselves a community policing department. Too often, programs are implemented in a vacuum, whereby they have little contact with other units and programs. Administrators fail to recognize that, for most problems, there is no quick fix, and that problems are complex, often requiring substantial effort to solve.

*Community policing is not merely problem-oriented policing.* Problem-oriented policing emphasizes social problems and holds the police solely accountable and responsible for addressing these concerns. Community policing recognizes that the police alone cannot solve social problems and that the community must be engaged in a meaningful way if change is to occur. Under the problem-oriented policing approach, the community may or may not be engaged in the identification and control of a community problem. Under community policing, there is always a collaborative level of cooperation between the police and the community. In fact under community policing the police mobilize the community for problem solving. Michael Scott (2000:98) summarized the difference in the following passage:

You can learn more about the various forms of community policing by going to www.cops.usdoj.gov

> Community policing strongly emphasizes organizing and mobilizing the community, almost to the point that doing so becomes a central function of the police; problem-oriented policing advocates such efforts only if they are warranted in the specific context of addressing a particular problem. Under community policing, certain features of police organizational structure and policy, like geographic decentralization and continuity in officer assignments to neighborhoods, are deemed essential; under problem-oriented policing, many of these features are seen as helpful, but not essential—problem-oriented policing can be done under a variety of organizational arrangements. Community policing emphasizes that the police share more decision-making authority with the community; problem-oriented policing seeks to preserve more ultimate decision making authority for the police.

Problem-oriented policing without community control retains the traditional authoritarian top-down approach to community problems and does not involve the power sharing necessary to make real changes in the community. If the police are not willing to share power and decision making with the community, there is little chance that the community will embrace the police, the problems the police deem necessary to address, or the solutions they come up with in isolation. Problem-oriented policing without community policing can quickly erode into aggressive law enforcement practices that foster conflict and divide the police from the community. In such a situation police are merely moving crime around like deck chairs on the Titanic, all the while ignoring that they are heading for an iceberg. Problem-oriented policing without community policing is merely the repackaging of traditional policing which has been shown to have devastating social consequences [...].

# Reconciling Law Enforcement with Community Policing

Community policing represents a departure from traditional reactive law enforcement. It de-emphasizes the law enforcement function and emphasizes service to the community, order maintenance, and community building. Indeed, only a small percentage of police activities and calls for service relate to the law enforcement function. There has been some criticism of community policing and its new direction. For example, Johnson (1997) notes that the community development goals of community policing are noble, but it is questionable whether the police can actually change value systems and cultural norms. He argues that family, peer, and community pressures and influences play a larger role in shaping identities than do surrogate associations with police officers. While there is truth to this assertion, values and culture are expressions of the real concrete living conditions within a community—not some ether that magically appears from abstract values. Changing the concrete conditions in which people live changes values, and police have an increasingly important role in changing community conditions. Regardless, the police must realize that they are confronting a monumental task when attempting to change a community's culture. Some would even argue that this falls outside the scope of law enforcement—but at some point, the scope of policing must be revolutionized.

The advent of community policing has witnessed resurgence in focused law enforcement activities. Police departments across the country are using saturation patrols, undercover operations, aggressive field interrogations, SWAT teams, and other highly visible enforcement tactics. Such tactics are being justified as a part of community policing and are being encouraged as part of the "war on terror." Police managers maintain that these tactics are efforts to "take back the streets" or regain control over areas that have been lost to crime or are in need of protection. The emergence of these aggressive tactics is grounded in a failed philosophy rooted in Wilson and Kelling's (2006) "broken windows" theory and the U.S. Justice Department's funding of "Weed and Seed" programs. **Broken windows** postulates that, if unchecked, a neighborhood in decline will continue to decline and the number of disorders and crime problems will increase. Therefore, the police and government must intervene and attempt to reverse neighborhood deterioration. **Weed and Seed** is an extension of broken windows. Under Weed and Seed, police departments across the country were funded to clean up drug-prone neighborhoods and, once the cleanup was complete, to engage the community and assist in revitalizing it. In other cases aggressive policing practices have been rationalized by the need to protect the community from potential terrorists, therefore justifying

You can learn more about the Weed and Seed program by going to www.csosa.gov/newsmedia/factsheets/weed-and-seed.pdf

the view that everyone, especially minorities, are suspects to be stopped and interrogated, or groups that warrant infiltration.

Decades of using aggressive law enforcement practices where the police wage a war against certain segments of the community have shown this to be a failed practice that only furthers community problems, reinforces the "crime-fighter" orientation of the police, and oftentimes leads to riots and civil unrest. Far too often, after police have aggressively "weeded" communities with law enforcement tactics, political leaders have failed to provide the promised "seed" to revitalize these communities, leaving the police with still another community relations nightmare. Worse yet, these tactics have been used in the interests of big business to displace residents for the purposes of development and gentrification (see Zimmer, 1997). Unfortunately, a number of police departments see aggressive law enforcement as a potent tool in the policing arsenal. These are, however, tools that are not in keeping with the spirit of community policing and were the hallmarks of the failed traditional model of policing.

Perhaps the best known of these aggressive programs is New York City's **zero-tolerance** policing. Here, the police lowered their tolerance and enforced the law in respect of many minor violations that historically were ignored by the police. The failed idea was that minor law violations ultimately lead to more serious crime, and, by attacking minor crime, the police can have an impact on serious crime (broken windows). At the same time, the department also began to target high-crime areas with highly aggressive law enforcement. The result was large numbers of arrests and a misguided belief that these practices resulted in a decline in serious violent crime. One must remember that almost every American city, even those that have not employed aggressive zero-tolerance practices, has experienced significant reductions in crime over the last four decades. Aggressive policing also resulted in an increase in complaints against the police. Greene (1999) questioned the effectiveness of New York's aggressive policing. She notes that other cities, particularly San Diego, experienced similar drops in crime without aggressive policing. San Diego was able to lower crime rates while adhering to a brand of community policing that emphasized community partnerships. The research is mixed regarding aggressive patrol's impact on crime. Novak and his colleagues (1999) found that it had no impact, while Sherman and Weisburd (1995) and Weiss and Freels (1996) found a very weak relationship. The research can be only marginally characterized as mixed, but the historical result of aggressive policing is more than clear. These police practices result in alienation of the community (Reisig & Parks, 2000; Sampson & Jeglum-Bartusch, 1998), riots and civil disorder, and a distrust of the police.

Law enforcement remains a central part of the police mission. Aggressive policing has become a frequently used tactic by departments that say they adhere to community policing. We would argue that aggressive law enforcement is anti-community policing. Others would argue that the police must take control of "lost" neighborhoods before more positive relationships and actions can develop. Police

## The Weed and Seed Strategy

In 1991, the U.S. Department of Justice established Operation Weed and Seed—a community-based multi-agency approach to law enforcement, crime prevention, and neighborhood restoration. The Community Capacity Development Office (CCDO), Office of Justice Programs, administers Operation Weed and Seed. The goals of Weed and Seed are to control violent crime, drug trafficking, and drug-related crime in designated high-crime neighborhoods and provide a safe environment free of crime and drug use for residents. The Weed and Seed strategy brings together federal, state, and local crime-fighting agencies, social service providers, representatives of the public and private sectors, prosecutors, business owners, and neighborhood residents under the shared goal of weeding out violent crime and gang activity while seeding in social services and economic revitalization. Weed and Seed began with three pilot sites in 1991 and has spread quickly to more than 300 high-crime neighborhoods across the nation.

The Weed and Seed strategy is a two-pronged approach to crime control and prevention:

- Law enforcement agencies and prosecutors cooperate in "weeding out" criminals from the designated area.
- "Seeding" brings prevention, intervention, treatment, and neighborhood revitalization services to the area.

The Weed and Seed approach is unique when compared with traditional crime prevention approaches of the past. The strategy is based on collaboration, coordination, community participation, and leveraging resources. Weed and Seed sites maximize existing programs and resources by coordinating and integrating existing federal, state, local, and private sector initiatives, criminal justice efforts, and social services. The strategy also puts heavy emphasis on community participation. Residents of Weed and Seed neighborhoods are actively involved in problem solving in their community. Neighborhood watches, citizen marches and rallies, cleanup events, drug-free zones, and graffiti removal are some of the common programs that encourage community participation and help prevent crime.

*Source*: Office of Justice Programs (2004). *The Weed and Seed Strategy*, pp. 1–2. Washington, DC: U.S. Department of Justice, Office of Justice Programs

## SPOTLIGHT ON COMMUNITY POLICING PRACTICE

### Broken Windows and Community Policing

The notion of broken windows has provided important insights and innovation to the field of policing. At times, however, these ideas have been misunderstood, misapplied, and often viewed outside the context of community policing. Broken windows is based on the notion that signs of incivility, like broken windows, signify that nobody cares, which leads to greater fear of crime and a reduction of community efficacy, which in turn can lead to more serious crimes and greater signs of incivility, repeating the cycle and causing a potential spiral of decay. For police, the insight of broken windows is that they are called on to address minor quality-of-life offenses and incidents of social disorder to prevent more serious crime, and that they must take specific steps to increase the capacity of communities to exert informal social control. Just as many have inaccurately reduced community policing to community relations, others have incorrectly reduced broken windows to merely zero-tolerance or order enforcement policies, with little regard for community concerns or outcomes. In fact, broken windows advocates for the careful implementation of these specific police tactics so that individual rights and community interests are respected. In addition, broken windows stresses the importance of including communities in the change process, with the primary goal being the development of informal social control mechanisms within the communities in question and not merely increased enforcement of minor offenses.

Later articulations of broken windows place it squarely within the context of community policing and attempt to address some of the legal and moral implications of its adoption. As Sousa and Kelling (2006:90) state, "we believe that order maintenance should represent a policy option in support of police and community efforts to be implemented as problem-analysis and problem-solving dictates." An application of a one-size-fits-all order maintenance program is unlikely to have universally positive effects on all of the various crimes and serious problems confronted by police departments and is not advocated for by broken windows theory. Rather, from the perspective of community policing, broken windows represents an important potential response to crime and disorder problems that may or may not be dictated through problem-solving processes, and broken-windows-style interventions should be conducted in partnership with community stakeholders.

Broken windows is more narrow in scope than the overarching community policing philosophy and fits well within the community policing context. For example, unlike the community policing philosophy, broken windows does not attempt to identify specific organizational changes in law enforcement agencies that are necessary to institutionalize these types of police interventions. Situating broken windows within the broader community policing philosophy can help to advance the organizational changes necessary to make broken windows interventions (when they are called for through careful analysis) successful and sustainable. For example, broken windows can benefit from community policing's focus on hiring different kinds of officers (who pay attention to disorder and have skills in community capacity building), building stronger analytical functions to support proper analysis, and making specific efforts to engage communities and increase trust to facilitate order-maintenance interventions.

When broken windows is correctly understood within a broader community policing philosophy, improper implementation of its central tenets through such things as ignoring community concerns, applying a zero-tolerance one-size-fits-all approach to minor offenses, and conducting cursory or no analysis of problems is less likely to occur. Appreciating the true scope of broken windows policing concepts within the context of community policing will enable these innovations to flourish and be most effective.

Matthew C. Scheider Ph.D.
Assistant Director
The COPS Office

*Source*: The e-newsletter of the COPS Office, Volume 2, Issue 1, January 2009 [citation omitted]

"Perhaps it is not true that history repeats itself; it is only that man remains the same."

—Walter Sorrell

executives must begin to take a cold, hard, and sober look at the politics underlying policing and crime control. They must ask some hard questions like: What public policies and political decisions led to the creation of communities that needed "weeding"? Did the very people who failed to provide the necessary "seed" to grow healthful communities make these decisions about weeding. Whose interests are really being served when long-time residents are pushed out of communities for development projects? Who benefits from promoting fear of crime and casting it in racist terms? Were the police abandoned to deal with the consequences of poor public policy and politically motivated decisions? Is aggressive policing a fix for communities or for political leaders?

## Summary

Community policing represents a new, bold approach to law enforcement. Not since the beginning of the 1900s has law enforcement moved back to its social service roots. Community policing represents a comprehensive attack on community problems. It signals a time whereby the police are concerned with people and their problems as opposed to focusing solely on responding to calls for service and making arrests. Community policing truly is a paradigm shift.

It is important for the police administrator to not mistake some strategy or tactic for community policing. While community policing employs a number of strategies and tactics, the essence of community policing (empowerment of the community, community engagement, problem solving, and community partnerships) represents the glue that holds these strategies and tactics together. Community policing requires that police work as closely as possible with people to identify and solve their problems. Under community policing, crime reduction and "crook-catching" are not primary objectives, but represent strategies that are a part of a rich, overarching philosophy of community service.

## KEY TERMS

aggressive tactics
broad police function
broken windows
community engagement
community focus
community input
community partnerships
community policing
community policing officer (CPO)
concern for people
creativity
decentralize
developing trust
face-to-face contact
fear of crime
geographic focus
hot spots
law enforcement function

neighborhood variation
order maintenance
organizational and personnel facet
organizational strategy
philosophical facet
prevention focus
proactive
problem-oriented policing
problem solving
professional model
programmatic facet
reoriented operations
sharing power
situational crime prevention
strategic facet
Weed and Seed
zero tolerance

# DISCUSSION QUESTIONS

1. Discuss the idea that community policing is little more than a continuation of police agencies telling communities what types of police services they need and will therefore receive.

2. Discuss and describe the sources of confusion surrounding the implementation of community policing.

3. Have a discussion on what exactly community policing is.

4. Discuss and describe major facets of community policing.

5. Briefly discuss how neighborhood variation can impact community policing efforts.

6. What is situational crime prevention, and how is it related to community policing?

7. Discuss the role of the CPO in community engagement. Include a discussion of the obstacles that may be present and how the officer can work to overcome them.

8. The text lists several concepts that are NOT a part of community policing. Discuss four.

9. Discuss "broken windows" theory. How does it relate to "Weed and Seed" programs? Is this an effective approach to helping communities?

10. Discuss the role community policing can play in homeland security. What are some of the pitfalls of a narrow police focus on terrorism?

# References

Bayley, D. H. (1988). Community Policing: A Report from the Devil's Advocate. In J. Greene & S. Mastrofski (Eds.), *Community Policing: Rhetoric or Reality?* (pp. 225–238). New York, NY: Praeger.

Bittner, E. (1970). *The Functions of the Police in Modern Society.* Rockville, MD: National Institute of Mental Health, Center for Studies of Crime and Delinquency.

Bracey, D. (1992). Police Corruption and Community Relations: Community Policing. *Police Studies, 15(4),* 179–183.

Braga, A., & Weisburd, D. (2010). *Policing Problem Places: Crime Hot Spots and Effective Prevention.* New York, NY: Oxford University Press.

Bursik, R. J. (2000). The Systemic Theory of Neighborhood Crime Rates. In S. S. Simpson (Ed.), *Of Crime & Criminality: The Use of Theory in Everyday Life.* Boston, MA: Pine Forge Press.

Carter, D. (1985). Hispanic Perception of Police Performance: An Empirical Assessment. *Journal of Criminal Justice, 13,* 487–500.

Chappell, A. (2009). The Philosophical Versus Actual Adoption of Community Policing: A Case Study. *Criminal Justice Review, 34,* 5–24.

Chermak, S., & Weiss, A. (2006). Community Policing in the News Media. *Police Quarterly, 9(2),* 135–160.

Clarke, R. V. (1992). *Situational Crime Prevention: Successful Case Studies.* New York, NY: Harrow and Heston.

Colvin, C. A., & Goh, A. (2006). Elements Underlying Community Policing: Validation of the Construct. *Police Practice and Research, 7(1),* 19–33.

Cornish, D. B., & Clarke, R. V. (1987). Understanding Crime Displacement: An Application of Rational Choice Theory. *Criminology, 25*, 933–947.

Crank, J. P. (2004). *Understanding Police Culture* (2nd ed.). Newark, NJ: LexisNexis Matthew Bender/ Anderson Publishing.

Eck, J., & Spelman, W. (1987). Newport News Tests Problem-Oriented Policing. *NIJ Reports*, (Jan.–Feb.), 2–8.

Famega, C. (2005). Variation in Officer Downtime: A Review of the Research. *Policing: An International Journal of Police Strategies & Management, 28*, 388–414.

Gaines, L. K., & Worrall, J. (2012). *Police Administration*. Clifton Park, NY: Delmar.

Gaines, L. K., & Kappeler, V. E. (2014). *Policing in America* (8th ed.). Waltham, MA: Elsevier (Anderson Publishing).

Gallup (1996). Community Policing Survey. October.

Goldstein, H. (1979). Improving Policing: A Problem-Oriented Approach. *Crime & Delinquency, 25*, 236–258.

Goldstein, H. (1990). *Problem-Oriented Policing*. New York, NY: McGraw-Hill.

Greene, J. A. (1999). Zero Tolerance: A Case Study of Police Policies and Practices in New York City. *Crime & Delinquency, 45(2)*, 171–188.

Greene, J. (2000). Community Policing in America: Changing the Nature, Structure, and Function of the Police. In *Criminal Justice 2000, Volume 3, Policies, Processes, and Decisions of the Criminal Justice System* (pp. 299–370). Washington, DC: National Institute of Justice.

Greene, J., & Klockars, C. (1991). What Police Do. In C. Klockars & S. Mastrofski (Eds.), *Thinking About Police: Contemporary Readings* (2nd ed.). New York, NY: McGraw-Hill.

Hale, C. (1996). Fear of Crime: A Review of the Literature. *International Review of Victimology, 4*, 79–150.

Jackson, J., & Gray, E. (2010). Functional Fear and Public Insecurities about Crime. *British Journal of Criminology, 50*, 1–22.

Johnson, R. A. (1997). Integrated Patrol: Combining Aggressive Law Enforcement and Community Policing. *FBI Law Enforcement Bulletin, 66(11)*, 6–11.

Kappeler, V. E., & Kraska, P. B. (1998a). Police Adapting to High Modernity: A Textual Critique of Community Policing. *Policing: An International Journal of Police Strategies and Management, 21(2)*, 293–313.

Kappeler, V. E., & Kraska, P. B. (1998b). Police Modernity: Scientific and Community Based Violence on Symbolic Playing Fields. In S. Henry & D. Milovanovic (Eds.), *Constitutive Criminology at Work*. Albany, NY: SUNY Press.

Kappeler, V. E., & Potter, G. W. (2005). *The Mythology of Crime and Criminal Justice* (4th ed.). Prospect Heights, IL: Waveland Press.

Kappeler, V. E., Sluder, R. D., & Alpert, G. P. (1998). *Forces of Deviance: Understanding the Dark Side of the Force* (2nd ed.). Prospect Heights, IL: Waveland Press.

Kasinsky, R. (1994). Patrolling the Facts: Media, Cops, and Crime. In G. Barak (Ed.), *Media, Process, and the Social Construction of Crime* (pp. 203–234). New York, NY: Garland Publishing, Inc.

Klockars, C. B. (1988). The Rhetoric of Community Policing. In J. Greene & S. Mastrofski (Eds.), *Community Policing: Rhetoric or Reality* (pp. 239–258). New York, NY: Praeger.

Kraska, P. B. (1996). Enjoying Militarism: Political/Personal Dilemmas in Studying U.S. Paramilitary Units. *Justice Quarterly, 13(3)*, 405–429.

Kraska, P. B., & Kappeler, V. E. (1997). Militarizing American Police: The Rise and Normalization of Paramilitary Units. *Social Problems, 44(1)*, 1–18.

Manning, P. K. (1988). Community Policing as a Drama of Control. In J. Greene & S. Mastrofski (Eds.), *Community Policing: Rhetoric or Reality* (pp. 27–46). New York, NY: Praeger.

Manning, P. K. (1997). *Police Work* (2nd ed.). Prospect Heights, IL: Waveland Press.

Mastrofski, S., & Ritti, R. R. (1999). *Patterns of Community Policing: A View from Newspapers in the United States. COPS Working Paper*. Washington, DC: USDOJ.

Morabito, M. (2010). Understanding Community Policing as an Innovation: Patterns of Adaptation. *Crime & Delinquency, 56*, 564–587.

National Institute of Justice (NIJ). (1997). *Criminal Justice Research under the Crime Act—1995 to 1996*. Washington, DC: U.S. Department of Justice.

Novak, K. J., Hartman, J. L., Holsinger, A. M., & Turner, M. G. (1999). The Effects of Aggressive Policing of Disorder on Serious Crime. *Policing: An International Journal of Police Strategies and Management, 22(2)*, 171–190.

Peak, K. J., & Glensor, R. W. (2007). *Community Policing & Problem Solving: Strategies and Practices* (5th ed.). Upper Saddle River, NJ: Prentice-Hall.

Reaves, B. (2010). *Local Police Departments, 2007*. Washington, DC: Bureau of Justice Statistics.

Reisig, M. D., & Parks, R. B. (2000). Experience, Quality of Life, and Neighborhood Context: A Hierarchical Analysis of Satisfaction with Police. *Justice Quarterly, 17*, 607–630.

Reisig, M. D., & Parks, R. B. (2004). Can Community Policing Help the Truly Disadvantaged? *Crime & Delinquency, 50(2)*, 139–167.

Reiss, A., & Bordua, D. (1967). Environment and Organization: A Perspective on the Police. In D. Bordua (Ed.), *The Police: Six Sociological Essays*. New York, NY: John Wiley.

Roh, S., & Oliver, W. (2005). Effects of Community Policing upon Fear of Crime: Understanding the Causal Linkage. *Policing, 28*, 670–683.

Rosenbaum, D., & Lurigio, A. (1994). An Inside Look at Community Policing Reform: Definitions, Organizational Changes, and Evaluation Findings. *Crime & Delinquency, 40*, 299–314.

Sampson, R. J., & Jeglum-Bartusch, D. (1998). Legal Cynicism and (Subcultural?) Tolerance of Deviance: The Neighborhood Context of Racial Differences. *Law & Society Review, 32*, 777–804.

Scaglion, R., & Condon, R. G. (1980). Determinants of Attitudes toward City Police. *Criminology, 17(4)*, 485–494.

Scott, M. (2000). *Problem-Oriented Policing: Reflections on the First 20 Years* (p. 99). Washington, DC: Office of Community-Oriented Policing Services, U.S. Department of Justice.

Scott, M. S., & Goldstein, H. (2005). *Shifting and Sharing Responsibility for Public Safety Problems. Problem-Oriented Guides for Police, Response Guide Series* (Vol. 3, pp. 1–53).

Sherman, L. (1987). Repeat Calls for Service: Policing the "Hot Spots." In *Crime Control Reports*. Washington, DC: Crime Control Institute.

Sherman, L., & Weisburd, D. (1995). General Deterrent Effects of Police Patrol in Crime "Hot Spots": A Randomized, Controlled Trial. *Justice Quarterly, 12*, 625–648.

Skogan, W. G., & Hartnett, S. M. (1997). *Community Policing: Chicago Style*. New York, NY: Oxford University Press.

Sousa, W. H., & Kelling, G. L. (2006). Of "Broken Windows," Criminology, and Criminal Justice. In D. Weisburd, & A. A. Braga (Eds.), *Police Innovation: Contrasting Perspectives* (pp. 77–97). Cambridge: Cambridge University Press.

Sparrow, M. (1988). *Implementing Community Policing. Perspectives on Policing* (No. 9). Washington, DC: National Institute of Justice and Harvard University.

Spelman, W. (2004). Optimal Targeting of Incivility-Reduction Strategies. *Journal of Quantitative Criminology, 20(1),* 63–89.

Stephens, D. (1996). Community Problem-Oriented Policing: Measuring Impacts. In L. Hoover (Ed.), *Quantifying Quality in Policing.* Washington, DC: PERF.

Suttles, G. D. (1972). *The Social Construction of Communities.* Chicago, IL: University of Chicago Press.

Taylor, R. B. (2001). *Breaking Away from Broken Windows.* Boulder, CO: Westview.

Trojanowicz, R. (1982). *An Evaluation of the Neighborhood Foot Patrol Program in Flint, Michigan.* East Lansing, MI: Michigan State University.

Van Maanen, J. (2006). The Asshole. In V. Kappeler (Ed.), *The Police & Society: Touch Stone Readings* (3rd ed.). Prospect Heights, IL: Waveland Press.

Velez, M. B. (2001). The Role of Public Social Control in Urban Neighborhoods: A Multi-Level Analysis of Victimization Risk. *Criminology, 39,* 837–864.

Weisburd, D., & Eck, J. (2004). What Can Police Do to Reduce Crime, Disorder, and Fear? *Annals of the American Academy of Political and Social Science, 593,* 42–65.

Weiss, A., & Freels, S. (1996). The Effects of Aggressive Policing: The Dayton Traffic Enforcement Experiment. *American Journal of Police, 15,* 45–64.

Williamson, T., Ashby, B., & Webber, R. (2006). Classifying Neighborhoods for Reassurance Policing. *Policing & Society, 16,* 189–208.

Wilson, J. Q. (1968). Dilemmas of Police Administration. *Public Administration Review,* (Sept./Oct.), 407–416.

Wilson, J. Q., & Kelling, G. (2006). Broken Windows. In V. Kappeler (Ed.), *The Police & Society: Touch Stone Readings* (3rd ed., pp. 154–167). Prospect Heights, IL: Waveland Press.

Wintersmith, R. F. (1976). The Police and the Black Community: Strategies for Improvement. In A. Cohn, & E. Viano (Eds.), *Police Community Relations* (pp. 422–433). Philadelphia, PA: J.B. Lippincott.

Wood, J., & Bradley, D. (2009). Embedding Partnership Policing: What We've Learned from the Nexus Policing Project. *Police Practice & Research, 10,* 133–144.

Zhao, J., He, N., & Lovrich, N. P (1999). Value Change among Police Officers at a Time of Organizational Reform: A Follow-up Study Using Rokeach Values. *Policing: An International Journal of Police Strategies and Management, 22(2),* 152–170.

Zhao, S., Scheider, M., & Thurman, Q. (2002). The Effect of Police Presence on Public Fear Reduction and Satisfaction: A Review of the Literature. *The Justice Professional, 15,* 273–299.

Zimmer, L. (1997). Proactive Policing against Street-level Drug Trafficking. In L. Gaines, & P. Kraska (Eds.), *Drug, Crime, and Justice* (pp. 249–296). Prospect Heights, IL: Waveland.

# The Criminal Profiling Illusion

## WHAT'S BEHIND THE SMOKE AND MIRRORS?

BRENT SNOOK, RICHARD M. CULLEN, CRAIG BENNELL,
PAUL J. TAYLOR, AND PAUL GENDREAU

There is a belief that criminal profilers can predict a criminal's characteristics from crime scene evidence. In this article, the authors argue that this belief may be an illusion and explain how people may have been misled into believing that criminal profiling (CP) works despite no sound theoretical grounding and no strong empirical support for this possibility. Potentially responsible for this illusory belief is the information that people acquire about CP, which is heavily influenced by anecdotes, repetition of the message that profiling works, the expert profiler label, and a disproportionate emphasis on correct predictions. Also potentially responsible are aspects of information processing such as reasoning errors, creating meaning out of ambiguous information, imitating good ideas, and inferring fact from fiction. The authors conclude that CP should not be used as an investigative tool because it lacks scientific support.

*Keywords:* criminal profiling; police investigations; belief formation; pseudoscience

Criminal profiling (CP) is the practice of predicting a criminal's personality, behavioral, and demographic characteristics based on crime scene evidence (Douglas, Ressler, Burgess, & Hartman, 1986; Hicks & Sales, 2006).[1] This practice is being utilized by police agencies around the world despite no compelling scientific evidence that it is reliable, valid, or useful (Snook, Eastwood,

Brent Snook, et al., "The Criminal Profiling Illusion: What's Behind the Smoke and Mirrors?," *Criminal Justice and Behavior*, vol. 35, no. 10, pp. 1257-1276. Copyright © 2008 by SAGE Publications. Reprinted with permission.

Gendreau, Goggin, & Cullen, 2007). This disparity between the use and the lack of empirical support leads one to consider the question Why do people believe CP works despite the lack of evidence? We explain this criminal profiling illusion in terms of the nature of the information about CP that is presented to the people and how they process that information.

Our article is divided into five sections. First, we outline current knowledge of CP techniques, the frequency with which CP is used in criminal investigations, and the extent to which police officers and mental health professionals perceive CP as a valuable tool. Second, we argue that CP has no basis in scientific theory and has meager empirical support as an investigative tool. The third and fourth sections are devoted to a consideration of how the discrepancy may have arisen between the lack of evidence supporting CP practices and beliefs about its effectiveness. Specifically, in the third section, we discuss some of the ways that information about CP is distorted as it is conveyed. In the fourth section, we discuss some cognitive tendencies that are useful for learning and reasoning but appear to have led police officers, profilers, and the rest of us to form an illusory belief about CP. Fifth, we conclude by arguing that CP should not be used as an investigative tool until it receives adequate scientific support.

## The Criminal Profiling Environment

Constructing a profile of an unknown criminal typically involves three stages (Hicks & Sales, 2006; Homant & Kennedy, 1998). Police officers collect crime scene data (e.g., photographs, detective reports, and autopsy results). These data are then forwarded to a profiler who makes predictions about the personality, behavioral, and demographic characteristics of the likely criminal. These predictions are then reported to the investigating officers. In principle, CP differs little from what so-called psychic detectives allegedly do in helping law enforcement agencies catch criminals or find missing persons (see Lyons & Truzzi, 1991; Nickell, 1994; O'Keeffe & Alison, 2000; Wiseman, West, & Stemman, 1996).

Although there are no standardized techniques for making these predictions, the different approaches to CP can be broadly classified as having a clinical or statistical orientation.[2] Clinically oriented profilers draw on their training, knowledge, experience, and/or intuition to predict offender characteristics (e.g., Ault & Reese, 1980; Copson, Badcock, Boon, & Britton, 1997; Douglas & Munn, 1992; Holmes & Holmes, 1996; Keppel & Walter, 1999; Turvey, 1999; West, 2000). By contrast, statistically oriented predictions are derived from an analysis of offenders who have previously committed crimes that are judged as similar to those being investigated (e.g., Canter & Fritzon, 1998; Davies, Wittebrood, & Jackson, 1997; Farrington & Lambert, 1997; Jackson, van den Eshof, & de Kleuver, 1997; Keppel & Weis, 1993; Santilla, Häkkänen, Canter, & Elfgren, 2003).

Published accounts testify to prolific growth in the utilization of CP techniques. For example, between 1971 and 1981, the FBI provided CP assistance on 192 occasions (Pinizzotto, 1984). A few years later, Douglas and Burgess (1986) indicated that FBI profilers were being asked to assist in 600 criminal investigations per year. A more recent account indicated that CP was applied by 12 FBI profilers in approximately 1,000 cases per year (Witkin, 1996). Police officers in the United Kingdom also appear to be incorporating CP into their investigations more frequently. Copson (1995), for instance, reported that 29 profilers were responsible for providing 242 instances of CP advice between 1981 and 1994, with the prevalence of CP increasing steadily during that period.

Other professionals, such as police psychologists, are also becoming involved in CP (Bartol, 1996). Although we do not have exact estimates of CP prevalence elsewhere, its use has been documented in numerous countries, including Canada, Finland, Germany, Sweden, and the Netherlands (Åsgard, 1998; Clark, 2002; Jackson, Herbrink, & van Koppen, 1997).

As the prevalence of CP has increased, there has been a simultaneous increase in the volume of published literature addressing the practice. For example, in a recent quantitative review of 130 CP articles, it was found that the number of published CP articles has increased from 5 articles between 1976 and 1980, to 9 between 1981 and 1985, 10 between 1986 and 1990, 22 between 1991 and 1995, 56 between 1996 and 2000, 27 between 2001 and 2005, and 1 in 2006 (Snook, Eastwood, et al., 2007; see also Dowden, Bennell, & Bloomfield, 2007). Moreover, the authors of many of these articles promote CP as a useful investigative tool.

The results of Snook, Eastwood, et al.'s (2007) examination accorded well with the views expressed by a significant number of police officers and mental health professionals. These views were identified from surveys about whether or not CP advice is valuable. In the earliest survey, Douglas (as cited in Pinizzotto, 1984) found that solving cases was attributed to CP advice in 46% of the 192 instances where FBI profiling was requested. Similarly, Jackson, van Koppen, and Herbrink (1993) found that five out of six surveyed police officers in the Netherlands reported some degree of usefulness for advice given by an FBI trained profiler. Likewise, Copson (1995) found that 82.6% of a sample of 184 police officers in the United Kingdom claimed that CP was operationally useful and 92.4% reported that they would seek CP advice again. Consistent with these results, Trager and Brewster (2001) showed that a significant portion of police officers in the United States believe that CP has value. Finally, Torres, Boccaccini, and Miller's (2006) recent survey of 92 forensic mental health professionals indicated that 86% believe that CP is a useful law enforcement tool.

# The Lack of A Scientific Basis to Criminal Profiling

Having established that CP is in widespread use and that people generally believe that CP works, we now present a critical review of the CP literature. This review reveals the blunt reality that (a) most of the typologies used to create criminal profiles are in fact false typologies, (b) the majority of CP approaches are based on an outdated theory of personality that lacks empirical support, and (c) there is no compelling evidence that predictions made by professional profilers are significantly more accurate than those made by nonprofilers.

## Are Commonly Used Profiling Typologies Actually False Typologies?

Current profiling practices typically involve some type of classification system, or typology, which is used to categorize both crime scene behaviors and offender background characteristics. By far the most routinely used typology is the FBI's organized–disorganized dichotomy, which was developed from interviews with offenders (Ressler, Burgess, Douglas, Hartman, & D'Agostino, 1986). The assumptions underlying this typology are that (a) offenses can be categorized as organized (e.g., well planned) or disorganized (e.g., unplanned) based on the behaviors present at a crime scene, (b) offenders can be categorized as organized (e.g., high functioning) or disorganized (e.g., low functioning) based on the background characteristics of the offender, and (c) there is a correspondence between offenses and offenders (i.e., organized offenders commit organized crimes and disorganized offenders commit disorganized crimes).

Although the organized–disorganized typology has been the driving force behind CP practices around the world for many years, it has only recently been the subject of empirical scrutiny. Preliminary evaluations of this typology suggest that it does not match the variations in offender behavior. For example, Canter, Alison, Alison, and Wentink (2004) examined whether 100 murders committed by serial killers in the United States could be categorized as organized or disorganized. Using a multidimensional scaling procedure, they analyzed 39 crime scene behaviors that had been categorized as organized or disorganized in the FBI's *Crime Classification Manual* (Douglas, Burgess, Burgess, & Ressler, 1992). In contrast to what would be predicted from the typology, the analysis did not reveal any distinct subsets of organized and disorganized behaviors, thus making it difficult to see how serial homicides may be categorized easily in this way.

Similar findings have been reported for other popular classification systems (Canter & Wentink, 2004; Melnyk, Bloomfield, & Bennell, 2007). For example, Melnyk et al.'s (2007) examination of Keppel and Walter's (1999) serial sexual homicide typology, which was borrowed from research on rape and refined on the basis of Keppel's experiences as a homicide investigator, failed to find any evidence supporting the hypothesis that offenses or offenders could be categorized as power–assertive, power–reassurance, anger–retaliatory, and anger–excitation. As with the organized–disorganized dichotomy, the credibility of Keppel and Walter's typology collapses under empirical scrutiny.

Nevertheless, there are signs that progress is being made. Several individuals are attempting to develop CP classification systems and are going through the steps required to validate those systems (e.g., Häkkänen, Lindof, & Santilla, 2004; Kocsis, 2006; Salfati, 2000). Others are taking a bottom-up approach to profiling by identifying individual behavior–offender associations and the condition in which these will arise (e.g., Goodwill & Alison, 2007). However, this research is in its infancy and the typologies emerging are still not used widely in CP circles. Unfortunately, that role is currently taken up by classification systems that are not largely supported by psychological science.

## Is CP Based on an Empirically Supported Theory?

In a similar way to the classic trait theory that was popular in personality psychology up until the late 1960s (Mischel, 1968), the majority of CP approaches (e.g., the organized–disorganized dichotomy) assume that criminal behavior is determined by underlying dispositions within offenders that make them behave in a particular way (e.g., Åsgard, 1998; Badcock, 1997; Boon, 1997; Canter, 1995; Douglas et al., 1992). The assumptions that emerge from this theory are fundamental to CP (Alison, Bennell, Mokros, & Ormerod, 2002; Woodhams & Toye, 2007). For example, the theory leads to the assumption that offenders will exhibit similar behaviors across their offenses as traits, versus situational factors, are the determinants of behavior. Perhaps more important for the practice of CP, the theory also suggests that offenders will display similar behaviors in their crimes and in other aspects of their lives (e.g., interpersonal relationships).

How do these assumptions manifest themselves in practice? Take, for example, the FBI's popular organized–disorganized dichotomy that was described above. This model of CP assumes that offenders are driven to behave either in an organized or disorganized fashion across all aspects of their lives. This supposedly allows the crimes committed by an individual to be correctly linked (i.e., a criminal committing an organized crime will continue to commit organized crimes) and the background characteristics of the offender to be accurately profiled (i.e., crime scenes consisting of organized behaviors reflect the fact that the offenses were committed by an organized individual; Ressler et al., 1986).

How valid are these assumptions? It is our contention that trait-based models of profiling are fundamentally flawed. Criminal profilers do not seem to have recognized that a consensus began to emerge in the psychological literature some 40 years ago that to rely on traits or personality dispositions as the primary explanation for behavior was a serious mistake. Situational factors contribute as much as personality dispositions to the prediction of behavior (Bowers, 1973; Mischel, 1968). This is equally true when predicting criminal behavior (Alison et al., 2002; Andrews & Bonta, 2006; Bennell & Canter, 2002; Gendreau, Smith, & French, 2006; Woodhams & Toye, 2007).

This importance of situational factors is apparent when one actually considers the empirical research in the profiling domain. For example, some studies report that offenders exhibit a reasonable degree of consistency across their crimes, but typically this is only found for a specific subset of behavior. In Bennell and Canter's (2002) study of serial commercial burglary, very low levels of consistency were observed for behaviors related to items stolen and entry methods (two domains that are heavily dependent on situational factors). However, a high level of consistency was found for crime site selection choices. Similar results (i.e., relatively high levels of consistency for some behaviors but low levels for many others) have been reported for residential burglary (Bennell & Jones, 2005), commercial robbery (Woodhams & Toye, 2007), and sexual offenses (Sjöstedt, Långström, Sturidsson, & Grann, 2004). In other cases, no evidence of across-crime consistency is found. For example, even when using liberal definitions of consistency and multiple methods for classifying and analyzing behaviors, Bateman and Salfati (2007) found no evidence of consistency across the crimes committed by serial killers. This finding is particularly alarming considering the frequency with which profiling is used in such cases (Snook, Haines, Taylor, & Bennell, 2007; Trager & Brewster, 2001).

A similar picture emerges when evaluating the degree to which offenders exhibit consistency across their crimes and other aspects of their lives. At best, small pockets of psychologically meaningful consistency have been identified, whereby a specific crime scene behavior is found to relate to a specific background characteristic. For example, Davies et al. (1997) found that rapists who forced entry into premises were four times more likely to have prior convictions for property offenses than those who did not engage in that behavior. Similarly, striking the victim twice or more during a rape indicated that the offender was three times more likely to have a prior conviction for a violent offense than those who did not display this degree of aggression. Other research, however, has not found these relationships. House (1997), for instance, tested the hypothesis that rapists who exhibit a high degree of criminality in their rapes (e.g., overt criminal acts indicative of attempts to conceal identity and avoid apprehension) would be more likely, than other types of rapists (e.g., sadistic, aggressive, or pseudointimate), to exhibit background characteristics related to criminality (e.g., previous incarceration). This was found not to be the case. Even when ignoring the requirement for an underlying theoretical account for a behavior-characteristic relationship, Mokros and Alison (2002) and Woodhams and Toye (2007) were still unable to find compelling evidence of consistency. In general, profilers seem unaware of this empirical research and its implications.

Profilers also appear to neglect research in closely related fields. For example, despite a massive effort to identify predictors of consistency in offender samples, within community and prison settings, research has failed to turn up anything of value to criminal profilers. Although it is possible to make reasonably accurate predictions of criminal behavior (with respect to recidivism) across a range of contexts (e.g., Andrews & Bonta, 2006; Andrews, Bonta, & Wormith, 2006; Gendreau, Little, & Goggin, 1996; Hanson & Morton-Bourgon, 2005), these predictions do not inform profiling practices. Indeed, well-established predictors of criminal behavior (e.g., antisocial attitudes and cognition) are quite unrelated to the sorts of variables typically focused on by profilers (e.g., crime scene behaviors and offender demographics). Unfortunately, instead of heeding this research, profilers continue to make predictions that have no basis in empirical research.

## Can Professional Profilers Make Accurate Predictions?

Douglas et al. (1986) stated that "The process used by an investigative profiler in developing a criminal profile is quite similar to that used by clinicians to make a diagnosis and treatment plan ... Investigators traditionally have learned profiling through brainstorming, intuition, and educated guesswork" (p. 405). This clinically based process is reminiscent of psychoanalytic approaches to therapy where mental health professionals diagnose their clients through subjective interpretations and unsupported methods (Dawes, 1997). Empirical research has shown that clinical experience has a limited effect on the accuracy of psychologists' and psychiatrists' judgments across a range of tasks (e.g., Garb, 1998; Garb & Boyle, 2003; Meehl, 1997). In addition, Faust and Ziskin (1988) found low intra- and interclinician consistency in judgments of mental health status and argued that when clinicians' predictions are compared against objectively determinable hard data their error rate often exceeds their accuracy rate.

A similar trend exists within the CP domain, where negligible quantitative differences have been found between the predictive ability of professional profilers and nonprofilers. The accuracy of profiler predictions has been tested by comparing the performance of the so-called professional profilers with that of the nonprofiler groups in mock profiling scenarios (Kocsis, 2004b; Kocsis, Hayes, & Irwin, 2002; Kocsis, Irwin, Hayes, & Nunn, 2000; Pinizzotto & Finkel, 1990). In a typical experiment, profilers and nonprofiler groups are asked to review details of a solved crime (or crime series) and then make predictions about the likely offender via a multiple choice questionnaire. Predictions are typically divided into four categories: cognitive processes, physical attributes, offense behaviors, and social history/habits (the results from these four categories are also combined to form an overall profile performance measure). The accuracy of the predictions is checked against the actual perpetrator's characteristics. Because of a lack of clear agreement on who should be considered a profiler, Snook, Eastwood, et al. (2007) conducted two meta-analyses of these studies.[3]

The first analysis compared the predictive accuracy of a group of self-labeled profilers and experienced investigators against nonprofilers (e.g., college students and psychologists). The profilers/investigators were more accurate than nonpolice personnel on an overall measure of profile accuracy ($r = .24$) and on the physical attribute category ($r = .10$). In contrast, the predictive accuracy of the profilers/investigators was marginally worse or no better than the non-profilers when it came to predictions of cognitive processes ($r = -.06$), offense behaviors ($r = .00$), and social history/habits ($r = -.09$). With respect to all comparisons, as the 95% confidence intervals (CI) about the point estimates were wide (e.g., two to five times the limit of .10), and often included 0, the estimates of the effect sizes were deemed imprecise.

In the second analysis, the experienced investigators were included in the nonprofiler group. In this analysis, the results favored the profilers across all the four predictor categories, but again the 95% CI were unacceptably wide. The best result came when the overall profile was considered ($r = .32$, 95% CI = .10 to .54). Even if one assumes that this optimistic result could be replicated, it warrants consideration that many variables included in this analysis are well known in the criminological literature (e.g., the likelihood that a serial offender will be of a particular age, have particular convictions, suffer substance abuse problems, etc.). This means, in our view, that any police professional with a good knowledge of the criminological literature should be able to achieve this level of success simply by relying on base rate information. In other words, success in CP may not be based on specialized knowledge of the peculiarities and idiosyncrasies found at a given crime scene.

In sum, there is no compelling scientific evidence to support the positive view of CP that dominates popular opinion. Far from cutting edge science, CP approaches are based on typologies that lack empirical support and are often based on an outdated understanding of human behavior. In addition, professional profilers often produce predictions that are not significantly more accurate than nonprofilers. Given this state of affairs, one might wonder why police officers continue to request the assistance of profilers. Whereas some police officers report using CP because they believe that it works (e.g., Copson, 1995; Jackson et al., 1993; Pinizzotto, 1984), there are likely other officers who use CP but do not believe that it works. We suspect that some of these officers might use CP because they believe (or are instructed) that it is their duty to use all available investigative techniques. Others may believe that they have nothing to lose in seeing what a profiler can offer to an investigation. It is not known, however, whether CP is helpful or harmful to police investigations.

As positive beliefs about the validity and reliability of CP are not supported by empirical evidence, the rest of this article is devoted to explaining why people might believe that CP works. We address eight reasons that can explain why criminal profilers, the police, and the public might believe CP works in the absence of scientific support. These reasons are divided into two categories: The first four are elements of the message that people receive about CP and the second four relate to human cognition. These reasons are neither exhaustive nor mutually exclusive.

## The Message

Research shows that second hand knowledge, such as that acquired from the media, often does not reflect the actual state of affairs (Sprott, 1996). Thus, unless people adopt a critical approach to information consumption, their judgments about the viability of practices like CP can be contaminated by the inaccurate or biased information that is being conveyed (Stanovich, 1992). The following are the four aspects of information from the CP environment (i.e., messages about CP) that have the potential to convince people that CP works.

### The Power of N = 1

Personal stories about exceptional incidents and experiences can be very seductive because they are concrete, vivid, and memorable (Borgida & Nisbett, 1977; Stanovich, 1992). However, their seductiveness has no relation to their credibility. A cornerstone of the scientific method is that conclusions should not be drawn from anecdotes that have no way of being replicated or understood in a way that permits generalization (Fearon, 2003; Wallston, 1983). Yet because anecdotes hold appeal in their concrete example and because most people are not trained to seek objective facts and reliable evidence (Carroll, 2003; Gilovich, 1991; Sagan, 1996; Shermer, 2003), people may automatically allow information obtained from anecdotes to form the foundation of their beliefs.

Unfortunately, many published accounts of CP rely on anecdotal evidence to illustrate how the technique is useful in catching criminals (e.g., Canter, 1994; Cook & Hinman, 1999). Snook, Eastwood, et al. (2007), for example, found that 60% of the 130 CP articles they reviewed used at least one anecdote as a source of knowledge. The most vivid and widely cited anecdote is undoubtedly that of New York's Mad Bomber, George Metesky (Brussel, 1968). In their attempts to catch the bomber, investigators requested the assistance of psychiatrist James A. Brussel to profile the criminal. Among other things, Brussel (1968) reportedly predicted that the bomber was a regular man, of ordinary fashions, who was foreign born and attended church regularly, and that he would be wearing a buttoned double-breasted suit when apprehended by authorities. It is often reported that Brussel correctly predicted a number of factors such as Metesky's demeanor, social activities, health condition, and even the double-breasted suit. However, certain details of this case are typically overlooked when it is discussed in CP accounts. For example, rarely is it mentioned that Brussel's profile was published in *The New York Times* during the investigation ("16-year," 1956) and that Metesky was acknowledged as following the media reports (Berger, 1957b), thus opening up the possibility that Metesky consciously or unconsciously altered his behavior based on what he had read. In addition, the profile did not actually solve the case as is commonly implied (Kocsis, 2004a). Information found on disgruntled employees in personnel files led investigators to inquire about Metesky (Berger, 1957a).

Of course, it is not the use of case studies per se that necessarily biases people's views of CP. Rather, it is the way case studies are used by advocates of CP that can result in problems. For example, nearly every published case study we have come across reports a success story, where a profiler provided an accurate profile that helped resolve a difficult criminal investigation. Many of these case studies have extremely seductive qualities, such as those highlighted by the Mad Bomber description provided above (e.g., extremely specific and seemingly accurate predictions, which are made with access to very limited information). In short, there is no element of balance in the presentation of case studies, despite the fact that much could be learned from cases where CP was employed unsuccessfully. Under such biased conditions it is not difficult to see why many people would believe that CP works. They simply generalize from the many success stories they read to the field of CP more generally.

## Repetition of the Message that Profiling Works

Empirical research shows that the likelihood of an individual's agreeing with a message generally increases as the message is repeated (Cacioppo & Petty, 1979). Thus, repeating the message that CP is an effective investigative tool may contribute to the CP illusion. In addition to repeated messages that CP works, people are often told that more and more people are becoming trained in CP. For example, one proponent of profiling stated that "As more and more personnel become trained and experienced in the application of the investigative technique of CP, more agencies will believe in its use" (Davis, 1999, p. 293). Repeated suggestions that police officers seek CP input for investigations because they find it helpful can also persuade people that CP is viable (Kocsis, 2003a).

It is not uncommon to read statements testifying to the value of CP, such as "criminal personality profiling has been used by law enforcement agencies with success in many areas" (Douglas & Burgess, 1986, p. 9), "more and more cases are being successfully analyzed, and criminal profiles are being constructed with remarkable accuracy" (Depue, 1986, p. 5), and "profiling has proven time and time again to be a valuable investigative tool in the arsenal of today's modern law enforcement cadre" (Davis, 1999, p. 293). Although such testimonials may provide an uncritical reader with the impression that CP works, the unfortunate reality is that the validity of such testimonials has yet to be empirically supported, and they are an inadequate basis for a belief. More importantly, as highlighted above, such statements fail to correspond to research that has examined the predictive ability of profilers (Snook, Eastwood, et al., 2007).

## Inappropriate Reliance on Correct Predictions

Profilers can create the impression that their trade is viable by overemphasizing their correct predictions (e.g., Canter, 1994; Douglas & Olshaker, 1995; McCrary & Ramsland, 2003) and by conducting studies that only measure accuracy as the number of correct predictions rather than the proportion of correct predictions (Kocsis, 2004b; Kocsis et al., 2002; Kocsis et al., 2000; Pinizzotto & Finkel, 1990). When all the necessary and pertinent information is not reported, readers may form beliefs based solely on the information that is presented to them (Gilovich, 1991; Paulos, 1988; Plous, 1993). Previous research in the judgment and decision-making domain (Chapman & Chapman, 1967; Crocker, 1981, 1982; White, 2003) suggested that the exclusive presentation of correct predictions can lead people to overestimate the accuracy and potential utility of profiles.

An article by Douglas et al. (1986) illustrates nicely how correct predictions are accentuated to promote the belief that CP is beneficial. Douglas and his colleagues presented a profile that predicted 29 criminal characteristics, but when discussing the accuracy of the profile, the authors emphasized just the 11 correct predictions (10 hits and 1 correct rejection). With some effort, one can collect all the evidence that is necessary (and should have been presented) for a reader to sufficiently assess the validity of that profile. If there were 11 correct predictions (hits and correct rejections), then there were 18 incorrect predictions (false alarms and misses). The profile was only 38% accurate! Because profilers focus their attention on their successes, they (and potentially the consumers of their profiles) appear to overattribute the causality of solved cases to their CP predictions (Lassiter, Geers, Munhall, Ploutz-Snyder, & Breitenbecher, 2002). It should not be overlooked that incorrect predictions have the potential to mislead an investigation.

## The Myth of Profiling Experts

Experts are people who have professional competence in a specialized area, usually acquired in the course of extensive theoretical and practical training (Kurz-Milcke & Gigerenzer, 2004). Because of this, people often accept information that is communicated to them by apparent authority figures or experts as being correct (Bochner & Insko, 1966; Milgram, 1964). This has been referred to in the literature as the use of an expertise heuristic (i.e., that experts' statements can be trusted; Reimer, Mata, & Stoecklin, 2004). Evidence for usage of the expertise heuristic is already available in the CP domain. For example, police officers viewing a profile rate it as more accurate when the production of the profile is attributed to an expert rather than a nonexpert (Kocsis & Hayes, 2004; Kocsis & Heller, 2004).

Experts in a criminal investigative context ought to provide the police with specialized skills or knowledge beyond that of the ordinary police officer (Gudjonsson & Copson, 1997). Some profilers claim that they possess accumulated wisdom, investigative and behavioral science experience, and training and/or knowledge of abnormal behavior that provides them with the necessary skills to predict offender characteristics from crime scene data, which is presumably beyond the ability of the average police officer and layperson (e.g., Ault & Reese, 1980; Blau, 1994; Cook & Hinman, 1999; Douglas & Burgess, 1986; Hazelwood, Ressler, Depue, & Douglas, 1995). Other profilers claim that their skills and knowledge have come from a long, formal scientific education that trained them to identify the statistical relationships between crime details and criminal personality and background characteristics (e.g., Canter, 1994; Godwin, 1999; Kocsis, Cooksey, & Irwin, 2002a, 2002b; Salfati & Canter, 1999). To date, however, profilers have failed to show that their training improves their ability to develop accurate profiles (Snook, Eastwood et al., 2007).

Other than the possession of specialized skills or knowledge, profilers might also be viewed as experts because they have testified as expert witnesses in court (McCann, 1992). Legal scholars, however, have been quick to challenge this notion because CP is not a generally accepted scientific technique, is not reliable, cannot prove the guilt of the defendant, and does not provide explanations that are outside the normal understanding of the jury (Ormerod, 1996a, 1996b; Risinger & Loop, 2002). Moreover, profile-based evidence has, on occasion, been found unacceptable by the courts because it is has been considered junk science (e.g., *State v. Fortin*, 1999). Also challenging the expert profiler label is the lack of consensus about who can be a profiler and a generally accepted regulatory body that provides professional profiling designations.[4]

## The Mind

People believe all kinds of strange things that are uncorroborated by scientific evidence. Prescient examples include the occurrence of alien abductions, the hot hand phenomenon in basketball, reincarnation, remote viewing, and the mystical power of the Egyptian pyramids (Gilovich, 1991; Hines, 1988; Vyse, 1997). Researchers have spent a great deal of time investigating how and why people might believe in unproven things. According to Shermer (2002), a consensus among many of these scientists is that the human mind evolved to identify patterns among environmental occurrences, a process that is believed to have been adaptive for the species, but which can lead to the identification of meaningless patterns. The identification of meaningless patterns can explain to a certain degree why people might believe that things such as psychic predictions, past-life regressions, and CP predictions are valid. Note that it is not our contention in this article to claim that these beliefs are irrational. Beliefs are merely a product of processing information from the environment. When the information is bogus, so will be the belief. Four aspects of human cognition that contribute to the CP illusion are discussed below.

# Reasoning Errors

People may believe in CP because of misguidance by natural human reasoning processes. People attempt to find order and meaning in an uncertain world and then form beliefs that can guide future behaviors (Gigerenzer, 2002; Shermer, 2003). From an evolutionary perspective, such cognitive processes allowed people to adapt to and control changing environments. However, in attempting to find useful patterns, people sometimes observe meaningless patterns. For example, a baseball player who does not shave before a game in which he hits two home-runs may infer that not shaving increases his performance and consequently never shave again before a game. This type of natural reasoning is often labeled superstition (Vyse, 1997). In the psychological literature, a variety of ways in which natural cognitive processing can lead to erroneous inferences have been documented (see Myers, 2002, for an overview of cognitive distortions). A consideration of these cognitive tendencies can help explain why profilers, police officers, and the public might believe CP works.

Judgment and decision-making research (e.g., Gilovich, 1991; Myers, 2002) suggests that profilers might assign more personal responsibility to investigative success than to investigative failure (i.e., self-serving bias) and be more confident in their ability to make accurate predictions than they should be (i.e., overconfidence). In addition, profilers and the public may attribute perceived successes to the profiler's abilities and discount the importance of the police officers' contribution (i.e., fundamental attribution error). Furthermore, profilers, police officers, and the public might be susceptible to misperceiving a profiler's competence if they evaluate the accuracy of a profile after the apprehension of the criminal (i.e., hindsight bias), or perceive a relationship between a profiler's predictions and the resolution of a case where one does not exist (i.e., illusory correlation).

After-the-fact reasoning is one particularly good example of how natural reasoning can lead to the detection of meaningless patterns (Carroll, 2003; Gilovich, 1991; Pope & Vasquez, 2005; Sagan, 1996; Shermer, 2002). Many events follow sequential patterns without being causally related; *after this* does not necessarily mean *because of this*. In some cases, criminal profiles appear to be the primary cause of the successful resolution of an investigation simply because a profile was obtained before the case was solved (e.g., Copson, 1995; Tenten, 1989; Wilson, Lincoln, & Kocsis, 1997). It might be the case that people believe in CP due to the inability to distinguish between meaningful and meaningless patterns.

A ubiquitous cognitive tendency that may also explain why profilers, law enforcement officers, and the rest of us believe in the veracity and predictive validity of CP is confirmation bias. Confirmation bias involves looking for, often unconsciously, evidence that confirms an existing belief and ignoring or filtering out evidence that disconfirms that belief (Nickerson, 1998; Shermer, 2003). This type of cognitive tendency has been shown to affect general public and scientists alike and, according to Shermer, is the most powerful of all cognitive biases that operates to confirm and justify many weird beliefs. He has argued that psychics, fortunetellers, palm readers, and astrologers all depend on confirmation bias to convince people of their abilities. Specifically, he believes that telling the client what to expect in the future (a one-sided event instead of a two-sided event) causes the client to notice the occurrence of a predicted event but ignore or filter out the nonoccurrence of a predicted event. By extension, it would not be surprising to discover that confirmation bias plays a role in the formation, and defense, of positive beliefs regarding CP. We suspect that there may be a tendency for those who have formed a positive belief about profiling to look for or remember confirmatory evidence (e.g., correct predictions or successful anecdotes, which are often evident in the literature and popular media) that supports their belief that profiling works and to ignore and/or forget contradictory evidence (e.g., incorrect predictions or unsuccessful anecdotes, which are rarely presented in the literature or popular media).

## Finding Meaning in Ambiguous Information

Clinical and personality research has consistently demonstrated that people are inclined to accept ambiguous, vague, and general statements as accurate descriptions of their own personalities (e.g., Dickson & Kelly, 1985; Johnson, Cain, Falke, Hayman, & Perillo, 1985; Sundberg, 1955). This phenomenon has been coined the Barnum effect, and within the psychological field it is believed to be especially problematic for the acceptance of clinical diagnoses (Snyder, Shenkel, & Lowery, 1977). Some researchers attribute the considerable acceptance rate of high base-rate feedback to human gullibility, whereas others note the importance of factors such as social desirability, situational insecurity, and interpreter prestige (Piper-Terry & Downey, 1998). Furthermore, Snyder, Larsen, and Bloom's (1976) results suggested that people are more inclined to accept a bogus personality description when it is believed to be based on a psychological assessment procedure rather than an alternate technique such as astrology, although in that study, differences in the degrees of acceptance were marginal.

In the CP context, a similar effect can occur when individuals evaluate whether or not an ambiguous profile describes a suspect accurately. Many profiles are so ambiguous that they can appear to describe any suspect (Alison, Smith, Eastman, & Rainbow, 2003). For example, Alison, Smith, Eastman, et al. (2003) analyzed 21 criminal profiles that were used in major criminal investigations and found a total of 3,090 statements. Of the 880 statements that contained predictions about the characteristics of the unknown criminal, 82% were unsubstantiated, 55% were unverifiable, 28% were falsifiable, and 24% were ambiguous. In a related study, Alison, Smith, and Morgan (2003) examined police officers' propensity to estimate the accuracy of an ambiguous profile. Two groups of officers were given the same ambiguous profile but substantially different descriptions of the criminal that the profile supposedly described (only one being that of the genuine offender). Accuracy judgments for both groups averaged 5.3 out of 7, suggesting that when a criminal is apprehended, any profile might retrospectively appear to describe him or her accurately.

A phenomenon related to the Barnum effect, known as the personal validation effect (e.g., Collins, Dmitruk, & Ranney, 1977), is concerned with changes in participants' attitudes when taking part in Barnum experiments. Personality research suggests that faith in psychological assessment methods and perceptions of diagnosticians' skills may increase as a result of exposure to ambiguous personality descriptions. For instance, Snyder et al. (1976) presented participants with a bogus personality interpretation and asked them to rate the acceptance of this interpretation as being personally relevant. As in previous studies, Snyder et al. found evidence for the Barnum effect. The more interesting contribution from this study, however, was that both faith in the assessment procedure and diagnostician's perceived skill were found to increase significantly after the participants evaluated the interpretation, regardless of whether the assessment procedure was based on astrology, graphology, or psychology. Their findings suggest that beliefs about CP methods and profiler skills may become more favorable after people are exposed to ambiguous profile material, even when the CP method is not actually valid and the profiler is not actually skilled.

## Imitation and Social Contagion

People often believe things, or do things a certain way, because they were believed or done that way by others (Dawkins, 2003). Dawkins (2003) contends that people form some beliefs without ever connecting them to evidence of their veracity. Simon (1990) has similarly argued that a large amount of what we know is naturally acquired from other people's behavior and instructions, and the tendency to accept the beliefs of others allows people to obtain knowledge and skills that may be useful in many of life's activities. Imitating others is adaptive because people do not need to expend much time or cognitive resources to carefully evaluate the consequences of everything they have observed (Simon, 1990). Believing things through imitation is the outcome of bounded human rationality in a complex world (Simon, 1990), but the consequence of uncritical acceptance of ideas is that people sometimes accept unhelpful information.

Police officers may believe CP is a valid investigative technique because they observe other police officers using it and accept messages promoting its effectiveness. Support for this argument comes from the results of a survey by Jackson et al. (1993). They found that police officers who used CP learned about it through informal policing networks within their police force and contact with colleagues who possessed knowledge about CP. Other ways by which officers learn about CP are through lectures, articles in police publications, and technical training at police academies and colleges (Jackson & Bekerian, 1997). As we have already described, most of these information sources present CP as a viable investigative tool.

Related to imitation is the phenomenon of social contagion. Social contagion research suggests that people will adopt others' beliefs after observing behavior that appeared to work. For example, suicide often occurs in clusters and is therefore thought to be contagious (Stack, 2000). According to Gould, Jamieson, and Romer (2003), fictional and nonfictional portrayals of suicide may make taking one's own life appear as an effective tool for achieving personal gain. Social contagion has also been documented for such phenomena as burnout among teachers (Bakker & Schaufeli, 2000), violence and aggression (Berkowitz & Macaulay, 1971; Goldstein, Arnold, & Rosenberg, 2001), military coups (Li & Thompson, 1975), mood (Neumann & Strack, 2000), and scratching in Japanese monkeys (Nakayama, 2004). Using CP and believing it works is likely contagious as well.

The importance of contagion to an account of why CP is believed to be a good idea is evidenced by numerous instances of public popularity. For example, according to Egger (1999), the Mad Bomber case ignited the notion that CP is a viable tool, but it was developments made by the FBI (e.g., training programs, extensive publications, television appearances) that led to the rapid growth in CP activities in the United States. In the United Kingdom, it appears that the apparent success of David Canter's profile in the Railway Rapist case led to an upsurge in both the interest and usage of CP. For instance, Copson (1995) found a tripling of the number of profile requests in the year following that case. Although it may be difficult to assess whether CP contagion exists, it is indisputable that there has been a steady rise, with intermittent dramatic increases, in CP use (e.g., see Copson, 1995, for data from the United Kingdom). This suggests that both imitation and social contagion may be contributing to the CP illusion.

## Mistaking Fiction for Fact

People are particularly attracted to phenomena that appeal to fantasy by focusing on the powers that ordinary people lack but desire (Sagan, 1996). Green, Brock, and Kaufman (2004) asserted that individuals generally want to be entertained and tend to seek out fiction rather than nonfiction to achieve this entertainment. They suggest that the main reason people appear to be attracted to the media is the desire to escape from the real world. They also maintain that people are susceptible to adopting beliefs about real world events that are entirely based on fictional accounts.

Because people are often intrigued by the criminal mind, CP activities tend to generate considerable public fascination. This observation is evidenced by the number of books, films, and television programs that deal with CP as well as the recent growth in college and university courses that address CP issues. Grubin (1995) has also suggested that CP appeals to fantasy because it conjures up the image of "the cerebral sleuth relying solely on his acute powers of observation and deductive reasoning to identify an elusive and much feared serial rapist" (p. 262). Indeed, some researchers have actually attributed, or at least associated, the origins of CP to fictional detectives such as Edgar Allan Poe's C. Auguste Dupin, Agatha Christies's Hercule Poirot, and Sir Arthur Conan Doyle's Sherlock Holmes (Blau, 1994; Campbell, 1976; Canter, 2000; McCann, 1992; Muller, 2000). The profiling fantasy is also the result of journalists who write about profilers with mystical powers of deduction, thereby increasing the public's belief in the validity of an unproven investigative method (Alison & Canter, 1999).

# Conclusion

There is a growing belief that profilers can accurately and consistently predict a criminal's characteristics based on crime scene evidence. This increased belief is evident from the fact that CP is becoming prevalent as an investigative technique, that positive opinions of CP are being communicated in published literature, and that police officers and mental health professionals support the use of CP. We contend that this belief is illusory because a critical analysis of research on CP showed that the field lacks theoretical grounding and empirical support. We proposed that belief in such a pseudoscientific practice is due to an interaction between the message and the mind—that is, the interaction between the information that people receive about CP and the way they process that information.

As CP has the potential to mislead criminal investigators, and thereby either hinder the apprehension of guilty criminals or lead to wrongful convictions, it is a practice that must be approached critically. Various information sources present fictional or nonfictional anecdotes involving the invaluable help of expert profilers in solving serious cases. The expert profilers use post hoc analysis of ambiguous predictions to create the impression that they reduced a detective's uncertainty about how to proceed with an investigation by providing a simple solution to a complex case. This has the potential of generating a reliance on a process that does not advance an investigation.

The belief that CP works is troubling because of the meager scientific evidence to support the practice. Nevertheless, we agree with Lilienfeld (2005) that there are at least three reasons for researchers to conduct proper scientific evaluations of practices that currently lack scientific support. First, CP may actually work. As Lilienfeld has argued, extraordinary claims may be shown to contain a core of truth that should not be automatically dismissed. In our opinion, the burden is on profilers, who make extraordinary claims about their abilities, to prove their worth by actually participating in controlled experimental studies. Second, people deserve to have an accurate view of CP. Conducting and disseminating scientific research is the best method to ensure that this occurs. Third, the effect of CP on police investigations is unknown. Research will be able to determine these effects, whether positive or negative. We anticipate that police officers might argue that they do not have time to wait for scientific evidence from CP research because they have to use something to assist them in their investigations. Such a response is justified, but, according to Lilienfeld, it is likely to cause tension between those who are skeptical about CP and those who believe that CP can contribute to an investigation.

More than 50 years of CP practice have passed without much rigorous scientific evaluation. We contend that it is now time to remove the shroud of secrecy in the CP field, evaluate it, and put the burden back on profilers to prove their worth.[5] We explored the CP illusion with the intention of providing a natural explanation for a belief that lacks scientific support. The next logical step is to test the various claims that we have made in this article. All currently uncorroborated statements we have made are testable and falsifiable by scientific research. Until this occurs, we advocate that readers approach CP, and even our article, with a critical mind.

# Notes

1. Although the scope of criminal profiling (CP) practice now goes beyond this original definition to include advice on interview strategies, media strategies, prioritizing resources, statement analysis, and so on, we believe that predicting offender characteristics remains the primary goal of CP. All of this additional advice is dependent on the type of person that the profiler believes committed the crime. Some CP advocates will no doubt argue that there are newer approaches to profiling that are based on empirical science (or that the field has moved on). However, research demonstrating how these new approaches are superior to existing profiling methods, or data illustrating their improved predictive validity, is nonexistent (see Hicks & Sales, 2006, for a similar view). Although some may consider geographic profiling as an integral part of criminal profiling, it is beyond the scope of the current article.

2. These two types are not necessarily mutually exclusive.

3. Although credit must be given to Richard Kocsis for collecting data that are suitable for a meta-analysis, that research (e.g., Kocsis, 2003b, 2004b; Kocsis, Hayes, & Irwin, 2002; Kocsis, Irwin, Hayes, & Nunn, 2000) has been criticized for a range of methodological and conceptual limitations such as the use of multiple choice questionnaires, variation in the length of time given to participants to complete the experiment, and aggregating data to favor the experimental group (see Bennell, Jones, Taylor, & Snook, 2006).

4. There is an existing regulatory body, the International Criminal Investigative Analysis Fellowship (ICIAF), which trains and accredits profilers. However, this organization has yet to gain widespread acceptance within the profiling and research communities.

5. Whether or not criminal profilers will readily come forward in sufficient numbers to have their skills assessed is questionable. Kocsis et al. (2000) reported that they requested 40 active profilers to take part in their experiments, but only 5 agreed to participate. We hope that profilers who read this article will contact us about participating in experimental tests of their abilities.

# References

Alison, L. J., Bennell, C., Mokros, A., & Ormerod, D. (2002). The personality paradox in offender profiling: A theoretical review of the processes involved in deriving background characteristics from crime scene actions. *Psychology, Public Policy, and Law, 8*, 115–135.

Alison, L. J., & Canter, D. V. (1999). Professional, legal, and ethical issues in offender profiling. In D. V. Canter & L. J. Alison (Eds.), *Profiling in policy and practice* (pp. 21–54). Aldershot, UK: Ashgate.

Alison, L. J., Smith, M. D., Eastman, O., & Rainbow, L. (2003). Toulmin's philosophy of argument and its relevance to offender profiling. *Psychology, Crime and Law, 9*, 173–183.

Alison, L. J., Smith, M. D., & Morgan, K. (2003). Interpreting the accuracy of offender profiles. *Psychology, Crime and Law, 9*, 185–195.

Andrews, D. A., & Bonta, J. (2006). *Psychology of criminal conduct.* Cincinnati, OH: Anderson.

Andrews, D. A., Bonta, J., & Wormith, J. S. (2006). The recent past and near future of risk and/or need assessment. *Crime & Delinquency, 52*, 7–27.

Åsgard, U. (1998). Swedish experiences in offender profiling and evaluation of some aspects of a case of murder and abduction in Germany. In Case Analysis Unit (BKA), *Method of case analysis: An international symposium* (pp. 125–130). Weisbaden, Germany: Bundeskriminalamt Kriminalistisches Institut.

Ault, R. L., Jr., & Reese, J. T. (1980). A psychological assessment of crime profiling. *FBI Law Enforcement Bulletin, 49*, 22–25.

Badcock, R. (1997). Developmental and clinical issues in relation to offending in the individual. In J. L. Jackson & D. B. Bekerian (Eds.), *Offender profiling: Theory, research, and practice* (pp. 9–42). Chichester, UK: Wiley.

Bakker, A. B., & Schaufeli, W. B. (2000). Burnout contagion processes among teachers. *Journal of Applied Social Psychology, 30*, 2289–2308.

Bartol, C. R. (1996). Police psychology: Then, now, and beyond. *Criminal Justice and Behavior, 23*, 70–89.

Bateman, A. L., & Salfati, C. G. (2007). An examination of behavioral consistency using individual behaviors or groups of behaviors in serial homicide. *Behavioral Sciences & the Law, 25*, 527–544.

Bennell, C., & Canter, D. V. (2002). Linking commercial burglaries by modus operandi: Tests using regression and ROC analysis. *Science & Justice, 42*, 153–164.

Bennell, C., & Jones, N. J. (2005). Between a ROC and a hard place: A method for linking serial burglaries using an offender's modus operandi. *Journal of Investigative Psychology and Offender Profiling, 2*, 23–41.

Bennell, C., Jones, N. J., Taylor, P. J., & Snook, B. (2006). Validities and abilities in criminal profiling: A critique of the studies conducted by Richard Kocsis and his colleagues. *International Journal of Offender Therapy and Comparative Criminology, 50*, 344–360.

Berger, M. (1957a, January 23). Bomber is booked: Sent to Bellevue for mental tests. *The New York Times*, pp. 1, 18.

Berger, M. (1957b, January 25). Twisted course of "Mad Bomber" vengeance traced in a deeply complex personality. *The New York Times*, p. 18.

Berkowitz, L., & Macaulay, J. (1971). The contagion of criminal violence. *Sociometry, 34*, 238–260.

Blau, T. H. (1994). Psychological profiling. In T. H. Blau (Ed.), *Psychological services for law enforcement* (pp. 261–274). New York: John Wiley.

Bochner, S., & Insko, C. A. (1966). Communicator discrepancy, source credibility, and opinion change. *Journal of Personality and Social Psychology, 4*, 614–621.

Boon, J. C. W. (1997). The contribution of personality theories to psychological profiling. In J. L. Jackson & D. B. Bekerian (Eds.), *Offender profiling: Theory, research, and practice* (pp. 43–59). Chichester, UK: Wiley.

Borgida, E., & Nisbett, R. E. (1977). The differential impact of abstract vs. concrete information on decisions. *Journal of Applied Social Psychology, 7*, 258–271.

Bowers, K. (1973). Situationism in psychology: An analysis and a critique. *Psychological Review, 80*, 307–336.

Brussel, J. A. (1968). *Casebook of a crime psychiatrist*. London: New English Library.

Cacioppo, J. T., & Petty, R. E. (1979). The effects of message repetition and position on cognitive responses, recall, and persuasion. *Journal of Personality and Social Psychology, 37*, 97–109.

Campbell, C. (1976, May). Portrait of a mass killer. *Psychology Today, 9*, 110–119.

Canter, D. V. (1994). *Criminal shadows: Inside the mind of the serial killer*. London: HarperCollins.

Canter, D. V. (1995). Psychology of offender profiling. In R. Bull & D. Carson (Eds.), *Handbook of psychology in legal contexts* (pp. 343–373). Chichester, UK: Wiley.

Canter, D. V. (2000). Offender profiling and criminal differentiation. *Legal and Criminological Psychology, 5*, 23–46.

Canter, D. V., Alison, L. J., Alison, E., & Wentink, N. (2004). The organized/disorganized typology of serial murder: Myth or model? *Psychology, Public Policy, and Law, 10*, 293–320.

Canter, D. V., & Fritzon, K. (1998). Differentiating arsonists: A model of firesetting actions and characteristics. *Legal and Criminological Psychology, 3*, 73–96.

Canter, D. V., & Wentink, N. (2004). An empirical test of Holmes and Holmes's serial murder typology. *Criminal Justice and Behavior, 20*, 1–26.

Carroll, R. T. (2003). *The skeptic's dictionary: A collection of strange beliefs, amusing deceptions, and dangerous delusions*. New York: John Wiley.

Chapman, L. J., & Chapman, J. P. (1967). Genesis of popular but erroneous psychodiagnostic observations. *Journal of Abnormal Psychology, 72*, 271–280.

Clark, D. (2002). *Dark paths, cold trails: How a Mountie led the quest to link serial killers to their victims*. Toronto, Ontario, Canada: HarperCollins.

Collins, R. W., Dmitruk, V. M., & Ranney, J. R. (1977). Personal validation: Some empirical and ethical considerations. *Journal of Consulting and Clinical Psychology, 45*, 70–77.

Cook, P. E., & Hinman, D. L. (1999). Criminal profiling. *Journal of Contemporary Criminal Justice, 15*, 230–241.

Copson, G. (1995). *Coals to Newcastle? Part 1: A study of offender profiling*. London: Home Office, Police Research Group.

Copson, G., Badcock, R., Boon, J., & Britton, P. (1997). Editorial: Articulating a systematic approach to clinical crime profiling. *Criminal Behavior and Mental Health, 7*, 13–17.

Crocker, J. (1981). Judgment of covariation by social perceivers. *Psychological Bulletin, 90*, 272–292.

Crocker, J. (1982). Biased questions in judgments of covariation studies. *Personality and Social Psychology Bulletin, 8*, 214–220.

Davies, A., Wittebrood, K., & Jackson, J. L. (1997). Predicting the criminal antecedents of a stranger rapist from his offence behaviour. *Science & Justice, 37*, 161–170.

Davis, J. A. (1999). Criminal personality profiling and crime scene assessment. *Journal of Contemporary Criminal Justice, 15,* 291–301.

Dawes, R. M. (1997). *House of cards: Psychology and psychotherapy built on myth.* New York: Free Press.

Dawkins, R. (2003). *A devil's chaplain: Reflections on home, lies, science, and love.* New York: Houghton Mifflin.

Depue, R. L. (1986). An American response to an era of violence. *FBI Law Enforcement Bulletin, 55*(12), 2–5.

Dickson, D. H., & Kelly, I. W. (1985). The "Barnum effect" in personality assessment: A review of the literature. *Psychological Reports, 57,* 367–382.

Douglas, J. E., & Burgess, A. E. (1986). Criminal profiling: A viable investigative tool against violent crime. *FBI Law Enforcement Bulletin, 55*(12), 9–13.

Douglas, J. E., Burgess, A. W., Burgess, A. G., & Ressler, R. K. (1992). *Crime classification manual: A standard system for investigating and classifying violent crime.* New York: Simon & Schuster.

Douglas, J. E., & Munn, C. (1992). Violent crime scene analysis: Modus operandi, signature, and staging. *FBI Law Enforcement Bulletin, 61*(2), 1–10.

Douglas, J. E., & Olshaker, M. (1995). *Mind hunter: Inside the FBI's elite serial crime unit.* New York: Simon & Schuster.

Douglas, J. E., Ressler, R. K., Burgess, A. W., & Hartman, C. R. (1986). Criminal profiling from crime scene analysis. *Behavioral Sciences & the Law, 4,* 401–421.

Dowden, C., Bennell, C., & Bloomfield, S. (2007). Advances in offender profiling: A systematic review of the profiling literatures published over the past 30 years. *Journal of Police and Criminal Psychology, 22,* 44–56.

Egger, S. A. (1999). Psychological profiling. *Journal of Contemporary Criminal Justice, 15,* 242–261.

Farrington, D. P., & Lambert, S. (1997). Predicting offender profiles from the victim and witness descriptions. In J. L. Jackson & D. B. Bekerian (Eds.), *Offender profiling: Theory, research, and practice* (pp. 133–158). Chichester, UK: Wiley.

Faust, D., & Ziskin, J. (1988). The expert witness in psychology and psychiatry. *Science, 241,* 31–35.

Fearon, P. (2003). Big problems with small samples. *Psychologist Special Statistics: Are You Behind the Times?, 16,* 632–635.

Garb, H. N. (1998). *Studying the clinician: Judgment research and psychological assessment.* Washington, DC: American Psychological Association.

Garb, H. N., & Boyle, P. A. (2003). Understanding why some clinicians use pseudoscientific methods: Findings from research on clinical judgment. In S. O. Lilienfeld, S. J. Lynn, & J. M. Lohr (Eds.), *Science and pseudoscience in clinical psychology* (pp. 17–38). New York: Guilford.

Gendreau, P., Little, T., & Goggin, C. (1996). A meta-analysis of adult offender recidivism: What works! *Criminology, 34,* 575–607.

Gendreau, P., Smith, P., & French, S. (2006). The theory of effective correctional intervention: Empirical status and future directions. In F. Cullen, J. Wright, & M. Coleman (Eds.), *Taking Stock: The status of criminological theory* (pp. 419–446). Piscataway, NJ: Transaction Press.

Gigerenzer, G. (2002). *Reckoning with risk: Learning to live with uncertainty.* London: Penguin.

Gilovich, T. (1991). *How we know what isn't so: The fallibility of human reason in everyday life.* New York: Free Press.

Godwin, M. G. (1999). *Hunting serial predators: A multivariate approach to profiling violent behavior.* Boca Raton, FL: CRC Press.

Goldstein, N. E., Arnold, D. H., & Rosenberg, J. L. (2001). Contagion of aggression in day care classrooms as a function of peer and teacher responses. *Journal of Educational Psychology, 93,* 708–719.

Goodwill, A. M., & Alison, L. (2007). When is profiling possible? Offense planning and aggression as moderators in predicting offender age from victim age in stranger rape. *Behavioral Sciences & the Law, 25,* 823–840.

Gould, M., Jamieson, P., & Romer, D. (2003). Media contagion and suicide among the young. *American Behavioral Scientist, 46,* 1269–1284.

Green, M. C., Brock, T. C., & Kaufman, G. (2004). Understanding media enjoyment: The role of transportation into narrative worlds. *Communication Theory, 14,* 311–327.

Grubin, D. (1995). Offender profiling. *The Journal of Forensic Psychiatry, 6,* 259–263.

Gudjonsson, G. H., & Copson, G. (1997). The role of the expert in the criminal investigation. In J. L. Jackson & D. B. Bekerian (Eds.), *Offender profiling: Theory, research, and practice* (pp. 61–76). Chichester, UK: Wiley.

Häkkänen, H., Lindof, P., & Santilla, P. (2004). Crime scene actions and offender characteristics in a sample of Finnish stranger rapes. *Journal of Investigative Psychology and Offender Profiling, 1,* 17–32.

Hanson, R. K., & Morton-Bourgon, K. E. (2005). The characteristics of persistent sexual offenders: A meta-analysis of recidivism studies. *Journal of Consulting and Clinical Psychology, 73,* 1154–1163.

Hazelwood, R. R., Ressler, R. K., Depue, R. L., & Douglas, J. E. (1995). Criminal investigative analysis: An overview. In A. W. Burgess & R. R. Hazelwood (Eds.), *Practical aspects of rape investigation: A multidisciplinary approach* (pp. 115–126). Boca Raton, FL: CRC Press.

Hicks, S. J., & Sales, B. D. (2006). *Criminal profiling: Developing an effective science and practice.* Washington, DC: American Psychological Association.

Hines, T. (1988). *Pseudoscience and the paranormal: A critical examination of the evidence.* New York: Prometheus Books.

Holmes, R. M., & Holmes, S. (1996). *Profiling violent crimes: An investigative tool.* Thousand Oaks, CA: Sage.

Homant, R. J., & Kennedy, D. B. (1998). Psychological aspects of crime scene profiling. *Criminal Justice and Behavior, 25,* 319–343.

House, J. C. (1997). Towards a practical application of offender profiling: The RNC's criminal suspect prioritization system. In J. L. Jackson & D. A. Bekerian (Eds.), *Offender profiling: Theory, research and practice* (pp. 177–190). Chichester, UK: Wiley.

Jackson, J. L., & Bekerian, D. A. (1997). Does offender profiling have a role to play? In J. L. Jackson & D. B. Bekerian (Eds.), *Offender profiling: Theory, research, and practice* (pp. 1–7). Chichester, UK: Wiley.

Jackson, J. L., Herbrink, J. C. M., & van Koppen, P. J. (1997). An empirical approach to offender profiling. In V. G. S. Redondon, J. Perez, & R. Barbaret (Eds.), *Advances in psychology and law: International contributions* (pp. 333–345). Berlin, Germany: De Gruyter.

Jackson, J. L., van den Eshof, P., & de Kleuver, E. E. (1997). A research approach to offender profiling. In J. L. Jackson & D. B. Bekerian (Eds.), *Offender profiling: Theory, research, and practice* (pp. 107–132). Chichester, UK: Wiley.

Jackson, J. L., van Koppen, P. J., & Herbrink, J. C. M. (1993). *Does the service meet the needs? An evaluation of consumer satisfaction with specific profile analysis and investigative advice offered by the Scientific*

*Research Advisory Unit of the National Criminal Intelligence Division (CRI)—The Netherlands.* Leiden: Netherlands Institute for the Study of Criminality and Law Enforcement.

Johnson, J. T., Cain, L. M., Falke, T. L., Hayman, J., & Perillo, E. (1985). The "Barnum effect" revisited: Cognitive and motivational factors in the acceptance of personality descriptions. *Journal of Personality and Social Psychology, 49,* 1378–1391.

Keppel, R. D., & Walter, R. (1999). Profiling killers: A revised classification model for understanding sexual murder. *International Journal of Offender Therapy and Comparative Criminology, 43,* 417–434.

Keppel, R. D., & Weis, J. G. (1993). *Improving the investigation of violent crime: The homicide investigation and tracking system. Research in Brief.* Washington, DC: National Institute of Justice.

Kocsis, R. N. (2003a). Criminal psychological profiling: Validities and abilities. *International Journal of Offender Therapy and Comparative Criminology, 47,* 126–144.

Kocsis, R. N. (2003b). An empirical assessment of content in criminal psychological profiles. *International Journal of Offender Therapy and Comparative Criminology, 47,* 38–47.

Kocsis, R. N. (2004a). Profiling the criminal mind: Does it actually work? *The Lancet, 364,* 14–15.

Kocsis, R. N. (2004b). Psychological profiling of serial arson skills: An assessment of skills and accuracy. *Criminal Justice and Behavior, 31,* 341–361.

Kocsis, R. N. (2006). *Criminal profiling: Principles and practice.* Totowa, NJ: Humana Press.

Kocsis, R. N., Cooksey, R. W., & Irwin, H. J. (2002a). Psychological profiling of offender characteristics from crime behaviors in serial rape offences. *International Journal of Offender Therapy and Comparative Criminology, 46,* 144–169.

Kocsis, R. N., Cooksey, R. W., & Irwin, H. J. (2002b). Psychological profiling of sexual murders: An empirical model. *International Journal of Offender Therapy and Comparative Criminology, 46,* 532–554.

Kocsis, R. N., & Hayes, A. F. (2004). Believing is seeing? Investigating the perceived accuracy of criminal psychological profiles. *International Journal of Offender Therapy and Comparative Criminology, 48,* 149–160.

Kocsis, R. N., Hayes, A. F., & Irwin, H. J. (2002). Investigative experience and accuracy in psychological profiling of a violent crime. *Journal of Interpersonal Violence, 17,* 811–823.

Kocsis, R. N., & Heller, G. Z. (2004). Believing is seeing II: Beliefs and perceptions of criminal psychological profiles. *International Journal of Offender Therapy and Comparative Criminology, 48,* 313–329.

Kocsis, R. N., Irwin, H. J., Hayes, A. F., & Nunn, R. (2000). Expertise in psychological profiling. *Journal of Interpersonal Violence, 15,* 311–331.

Kurz-Milcke, E., & Gigerenzer, G. (2004). *Experts in science and society.* New York: Kluwer Academic/ Plenum.

Lassiter, G. D., Geers, A. L., Munhall, P. J., Ploutz-Snyder, R. J., & Breitenbecher, D. L. (2002). Illusory causation: Why it occurs. *Psychological Science, 13,* 299–305.

Li, R. P., & Thompson, W. R. (1975). The "coup contagion" hypothesis. *Journal of Conflict Resolution, 19,* 63–88.

Lilienfeld, S. O. (2005). The 10 commandments of helping students distinguish science from pseudoscience in psychology. *The Observer, 18,* 39–51.

Lyons, A., & Truzzi, M. (1991). *The blue sense: Psychic detectives and crime.* New York: Mysterious Press.

McCann, J. T. (1992). Criminal personality profiling in the investigation of violent crime: Recent advances and future directions. *Behavioral Sciences & the Law, 10,* 475–481.

McCrary, G. O., & Ramsland, K. M. (2003). *The unknown darkness: Profiling the predators among us.* New York: HarperCollins.

Meehl, P. E. (1997). Credentialed persons, credentialed knowledge. *Clinical Psychology: Science and Practice, 4,* 91–98.

Melnyk, T., Bloomfield, S., & Bennell, C. (2007, September). *Classifying serial sexual homicide: Validating Keppel and Walter's (1999) model.* Poster session presented at the annual meeting of the Society for Police and Criminal Psychology, Springfield, MA.

Milgram, S. (1964). Issues in the study of obedience. *American Psychologist, 19,* 848–852.

Mischel, W. (1968). *Personality and assessment.* New York: John Wiley.

Mokros, A., & Alison, L. (2002). Is offender profiling possible? Testing the predicted homology of crime scene actions and background characteristics in a sample of rapists. *Legal and Criminological Psychology, 7,* 25–43.

Muller, D. A. (2000). Criminal profiling: Real science or just wishful thinking? *Homicide Studies, 4,* 234–264.

Myers, D. G. (2002). *Intuition: Its powers and perils.* New Haven, CT: Yale University Press.

Nakayama, K. (2004). Observing conspecifics scratching induces a contagion of scratching in Japanese monkeys (*Macaca fuscata*). *Journal of Comparative Psychology, 118,* 20–24.

Neumann, R., & Strack, F. (2000). "Mood contagion": The automatic transfer of mood between persons. *Journal of Personality and Social Psychology, 79,* 211–223.

Nickell, J. (1994). *Psychic sleuths.* Buffalo, NY: Prometheus Books.

Nickerson, R. S. (1998). Confirmation bias: A ubiquitous phenomenon in many guises. *Review of General Psychology, 30,* 395–406.

O'Keeffe, C., & Alison, L. J. (2000). Rhetoric in "psychic detection." *Journal of the Society for Psychical Research, 64,* 26–38.

Ormerod, D. (1996a). The evidential implications of psychological profiling. *Criminal Law Review, 717,* 863–877.

Ormerod, D. (1996b). Psychological profiling. *The Journal of Forensic Psychiatry, 7,* 341–352.

Paulos, J. A. (1988). *Innumeracy: Mathematical illiteracy and its consequences.* New York: Hill and Wang.

Pinizzotto, A. J. (1984). Forensic psychology: Criminal personality profiling. *Journal of Police Science and Administration, 12,* 32–40.

Pinizzotto, A. J., & Finkel, N. J. (1990). Criminal personality profiling: An outcome and process study. *Law and Human Behavior, 14,* 215–233.

Piper-Terry, M. L., & Downey, J. L. (1998). Sex, gullibility, and the Barnum effect. *Psychological Reports, 82,* 571–576.

Plous, S. (1993). *The psychology of judgment and decision-making.* New York: McGraw-Hill.

Pope, K. S., & Vasquez, M. J. T. (2005). Avoiding logical fallacies in psychology. In K. S. Pope (Ed.), *How to survive and thrive as a therapist: Information, ideas, and resources for psychologists in practice* (pp. 101–107). Washington, DC: American Psychologist.

Reimer, T., Mata, R., & Stoecklin, M. (2004). The use of heuristics in persuasion: Deriving cues on source expertise from argument quality. *Current Research in Social Psychology, 10,* 70–83.

Ressler, R. K., Burgess, A. W., Douglas, J. E., Hartman, C. R., & D'Agostino, R. B. (1986). Sexual killers and their victims: Identifying patterns through crime scene analysis. *Journal of Interpersonal Violence, 1,* 288–308.

Risinger, D. M., & Loop, J. L. (2002). Three card monte, monty hall, modus operandi and "offender profiling": Some lessons of modern cognitive science for the law of evidence. *Cardozo Law Review, 24*, 193–285.

Sagan, C. (1996). *The demon-haunted world: Science as a candle in the dark*. New York: Ballantine Books.

Salfati, C. G. (2000). The nature of expressiveness and instrumentality in homicide: Implications for offender profiling. *Homicide Studies, 4*, 265–293.

Salfati, C. G., & Canter, D. V. (1999). Differentiating stranger murders: Profiling offender characteristics from behavioral styles. *Behavioral Sciences & the Law, 17*, 391–406.

Santilla, P., Häkkänen, H., Canter, D. V., & Elfgren, T. (2003). Classifying homicide offenders and predicting their characteristics from crime scene behavior. *Scandinavian Journal of Psychology, 44*, 107–118.

Shermer, M. (2002). *Why people believe weird things: Pseudoscience, superstition, and other confusions of our time*. New York: Henry Holt.

Shermer, M. (2003). *The borderlands of science. Where sense meets nonsense*. Oxford, UK: Oxford University Press.

Simon, H. A. (1990, December 21). A mechanism for social selection and successful altruism. *Science, 250*, 1665–1668.

16-year search for madman. (1956, December 25). *The New York Times*, pp. 1, 31.

Sjöstedt, G., Långström, N., Sturidsson, K., & Grann, M. (2004). Stability of modus operandi in sexual offending. *Criminal Justice and Behavior, 31*, 609–623.

Snook, B., Eastwood, J., Gendreau, P., Goggin, C., & Cullen, R. M. (2007). Taking stock of criminal profiling: A narrative review and meta-analysis. *Criminal Justice and Behavior, 34*, 437–453.

Snook, B., Haines, A., Taylor, P. J., & Bennell, C. (2007). Criminal profiling belief and use: A survey of Canadian police officer opinion. *Canadian Journal of Police and Security Services, 5*, 169–179.

Snyder, C. R., Larsen, D. L., & Bloom, L. J. (1976). Acceptance of general personality interpretations prior to and after receipt of diagnostic feedback supposedly based on psychological, graphological, and astrological assessment procedures. *Journal of Clinical Psychology, 32*, 258–265.

Snyder, C. R., Shenkel, R. J., & Lowery, C. R. (1977). Acceptance of personality descriptions: The "Barnum effect" and beyond. *Journal of Consulting and Clinical Psychology, 45*, 104–114.

Sprott, J. B. (1996). Understanding public views of youth crime and the youth justice system. *Canadian Journal of Criminology, 38*, 271–290.

Stack, S. (2000). Media impacts on suicide: A quantitative review of 293 findings. *Social Science Quarterly, 81*, 957–971.

Stanovich, K. E. (1992). *How to think straight about psychology*. New York: HarperCollins.

*State v. Fortin*, 724 A.2d 818 (N.J. Super. Ct. App.Div. 1999).

Sundberg, N. D. (1955). The acceptability of "fake" versus "bona fide" personality test interpretations. *Journal of Abnormal and Social Psychology, 50*, 145–147.

Tenten, H. (1989). Offender profiling. In W. Bailey (Ed.), *Encyclopedia of police science* (pp. 365–376). New York: Garland.

Torres, A. N., Boccaccini, M. T., & Miller, H. A. (2006). Perceptions of the validity and utility of criminal profiling among forensic psychologists and psychiatrists. *Professional Psychology: Research and Practice, 37*, 51–58.

Trager, J., & Brewster, J. (2001). The effectiveness of psychological profiles. *Journal of Police and Criminal Psychology, 16*(1), 20–28.

Turvey, B. (1999). *Criminal profiling: An introduction to behavioral evidence analysis.* San Diego, CA: Academic Press.

Vyse, S. A. (1997). *Believing in magic: The psychology of superstition.* London: Oxford University Press.

Wallston, K. A. (1983). Problems of generalizing from small samples: Comment on Larde and Clopton. *Psychological Reports, 53,* 573–574.

West, A. G. (2000). Clinical assessment of homicide offenders: The significance of crime scene in offense and offender analysis. *Homicide Studies, 4,* 219–233.

White, P. A. (2003). Making causal judgments from the proportion of conforming instances: The pCl rule. *Journal of Experimental Psychology: Learning, Memory, and Cognition, 29,* 710–727.

Wilson, P., Lincoln, R., & Kocsis, R. (1997). Validity, utility and ethics of profiling for serial violent and sexual offenders. *Psychiatry, Psychology and Law, 4,* 1–12.

Wiseman, R., West, D., & Stemman, R. (1996). An experimental test of psychic detection. *Journal of the Society for Psychical Research, 61,* 34–44.

Witkin, G. (1996, April 22). How the FBI paints portraits of the nations most wanted. *U.S. News & World Report, 120,* 32.

Woodhams, J., & Toye, K. (2007). An empirical test of the assumptions of case linkage and offender profiling with serial commercial robberies. *Psychology, Public Policy, and Law, 13,* 35–58.

# Law, Courts, and Judicial Process

# Criminal Prosecution

JOYCELYN M. POLLOCK

There are 50 different state court systems (as well as the court systems in Puerto Rico, Guam, and American Samoa), and a parallel federal court system. In this chapter, we will focus specifically on criminal courts, but remember that states may also have civil courts, family courts, probate courts, and a host of other limited jurisdiction courts. Our inquiry will include an objective look at some of the new court processes to see whether these innovations improve the system.

## What are the Different Levels of Courts?

Generally, each state has trial courts, intermediate appellate courts, and a supreme court or court of last resort that hears final appeals. Trial courts can be further separated into courts of general jurisdiction and courts of limited jurisdiction.

The names of each level of the court system can vary considerably from state to state. "Supreme" may refer to the court of last resort, or, in some states, this term refers to trial courts. "Circuits" may refer to the intermediate appellate courts or the trial courts. That is why it is best to become familiar simply with the general categories of:

- trial courts (limited jurisdiction and general jurisdiction)
- intermediate appellate courts
- courts of last resort (final appeal).

Courts have subject matter jurisdiction and geographic jurisdiction. **Subject matter jurisdiction** refers to the type of case that can be heard in each type of court; this is defined by legislation. Municipal courts, for instance, can only adjudicate certain types of cases. Courts must also have **geographic jurisdiction** over the case. In criminal cases, this means that the crime must have taken place in the court's geographic jurisdiction. If the prosecutor does not prove this essential fact, the defendant must be acquitted. In California and many other states, the geographic boundary for each court is the county; however, in some states, a district or circuit may encompass more than one county.[1] In larger jurisdictions, there may be many judges, each with their own courtroom, for that jurisdiction. Each of the courts receives incoming cases on a random or rotating basis.

**General jurisdiction courts** are the courtrooms of television and movies, and they are what most people think of when they think of criminal courts. These courts typically try felonies and have the power to sentence to state prison. General jurisdiction courts also try civil cases, although the courts are usually divided, so that there are civil trial courts and criminal trial courts. These general jurisdiction courts may be called district courts, superior courts, or some other name. **Courts of limited jurisdiction** can be found in all but five states.[2] Their jurisdiction is limited to specific types of cases. For instance, municipal courts may only adjudicate city ordinances and misdemeanors. There may be special traffic courts that only hear traffic violations up to a certain level of seriousness. Justices of the peace exist in some states and may hear minor misdemeanors and ordinance violations as well as civil cases. The judges/magistrates in such courts may also hold first appearances and arraignments for felony cases. The powers of such courts are set by legislation, and their jurisdiction may be limited to a county, part of a county, city, or municipality. In Figure 13.1, the criminal court system of New York is presented as an example of one criminal court system.

**Trial courts**. The trial courts as represented on television may not be what you see if you go into a criminal court, since the majority of time, other things are happening. On any given day in a trial courtroom you may see judges taking pleas, having docket calls, listening to pre-trial motions, or conducting other court business. Trials are not always underway and, in fact, there is tremendous variation, even within the same jurisdiction, among judges in how many trials are conducted each

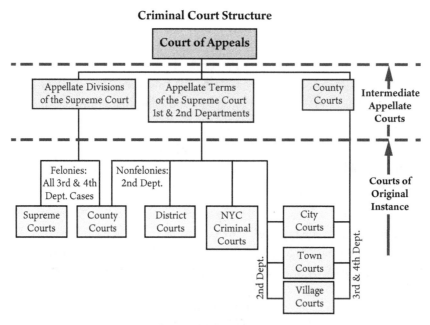

FIGURE 13.1 Court structure of New York State
*Source*: https://www.nycourts.gov/courts/structure.shtml.

year. While some judges may clear up to a dozen cases off their **docket** (cases assigned to their court) each month, others take a more leisurely pace.

Many states now allow cameras and audio equipment in the courtroom, but jury deliberations continue to be held in private. Despite news footage and reality programming, most people's perception of what happens in a courtroom is shaped by the countless television shows and movies that find courtroom drama so compelling.

The combined state and federal criminal trial courts produce convictions from well over one million offenders each year. In 2006, 1,132,290 defendants were convicted of a felony in state trial courts, and 69 percent were sentenced to jail or prison. Of these, 18 percent were convictions for a violent crime, 28 percent were convictions for a property crime, and 33 percent were convictions for a drug offense. Unfortunately, this seems to be the last year that the Bureau of Justice Statistics has provided statistics of felony processing.[3] In another data series source, it was reported that state prosecutors' offices reported closing 2.9 million cases charged as felonies in 2007 through convictions, acquittals, dismissals, or other dispositions.[4]

**Appellate courts**. Defendants who are convicted may appeal only if there has been some error in the trial or the process leading up to the trial. If, for instance, police officers interrogated the defendant and obtained a confession without giving him the Miranda warnings, that would be grounds for an appeal. Or, if, during trial, the judge made incorrect legal rulings, or if there was some attempt to improperly influence the jury, that would be grounds for appeal. The defense attorney must "preserve" the error by objecting to it during the trial. If he or she does not object, then in most cases the error will not be able to be used as grounds for an appeal. All defendants have a right to an attorney for the first "direct" appeal. If there are subsequent appeals, then the defendant must pay for the attorney. If there is an alleged violation of the Constitution then, after state appeals are exhausted, there can be an appeal to the Supreme Court. Generally, this is done through the writ of **habeas corpus**, which basically alleges unlawful imprisonment. In some cases, the writ is used when a prisoner believes the prison or the holding facility is operated in a way that is violative of the Constitution, but in other cases, it is used when the allegation is that the person ought not to be held at all because of an error at trial.

The appellate courts evaluate the alleged error and determine whether to take the case and, if they do, both parties will file a written brief and engage in oral argument before the court. If the appellate court does not find for the appellant (defendant), then that decision can be appealed to a higher court up to the state's highest court. If the appellate court does find for the appellant (defendant), then the state can appeal the decision. Sometimes, the appellate court agrees with the appellant but determines that the error was "harmless" and did not affect the outcome of the trial. **Harmless error** means that there was a legal error, but the

For an interesting website that provides information about state courts, go to the National Center for State Courts' website at www.ncsc.org/

evidence was so substantial in other ways that even if the error hadn't occurred, the result would have been the same.

In some states, there are several intermediate courts of appeal, distributed geographically across the state. In most states, the intermediate appellate court must review all appeals filed from trial courts (at least in criminal cases). That does not necessarily mean that there is any type of hearing. The court may review the appellate brief and find it is without merit and deny a full hearing.

While the **court of last resort** in any state is usually a very old institution, probably dating back to the beginning of statehood and the state constitution, intermediate appellate courts are more recent additions and serve to reduce the highest court's caseload. About forty states have these intermediate courts.[5] California has the largest number of intermediate courts, divided into nine divisions with more than 100 judges. Most of the time cases are heard by a panel of three judges, rather than the total number of judges in each division.

The highest court in the state, or court of last resort, is often called the state supreme court. Texas and Oklahoma are the only two states that split their court of last resort into two courts, including one that hears criminal appeals (court of criminal appeals), and one that hears civil appeals (supreme court).[6] If appellants also lose at the highest state level, and when there is an issue of constitutionality, the appellate attorney may file a **writ of certiorari** to the United States Supreme Court. The U.S. Supreme Court only hears about 1 percent of cases that are appealed in this way.

A good rule of thumb is that trial courts decide upon facts, and appellate courts rule on points of law. However, this is not completely accurate because trial courts also make rulings on interpretations of law. The most important thing to remember is that an appeal can only be filed because of an error of law. Appellate courts never retry facts. Thus, the guilt or innocence of a defendant is never the issue, only whether there was some legal procedural error, or violation of a state or federal constitutional right, during the proceedings.

# What are Specialized Courts?

There are also a growing number of **community courts**,[7] or problem-solving courts, which may be courts of limited jurisdiction, but more often are courts of general jurisdiction, meaning that they may handle up to and including felony criminal matters. The defining feature of this type of court is a focus on "problem solving." Community courts focus on less serous criminal offenses and attempt to divert offenders from the criminal justice system. The concept fits well with community policing because both are interested in strengthening the community's ability to respond to such problems as delinquency and crime. Typically, community courts use alternative sentencing models to achieve the restorative justice goals. Community courts or problem-solving courts might include drug courts (dealing specifically with drug offenders or offenders who are drug addicted), veteran's courts (dealing specifically with offenders who have served in the military), domestic violence courts (dealing specifically with crimes involving family member victimization), and so on. An important question to ask is if these types of courts are more effective than traditional prosecution and our focus on data section looks at this question.

# Focus on Data: Are Specialized Courts Effective?

One type of problem-solving court is the **drug court**, which is typically a court of general jurisdiction but with a specialized caseload of drug cases. Since the first drug court was established in 1989, hundreds of drug courts have been established across the country. The judges in these alternative courts identify first-time drug offenders, sentence them to drug testing and treatment programs, and then monitor the offender's progress through the program. If the offender successfully completes the program, he or she may be diverted from incarceration and their conviction may also be erased.[8] The major goal of drug courts is to break the cycle of drug use rather than simply administer punishment.

Some studies have shown that offenders who go through drug courts are more likely to complete drug treatment programs and have lower recidivism rates than offenders who are sentenced through regular court processes. However, at this point, the research is mixed, with just as many evaluations showing no difference as those that find that drug courts reduce recidivism, as compared to regular court processing.[9] In a study of a Cincinnati drug court, researchers found that drug court participants were more likely to get probation than a comparison group, and the comparison group was more likely to receive intensive supervision probation. While there was no difference in drug arrests between the drug court participants and the control group (30.8 percent versus 37.4 percent were re-arrested), there was a significant difference in theft/property arrests (18.4 percent versus 31.7 percent).[10]

Another study looked at whether biweekly review sessions with the judge had an effect on recidivism. In some drug courts, there is minimal interaction between the offender and the judge, but this study looked at a program where the judge met much more frequently with the offenders. The findings indicated that biweekly hearings reduced recidivism among high-risk offenders, but not low-risk offenders.[11] In a cost-effectiveness study, researchers concluded that cost savings in a drug court in Multnomah County, Oregon, saved taxpayers close to $500,000 for every 100 participants.[12] In one review of several drug court evaluations, the authors concluded that effectiveness would be increased if the courts:

- used objective risk and need instruments
- used behavioral and cognitive treatment strategies
- made sure the level of treatment was matched to the offender
- provided aftercare
- maintained quality control over treatment options.[13]

A more recent study conducted by Urban Institute researchers utilized twenty-three drug courts and six comparison jurisdictions covering eight states in a five-year study that interviewed participants and examined criminal records. They found that drug courts did significantly reduce substance abuse and crime. Offenders in drug court caseloads reported committing half as many crimes as those in regular courts. Researchers also found that positive effects were correlated with perceptions of the judge. Those who perceived the judge treated them fairly and with respect, and allowed them to talk in court, were likely to do better than those without such perceptions. The final analysis showed that drug courts saved the jurisdiction $2.00 for every $1.00 spent.[14]

Domestic violence courts deal with assaults that occur between intimates, either in a spousal (husband–wife), familial (parent/caregiver–child/dependent), or intimate (boyfriend–girlfriend or same-sex partners) relationship. These courts have developed because of the growing awareness of the problem of domestic violence and the system's reaction to it. Mandatory arrest policies, for instance, have led to an increase in prosecutions for domestic assaulters, taxing the courts and filling jails and prisons with offenders. The impetus for domestic violence courts came from the Violence Against Women Act, which created federal funding for the implementation of the courts. Domestic violence courts increase coordination among the courts, police, and social service agencies, and adopt a "therapeutic approach" to justice.[15] The concept of a specialized court recognizes the unique interpersonal issues involved in domestic violence and emphasizes treatment for the batterer and services for the victim. These courts employ both sanctions (punishment) and services for greater effect. Recognizing the unique nature of domestic violence, these courts may also handle restraining or protective orders and even child custody and visitation issues to provide a comprehensive judicial response to the problem of violence in the home.

In the few studies that have been undertaken, domestic violence courts were found to reduce recidivism over traditional court processing. In one study, recidivism in the domestic violence court sample was 6 percent compared to a control sample of 14 percent. On the other hand, another study showed that the creation of a domestic violence court increased the number of arrests for domestic violence. This was explained as the result of law enforcement becoming sensitized to the issue, as well as being more likely to arrest, knowing that the domestic violence court was available as a resource. The study also found that participants in the domestic violence court were significantly less likely to recidivate than those who went through traditional court processing. The conclusion of the study described earlier was that a "coordinated community response" to domestic violence, involving the police, courts, and social services, reduces recidivism.[16] In another study, a court program for domestic violence offenders in Albuquerque, New Mexico, was found to reduce recidivism as compared to a matched sample who did not go through the court program.[17]

Although findings are mixed, specialized problem-solving courts seem to be helpful in reducing recidivism over traditional court processing. The studies that exist seem to indicate that certain elements, e.g., closer judicial supervision, may improve the success of such courts so it would be important to carefully evaluate programs noting differences between them.

## How Do Prosecutors Decide Whether and What to Charge?

A district attorney (prosecutor) is usually an elected official (except in Alaska, Connecticut, the District of Columbia, and New Jersey).[18] In all but the smallest jurisdictions, there are also assistant prosecutors who also try cases, but are hired and not elected. In larger jurisdictions, they may number in the hundreds, and the elected district attorney never actually prosecutes a case, but rather acts as the policy director and CEO of the office. There are about 2,330 state court prosecutors' offices, employing 78,000 attorneys, investigators, and support staff. This does not include county or city prosecutors who prosecute in courts of limited jurisdiction.[19]

Our conception of prosecutors' offices is probably shaped by television and movies, which tend to portray large jurisdictions such as New York City and Los Angeles. In reality, most offices are quite small. Most prosecutors' offices receive both state and county funding. Most prosecutors' offices employ ten or fewer people. In some offices, prosecutors serve on a part-time basis, maintaining their own private law practice as well. The role of a part-time prosecutor in a small town is very different from the district attorneys in large cities like New York, Chicago, or Houston, which have hundreds of assistant prosecutors.[20]

In very rare cases, special prosecutors are appointed by the governor or attorney general when it is believed that a local prosecutor has a conflict of interest or the prosecution involves a case that crosses jurisdictional lines. Such special prosecutors can also be found at the federal level. Currently, there is discussion nationwide as to whether special prosecutors should be appointed by state attorneys' general offices when a police officer is charged with a crime. The argument is that local prosecutors' offices have too close of a relationship with police departments to be unbiased in decisions of charging or trial strategy.

In some larger jurisdictions, the prosecutor's office is divided into divisions. The most common divisions are the misdemeanor division and the felony division. There may also be specialized caseloads, such as sexual assault or domestic violence caseloads. Prosecutors may be attached to a specific court and always appear before the same judge in the same courtroom, following a case from first appearance through sentencing. Alternatively, prosecutors may be assigned different stages of the process, so that they may deal with only preliminary hearings or only first appearances and pass the case on to those who specialize in litigation for the trial portion.

In some states, counties and cities also each have either appointed or elected attorneys who handle cases for these jurisdictions. The majority of their caseloads may be civil, but city attorneys, for instance, may enforce code violations and infractions.

Each state also has an attorney general who is the state's chief legal officer. Attorneys general may have personnel who enforce child support enforcement; they may have lawyers that represent the state's citizens in consumer protection, antitrust, and utility litigation; they enforce federal and state environmental laws and represent the state and state agencies in criminal appeals and statewide criminal prosecutions.

The role of any prosecutor is quite different from that of the defense attorney. While the defense attorney's role is to protect the rights of the accused, the prosecutor has the ethical duty to "seek justice"—and this does not necessarily translate into "get a conviction." Prosecutors must balance office resources, the relative seriousness of the crime, and the desires/needs of the victim and community when making decisions about whether and how to prosecute. Not all cases that begin with arrest are prosecuted. In fact, prosecutors drop many cases without prosecution, and this decision-making ability is one of the least studied areas of the criminal justice system.

A study of prosecutors' discretion in two large counties utilized interviews and a survey that included hypothetical cases. The results were then analyzed to determine the elements of prosecutors' decisions. Research showed that outcomes are affected by legal factors (e.g., strength of the evidence, type and seriousness of the offense, and defendant's culpability), quasi-legal factors (e.g., legally

To read a news story about this issue, go to http://www.nytimes.com/2015/07/08/nyregion/cuomo-to-appoint-special-prosecutor-for-killings-by-police.html?_r=0

For a website that further describes attorneys general, go to www.naag.org/

To find information on the staffing and salaries of prosecutors, go to the most recent national statistics from the Bureau of Justice Statistics at http://www.bjs.gov/content/pub/pdf/psc07st.pdf

non-relevant though potentially influential factors, such as defendant–victim relationship, victim age, and defendant age), and extra-legal factors (e.g., legally impermissible factors pertaining to defendant and victim, such as race, ethnicity, or gender).[21] Organizational factors also influence prosecutors. Rules, the availability of resources, and personal relationships, perhaps with police officers involved, sometimes are more important than evaluations of the strength of the evidence, the seriousness of the offense, and the defendant's criminal history.

## What are the Duties of a Defense Attorney?

Defense attorneys are favorite characters for television and movie script writers. They are portrayed as tireless crusaders for the downtrodden or sleazy "hacks" willing to do anything to help their clients avoid their just punishment. The reality, of course, resembles neither of these two extremes. Defense attorneys, for the most part, help the system work by helping individual defendants navigate the complex and confusing world of the justice system. Clients are more likely to receive due process because of defense attorneys. Criminal law is not a favored specialty of lawyers; less than 10 percent of all lawyers have a full-time criminal practice. Most attorneys who do take criminal cases also carry a general law practice.

To find information about your own state's method for delivering indigent defense services, go to http://public.findlaw.com/library/state-public-defenders.html

The Supreme Court holding in *Gideon v. Wainwright* (1963)[22] recognized a 6th Amendment right to an attorney when a defendant was facing a felony conviction, and later, in *Argersinger v. Hamlin* (1972)[23] the Supreme Court held that all indigent offenders facing incarceration had a 6th Amendment right to counsel (an attorney). This requirement meant that states needed to develop ways of providing defense counsel to all defendants facing jail or prison. The two most common ways are appointed counsel systems and public defender offices. All states except Maine have either a state or county public defender system (although most states also have appointed attorneys to supplement the public defenders).[24]

Appointed counsel systems operate with a list of attorneys approved to be appointed to indigent defendants. Assignments are given on a rotating or other basis. Attorneys get on this list by volunteering or, in a few cases, all attorneys in the jurisdiction are on the list. These attorneys are in private practice and have private clients as well as court appointments.

To read an interesting article about a day in the life of a public defender, go to http://www.courier-journal.com/story/news/crime/2015/11/19/kentucky-public-defenders-risks/76046976/?from=global&sessionKey=&autologin=

In public defender systems, the defense attorneys are full-time employees of a public defender office. They may be either county or state employees, or employees of a private nonprofit agency that holds a contract from the state for indigent defense. Public defender systems are more common in urban areas, while appointed counsel systems are more common in suburban and rural areas.[25]

A third form of indigent defense is the contract attorney model. This is similar to the appointed counsel model, except that, instead of distributing cases to all the attorneys on a list, one or two attorneys take all of the indigent cases for a set contract amount. These attorneys may or may not also have a separate private practice, depending on how large is the indigent caseload. This model has proven to be attractive to some jurisdictions because it may be less expensive than the appointed counsel model and is useful in jurisdictions that do not have enough indigent cases to justify a public defender office.

The general thought is that individuals who are defended by a public defender or appointed counsel do not receive the same quality of legal assistance as those who are able to hire their own private attorneys. While the findings of researchers are mixed, it seems to be the case that indigents are more likely to receive a sentence to jail or prison and are more likely to plead guilty when they have counsel provided to them, but they receive shorter terms than those with privately retained attorneys.[26]

Other research indicates that, at least in the federal system, appointed attorneys perform considerably worse than public defenders. They evidently bill for more hours per case, are less qualified, and achieve worse results for their clients. They cost the public, in the aggregate, about $61 million more than if public defenders had taken the cases. Suggested reasons for the difference between appointed attorneys and public defenders are that public defenders have more experience in criminal law and have a better relationship with prosecutors.[27] Another study found that about 29 percent of cases with private attorneys resulted in a prison sentence, 32 percent with a public defender did so, but 46 percent of cases with appointed counsel did, indicating that there was a lower standard of representation with appointed counsel.[28]

About 80 percent of all criminal defendants are indigent. **Indigency** requires the provision of publicly funded defense. One study reports that when the federal public defender system began in the 1960s about 30 percent of defendants were indigent and needed services, but now that figure is 90 percent.[29] Unfortunately, the system of public defense has been chronically underfunded.[30] In a 2008 report concerning public defense sponsored by the Department of Justice, the Bureau of Justice Assistance, and the National Legal Aid and Defender Association, it was noted that in the last 30 years there had been substantial improvement in the coverage of public defender programs; however, many indigent defendants do not receive adequate legal aid before pleading because of resource deficits in the states.[31] In a study of how states spent their Byrne Justice Assistance Grant funds from the Department of Justice, it was found that in Fiscal Year 2009, $20.8 million went toward prosecution, and only $3.1 million went to public defense. A total of $1.2 billion was allocated for all programs, meaning that the public defense allocation amounted to roughly 0.25 percent.[32] Costs of criminal defense represent a very small portion of criminal justice costs: about one-twentieth the costs of police and about one-fifteenth the cost of corrections.[33] One study in Tennessee showed that prosecution costs were between $130 and $139 million for the same set of cases for which public defense received $56.4 million.[34] Other countries spend more on public defense than the United States. While the UK spends 0.2 percent of its GNP on public defense, the US spends only 0.0002 percent.[35]

About twenty-two states administer and fund at the state level; eighteen rely primarily on county funding with some state support, and the remaining states have some hybrid system.[36]

To see states' funding for indigent defense, go to a 2016 Bureau of Justice report at http://www.bjs.gov/content/pub/pdf/idsuso812.pdf

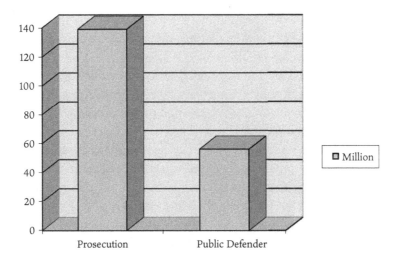

**FIGURE 13-2** Public defender costs in tennessee
*Source*: Justice Policy Institute, *System Overload: The Costs of Underresourcing Public Defense*. Washington, DC: Justice Policy Institute, 2011, p. 8.

In 2012, U.S. Attorney General Eric Holder announced that significant new resources would be directed to indigent aid. A number of private and public advocacy groups (6th Amendment Center, Brennan Center, The Constitution Project, the Gideon at 50 Project, the American Bar Association) have recently brought attention to the fact that indigent legal aid is so overburdened that representation likely falls below constitutional requirements. Studies show that public defender caseloads are often twice what ABA standards indicate they should be. Another source indicated that 79 percent of state public defender offices did not have enough attorneys to meet ABA recommended caseload sizes and that public defenders in large cities often handle 2,000 misdemeanor cases a year, which is five times the recommended number.[37] This means that public defenders or appointed counsel meet with their clients sometimes minutes before court appearances, don't have the resources to hire investigators, and miss the opportunity to obtain bail or pre-trial release for their clients. Underresourcing public defenders may result in higher costs to the system because offenders stay in the system longer unnecessarily.

In 2012, the American Bar Association's Standing Committee on Legal Aid and Indigent Defendants and the National Association of Criminal Defense Lawyers completed an examination of indigent defense and produced five core principals to improve indigent defense:

- Reclassify petty and nonviolent offenses to reduce "overcriminalization" that leads to unmanageable caseloads.
- Ensure counsel is provided to defendants at all initial court appearances, particularly when it comes to decisions about bail, to cut down on cost of detaining, especially those charged with minor offenses.
- Ensure access to effective counsel.
- Consult with defense bars before new law enforcement initiative are launched.
- Foster greater private–public involvement in indigent defense under a structured system.[38]

There is currently also interest in creating a more holistic approach to public defense. This involves the participation of other professionals who work with the defense attorney, such as social workers, community outreach workers, and others, who develop a more comprehensive response to the offender rather than merely a legal response to the charge. For instance, social workers may be in court and begin the process of finding a drug treatment program immediately as well as helping the offender with housing and jobs. In the long run this approach may have the potential to reduce the offender's involvement in the criminal justice system by addressing underlying problems, but it is time- and cost-intensive and requires adequate resources to be effective.[39]

## What is the Role of a Judge? How are They Selected?

As described earlier, judges may be either trial judges in courts of general juris-diction or courts of limited jurisdiction, or they may be appellate judges in intermediate courts or the court of last resort in the state (the state supreme court). Judges may be either elected or appointed. About one-third of all state trial judges receive their position through a general nonpartisan election (33.3 percent). Roughly another third (31.4 percent) are chosen through some form of merit selection process. Another 17.6 percent are elected through partisan elections. The rest obtain their judgeships through legislative appointments, gubernatorial selection, or other means.[40]

They typically serve fixed terms, although in a few states their terms are for life or at least until retirement age. The **Missouri Plan** is a merit selection pro-cess of appointing judges that involves a nominating process by statewide (for appellate) and local (for trial judges) committees. These committees send the nominees' names to the governor, who makes the appointment. The appointee then faces an election after one year, running against his or her own record. While 37 states use some form of nomination process, the remaining states still use general elections. In some of those states, the elections are partisan (with judges running as Democratic, Republican, or Independent), and in others the elections are nonpartisan.

There is increasing criticism of judges being elected through partisan elections. Critics argue that judges should be guided by the law, not popular opinion and they should not be elected in the same way as other politicians. More impor-tantly, the public is not knowledgeable about the candidates or what should be considered as qualifications, i.e., legal expertise, conscientious or ethical behavior. Even retired Supreme Court Justice Sandra Day O'Connor has weighed in on this important topic and favors a hybrid system whereby a judicial nominating commission presents a recommendation to the governor who appoints the judge, a judicial performance evaluation is then done and publicized followed by a retention election.

To read about how judges are selected in your state, go to the National Center for State Judges website and click on your state on the map: http://www.judi cialselection.us/

To read this report go to http://iaals.du.edu/quality-judges/projects/oconnor-judicial-selection-plan

## Trial Judges

Trial judges may preside over courts of general jurisdiction or limited jurisdiction. They may be family court judges, juvenile judges, criminal judges, or civil judges; or, in other jurisdictions, they may try all these kinds of cases in the same courtroom. Judges of limited jurisdiction (county courts, municipal courts, justices of the peace) may sit only part-time. Some of these magistrates may not even need to be lawyers to hold the judicial position (although this is rare). Some jurisdictions may occasionally hire retired judges to help with overloaded dockets.

Trial judges are basically like umpires in the justice process. They make decisions on rules of evidence and procedure. If a defendant decides to plead guilty (as the vast majority of defendants do), the judge must ensure that the confession is voluntary and that there is other evidence, in addition to the confession, upon which to convict the defendant. The judge, in these cases, must decide whether to agree with the prosecutor's recommendation for sentencing. Over 90 percent of all cases are resolved through a **plea bargain**, in which the defendant agrees to plead guilty in return for a favorable sentencing recommendation.

In cases that go to trial, the defendant may choose to have a **bench trial**, which means that there is no jury and the case is tried solely by the judge. The judge not only ensures that rules are followed, but also determines guilt or innocence in these trials. Most felony trials, however, include a jury.

Judges carry great weight with the jury and jurors may be influenced by any obvious bias the judge displays toward either the defense or the prosecution. The judge may be called upon to rule on pre-trial motions, which may include motions to exclude evidence because of alleged 4th Amendment violations by police officers. During the trial, judges rule on objections made by either the prosecution or defense attorney, based on rules of procedure in that jurisdiction. Some of the more common objections made during a trial are that the evidence does not have a proper foundation (meaning that the attorney has not obtained, through questioning witnesses, the proper level of proof that the item is what it is purported to be), the question asks something that is irrelevant or prejudicial, or the attorney was "leading" the witness (meaning that they were answering the question or suggesting the answer to the witness).

Although the jury determines guilt or innocence, the judge does have the power to throw out a guilty verdict if he or she finds that there is not sufficient evidence to support a judgment of guilt, as a matter of law. If a guilty verdict occurs, the judge may also be obliged to sentence the offender; although in some states juries have this function. Judges (or juries) must sentence within the statutory guidelines for sentencing.

If an offender is sentenced to probation, the judge maintains control over the defendant. Probation officers periodically submit progress reports to the court. The sentencing judge will ultimately be the one to close the case, either by revoking probation and sending the person to prison, by agreeing to an early release, or by recognizing that the offender has served the full term of probation.

## Appellate Judges

There are about 1,335 appellate judges in the country. Their terms range from four to sixteen years, but Rhode Island judges have a term for life, and judges in Massachusetts and Puerto Rico have terms that last until age 70 (the mandatory retirement age).[41] Appellate judges may not be as newsworthy as their brethren in trial courts, but their decisions are, in some ways, much more powerful. Appellate courts overturn trial verdicts when they recognize errors of law and/ or constitutional violations. Much of their caseload consists of civil appeals, but they also hear criminal appeals. Typically, appeals are heard by three-judge panels, and, if the three-judge panel denies relief, the petitioner may appeal to have the case heard **en banc**, meaning with the full number of appellate judges, or, in a state with more than one appellate jurisdiction, with all of the justices in that jurisdiction. It is typically from the ranks of state appellate judges that federal justices are selected.

## What is the Jurisdiction of Federal Courts?

The federal court system is a parallel to what we have described here for state court systems. Figure 13.3 illustrates the organization of the federal court system. There are trial courts and appellate courts. Federal trial courts (called federal district courts and magistrate courts) hear criminal cases prosecuting alleged violations of federal laws. If convicted, these federal convictions can be appealed. The federal system has appellate courts (circuit courts) to hear appeals if there have

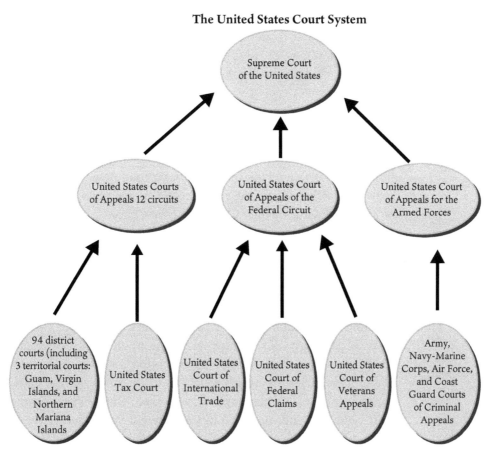

**FIGURE 13.3** Federal court system
*Source*: http://www.uscourts.gov/about-federal-courts/court-role-and-structure

been legal errors or constitutional violations, and, ultimately, these cases may also be appealed to the U.S. Supreme Court.

The United States military has its own judicial system. Each of the branches of the military has its own court of military review. Military law is set out in the Uniform Code of Military Justice. Decisions may be appealed to the United States Court of Military Appeals and, ultimately, to the Supreme Court. Procedures, rules of evidence, and even crimes are different in the military justice system. One of the interesting differences is that the defense and the prosecutor for a case are assigned out of the same office (the adjutant general's office).

The United States attorney is the federal equivalent of a district attorney or state prosecutor. There are about ninety-four U.S. attorneys attached to the ninety-four U.S. federal district courts, which are the federal trial courts.[42] There are also specialized courts that have limited jurisdiction over matters such as tax and patent law. A federal case can be appealed to the court of appeals. The country is divided into twelve circuits, each with its own court of appeals.

For an interesting website on the Supreme Court, go to http://www.supremecourt.gov/

All federal judges are nominated by the president after receiving recommendations from the U.S. senators in that jurisdiction. The nominees must go through a confirmation process by the United States Senate. Once confirmed, they may hold their position for life, unless they are impeached by Congress.

The United States Supreme Court is the highest court in the land. The Justices on the Supreme Court hold their position for life. The Supreme Court is the only court that was established by the United States Constitution. Article III states:

> The judicial Power of the United States, shall be vested in one supreme Court, and in such inferior Courts as the Congress may from time to time ordain and establish. The Judges, both of the supreme and inferior Courts, shall hold their Offices during good Behavior, and shall, at stated Times, receive for their Services a Compensation which shall not be diminished during their Continuance in Office.

Article III also specifies the jurisdiction of the court.

> The judicial Power shall extend to all Cases, in Law and Equity, arising under this Constitution, the Laws of the United States, and Treaties made, or which shall be made, under their Authority;—to all Cases affecting Ambassadors, other public Ministers and Consuls;—to all Cases of admiralty and maritime Jurisdiction;—to Controversies to which the United States shall be a Party;—to Controversies between two or more States;—between a State and Citizens of another State;—between Citizens of different States;—between Citizens of the same State claiming Lands under Grants of different States, and between a State, or the Citizens thereof, and foreign States, Citizens or Subjects.

Article III goes on to specify that, in some cases, the jurisdiction of the Supreme Court shall be original (meaning that the case can be brought directly), but in other cases the jurisdiction is appellate (meaning that the Court can only hear appeals after the case has been litigated in a lower court).

> In all Cases affecting Ambassadors, other public ministers and Consuls, and those in which a State shall be Party, the supreme Court shall have original Jurisdiction. In all the other Cases before mentioned, the supreme Court shall have appellate jurisdiction, both as to Law and Fact, with such Exceptions, and under such Regulations as the Congress shall make.

The Court rarely exercises original jurisdiction and almost all case decisions are those that occur when the Court issues a writ of certiorari, which means to bring the case forward. Because most of the cases appealed to the Supreme Court fall into the area of discretionary review, the Court does not have to hear them. When four or more justices agree to hear a case, the Court issues the writ of certiorari. Typically, the Court receives thousands of appeals each year but issues written opinions in only a hundred or so cases.

It is important to note that only decisions of the Supreme Court are clearly and absolutely "the law of the land." In all other legal questions or issues, you cannot assume that you know the law in your state and jurisdiction unless you research case decisions in your particular jurisdiction. In textbooks, for instance, you may read cases from a court opinion from a federal circuit that does not encompass your state, or the supreme court of another state, or from a state intermediate court of appeals from a jurisdiction in your state, but one that does not include your city or town. In these cases, the holding or the principle of law that is set by the court may or may not be the law in your jurisdiction. The holdings in other jurisdictions are only "persuasive," not "authoritative" when the same legal issue comes up. The Supreme Court's opinions, however, apply instantly and absolutely to all jurisdictions in the country. For this reason, these nine individuals on the Court are sometimes called the most powerful people in the country.

When Justice Atonin Scalia passed away in February 2016, the Supreme Court was reduced to eight from its normal nine members. The current members of the court are:

- Chief Justice John Roberts
- Samuel Alito
- Ruth Bader Ginsburg
- Stephen Breyer
- Clarence Thomas
- Anthony Kennedy
- Sonia Sotomayor
- Elena Kagan.

# How Does Due Process Protect Individuals Against Error in the Criminal Justice Process?

Recall that due process refers to procedural protections that guard against errors when the government seeks to deprive anyone of life, liberty, or property. Elements of due process include:

- notice of charges
- right of counsel
- right to confront and cross-examine witnesses and evidence
- right to present witnesses and evidence
- right of impartial fact finders
- right to a statement of fact findings
- right of appeal.

**Due process** is perhaps the most important civil right guaranteed to us by our Constitution. We have certain protections when governmental actors want to take something from us, whether it is life, liberty, or property. These protections don't stop the deprivation, but they do make it more likely that government actors make these decisions in a fair, unbiased, and nonarbitrary manner. Due process applies in other contexts besides the criminal justice system; whenever the government seeks to deprive an individual of some protected liberty interest, due process applies. For instance, denial of social security payments, **eminent domain**, and involuntary mental commitments are all examples where due process protections are in place to protect individuals from governmental power. Due process is not a static concept. What is considered necessary due process depends on the nature of the deprivation. The deprivation of life, for instance, is the most extreme of all deprivations, which is why extreme procedural protections are in place for capital trials. The more serious the deprivation, the more important it is to make sure that no errors are made. Recall that due process clauses exist in the 5th and 14th Amendments, but the 6th Amendment can be considered to provide specific elements of due process and is often called the "trial rights" amendment.

The 6th Amendment states that the accused deserves a speedy and public trial, by an impartial jury. Further, each defendant has a right to be informed of the nature of the charges, to have the opportunity to confront and cross-examine the accusers and witnesses, and to have the assistance of counsel. It should be understood, however, that the 6th Amendment "trial rights" are only an example of due process. The framers of the Constitution evidently thought it necessary to specifically identify the rights of the individual when facing the awesome power of the government in the 6th Amendment.

> In all criminal prosecutions, the accused shall enjoy the right to a speedy and public trial, by an impartial jury of the State and district wherein the crime shall have been committed, which district shall have been previously ascertained by law, and to be informed of the nature and cause of the accusation; to be confronted with the witnesses against him; to have compulsory process for obtaining witnesses in his favor, and to have the Assistance of Counsel for his defence.

Due process applies before and after the trial. Pre-trial diversion, being held before booking, and being arrested implicate due process rights because they involve various types of deprivations. Sentencing and treatment in prison also may implicate due process rights. In fact, due process applies at each step in the justice process from investigatory detentions through release from prison.

## Arrest

Due process mandates that **probable cause** must exist before a warrant can be issued or an arrest made. If the police officer does not meet the probable cause standard, then the arrest is an illegal deprivation of liberty. The legal remedy for an improper arrest is that any evidence obtained directly from that arrest can be excluded under the exclusionary rule. If maliciousness can be proven, an individual subject to a false arrest may also pursue a civil judgment against the individual officer, and even the department if there was complicity on the part of superiors. The charging document for an arrest is a "complaint"—which sets out the facts that make up probable cause.

## Booking

Booking typically involves transporting the suspect to the lockup or county jail and filling out appropriate paperwork before the individual enters the facility. Booking is a due process step only in the sense that some errors of identity may be discovered at this point when fingerprints are taken. In rare cases, individuals are arrested because of outstanding warrants for others with the same name and birth date. If fingerprints are on file for the true offender, the booking process may be instrumental in discovering this mistake. Individuals may also be kept in **lockups** for a short period. These temporary holding cells are in police stations.

## Initial Appearance

Due process requires that every person taken into custody must see a magistrate within a reasonable period. In *Riverside v. McLaughlin*,[43] the Supreme Court ruled that, unless there were special circumstances, the initial hearing must take place within forty-eight hours of arrest. This is in order to ensure that the detention of the individual is legal, that is, that the charging documents are in order, there is probable cause for the arrest, and there is no clear abuse of power.

One of the major functions of the initial appearance is to notify the accused of the charges against him or her. Recall that one of the first elements of due process is notice. It is impossible to defend yourself unless you know what it is you are being accused of. The accused is usually provided with a copy of the complaint or charging document at this point. The magistrate also recites the Miranda warnings again to make sure that the defendant understands them. The hearing magistrate, who may be a judge of any level from municipal court to state district court, will begin to assess whether the accused is indigent and will need an attorney provided by the state. Jurisdictions typically use some form of a questionnaire that asks the defendant to show assets and debts in order to determine indigency, which simply means without appreciable assets. The other major function of the hearing is to assess bail or offer some other **pre-trial release program**.

## Bail

**Bail** or **release on recognizance** allows the accused to spend the time before trial out in the community. The adjudicatory process sometimes takes months or even years to complete. Until it is over, it is obviously important that the suspect/defendant remain in the jurisdiction. For this reason, many are kept in jail until a conviction, dismissal, or acquittal occurs. However, if other means are sufficient to ensure that the individual does not disappear, then pre-trial detention is unnecessary. The bail hearing is the due process designed to minimize error in the decision regarding this deprivation of liberty. The judge determines how likely it is that the defendant will **abscond** (escape the jurisdiction), and then determines whether to offer a pre-trial release option, and/or what level of bail is the lowest necessary to ensure presence at trial. There is no constitutional right to bail, although the 8th Amendment prohibits excessive bail.

> Excessive bail shall not be required, nor excessive fines imposed, nor cruel and unusual punishments inflicted.

The individual pledges money and/or property that is forfeited if they do not appear. More serious crimes carry with them more serious punishments; therefore, bail is set higher because it is assumed that defendants have more reason to run when facing more serious punishments. The amount of bail for each suspect is determined not only by the seriousness of the crime, but also by the characteristics of the defendant. Home ownership, employment, and residential stability indicate that the suspect is a low risk for flight (unless the crime is very serious); however, if the offender is unemployed, has no family in the area, and has no place to stay prior to trial, there is a high probability that he or she will flee. Of course, there is also the high probability that they cannot afford bail either, and so these individuals would probably remain in jail.

There are a variety of bail/surety alternatives involving the courts and/or private bail bonds providers:

1. Direct/full bail
2. Private bail bonds—secured (requiring collateral) or unsecured
3. Court surety programs—secured (requiring collateral) or unsecured
4. Release on recognizance.

Some defendants may be able to post the full amount of bail; however, most do not have the ability to offer that amount of cash. Most often, defendants or their families contract with bail bonds agents who often demand collateral from the defendant (i.e., house, car, money) in return for the bond agent signing a promissory note to the court. If the defendant does not appear, the bond agent must pay the full amount of the bail. Bond agents receive a fee even if the defendant appears; thus, even if the defendant is acquitted of all charges or the charges are dropped, they still have to pay the bond agent for the right to be released prior to court proceedings. In other instances, bond agents do not require collateral;

To read an interesting *New York Times* article about bail in New York City that describes typical cases and how the process works, go to http://www.nytimes.com/2015/08/16/magazine/the-bail-trap.html

they take on the risk of having to pay the court the full amount if the defendant absconds. In return for their assumption of this risk, the bond fee may be higher.

In some jurisdictions, the court cuts out the private bond agents and allows the defendant to offer the collateral directly to the court, along with a percentage (typically 10 percent) of the full amount of bail. If the defendant does not appear, then the deposit and the property are forfeited. In a very few jurisdictions, courts offer an unsecured bond option where the defendant promises to pay the full amount, but it is unsecured by collateral. In both types of these **court surety programs**, if the defendant does appear, he or she pays only a small administrative fee. These programs, where they exist, save defendants quite a bit of money. Even in the areas where there are court surety programs, private bail bond agents still have a role because defendants typically must meet fairly stringent background characteristics in order to be eligible for the court surety program, and all others who have bail granted must resort to the private vendor if they want to be released prior to trial. The problem is that many defendants do not have any collateral. They do not have financial resources to equal the bail amount and, therefore, are not eligible for programs that require collateral. Thus, it is argued that the poor spend pre-trial time in jail while those who have money do not, regardless of their risk of flight.

In the 1960s, the Vera Institute of Justice funded the Manhattan Bail Project. This was the first formal **release on recognizance** (ROR) program. Defendants who could not afford bail but who seemed to be good risks were identified. In the course of one study period (1961–64), the project evaluated 10,000 defendants for release; 4,000 were recommended for release; 2,195 were released; and only 15 did not show up for a court appearance. In general, ROR programs find that the failure-to-appear rates for those in the program are similar to those on bail.[44]

Current studies are also finding that unsecured bonds can be an effective release mechanism. For instance, one study, utilizing court data from Colorado, found that for low-risk, moderate-risk, and high-risk offenders, unsecured bonds were as effective (in not resulting in new crimes) as secured bonds and unsecured bonds were as effective in ensuring court appearances as secured bonds. The use of unsecured bonds freed up more jail beds by allowing booked defendants to be released and released faster. Another interesting finding of this study was that the cost of the bonds was associated with pre-trial detention (that is, the higher the bond, the less likely the defendant was to pay it and be released), but it was not related to increased court appearance rates.[45] The policy implications of this study and others is that unsecured bonds can reduce jail populations without sacrificing public safety.

In 1984, Congress passed the Federal Bail Reform Act.[46] This bill allowed for the preventive detention of federal defendants. **Preventive detention** is when the individual is incarcerated before trial, not because of a fear that they will abscond, but because of a perceived risk to the public if they are in the community. With the federal preventive detention measure, judges can consider the offense, the weight of the evidence, the history and character of the defendant, ties to the community, drug history, and the nature and seriousness of danger to the community. They may determine that the risk to the public is too great to allow the offender to remain in the community prior to trial, and the offender will be held without bail. This seems to be contrary to the due process concept of "innocent until proven guilty," but there is at least some due process in that there is a separate preventive detention hearing where the magistrate weighs the risk and makes the determination.[47]

Your state probably has similar legislation allowing for the preventive detention of suspects in state prosecutions.

## Grand Jury Indictment or Information

Arrests generally are based on criminal complaints issued against the accused, however, before the process goes further, a formal charging document must exist—the two charging documents are an **indictment** issued by a grand jury or an **information** issued by the prosecutor's office. The 5th Amendment guarantees the right of grand jury review to federal defendants, but the right has not been "incorporated" to state citizens (those facing prosecution by states). Only about half of the states use **grand juries**. In some of these states, the right, at least for felony defendants, is guaranteed by the state constitution (New York, Ohio, and Texas). In other states, there is an option to go to the grand jury for indictment; otherwise, the prosecutor will issue the charging instrument.

Many people are confused about the difference between a grand jury and a **petit (or trial) jury**. You will not usually ever see a grand jury. Grand jury members are selected by the presiding or administrative judge and tend to be "good citizens known to the court." They sit for a month, six months, or even a year, for one day or an afternoon a week. The grand jury listens to cases brought before them by the prosecutor. The prosecutor may bring in witnesses to question, or just describe the evidence in the case, and then they determine whether there is probable cause to go forward. If a grand jury decides that there is probable cause, they return an indictment. If they do not believe that the prosecutor has proven probable cause, they will **no bill** the case, meaning that there is no indictment.

## Preliminary Hearing

The preliminary hearing may also be called the preliminary examination, probable cause hearing, bindover hearing, or some other term. This type of hearing is sometimes combined with the initial hearing, but more often it takes place several days later. While defendants would not necessarily have an attorney at the initial appearance, they must have one at the preliminary hearing. In the preliminary hearing, a judge rules on the strength of evidence by determining whether the prosecutor has shown that there is probable cause the defendant committed the crimes charged. The defense is not obligated to do anything at a preliminary hearing. If they choose, they can present evidence or witnesses, and they may cross-examine prosecution witnesses, but it is solely the prosecutor's burden to prove that there is enough evidence to go forward with the prosecution.

If the charges are dismissed at this point, the prosecutor is free to continue to try to make a case. **Double jeopardy**—the right not to be tried for the same offense—does not "attach" or become an issue until a jury is empaneled. About half of cases are dismissed before trial, although some are refiled when there is more evidence.[48] If the prosecutor is successful in showing probable cause, then an information is issued, which is the charging document to go forward.

## Arraignment and Plea Bargaining

The next step in the proceedings is the arraignment. Here, the defendant is formally notified of the charges against him or her and asked for a plea. If the defendant accepts a plea bargain, the arraignment may become the end of the process with the judge accepting the plea and setting punishment. As you probably know, over 90 percent of criminal defendants plead guilty. Most do so in return for a recommendation for a reduced sentence. Judges are not bound to accept the prosecutor's recommendation for sentencing, but they do so in the vast majority of cases. If a judge takes a plea, typically, the only evidence is an affidavit of the defendant admitting guilt. Attached to this legal document is the prosecutor's recommendation for sentencing. The judge should ensure that the defendant is knowingly and voluntarily agreeing to the plea bargain. If the judge does not agree to the recommendation, the defendant has a right to withdraw the confession. The prosecutor is also barred from agreeing to a sentence and then retracting the agreement once he or she has obtained a confession. On the other hand, the Supreme Court has generally upheld cases where the defendant was forced to choose between a plea bargain and the possibility of the death penalty. Plea bargaining allows the system to dispose of a tremendous number of cases without the expense of further adjudication.

## Pre-trial Motions

Typically, after the arraignment, but before the beginning of the trial, if the case isn't plea bargained, there may be a number of pre-trial motions. A **motion** is simply a request that the judge order something to be done or not done. For instance, the defense may file a motion to exclude evidence. The defense attorney would have to show either that the evidence was obtained illegally and should be excluded, or that the evidence is more prejudicial than probative (meaning helpful to prove). Generally, prior prison sentences or prior accusations are excluded because they are highly prejudicial and don't prove that the defendant did this particular crime, although, in some cases such evidence might come in as evidence of a pattern of criminal behavior. The **motion in limine** requests the judge to bar the mention of something that might be prejudicial during the trial, but has no bearing on guilt or innocence in the case, such as a prior prison term.

Another pre-trial motion is a **change of venue**, which is a request for the trial to be moved to another jurisdiction because of a belief that any jurors from the locale where the crime took place would be too biased to render a fair verdict. This is also a motion typically filed by the defense.

Either side might, but rarely does, file a motion for the judge to **recuse** himself (**recusal**). This motion basically argues that the judge is not able to conduct the trial in a fair and unbiased manner because of some conflict of interest. The attorney who files a recusal motion hopes that the judge will grant it and remove him- or herself from the case and give it to another judge.

**Brady motions** have become well-known because of cases of prosecutorial misconduct in not providing exculpatory evidence to the defense. The motion comes from *Brady v. Maryland*,[49] a case where the Supreme Court held that prosecutors must share with defense when asked for any evidence that might lead to a finding of innocence. In some of the most notorious exonerations where innocent people have been released from prison, it was discovered that prosecutors did not turn over exculpatory information that might have prevented the conviction and incarceration of the innocent person.

Other pre-trial motions judges may be called upon to decide are motions for severance of defendants when two or more defendants are being charged and tried together, but a defense attorney wants to separate out his or her defendant to be tried separately. Another motion is to force discovery, when the defense believes the prosecution has something that they are not sharing and the defense has a legal right to have access to it. Finally, perhaps the most common motion is a motion for continuance when one side or the other requests that the trial date be delayed for some reason. It is not at all uncommon to have a dozen or more continuances delaying the trial for a year or more from its originally scheduled date.

# What are the Steps of a Trial?

If one were to enter a criminal trial court in most states, it would be easy to identify the judge, the prosecutor(s), and perhaps the defense attorney(s). One could also identify the bailiff, who may be either a sheriff's deputy or a court employee. Typically, there is also a court administrator who handles the non-judicial aspects of the court, including scheduling and caseload processing. The court clerk handles legal filing of court orders, may collect court fees, and schedules the trial docket. In larger jurisdictions where there are many judges, one of the trial judges also serves as a presiding or administrative judge and handles the managerial and the budgetary aspects of the court system in that jurisdiction. Most cases that go to trial are serious crimes such as murder, rape, or another serious crime where the defendant is facing a long prison sentence or perhaps even a death sentence.

For an interesting website about famous trials throughout history, go to http://www.law.umkc.edu/faculty/projects/ftrials/ftrials.htm

In a criminal case, the state has the burden of proving the guilt of the accused beyond a reasonable doubt. That means that the prosecution has the responsibility to prove each of the elements of the crime with which the accused is charged. For example, the crime of burglary generally has these elements: breaking and entering the dwelling of another with intent to commit a felony therein. If the prosecution fails to prove any element of the crime beyond a reasonable doubt, but proves the other elements, the accused may sometimes be found guilty of a lesser crime. But ordinarily, if the prosecutor is unable to prove all elements beyond a reasonable doubt, the person charged cannot be convicted of the crime. Also, recall that the prosecutor must also prove that the offense took place within the geographic jurisdiction of the court.

In a civil case the degree of proof is a "preponderance of the evidence"; but in a criminal case, the degree of proof is "beyond a reasonable doubt." In some states, the exact wording of the charge to the jury dealing with the standard of proof is stated by statute. In other states, there is no such requirement, and in fact, the judge may not allow the prosecutor's or defense attorney's suggested definitions, preferring the jury to decide themselves what it means. The "beyond a reasonable doubt" standard is a constitutional requirement. In 1970, the Supreme Court left no doubt about the requirement in the holding of *In re Winship*:

> Lest there remain any doubt about the constitutional stature of the reasonable-doubt standard, we explicitly hold that the Due Process Clause protects the accused against conviction except on proof beyond a reasonable doubt of every fact necessary to constitute the crime with which he is charged.[50]

In most cases, the defense has no burden of proof at all, and can merely remain silent and argue that the prosecutor has not proven beyond a reasonable doubt that the defendant committed the crime. In certain cases, however, the defense may argue an **affirmative defense**, such as coercion, self-defense, entrapment, mistake, alibi, or insanity. In these cases, the defendant's attorney must offer proof (usually by a preponderance) before the jury can consider the defense.

## Jury Selection

As noted above, there may be pre-trial motions and many continuances before a trial actually starts. The first step in the trial itself is jury selection.

As you know, the 6th Amendment gives criminal defendants the right to a trial by a jury of their peers. This has been interpreted by a line of court cases to mean that the jury pool must be pulled in such a way as to not clearly exclude any particular group, not necessarily that the jury panel represent the demographic characteristics of the defendant.

Typically, jurisdictions use voter registration, driver's licenses, or motor vehicle registration lists to pull jury panels. Once called to perform jury duty, you may or may not actually serve on a jury. Depending on the jurisdiction, you may be on call for a day or a week (perhaps having the option to call in each morning to check to see if you are needed). If a judge in that jurisdiction is starting a trial, he or she will call for a jury panel of up to 50 people (depending on the case, the number of peremptory challenges, and the size of the jury in that jurisdiction).

Most jurisdictions allow for certain exemptions from jury duty. If one has minor children at home, is a full-time student, or is past a certain age, they are generally exempt. Some states have automatic occupation exemptions; others do not. Typically, jury members must be citizens, not have a criminal record, and be of "sound mind."

We tend to think that juries must be twelve individuals who vote unanimously to convict the defendant, but there is no constitutional right to a twelve-person jury.[51] States may require only eight people to be on a jury (Arizona and Utah), or six (Connecticut and Florida), at least in noncapital cases. There is also no constitutional right to have a unanimous verdict. Some states do not require unanimous jury verdicts (Louisiana and Oregon).[52]

After the jury panel has been seated, the defense and prosecuting attorneys have a chance to examine the jury cards that jury panel members have filled out. These provide quite a bit of information about each panel member, including marital status, age, occupation, income, number of children, and so on. The process by which the prosecutor and defense attorney question the jury panel to determine if they need to request any members of the panel be removed is called **voir dire**. A translation of voir dire is something like "to see to say," but it basically means to speak the truth. The first question that is asked is whether jury members know any of the principal players in the trial, such as the victim, the offender, either attorney, or the judge. Then attorneys ask questions relevant to the particular case. For instance, if the defendant was charged with negligent manslaughter because he killed someone in an accident after a night of drinking, the defense attorney is going to want to know the drinking habits of the prospective jurors and whether any of them had a relative who had been killed by a drunk driver. Attorneys may ask any questions that may uncover any biases that prospective jurors may have either for or against the defendant.

State statutes set the number of **peremptory challenges** for the prosecutor and the defense attorney. Peremptory challenges allow the attorney to reject the juror without having to show a particular reason. However, the attorney cannot use race as a reason to reject someone. The Supreme Court said in *Batson v. Kentucky*[53] that attorneys who used race as a reason to reject prospective jurors violated the equal protection clause of the 14th Amendment. In subsequent cases, the Court also rejected the use of race by the defendant (as opposed to the prosecutor as in *Batson*) and gender. **Challenges for cause** are unlimited, but there must be a reason why the juror would be biased in the trial. The attorney has to state what the objection is, and the judge will consider the challenge and agree and dismiss the juror, or disagree and allow the juror to remain.

After each attorney has identified the jurors he or she has rejected under the peremptory challenges, and the judge has dealt with any requests to strike jurors for cause, the remaining jurors are called up one at a time to the jury box until it is filled with the appropriate number and, in some instances, alternates. Once the jury is seated, the trial can begin.

## Opening Statements

The opening statements are the attorneys' opportunity to address the jury as to what they should be looking for in the presentation of evidence. Each attorney seeks to educate the jury as to his or her version of the events. They need to convince the jury of their version through evidence that consists either of witnesses who testify to what they have seen, heard, or experienced, and/or expert witnesses who can offer opinions and judgments, at least within the confines of their expertise. The opening statement gives the attorney a chance to talk directly to the jury and tell them what they are going to hear. The defense often asks that their opening be deferred to the beginning of the defense's case.

## Presentation of Evidence

You have probably seen innumerable trials on television shows and movies. Some are fairly accurate and some are not. The prosecution presents the state's case first. Witnesses are put on the stand, and the prosecutor goes through a **direct examination**, which is the questioning of his or her own witness. The questions cannot be leading (telling the witness the answer or making a statement); they cannot ask for an opinion, they cannot ask for **hearsay** (something that the witness did not hear, see, or experience directly), although there are many exceptions to this rule. They also cannot ask for something that would be unduly prejudicial or otherwise not be allowed into evidence.

After the prosecutor has finished questioning a witness, the defense may cross-examine the witness. These questions have pretty much the same rules, but there is the opportunity to ask leading questions, such as, "Isn't it true that on the night of July 15, you had so much to drink that you were not able to see the defendant clearly across the parking lot of the bar?" After the defense has finished the cross-examination, the prosecutor has the opportunity to question the witness again over any material that was brought up in the cross-examination. This process continues until all witnesses have been examined. Then, the prosecutor has the chance to present any rebuttal witnesses that might be appropriate. This might occur if the defense has elicited some information from one of the witnesses that the prosecutor can show is irrelevant or untrue or just to shed additional light on the information. Rebuttal witnesses respond directly to the facts already in evidence.

The presentation of the defense's case comes next, beginning with the opening statement if the attorney reserved the right to give one. The direct examination, cross-examination, and rebuttal witnesses occur in the same order, only this time the witnesses are defense witnesses and the prosecutor cross-examines. After all witnesses are finished testifying, there are closing arguments.

## Closing Arguments

An instance where the prosecutor has an advantage over the defense is that they are allowed to have the first closing statement and then are able to speak to the jury again after the defense's closing statement. This is because prosecutors have the burden of proof in a trial. In the closing, each side summarizes the evidence in a way that supports their version of the case. They emphasize certain portions of the evidence, and they comment on the weight of the evidence. Attorneys cannot mention any facts not in evidence.

## Jury Instructions

After the closing, the judge reads to the jury an instruction. The instruction to the jury is written by the judge with both attorneys suggesting text. It may include definitions of legal terms. It may ask them to choose between two or more different levels of culpability. For instance, in a homicide case, the instructions may give the jury the choice between finding the defendant guilty of murder in the first degree, second degree, or even manslaughter. The rules for instructions are different among the states, but it is basically the guidelines, rules, or verdict available for the jury to follow in their deliberation.

## Jury Deliberation

You may have seen movies where the jury is sequestered, meaning that they stay in hotel rooms until they reach a verdict. Ordinarily, they are allowed to go home in the evening until the verdict is reached although they are instructed not to watch news or discuss the case. If the jury cannot reach a verdict, it is called a "hung jury" and the prosecutor may decide to try the case again. This would not be double jeopardy because the trial is not officially over yet. If the jury comes back with an acquittal, it does not mean the jury members necessarily believe the defendant is innocent, it means that they did not believe the prosecutor proved the case beyond a reasonable doubt. If the jury comes back with a guilty verdict, the next step is sentencing.

## Sentencing

Depending on the state, judges or juries may sentence convicted felons and misdemeanants. In both cases, statutory guidelines limit the discretion of the judge or jury in what type of sentence can be imposed, and how long the sentence may last. A sentencing hearing is a "critical stage" of the trial process, meaning that the courts have held that a defendant must have an attorney present if they are facing the possibility of a jail or prison sentence. There are, however, relaxed rules of evidence. Hearsay may be admitted, as when people testify about the character of the offender. Victim statements may be read, which allow the victim or the victim's family to state how the crime has affected them.

In most states, pre-sentence reports are also used in order to give the judge or the jury more information about the offender before a sentence decision is made. A pre-sentence division in a probation agency conducts pre-sentence investigations, and they provide information on the offender's criminal, educational, family, and work history. Sentencing can be considered the last step of the trial process and the first step in the corrections process.

# Summary

### What are the Different Levels of Courts?
State systems typically involve state trial courts of general and limited jurisdiction, intermediate appellate courts, and state courts of last resort. Specialized courts exist, such as family or juvenile court, community courts, drug courts, and domestic violence courts.

### What are Specialized Courts?
Specialized, community or problem-solving courts refer to courts that have specialized caseloads and their objective is not to simply administer a verdict and punish, but to address the underlying causes of the defendants' criminality, e.g., drug addiction, PTSD, or some other issue.

### How Do Prosecutors Decide Whether and What to Charge?
District attorneys (prosecutors) are usually elected, but their assistant prosecutors are not. Most prosecutors' offices employ less than ten people, but some large cities have hundreds of prosecutors. Prosecutors are not legally obligated to bring charges and do so typically on the basis of the strength of the evidence, although other factors also play a part, such as victims' wishes.

### What are the Duties of a Defense Attorney?
Defense attorneys for indigents are provided through a public defender system, an appointment system, or by contract attorneys. Their duty is to zealously pursue the interests of their client without subverting the legal process.

### What is the Role of a Judge? How are they Selected?
Judges may be elected or appointed. If appointed, typically a form of the Missouri Plan is utilized. The role of a judge is somewhat like an umpire. He or she rules on pre-trial motions and trial objections, and ensures the legal process proceeds without error. In bench trials, the judge decides guilt or innocence because there is no jury.

### What is the Jurisdiction of Federal Courts?
The federal court system operates in parallel to state systems, and federal crimes (and civil matters relevant to federal laws or that cross state lines in jurisdiction) are prosecuted in these courts. There are 94 federal districts, each with their own trial court and a U.S. attorney (and assistants) to prosecute federal crimes. Federal cases (and some state cases that allege constitutional issues)

can be appealed to federal courts of appeals and, ultimately, to the Supreme Court. The Supreme Court hears only a small fraction of the cases that are appealed to it. When the Court chooses to hear a case, a writ of certiorari is issued.

## How Does Due Process Protect Individuals Against Error in the Criminal Justice Process?

Due process protections come to us through the 5th and 14th Amendments. The 6th Amendment gives us specific due process rights when faced with criminal prosecution, including a right to a jury of peers, and counsel. It is important to remember, however, that our due process rights go far beyond the Sixth Amendment, and are implicated any time the government attempts to deprive us of life, liberty, or property. The steps of the criminal process begin with arrest and booking, continue through initial appearance, preliminary hearing, indictment or information, arraignment, and trial and sentencing. At each step, the process is designed to minimize or eliminate any errors that the government may make.

## What are the Steps of a Trial?

A trial includes pre-trial motions, jury voir dire, opening statements, direct examinations, cross-examinations, rebuttal witnesses, and closing statements. A sentencing hearing follows if the defendant is convicted.

## CRITICAL THINKING EXERCISES

1. Utilize any movie or television show that portrays a criminal prosecution through trial. Try to identify as many errors as you think the scriptwriters commit after reading this chapter.
2. Plea bargaining continues to be a controversial element of our criminal justice system. Do some research and construct an argument for plea bargaining and an argument against it.

## Notes

1. D. Rottman and S. Strickland, *State Court Organization*. Washington, DC: Bureau of Justice Statistics, 2006, p. 4.
2. R. Malega and T. H. Cohen, *State Court Organization, 2011*. Washington, DC: Bureau of Justice Statistics, 2013, p. 4.
3. S. Rosenmerkel, M. Durose and D. Farole, *Felony Sentences in State Courts, 2006, Statistical Tables*. Washington, DC: Bureau of Justice Statistics, 2009.
4. S. Perry, D. Banks, *Prosecutors in State Courts, 2007—Statistical Tables*. Washington, DC: Bureau of Justice Statistics, 2011, p. 1.
5. R. Malega and T. H. Cohen, *State Court Organization, 2011*. Washington, DC: Bureau of Justice Statistics, 2013, p. 4.

6. D. Rottman and S. Strickland, *State Court Organization*. Washington, DC: Bureau of Justice Statistics, 2006.

7. P. Casey and D. Rottman, *Problem Solving Courts: Models and Trends*. Washington, DC: National Center for State Courts, 2003.

8. J. Petersilia, *Reforming Probation and Parole*. Lanham, MD: American Correctional Association, 2002, p. 4; S. Listwan, J. Sundt, A. Holsinger and E. Latessa, "The effect of drug court programming on recidivism: The Cincinnati experience." *Crime and Delinquency* 49 (3) (2003): 389–411.

9. J. Petersilia, *Reforming Probation and Parole*. Lanham, MD: American Correctional Association, 2002, p. 5.

10. S. Listwan, J. Sundt, A. Holsinger and E. Latessa, "The effect of drug court programming on recidivism: The Cincinnati experience." *Crime and Delinquency* 49 (3) (2003): 389–411.

11. D. Marlow, D. Festinger, P. Lee, K. Dugosh and K. Benasutti, "Matching judicial supervision to clients' risk status in drug court." *Crime and Delinquency* 52 (1) (2006): 52–76.

12. M. Carey and W. Finigan, "A detailed cost analysis in a mature drug court setting." *Journal of Contemporary Criminal Justice* 20 (3) (2004): 315–338.

13. S. Johnson, D. Hubbard and E. Latessa, "Drug courts and treatment: Lessons to be learned from the 'what works' literature." *Corrections Management Quarterly* 4 (4) (2000): 70–77.

14. S. Rossman, J. Roman, et al., *A Multi-site Adult Drug Court Evaluation*. Washington, DC: Urban Institute, 2011.

15. A. Gover, J. MacDonald and G. Alpert, "Combating domestic violence: Findings from an evaluation of a local domestic violence court." *Criminology and Public Policy* 3 (1) (2003): 109–132. Also see L. Levy, M. Steketee and S. Keilitz, *Lessons Learned in Implementing an Integrated Domestic Violence Court*. Williamsburg, VA: National Center for State Courts, 2001.

16. A. Gover, J. MacDonald and G. Alpert, "Combating domestic violence: Findings from an evaluation of a local domestic violence court." *Criminology and Public Policy* 3 (1) (2003): 111.

17. W. Pitts, E. Givens and S. McNeeley, "The need for a holistic approach to specialized domestic violence court programming: Evaluating offender rehabilitation needs and recidivism." *Juvenile and Family Court Journal* 60 (3) (2009): 1–22.

18. C. DeFrances, *Prosecutors in State Courts*. Washington, DC: Bureau of Justice Statistics, 2001.

19. S. Perry and D. Banks, *Prosecutors in State Courts, 2007—Statistical Tables*. Washington, DC: Bureau of Justice Statistics, 2011, p. 1.

20. D. Rottman and S. Strickland, *State Court Organization*. Washington, DC: Bureau of Justice Statistics, 2006.

21. B. Frederick and D. Stemen, *The Anatomy of Discretion: An Analysis of Prosecutorial Decision Making—Technical Report*. Washington, DC: National Institute of Justice, OJP, 2012.

22. *Gideon v. Wainwright*, 373 U.S. 335, 1963.

23. *Argersinger v. Hamlin*, 407 U.S. 321, 1972.

24. L. Langton and D. Farole, *State Public Defender Programs*. Washington, DC: Bureau of Justice Statistics, 2010.

25. Justice Policy Institute, *System Overload: The Costs of Underresourcing Public Defense*. Washington, DC: Justice Policy Institue, 2011.

26. C. Harlow, *Defense Counsel in Criminal Cases*. Washington, DC: Bureau of Justice Statistics, 2000.

27. A. Liptak, "Study reveals gap in performance of public defenders." *Austin American-Statesman*, July 14, 2007, A9.

28. T. Cohen, "Who's better at defending criminals? Does type of defense attorney matter in terms of producing favorable case outcomes." Social Science Research Working Paper series, 2011. Available at: https://nationalcdp.org/docs/defense-counsel-and-ajudication.pdf

29. National Association of Criminal Defense Lawyers. *Federal Indigent Defense, 2015: The Independence Imperative.* Washington, DC: NACDL, 2015.

30. K. Goetz, "Ky public defenders: Thin ranks, high risks." *St Louis Courier,* November 22, 2015. Retrieved from: http://www.courier-journal.com/story/news/crime/2015/11/19/kentucky-public-defenders-risks/76046976/?from=global&ses-sionKey=&autologin=

31. Bureau of Justice Assistance, *Public Defense Reform since Gideon: Improving the Administration of Justice by Building on Our Successes and Learning from Our Failures.* Washington, DC: Bureau of Justice Assistance, 2008.

32. N. Mariano, "Justice denied: The high price of justice." TheSouthern.com, April 19, 2015, http://thesouthern.com/news/local/justice-denied/the-high-price-of-justice-sixth-amendment-guarantee-deteriorating-under/article_2992e476-c4ca-5124-a433-23a025a26bf8.html

33. Justice Policy Institute, *System Overload: The Costs of Underresourcing Public Defense.* Washington, DC: Justice Policy Institue, 2011, p. 7.

34. Quoted in Justice Policy Institute, *System Overload: The Costs of Underresourcing Public Defense.* Washington, DC: Justice Policy Institute, 2011, p. 8.

35. Quoted in Justice Policy Institute, *System Overload: The Costs of Underresourcing Public Defense.* Washington, DC: Justice Policy Institute, 2011, p. 7.

36. N. Mariano, "Justice denied: The high price of justice." TheSouthern.com, April 19, 2015, http://thesouthern.com/news/local/justice-denied/the-high-price-of-justice-sixth-amendment-guarantee-deteriorating-under/article_2992e476-c4ca-5124-a433-23a025a26bf8.html. Note that another source (Justice Policy Institute, note 33) reported 30 public defender systems were state funded, 18 were county and state funded, and only 1 state—Pennsylvania—was entirely county funded.

37. Quoted in Justice Policy Institute, note 33, p. 11.

38. Quoted in N. Mariano, note 35.

39. Justice Policy Institute, note 33.

40. American Judicature Society, *Judicial Selection in the States.* Des Moines, IA: American Judicature Society, 2004.

41. Bureau of Justice Statistics. Retrieved 6/1/2007 from http://www.ojp.usdoj.gov/bjs/.

42. U.S. Department of Justice, United States Attorneys. Retrieved 6/1/2007 from http://www.usdoj.gov/usao/offices/usa_listings2.html#n.

43. *Riverside v. McLaughlin,* 500 U.S. 44, 1991.

44. S. Maxwell, "Examining the congruence between predictors of ROR and failures to appear." *Journal of Criminal Justice* 27 (2) (1999): 127–141. Also see, T. Cohen and B. Reaves, *Pretrial Release of Felony Defendants in State Courts.* Washington, DC: Bureau of Justice Statistics, 2007.

45. M. Jones, *Unsecured Bonds: The As Effective and More Efficient Release Option.* Pretrial Justice Institute, 2013. file:///C:/Users/jp12/Desktop/INTRO3RD/COURTS/Unsecured+Bonds,+The+As+Effective+and+Most+Efficient+Pretrial+Release+Option+-+Jones+2013.pdf

46. 18 U.S.C.A. § 3141 et seq. 1996.

47. See *United States v. Salerno,* 481 U.S. 739, 1987.

48. B. Boland, P. Mahanna and R. Sones, *The Prosecution of Felony Arrests, 1988*. Washington, DC: Bureau of Justice Statistics, 1992.

49. *Brady v. Maryland*, 373 U.S. 83, 1963.

50. *In re Winship*, 397 U.S. 358, 1970.

51. *Williams v. Florida*, 399 U.S. 78, 1970.

52. *Apodaca v. Oregon*, 406 U.S. 404, 1971.

53. *Batson v. Kentucky*, 476 U.S. 79, 1986.

# Due Process of Law

BRUCE E. ALTSCHULER, CELIA A. SGROI, AND
MARGARET RYNIKER

## Introduction

The Fifth Amendment prohibits the federal government from depriving anyone of
life, liberty, or property without due process of law, a protection the Fourteenth
Amendment extended to apply to the states. The familiarity of the phrase "due
process," however, can hide its complexity. As Justice Felix Frankfurter put it in
the case of *Joint Anti-Fascist Refugee Committee v. McGrath*, 341 U.S. 123 (1951),
"'Due process,' unlike some legal rules, is not a technical conception with a fixed
content unrelated to time, place, and circumstances. ... Due process is not a
mechanical instrument. It is not a yardstick. It is a delicate process of adjustment
inescapably involving the exercise of judgment by those whom the Constitution
entrusted with the unfolding of the process."

How can we understand a concept without a fixed meaning? Fortunately,
that concept is so fundamental to our freedom and its history so rich with detail
that we can set out standards for judgment even if exact definition is impossible.

## The Limits of Due Process

Due process is basically a guarantee of government fairness. Government cannot
take our lives, liberty, or property unless it provides us with the chance to protect
our interests that is called due process. In other words, the due process clauses
protect us from arbitrary and unreasonable actions by government. This sets
out the first limit of the concept. It applies to government actions, not private
ones. When the Fifth Amendment was ratified, government played a relatively
small role in the lives of most citizens, so the distinction was clear and cases
few. Between the adoption of the Constitution and the end of the Civil War, the
Supreme Court decided only one case based on due process! One of the major

changes in our society since then, however, has been the growth of government into virtually all areas of life. This has often created situations intertwining public and private action, making the boundary between the two more difficult to draw. Thus, the actions of a public college are covered by due process, but what about a private college that gets a substantial amount of government funding? What if the government outsources what had previously always been a public function? For example, private companies now operate prisons under contracts with the government. Do their prisoners have the same rights to due process as those in government-run prisons? In one of the cases presented in this chapter, a court has to determine whether an employee of a privately run but largely publicly funded library has the same due process rights as a public employee. Such examples can be easily multiplied.

The second limit is that due process applies only to something—life, liberty, or property (not the pursuit of happiness, which is in the Declaration of Independence but was replaced by property in the Constitution)—that belongs to the person alleging its deprivation. If there is no such entitlement, there can be no deprivation, hence no requirement of due process. Thus, the government cannot execute you, incarcerate you, or take something you own unless it acts within the guidelines of due process. However, a public hospital could ban smoking without violating due process because there is no right to smoke. Even though smokers may be significantly inconvenienced, they are not being denied life, liberty, or property. [...]

## Procedural and Substantive Due Process

Traditionally, due process has been divided into two areas: procedural and substantive. Originally, due process referred to the procedures by which laws were carried out. Procedural due process requires that before any deprivation there must be notice and opportunity for a fair hearing before someone neutral and competent. In the mid-nineteenth century the concept was expanded to include substantive due process, which requires that laws be reasonable attempts to achieve legitimate government goals while putting the least burden on people's rights. It also requires laws to be clear enough so that citizens know what is allowed and what is not. Under the doctrine of substantive due process, the courts examine the content of laws to ensure that they do not violate traditional notions of fairness. This may require courts to protect rights that are not explicitly stated in the Constitution, giving judges significant discretion in determining what these rights are. Today, most legal scholars agree that the Supreme Court went overboard during the early twentieth century, using substantive due process to overturn economic reforms that the justices disagreed with. These decisions so discredited the concept that it nearly disappeared for a time. That is why Justice Douglas included language specifically refusing to base his decision in *Griswold v. Connecticut* (see p. 62 in chap. 2) on substantive due process.

This caution has not prevented courts from continuing to use substantive due process, but the major change has been that it is now used more to protect civil rights than economic ones. During the first decades of the twentieth century, the Supreme Court invalidated minimum wage, maximum hour, and child labor laws on the basis of "rights," such as that of entering into a contract. Today society's values have changed so much that these decisions appear mistaken to most people. Courts are more likely to use such civil rights as the right to privacy to limit what government can do. The concept of substantive due process is one of the clearest examples of how such changes in society result in changes in the meaning and application of legal doctrines.

Procedural due process is the more frequently invoked and more familiar of the two types of due process. It requires fair procedures before government can deprive someone of life, liberty, or property; however, the Constitution makes little attempt to define these procedures except in criminal cases for which the Bill of Rights provides specific guarantees, such as the rights to counsel, to confront witnesses, and to avoid compelled self-incrimination. As indicated by the quote from Justice Frankfurter at the beginning of this chapter, the courts have held that the procedural requirements of due process vary with the situation. In general, the person being deprived must be given adequate notice and a fair hearing at which to present his or her side to a disinterested party. In general, the greater the deprivation, the more formal the hearing, with criminal trials providing the greatest protection and minor deprivations the least. Conversely, emergency situations can justify more expedited procedures. As of this writing the courts are wrestling with the issue of what procedures to require for those captured in Afghanistan and subsequently held in Guantanamo Bay who are challenging their detention as what the Bush administration has termed "illegal combatants." The materials in this chapter help clarify what procedural process is required in a variety of circumstances by looking at specific issues.

This introduction provides a basic understanding of the main points of due process. Although it cannot be defined with precision, it is a basic guarantee requiring that when government deprives someone of life, liberty, or property, it must do so in a manner that both is and appears to be fair. This may give courts considerable discretion, but it also provides the flexibility necessary to avoid injustice.

# The Meaning of Due Process

In the first reading, Judge Edward D. Re explains the role of courts in protecting the due process rights of individuals. In doing this he stresses both the importance and flexibility of due process. Note that the lack of a specific definition of due process has not prevented courts from providing guidelines to help apply the concept. Also, pay close attention to his discussion of Section 1983 of the 1871 Civil Rights Act, which is frequently used to authorize lawsuits seeking to protect individual rights threatened by government action.

*Due Process, Judicial Review, and the Rights of the Individual Edward D. Re*

In Anglo-American law probably no concept is more important than that of due process of law. It is from the guarantee of due process that all of the substantive and procedural rights embodied in the Constitution and laws acquire meaning and vitality. Indeed, it is at the heart of the common law system of jurisprudence.

The phrase "due process of law" implies that a person will receive fair treatment, and a procedure designed to achieve just result. In the judicial context, it connotes an opportunity to be heard before a decision is made that will affect one's rights or legally protected interests. It applies both to personal rights, sometimes termed "liberty interests," and to property rights. The type or nature of the hearing to which one will be entitled and when it will be granted, will depend upon the nature of the interest affected and the degree or severity of the deprivation that may be imposed. To say that a person has been deprived of due process of law implies that the person has not been granted or has not received those protections or safeguards that are guaranteed to all persons under the law.

The guarantees of due process of law are specifically set forth in the Fifth and Fourteenth Amendments to the Constitution. The Fifth Amendment provides that "No person shall be ... deprived of life, liberty, or property without due process of law. ..."

The Fifth Amendment, adopted as part of the Bill of Rights, was originally interpreted to serve as a check upon the acts of the federal government only. The Fourteenth Amendment, adopted over three-quarters of a century later in the aftermath of the Civil War, applies expressly to the state government. In more recent years, in a series of landmark decisions, the Supreme Court has held that most of the protections contained in the Bill of Rights have been incorporated into the Fourteenth Amendment and, therefore, are also binding upon the states. In addition to these constitutional provisions, there are specific statutory enactments that are designed to promote the enforcement of these constitutional guarantees.

In the American constitutional system, the judiciary plays a unique role in interpreting and applying the guarantees and freedoms enumerated in the Constitution. On judicial review, it is the role of the courts to determine whether the enactments of the legislature, or the actions of an administrative or executive agency, comport with requirements of due process of law. If the challenged government actions do not meet the constitutional standards of due process, the courts will overturn those actions in order to ensure that the aggrieved party receives the "due process" to which that party is entitled.

The courts have developed a body of case law that embodies the standards of due process that must be followed in particular cases. This body of case law, developed over time, provides guidance not only for all of the courts of the land, but also for all branches of government in defining and applying due process in different situations and cases.

The basic premise of due process of law is that all persons are entitled to the benefits, protections, and privileges of the law of the land. As Chief Justice John Marshall stated in the landmark case of *Marbury v. Madison*: "the very essence of civil liberty certainly consists in the right of every individual to claim the protection of the laws ..." However, while it is clear that everyone is entitled to the protections of due process of law, the difficulty arises in the application of due process of law in the particular case or circumstance. It is therefore difficult, if not impossible, adequately and accurately to define due process because the concept is elastic and flexible, and must be adaptable to countless different contexts.

There is a reluctance to define due process for fear that the definition may be interpreted in a way that would limit or restrict its application in a particular case.

The guarantees and protections of due process apply to both criminal and civil cases, as well as the countless civil matters in which a person comes into contact with administrative agencies and government officials. In criminal cases, what is termed a "liberty interest" is usually at stake. In civil matters, a liberty interest or a property right may be at issue. Although due process applies in all cases, the specific degree of protection may vary depending on the nature of the interest threatened, and the competing governmental or other interests that must also be considered.

In our constitutional system, it is fundamental that persons are entitled to due process of law before they are deprived of a liberty interest or a property right. Property rights can take on many forms, from tangible things such as land or money to intangible interests such as the right to a public education or an interest in continued employment. In order to pursue a claim based on a deprivation of a property right without adequate due process, a person must show a "legitimate claim of entitlement" to the interest affected by governmental action. It is important to remember, however, that generally "[p]roperty interests are not created by the Constitution, 'they are created and their dimensions are defined by existing rules or understandings that stem from an independent source such as state law'" *Cleveland Board of Education v. Loudermill,* 470 U.S. 532 (1985).

Since the due process clauses of the Fifth and Fourteenth Amendments govern only the federal and state governments, respectively, there must be some type of "state action" for a court to grant relief. Hence, the actions of a private party acting in a purely personal capacity are generally not restricted or restrained by the requirements of due process. The Supreme Court has held that, for the purposes of determining whether an action is subject to the due process requirements of the Constitution, "a State normally can be held responsible only when it has exercised coercive power or has provided such significant encouragement, either over or covert, that the choice must in law be deemed to be that of the State" *Blum v. Yaretsky,* 457 U.S. 991 (1982).

A federal court of appeals has stated that, "[w]henever a governmental body acts so as to injure an individual, the Constitution requires that the act be consonant with due process of law" *Dixon v. Alabama State Board of Education,* 294 F.2d 150, 5th Cir., cert. denied 368 U.S. 930 (1961). Thus, courts have found state action and property interests sufficient to activate or require due process in situations such as the firing of a government employee, the termination of welfare benefits, and the suspension of a student from a public school or state university.

After a court has decided that there has been a deprivation of life, liberty, or property interest, and sufficient state or official government action to invoke the due process clause, the court must determine whether the person has been denied or deprived of due process of law. At a minimum, a deprivation of life, liberty, or property must be accompanied by "notice and opportunity for hearing appropriate to the nature of the case" *Mullane v. Central Hanover Bank & Trust Co.,* 339 U.S. 306 (1950). Usually, the hearing must be held prior to the deprivation because it should occur "at a time when the deprivation can still be prevented" *Fuentes v. Shevin,* 407 U.S. 67 (1972). When there is a significant government interest in postponing a hearing, a post-deprivation hearing may be sufficient to satisfy due process requirements, although at some point the delay may be considered a constitutional violation.

A hearing serves several purposes. First, the opportunity for the aggrieved or threatened party "to present his side of the case is recurringly of obvious value in reaching an accurate decision" (*Loudermill* at 543). Thus, by allowing or requiring both sides to present their cases, the risk of factual error or mistake is reduced. Second, even when no facts are in dispute, allowing the affected party to respond or explain permits the responsible administrator or official to make a more informed decision, and permits a sounder exercise of discretion.

Whether the hearing or procedure involved was fair depends upon the nature of the interest affected and all of the other facts and circumstances of the particular case. In *Mathews v. Eldridge,* 424 U.S. 319 (1976), the Supreme Court identified three factors that a court must balance or consider in evaluating a due process claim:

"First, the private interest that will be affected by the official action; second, the risk of an erroneous deprivation of such interest through the procedures used; and the probable value, if any, of additional or substitute procedural safeguards; and finally, the [state] interest, including the function involved and the fiscal and administrative burdens that the additional or substitute procedural requirement would entail."

These formulations reflect the efforts of the courts to ensure the fairness of any government action while recognizing, at the same time, the need for a governmental body to function efficiently and economically. Thus, a student faced with disciplinary action by a public university would not be entitled as a matter of due process to the full panoply of procedural protections afforded a criminal defendant. Similarly, a government employee who has been discharged for cause has a right to be informed of the nature of the charges and to respond to the charges. Normally, however, the employee would not be entitled to a full-blown adversary hearing conducted under strict rules of evidence and procedures appropriate for the trial of criminal cases.

A crucial function of the due process clauses is to give full force and effect to the ideal of fairness enshrined in the Constitution. In attempting to effectuate and implement the ideals of equal justice and non-discrimination, Congress has enacted certain civil rights statutes prohibiting discrimination in voting, education, housing, employment, and other areas on the basis of race, color, religion, national origin, gender, age, or handicap. These statutes are specific and go beyond the constitutional protections in that they have a broad application to the discriminatory actions of private individuals, as well as governmental agencies and officials.

An enforcement mechanism is the Civil Rights Act of 1871, 42 U.S.C. Section 1983. This act, which was passed in response to post-Civil War racial abuses and terrorism, "provides for a broad and comprehensive civil rights jurisdiction, and was intended 'to ensure that individuals whose federal constitutional or statutory rights are abridged may recover damages or secure injunctive relief'" *Freeman v. Rideout*, 808 F.2d 949 (2d Cir. 1986).

In essence, section 1983 provides jurisdiction and a right of action in a federal court for a person whose constitutional rights have been abridged or denied under the color of state law. It is not limited to constitutional violations involving racial discrimination, but functions as a source of relief for persons who have been deprived of a host of constitutional rights under color of state law.

Section 1983 provides a right of action, for example, for someone whose home, in an outrageous manner, has been illegally searched in violation of the Fourth Amendment by police officers acting under color of state law.

In a federal system founded upon the separation of powers and the role of law, all branches of government perform indispensable functions. Nevertheless, without the beneficial scrutiny of judicial review, government officials may on occasion forget that all public servants are duty bound to obey the law, and protect the rights of the persons whom they are to serve.

The guarantee of due process of law, as embodied in the Fifth and Fourteenth Amendments to the Constitution, and, as interpreted by the courts, provides for fair treatment for all who are affected by government action. It implies that a person will receive fairness of treatment, and a procedure designed to achieve a just and equitable result. The guarantee of due process serves to check or control the misuses of abuse of power, and ensures that other rights and privileges protected by the Constitution and laws are given force and effect. By confining the agents of government to their properly delegated authority under the Constitution and laws, due process of law provides a fundamental cornerstone for a free and lawful society.

# Note

1. Chief Judge Emeritus, U.S. Court of International Trade; Distinguished Professor of Law, St. John's University School of Law. Originally published in *Cleveland State Law Review* 39 (1991): 5–13. Reprinted by permission.

## FOR DISCUSSION

1. Judge Re states that in our law, "no concept is more important than that of due process of law." Why does he believe it is so significant? Do you agree or is there another concept that you think is more important?

2. The courts have deliberately chosen not to define due process. Explain why. What are the advantages and disadvantages of this lack of a specific definition?

3. What is a "liberty interest"? Why is it important?

4. Explain the steps taken by a court in determining whether or not procedural due process has been violated.

5. How does Section 1983 of the 1871 Civil Rights Act help to enforce the due process guarantee?

6. According to Judge Re, in due process cases, "the specific degree of protection may vary depending upon the nature of the interest threatened, and the competing governmental or other interests that must also be considered." Why should there be such variations in due process protection? Would you prefer a single standard for every case?

## Government Action

When an employee of a privately run library is fired, she files a Section 1983 lawsuit, claiming that the fact that more than 85 percent of the library's funding comes from government makes her a public employee protected by due process. By examining past cases, the court determines which factors can convert the actions of a private entity into state action. Note how they apply these factors to the Westport Library Association.

*Horvath v. Westport Library Association U.S. Court of Appeals, Second Circuit (2004) 362 F.3d 147*

POOLER, Circuit Judge: Horvath began working for the Westport Library Association ("the Library"), located in Westport, Connecticut ("the Town"), in October 1989 as a "business manager assistant." She was discharged on December 29, 2000. The Library contends that Horvath was terminated because of her resistance to the implementation of new payroll technology and because of general incompetence.

Horvath's Section 1983 claim is based upon her contention that the Library violated her right to due process by not affording her notice and an opportunity to be heard prior to termination. The district court, however, rejected Horvath's Section 1983 claim because the Library was not a state actor, and was therefore not charged with affording its employees due process before terminating them. Because Horvath has dropped her ADEA [Age Discrimination in Employment Act] claim, the only facts germane to this appeal are those that are relevant to the Library's status as a state actor.

We note at the outset that both parties rely heavily upon factual findings contained in two written decisions of the Connecticut State Board of Labor Relations ("the Board"), one from 1977 and one from 1989, issued in cases in which the Library was a party. Both of these cases involved disputes between the Library and the labor union representing its staff members regarding whether the Library was a "municipal employer" within the meaning of Connecticut law. The Library states in its brief on this appeal that these factual findings are "consistent with the Library's current status," except to the extent set forth in an affidavit filed in the district court by the Library's current Director.

We emphasize, however, that, although both the 1977 and 1989 Board opinions concluded that the Library was not a "municipal employer" under Connecticut law, these conclusions are clearly irrelevant to our consideration of whether Horvath should have been afforded the due process protections available to public employees under federal law. As the magistrate judge correctly noted, the Library "cannot transform the legal conclusions reached in 1977 and 1989 into facts by reiterating them ... as if they were facts." Thus, while the paucity of the record gives us no alternative to relying upon the factual findings set forth in the Board decisions, we emphasize that our legal conclusions regarding Horvath's Section 1983 claim are independently derived.

The 1977 Board decision contains the following factual findings that we believe are relevant to the instant appeal:

1. The Westport Library Association is a non-stock corporation created by a special act of the [Connecticut] General Assembly in 1907 with the right to acquire, hold, and manage such property as may be necessary for establishing and maintaining a public library in the Town of Westport, and to "make such by-laws, rules, and regulations ... as it shall deem best for the management of the property and affairs of said Association."

\* \* \*

3. Under the Library by-laws the Library director is appointed by its board of trustees and has charge of the administration of its affairs under the direction and review of a board of trustees. This includes the responsibility for the care of the building and equipment; the hiring, disciplining, and promotion of employees, and the supervision of their duties; responsibility for the service to the public and the operation of the library under the financial conditions set forth in the budget.

\* \* \*

5. One half of the trustees of [the] Library are designated by the Town.
6. [The] Library has some income from investments, gifts, and fines and rentals, but the bulk of its annual income comes from an appropriation from the general funds of the Town. The operating budget for 1976–7 was $545,210 of which the Town appropriation was $489,345.

\* \* \*

12. None of the current trustees of [the] Library is an employee or official of the Town.

The 1989 Board decision contains the following additional relevant findings of fact:

2. The Library is governed by a Board of Trustees composed of 14 voting members.

3. Seven (7) members of the Library's Board of Trustees are appointed by the Representative Town Meeting of the Town of Westport. ... The other seven (7) Trustees are appointed by the Board of Trustees themselves.

* * *

4. None of the current seven (7) Trustees who were appointed by the Representative Town Meeting are elected or appointed officials of the Town of Westport.

5. The Director of the Library is appointed by the full Board of Trustees. The Director is responsible for hiring the Library's Department Heads who in turn hire the members of the staff.

6. The operations of the Westport Public Library are funded by a budget (1988–89) that is composed of (1) grants from the Town of Westport, (2) gifts, (3) investments, (4) fines, and (5) rentals. 88% of the budget is composed of grants from the Town of Westport.

7. The Library's budget process entails creation of a preliminary budget request by the Library staff which is presented to the Board of Trustees for their approval. If approved, the Library staff and Board of Trustees present the budget request to and participate in meetings with the Town's Board of Finance. The Town's Board of Finance ultimately recommends a budget to the Representative Town Meeting for final approval. The final budget allocation is in a lump sum and is without restriction as to expenditure by the Library.

As already noted, the 1977 and 1989 Board decisions have been supplemented by an affidavit of the Library's current Director. The affidavit contains the following information concerning the Library's budget: The Library's budget for FY 2000–2001 was $3,187,644 with 86.5% of $2,777,494 coming from the Town of Westport. The remainder of the Library's funding comes from private fund-raising, fines, late fees and profits derived from a cafe, which it owns and runs on premises.

In her own affidavit, Horvath discloses that she, along with the rest of the Library's staff, is a member of a union which is only identified in the record as the Brotherhood of Municipal Employees ("the Union"). Also in the record is a copy of the collective bargaining agreement between the Library and the Union in force at the time of Horvath's discharge. The agreement provides that a staff member may only be discharged "for just cause" and that, if discharged, the staff member "shall be given the reason therefore, in writing, within three (3) days with a copy to the Union President." The agreement also provides for a three-stage grievance procedure for "any grievance or dispute which may arise between the parties concerning the interpretation or application of any provision" of the collective bargaining agreement. The first two stages involve internal dispute resolution procedures and the third is an appeal to the Board. We also note that the agreement enrolls Library staff members in the Town's municipal employee pension plan.

It is unclear whether Horvath followed the first two stages of the collective bargaining agreement's grievance procedure, but she did appeal her discharge to the Board. A three-member panel of the Board—composed of a "Public Member," a "Management Member," and a "Labor Member"—held a hearing on the matter on January 8, 2001. Horvath was represented at the hearing by the President of the Union, and a decision was issued on February 15, 2001. The decision states that "the ultimate issue" for the panel's consideration is whether Horvath was discharged for just cause, but that "a threshold question [was] whether the Westport Public Library [was] a municipal employer and thus subject to the due process requirement of the Fourteenth Amendment of the U.S. Constitution." As to the latter issue, the panel majority summarily reaffirmed the 1977 and 1989 Board decisions holding that the Library was not a municipal employer. The majority also found that the evidence of Horvath's "shortcomings" was so extensive as to make it "self-evident" that she was discharged for just cause.

The "Labor Member" of the panel issued a dissenting opinion. In his view, the Library qualified as a municipal employer because "it [was] clear that a symbiotic relationship existed between the Westport Public Library and the State of Connecticut, because the Library received appropriations from the Town and the State." In addition, he believed that the evidence demonstrated that Horvath was "a loyal employee with twelve years of service [who] was given a constructed [sic] termination."

Again, the substance of Horvath's § 1983 claim is that the Library violated her right to due process when it terminated her without prior notice and an opportunity to be heard. There is no question that "[a] public employee who has a right not to be fired without 'just cause' ... has a property interest in her employment that qualifies for these protections of procedural due process." *Otero v. Bridgeport Hous. Auth.*, 297 F.3d 142, 151 (2d Cir. 2002) (internal quotations and brackets omitted). As already noted, the collective bargaining agreement between the Library and the union representing Horvath provides that members of the Library staff can be fired only for just cause.

The issue that remains for us is whether Horvath was a public employee when she worked for the Library. The right to due process established by the Fourteenth Amendment applies only to government entities, and an attempt to vindicate that right through a Section 1983 claim can be lodged only against a government entity. Accordingly, "the ultimate issue in determining whether a person [may bring] suit under § 1983 is the same question posed in cases arising under the Fourteenth Amendment: is the alleged infringement of federal rights 'fairly attributable to the State?'" *Rendell-Baker v. Kohn*, 457 U.S. 830 (1982). The magistrate judge answered this question in the negative, although it noted that "the question appears closer than defendants allow." We believe that the question must be decided in Horvath's favor.

As a general matter, defining the limits of the State's presence tends to be a difficult endeavor because of the protean character of contemporary government activity. The Supreme Court has noted something like this in its most recent substantial statement on state action doctrine:

> What is fairly attributable [to the government] is a matter of normative judgment, and the criteria lack rigid simplicity. From the range of circumstances that could point toward the State behind an individual face, no one fact can function as a necessary condition across the board for finding state action; nor is any set of circumstances absolutely sufficient, for there may be some countervailing reason against attributing activity to the government. *Brentwood Academy v. Tennessee School Athletic Ass'n.*, 531 U.S. 288 (2001) ("Brentwood Academy").

Not surprisingly, therefore, "there is no single test to identify state actions and state actors." Rather, there are "a host of facts that can bear on the fairness of ... an attribution" of a challenged action to the State.

State action may be found in situations where an activity that traditionally has been the exclusive, or near exclusive, function of the State has been contracted out to a private entity. For example, only the State may legitimately imprison individuals as punishment for the commission of crimes. Acts of prison employees will therefore almost certainly be considered acts of the State whatever the terms of their employment. But it can hardly be said that the provision of library services is similarly a "traditionally exclusive public function." *American Mfrs. Mutual Ins. Co. v. Sullivan*, 526

U.S. 40 (1999). On the contrary, a private individual or enterprise certainly could provide library services to the citizens of the Town in just the same manner as Benjamin Franklin provided library services to the citizens of Philadelphia two hundred and fifty years ago. It cannot be said "that the operation of a library constitutes ... a function traditionally associated with sovereignty." *Hollenbaugh v. Carnegie Free Library, of Connellsville, Pa.,* 545 F.2d 382 (3rd. Cir. 1976).

Further, Horvath's argument in favor of a finding of state action focuses most heavily on the fact that the Library's budget is almost exclusively composed of public funds. It is almost self-evident that this weighs in favor of Horvath's claim, but the Supreme Court has cautioned that it is far from the case that a predominance of public funding is conclusive evidence of state action. In *Rendell-Baker v. Kohn,* a privately operated school for students with disciplinary problems was sued by various former employees over the circumstances of their discharges. Most of the school's students had their tuition paid by public school districts, and the school also received aid from various federal and state education agencies. For several years, therefore, public funds accounted for more than ninety percent of the school's operating budget. In short, public entities were by far the school's biggest customer and source of funds.

The Supreme Court held, however, that the school was not a state actor, at least for the purposes of the petitioners' claims. The decisive factor in the Court's view was that the school's personnel decisions were uninfluenced by public officials and that "the decisions to discharge the petitioners were not compelled or even influenced by any state regulation." In light of the autonomy with which it made its decisions as to whom to hire and fire, the school was not "fundamentally different from many private corporations whose business depends primarily on contracts to build roads, bridges, dams, ships, or submarines for the government. Acts of such private contractors do not become acts of the government by reason of their significant or even total engagement in performing public contracts."

Thus, it is plain that the Library is not a state actor by virtue of public funding alone. But we do not believe that *Rendell-Baker* controls this case, because it is also plain that the Library is not merely a private contractor whose internal management decisions are beyond state regulation. Nor is the Library merely an entity that has the State for its biggest customer. Rather, as noted above, the Library is governed by a Board of Trustees, half of whose members are appointed by the Town. The significance of this fact in the state action inquiry is most extensively set forth in *Lebron v. National Railroad Passenger Corp.,* 513 U.S. 374 (1999), a case not cited by either of the parties.

In *Lebron,* the Supreme Court considered the state actor status of the National Railroad Passenger Corporation, commonly known as Amtrak. Amtrak was established by a Congressional statute, which explicitly states that it "'will not be an agency or establishment of the United States Government.'" This designation, however, was held to be anything but conclusive because "it is not for Congress to make the final determination of Amtrak's status as a Government entity for purposes of determining the constitutional rights of citizens affected by its actions." Rather, the Court looked to the fact that the statute creating Amtrak also "provided for a board of nine members, six of whom [were] appointed directly by the President of the United States." Two other members of the board are appointed by Amtrak's preferred shareholders, and the final member was appointed by the other eight members. The Court concluded that "where ... the Government creates a corporation by special law, for the furtherance of government objectives, and retains for itself permanent authority to appoint a majority of the directors of that corporation," the corporation would be considered a state actor.

Following *Lebron*, we have utilized the following standard to determine whether or not a corporate entity qualifies as a state actor: "only if (1) the government created the corporate entity by special law, (2) the government created the entity to further governmental objectives, and (3) the government retains 'permanent authority to appoint a majority [of] the directors of the corporation' will the corporation be deemed a government entity for the purpose of the state action requirement." *Hack v. President & Fellows of Yale Coll.*, 237 F.3d 81, 84 (2d Cir. 2000) (quoting *Lebron*). In *Hack*, we considered whether Yale qualified as a state actor. Although we found that the first two elements of the *Lebron* standard were "easily satisfied," the fact that the State of Connecticut retained the right to appoint only two of Yale's nineteen board members meant that the school was "a long way from [being] controlled" by the state.

Here we believe that the *Lebron* standard has been satisfied. It is plain that the first two elements are present; as noted above, the Library was created by a special act of the Connecticut State legislature and there is no doubt that the provision of library services is a legitimate statutory objective. As to the third element, it is correct that only one-half, and not a majority, of the Library's trustees are appointed by the Town. However, we do not believe that this precludes a finding that the third element of Lebron has been satisfied. The additional fact that only a little more than a tenth of the Library's funding comes from sources other than the Town convinces us that the Town maintains sufficient control over the Library to qualify it as a state actor for the purposes of Horvath's claim. Thus, we conclude that the argument that the Library is a private entity "is overborne by the pervasive entwinement of public institutions and public officials in its composition and workings, and there is no substantial reason to claim unfairness in applying constitutional standards to it." *Brentwood Academy*, 531 U.S. at 289.

Two arguments to the contrary do not persuade us. The Library urges that the decision to terminate Horvath was made solely by the Library's Director who, although appointed by the trustees, is not herself a public official. This is significant because a finding of state action must be premised upon the fact that "the State is *responsible* for the *specific conduct* of which the plaintiff complains." *Blum v. Yaretsky*, 457 U.S. 991 (1982) (first emphasis in original; second emphasis added). In *Brentwood Academy*, however, the Supreme Court has cautioned that the concept of responsibility is not to be read narrowly in the context of the state action inquiry. That is, the State need not have coerced or even encouraged the events at issue in the plaintiff's complaint if "the relevant facts show pervasive entwinement to the point of largely overlapping identity" between the State and the entity that the plaintiff contends is a state actor. The combination of pervasive public funding of the Library and control of one-half of its governing board persuade us that such "pervasive entwinement" is present here.

We also note that none of the trustees appointed by the Town to the Library's board at the time of Horvath's discharge were themselves public officials. But this fact certainly does not preclude a finding of state action because, pursuant to *Lebron*, it is the Town's "authority to appoint" trustees, and not the identity of the trustees appointed, that is relevant to the state action inquiry.

For the forgoing reasons, we reverse the district court's grant of summary judgment. We note that the district court's holding was limited to a finding that the Library was not a state actor for the purposes of Horvath' s Section 1983 claim, and that the court made no factual findings regarding Horvath's assertion that she was denied notice and an opportunity to be heard prior to her discharge. Our decision is similarly limited to the question of the Library's status as a state actor, and we express no opinion as to whether the Library satisfied the requirements of due process when it terminated Horvath.

## FOR DISCUSSION

1. Why is it so important to determine whether or not the library is a "state actor"?

2. What is Horvath's basis for concluding that even though it is a private entity the library is really a state actor? How does the library reply?

3. In 1977 and 1989 the State Board of Labor Relations ruled that the library was not a "municipal employer." How did these rulings affect Judge Pooler's decision?

4. Judge Pooler compares the library to Amtrak and to Yale University. Explain how she uses these comparisons in her decision.

5. What are the crucial factors in determining whether the library's actions are subject to due process?

6. What happens next? What do you think the likely outcome of the case will be?

### YOU BE THE JUDGE

Margaret Apao obtained a $280,000 mortgage on her Honolulu home from San Diego Home Loans, Inc. After three years she notified the bank that she intended to cancel the mortgage and make no further payments because of her belief that the mortgage violated the federal Truth in Lending Act. The bank moved to foreclose based on provisions of the mortgage contract and a Hawaii statute that authorized a private nonjudicial foreclosure sale provided the borrower is notified through publication in a widely read newspaper over three weeks and posting notice on the premises three weeks before the property is sold. Copies of this notice must also be filed with the state director of taxation. The provisions of this law and the mortgage contract were followed, resulting in a foreclosure sale of the property.

Apao sued under the Fourteenth Amendment, arguing that the sale deprived her of her property without due process of law as she had no opportunity to challenge the provisions of the contract. She noted that the sale was authorized by statute, that it was conducted by a self-interested lender, and that the mortgage business is regulated by both state and federal law. Was the sale of her property state action that she can challenge in court as a violation of her due process rights?

For the decision of the U.S. Court of Appeals, see *Apao v. The Bank of New York* in the You Be the Judge Key at the end of the chapter.

# Property Rights and Liberty Interests

In his essay, Judge Re wrote that "persons are entitled to due process of law before they are deprived of a liberty interest or a property right." In the next case, Michael Winbush was relieved of his duties as assistant football coach and head women's softball coach, denied a promised raise, and reassigned as intramural coordinator without change to his existing paygrade.

The Court of Appeals of North Carolina has to decide whether he has been deprived of property. If he has, he can challenge the dismissal on due process grounds. If you are wondering why, despite overturning the trial court order to reinstate Winbush, the appellate court affirmed in part and reversed in part, that is because it agreed that the Office of Administrative Hearings and State Personnel Commission did have jurisdiction.

*Winbush v. Winston-Salem State University Court of Appeals of North Carolina (2004) 598 S.E.2d 619*

BRYANT, Judge. Winston-Salem State University (respondent) appeals a superior court order filed 17 March 2003 reversing an order by the State Personnel Commission (SPC) and ordering the reinstatement of Michael T. Winbush (petitioner) to his duties as Assistant Football Coach and Head Women's Softball Coach.

On 2 October 2000, petitioner filed a petition for a contested case hearing with the Office of Administrative Hearings (OAH). The petition alleged petitioner had been discharged or reassigned from his coaching duties without just cause. Attached to the petition was a statement by petitioner that he had been "relieved of [his] athletic duties and privileges effective June 30, 2000" by respondent's Athletics Director. In a recommended decision, the administrative law judge (ALJ) who initially heard the case concluded: (1) the OAH had "jurisdiction over this contested matter" and (2) petitioner was demoted without just cause. The SPC, however, rejected the ALJ's findings of fact and conclusions of law as "erroneous as a matter of law." In rejecting the ALJ's recommended decision in its entirety, the SPC stated: "The Commission finds that neither the ALJ nor the Commission have jurisdiction under Chapter 126 over petitioner's complaint, as an employee subject to the State Personnel Act, that he was not assigned the job duties of his choice, i.e. specifically certain coaching duties and responsibilities." Petitioner appealed the SPC ruling to the superior court.

In an order filed 17 March 2003, the superior court in turn reversed the SPC decision, finding jurisdiction and making the following pertinent findings of fact:

33. As a result of the disciplinary action … , [petitioner] did not receive the 10% raise in salary in July[] 2000, which he had been told that he would receive for his coaching accomplishments.

\*\*\*

35. [Petitioner] is still employed at WSSU as a recreation worker, and his pay grade has not changed. [Petitioner] was hired as a coach, has excelled as a coach and has developed a reputation as an excellent coach; however, he has not been allowed to coach at WSSU since June 30, 2000.

The superior court concluded petitioner had been demoted or discharged for disciplinary reasons without just cause from his position as coach. The superior court also concluded that petitioner had been denied a 10% pay raise for his coaching responsibilities.

The issues are whether: (I) the allegations in the petition invoked the jurisdiction of the OAH and SPC and (II) the superior court erred in concluding petitioner had been demoted or discharged from his coaching duties in violation of N.C. Gen. Stat. § 126–34.1(a)(1).

The rights of university employees to challenge any employment action in the OAH arise solely from the State Personnel Act (SPA). Thus, the OAH's jurisdiction over appeals of university employee grievances is confined to the limits established by the SPA. In 1995, N.C. Gen. Stat. § 126–34.1 was enacted to specifically define the types of employee appeals that constitute contested case issues of which the OAH may hear. N.C. Gen. Stat. § 126–34.1 provides in pertinent part that a State employee or former State employee has the right to challenge his "dismissal, demotion, or suspension without pay based upon an alleged violation of G.S. 126–35, if the employee is a career State employee." Pursuant to N.C. Gen. Stat. § 126–35, "no career State employee subject to the [SPA] shall be discharged, suspended, or demoted for disciplinary reasons, except for just cause." Therefore, an employee petition filed with the OAH that alleges the employee has been dismissed, demoted, or suspended without just cause is sufficient to invoke the jurisdiction of the OAH and SPC.

In this case, the petition filed by petitioner alleged he had been discharged without just cause or reassigned without just cause when he was "relieved of [his] athletic duties and privileges effective June 30, 2000" by respondent's Athletics Director. Under our liberal rules of construction for allegations raised in a party's pleading, the petition thus alleges either a discharge or demotion. Accordingly, the superior court properly concluded that the OAH and SPC had jurisdiction to hear the petition.

We next consider whether the superior court erred in concluding that petitioner had been demoted or discharged from his coaching duties in violation of N.C. Gen. Stat. § 126–34.1(a)(1).

The evidence establishes that petitioner was neither dismissed nor demoted from his respondent employment. In 1994, respondent's Student Affairs Department hired petitioner to fill the position of "Recreation Worker II." Petitioner's annual salary was $22,557.00, which was equivalent to a "paygrade 64" on the N.C. State Salary Schedule. As a respondent employee, petitioner's primary responsibility was to coach football and women's softball. In April 2000, petitioner was commended for his coaching accomplishments and told he would receive an additional 10% raise in salary effective 1 July 2000.

In June 2000, a dispute arose over petitioner's coaching performance: Petitioner had organized a youth football camp to occur on 18 and 19 June 2000. After having scheduled the football camp, petitioner learned he was required to attend a respondent staff retreat on 17 and 18 June 2000. Petitioner made arrangements for his staff to operate the football camp while he attended the required respondent staff retreat. However, against the instructions of his supervisor, petitioner failed to obtain prior, written approval to conduct the football camp. Consequently, effective 1 July 2000 petitioner was removed from his coaching duties and began serving as intramural coordinator, without change to his paygrade or Recreation Worker II status. In addition, he failed to receive the promised raise in salary for his coaching accomplishments.

This evidence shows petitioner was neither dismissed nor demoted in his Recreation Worker II position at respondent. At most, the evidence speaks to a reassignment, as petitioner claims to have lost his more significant coaching responsibilities. "Because petitioner [is] a permanent State employee, it is well-settled that he [has] a 'property interest of continued employment created by state law and protected by the Due Process Clause.'" *Nix v. Dep't of Administration,* 417 S.E.2d 823, 825 (1992). That interest "does not extend to the right to possess or retain a particular job or to perform particular services." *Fields v. Durham,* 909 F.2d 94, 98 (4th Cir. 1990), cert. denied, 498 U.S. 1068, (1991).

As previously stated, a demotion is defined as a "lowering in rank, position, or pay," Black's Law Dictionary 444. Rank is defined as "relative standing or position" within a group. *Webster's Third New International Dictionary* 1881 (3d ed. 1966). A reduction in position under the SPA has been construed by this Court to mean the placement of an employee "in a lower paygrade." *Gibbs v. Dept. of Human Resources,* 335 S.E.2d 924, 927 (1985) (rejecting a petitioner's contention that she had been demoted under the SPA when she was reassigned to a position with fewer responsibilities but which was subject to the same paygrade). In the instant case, petitioner's paygrade remained the same. Furthermore, as the promised raise in salary had not yet come into effect at the time of his reassignment, petitioner has also failed to show a demotion through a decrease in pay. As such, petitioner was neither discharged nor demoted and is not entitled to relief under the SPA. Accordingly, the superior court erred in concluding that petitioner had been discharged without just cause.

Affirmed in part, reversed in part.

## FOR DISCUSSION

1. In order to invoke his due process right, Winbush must show that he has been deprived of something he is entitled to. What does he claim he was deprived of? What did the Office of Administrative Hearings rule? On what basis? Why did the State Personnel Commission overturn that ruling?

2. The trial court ordered Winbush reinstated as assistant football coach and head women's softball coach. What was the basis for that decision?

3. Why does the Court of Appeals of North Carolina overturn the lower court order reinstating Winbush? Why is his failure to receive the promised 10 percent increase not a loss of property?

4. If you were deciding this case, how would you rule?

5. 5. Why does the court never evaluate the reasons for Winbush's reassignment? Does that seem fair to you?

## Substantive Due Process

Unlike procedural due process, substantive due process looks at the content of the law. One of the most common uses of substantive due process is to protect against vagueness. A law must define what conduct is required or prohibited clearly enough so that people know how to conform their conduct to it. Laws that fail to do so violate substantive due process. The next case shows how courts evaluate claims that laws are unconstitutionally vague.

*Bell v. Arlington County, Virginia U.S. District Court, E.D. Virginia, Alexandria Division (1987) 673 F. Supp. 767*

CACHERIS, District Judge The issue in this case is the constitutionality of the Arlington County Code Sections which prohibit cross-sexual massages.

Both plaintiff and defendant Arlington County, Virginia, moved for summary judgment on the constitutionality of Arlington County Code Chapter 49. The court finds that the statute is unconstitutionally vague and grants plaintiff's Motion for Summary Judgment.

Plaintiff Gail Bell has brought suit under 42 U.S.C. § 1983, alleging a violation of her Fourth Amendment right to be free from unreasonable search and seizure, defamation, intentional infliction of emotional distress, false arrest and imprisonment, negligence and malicious prosecution.

Plaintiff is a trained masseuse who has all the necessary business licenses and permits to provide massage services as a massage therapist. In May, 1986, the defendants began an investigation of plaintiff's massage therapy practice. Despite her status as a licensed massage therapist, plaintiff was arrested under Chapter 49 of the Arlington County Code and charged with violating the Code section which prohibits a massage technician from giving a massage to a member of the opposite sex.

On October 1, 1986, the Arlington County Commonwealth's Attorney dismissed the charge against the plaintiff. On November 14, 1986, the Arlington County Circuit Court expunged all police and court records relating to the criminal charge filed against Bell.

Plaintiff has moved for summary judgment on her claim for declaratory injunctive relief relative to Chapter 49 of the Arlington County Code, requesting the court to declare that the Code Section is unconstitutionally vague. The defendant Arlington County has opposed the motion and asked for summary judgment on the grounds that the statute is not unconstitutionally vague.

The court recognizes that when a statute is fairly susceptible to more than one interpretation, the interpretation most consistent with constitutionality should be adopted. The court should determine whether a constitutional construction of the ordinance is possible in order to avoid a question of an unconstitutional construction.

In Arlington County's Motion, the County argues that the ordinance sets up two distinct categories, massage therapist and massage technician. The former could perform a cross-sexual massage, while the latter was prohibited. However, prior to Bell's arrest, the Police Department operated on the understanding, given to them by Henry Hudson, Arlington County Commonwealth's Attorney, that neither massage therapists nor massage technicians could give cross-sexual massages.

As the basis for Bell's arrest, the police department had interpreted the ordinance to state that massage therapists were a subclass of massage technicians, and therefore, were prohibited from giving cross-sexual massages.[1]

Police Chief Stover, who was charged with the responsibility of enforcing the ordinance, had several problems understanding the statute. Stover believed the ordinance was "too vague," could only be understood by a lawyer, "unfair" to Ms. Bell, unclear "to a reasonably ordinary intelligent person of what is and what is not permissible," and that "it fails to give reasonable notice to a lay person as to what is lawful and what is not lawful for a massage therapist."

Lt. John Karinshak, who was in charge of the Police's vice-control section, was under the belief that until last year all cross-sexual massages were illegal under the Arlington County Code. Karinshak thought that, based on his interpretation of law, the statute had problems and that it was vague. He felt it was not clear as to who could or could not give cross-sexual massages. As a result

---

1 § 49–2 defines massage technician as "any person who administers a massage to another person for pay," and a massage therapist is defined as a massage technician with certain specified training.

of problems with the Bell case, he found it necessary to draft a policy statement for the vice-squad in 1986 to prevent a repetition of an arrest similar to the one that occurred in this case. Karinshak's memorandum indicated that massage technicians could not engage in cross-sexual massages, however, massage therapists could. Nevertheless, even after the County clarified its policy, Detective Kozich was still unclear as to whether Bell was entitled to massage men under the current ordinance.

The standard for determining whether the ordinance is unconstitutionally vague is where "its prohibitions are not clearly defined" and where a "person of ordinary intelligence" is not given a "reasonable opportunity to know what is prohibited so that he may act accordingly." *Grayned v. City of Rockford*, 408 U.S. 104 (1972). The court continued in *Rockford* to state:

> [A] vague law impermissibly delegates basic policy matters to ... [officials charged with enforcement] for resolution on an ad hoc and subjective basis, with attendant dangers of arbitrary and discriminatory applications.

It is quite obvious that the statute is unconstitutionally vague. The County's argument that the statute sets up one standard for massage technicians and another for massage therapists fails because the police officers who were charged with the responsibility of enforcing the ordinance have found that they themselves have difficulty in interpreting it. Reading § 49–2's definition of massage technician together with § 49–7(2)'s prohibitions against cross-sexual massages, the statutes appear to say that any person who receives money from massages cannot give cross-sexual massages. This interpretation would include licensed massage therapists who receive money for massages. Yet, the Chapter appears to contemplate that massage therapists can give cross-sexual massages. Obviously the ordinance is confusing because the officers who were charged with the responsibility for enforcement are confused over its interpretation. If the officers are confused, it is too much to ask the citizenry to know what is prohibited. Therefore, the court finds that § 49–7(2) is unconstitutionally vague. Plaintiff's Motion for Summary Judgment is GRANTED and defendants' Motion for Summary Judgment is DENIED.

## FOR DISCUSSION

1.  The Court never discusses the purpose of this law. What do you think it is? If you need some help, review the *Stidwell* case in the You Be the Judge section [...].

2.  Judge Cacheris gives a great deal of weight to the confusion of the police about the meaning of the law. If all of the police officers who had testified in this case had agreed on the law's meaning, do you think it would have changed the result?

3.  Can you articulate a standard for deciding when a law is too vague to meet the test of substantive due process?

4.  Can you write a law that would accomplish the goals of Arlington County Code Chapter 49 and not be unconstitutionally vague? Examine Judge Cacheris's footnote to see the definition used in the statute being challenged.

5.  Could your law be challenged as discriminating on the basis of gender?

Substantive due process also requires that laws not be arbitrary. This case is a good example of how courts are generally reluctant to overturn legislation as arbitrary as long as it can be argued that the law is a reasonable, even if not necessarily the best, method of achieving a legitimate goal of government. At the time of this decision, Donna Shalala was the Secretary of Health and Human Services, the cabinet department that oversees Social Security.

*Muriel Lauger on Behalf of John Lauger v. Shalala U.S. District Court, S.D. California (1993) 820 F.Supp. 1239*

HUFF, District Judge.

The plaintiff appeals the Secretary's denial of her application for disability benefits. Both the plaintiff and the defendant move for summary judgment. Because the court finds the denial of benefits did not violate substantive or procedural due process, the court grants the defendant's cross-motion for summary judgment.

The plaintiff's husband died on August 8, 1990. At the time of his death, the plaintiff was suffering from neck pain and was recovering from a hysterectomy performed in April 1990. In December 1990, she learned of social security burial benefits and contacted the social security office. An interview was arranged with the social security office in Oceanside for February 20, 1991. Prior to that time, a social security employee contacted the plaintiff and informed her that, in addition to burial benefits, she may be entitled to Title II social security disability benefits. On February 15, 1991, she submitted an application for the disability benefits, but her application was denied on February 20, 1991, due to untimeliness.

The plaintiff seeks reconsideration of the denial of disability benefits. After a hearing, an ALJ [Administrative Law Judge] reaffirmed the denial of benefits, and the Appeals Council affirmed the decision. The plaintiff now seeks judicial review from this court. 42 U.S.C. § 423(a)(1) provides for the payment of disability benefits if an application is filed within three months from the date of death. The section makes no exceptions for late filings. The plaintiff argues this time limitation is arbitrary and, thus, unconstitutional. Specifically, the plaintiff argues there is no rational basis for refusing to excuse late filings based on good cause.

The court must uphold economic regulations against constitutional challenge if the statute "has a rational relationship to a legitimate goal of government." *Price v. Heckler,* 733 F.2d 699, 701 (9th Cir. 1984). Courts generally must be deferential to the government's determination of preferable means of regulation and will overturn such a determination only if it is "wholly arbitrary." *City of New Orleans v. Dukes,* 427 U.S. 297 (1976). The Supreme Court has granted a strong presumption of constitutionality to legislation conferring monetary benefits because the Court believes that Congress should have discretion in deciding how to expend necessarily limited resources.

The court cannot hold that Congress's imposition of a time limit upon the receipt of benefits is arbitrary. The imposition of a time limitation ensures that the Social Security Administration will know with certainty the demands made upon a particular fund. The amount necessary to pay disability benefits would become substantially less certain if a good cause exception was allowed. Section 423(a)(1) does not become arbitrary merely because Congress has allowed longer time limitations in other sections governing the receipt of social security benefits. 42 U.S.C. § 402 provides for a "lump-sum death payment" if an application is filed within two years after the date of death. This longer time limitation does not necessarily render more restrictive time limitations irrational. For example, the payment under section 402 is limited to $255 per person. Disability benefits, however, are determined according to a complex formula set forth in 42 U.S.C. § 415. These payments could substantially exceed $255 per person. Thus, Congress may have determined a more restrictive time limitation is necessary in order to budget for larger expenditures. The court, therefore, finds the three-month time limitation is not arbitrary.

The court also finds the statutory section comports with procedural due process. To determine the procedures needed to comply with due process, the court must consider (1) the private interest affected by the governmental action, (2) the risk of an erroneous deprivation of such interest through the procedures used, and (3) the government's interest, including the fiscal and administrative burdens, that the additional procedure would entail.

The plaintiff has received full hearings on whether she in entitled to disability benefits and, specifically, the constitutionality of section 423 before an ALJ and this court. Contrary to the plaintiff's allegation, due process does not require the Social Security Administration to provide notice to all individuals who may be entitled to some payment of social security benefits.

First, it is the plaintiff's burden to demonstrate eligibility for benefits. Further, the cost in terms of resources and money to the Administration would be astronomical. This cost would substantially reduce the amount of benefits available for disabled individuals. Although the court is sensitive to the plaintiff's situation, the court finds procedural due process has been satisfied in this case.

Accordingly, the court grants the defendant's cross-motion for summary judgment and denies the plaintiff's motion for summary judgment.

## FOR DISCUSSION

1.  What provision of law is Muriel Lauger challenging? How does she believe it hinders her right to substantive due process?

2.  What governmental interest does the law further? Is this a legitimate interest of government?

3.  The time limit in the law provides for no exceptions. What reasons might Ms. Lauger have for filing late? Does the court find this particular time limit a due process violation as applied to this case? Explain whether you agree.

4.  Congress has allowed more time to file for other types of Social Security benefits. Does that affect this case? Evaluate Judge Huff's reasoning on this point.

5.  Can you think of a situation where a time limit would be so arbitrary as to violate due process?

6.  Why do you think courts are so reluctant to overturn laws as arbitrary? [...]

## Procedural Due Process

A good way to understand the concept of procedural due process is to look at a specific area familiar to most readers, due process in schools. In the following essay, Donald Gehring describes and criticizes current student disciplinary procedures. He argues for a less legalistic and adversarial process that would be more educational for those students involved. Because he is discussing due process rights, it is important to remember that the court decisions he refers to are for public schools. Private colleges and universities are not legally bound to follow due process, although most do, mainly because any that arbitrarily disciplined students would likely see a decline in student applications.

# Reading

*The Objectives of Student Discipline and the Process That's Due: Are They Compatible? Donald D. Gehring*

## Purpose

How can campus judicial officers teach while ensuring enforcement of campus rules? Are the two tasks compatible? What does the law have to say about what public institutions need to do in order to discipline students? The purpose of this article is to burn off the blanket of legal ground fog by exposing it to the light of judicial opinion, which not only finds the teaching function compatible with the law, but also actually encourages it. It is the intention of this article to use the actual words of the courts to dispel the need for formalism and to illustrate how a simpler process can rise to the level of what is constitutionally due while meeting our objective of enhancing development.

## The Process That's Due

The best place to begin is with the opinion of the Fifth Circuit Court of Appeals in *Dixon v. Alabama State Board of Education* (294 F.2d 150, 5th Cir. 1961; cert. den. 386 U.S. 930, 1961). The court was considering the expulsion of students who had been denied both a notice of the reason they were expelled and an opportunity to speak in their own defense. While the court said the students were entitled under the Constitution to "... notice and some opportunity for hearing before ... [being] expelled for misconduct" it also made it clear that "This does not imply that a full-dress judicial hearing with the right to cross-examine witnesses is required." The Supreme Court denied certiorari. Normally the denial of certiorari does not tell us whether the Court agreed or disagreed with the opinion. However, in a subsequent case considering the 10-day suspension of school children, the Supreme Court referred to *Dixon* as the "landmark case" in the area of student discipline. *Dixon* has since been cited by two U.S. Courts of Appeals as "the pathbreaking decision recognizing the due process rights of students at a state university" (*Blanton v. State University of New York*, 489 F.2d 377, 2d Cir. 1973) and "The classic starting point for an inquiry into the rights of students at state educational institutions" (*Jenkins v. Louisiana State Board of Education*, 506 F.2d 992, 5th Cir. 1975). Thus, it seems that *Dixon* is good law and a standard to be followed.

To say that due process is required in student disciplinary cases is only the beginning of the inquiry. However, due process is not well defined, but is a flexible concept.

Justice Holmes referred to the process as "... the rudiments of fair play ..." (*Chicago, Milwaukee & St. Paul R.R. Co. v. Polt*, 235 U.S. 165, 1914). The Supreme Court has provided further guidance when it told us that:

Considerations of what procedures due process may require under any given set of circumstances must begin with a determination of the precise nature of the government function involved as well as the private interest that has been affected by governmental action (*Cafeteria & Restaurant Workers Union v. McElroy*, 367 U.S. 886, 1961).

## The Nature of the Government Function in Student Discipline

What is the "precise nature of the government function involved" in student discipline? There are those who would analogize the "nature of the government function involved" in student disciplinary situations to the prosecution of crimes.

Recently, the federal Congress passed the Higher Education Amendments of 1998 mandating that institutions keep statistics on students "referred for campus disciplinary action for liquor law violations …" Other federal legislation equally confuses violations of law (criminal behavior) with violations of campus community standards. Those who confuse crimes and campus rule violations fail to understand that to be considered a violation of law, specific elements must be proven beyond a reasonable doubt whereas a violation of a community standard only requires that it be shown the person more likely than not engaged in the prohibited behavior. While a crime may be a violation of campus rules, a violation of campus rules is not necessarily a crime. It is often the case that students found responsible for violating campus rules are not prosecuted and are never convicted of a violation of law, thus, they are not guilty of a crime.

When care is not taken to separate legalistic language from campus codes confusion arises, and there is a misunderstanding on the part of students, attorneys and others. While it is true that one infraction, such as a rape, may be a violation of the law (a crime), and also a violation of campus regulations, only the local prosecutor has the authority to prosecute the crime. Colleges and universities do not prosecute crimes, but simply discipline students who violate their rules. Any analogy of criminal prosecution and crimes to campus proceedings and violations of campus rules is simply not valid.

The courts have consistently reiterated that they "… do not believe there is a good analogy between student discipline and criminal procedure" (*Norton v. Discipline Committee, East Tennessee State University*, 419 F.2d 195, 6th Cir. 1969). Four other United States Courts of Appeals have echoed this sentiment.

## Essential Elements of Due Process

If criminal procedures are not the model to follow in student disciplinary actions where the individual could be suspended or expelled ("the private interest affected …"), then what standards of process are due? Again, the 1961 "landmark case" of *Dixon* provides counsel and it is instructive to revisit the court's words.

> For the guidance of the parties in the event of further proceedings, we state our views on the nature of the notice and hearing required by due process prior to expulsion from a state college or university. … The notice should contain a statement of the specific charges and grounds which, if proven, would justify expulsion under the regulations … a hearing

which gives the Board or the administrative authorities of the college an opportunity to hear both sides in considerable detail. ... [T]he student should be given the names of the witnesses against him and an oral or written report on the facts to which each witness testifies. He should be given an opportunity to present to the Board or the administrative official of the college his own defense against the charges and to produce either oral testimony or written affidavits in his behalf.

In this case when the court referred to the "Board," it meant the Board of Education and not a campus judicial board. It is interesting to note that the *Dixon* court said that if these procedures were followed, "... the rudiments of an adversary proceeding may be preserved without encroaching upon the interests of the college." Note first that the court spoke of the "rudiments of an adversary proceeding" not an adversarial environment like a criminal trial which is confrontational and contentious. Thus, a hearing before an administrative official would preserve the elements of an adversary proceeding (one against the other) but would not necessarily create an adversarial environment (permeated with confrontation and contentiousness) in which the educational value of the experience might be lost. It is also of consequence to observe that the court specifically pointed to the college's interests and said those could be preserved. In other words the court is saying that even in an expulsion hearing, following the procedures it has outlined would allow the institution to take advantage of an opportunity to teach valuable lessons.

As noted in the facts of the case and the court's language, these procedures were confined to expulsions and allowed for an administrative official of the college to hear the student's defense.

While allowing an administrator to hear the student's defense is legally defensible, including students on a hearing panel has certain educational benefits. However, excluding the maturity and wisdom administrative officials bring to the hearing can preclude taking advantage of a "teachable moment" for the student accused of violating community standards.

## The Process That's Not Due

These "essential elements of due process" are those noted in *Dixon,* and do not include a right to be represented by counsel, to cross-examine witnesses, or even, in some cases, to confront them physically, nor to appeal the decision. Although there is no general right to counsel, when the college or university is represented by counsel it is only "fair" to allow the student the same right. But, there is no legal or other reason for the institution to use counsel, thereby complicating the procedures and moving to an adversarial rather than a teaching mode, and thus giving up the opportunity for a positive learning experience to take place. However, students who are also charged with criminal conduct arising from the same set of facts should be allowed to have counsel advise, but not represent them at the hearing. This would not necessarily create an adversarial environment since counsel would have a limited role "... only to safeguard appellee's rights at the criminal proceeding, not to affect the outcome of the disciplinary hearing" (*Gabrilowitz v. Newman,* 582 F.2d 100, 1st Cir. 1978).

Cross-examination of witnesses by accused students can turn disciplinary hearings into invective proceedings that are ill suited to teaching or even to civility. Often students accused of violating campus rules who appear before judicial boards to claim their innocence are angry and are certainly not trained to cross-examine witnesses who may be reluctant to testify in the first place. In most student disciplinary actions there is generally no legal or other reason for accused students to engage in cross-examination of witnesses since the judicial board can ask questions of anyone giving testimony in order to get at the truth. Even where the consequence of the hearing may be expulsion, the courts, beginning with *Dixon* have said there is no right to cross-examine witnesses. Two disciplinary hearings contested in court because of the failure to allow the accused student to directly cross-examine adverse witnesses were resolved in favor of the institution. Once case dealt with an act of academic dishonesty (*Nash v. Auburn University*, 812 F.2d 655, 11th Cir. 1987) and the other a date rape (*Donohue v. Baker*, 976 F. Supp. 136, N.D. NY 1997). The Eleventh Circuit Court of Appeals said in the academic dishonesty case that there was "… no denial of applicant's constitutional rights to due process by their inability to question the adverse witnesses in the usual adversarial manner." In the situation involving a date rape where credibility was an issue and the facts were disputed, the federal district court said due process was satisfied if the student was allowed to question his accuser through the disciplinary panel.

There are also institutions that permit multiple levels of appeals beyond the original decision. While it may be reasonable to have an expulsion or long-term suspension reviewed by an administrative official to ensure that the institution followed its own procedures and the violation merited the sanction, there is no legal basis for an appeal. The Supreme Court has made it clear that "Due process does not comprehend the right of appeal" (*District of Columbia v. Clawans*, 300 U.S. 617, 1936). The Court's logic in stating that due process does not include the right of appeal was explained in one of its earliest cases when it said "If a single hearing is not due process doubling it will not make it so" (*Reetz v. Michigan*, 188 U.S. 505, 1903).

## The Process That's Due for Lesser Offenses

In instances where students are not in jeopardy of being expelled or suspended for a long period of time, "the private interest that has been affected by government action" (*McElroy*) is minimal and thus the requirements of due process are lower. The Supreme Court has said that even in the case of a student suspended for 10 days there was only required "some kind of notice and … some kind of hearing." The Court characterized this as an "… informal give-and-take between student and disciplinarian …" (*Goss v. Lopez*, 419 U.S. 565, 1975).

The Supreme Court also recognized that "the educational process is not by nature adversarial, instead it centers around a continuing relationship between faculty and students, 'one in which the teacher must occupy many roles—educator, advisor and at times parent-substitute'" (*Board of Curators of University of Missouri v. Horowitz*, 435 U.S. 78, 1978). The Court has thus even permitted school administrators to suspend students for short periods if they engage in a "give-and-take" conversation, which would allow for taking advantage of the teachable moment a disciplinary hearing presents.

The "essential elements of due process" as the Supreme Court pointed out, are "some kind of notice and … some kind of hearing." These two essential aspects of due process need not be overly formalized in lesser disciplinary sanctions but are amenable to a simple and straightforward administrative notice and hearing in which the student and the administration engage in a "give-and-take" discussion.

# Discussion

The "creeping legalism" described by Dannells[2] has gone far beyond what the courts have actually required in order to provide students with due process. Institutions have unnecessarily formalized their procedures to incorporate the right to counsel, confrontation and cross-examination of witnesses and multiple appeals. These types of procedures are confusing to students, preclude the "opportunity for development efforts" (Dannells 1997: 79) and even "... create an adversarial atmosphere likely to produce harsher, not more lenient results."[3]

Whether the relationship between a student and an institution is characterized as one of contract or association, the institution must substantially follow its own rules. Thus, the more straightforward and clear the disciplinary procedures are, the easier they will be for students to understand and for the institution to follow. Adversarial procedures that pit one antagonist against another, like criminal procedures, are complex but even worse, do not provide the support necessary for personal and social development.

Institutions would be well served by a comprehensive review of their disciplinary procedures. Legalistic language and structure should be eliminated and procedures streamlined. Hearings should be designed as fact-finding procedures and a time to raise ethical questions. Minor offenses, which could result in less than a suspension, should be dealt with at the lowest level possible and provide the student with an oral or written notice and an opportunity to present his or her side of the story. Decisions about responsibility for violating rules of conduct can be based on whether it is more likely than not that the student engaged in the behavior. There would be no need for confrontation or cross-examination of witnesses or representation or advice of counsel (unless there is a pending criminal charge). A letter to the student should state the outcome of the hearing and the basis for the findings. One level of review of the decision could be provided if requested and justified.

Major offenses where the result could be suspension or expulsion could be handled in a similar procedural manner, since the essential elements of due process are present. Of course, if there is a question of credibility of a witness, cross-examination should be allowed, and even then this can be accomplished by having questions directed through the hearing officer or panel. If criminal charges are pending as a result of the same incident, the students should have counsel to advise them. Even where the outcome is expulsion, there is no need for more than one level of appeal and it should be granted only where it can be shown either that there is new evidence which clearly was not available at the time of the hearing, that there has been a substantial and prejudicial departure from the procedures, or that the student's rights were in some way violated. These added measures would be called into play only in unusual circumstances. For most cases a one-on-one dialogue can take place which allows the administrator to hear both sides in considerable detail and make a decision of responsibility. This type of dialogue may also permit the administrator to assess the individual's level of development and ask questions that require the student to reflect on a higher level. Finally, administrators may also want to include students as members of hearing panels for the educational benefits such service provides. While this is an excellent educational opportunity, it requires a great

2    M. Dannells, *From Discipline to Development: Rethinking Student Conduct in Higher Education* (Washington, DC: Association for the Study of Higher Education, 1997).

3    G. Pavella, "Due Process at Private Colleges," Synfax Weekly Report, Oct. 18, 1999, 906.

deal of preparation and training and should not be undertaken unless appropriate resources are available to provide the support required.

If institutions review their disciplinary procedures with the objective of providing a system that both aides in the development of students and meets what the courts have defined as due process in student discipline without excessive formalism, then everyone involved will benefit.

## Note

1. Originally published in *NASPA Journal* 38 (Summer 2001): 466–81. Reprinted by permission.

## FOR DISCUSSION

1. Gehring is particularly critical of "those who confuse crimes and campus rule violations." Explain his criticisms and whether you agree.

2. What should be the goals of student disciplinary hearings? How, if at all, do they differ from the goals of a criminal trial?

3. What procedures have the courts required colleges to use in student disciplinary hearings to meet the requirements of due process? What procedures that are required in criminal trials are not required for disciplinary hearings? Explain the reasoning behind this and whether you agree.

4. According to Gehring many colleges have "gone far beyond what the courts have actually required." Why do you think they have done so? Do you agree with Gehring that this is not a good thing? Explain.

5. How does Gehring think disciplinary hearings should be conducted? If you were charged with violating your college's disciplinary code would you find these procedures fair? Would you feel differently if you were bringing a complaint against someone?

6. Compare your college's disciplinary rules with those advocated by Gehring. Explain which you prefer.

The next case presents an example of what happens when a university disciplinary hearing is challenged in court as violating due process. Note the standards that the court uses to determine whether the school's actions met the minimum requirements of due process.

*Osteen v. Henley U.S. Court of Appeals, Seventh Circuit (1993) 13 F.3d 221*

POSNER, Chief Judge. Late one night, as Thomas Osteen, an undergraduate at Northern Illinois University, was leaving a bar in the company of two male friends and the girlfriend of one of them, the girlfriend began "mouthing off to a male [another student] who was outside of a bar who decided to mouth off to her and the two of them mouthed out to each other and he didn't realize she was with three football players so when he realized that he was mouthing off to a young lady that was being accompanied by three football players one of which was her boyfriend, it was a little bit too late for him." (We are quoting, not Gertrude Stein, but one of the defendants, university judicial officer Larry Bolles.) "I'm told without one word, Mr. Osteen, not one word out of his mouth he stomps this guy in the head with some cowboy boots. This is what the guy said, he had on some boots and he stomped him." Osteen's kick or stomp broke the other student's nose. Another student, apparently a friend of the one whom Osteen had just assaulted, approached Osteen, who again without a word "broke his face with one punch." Osteen had broken his second nose for the night. The incident, aggravated in Bolles's mind by the fact that the woman whose honor Osteen was defending in this violent manner was not even Osteen's own girlfriend, led to Osteen's expulsion for two years and to this lawsuit (dismissed by the district court), in which Osteen challenges the expulsion as a deprivation of property without due process of law, in violation of the Fourteenth Amendment.

Bolles mailed Osteen a notice of charges and a copy of the university's student judicial code, thus initiating disciplinary proceedings. According to the code, Bolles's function as university judicial officer was to meet with Osteen and attempt to resolve the matter without a hearing, but if this failed he was to present the case against Osteen at a hearing. The two met and in Bolles's presence Osteen signed a form in which he pleaded guilty to the charges but requested a hearing on Bolles's proposed sanction, which was a two-year expulsion. The hearing was held before an appeals board consisting of the university's assistant judicial officer (i.e., assistant to Bolles) presiding and in addition one faculty member and two students. The case against Osteen was presented by Bolles, Osteen being represented by a student advocate. Osteen, his advocate, and Bolles addressed the board (we quoted part of Bolles's statement earlier), which in addition considered character references and other documents and concluded that the two-year expulsion was the proper sanction. Osteen attempted to appeal to the university's vice-president for student affairs but was told that the vice-president's authority under the judicial code had been delegated to an associate vice-president. After considering Osteen's appeal that officer upheld the expulsion but postponed it to the end of the semester.

The suit attacks a number of features of the disciplinary proceeding. Bolles had played a dual role as judge and prosecutor. The presiding officer of the appellate tribunal was Bolles's assistant. She cut off Osteen's advocate on the ground that the issue of guilt was not before the board, just the issue of sanction, when the advocate was trying to give Osteen's version of the assaults. Osteen was not allowed to cross-examine. His lawyer (his real lawyer, not the student advocate) was not permitted to participate in the proceedings. At the oral argument before us Osteen's counsel repeated, what had been in his complaint but not in his briefs, the alarming further charge that Bolles had induced Osteen to plead guilty on the representation that on appeal the two-year expulsion would be rescinded—then (as we know) turned around and argued passionately to the appeals board for expulsion.

In his opening brief in this court Osteen raised just three issues; the others are therefore waived, and we will not consider them. The issues he raised are the defendants' failure to comply with all the requirements of the student judicial code, the interruption of himself and his advocate by the appeals board, and the denial of a right to counsel. The first point has no possible merit. As we tirelessly but unavailingly remind counsel in this court, a violation of state law (for purposes of this case the student judicial code may be treated as a state law) is not a denial of due process, even if the state law confers a procedural right. The standard of due process is federal. *Cleveland Board of Education v. Loudermill*, 470 U.S. 532 (1985).

As for the interruption of his student advocate, Osteen had by pleading guilty to the charges against him conceded his guilt, so the presiding officer was entitled to cut off what appeared to be an attempt to reopen the issue. Osteen was allowed to make a statement in mitigation; his advocate was interrupted only when it appeared that she was trying to revisit the issue of guilt. The interruption, designed to confine the proceeding to relevant matters, was well within the outer bounds of the presiding officer's discretionary authority over the scope of the hearing—and it is the outer bounds that the due process clause patrols.

The most interesting question is whether there is a right to counsel, somehow derived from the due process clause of the Fourteenth Amendment, in student disciplinary proceedings. An oldish case (by the standards of constitutional law at any rate) says yes, *Black Coalition v. Portland School District No. 1*, 484 F.2d 1040 (9th Cir. 1973), but the newer cases say no, at most the student has a right to get the advice of a lawyer; the lawyer need not be allowed to participate in the proceeding in the usual way of trial counsel, as by examining and cross-examining witnesses and addressing the tribunal. E.g., *Gorman v. University of Rhode Island*, 837 F.2d 7, 16 (1st Cir. 1988). Especially when the student faces potential criminal charges (Osteen was charged with two counts of aggravated battery; the record is silent on the disposition of the charges), it is at least arguable that the due process clause entitles him to consult a lawyer, who might for example advise him to take the Fifth Amendment. In fact *Gabrilowitz v. Newman*, 582 F.2d 100 (1st Cir. 1978), so holds, though over a dissent which points out that the Supreme Court had rejected the same argument in the parallel context of prison disciplinary proceedings. *Baxter v. Palmigiano*, 425 U.S. 308 (1976).

Even if a student has a constitutional right to consult counsel—an issue not foreclosed by *Baxter*, as we shall see—we don't think he is entitled to be represented in the sense of having a lawyer who is permitted to examine or cross-examine witnesses, to submit and object to documents, to address the tribunal, and otherwise to perform the traditional function of a trial lawyer. To recognize such a right would force student disciplinary proceedings into the mold of adversary litigation. The university would have to hire its own lawyer to prosecute these cases and no doubt lawyers would also be dragged in—from the law faculty or elsewhere—to serve as judges. The cost and complexity of such proceedings would be increased, to the detriment of discipline as well as of the university's fisc [budget]. Concern is frequently voiced about the bureaucratization of education, reflected for example in the high ratio of administrative personnel to faculty at all levels of American education today. We are reluctant to encourage further bureaucratization by judicializing university disciplinary proceedings, mindful also that one dimension of academic freedom is the right of academic institutions to operate free of heavy-handed governmental, including judicial, interference. The danger that without the procedural safeguards deemed appropriate in civil and criminal litigation public universities will engage in an orgy of expulsions is slight. The relation of students to universities is, after all, essentially that of customer to seller. That is true even in the case of public universities, though they are much less dependent upon the academic marketplace than private universities are. Northern Illinois University can't have been happy to lose a student whom it had wanted so much that it had given him a football scholarship, and who had made the team to the greater glory of the institution.

The canonical test for how much process is due, laid down by the Supreme Court in *Mathews v. Eldridge*, 424 U.S. 319 (1976) requires consideration of the cost of the additional procedure sought, the risk of error if it is withheld, and the consequences of error to the person seeking the procedure.

The cost of judicializing disciplinary proceedings by recognizing a right to counsel is nontrivial, while the risk of an error—specifically the risk that Osteen was unjustly "sentenced"—is rather trivial. Not only has the university, as we have said, no incentive to jerry-rig its proceedings against the student—and there is no indication of that here, for even permanent expulsion would not have been an excessive sanction for Osteen's brutal and gratuitous misuse of his football player's strength. In addition the issue of the proper sanction generally and here involves no subtleties of law or fact, being judgmental rather than rule-guided, like federal sentencing before the Sentencing Guidelines. Finally, the consequence for Osteen—a nonpermanent expulsion that did not prevent him from enrolling in another college—is not so grave as to entitle him to the procedural protections thought necessary in litigation because large interests of liberty or property may be at stake.

The last point gives us the most pause, as we suspect, though the record is barren on the point, that the expulsion cost Osteen scholarship assistance that he or his family needed. But when we consider all the factors bearing on his claim to a right of counsel, we conclude that the Constitution did not confer such a right on him. We doubt that it does in any student disciplinary proceeding. After *Walters v. National Association of Radiation Survivors*, 473 U.S. 305 (1985), the scope of the due process right to counsel seems excruciatingly narrow. *Gabrilowitz v. Newman* may survive, because "right to counsel" is rather a misnomer for the far more limited, and hence less costly and disruptive, right of consultation recognized there and not at issue in *Baxter v. Palmigiano*, where the prisoners were seeking the full right of counsel. But Osteen was not denied the right to consult counsel; and he had no greater right.

We do not condone trickery and coercion, alleged by Osteen but abandoned in this court. And we are sensible of the anomaly of having one's own assistant (Bolles's) sitting in judgment on one's case (Bolles was the "presenter"—in effect the prosecutor), although this kind of conflict of interest has not been thought in the previous cases involving school disciplinary action to violate due process. We need not decide today at what point informality of disciplinary procedures crosses the line drawn by due process. It is enough for the decision of this case that none of Osteen's nonwaived complaints about the procedure to which he was subject, signally including the limitations on the participation of counsel, crosses it. AFFIRMED.

## FOR DISCUSSION

1.  Osteen has a number of complaints about the process, yet his appeal raises just three. What were the other issues, and why do you think he failed to raise them? Was the court correct in not considering these other matters, one of which Judge Posner calls "an alarming further charge"?

2.  Judge Posner rejects the argument that the university's failure to comply with its own rules violated due process as having "no possible merit." Why does he dismiss it so quickly?

3.  What does the court have to say about the interruption of Osteen's student advocate? Explain what Judge Posner means when he states that "it is the outer bounds [of the presiding officer's discretionary authority] that the due process clause patrols."

4.  The most difficult issue for the court is whether Osteen had a right to counsel, especially considering that he was also facing criminal charges for the incident. What right to counsel does the court believe the due process clause requires for student disciplinary hearings? How does that apply in this case?

5.  How do you think Gehring would react to this decision? Explain your answer.

Of course student disciplinary hearings are not the only situations in which procedural due process must be followed. Any time the state seeks to take away someone's life, liberty, or property, it can only do so in accord with due process. Taking custody of a child from a parent is a deprivation

## UPDATE

Before his appointment to the U.S. Court of Appeals in 1981, Richard A. Posner was a longtime professor at the University of Chicago law school. During that time, he wrote extensively, especially concerning the application of economics to the law. He served as chief judge of the Seventh Circuit from 1993 to 2000. While serving as a judge he has continued his prolific writing with more than thirty books and three hundred articles and book reviews to his credit.

One of his recent books, *An Affair of State: The Investigation, Impeachment, and Trial of President Clinton*, raises the question of the boundaries of sitting judges writing about contemporary legal and political controversies. Writing in the *New York Review of Books* (vol. 47, March 9, 2000), Ronald Dworkin claims that Posner's ethics "are open to question because judges are not meant to enter political controversies." He is particularly critical of Posner's assertion that "it is clear Clinton perjured himself."

In the book's introduction, Posner points out that except for the Chief Justice of the Supreme Court, the judiciary is excluded from the impeachment process. Because no cases involving impeachment were pending when the book was written, he does not believe he has violated the rules of ethics of the federal judiciary. He writes that he is "unapologetic ... about my decision to write about the struggle to impeach and remove Clinton, despite its partisan overtones and its origins in a sexual relationship widely regarded as tawdry."

What do you think? Is it appropriate for a federal judge to weigh in with his opinions on matters as controversial as the Clinton impeachment?

that requires due process. In the next case, the Court of Appeals of Kentucky rules that when a court orders a significant change in child custody arrangements, the appearance of fairness can be as important as the correctness of the decision.

*Sherryl Frey Lynch v. Boyd Lee Lynch Court of Appeals of Kentucky (1987) 737 S.W.2d 184*

REYNOLDS, Judge. This appeal arises from an order of the Fayette Circuit Court which changed appellant's sole custody of the parties' two minor children into a "joint reciprocal custody" arrangement in favor of both parents. Appellant maintains she was denied due process of law and a fair trial. We reverse as the record reflects, at a minimum, the appearance of a denial of due process.

Both parties are aware of the underlying facts behind this long-running dispute, and we therefore find it unnecessary to provide more than a brief recitation of the background. Sherryl Frey Lynch (appellant) and Boyd Lee Lynch (appellee) were married on August 4, 1973. Two children were born of this marriage, John (approximately 13 years old), and Leanne (approximately 8 years old). On October 13, 1982, appellee filed a petition for divorce. A decree of dissolution was entered by the Fayette Circuit Court on May 13, 1983. This decree, pursuant to a separation agreement, gave custody of the two children to appellant and provided appellee with open visitation.

However, this policy of open visitation was not successful and, within four months, appellee made his first motion for specific visitation. The parties' inability to reach any sort of understanding on visitation is amply illustrated in the over 400 pages of record which accompanied this action. The current dispute began on April 21, 1986, when appellee filed a motion for a change of custody.

A hearing on this motion began on September 2, 1986, and continued into the next day. During these two days, appellee presented most of his case-in-chief. By agreement, one of appellant's witnesses, a licensed psychologist, testified out of order. The hearing was then continued to October 3, 1986.

Appellee concluded his case-in-chief on that day. Appellant then began her argument and completed all of her evidence, except for one witness who the trial court deemed unnecessary. It was at this point in time that the court presented each party with a 16-page document explaining:

> I have heard all of this testimony and I strongly believe that the decision should be made immediately in this case. I have undertaken to draw up Findings of Fact and Conclusions of Law and an Order in anticipation of not learning anything new today. I will give you copies of it, copies so that you and your clients may read it. ...

Over appellant's objection, this order was subsequently entered.

The order, citing the inability of the parties to work out their visitation disagreements, set up a system known as "joint reciprocal alternating custody." Briefly, this procedure divides the year into four three-month periods. During the first three months, one party (in this situation appellant) would have custody for three weeks, followed by one week in which the other party (appellee) would have custody, followed by three weeks for appellant, followed by one week for appellee, and so on. At the end of the first three-month period the times switch, giving appellee custody for three weeks, followed by appellant for one week, and so on. The sequence continues to reverse with each quarter.

It is not necessary for this Court to decide the appropriateness of such a system at this time. Appellant's primary argument is concerned with the manner in which this order was entered.

It is clear from the record that the trial court had prepared its findings, conclusions and order prior to the final day of testimony. Except for one witness, previously taken out of order, appellant had not presented any evidence until after the document had been prepared. Due process requires, at the minimum, that each party be given a meaningful opportunity to be heard. Hearings should be conducted in a manner which leaves no question to their regularity. Although the trial court retained the option of not releasing its previously prepared order, its action in this situation creates the appearance that it had made up its mind before it had all of the evidence.

The record does contain information which might explain the trial court's desire for a quick solution. The two children had been in a state of uncertainty, because of their parent's inability to work together, since the divorce. We understandingly sympathize with the trial court's attempt to bring this matter to an equitable solution as soon as possible, but due process cannot be ignored.

Appellant has directed us to a recent criminal case which somewhat parallels our situation. In that action, the trial court had prepared the final judgment prior to a sentencing hearing. The Kentucky Supreme Court held that this was an abuse of discretion, even though the trial court retained the option of changing the judgment if the defendant produced some compelling evidence. *Edmonson v. Commonwealth, Ky.*, 725 S.W.2d 595 (1987). The trial court's discretion "must be exercised only after the defendant has had a fair opportunity to present evidence at a meaningful hearing ..."

In *Edmonson*, the Kentucky Supreme Court vacated the judgment and returned the case for action by a different circuit judge. We conclude that this would also be the correct procedure in this situation. There is a complete record, including video transcripts of the hearing, making additional testimony unnecessary.

Although we decline to discuss the merits of the trial court's decision, two of appellant's other points merit a brief discussion. Appellant claims that the trial court considered material outside the evidence. It is well settled that extra-judicial evidence, not part of the record, cannot form the basis of a decision. Appellant also contends that the trial court erred in not making the specific findings required by KRS 403.340. We agree. While this Court has concluded that such findings are unnecessary when changing from joint custody to sole custody, such findings are always required when changing single custody into another arrangement.

For the foregoing reasons, the order of the Fayette Circuit Court is vacated and this action is remanded with directions that it be assigned to a different circuit judge for new findings and conclusions, based on the present record.

## FOR DISCUSSION

1. Does the Court of Appeals conclude that there is anything wrong with the order of the trial court?

2. Is there any evidence that the trial court judge was concerned with anything other than the welfare of the Lynch children? If not, why does Judge Reynolds conclude that Sherryl Frey Lynch's due process rights were violated?

3. According to Judge Reynolds, procedural due process requires "that each party be given a meaningful opportunity to be heard." Since Ms. Lynch presented her case before the trial court, how were her rights violated?

4. The trial judge could have changed his opinion if Ms. Lynch had presented strong arguments. Does this repair any due process violations?

5. If the trial judge had waited a day or two before releasing his decision, would there have been any violation of Ms. Lynch's procedural due process rights?

6. When a court order is vacated, the case is often returned to the original trial judge who is likely to be the most familiar with the case. Why does the Court of Appeals direct that this case be assigned to a different judge who will have to rely on a videotaped transcript of the original hearing?

## YOU BE THE JUDGE

Shortly after their child was born, father O.A.H. was divorced from mother E.P.A. Since that time, the father has had little contact with his child. The parents dispute whether the child was abandoned by its father or concealed by its mother, who is now remarried. E.P.A. went to court seeking termination of O.A.H.'s parental rights and adoption by the child's stepfather. O.A.H., who is incarcerated and indigent, requested that counsel be appointed to represent him. The trial judge refused. After a hearing that O.A.H. was unable to attend in person, separate orders were entered terminating his parental rights and granting the stepfather's adoption of the child.

The statute involved does not require appointment of counsel for those unable to afford it. Does procedural due process require that indigents like O.A.H. be furnished with counsel at court proceedings to terminate parental rights? For the appellate court ruling, see *O.A.H. v. R.L.A.* in the You Be the Judge Key at the end of the chapter.

# Legal Terms to Know

liberty interest
procedural due process
Section 1983
substantive due process
state action

# For Further Reading

Bach, Jason. "Students Have Rights Too: The Drafting of Student Conduct Codes." *Brigham Young University Education and Law Journal* 2003 (2003): 1–35.

Berger, Curtis, and Vivian Berger. "Academic Discipline: A Guide to Fair Process for the University Student." *Columbia Law Review* 99 (March 1999): 289–362.

Metzger, Gillian. "Privatization as Delegation." *Columbia Law Review* 103 (October 2003): 1367–502.

Orth, John V. *Due Process of Law: A Brief History.* Lawrence: University of Kansas Press, 2003.

Rubin, Peter. "Square Pegs and Round Holes: Substantive Due Process, Procedural Due Process, and the Bill of Rights." *Columbia Law Review* 103 (May 2003): 833–927.

Vance, Virginia T. "Applications for Benefits: Due Process, Equal Protection, and the Right to Be Free From Arbitrary Procedures." *Washington and Lee Law Review* 61 (Spring 2004): 883–927.

# You Be the Judge Key

**1.** In *Apao v. The Bank of New York,* 324 F.3d 1091 (9th Cir. 2003), the U.S. Court of Appeals upheld the trial court's dismissal of Apao's lawsuit on the grounds that the foreclosure sale did not involve state action. Merely because a business is subject to government regulation does not convert its actions into the state action required to invoke due process. So much of business is regulated by government in some fashion that accepting Apao's argument would nearly destroy the distinction between government and private action. The foreclosure sale was a purely private remedy for a contract violation. Without "overt official involvement" in the foreclosure, there was no state action.

2. The Court of Appeal of Florida, Second District overturned the trial judge's denial of counsel in *O.A.H. v. R.L.A.*, 712 So.2d 4 (1998). It noted that there had been a trend in other states in favor of appointing counsel, with a majority of states now requiring it in parental termination proceedings. Because this proceeding ends all legal relationships between the adopted person and his birth father, it is such a severe deprivation as to require counsel to protect the fundamental rights of the parent.

# Bail

PIETRO TOGGIA

Bail is a pretrial release with or without conditions while a defendant is awaiting his or her criminal trial. There is also postconviction bail, in which conditional and nonconditional release may also be considered for convicted offenders while they are waiting for their sentences and while their appeals are pending. Release on bail is often weighed as an alternative to pretrial detention of suspects or defendants.

Bail decisions invariably fall within the purview of the judiciary; judicial officers, also referred to as bail authorities, determine and decide pretrial release or pretrial detention. The twofold criteria for all forms of release on bail are flight risk and future dangerousness to society.

There are legislative or statutory laws that extend conditional rights to defendants to be released on bail, as well as constitutional safeguards to these rights that the bail shall not be excessive. This is a universally and formally acclaimed due process right, which evokes presumption of innocence and humanitarian consideration. Hence, bail shall be viewed not only as a matter of legal rights but also as an ethical issue. It is an issue of justice, fairness, equity, respect, equal protection, and sensibility.

Release on bail provides suspects or defendants of nonviolent crimes the opportunity to be free while effectively preparing cases for their defenses, fulfilling their family responsibilities, continuing working, maintaining their community ties, and suspending punishment until found guilty beyond reasonable doubt.

The most extensively utilized type of bail in the United States is a secured, bail in which a financial guarantee or surety bond is promised or posted to the court by a third party. In the United States, commercial bail is the principal form in which a licensed and insured bond agents facilitate the release as surety or guarantor, after collecting a 10 percent (of the total posted bail amount) nonrefundable payment from the defendant. The bond agent assumes responsibility to ensure the appearance of the defendant in court, risking forfeiture of the money bond they posted on behalf of the defendant. The court also verifies that the source of the bond money is clean and was not obtained with any type of illegal means. The other variations as alternative to commercial bail are (1) release on recognizance (ROR), in which low-risk, defendants are released without financial bond with only a promise to appear in courts; (2) refundable cash bail and deposit bail, which are posted with county and district courts; (3) use of summons in lieu of arrests; and rarely (4) property bail in which real property, such as a home, is used to post bail.

The history of bail goes back a little more than seven centuries, and is traced to the English Common law tradition in the 13th century. In 1275, the Stature of Westminister for the first time classified crimes as bailable and nonbailable offenses and limited the unchecked power to issue detention orders of the local sheriff. Subsequently, the English Parliament enacted the Habeas Corpus Act in 1677. The act empowered the magistrates as bail authorities, permitted the release of defendants who committed bailable offenses on recognizance with surety, as well as brought focus for the first time on the characteristics of offenders and the gravity of the offenses as conditions for release on bail.

Most important, the 1689 English Bill of Rights, the precursor to the U.S. Bill of Rights, prohibited the setting of bail with an excessive monetary value. The Eighth Amendment to the U.S. Constitution echoes this constitutional protection of due process rights by regulating unlimited judicial discretionary power. Similarly, both Pennsylvania's and Virginia's constitutions, ratified in 1776, prohibit excessive bail. It has been observed that the right to bail is explicitly guaranteed by federal and state legislation, while these rights are implicitly safeguarded by the U.S. and state constitutions, limiting the power of the judiciary in setting excessive bail. This means that the Eighth Amendment is not executable without attendant and specified statutory (substantive) laws pertaining to release on bail. The statutes affirm bail as a fundamental but a qualified right; whereas, the constitutional amendments safeguard the reasonable implementation of the right.

In this respect, the 1789 Judiciary Act provided a general framework of bail laws in the United States. It stipulated which types of offenses were to be bailable, and it ascertained judicial discretion about the pretrial release or pretrial detention of defendants even on capital offense cases. The act also highlighted factors, such as the seriousness of the crime and the strength of incriminating evidence, to be accounted for the determination and decision of pretrial release on bail.

Particular attention was given to bail reform in the criminal justice system beginning in the 1960s. Much of the credit for invigorating such concern goes to Arthur Beeley and Caleb Foote, who had critically examined the bail system and process in Chicago in the 1920s and in Philadelphia and New York in the 1950s, respectively. Their studies showed the unnecessary and unfair overuse of pretrial detentions, particularly against poor defendants for nonviolent offenses in overcrowded jails.

The Manhattan Bail Project was launched in 1961 in New York City under the Vera Institute, with a budget of $95,000 to address such serious concerns as the bail rights of poor defendants and jail overcrowding. The project primarily assisted poor and low-risk youth detainees. These detainees, who were identified for pretrial release, were identified through interviews on the basis of strong community ties.

The Bail Reform Act was enacted by the U.S. Congress on June 22, 1966. The act addresses the release on recognizance or release on personal bond in noncapital federal cases with a guarantee to appear at a future trial. It also enumerates factors, such as the nature of the offense and the offender, ties to his or her family or community, employment history, and mental condition, for judges to consider for bail release with or without financial bond. Furthermore, imposition of travel restrictions, pretrial supervision, and regular reporting were stipulated as control conditions of the defendant, addressing public safety concerns while defendants are free on bail. The 1974 federal reform to achieve constitutionally mandated speedy trials with the 100-day rule also complemented bail reforms.

The federal bail reforms culminated in comprehensively revised and additional statutes in 1984. The Bail Reform Act of 1984 legitimized pretrial detention so long as the release of the defendant "will not reasonably assure the appearance of the person as required or will endanger the safety of any other person or the community" (§3141(c)). The act also requires a mandatory pretrial detention hearing and a revocation hearing in open court, in which the defendant enjoys the rights to a defense counsel, to cross-examine government witnesses, and to present evidence in his or her favor, as well as appeal rights in case of denial of bail. The act further sets the procedural parameters of "standard of proof" (preponderance of evidence), admissibility of "hearsay evidence," and "burden of persuasion" (on the government) about flight risk and future dangerousness. The act also requires that detention orders shall be provided in writing with clear and convincing "finding of facts" and "statements of reason." One of the unique features in the act is the incorporation of sentence enhancing provisions for new crimes committed while free on bail, that is, up to one year for a misdemeanor and up to 10 years for a felony to be added to the penalty of the new crime.

According to the act, the conditions for freedom on bail include, among other things, custodial supervision, abstention from commission of crime, abstention from drugs and alcohol, enrollment in educational and rehabilitation programs, staying away from victims and witnesses in the case, no possession of firearms, and forfeiture of cash deposit or property in case of "jumping" bail. The local and state court jurisdictions, by far and large, have salient features about the substantive and procedural aspects of release on bail similar to the federal laws, including such release criteria as flight risk and future dangerousness, detention and bail revocation hearings, and preconditions of release while awaiting trial or sentencing or pending appeals.

In *United States v. Salerno* (1987), the Bail Reform Act of 1984 was challenged in the U.S. Supreme Court for violation of the due process rights of the two defendants who were charged with multiple offenses of racketeering. At issue was whether the defendants' pretrial detention (denial of bail) was a violation of their due process rights protected under the Fifth and Eighth Amendments, and that the defendants were punished before convicted or found guilty. The U.S. Supreme Court decided the pretrial detention by the district court was constitutional because (1) the legislative intent of the U.S. Congress was "regulatory" (protection of public safety) and not "punitive," community safety outweighs the freedom of high-risk individuals, and analogously, the government has "compelling interest" to maintain public order, and (2) the Eighth Amendment does not accord individuals with the right to be released on bail.

# Further Readings

Foote, Caleb. "The Coming Constitutional Crisis in Bail: Part I." *University of Pennsylvania Law Review,* v.113/7 (May 1965).

Friedman, Lee. "The Evolution of a Bail Reform." *Policy Sciences,* v.7/3 (September 1976).

The Federal Judicial Center, 2nd ed. The Bail Reform Act of 1984 (18 U.S.C. §§ 3141–3150, 3156). http://www.fjc.gov/public/pdf.nsf/lookup/bailref.pdf/$file/bailref.pdf (Accessed March 2013).

*U.S. v. Salerno,* 481 U.S. 739 (1987). Cornell University Law School. http://www.law.cornell.edu/supct/html/historics/USSC_CR_0481_0739_ZO.html (Accessed March 2013).

Wice, Paul. *Freedom for Sale: A National Study of Pretrial Release.* Lansing: University of Michigan Press, 1974.

# Plea Bargaining

MÁXIMO LANGER

Plea bargaining is a procedural mechanism through which the prosecution and defense in a criminal proceeding can reach an agreement for the disposition of a case, subject to the approval of the court. The agreement may take several forms, but usually requires the defendant to plead guilty to one or more offenses. In exchange, the prosecutor drops other charges, accepts that the defendant pleads guilty to a lesser offense, and requests a certain sentence for the defendant or does not oppose the defense's sentence request.

## Types and Use in the United States

In the United States, under the Federal Rules of Criminal Procedure, rule 11 requires that the court ensure that the plea agreement is intelligent and voluntary and determine that there is a factual basis for the plea. Nevertheless, the judge must not participate in plea negotiations. There are different kinds of plea agreements, but the two main types are *charge* bargains—in which the prosecutor drops one or more charges or charges the defendant with a less serious offense in exchange for a guilty plea—and *sentencing* bargains—in which the prosecution agrees to, recommends, or does not oppose a certain sentence or the consideration of certain sentencing factors. Prosecutors use plea agreements not only to save human and material resources by obtaining convictions without trial, but also as investigative tools. As part of a plea agreement, the defendant may have to provide information and testify at trial for its prosecution against his former confederates.

There have been extensive criticisms against plea bargaining that come from different perspectives. From a *crime-control* perspective, critics argue that the practice leads prosecutors and judges to be soft on defendants, which undermines the deterrence effect of punishment. From a *due-process* perspective, critics argue that it generates perverse incentives for prosecutors to overcharge and ask for harsher sentences as a way to obtain an advantage in plea negotiations. It also offers defendants pleas that are more convenient when the evidence is weak. Finally, defense attorneys and public defenders encourage their clients to accept agreements so that they save time and reduce their caseload, while judges abdicate their adjudicative role in favor of prosecutors' decisions.

Some scholars consider plea bargaining to be in conflict with the federal constitutional rights to a trial by jury, confrontation, cross-examination, and proof beyond a reasonable doubt, among others, because it is prosecutors who, in fact, determine which defendants are convicted, and of which sentence, based on criteria not necessarily related to the merits of the case. Worse, those defendants who exercise these rights face potentially harsher punishments. This dilemma would be especially tough for innocent defendants who, in many cases, have to choose between a mild sentence offered by the prosecutor in plea negotiations and a much harsher sentence that could come after a conviction at trial. The same holds for defendants who are in pretrial detention and the courts would release if they accepted the plea agreement. Because plea bargaining generates these kinds of dilemmas, many consider it to be a coercive mechanism against defendants. In 1978, John Langbein even compared it to medieval torture.

Despite their differences, both crime-control and due-process critics agree that the main beneficiaries of plea bargaining are the professional actors of the criminal-justice system, rather than society, victims, or defendants. In addition, from both perspectives, plea bargaining may compromise the truth-determination function of criminal justice by resulting in guilty pleas even in cases where the defendant does not admit his guilt. It may also distort the facts of a case as part of an agreement, for instance, if the defendant pleads guilty to assault when he actually committed rape. Finally, Albert Alschuler argued that plea bargaining depreciates the value of human liberty and diminishes the purposes of criminal sanctions by treating these principles as commodities to be traded for economic savings.

## Reform Proposals

There are many proposed reforms to address these problems. Some of the more common include the following: (1) Increase the budget of the criminal-justice system so that more trials occur. (2) Give financial incentives to prosecutors to limit their discretion and make plea negotiations between prosecution and defense better balanced. (3) Screen prosecutors more closely in the charging decision. (4) Restructure the economic relationship between attorneys and their clients so that the former have better capacities and incentives for zealous representation. (5) Require preplea disclosure to make negotiations more equal and a defendant's decision to plead guilty better informed. (6) Make judges take a more active role in plea negotiations so that prosecutors, in fact, do not determine sentences. (7) Enforce more strictly government concessions in plea agreements, which will protect defendants against defense-attorney errors in plea agreements and limit prosecutorial manipulation of broad mandatory-sentencing statutes. (8) Replace misdemeanor trials with the German system of penal orders. (9) Offer defendants incentives to choose bench trials. (10) Simplify the current trial by jury or replace the trial by jury with trial before mixed courts so that there are fewer incentives for plea agreements. (11) Abolish plea bargaining altogether.

Defenders of plea bargaining argue that the mechanism is a fair way of disposing of cases because the prosecutor takes into consideration the chances to win the trial when she makes her offer. In addition, the prosecutor is probably in a better position than jurors are to determine whether the defendant is guilty or innocent, because the prosecutor has access to information that may not be admissible or produced at trial. Plea-bargaining defenders also claim that even if the practice presents serious problems, trials themselves often have problems and one should not idealize them. In addition, they claim that in plea agreements, both society and defendants benefit. Society secures convictions at a lower cost, and thus can prosecute and punish more offenders. Moreover, plea bargains are a powerful tool that enables society to deal with organized crime. Defendants benefit by obtaining sentences that are lower than those they would have received had the judge or jury convicted them at trial; in addition, defendants avoid the anxieties and uncertainties of a trial. Finally, defenders maintain that a plea agreement contributes to a defendant's rehabilitation and victims avoid the rigors of testifying at trial and the possibility that the prosecution will not get a conviction. One of the assumptions of many plea-bargaining defenders is that both parties have, in most cases, equal bargaining power.

## Origin and Acceptance

Whatever the merits and demerits of plea bargaining, there is no question that it is a well-established practice of the American criminal-justice system. Although plea bargaining has been widely criticized, the U.S. Supreme Court upheld it as constitutional in *Brady v. United States* (397 U.S. 742, 1970) and stated in *Santobello v. New York* (404 U.S. 257, 260, 1971) that the practice was "an essential component of the administration of justice." In addition, despite reforms intended to eliminate or limit the mechanism, about 90 percent of federal cases and 95 percent of state cases are disposed through guilty pleas, the vast majority of which occur through plea agreements.

Despite its entrenchment, the extensive use of plea bargaining in the United States is a relatively new phenomenon. There may have been some examples of this practice before the nineteenth century, but prosecutors did not begin to use plea bargaining widely until around 1900. Historians do not agree on what caused plea bargaining's rise and wide spread; explanations vary from jurisdiction to jurisdiction. They point to factors such as an increase in criminal dockets, at least partially caused by an expansion of substantive criminal law; an increase in civil dockets; the bureaucratization and professionalization of the police, prosecution, and defense functions; the increasing complexity of criminal trials; favoring the individualization of a sentence that would be more appropriate for the needs of the offender; political corruption; and the development of plea bargaining as a legal tool to promote and legitimize a certain social order.

## Other Common Law Countries

Even if plea bargaining is considered a distinctive feature of the American criminal-justice system, the practice is not unique to the United States. Other common law jurisdictions have also made use of this tool, though in some cases their practices present differences from the American system. For instance, in England fewer cases are disposed through guilty pleas (an average of 63 percent in crown court circuits in 1994) and the incidence of plea bargaining is less substantial than in the United States. In addition, many English guilty pleas occur without explicit plea bargains between prosecution and defense such as those that prevail in the United States. Rather, they involve implicit plea bargaining, in which a defendant who pleads guilty gets a substantial discount in sentence as a matter of course, even if there is not a concrete ex ante promise by the prosecutor or the judge. Despite these differences, plea bargaining in England has received important criticisms similar to many of those already mentioned regarding American plea bargaining.

# Civil Law Countries

Until recently, comparatists considered civil law jurisdictions to be "lands without plea bargaining," as Langbein put it in 1979. The very concept of the guilty plea did not exist in inquisitorial systems of civil law tradition. If defendants admitted their guilt, judges considered the acknowledgments confessions that may have been helpful in determining the truth at trial, but the admissions did not dispose of the cases. In addition, since in inquisitorial systems the prosecutorial role is one of an impartial official who has a duty to determine the truth, the act of negotiating with the defendant traditionally would be improper conduct by these officials. However, in the past three decades, and especially in the past decade, this situation has changed, and civil law jurisdictions have adopted consensual mechanisms to dispose of criminal cases in ways that are similar to plea bargaining. For example, Germany incorporated the *Absprachen* during the 1970s, Italy adopted the *patteggiamento* in 1989, Argentina adopted the *procedimiento abreviado* or *juicio abreviado* in 1997, and France brought in the *composition pénale* in 1999 and the *comparution sur reconnaissance préalable de culpabilité* in 2004.

The reasons for the introduction of these reforms vary from jurisdiction to jurisdiction, but they include an increase in crime rates and court caseloads, the development of new legal tools to deal with complex criminal cases, and the influence of the American criminal-justice system on civil law jurisdictions.

Judges, practitioners, and commentators have resisted these mechanisms in many civil law jurisdictions, usually because they consider them an intolerable reduction of the sentencing powers of trial judges, a violation of due process, or out of fear of Americanization. However, in most cases courts uphold these practices and use them widely. For instance, 22 percent of the cases before misdemeanor trial courts and 52 percent of the cases of crime trial courts in Buenos Aires (Argentina) are disposed through the *procedimiento abreviado*, and every fourth criminal trial in Germany is settled.

Even if American plea bargaining has inspired some of these consensual mechanisms, many present substantial differences from the American system. For instance, in Germany, unlike the United States, the trial judge has an active role in the negotiations. In Italy, in the *patteggiamento*, the defendant does not explicitly admit his guilt, and the Italian mechanism is more similar to an American nolo contendere than to plea bargaining. In Argentina, the *juicio abreviado* only permits sentencing bargains, not charge bargains. In France, the judge many only apply the *composition pénale* and the *comparution sur reconnaissance préalable de culpabilité* to offenses that carry a maximum potential punishment of five years imprisonment.

# International Courts

Plea bargaining has reached international criminal jurisdictions. Though initially excluded from the International Criminal Tribunal for the former Yugoslavia (ICTY), plea bargaining was later incorporated by the ICTY to its rules of procedure and evidence (rule 62 *ter)*, and it is now widely practiced in that jurisdiction. Nancy Combs attributed the growing reliance on ICTY plea bargaining to trial complexity, but other factors, such as an increasing caseload, case complexity, and external pressures to process cases more swiftly, have all played roles that are at least as important. The International Criminal Tribunal for Rwanda also has accepted plea bargaining and expressly regulates it in rule 62 *bis* of its rules of procedure and evidence. Finally, the drafters of the Rome Statute of the International Criminal Court tried to exclude plea bargaining from the court's jurisdiction by establishing, in article 65.5, that any discussions between the prosecutor and the defense regarding modification of the charges, an admission of guilt, or the final penalty must not be binding on the court. It is still unclear, though, whether this entry will dissuade the use of plea bargaining in the International Criminal Court once it begins to prosecute and try actual cases.

—*Máximo Langer*

*See also* Confessions and Interrogation; Consensual Penal Resolution; Defense Lawyers; International Criminal Tribunals; Penal Court Procedures, Doctrinal Issues in; Plea Bargaining, Economics of; Prosecutorial Discretion; Prosecutors; Victims' Rights

# Further Readings

Alschuler, Albert W. (1981). "The Changing Plea Bargaining Debate:' *California Law Review* 69: 695–703.

_____. (1983). "Implementing the Criminal Defendant's Right to Trial: Alternatives to the Plea Bargaining System." *University of Chicago Law Review* 50: 937–48.

Bibas, Stephanos. (2004). "Plea Bargaining Outside the Shadow of Trial." *Harvard Law Review* 117: 2463–2547.

Combs, Nancy Amoury. (2006). *Guilty Pleas in International Criminal Law: Constructing a Restorative Justice Approach.* Stanford, CA: Stanford University Press.

Conference on Plea Bargaining. (1979). *Law and Society Review* 13: 189–582. [Articles on historical and comparative perspectives, reform, empirical research, and philosophical implications; see especially articles by Albert Alschuler (211–46), Lawrence Friedman (247–60), Mark Haller (273–80), John Baldwin and Michael McConville (287–308), William Felstiner (309–26), and Thomas Church (509–26)].

Ferrua, Paolo. (1997). "La Giustizia Negoziata nella Crisi della Funzione Cognitiva del Processo Penale." In *Studi sul Processo Penale,* edited by Paolo Ferrua, vol. 3. Torino: G. Giappichelli, 131–61.

Fisher, George. (2003). *Plea Bargaining's Triumph: A History of Plea Bargaining in America.* Stanford, CA: Stanford University Press.

Langbein, John H. (1978). "Torture and Plea Bargaining." *University of Chicago Law Review* 46: 3–22.

_____. (1979). "Land without Plea Bargaining: How the Germans Do It." *Michigan Law Review* 78: 204–25.

Langer, Máximo. (2001). "La Dicotomía Acusatorio-Inquisitivo y la Importación de Mecanismos Procesales de la Tradición Jurídica Anglo-Sajona." In *Procedimiento Abreviado,* edited by Julio B. J. Maier and Alberto Bovino. Buenos Aires: Editores del Puerto, 97–134.

———. (2004). "From Legal Transplants to Legal Translations: The Globalization of Plea Bargaining and the Americanization Thesis in Criminal Procedure." *Harvard international Law Journal* 45: 1–64.

McConville, Mike, and Chester Mirsky. (1995). "The Rise of Guilty Pleas: New York, 1800–1865." *Law & Society Review* 22: 443–74.

Nasheri, Hedieh. (1998). *Betrayal of Due Process: A Comparative Assessment of Plea Bargaining in the United States and Canada.* Lanham, MD: University Press of America.

Pizzi, William T., and Mariangela Montagna. (2004). "The Battle to Establish an Adversarial System in Italy." *Michigan Journal of International Law* 25: 429–66.

Schulhofer, Stephen. (1992). "Plea Bargaining as Disaster." *Yale Law Journal* 101: 1979–1117.

Schünemann, Bernd. (2002). "Die Absprachen in Strafverfahren." In *Festschrift für Peter Riess zum 70. Geburtstag,* edited by Ernst-Walter Hanack et al. Berlin: W. de Gruyter, 525–46.

Scott, Robert E., and William Stuntz. (1992). "Plea Bargaining as Contract." *Yale Law Journal* 101: 1909–68, 2011–15 (reply).

# Juvenile Justice

## AN OVERVIEW

### ROSEMARY C. SARRI

## 17

## Abstract and Keywords

The juvenile justice system was established with the founding of the Juvenile Court in Chicago in 1900, an institution that spread to all the states in a short period of time. The history, organization, structure and operations of the system are described along with its growth along with increasing Among the key issues examined are: gender, overrepresentation of children of color, placement of mentally ill and abused or neglected children, human rights and reintegration of juvenile offenders after their returning home.

**Keywords:** history, court processing, disposition and placement, gender, overrepresentation, social justice issues

The establishment of the juvenile court in Illinois in 1899 led to the development of the United States juvenile justice system, which was mandated to provide for the processing, adjudication, and rehabilitation of juveniles charged with criminal violations, as well as for the care and treatment of abused and neglected children. Social advocates such as Jane Addams as well as crusading judges like Ben Lindsey (Tanenhaus, 2002) established the system, emphasizing care and treatment rather than punishment and control. The response to this new social invention was rapid, and the juvenile court spread throughout the United States in less than 25 years. Since that time it has become a model for the legal processing of children in much of the developed world. Although the juvenile court still retains jurisdiction over the processing of abuse and neglect cases, most of the processing care and supervision of those cases lie within the child welfare system while the juvenile justice system focuses primarily on youth charged with delinquency or status offenses. As of 2002, more than 3.1 million youth were under juvenile court supervision annually with ~1.6 million new cases processed each year (Snyder & Sickmund 2006).

# History

The principles underlying the creation of this social institution were that children were developmentally immature and required protection; they were malleable and could be habilitated or rehabilitated; and the court should aid children suffering from a broad range of problems different from adults. Children were assumed to be dependent, developing physically and psychologically, in need of care and nurturance. They differed from adults by having lesser capacity for reasoning and moral judgment; thus they were less culpable for their behavior (Tanenhaus, 2002). Because the focus was on the rehabilitation of offenders, its development had an impact on court procedures, and resulted in a theory of state responsibility for children as represented in the concept of *parens patriae*.

Prior to the establishment of the juvenile court, juveniles charged with delinquent acts were primarily tried in the criminal justice system, but even then age played a role in presumptions of guilt because juveniles below the age of 14 were presumed not to possess sufficient criminal responsibility to commit a crime. The creation of the juvenile court altered this presumption in part, providing almost exclusive jurisdiction over individuals below the age of 18 who were charged with violating criminal laws in most states. Hearings were to be informal, private, "in the best interest of the child," and civil rather than criminal. These tenets constituted a separate system of justice that recognized the differences between children and adults (Zimring, 2002).

State legislation permitted judges to use their discretion in conducting hearing and prescribing interventions. To meet their statutory goals, the juvenile justice system employed a range of programs and services—including prevention, diversion, detention, probation, community services, and residential treatment (Rosenheim, 2002). For most of the 20th century, judges heard juvenile cases and then diverted them to community services outside the court, but substantial numbers were institutionalized even for extended periods.

*1960–1980.* In many communities, the court failed to meet the goals of its founders to be responsible for the provision of rehabilitation. Beginning in the 1960s, the human rights movement influenced developments in juvenile justice because of growing concern that juveniles receive due process and protection of their civil liberties. Decisions of the Supreme Court in cases such as *Kent v. U.S. 383 U.S. 541 (1966)*, *In re Gault 387 U.S.1 (1967)*, and *In re Winship 397 U.S. 352 (1970)* led to many new social policy initiatives to protect children's rights to challenge arbitrary dispositions. A series of national commission reports (Presidential Commission on Law Enforcement and Criminal Justice and the Task Force on Juvenile Delinquency and Youth Crime, 1974) had positive effects, extending human rights along with policies of decriminalization, deinstitutionalization, and diversion. By the 1970s passage of the first federal juvenile justice legislation, the Juvenile Justice and Delinquency Act of 1974, funded state efforts to reduce institutionalization and increase local community-based programming.

*1980–2000.* The progress of the 1960s and 1970s was dramatically reversed in the 1980s and 1990s, with the passage of federal and state legislation that emphasized incarceration and punishment, along with withdrawal of the distinction between juveniles and adults as far as certain criminal behavior was concerned. As a century of the juvenile court was celebrated in 2000, laws and philosophy had returned to many practices in place before the invention of the juvenile court. Thousands of juveniles were held in adult prisons and jails, often under very punitive conditions (Lerman, 2000). Feld (1999) argues that judicial, administrative, and legislative decisions transformed the court into a second-class criminal court that did not serve the interests of children. Much of the transformation appeared to be "justified" by the increase in juvenile crime between 1985 and 1995 (Bishop, 2000). However, after 1995 there was a dramatic decline in juvenile crime that continued through 2005, especially serious violent crime, but there has not been a corresponding reduction in the numbers of juveniles processed (Snyder & Sickmund 2006).

*Since 2000.* Much of the discussion about the juvenile justice system in the early 21st century neglects the changes in the societal context in which it operates. Garland (2001) and Beckett and Western (2000) point to the increasing culture of control and the declining provision of social welfare benefits for the population at risk for involvement in the justice system. Family structure has undergone and is undergoing substantial changes that affect children because single parents are unable to provide the necessary supervision and support, especially in critical adolescent years. The increasing rates of poverty, the decline of public school education, the lack of physical and mental health care, and the changing economic structure in which well-paying blue collar jobs are unavailable for young adults have had a pronounced effect on these vulnerable youth since the mid-1990s. Millions are spent on incarceration and control but little is available to prepare the middle- and working-class youth population for successful adulthood (Osgood, Foster, Flanagan, & Ruth 2005; Setterstein, Furstenberg, & Rumbaut 2005). All these factors affect juvenile crime in the society and thereby the operation of the juvenile justice system.

## Organization and Structure

The juvenile justice system is composed of the statutes and policies as well as organizations charged with responsibility for the processing of juveniles who violate state laws and local ordinances (Roberts, 2004). The legal definition of delinquency and crime varies from state to state as to age of juvenile court jurisdiction and the roles of the various court officials responsible for the processing of juveniles into and through the court. The processing typically includes the following:

1. Arrest and referral of a juvenile to the court for a law violation; some police may have warning and diversion alternatives.
2. Juvenile court intake includes referral for trial, diversion of minor offenders, detention, and preliminary assessment.
3. Filing of a formal petition and deciding to try the youth in juvenile court or transfer the youth to adult court for criminal processing.
4. Hearing or trial by the court and determination of innocence or guilt.
5. Disposition decision making by the judge and placement in a program for those adjudicated as delinquent for an indeterminate or specific period of time, depending upon state laws or judicial discretion, and release or special sanctions for the others.
6. Reintegration or reentry programming, which is formalized as parole, but may also be informally and unevenly provided.

# Demographics

## Court Processing

More than 2.2 million youth below the age of 18 were arrested in 2003, but only 25% were arrested for serious person or property crimes or "index" crimes as these are defined (Snyder & Sickmund 2006). The remaining offenses were misdemeanors, drug offenses, and public order or status offenses. Juvenile crime increased substantially in the late 1980s, but by 2003 most violent crime had fallen below that observed in 1980 (Stahl et al., 2005). Of those arrested 1.615 million cases were referred to the juvenile court in 2002. Cases not referred may be diverted to other agencies, particularly "status offenses;" those behaviors that are included in the jurisdiction of the juvenile court in many states but are not classified as crimes. Status offenses include running away, incorrigibility, truancy, and liquor law violations.

Fifty-eight percent of the all cases are formally petitioned and 42% are dismissed or referred to a variety of social agencies for services. If petitioned 67% can be expected to be adjudicated delinquent and subsequently 62% are placed on probation and 22% receive an out-of-the-home placement, most often in a residential institution. Even at the final disposition stage, juvenile cases are dismissed, and youth are released or given other sanctions outside the formal justice system. Waiver to adult court will result for about 1% of the cases, but that number declined since 2002 (Bishop, 2000). However, it varies widely among the states reflecting the differences in state statutes. Overall, fewer than 10% of the youth who enter the court ultimately end up in a correctional institution.

Delinquency case rates overall were 51.6 per 1,000 youth aged 10–17 years in 2002, but there were marked variations by age from 4.6 per 1,000 for 10-year-old youth to 109.1 per 1,000 for those 17 years old. The overall rate was far lower than the rate of 81.6 in 1994, a reflection of the decline in crime by juveniles during a period of substantial population growth (Snyder & Sickmund 2006). There are sex differences by age in that female crime peaks at 16 years while the peak age for males is 17.

As Table 17.1 indicates, the largest number of youth held in custody out of their homes is held in detention. The rate of 10.2 per 1,000 youth is nearly 3 times the rate of those in placement following adjudication. Placement in detention is important because it is predictive of subsequent adjudication and referral to an institution. The numbers in detention increased substantially after 1985, with drug cases explaining most of the increase (140%). Frequently arrested for drug violations, African American males are 37% of all detainees and their detention is a key factor in their overall disproportionate representation in the juvenile justice system (Snyder & Sickmund 2006).

In the decade between 1990 and 2000 formal handling of juvenile court cases increased from 49.8% to 57.7% (McNeece & Jackson 2004). Not surprisingly, there were subsequent increases in adjudications, waivers, and placements as formalization increased.

# Dispositions

On a given day in 2004, 96,655 youth were held in public and private correctional facilities (Snyder & Sickmund 2006). Annually more than 145,000 youth adjudicated for delinquency are sent to an out-of-home placement for a specified period or an indefinite stay. This is a small percentage of the more than 2.2 million youth arrested, and the numbers in placement declined after 2000, following the increases in most states during the 1990s when the juvenile crime rate was substantially higher.

TABLE 17.1   Youth Population and Processing Rates

|  | Number | Rate |
|---|---|---|
| Population, 10–17 years | 33,352,224 | |
| Juvenile arrests (2004) | 2,202,000 | 66.2 |
| Referrals to juvenile court—delinquency | 1,620,800 | 48.8 |
| Petitions to juvenile court | 934,900 | 28.1 |
| Detention | 339,800 | 10.2 |
| Adjudications | 634,500 | 19.1 |
| Assigned to probation | 385,400 | 11.6 |
| Placed out of home | 144,000 | 4.3 |
| Waived to adult criminal court | 6,900 | 0.21 |

Rates are calculated at the numbers per 1,000 youth processed during the year 2002.

Females account for 15% of the juveniles in custody in public and private facilities, but of that total 40% are placed for status offenses as their most serious offense. As Table 17.2 indicates, male youth in custody have a more serious crime profile than do females, and they tend to remain longer in placement. The majority of youth are held in public facilities, but one-third is placed in private institutions.

Youth charged with person crimes have a higher probability of postadjudication placement than those charged with property or public order crimes. Among the person crimes, there has been a substantial increase in processing and institutionalization of juveniles as sexual offenders for extended periods followed by placement of their names on a public registry. Zimring (2004) strongly criticizes the punitiveness of some of these practices. Although a relatively small percentage of youth are

TABLE 17.2   Delinquency Offense and Placement Profile, 2002

| Type of Crime | Referral to Court | Postadjudication placement | | | | |
|---|---|---|---|---|---|---|
|  | Male | Female | Male | Female | Public | Private |
| Person | 23% | 26% | 35% | 14% | 35% | 32% |
| Property | 34 | 39 | 29 | 12 | 28 | 27 |
| Drugs | 13 | 8 | 8 | 7 | 8 | 10 |
| Public Order | 25 | 27 | 10 | 12 | 26 | 20 |
| Status | – | – | 4 | 40 | 3 | 11 |

From *Juvenile Offenders and Victims: 2006 National Report*, by Snyder, H. N., and Sickmund, M., 2006, Washington, DC: OJJDP, Office of Justice Programs, U.S. Department of Justice. Copyright 2006 by the U.S. Department of Justice. Reprinted with permission.

charged with drug crimes, they are likely to be placed out of the home because of the lack of drug treatment facilities in many communities. The profile of offenders in public versus private facilities does not vary significantly. Out-of-home placement rose by 44% during the late 1990s but since 2000 has declined by 12%, primarily among property and person offenders. Increases in placement on probation appear to be the explanation.

## Gender

Young females' rising rates of involvement with the juvenile justice system now receive increased attention. Their rate of arrest rose to 29% of total juvenile arrests in 2002, and the involvement of young women in certain crimes (larceny, drugs and simple assault) has risen more sharply than that of males (Snyder, 2006). Because the number of male offenders is so much larger, percentage comparisons are misleading. It is less clear that female crime has increased commensurate to their involvement in the justice system, for example, their detention and placement in residential programs for status offenses, primarily involving family conflict. The rising rate of their involvement may be partly the result of changing policies and practices that serve to bring more young women under the care and control of the justice system, for example, the referral of girls in need of mental health services to the justice system. It has been noted that 60–70% of the youth in juvenile justice have a diagnosable mental health problem with more females than males so diagnosed (Coalition for Juvenile Justice, 2000; Grisso, 2004).

## Evidence-Based Models of Intervention

Because it has been shown that there is a wide range of factors that cause or are associated with delinquency, it is not surprising that there are many programs for prevention, early intervention, alternatives to incarceration, community-based intervention, and residential treatment. Using meta-analysis techniques, Lipsey and Wilson (1998) found the following characteristics to be associated with greater effectiveness:

- The integrity of the treatment model implementation.
- Longer duration of treatment produces better results.
- Results from well-established programs exceed new programs.
- Treatment administered by mental health professionals.
- Emphasis on interpersonal skills training.
- Use of the teaching family home methods.

Overall, they found community-based programs to be more effective than programs in custodial settings, so the context for the treatment is important. Voluntary participation was shown to be more effective than that which is coerced, and there are ways by which voluntary assent can be achieved. Greenwood (2006) shows that balanced and restorative justice (BARJ) programs can integrate restitution and community service by which an offender can repair the harm he or she may have caused. A report of the U.S. Surgeon General on Youth Violence (2001) concurs that many programs are effective with delinquent youth, but they emphasize the importance of the quality of implementation.

Elliot and his colleagues at the Center for the Study and Prevention of Youth Violence have developed "Blueprints" of 10 programs meeting rigorous criteria that include demonstrated positive outcomes on problem behavior that persists beyond a youth's involvement in a program. They can be consulted at http://www.colorado.edu/cspu/blueprints for technical assistance regarding the programs that they regard as effective. (Michalic, Fagan, Irwin, Ballard, & Elliot 2002).

Greenwood (2006) has identified a large number of programs that have been shown to be effective for working with youth from preschool age through adolescence. For example, the Perry School Pre-School program was shown to reduce delinquency when the participants reached adulthood in contrast with a comparable control group. Programs targeting the youth and his or her family have been shown to be effective, including functional family therapy, multisystemic therapy, the Seattle Social Development Program, and Big Brothers/Big Sisters. If cost benefit issues are of concern, Greenwood (2006) shows that cost-effective programs ultimately reduce crime.

Because of the lack of systematic evaluation the effectiveness of most juvenile justice program is unknown. However, residential programs that include only delinquent youth are seldom effective in reducing recidivism. Other popular programs that have been shown not to be effective include boot camps, substance abuse programs such as DARE, and "scared straight" programs.

# Social Justice Issues

Some important social justice issues include overrepresentation of youth of color, prosecution of juveniles as adults, child welfare and juvenile justice, mental health of offenders, reintegration, and human rights.

# Overrepresentation of Youth of Color

One of the most critical issues facing the entire justice system in the United States in the disproportionate representation of persons of color in all phases of the system, despite the fact that the United States has ratified the U.N. Convention on the Elimination of all Forms of Racial Discrimination. The juvenile justice system is not an exception in that youth of color are disproportionately represented in all phases of the justice, child welfare, and public assistance systems, particularly African American youth. The Juvenile Justice and Delinquency Prevention Act of 1974 was amended in 1988 to mandate that states who participate in its programs make "every effort" to achieve proportional representation of youth of color in the juvenile justice system. As of 2003, youth of color comprised 36% of the total juvenile population, but 62% of those in detention and 67% of those in other types of residential facilities. The overrepresentation of youth of color in the early stages of processing has profound effects, because if a youth is detained, there is an increased probability of being found guilty and sentenced to an out-of-home placement. As youth of color move through the justice system there are amplification effects in the subsequent processing that add to the overrepresentation (Kempf-Leonard & Sontheimer 1995).

A variety of factors have been identified as causes of this disproportionality, including:

- Crime rates are higher in neighborhood of high levels of deterioration and segregation where youth of color reside and where police are likely to do more surveillance (Sampson, Morenoff, & Raudenbush 2005).
- Juvenile justice agencies treat youth of color more severely than white youth, particularly early in processing (Bishop & Frazier 2000; Bridges & Steen 1998).
- Nunn (2002) argues that the oppression of African American youth (especially males) appears normal because decision makers have been socialized to undervalue the lives of these youth.
- Diversion and other alternatives to incarceration are more available in suburban areas with lower proportions of youth of color (Sarri, Shook, & Ward 2001).

The highest rates of incarceration of youth of color are found in public residential facilities reaching 90% in some states (Snyder & Sickmund 2006). Overall, as of 2004, 754 African American, 496 American Indian/Native American, 348 Hispanic, 190 white, and 113 Asian youth per 100,000 were incarcerated.

## Prosecuting and Incarcerating Juveniles as Adults

The shift toward the punitive handling of children and youth in the justice systems is best exemplified by the increased transfer of juveniles to adult criminal courts and their subsequent incarceration in adult prisons. During the 1990s, there was a proliferation of transfer legislation: 44 states and the District of Columbia enacted at least one change easing the processing of juveniles as adults (Torbet & Szymanski 1998). By the end of the decade, all 50 states permitted the transfer to adult courts. Although the legislative changes were made to address growing youth violence, by 2000 the majority of youth sentenced to the adult system were there for property, drug, and public order offenses. This legislation also decreased the power of the juvenile court judge and expanded that of the prosecutor. This change represented a significant shift in the role of the judge that had existed since 1900, about when the court was founded.

There are three procedures by which juveniles are transferred for trial as adults: judicial discretion, prosecutorial discretion, and statutory exclusion of certain youth from the juvenile court based on offense and age. Some states do not maintain minimum age limits for trying juveniles as adults while other states set the lower age limit between 10 and 16 years. Some states allow for a case to be designated for trial in the juvenile court with adult court rules. The juvenile may receive a "blended sentence" that permits a youth to remain in the juvenile system, provided he or she commits no subsequent crime.

Accurate information on the numbers of youth processed as adults is not available. Bishop (2000) reviewed a large number of studies and was unable to arrive at a sound estimate. Conservative estimates placed the number processed under the age of 18 at 200,000 per year, but the numbers convicted were far smaller (Sickmund, Snyder, & Poe-Yamagata, 2000). There has been a decline since 2000 because of the dramatic decline in serious and violent crime by juveniles, but the amount of the decline remains unknown. The U.S. Justice Department reported that as of 2004 there were 2,800 youth under 18 in adult prisons; however, this number excludes adults who were sentenced as juveniles, often with long sentences, so nationally the number may well exceed 100,000 individuals

(Harrison & Beck 2006). In 1997 there were 7,400 juveniles below 18 in state and federal prisons; so there has been a substantial decline as of 2004.

Juveniles of color and males are the overwhelming majority of those tried as adults (Bortner, Zatz, & Hawkins 2000). Most of the youth in adult prisons will be released in their mid-20, but they will be ill-equipped to meet the demands of society for successful adulthood and parenting because of the stigma of incarceration and because of the lack of education, health care, and social services while incarcerated. Moreover, charges of human rights violations have been and are being made with respect to the conditions of incarceration (Human Rights Watch, 2005). Studies of recidivism indicate that juveniles released from adult facilities have higher rates of recidivism than similar youth released from juvenile facilities (Bishop & Frazier 2000; Fagan, 1996). Thus, the transfer of juvenile s to the adult criminal justice system is counterproductive as a crime control policy.

## Child Welfare and Juvenile Justice

The juvenile court serves both abused and neglected children as well as those charged with delinquency, but it was expected that the two areas would be separately addressed since child welfare clients are initially victims of parental abuse or neglect while juvenile delinquents are viewed as primarily responsible for their behavior as perpetrators of crime. This distinction has become increasingly ambiguous as studies have shown the "drift" of child welfare clients to the juvenile justice system (Jonson-Reid & Barth 2000; Kaufman & Widom 1999; Smith & Thornberry 1995). A large study by Kelly (2002) in the Cook County, Illinois, juvenile court, observed that more than a third of maltreated children ended up in the juvenile justice system as delinquents.

Overall, African American and Hispanic youth with experience in foster care have been shown to be at high risk for subsequent transfer to the justice system. Although the numbers of male victims are greater than those of females, most of those who "drift" to the justice system are reported to be female, largely for status offenses and property crime. With a large sample in California, Jonson-Reid and Barth (2000) followed youth from child welfare to entrance into the California Youth Authority. They observed that if youth were transferred to probation, the risk for subsequent transfer to the CYA for a serious felony increased significantly. Having multiple placements was correlated with transfer to the justice system.

A recent study in Michigan of adolescents who aged out of foster care reported several negative outcomes: homelessness, inadequate education, lack of employment, mental health problems, substance abuse, and experience in the justice system (Fowler & Toro 2006). These youth also reported being physically and sexually abused. To delineate the process by which child welfare youth "drift" to the justice system, youth frequently run away from placements, more often from congregate care than individual foster care or kin care. Some of these youth may engage in delinquent behavior as they attempt to survive "on the street." When they are apprehended by police, they may be taken to a detention facility pending a hearing by the court. Depending upon the outcome of that placement a juvenile may then be moved to juvenile justice system status, and the child welfare system may cease involvement with the case. Because a youth may be an older adolescent at this point, there is a tendency to view them more as a delinquent than a victim of abuse or neglect.

## Mental Health and Juvenile Competency

The collapse of the mental health system serving children and youth in the 1990s resulted in a gradual movement of mentally ill juveniles into the justice system. The inappropriateness of these placements was exacerbated by the lack of adequate legislation in many states for the assessment of competency for trial as a delinquent or as an adult. Prior to the 1990s, the issues of juvenile competence were seldom raised, but findings from research on brain development and developmental maturity, as well as concerns about due process protection of youth, raised concerns in both the mental health and legal professions (Scott & Grisso 1997). Findings from brain development research are directly relevant to the criminal justice processing of juveniles for both the individual's culpability and ability to participate effectively in his or her defense. Recent neuroimaging studies indicate that the brain, specifically the pre-frontal lobe (PFC), continues to grow and change throughout adolescence and into the 20s. The PFC controls higher-order cognitive processes, which include motivation, inhibition, logical decision making, risk taking, problem solving, planning, emotional regulation, sexual urges, and anticipation of consequences (Spear, 2000). Past and current trauma and stress have detrimental effects on adolescent brain functioning, and delinquent adolescents are significantly more at risk for limited cognitive development (Arnsten & Shansky 2004).

In trying to estimate the number of juveniles with a diagnosable mental disorder, Grisso (2004) reported that findings from several studies indicated that 60–70% of juveniles in correctional facilities have at least one disorder. Relatively few receive professional evaluations or treatment in most settings. Grisso (2004) suggests reasons for attention to these youth: (a) agencies have a legal and moral responsibility to attend to the mental health needs of juveniles; (b) juveniles are entitled to due process and equal protection under the law, including determination of their competency to participate in their own defense; and (c) protection of the public requires that juveniles with mental disorders be treated and managed in ways that maintains protection.

## Reintegration and Aftercare

Each year nearly 100,000 juvenile offenders in correctional facilities are returned to their home communities, and an even larger number are released from probation, but reintegration services are poorly developed and reach a small proportion of returning youth (Griffin, 2005). In many states juveniles are released from correctional facilities under state supervised parole, and so there is little adaptation to the circumstances of the youth or the community.

Griffin (2005) describes three court-directed programs for aftercare and reintegration in Pennsylvania, West Virginia, and Indiana, which offered comprehensive services for education, employment, and treatment as needed along with mentoring and monitoring. Altschuler, Armstrong, & MacKenzie (1999) developed a model for intensive aftercare by institutional and parole staff that is now being tested in several communities. Spencer and Jones-Walker (2004) offer a theory-based reintegration model that focuses on identity formation recognizing that being in a correctional program is a life-changing experience. They present a cognitive behavioral approach that addresses the individual's environment as well as their personal characteristics. Their research and that of Barton (2006) found very low rates of recidivism among youth who completed programs that promoted competency, a positive sense of self, and transition programming with strong social support necessary for the youth to achieve success and stability.

## Human Rights

The United States strongly advocates for the extension of human rights enforcement throughout the world, but when it relates directly to the United States, there is resistance not only to the adoption but also to enforcement of those rights by United Nations agencies. Nowhere are the principles of human rights more at risk than in the U.S. processing of juveniles in the justice system. The International Convention on the Rights of the Child has not been ratified and several of its provisions were ignored. The United States has signed and ratified four other conventions, which are often negated by our practices of processing juveniles as adults, in the conditions of confinement in many facilities, in the incarceration of juveniles when community services would be more effective, and in the overrepresentation of youth of color in all levels of the juvenile justice system. The four other conventions include the following: Convention on the Elimination of All Forms of Racism, the Covenant on Civil and Political Rights, the Convention against Torture, and the Convention on Human Rights. The relevance and importance of international law and customs was acknowledged by Justice Arthur Kennedy of the U.S. Supreme Court in his decision in the *Roper v. Simmons* case 543 U.S., in which the Court acknowledged that the juvenile death penalty was unconstitutional. In 2005 writing for the majority Justice Kennedy stated that international law provided guidance for the Supreme Court because execution of juveniles was prohibited in many Western countries many years prior to 2005.

Human rights conventions set limits on state punishment and control, specify what is required in legal representation of children in the justice systems, reject the transferring children to the adult justice system, mandate states to make "every effort" to achieve proportional representation of youth of color in the juvenile justice system, and specify appropriate conditions of confinement (Sarri & Shook 2005). Attention to international law and custom is increasingly recognized in the United States as are the more humane policies and practices in other countries (Amnesty International, 1998). Human rights frameworks provide powerful tools for effecting the processing of juveniles in the United States. It is probable that in the near future we will see a challenge to the "life without parole" sentences of juveniles, using international law as a conceptual framework for the complaint.

# Future Trends and Directions

Greater attention to community-based intervention is essential if juvenile justice in the United States is to increase in effectiveness (Tyler, Zeidenberg, & Lotke 2006). The efforts of the founders of the juvenile court along with those who advocated for juvenile rights in the 1960s and 1970s need reexamination, including the goals of the Juvenile Justice and Delinquency Prevention Act, which strongly asserted that juveniles were to be primarily treated in the community. Moreover, that Act has emphasized priorities to reduce overrepresentation of youth of color, achieve gender equity, and increase community-based intervention. Edelman's presentation of the four circles for intervention in a comprehensive approach to youth policy comes the closest to recognition of the earlier priorities—reduction of poverty, universalistic approaches to youth development, education and after-school programming, and parsimony in punitive intervention (Edelman, 2002). He argues for approaches that "do no harm" as a minimum requirement.

Public opinion surveys report that a majority of the public (91%) believe that rehabilitative services and treatment for incarcerated youth can help prevent future crimes (Krisberg & Marchionna 2007). The public also think that spending on rehabilitative services will save tax dollars in the long run. These attitudes suggest that in the future we may see a return to the goals of the original juvenile court, as Mears, Hay, Gertz, and Mancini (2007) suggest. The character of the justice system is shaped by the attitudes and behavior of local communities. The newly developing programs of restorative justice, community service, and conflict resolution may provide the mechanisms for restoring community values regarding children and youth.

# References

Altschuler, D., Armstrong, T., & MacKenzie, D. (1999). Reintegration, supervised release and intensive aftercare. Washington, DC: U.S. Department of Justice, Office of Justice Programs, OJJDP Juvenile Justice Bulletin. Find this resource:

Amnesty International. (1998). Betraying the young: Human rights violations against children in the U.S. justice system. New York: Amnesty International. Find this resource:

Arnsten, A., & Shansky, R. (2004). Adolescence: Vulnerable period for stress-induced prefrontal cortical function. Annals of the New York Academy of Sciences, 1021 (Adolescent brain development: Vulnerabilities and opportunities) 143–147.Find this resource:

Barton, W. (2006). Incorporating the strengths perspective into intensive juvenile aftercare. *Western Criminology Review,* 7(2) 48–61.Find this resource:

Beckett, K., & Western, B. (2000). The institutional sources of incarceration: Deviance, regulation and the transformation of state policy. Paper presented at the American Criminology Society Annual Meeting, Toronto, Ontario, Canada. Find this resource:

Bishop, D. (2000). Juvenile offenders in the adult criminal justice system. In M. Tonry (Ed.), Crime and Justice: A Review of Research. Chicago: University of Chicago Press. Find this resource:

Bishop, D., & Frazier, C. (2000). Consequences of Transfer. In J. Fagan & F. Zimring (Eds.), The changing borders of juvenile justice. (pp. 227–276). Chicago: University of Chicago Press.Find this resource:

Bortner, M., Zatz, M., & Hawkins, D. (2000). Race and transfer: Empirical research and social context. In J. Fagan & F. Zimring (Eds.), The changing borders of juvenile justice (pp. 277–320). Chicago: University of Chicago Press. Find this resource:

Bridges, G. S., & Steen, S. (1998). Racial disparities in official assessment of juvenile offenders; attributional stereotypes as mediating mechanisms. *American Sociological Review,* 63(4), 554–570.Find this resource:

Coalition for Juvenile Justice. (2000). Serving the mental health needs of young offenders. Washington, DC: Author. Find this resource:

Edelman, P. (2002). American government and the politics of youth. In M. Rosenheim (Eds.), A century of juvenile justice(pp. 310–339). Chicago: University of Chicago Press. Find this resource:

Fagan, J. (1996). The comparative advantage of juvenile versus criminal court sanction among adolescent felony offenders. *Law and Society,* 18(1), 77–114.Find this resource:

Feld, B. (Ed.). (1999). Bad kids: Race and the transformation of the juvenile court. New York: Oxford University Press. Find this resource:

Fowler, P., & Toro, P. (2006). Youth aging out of foster care in southeast michigan. Detroit, MI: Dept. of Psychology, Wayne State University. Find this resource:

Garland, D. (2001). The culture of control. Chicago: University of Chicago Press. Find this resource:

Greenwood, P. (2006). Changing lives: Delinquency prevention as crime-control policy. Chicago: University of Chicago Press.Find this resource:

Griffin, P. (2005). Juvenile court-controlled reentry: Three practice models. Special Project Bulletin. Pittsburgh, PA: Office of Juvenile Justice and Delinquency Prevention, National Center for Juvenile Justice. Find this resource:

Grisso, T. (2004). Double jeopardy: Adolescent offenders with mental disorders. Chicago: University of Chicago Press. Find this resource:

Harrison, P., & Beck, A. (2006). Prisoners in 2005. Washington, DC: U.S. Dept. of Justice, Bureau of Justice Statistics. NCJ 215092.Find this resource:

Human Rights Watch. (2005). The rest of their lives: Life without parole for child offenders in the U.S. New York: Human Rights Watch & Amnesty International. Find this resource:

Jonson-Reid, M., & Barth, R. (2000). From treatment report to juvenile incarceration. The role of child welfare services. *Children and Youth Services Review*, 22(7), 493–516. Find this resource:

Kaufman, J., & Widom, C. (1999). Childhood victimization, running away and delinquency. *Journal of research in crime and delinquency*, 36(4), 347–370.Find this resource:

Kelly, K. (2002). Abuse/neglect and delinquency: Dually involved minors in the juvenile court. Paper presented at the American Society of Criminology Annual Meeting, Chicago. Find this resource:

Kempf-Leonard, K., & Sontheimer, H. (1995). The role of race in juvenile justice in Pennsylvania. In C. E. Pope & W. H. Feyerherm (Eds.), Minorities in juvenile justice (pp. 98–128). Thousand Oaks, CA. Find this resource:

Krisberg, B., & Marchionna, S. (2007, February). Attitudes of US voters toward youth crime and the justice system. Focus. San Francisco: National Council on Crime and Delinquency. Find this resource:

Lerman, P. (2000). Twentieth century developments in America's institutional system for youth in trouble. In M. Rosenheim (Ed.), A Century of Juvenile Justice (pp. 74–110). Chicago: University of Chicago Press. Find this resource:

Lipsey, M., & Wilson, D. (1998). Effective intervention for serious delinquency in adolescence and early adulthood. In R. Loeber & D. Farrington (Eds.), Serious and violent juvenile offenders. Thousand Oaks, CA: Sage. Find this resource:

McNeece, C. A., & Jackson, S. (2004). Juvenile justice policy: Current trends and 21st century issues. In A. Roberts (Ed.), Juvenile Justice Sourcebook (pp. 41–68). New York: Oxford University Press. Find this resource:

Mears, D., Hay, C., Gertz, M., & Mancini, C. (2007). Public opinion and the foundation of the juvenile court. *Criminology*, 45(1), 223–258. Find this resource:

Michalic, S., Fagan, A., Irwin, K., Ballard, D., & Elliot, D. (2002). Blueprints for violence prevention replications: Factors for Implementation Success. Boulder, CO: Center for the Study and Prevention of Violence, Institute of Behavioral Science, University of Colorado. Find this resource:

Nunn, K. (2002). The child as other: Race and differential treatment in the juvenile justice system. *DePaul Law Review*, 51 (Spring), 134–146. Find this resource:

Osgood, D. W., Foster, M., Flanagan, C., & Ruth, G. (2005). On your own without a net: The transition to adulthood for vulnerable populations. Chicago: University of Chicago Press. Find this resource:

Roberts, A. R. (2004). Juvenile justice sourcebook. New York: Oxford University Press. Find this resource:

Rosenheim, M. (2002). The modern American juvenile court. In M. Rosenheim, F. Zimring, D. Tanenhaus, & B. Dohrn (Eds.), A century of juvenile justice (pp. 341–360). Chicago: University of Chicago Press. Find this resource:

Sampson, R., Morenoff, J., & Raudenbush, S. (2005). Social anatomy of racial and ethnic disparities in violence, *American Journal of Public Health*, 95(2), 224–232. Find this resource:

Sarri, R., & Shook, J. (2005). Human rights and juvenile justice in the United States: Challenges and opportunities. In M. Ensalaco & L. Majka (Eds.), Children's human rights (pp. 197–228). New York: Rowman and Littlefield. Find this resource:

Sarri, R., Shook, J., & Ward, G. (2001). Decision making in juvenile justice: A comparative study of four states. Ann Arbor: Institute for Social Research, University of Michigan. Find this resource:

Scott, E., & Grisso, T. (1997). The evolutions of the adolescence: A developmental perspective on juvenile justice. *Journal of Criminal Law and Criminology*, 88, 137–138. Find this resource:

Setterstein, R., Furstenberg, F., & Rumbaut, R. (2005). On the frontier of young adulthood: Theory, research and public policy. Chicago: University of Chicago Press. Find this resource:

Sickmund, M., Snyder, H., & Poe-Yamagata (2000). Juvenile Transfers to Criminal court in the 1990's: Lessons Learned from Four States. Washington, DC: U.S. Department of Justice Office of Juvenile Justice and Delinquency Prevention. Find this resource:

Smith, C., & Thornberry, T. P. (1995). The relationship between childhood maltreatment and adolescent involvement in delinquency. *Criminology*, 33(3), 451–481. Find this resource:

Snyder, H. N. (2006). Juvenile Arrests, 2004. Washington, DC: OJJDP, Office of Justice Programs, U.S. Department of Justice. Find this resource:

Snyder, H. N., & Sickmund, M. (2006). Juvenile offenders and victims: 2006 national report. Washington, DC: OJJDP, Office of Justice Programs, U.S. Deptartment of Justice. Find this resource:

Spear, L. (2000). The adolescent brain and age-related behavioral manifestations. *Neuroscience Biobehavior*, 24, 417–463. Find this resource:

Spencer, M. B., & Jones-Walker, C. (2004). Interventions and services offered to former juvenile offenders reentering their communities: An analysis of program effectiveness. *Youth Violence and Juvenile Justice*, 2(1), 88–89. Find this resource:

Stahl, A., Puzzanchera, C., Sladky, A., Finnegan, T., Tierney, N., & Snyder, H. (2005). Juvenile court statistics 2001–2002. Pittsburgh, PA: National Center for Juvenile Justice. Find this resource:

Tanenhaus, D. (2002). The evolution of the juvenile court in the early twentieth century. In M. Rosenheim, F. Zimring, D. Tanenhaus, & B. Dohrn (Eds.), A century of juvenile justice (pp. 42–74). Chicago: University of Chicago Press. Find this resource:

Torbet, P., & Szymanski, L. (1998). State legislative responses to violent juvenile crime: 1996–1997 update. Washington, DC: OJJDP, Office of Justice Programs, U.S. Department of Justice. Find this resource:

Tyler, J., Zeidenberg, J., & Lotke, E. (2006). Cost effective youth corrections: The fiscal architecture of rational juvenile justice systems. Washington, DC: Justice Policy Institute. Find this resource:

U.S. Surgeon General (2001). Delinquency prevention programs that do not work. Washington, DC: U.S. Department of Health and Human Services. Find this resource:

Zimring, F. E. (2002). The common thread: Diversion in the jurisprudence of juvenile courts. In M. Rosenheim, F. Zimring, D. Tanenhaus, & B. Dohrn (Eds.), A century of juvenile justice (pp. 142–158). Chicago: University of Chicago Press. Find this resource:

Zimring, F. E. (2004). An American travesty. Chicago: University of Chicago Press. Find this resource:

## Further Reading

Andrews, D., Zinger, I., Hoge, R., & Bonta, J. (1990). Does correctional treatment work? A clinically relevant and psychologically informed meta-analysis. *Criminology*, 28, 369–404. Find this resource:

Pope, C., & Feyerherm, W. H. (1995). Minorities in juvenile justice. Thousand Oaks, CA: Sage. Find this resource:

# Corrections

# Prison

## PETER B. WOOD

## 18

In 21st-century America, imprisonment has become a $60+ billion per year industry, and will continue to increase in scope in the coming decades. The "prison industrial complex" includes not only those agencies directly involved in delivering punishment (courts, corrections, parole and probation agencies, etc.), but also a widening array of vested interests that depend for their political and economic well-being on an ever-increasing supply of inmates. This new constellation of interests includes financial institutions that bankroll and finance construction and management of correctional institutions; political action committees that lobby for new prisons; politicians who run on law-and-order platforms that emphasize punishment for criminal offenders; local development authorities that compete for prisons, believing they will be economic development catalysts for their communities; the many for-profit firms engaged in prison privatization; architectural and construction firms that specialize in large institutions; and a broad range of service providers that seek to secure long-term contracts to provide telecommunications, transport, correctional technologies, food and beverage, clothing, computers, and personal hygiene products to the 2.4 million inmates that currently reside in American prisons and jails.

Beyond the tremendous recent growth in the number of inmates and facilities associated with imprisonment, several developments unique to this new era of punishment deserve notice. But before they are introduced, it is instructive to provide some information about how the scope of imprisonment has changed in the last 30 years.

# The Transition From 20th- to 21st-Century Imprisonment

For several decades prior to the 1970s, what was most notable was the remarkable stability of the incarceration rate, averaging about 110 per 100,000 (excluding jail populations). While there were minor fluctuations in this period, the rate remained very stable, which led some criminologists to hypothesize a "theory of the stability of punishment," suggesting that a given society develops a certain culture regarding the level of punishment with which it is comfortable, and then, consciously or not, adjusts its policies and practices to meet this desired outcome. In 1972, federal and state prisons held 196,000 inmates for a prison incarceration rate of 93 per 100,000. In addition, about 130,000 inmates were held in jails, resulting in about 1 out of every 625 adults serving time in jails or prisons.

At the time, this level of imprisonment was viewed as egregiously high among those supporting a moratorium on prison construction, and in 1972, the National Council on Crime and Delinquency passed a policy statement calling for a halt to prison construction in the United States. In 1973, the National Advisory Commission on Criminal Justice Standards and Goals recommended that "no new institutions for adults should be built and existing institutions for juveniles should be closed," and concluded that "the prison, the reformatory, and the jail have achieved only a shocking record of failure. There is overwhelming evidence that these institutions create crime rather than prevent it" (National Advisory Commission on Criminal Justice Standards and Goals, 1973, p. 1).

Despite these sentiments, a prison expansion unprecedented in human history was about to take place. No one would have predicted that a large-scale imprisonment binge would characterize the next three decades. Many scholars point to the 1974 "Martinson report" (known for finding that "nothing works" to rehabilitate criminals) as signaling the death knell of the rehabilitation ideal in the United States, and since the late 1970s policy and public opinion has shifted toward more certain and severe punishment characterized by longer prison terms for an ever-increasing number of offense types.

The imprisonment binge over the past 30 years has resulted in a 700% increase in the U.S. incarceration rate to 762 per 100,000 and approximately 2.3 million in prisons (1.5 million) and jails (800,000) in 2007 (The Sentencing Project). With 1 out of every 100 adults incarcerated, the United States boasts the world's highest incarceration rate (well ahead of the Russian rate of 635 per 100,000) and accounts for about 25% of the entire world's imprisoned population. At present, this trend shows no sign of reversing. In addition, nearly 800,000 prisoners per year are now being released from prisons and jails into communities across the United States—the majority of whom will be readmitted within 3 years. The staggering growth in imprisonment in the United States and its scope compared to the past has generated several unique situations and circumstances not previously seen or anticipated. These include but are not limited to prison hosting, coercive mobility and its effects, issues associated with prisoner reentry, a host of "invisible punishments" and their consequences, and the impact of mass imprisonment on minority groups—particularly African Americans.

# Prison Hosting in the 21st Century

In the past, prisons have been viewed as undesirable, and communities have traditionally lobbied against the placement of correctional facilities in their midst. Such institutions were regularly a focus of the NIMBY (Not In My Back Yard) and LULU (Locally Unwanted Land Uses) literatures, along with community mental health centers, mental institutions, free health and methadone clinics, homeless shelters, and other agencies or institutions that residents viewed with concern and even fear.

Such concerns have faded as communities now lobby fiercely for the opportunity to host prisons. Particularly for counties and communities that have fallen on hard economic times, a new prison offers the prospect of a new industry, new jobs, and a potential economic catalyst that will spark community growth and development. Most new prisons in the past 20 years have been built in rural communities characterized by high unemployment and low wages, as local development agencies and authorities are lobbied by correctional firms and interests with the promise of higher wages, job opportunities, and so-called "multiplier effects" that are presumed to enhance quality of life for local residents (Wood & Dunaway, 2003).

Over 1,000 new correctional facilities were built in the United States in the last two decades of the 20th century—most in poor rural communities. Between 1980 and 2003, over 350 rural counties built prisons, and some counties boasted several. Nearly 250 prisons opened in 212 of the nation's 2,290 rural counties in the 10-year period between 1991 and 2001 alone (Beale, 2001). In short, one (or more) prison(s) opened in approximately 10% of all rural counties in the United States in just those 10 years. Currently, nearly 60% of prisoners residing in prisons live in facilities built since 1980 in rural areas, and the average of 25 new rural prisons opening each year in the 1990s (in 1998, a total of 38 new rural prisons opened, the peak year for new rural prisons) is a significant departure from a yearly mean of 16 in the 1980s and 4 in the 1970s.

Correctional facilities are particularly attractive to local legislators and development authorities who seek to "bring home the bacon" to their constituents and hopefully promote economic development in their communities. In addition to the hope that jobs will be created during construction as well as service and supply jobs once the facility is in operation, counties typically charge the state for each inmate/day that a state inmate is housed at the county-level facility. Further, rural counties use minimum-security inmates for municipal and public works. For many rural counties, the majority of municipal and public work is conducted by state inmate road crews. The expense of local municipal services (trash and debris removal, construction work, road maintenance, etc.) is significant, and can be offset by requiring that inmates perform these services as part of their sentence—at no cost to the county. Thus, counties anticipate several payoffs; a new facility may serve as an economic catalyst, counties charge the state to house inmates, and counties use inmates to perform municipal services. In addition to publicly funded facilities, private prisons are increasingly likely to be located in economically distressed rural areas. Prison expansion has spawned a new and powerful coalition of vested interests with stakes in keeping prisons full and building more of them. The result has been a financial and political bazaar with prisoners as the prize.

Any new prison is likely to remain operating in place for at least 50 years, which appeals to communities as a secure source of employment. But there is little evidence that prison hosting stimulates economic development at the local level (Herival & Wright, 2007). Several national and regional studies have demonstrated that rural counties that host prisons typically show no positive benefits in per capita income or reduced unemployment compared to nonprison areas. Why is this the case?

While prisons create jobs, they don't usually go to people in those communities, who don't have the skills or civil service rating to become a correctional officer. And in rural communities, people are used to commuting long distances to work, so guards at nearby prisons may choose to transfer to the new ones. Also, aggressive pursuit of new prisons can create an imbalance in a county's economic development strategy. Energies devoted to prison lobbying can detract from other pursuits that might create more jobs. In addition, there is a stigma attached to becoming viewed as a prison town. How many people think of a family trip to Attica as a summer vacation option?

The prison-building binge may have slowed in recent years, but given the projected increases in national prison populations, other states may soon follow the lead of California, which recently established a plan to add another 53,000 prison, jail, and juvenile detention beds for an estimated cost of $7.9 billion. Though current economic woes have caused federal and state governments to reduce their investments in punishment, the expected future increase in the number of inmates, correctional institutions, and costs associated with the decades-long expansion has enough momentum to carry well into the mid-21st century.

## Coercive Mobility in the 21st Century

The aim of get-tough sentencing policies was to reduce crime and improve community life, but neither policymakers nor the public anticipated how putting so many people in prison would damage the communities from which they were removed. While mass imprisonment has indeed incapacitated many who would otherwise have an overall negative effect on community life, it has also removed thousands of people who had a net positive effect on the economy, families, and the community as a whole. Many communities now face economic hardship, family disruption, and more crime due to high levels of incarceration.

A growing literature has begun to document the effects on community life of America's 30-year incarceration binge, but only a few studies have analyzed the complex relationship between incarceration and crime. Most scholarship that examines the incarceration-crime relationship has applied a social disorganization framework. In their seminal Chicago Area Project, Shaw and McKay (1942) found that the highest crime rates were in neighborhoods marked by social disorganization: dilapidated housing and infrastructure; unemployment; poverty; and most important, high residential mobility—people moving in and out of the neighborhood at a high rate. Much subsequent research confirms that crime is disproportionately concentrated in these types of neighborhoods. Because of conditions in these neighborhoods, those who "make it" move out, eroding a community's ability to maintain primary institutions like schools, churches, and neighborhood associations. Social disorganization theorists argue that high residential mobility limits the formation of strong social networks essential in controlling crime, undermining the stability necessary to establish the elements of social capital (i.e., trust, empowerment, norms, and reciprocity) that serve as the backbone of effective mechanisms of informal social control.

Coercive mobility (incarceration and prisoner reentry) is concentrated in poor, urban, and predominantly minority neighborhoods and is an important source of residential mobility that leads to social disorganization and crime. But unlike voluntary mobility, coercive mobility has profound negative effects on other aspects of social life such as labor market participation, family functioning, and political participation. While not all coercive mobility results in social disorganization, at some level (a "tipping point") the benefit of removing those disruptive to the community (criminals) is outweighed by the costs of removing parents, workers, and family members who provide a net positive effect on social capital and informal social control. When the tipping point is reached, too much incarceration can weaken community economies, family relationships, and overall social capital and lead to higher crime rates.

Clear, Rose, Waring, and Scully (2003) collected community-level data regarding prison admission rates, prison release rates, and crime rates for several neighborhoods in Tallahassee, Florida, and Renauer, Cunningham, Feyerherm, O'Connor, and Bellatty (2006) collected similar data on 95 communities in the Portland, Oregon, area. Both research efforts found coercive mobility concentrated in poor communities with large minority populations, and communities with extremely high coercive mobility had higher subsequent crime rates even when controlling for other indicators of social disorganization. As expected, the relationship between coercive mobility and crime was curvilinear—incarceration reduced crime at moderate levels, but began to increase crime rates when they reached a tipping point of about 1.7 per 100 people in Tallahassee and about 2.75 per 100 in Portland.

High levels of incarceration may not lead to less crime because communities with the highest levels of incarceration (poor, predominantly minority ones) are actually weakened by the very thing that is supposed to make them safer. Research described above supports the idea that, at the community level, low and moderate levels of incarceration can reduce crime, but high levels of incarceration can increase it by reducing social and neighborhood capital.

## Coercive Mobility and Counting Prisoners

In 21st-century America, imprisonment typically moves people out of large urban centers and into rural communities. This has major implications for electoral apportionment and financial distributions. The census general rule is to count people in their usual residence, "the place where they live and sleep most of the time." The usual residence need not be the same as a person's legal or voting residence, and a person need not be there at the time of the literal census. The person can take a vacation and still count at home, or even work overseas and still count at home.

The Census Bureau counts prisoners as residents of the town that contains the prison in which they are housed. This practice reduces the population of communities where most prisoners originate (usually urban, low-income, minority communities) and swells the population of rural communities that host prisons. When prisoners are counted as residents of the prison town, it leads to misleading portrayals of which counties are growing or declining. Urban and black communities are the losers in the census count, since congressional apportionment of services, grants, funds, poverty relief, welfare, and so forth are based on census figures.

An accurate count of the population is used to apportion voting representation, draw political boundaries, and allocate state and federal funds among local and state governments. Mass incarceration distorts this fundamental tool of representative democracy. In the 1990s, 30% of new residents in upstate New York were prisoners. About 200 counties in the United States have more than 5% of the population in prison. Many have more than 20% of their population in prison. (In at least 21 Texas counties, inmates account for over 20% of the local population.) But when released, prisoners usually return to the community they call home. Whatever benefits accrue to a jurisdiction by virtue of its population, urban communities with high incarceration rates are losing. Conversely, rural counties with prisons are getting more than their fair share.

The official constitutional purpose of the census is political apportionment. About 12% of all African American men live in prison. Most of them are apportioned to districts that do not reflect the interests of their home communities or their personal political concerns. Significant densities of prisoners in state legislative districts are important because most criminal justice policy is made at the state level. Each free resident of a rural district with prisons gets a larger voice in the state capital than free residents in urban districts that have high numbers of residents in prisons. Prisons inflate the political clout of every real rural constituent. And at the state level, counting urban residents as rural residents dilutes urban voting strength and increases the weight of a vote in rural districts.

Larger places (those with larger populations) receive a correspondingly larger share of government resources. The primary measure of size for determining resource distribution is the official census count. The coercive mobility of offenders creates a consistent distortion in funding formulas such that rural counties come out ahead of urban counties that send them prisoners. For example, the U.S. Department of Agriculture (USDA) distributes some $60–70 million annually to poor Appalachian communities via the Appalachian Regional Commission, and population is a distribution factor—so rural communities with prisons have an advantage over those without prisons. The USDA does not intend to reward prison construction, but that is the result.

It is estimated that the total cost of counting prisoners in their prison communities rather than their home communities runs between $50 and $250 per person, and averages about $100 or more per prisoner for the local community where they are housed. When a jurisdiction plans to open a new 1,000-bed prison, it can generate at least $100,000 in new "unearned" revenues that accrue simply from counting the prisoners. That $100,000 doesn't sound like much, but it can mean a new fire truck, a renovation for a youth center, or a computer upgrade for a municipality. In sparsely populated areas, large prisons in small towns can result in significant distortions of the local population. A new 500-bed prison can yield $50,000 in new revenue. The most dramatic impact can be seen in towns like Florence, Arizona, with a free population of about 5,000 and another 12,000 in at least three prisons. State and federal funds specifically linked to the prison population are estimated at $4 million annually. This has tempted other towns to follow the path toward prison hosting.

Another effect of coercive mobility and counting prisoners where they are held is on the calculation of per capita income, which is figured by dividing the total community income by the total population. When prisoners account for a substantial proportion of the population, the apparently low per capita income makes that community more competitive for U.S. Housing and Urban Development (HUD) grants aimed at low-income areas. The appearance of greater need results in those communities getting more than their fair share. For example, in Virginia, distribution of K–12 education aid uses a formula based on county population. Several years ago, according to the Census Bureau, Rural Sussex County, which has a population that is 19% inmates, received $115,000 extra as a result of the imprisoned population. Henrico County (Richmond) loses roughly $200,000 as a result of the "exported" prisoner population. And because Latinos and blacks are imprisoned at 4–8 times the rate of whites, where incarcerated people are counted has significant implications for how black and Latino populations are reflected in the census.

Prison towns gain political clout through enhanced population, while the urban areas from which they come are further deprived through the loss of political influence and resources. When prison communities are credited with large, externally sourced populations of prisoners—who are not local residents—it turns the "one person, one vote" principle on its head. Prison towns do not share a "community of interest" with urban prisoners or their loved ones or neighborhoods. This phenomenon is unique to the new landscape of 21st-century corrections.

# Prisoner Reentry in the 21st Century

Over the past 15 to 20 years, a significant body of scholarship has addressed the issue of prisoner reentry into society, a focus that evolved due to the rapidly increasing number of prisoners being released—now nearly 800,000 per year—as well as the high rate of recidivism. (About two thirds of prisoners are readmitted to prison within 3 years of release.) This issue has become a major concern among those who study issues associated with reentry, deterrence, rehabilitation, and the possible criminogenic effects of imprisonment. Some scholars are convinced that the return of so many offenders—many who are committed to a criminal lifestyle—has a significant independent effect on crime rates.

In 2000, researchers at the Urban Institute launched an ongoing inquiry into prisoner reentry research to better understand the pathways to successful reintegration; the social and fiscal costs of current policies; and the impacts of incarceration and reentry on individuals, families, and communities. Their findings focus on several key dimensions of reentry.

## Housing and Reentry

Perhaps the most immediate challenge facing returning prisoners is to secure housing. Many plan to stay with families, but those who don't face limited options. The process is complicated by scarcity of affordable and available housing, legal barriers and regulations, prejudices that restrict housing options, and strict eligibility requirements for federally subsidized housing. Research shows that those without stable housing are more likely to return to prison, and the majority of released prisoners themselves believe that having stable housing is important for successful reentry.

The majority of returning prisoners live with family members or intimate partners after release. Three months after release, 60% to 85% of returning prisoners live with families or partners. Many return home to living arrangements that are only temporary, and 6 to 8 months after release about one third had lived at more than one address. More than half of returning prisoners in Illinois thought they would not be staying in their current neighborhood for long, and in Maryland over half expected to be moving within weeks or months (Lynch & Sabol, 2001). Those who do not stay with family face limited options—many of which are unavailable to formerly incarcerated people. The shortage of affordable and available housing is a serious problem for returning prisoners.

## Employment and Reentry

Finding and maintaining employment is critical to successful prisoner reentry. Employment is associated with lower rates of reoffending, and higher wages are associated with lower rates of criminal activity. But prisoners face enormous challenges in finding and maintaining legitimate job opportunities—including low levels of education, limited work experience, and limited vocational skills. This is further compounded by the incarceration period during which they forfeit the opportunity to gain marketable work experience and sever professional connections and social contacts that might lead to employment on release. In addition, the general reluctance of employers to hire former prisoners serves as a barrier to job placement.

While prisoners believe that having a job would help them stay out of prison, on average only about 1 in 5 reported that they had a job lined up immediately after release. Moreover, despite the need for employment assistance, few prisoners receive employment-related training in prison. Even ex-cons who do find work do not necessarily have full-time or consistent work. At 4 to 8 months after release, 44% of Illinois respondents reported having worked for at least 1 week since their release. But less than one third were employed at the time of the interview, and only 24% of all respondents were employed full-time. At their first post-release interview, nearly 60% of ex-cons in Maryland were either unemployed or working less than 40 hours per week (Lynch & Sabol, 2001). Making things more difficult, transportation is a significant barrier to employment. More than one third of released prisoners had problems obtaining a car for work, and nearly one quarter reported problems accessing public transportation. It is widely accepted that finding and maintaining employment reduces recidivism, and an increase in levels of employment serves to reduce drug dealing, violent crime, and property crime.

## Health and Reentry

Released prisoners have an extremely high prevalence of mental disorders and chronic and infectious diseases—much higher than in the general population. Ex-cons face limited and insufficient access to community-based health care upon release. Further, incarceration disqualifies inmates from Medicaid eligibility, and restoring eligibility can take several months—interrupting access to prescription drugs and health care. Between 30 and 40% of released prisoners reported having a chronic physical or mental health condition—most commonly depression, asthma, and high blood pressure. In New Jersey, one third of those released in 2002 had at least one chronic or communicable medical condition. Many more released offenders report being diagnosed with a medical condition compared to those who received medication or treatment for the condition while incarcerated. Only 12% report having taken medication regularly in prison. In Ohio, over half reported depression, but only 35% reported receiving treatment or medication. While 27% reported having asthma, less than 14% received treatment for it (Lynch & Sabol, 2001). Corrections agencies often lack discharge planning and preparation for health care needs upon release. Less than 10% of Illinois ex-cons received referrals to services in the community. Securing health care is a major concern for many released prisoners. At least 75% of those interviewed said they needed help getting health care after release. As might be expected, the vast majority of returning prisoners have no medical insurance—only 10% to 20% reported having private insurance.

## Substance Use and Reentry

Research shows that while 83% of state prisoners have a history of drug use, only about 15% of this group receives treatment in prison, and even fewer continue to receive appropriate treatment once released. The majority of those released have extensive substance use histories. In Maryland, in the 6 months before entering prison, over 40% of offenders reported daily heroin use, while nearly

60% of returning prisoners in Texas reported daily cocaine use. Prisoners identify drug use as the primary cause of their past and current problems, but few prisoners receive drug treatment while incarcerated. In New Jersey, though 81% of inmates had drug or alcohol problems, program capacities were limited to only 6% of the state prison population. In Texas, substance abuse program capacity can only serve 5% of the potential population in need (Lynch & Sabol, 2001).

Researchers agree that in-prison treatment is much more likely to effectively sustain a decline in substance use if it is tailored to an individual's need and level of risk, and if it is linked to drug treatment aftercare in the community. Those with substance use histories and who engage in substance use after release are very likely to reoffend.

## Families and Reentry

Well over half of U.S. prisoners are parents of minor children, and up to 75% of incarcerated women are mothers of minors. Nearly 3% of all minor children in the United States, and nearly 10% of children of color, have a parent in prison. When a parent is sent to prison, the family structure, financial responsibilities, emotional support systems, and living arrangements are all affected. Incarceration can drastically disrupt spousal relations, parent-child relations, and family networks. There are significant challenges to maintaining family contact while in prison, including visiting regulations, transportation costs to distant facilities, other financial barriers, and emotional strains. More than half of incarcerated parents report never having received a visit from their children.

Nearly 75% of returning prisoners in Illinois and Maryland felt that family support had been important in helping them to avoid prison after release, and strong family support before prison may also reduce likelihood of recidivism. Those who reported positive family relations were less likely to be reconvicted, while those who reported negative family relations were more likely to be reconvicted and reincarcerated. Those with closer family relations and strong family support were less likely to have used drugs since release. Most prisoners have contact with family and children, but it is usually through phone and mail. In Illinois, only 13% of returning prisoners had had in-person contact with family members or children; 29% had visits from spouses/partners.

Distance to the correctional facility is one of the greatest challenges to maintaining contact. Three quarters of family members surveyed said the distance to the facility was the main problem with visitation. For the two thirds who did not visit family in prison, the median estimated travel time to the prison was 4 hours longer than those who did visit. This issue of distance and visitation is exacerbated in the context of coercive mobility. The 500 Hawaiian prisoners housed in Mississippi are unlikely to receive any visitation during their prison stay, and neither are the 1,500 Californian prisoners due there. States routinely exchange hundreds and thousands of prisoners in order to minimize the cost of housing them in-state.

Close family relationships can improve employment outcomes for returning prisoners, and closer family and partner relations and stronger family support result in more employment after release—likely because many releasees are hired by family members. But it has become increasingly common to export and import prisoners across state lines in order to save money, and more difficult for prisoners to maintain family ties and support systems while incarcerated.

## Communities and Reentry

Released prisoners are returning in high concentrations to a small number of communities in urban areas—having a profound and disproportionate effect on community life, family networks, and social capital in these neighborhoods. These places are characterized by social and economic disadvantage, which compounds the problems associated with reentry. In addition, research shows that high rates of incarceration and reentry may destabilize these communities and result in higher crime rates.

A relatively large number of prisoners return to a small number of cities in each state. For example, recent data show that Chicago and Baltimore received more than half of all prisoners returning to Illinois and Maryland, respectively. Houston received one quarter of all prisoners returning to Texas. Two of New Jersey's 21 counties accounted for one third of all returning prisoners. Nearly 49% of prisoners returning to Massachusetts returned to just two counties. Five of Idaho's 44 counties accounted for three quarters of returning prisoners. Returning prisoners are often clustered in a few neighborhoods in these cities. For instance, 8% of Chicago communities accounted for over one third of all prisoners returning to Chicago; 7% of the zip codes in Wayne County, Michigan (8 of 115)—all of which are in Detroit—accounted for over 40% of all prisoners being released in that state.

High levels of social and economic disadvantage characterize communities to which prisoners return. These communities have above-average rates of unemployment, female-headed households, and families living below the federal poverty level. Former prisoners who relocate tend to move to neighborhoods similar to the ones they left, with similar disadvantages, and prisoners returning to neighborhoods that are unsafe and lacking in social capital are at greater risk of recidivism and reincarceration.

## Public Safety and Reentry

Over two thirds of released prisoners are arrested for a new crime within 3 years of release—many within the first year. Released prisoners make a substantial contribution to new crimes. Most returning prisoners have extensive criminal histories. Most returning prisoners (80%–90%) had at least one prior conviction, and at least two thirds have previously served time in prison. In Massachusetts, 99% of those released in 2002 had been previously incarcerated in a state or county facility. About 80% of those released from the Philadelphia prison system had been previously incarcerated there.

Many released prisoners are reconvicted or rearrested for new crimes—many within the first year of release. About one third are reconvicted or reincarcerated within 1 year. In Maryland, about one third had been rearrested for at least one new crime within 6 months of release, 10% had been reconvicted, and 16% had been returned to prison/jail for a new crime conviction or parole/probation violation. Releasees with substance use histories and who use substances after release are at high risk to recidivate.

## Community Supervision and Reentry

The vast majority of released prisoners (over 80%) are subject to a period of community supervision. There are now over 800,000 parolees in the United States, up from about 200,000 in 1980. And there are many more offenders under probation or some other community-based sanction—of the 8 million under correctional supervision, about 70% are in the community. Resources have not kept up with the increase. Most probation and parole officers average 70 or more cases—about twice the recommended number. Persons on community supervision account for nearly 40% of new prison admissions nationally. Parole and probation violations have increased significantly over the past 25 years, and the number of persons returning to prison for a violation increased 1,000% between 1980 and 2000. About 40% of prisoners in state prison/jail are serving time for a probation and parole violation. Probation and parole officers appear to have little effect on rearrest rates of released prisoners. Findings show that prisoners who are released under supervision fare no better than those without supervision—their rearrest and reconviction rates are not significantly different.

What does all this tell us? Prisoner reentry is fraught with problems, the numbers are increasing rapidly, and not enough resources are being put into the process—particularly given the increase in the number of returning prisoners. This is a growing and difficult problem that has no easy solution and that requires significant investment in time and energy to address.

# Invisible Punishments in the 21st Century

Entering the 21st century, a new set of dynamics has come into play that calls for an understanding of the ways in which the effects of prison on society are both quantitatively and qualitatively different from previous times. These effects have been conceptualized as collateral consequences of imprisonment and have been dubbed "invisible punishments" by scholars (see Mauer & Chesney-Lind, 2002, for an overview). They are invisible in that they are rarely acknowledged in the courtroom when they are imposed, and equally rarely assessed in public policy discussions. These themes, and their impact on individuals and communities, should be the subject of careful scrutiny by those who study prison dynamics in the 21st century. While prison has always affected the individuals who are imprisoned and their families, the scale of imprisonment now magnifies these effects and expands their scope. Further, the racial dynamics of imprisonment have become a central component of this social policy.

## Barriers to Reintegration Among Released Offenders

Once a prison term is completed, the transition back into the community is almost always difficult. Having limited connections with the world of work, for example, becomes even more problematic with the stigma of imprisonment attached to former offenders. In an economy increasingly characterized by a division between high skills/high technology and a low-skill service economy, few offenders have promising prospects for advancing up the job ladder—or even finding a spot at the bottom of it.

Over the past 30 years, policymakers have expanded the reach of punishments beyond sentencing enhancements, and have enacted a new generation of collateral sanctions that impose serious obstacles to a person's life chances long after a sentence has been completed. Many of these obstacles are related to the war on drugs, and include a seemingly endless series of restrictions placed on those convicted of a drug offense. Depending on the state, an 18-year-old with a first-time conviction for felony drug possession now may be barred from receiving welfare benefits for life, prohibited from living in public housing, denied student loans to attend college, permanently excluded from voting, and may be deported if not a U.S. citizen. Ironically, many of these sanctions pertain only to drug offenders, not those convicted of murder, rape, and other serious violent offenses.

## Impact on Families and Communities

A growing number of children have a parent in prison, and current estimates place this number at well over 1.5 million. But the racial dynamics of imprisonment produce a figure of between 7% and 10% or up to 1 in 10 for black children. Since this reflects a 1-day count, the proportion of black children who have experienced parental incarceration at some point in their childhood is considerably greater. Being the child of a criminal is not a status worth boasting about; shame and stigma are still the norm. One common consequence of this stigma is the severance of social ties to family and friends, which low-income families rely upon to cope with poverty and other hardships. The impact of parental incarceration will vary depending on which parent is imprisoned. Mothers in prison are far more likely to have been primary caretakers of children prior to imprisonment and were often single parents, and this dramatically impacts the children they leave behind.

In addition to the experience and stigma of parental incarceration, children in low-income minority communities now grow up with a strong likelihood of spending time in prison themselves. An estimated 1 in 3 black males born today can expect to go to prison. While they may not know these odds, their life experiences communicate this reality as they witness older brothers, cousins, parents, and neighbors cycling in and out of prison. Some contend that prison has become a "rite of passage" for young black men today and is almost welcomed as a badge of honor in certain communities. Prison is increasingly viewed as an inevitable part of the maturation process for many low-income minority children—in the same way that going to college is the norm in many middle- and upper-class communities. When there is little chance of traditional success (schools, college, jobs, marriage, etc.), the often-taught value of hard work leading to success may seem unrealistic to many children in these communities.

## Mass Imprisonment and Voter Disenfranchisement

When the nation was founded in the late 1700s, the vast majority of people in the United States were ineligible to participate in democratic life. Excluded were women, blacks, Native Americans, and other minorities, as well as illiterates, poor people, and felons. Only white males were "citizens" with the right to vote. Over the course of 200 years, restrictions for all these categories have been lifted—save for those with felony convictions.

Today, some 5 million Americans are ineligible to vote as a result of a felony conviction in the 48 states and D.C. that employ disenfranchisement policies for varying degrees of felons and ex-felons. If there was any doubt about the effect of these laws, consider the 2000 presidential election in Florida. That election was decided by less than 1,000 votes in favor of George W. Bush, while an estimated 600,000 former offenders—people who had already completed their sentences—were ineligible to vote due to that state's restrictive policies. One wonders who most former inmates would have supported.

While an estimated 2% to 3% of the national population is disenfranchised, the rate for black men is 13%, and in some states is well over 20%. When such high numbers of men in urban communities can't vote, the voting power/efficacy of that whole community is reduced in relation to communities with low rates of incarceration. New evidence indicates that disenfranchisement effects go well beyond the legally disenfranchised population. Studies of voter turnout show that in the most restrictive states, voter turnout is lower, particularly among African Americans, and even among persons who themselves are not disenfranchised as a result of a felony conviction. Voting is a civic duty, and a process engaged in with families and communities. Family members talk about elections at home, drive to polls together, and see their neighbors there. When a substantial number of people In a community are legally unable to vote, it is likely to dampen enthusiasm and attention among others as well. Forty years after the Voting Rights Act was passed, mass imprisonment and disenfranchisement results in a greater proportion of African American and other minority communities losing the right to vote each year.

## Mass imprisonment and State Budgets

Regarding the impact of mass imprisonment on state economies, specifically higher education, a recent report by Grassroots Leadership shows how massive spending on Mississippi prisons has siphoned funds from classrooms and students, leaving higher education appropriations stagnant and African Americans shouldering the burden. The report documents a startling shift in Mississippi budget priorities. In 1992, the state spent most of the discretionary portion of its budget on higher education. By 2002, the majority of discretionary funds went to build and operate prisons. Between 1989 and 1999, Mississippi saw per capita state corrections appropriations rise by 115%, while per capita state higher education appropriations increased by less than 1%. Mississippi built 17 new prisons between 1997 and 2005, but not one new state college or university. And several more Mississippi prisons are under construction or consideration. There are now almost twice as many African American men in Mississippi prisons as in colleges and universities, and the state spends nearly twice as much to incarcerate an inmate as it takes to send someone to college. Moreover, due to new drug laws and a "truth-in-sentencing" bill passed in the mid-1990s, nearly 70% of those imprisoned in the state are nonviolent offenders. Mississippi is not unique in this situation—most states have followed this path and are facing serious budget shortages due to multiyear commitments to expand their correctional systems.

These and other dynamics of mass imprisonment make up what are called invisible punishments or collateral consequences. Changing the trends noted here are difficult for several reasons. First, it is very difficult to alter prevailing sentencing policies and practices, which can be legislated in a matter of hours but take years to undo. In a broader sense, the national commitment to mass imprisonment is deeply embedded in a punitive and individualistic approach to social policy. This has not always been the case in the United States, and is certainly not the style adopted in many other countries. Changing this political and social environment remains the real obstacle to a more effective and humane crime policy.

# Race and Imprisonment in the 21st Century

In the 50-plus years since the historic *Brown* v. *Board of Education* decision that ordered desegregation of public education, no American institution has changed more than the criminal justice system, and in ways that have profound effects on the African American community. Mass imprisonment has produced record numbers of Americans in prison and jail (now approaching 2.5 million) and has had a disproportionate effect on African Americans. There are now about 10 times as many African Americans in prison/jail as on the day of the *Brown* decision (98,000 in 1954; nearly 1,000,000 in 2007).

Today, 1 out of every 21 black men is incarcerated on any given day. For black men in their twenties, the figure is 1 in 8. Given current trends, 1 of every 3 (32%) black males born today can expect to go to prison in his lifetime (U.S. Bureau of Justice Statistics [BJS] Web site). More than half of black men in their early 30s who are high school dropouts have a prison record. With regard to black women, 1 of every 18 black females born today can expect to go to prison—6 times the rate for white women. Moreover, black women born today are 5 times more likely to go to prison in their lifetimes than black women born 30 years ago.

Factors contributing to the dramatic increase in the number of African Americans in prison/jail are complex, and involve dynamics both within and outside the criminal justice system. Incarceration rates are about 8 times higher for blacks overall than for whites, and high school dropouts are more than twice as likely to end up in prison than are high school graduates. Consequently, much of the growth in imprisonment has been concentrated among minority young men with little education. By the late 1990s, two thirds of all prison inmates were black or Hispanic, and about half of all minority inmates had less than 12 years of schooling.

Imprisonment has become so pervasive among young black men that it is now viewed as a common stage in the life course by some researchers (Pettit & Western, 2004). Among all men born between 1965 and 1969, an estimated 3% of whites and 20% of blacks had served time in prison by their early thirties. Among black men born, during this period, 30% of those without a college education and nearly 60% of high school dropouts went to prison by 1999. For black men in their mid-30s at the start of the 21st century, prison records were nearly twice as common as bachelor's degrees, and imprisonment was more than twice as common as military service. Imprisonment has become a common life event for black men that sharply distinguishes their transition to adulthood from that of white men.

Black/white inequality is obscured by using employment and wage figures that fail to include inmates. From a life course perspective, the earnings of ex-convicts diverge from the earnings of non-convicts as men get older. By their late 20s, non-convicts have usually settled into a stable path of earnings growth, while ex-convicts follow an unstable trajectory of irregular/transitory employment and low earnings. Research notes that white offenders tend to age out of crime earlier than do black offenders, suggesting that employment and wage earning deficits experienced by black ex-convicts may endure for a longer period of time than for white ex-convicts.

Changes in the criminal justice system over the past 25 years have been wide-ranging, affecting policing, sentencing, prison construction, post-release supervision, and a variety of other policy areas at the state and federal levels. The sheer magnitude of the commitment of public resources is comparable to that expended in the social welfare efforts of the 1960s and 1970s. Unlike anti-poverty policy, however, the punitive trend in criminal justice policy serves to conceal and deepen economic inequality between blacks and whites. Whereas it has often been considered how welfare, employment, and education policy affects inequality, it is now known that criminal justice policy over the past 25 years has impacted racial economic inequality in a significant way, to the point where inequality can be seen as a product of the expansion of mass imprisonment.

# Conclusion

Over the past 30 years, a complex set of social and political developments has produced a wave of building and filling prisons unprecedented in human history. Beginning with less than 200,000 in 1972, the number of inmates in U.S. prisons has increased to over 1.5 million today. Add to this the over 800,000 inmates in local and regional jails either awaiting trial or serving sentences, and a remarkable 2.4 million (and counting) Americans are behind bars as of 2008.

These figures take on more meaning in comparison with other nations. The United States locks up offenders at a rate 6 to 10 times that of other industrialized nations. The next-closest nation to ours in incarceration rates is Russia—which has been de-incarcerating for several years now. The nature and meaning of incarceration in the United States have changed in a variety of profound ways with far-reaching implications.

Among these is the institutionalization of a societal commitment to the use and expansion of a massive prison system. Nearly two thirds of prisons today have been built in the past 20 years. These prisons are expected to hold offenders for at least the next 50 years, guaranteeing a national commitment to a high rate of incarceration. The growth of the system has spawned a set of vested interests and lobbying forces that perpetuate a societal commitment to imprisonment. The nearly 1,000,000 prison and jail guards, administrators, service workers, and other personnel represent a potentially powerful political opposition to any scaling down of the system.

The idea of prisons as sources of economic growth appeals to many communities that have lost jobs in recent years. Communities that once organized against the location of prisons now beg state officials and private prison companies to construct new prisons in their backyards. But the scarce research available questions the promise of prisons as economic development catalysts. There is also a rapidly expanding prison privatization movement focused on the bottom line of profiting from imprisonment. Privatization has produced a new dynamic in mass imprisonment that encourages the production of more inmates—which means more money and more profits.

The near permanent status of mass imprisonment is evidenced despite expressed concerns that often focus on the problem of funding for an expanding prison system that diverts resources from other public spending. Vast expenditures on corrections systems are now considered the norm, and represent the largest growth area in most state budgets. Virtually every state has engaged in a significant if not massive prison construction program over the past 20 years, financed through general funds; bonds; and more recently, public-private venture arrangements, which put communities into further long-term debt.

The impact of incarceration on individuals can be understood to some degree, but the effect of mass imprisonment on African American communities is a phenomenon that has only recently been investigated. Marc Mauer (Mauer & Chesney-Lind, 2002) of The Sentencing Project has asked what it means to a community to know that 4 out of 10 boys growing up will spend time in prison; what it does to family and community to have such a substantial proportion of its young men enmeshed in the criminal justice system; what images and values are communicated to young people who see the prisoner as the most prominent or pervasive role model in the community; and what the effect is on a community's political influence when one quarter of black men cannot vote as a result of a felony conviction.

New prison cells are increasingly being used for drug and nonviolent offenders. About 3 of every 5 (61%) new inmates added to the system in the 1990s were incarcerated for a nonviolent drug or property offense. In the federal system, three quarters (74%) of the increase in the inmate population are attributed to drug offenses alone. Incarcerating ever-increasing numbers of nonviolent property and drug offenders is not the only option open to policymakers, nor is it the most cost-effective. A large proportion of these offenders would be appropriate candidates for diversion to community-based programs—if policy could be diverted away from imprisonment.

Direct consequences of the wars on drugs and crime include the imprisonment of literally millions of people, most of whom are guilty of relatively petty crimes; their lengthy and debilitating incarceration; and their ejection (reentry) back into society—ill-prepared and handicapped by their stigmatized social status. The direct financial cost of the imprisonment binge has been well publicized, and exceeds $60 billion per year. What has not been emphasized enough are the invisible or collateral damages of mass imprisonment, including the harm done to other social programs because so much money has been siphoned off into corrections, the diminution of civil rights of many kinds, the erosion of traditional values of fairness and tolerance, the damage done to families and communities, and the creation of new and powerful lobbying groups with vested interests in more imprisonment. Imprisonment in the 21st century has generated far-reaching consequences that touch virtually every aspect of life, for prisoners and non-prisoners alike, and will continue to do so into the foreseeable future.

# References and Further Readings

Beale, C. (2001, August). *Cellular rural development: New prisons in rural and small town areas in the 1990s.* Paper presented at the Annual Meeting of the Rural Sociological Society, Albuquerque, New Mexico.

Clear, T. R., Rose, D. R., Waring, E., & Scully, K. (2003). Coercive mobility and crime: A preliminary examination of concentrated incarceration and social disorganization. *Justice Quarterly, 20*(1), 33–64.

Herival, T., & Wright, P. (2007). *Prison profiteers: Who makes money from mass incarceration?* New York: The New Press.

Hooks, G., Mosher, C., Rotolo, T., & Lobao, L. (2004). The prison industry: Carceral expansion and employment in U.S. counties, 1969–1994. *Social Science Quarterly, 85,* 37–57.

Justice Policy Institute: http://www.justicepolicy.org

Lotke, E., & Wagner, P. (2004). Prisoners of the census: Electoral and financial consequences of counting prisoners where they go, not where they come from. *Pace Law Review, 24,* 587–607.

Lotke, E., & Ziedenberg, J. (2005, March). *Tipping point: Maryland's overuse of incarceration and the impact on public safety* [Policy brief], Washington, DC: Justice Policy Institute.

Lynch, J. P., & Sabol, W. J. (2001, September). *Prisoner reentry in perspective* (NCJ 191685). Washington, DC: Urban Institute.

Mauer, M., & Chesney-Lind, M. (Eds,). (2002). *Invisible punishment: The collateral consequences of mass imprisonment.* New York: The New Press.

National Advisory Commission on Criminal Justice Standards and Goals. (1973). *Corrections.* Washington, DC: U.S. Government Printing Office.

National Criminal Justice Reference Service: http://www.ncjrs.gov

Pettit, B., & Western, B. (2004). Mass imprisonment and the life course: Race and class inequality in U.S. incarceration. *American Sociological Review, 69,* 151–169.

Prison Policy Initiative: www.prisonpolicy.org

Renauer, B. C., Cunningham, W. S., Feyerherm, B., O'Connor, T., & Bellatty, P. (2006). Tipping the scales of justice: The effect of overincarceration on neighborhood violence. *Criminal Justice Policy Review, 17(3),* 362–379.

Rothfield, M. (2008, May 7). Foes sue over prison bond sale. *Los Angeles Times.* Retrieved April 1, 2008, from http://www.latimes.com

Seiter, R., & Kadela, K. (2003). Prisoner reentry: What works, what does not, and what is promising. *Crime & Delinquency, 49,* 360–388.

Sentencing Project, The: http://www.sentencingproject.org

Shaw, C., & McKay, H. (1942). *Juvenile delinquency and urban areas.* Chicago: University of Chicago Press.

Uggen, C., & Manza, J. (2002). Democratic contraction? Political consequences of felon disenfranchisement in the United States. *American Sociological Review, 67,* 777–803.

Uggen, C., Manza, J., & Thompson, M. (2006). Citizenship, democracy, and the civic reintegration of criminal offenders. *Annals of the American Academy of Political and Social Sciences, 605,* 281–310.

Urban Institute: http://www.urbaninstitute.org

U.S. Bureau of Justice Statistics (BJS): http://www.ojp.usdoj.gov/bjs

Western, B. (2002). The impact of incarceration on wage mobility and inequality. *American Sociological Review, 67,* 526–546.

Western, B., Kling, J., & Weiman, D. (2001). The labor market consequences of incarceration. *Crime & Delinquency, 47,* 410–427.

Wood, P., & Dunaway, R. G. (2003). Consequences of truth-in-sentencing: The Mississippi case. *Punishment & Society, 5,* 139–154.

# The Scale of Imprisonment in the United States

## TWENTIETH CENTURY PATTERNS AND TWENTY-FIRST CENTURY PROSPECTS*

FRANKLIN E. ZIMRING**

## Introduction

The prison has been far more important to criminal justice practice than to academic theory in the century examined by this Symposium. Imprisonment is the dominant severe criminal sanction worldwide and there is no evidence that its hegemony at the deep end of crime control will change. But the study of imprisonment has not been a major feature of criminal law theory at any time, while some aspects of prisons have commanded attention in the literature of criminology. So imprisonment has played a dominant role in American criminal justice but a minor role in the discourse about criminal law. The *Harvard Law Review*, for example, listed twenty-seven articles with "prison" or "imprisonment" in the title in one hundred years of publication beginning in 1910.

The interdisciplinary character of the *Journal of Criminal Law and Criminology* and its crime focus made it into the leading forum in law-related scholarship covering issues of prison operation and function. No fewer than 155 main articles

*I thank Ginger Jackson-Gleich and Stephen Rushin for research assistance, David Johnson for comments, and the participants in the January 29, 2010 Symposium for questions and commentary. Jeff Fagan introduced me to the statistical tests of the normality of distributions and performed the calculations reported in Table 19.1. The efforts reported […] of this essay were inspired by a conversation with Justin McCrary, who must therefore share responsibility for some of the resulting analysis.

**William G. Simon Professor of Law and Wolfen Distinguished Scholar, University of California, Berkeley School of Law.

were published with "prisons" or "imprisonment" in their titles in a century of publications, by far the largest concentration one would find in any scholarly journal closely linked to legal education.[1] And prisons played a prominent part in the scholarly portfolio of the *Journal* from the very beginning, with slightly more articles on prisons in the first half of its volumes than in the second. The range of prison-related topics covered from the beginning—including comparative and empirical work—was impressive.

But little of the first half-century of the *Journal* touched on the central issue in this analysis—what I shall call *the scale of imprisonment*. Zimring and Hawkins define the issue of scale as analysis of the appropriate "size of a society's prison enterprise in relation to other criminal sanctions and to the general population. How many prisoners? How many prisons? What criteria should govern decisions about how large a prison enterprise should be constructed and maintained?"[2]

Only one of the more than seventy articles with prison in its title that appeared in the *Journal* in its first half-century was principally concerned with rates of imprisonment: an article by Edwin Sutherland describing the decline in rates of imprisonment in England.[3] One important reason for the lack of scholarly attention to variation in the rate of imprisonment in the United States is that there was not a great deal of variation over time in the rate of imprisonment.

Indeed, the lack of dramatic variation in rates of imprisonment inspired Alfred Blumstein and Jacqueline Cohen to construct what they called "A Theory of the Stability of Punishment"[4] in the *Journal* in 1973, probably the most important and certainly the most ironically timed article on imprisonment in the *Journal's* first century. Blumstein and Cohen posit that levels of severe criminal

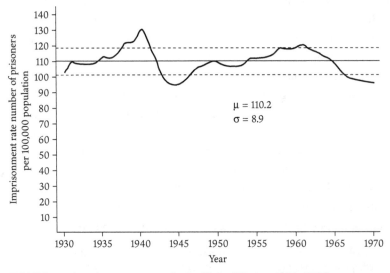

**FIGURE 19.1** Imprisonment rates in the United States, 1930–1970[5]

1    The *Journal of Criminal Law and Criminology* search was conducted by *Journal* staff while the Harvard search was conducted on January 22, 2010, by Ellen Gilmore, a reference librarian at the University of California, Berkeley Law Library.

2    Franklin E. Zimring & Gordon Hawkins, *The Scale of Imprisonment* xi (1991).

3    Edwin H. Sutherland, *The Decreasing Prison Population of England*, 24 J. Crim. L. & Criminology 880 (1934).

4    Alfred Blumstein & Jacqueline Cohen, *A Theory of the Stability of Punishment*, 64 J. Crim. L. & Criminology 198 (1973).

5    Blumstein & Cohen, *supra* note 4.

punishment trend toward stability over time and they offered as evidence of this phenomenon the rather stable rates of imprisonment in the national aggregate over the years 1930–1970. Their Figure 2 is reproduced from Blumstein and Cohen as my Figure 19.1. The interpretation of this data was straightforward:

> It can be seen from Figure 2 that over that period the imprisonment rate was reasonably constant, having an average value of 110.2 prisoners per 100,000 population and a standard deviation during that time ... of 8.9 prisoners per 100,000 population. ... The stability of the time series is especially noteworthy when it is considered that the population of the United States increased by over 50 percent in the same period.[6]

Twice more in the 1970s, Blumstein and his associates would produce data and analysis to augment their stability of punishment theory,[7] but then their entire theoretical structure was overtaken by events. From its low point in 1972, U.S. prison populations had begun a consistent and unprecedented climb. Figure 19.2, taken from U.S. Bureau of Justice Statistics data, shows an uninterrupted increase in aggregate imprisonment rates that lasted the full generation after 1972.

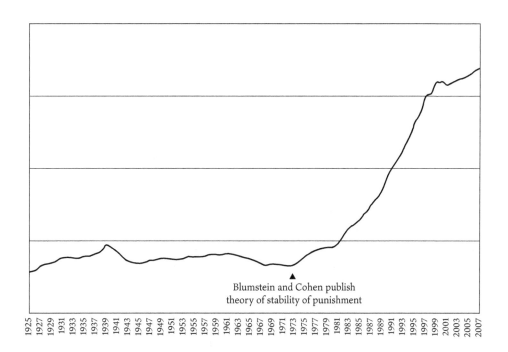

Blumstein and Cohen publish
theory of stability of punishment

**FIGURE 19.2** Imprisonment rates per 100,000 population, United States, 1925–2007[8]

---

6    *Id.* at 201.

7    Alfred Blumstein, Jacqueline Cohen & Daniel Nagin, *The Dynamics of a Homeostatic Punishment Process*, 67 J. Crim. L. & Criminology 317 (1977); Alfred Blumstein & Soumyo Moitra, *An Analysis of the Time Series of the Imprisonment Rate in the States of the United States: A Further Test of the Stability of Punishment Hypothesis.* 70 J. Crim. L. & Criminology 376 (1979).

8    Blumstein & Cohen, *supra* note 4.

The contrast between the four decades after 1930 and the three and a half decades after 1972 is stark. The highest annual imprisonment rate in the 1930–1970 period was 38% above the lowest (131.5 versus 95.5 per 100,000) and there was no clear trend over time. In the thirty years after 1972, the rate of imprisonment grew every year and the rate of imprisonment by 2007 was five times greater than at the beginning.

The first impact on scholarship of this unprecedented increase in the use of prisons in the United States was to end any serious discussion of "stability of punishment." That theory was produced by flat trends over time in the United States after 1925 and was destroyed by the imprisonment boom that followed 1972.

The second product of the sharp increase in American prison population was academic interest in what features of society and government might influence rates of imprisonment over time. Once the dynamic and non-homeostatic qualities of imprisonment rates were established by the history of imprisonment after 1975, the causes of variation in imprisonment over time and cross-sectionally became an important topic for empirical analysis. The same upward march in prison population that ended interest in stability of punishment generated curiosity about the scale of imprisonment as a variable in crime policy and governance.

There are two parallels between the "stability of punishment" exercises of the 1970s and the more recent efforts to comprehend and measure what determines the scale of imprisonment in the United States. The first important shared characteristic of these two lines of inquiry is that each theory was derived from and driven by empirical data. For all its Durkheimian analysis, the inspiration for Blumstein and Cohen's stability of punishment insight was the flat distribution of imprisonment rates over time in the United States, a pattern that invited speculation about its potential causes. In that sense, the stability pattern was a practice in search of a theory before any explanation was produced. The more recent work on the scale of imprisonment was also provoked by the changing trends that demanded explanation and analysis. All of the recent studies of imprisonment scale have been inspired by these sharp increases, so here again the data to be explained arrive prior to the theories to be tested.

The second parallel is an unjustified assumption of temporal normality. Despite the fact that theories of stability and then of variability were inspired by provocative empirical trends, the analysis of historical data testing these theories has assumed that the periods to be analyzed are normal and typical. In the earlier work, the observed stability was assumed to be representative of other periods as well, so that the generality of patterns observed could be expected. Again, in the statistical explanations of the period after 1972, the empirical analysis has been assuming that the prison trends of the thirty years after 1972 are representative of other periods and public moods so that the statistical relationship and magnitude of effects noted in this period will hold for other times and conditions.

This Article focuses on three aspects of the prison trends in the United States since 1975. First, I discuss the size and generality of the increase in prison population with special emphasis on the features of government that make the pattern of growth so surprising. Second, I identify and discuss two central empirical questions about the imprisonment boom after 1972. [In the section "Does Crime Matter"] explores the effects of the analysis in [the section "Two Fundamental Questions"] on the proper method of testing whether crime rates are important in predicting imprisonment. The final section of this Article asks whether and to what extent the volatility in the growth of prison populations might also signal that major drops in the scale of imprisonment might happen soon.

# The Magnitude of Prison Growth

The thirty-five years after 1972 produced a growth in rates of imprisonment that has never been recorded in the history of developed nations. Figure 19.3 compares the rate of imprisonment in 1972 with the rate in 2007.

The 502 per 100,000 rate of state and federal imprisonment is not only five times the rate of imprisonment in the base year of 1972 but also almost four times the highest level of imprisonment in the four decades prior to 1970. By the early 1980s, the U.S. prison population passed its previous high rate and continued a sharp increase without any pause for more than two additional decades. In the generation after 1970, the rate of imprisonment in the United States doubled (between 1972 and 1988) and then doubled *again*.

When this growth began in the 1970s, the rate of imprisonment in the United States was on the high end of western democracies but not what statisticians would call an "outlier" totally apart from the other nations in the G7.[9] But the rate of imprisonment achieved by 2007 in the United States was three times that of any fully developed nation at any point in the post World War II era. So the extent of growth experienced by the United States in the thirty-five years after 1970 would be remarkable for any nation in any era. But there are three aspects of the governmental and legal structure of the United States that make the uninterrupted upward march of prisoners nothing short of astonishing.

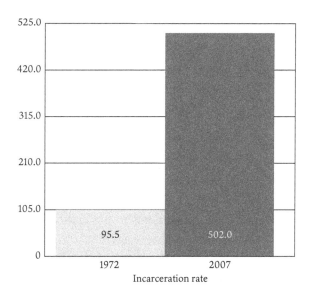

**FIGURE 19.3** Imprisonment in 1972 and 2007, U.S. Rates per 100,000
*Source*: Bureau of Census and Bureau of Justice Statistics

---

9    Zimring & Hawkins, *supra* note 2, at 150 tbl.6.6; *see also* Franklin E. Zimring & Gordon Hawkins, *Crime Is Not the Problem* 31 tbl.2.2 (1997).

The first distinct feature of U.S. government that should even out variations in prison population over time is the decentralized structure of criminal law and criminal punishment. The national government is responsible for less than 10% of the persons incarcerated in the United States, with the fifty states each responsible for determining definitions of crimes and schedules of punishment and typically administering and funding prison systems. This decentralized punishment policy means that the aggregate "rates of imprisonment" in Figure 19.1 and Figure 19.2 of this article are really an aggregate average from fifty-one different systems, each of which has responsibility and power to set autonomous policy for prisons. These multiple decision points should moderate the extreme values of individual states and produce modest aggregate changes over time. Except that the moderating influence of aggregating fifty-one different systems was not very substantial in the generation after 1970. While there was some variation in rates of growth from state to state, the overpowering trend was toward sustained high rates of growth. Zimring and Hawkins identify the 1980s as the period when the push toward and beyond historically high rates of imprisonment became clear:

> As of 1980 only eleven states reported rates of imprisonment higher than at any previous point in the century. But a cyclical hypothesis has been decisively disproved by prison population trends since 1980. Forty-six of the fifty states report rates of imprisonment between 1985 and 1987 which are the highest they have experienced in a century.[10]

The near unanimity of century-high imprisonment mentioned in the previous paragraph was noted in the mid-1980s, when the aggregate rate of imprisonment had only come near to completing its first doubling. By the early 1990s the journey of state governments into unprecedented high rates of imprisonment had become universal if not uniform. So decentralized power and multiple autonomous centers of policy power became the first structural feature of the American system that should have moderated the expansion of rates of imprisonment but didn't to any significant degree.

The second element of the U.S. system in the 1970s and 1980s that one would expect to moderate the growth of imprisonment was the absence of significant change in penal legislation during the first two decades of the great American prison expansion. There was no general trend toward either increasing the number of crimes or escalating either minimum or maximum terms of imprisonment during the period from 1970 to 1985. A few states shifted from indeterminate to determinant sentencing systems (including California and Illinois) in the 1970s, but there is no evidence that these structural changes had any significant impact on the growth of imprisonment during the period.[11]

The wide discretion in determining punishments in the prosecution and sentencing systems of the United States mean that substantial changes in aggregate punishment policy can take place without any substantial change in the legislation governing the levels of punishment available or the choice of punishments in individual cases. The first doubling of the U.S. prison population after 1972 is decisive evidence that the extraordinary latitude for exercise of discretion in American systems of criminal justice can produce very large changes in rates of imprisonment with no important changes in the legal framework of criminal punishment. Because there are so few restrictions on discretionary choices in individual cases, a substantial shift in the choices made by prosecutors and judges and police can produce very sharp shifts in policy. Certainly for the first fifteen years of the prison population expansion, this model of collective change in discretionary decisions is a much

---

10    Zimring & Hawkins, *supra* note 2, at 152.

11    1 *Research on Sentencing: The Search for Reform* 206 (Alfred Blumstein et al. eds., 1983).

better model for explaining increases that any pattern of significant legal change. The legal structures in place in the United States when it had a state prison population of 205,000 in 1972 were not greatly different from the legal structures that were responsible for 800,000 prisoners in 1991.

The third systemic element that might be expected to moderate the rate of prison growth in the United States is the relatively fixed number of prisons and space for prisoners in the United States. Prisons are capital goods with high fixed costs, long useful lives, and substantial lead times between authorization and completion. By the mid-1980s, over 90% of all the states in the United States were at the high point of the century for rates of imprisonment so that the relatively fixed resources in these places to house inmates were presumably close to their usual capacities. Under these circumstances, the crowding of existing prison facilities would be expected to restrain the rate at which still more prisoners were sent to penal facilities. The highly discretionary processes that produce commitments to prison should be sensitive to population pressure without delay. So the rate of prison population growth should have moderated after the first doubling of rates in the 1970s and 1980s as crowding pressures restrained prosecutors and judges from unlimited expansion policies, but this did not happen. Even with the population of prisoners swelling to unprecedented numbers in the 1990s, the expansion of incarceration continued, new facilities were constructed, and old prisons were retrofitted to accommodate larger populations. The single cell became the double cell and, not infrequently, the triple cell. So inertial forces which would ordinarily be expected to substantially slow the expansion of prison populations were overwhelmed by whatever systemic and political forces were driving prison expansion.

Perhaps the continual expansion of prisons tells us that capacity restraints and decentralized punishment power were overestimated as moderating forces on prison growth. But the unrestrained momentum of prison population growth after 1970 shows also that the political forces which drove the penal expansion were substantial and had substantial impact. This may be of some importance in predicting the size and speed of any future downward pressure on imprisonment.

# Two Fundamental Questions

The thirty-five annual entries in the national portrait of rates of imprisonment after 1972 in Figure 19.2 give the impression of a single national pattern and a continuous upward trajectory. But looks can be deceiving. This section addresses two fundamental questions about the character of the thirty-five-year growth in rates of imprisonment. The first part of this section discusses whether the aggregate growth of imprisonment in the fifty states and the federal system is best viewed as (a) a single process with fifty-one different levels of government participating in essentially similar transformations of policy or (b) an aggregation of different levels or types of policy change. The second part of the section addresses whether the thirty-five years of increase are a single era of growth or are composed of two or three distinct and discrete eras with different causes and magnitudes.

## One Process or Many?

The aggregate growth rates portrayed in Figure 19.2 are the sum of data from fifty-one different governmental systems. As a matter of political science and perhaps of logic, it is inaccurate to speak of the rate of imprisonment in the United States as a single measure or to speak of the growth rate of imprisonment in the United States as a unitary phenomenon. But noting the multiplicity of different components of policy in American penality is the beginning, rather than the end, of the analysis that I am suggesting is required. Despite the large number of states and the diversity of their social and demographic composition, it is not unusual for nationwide trends to be evident in matters relating to crime and punishment. One recent example of a plenary national trend was the sharp decline in reported serious crime in the United States during the 1990s.[12] Zimring and Hawkins noted in 1991, "one of the most puzzling features of recent decades is the way in which the many political units that share power in the American criminal justice system altered their policies in a way that increased prison populations at the same time and with similar intensity."[13]

The fourfold increase in the imprisonment rate in the United States obviously must be a broad trend to produce an aggregate impact that large. But there are two rather different patterns that can produce large growth in the aggregate. The large growth numbers can mask very large differences between highest growth and lowest growth jurisdictions where there are significant differences between one cluster of jurisdictions and another. In that case, aggregate growth levels are not the best way to study the causes of differential growth. The differences between states will be at least as important as national trends over time.

But the large number of states might all be more or less evenly participating in a national trend, in which case studying the factors associated with different rates of growth in different states will not provide an obvious key to the states' shared characteristics that are the main causes of growth in all states. This methodological point was argued by Zimring and Hawkins:

> At stake ... is the appropriate unit of analysis for imprisonment policy. To the extent that the United States is a single social system, approaches that view variations in imprisonment as an outgrowth of social and economic processes would emphasize the national scale as a unit of analysis ... [t]o the extent that prison population is best viewed as an outcome of conscious governmental choice ... the most significant political power over imprisonment is exercised at the state level and the state should be the significant unit of analysis.[14]

While Zimring and Hawkins spotted an important issue, their analysis jumps to premature conclusions about the appropriate level of government for studies of the scale of imprisonment. Even if the major influences on rates of imprisonment are political, the mechanisms that produce political change at the state level may be national in scope and might best be studied at the national aggregate level. If most states respond in relatively uniform ways to a national-level stimulus, interstate variation should not be the central focus of the search for causal factors.

Figure 19.4 shows the distribution of percentage growth in rates of imprisonment for the U.S. federal system and the fifty states.

---

12    Franklin E. Zimring, *The Great American Crime Decline* 3–24 (2007).

13    Zimring & Hawkins, *supra* note 2, at 137.

14    *Id.* at 137–38.

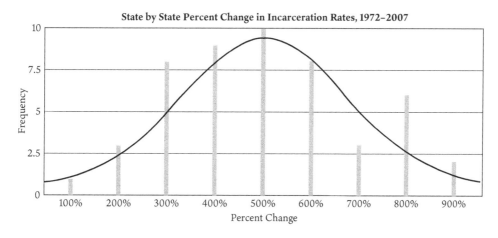

**FIGURE 19.4** The almost bell curve distribution of state imprisonment growth rates

The pattern of state rate growth most consistent with a unitary national trend over the time period would show the largest concentration of states in the middle of the distribution with very few states at both extremes. The model for this type of pattern is a normal distribution around a mean value. To the extent that extreme values are found, they should tend to be in smaller states, and there should not be any clear pattern of regional clustering in one part of the distribution. That pattern would be a distribution consistent with a unitary national trend.

A pluralistic distribution would not concentrate in the center of the growth rate scale, would have clusters of cases at some distance from the mean, and would produce clusters of cases with apparent similarities in geography, crime, or politics and different characteristic growth rates. To the extent that a distribution suggests a unitary pattern, the appropriate level of analysis is the national aggregate. To the extent that plural clustering is evident in the distribution, the explanation of patterns of state variation becomes an important focus of inquiry. But which is distribution is present in Figure 19.4?

A formal statistical analysis confirms the visual impression that the pattern of state growth rates over 1972–2007 is consistent with a normal distribution. We use the fifty state growth rates as our sample set because they were produced in the same fashion. The federal data are excluded from this analysis. Two statistical tests analyze how often a distribution of fifty outcomes (in this case percent growth in state imprisonment rate) like that shown in Figure 19.4 would be likely to occur as chance variations from a normal distribution. They are the Shapiro-Wilk and Shapiro-Francia tests each named after its creators.[15] Table 19.1 shows the fifty state results for the growth rates reported in Figure 19.4.

---

15    J.P. Royston, *A Simple Method for Evaluating the Shapiro-Francia W' Test of Non-Normality*, 32 *Statistician* 297 (1983); Patrick Royston, *Estimating Departure from Normality*, 10 *Stat. Med.* 1283 (1991); S.S. Shapiro & M.B. Wilk, *An Analysis of Variance Test for Normality (Complete Samples)*, 52 *Biometrika* 591 (1965); S.S. Shapiro & R.S. Francia, *An Approximate Analysis of Variance Test for Normality*, 67 J. Am. Stat. Ass'n 215 (1972).

**TABLE 19.1  The Probable Normality of Distribution of Imprisonment Growth Rates of Fifty U.S. States**[16]

| Test | Obs. | W | V | Z | Probability > Z |
|------|------|-----|-----|-----|------|
| Shapiro-Wilk | 50 | 0.97322 | 1.259 | 0.492 | 0.31151 |
| Shapiro-Francia | 50 | 0.97985 | 1.045 | 0.085 | 0.46612 |

The smaller the probability that this is a fifty-case sample from a normal distribution, the more likely the pattern of difference observed is not normal, with a probability of 0.05 or less a usual benchmark for strong statistical evidence of non-normal distribution. But using a Shapiro-Wilk test produces a probability of normal distribution of 0.31151 and the Shapiro-Francia test probability is 0.46612. The question these tests address is "how likely" it is that a distribution like the one being tested could be the outcome of sampling fifty readings from a normal distribution. The answer is "pretty likely." There are thus no indications in these analyses of anything other than fifty different outcomes of a uniform process.

## One Policy Era or Three?

When trends in national rates of imprisonment are charted over time in Figure 19.2, the visual image is of two discrete trends—a flat and relatively stable period from 1930 to about 1970 and a second continuously upward period of uninterrupted growth. While the upward trajectory of increased rates of imprisonment moderates as the base rate of prison population increased in the 1980s and early 1990s, the number of prisoners added to the U.S. population remained between 300,000 and 437,000 for each five year period between 1985 and 2000.[17] So the visual temptation in a graph like Figure 19.2 is bifurcation into a single era of stability and a single era of growth.

It is however one thing to note that a growth rate has been constant over a long period of time and quite another to assume that the substantive influences that were driving increases in prison population in the late 1970s are the same that were operating in the 1980s and remained stable in the 1990s. There are some indications that policy emphasis changed over the generation of growing rates with higher rates of commitment for a wide range of felonies being more important in the period prior to 1986, greater proportionate growth in drug and sex crimes being of greater significance from the mid 1980s to the mid-1990s, and with legislative increases in prison terms and longer prison sentences showing a more important role in the decade after 1995.[18]

Without a doubt the changes in emphasis and priority over time during the different eras turn generalization over the entire growth period about causes of imprisonment growth into a hazardous occupation. The sharp growth not only in drug prisoners, but in the percentage of state prisoners

16    Bureau of Justice Statistics, Key Facts, http://bjs.ojp.usdoj.gov/index.cfm?ty=tp&tid=13#key_facts; Nat'l Criminal Justice Reference Serv., http://www.ncjrs.gov/App/Topics/Topic.aspx?TopicID=1.

17    See the comparison of growth rates and numbers in *Zimring, supra* note 12, at 50 fig.3.5.

18    Franklin E. Zimring, *Penal Policy and Penal Legislation in Recent American Experience*, 58 Stan. L. Rev. 323, 329–34 (2005).

sentenced for drug crime between 1987 and 1991[19] suggest different causal paradigms for earlier prison growth than during the drug war's peak years.

But there may be more unity in the process of prison growth than preoccupation with the changing characteristics of crimes and sentences would allow. To the extent that a relatively fixed expansion of imprisonment might be either desired or tolerated in the years after 1972, the crimes or sentence lengths that are added to reach that level may not be an important influence on the motivation or tolerance for prison growth. To the extent, then, that the relatively constant growth of imprisonment before and after the peak emphasis on the war on drugs indicates that drug offenders simply crowded out marginal property offenders or restrained longer prison sentences for street criminals when they took priority in the late 1980s, the drug panic was not itself a primary cause of change in the growth rate of imprisonment. To the unknown extent that the pace of national prison expansion operated independently of the categories of cases that were given emphasis in filling the new space, the conception of the post-1972 growth of imprisonment as a unitary trend across thirty-five years is plausible.

## Does Crime Matter?

This section of the analysis will apply the perspectives discussed in Part III to review the published work discussing the role of variations in crime rates as explanations for variations in the rate of imprisonment cross-sectionally and over time. Of the potential hypotheses to use in applying analytic tools for study of the scale of imprisonment, the link between variations in crime and variations in imprisonment is a natural priority for two reasons. The link between crime volume and imprisonment volume should be a fundamental one, because criminal conviction is a necessary condition for eligibility for prison. All prisoners at any time are convicted criminals so that variations in the supply of crime and presumably criminals is one obvious source of variation in the amount imprisonment is used or demanded. This essential linkage has produced a second condition that recommends the crime/imprisonment issue as a demonstration example—the relatively large number of empirical studies published in this and other journals that have explored the topic and reported significant findings when crime rates are tested as an influence on relative growth of imprisonment in the era of prison expansion. There have not been many published studies on the scale of imprisonment nor have a wide variety of different analytic strategies been used, but the crime/imprisonment relationship has still received as much attention as any other potential cause.

Since criminal convictions are necessary (but not sufficient) conditions for imprisonment, an increase in convictions is one obvious reason why more people would be sent to prison, and one natural influence on the volume of convicted offenders is the volume of reported crimes. Several published studies have found that variation in crime at the state level predict variations in the growth of imprisonment at the state level. But a detailed comparison of the data analyzed suggests several limits to existing studies of the crime versus rates of imprisonment relationship.

One limit of the current studies is that the time periods studied were during the post-1972 uninterrupted growth in rates of imprisonment. Does growth in crime predict growth in imprisonment during periods with less growth to explain? If not, the relationship of crime trends and prison trends

---

19    *See* Franklin E. Zimring & Bernard E. Harcourt, *Criminal Law and the Regulation of Vice* 219 fig.3 (2007).

may be much weaker in more "normal" periods of relative stability in imprisonment rates in which variations in rates of many crimes are not predictive of differential imprisonment growth.

And even in periods of high growth in imprisonment, the type of growth most clearly associated with increasing prison numbers may have a large effect on the impact of crime rates on prison growth. In the first era of growth from 1974 to 1987, the most prominent cause of incarceration growth was the increasing rate of imprisonment for high volume felonies at the margin between prison and lesser sanctions—burglary, auto theft, unarmed robbery, assault.[20] Variations in crime rates might have a strong influence on prison use by increasing the number of such offenses just when the prison risk for such crimes was going up—the two forces might interact to redouble the risk increase that was occurring independently. But variations in reported part I or index crime (property crimes with victims and violent crimes of some seriousness) levels would not have as strong an influence during an imprisonment policy focus driven by increases in sentenced drug offenders and non-rape sex offenders—the special features of the increase in imprisonment over the period 1987–1995, because there is no count of drug offenses or of non-rape sex offenses that would measure variations in the rate of these types of offenders. So the relationship of variations in official crime rates to differential growth rates of state imprisonment should be much weaker in an era of special emphasis on these non-index crimes. In fact, many of the studies that find strong crime/imprisonment links involved data from the first period of increasing prison risk for marginally serious index crimes (e.g., Table 19.1 in Pfaff).[21] For this reason, such studies probably overestimate the impact on official rates of index crime and prison population even for the entire set of high growth eras.

And because these studies were only attempting to access the role of differential crime growth in explaining state-to-state differences in growth of imprisonment, the studies that were conducted produce no direct evidence on the question of how much of the growth in imprisonment at the national level was driven by the growth of crime. The greater the likelihood that a single national-level process was taking place during the period beginning in the 1970s, the more appropriate it becomes to explore the relationships between crime and imprisonment over time at the national level.

Figure 19.5 uses homicide rates over time as a proxy for crime trends nationally and compares temporal trends for homicide and imprisonment rate per 100,000 for the United States as a whole.

Homicide is selected as one proxy for serious crime because it is reliably reported and a good index of variation in rates of life threatening violence.[22] Over the forty-three years after 1964, the observed rates of homicide and imprisonment are on very different trend lines. Homicide rates double between 1964 and 1974 in the United States, while imprisonment rates continue to decline until 1973. When imprisonment rates begin to rise over the late 1970s, homicide rates first fall then increase back to just above the 1974 high in 1980, then drop substantially until 1984, increase from 1986 to 1991, then drop steadily throughout the 1990s and level off in the years after 2000.

The temporal pattern for imprisonment shows little of the cyclical variations of homicide. Imprisonment drifts downward for eight years and then turns up for thirty-five years. One might argue that the increase in homicide in the late 1960s starts to drive imprisonment upward after a long lag, but an eight-year gap between the increase in killings and the increase in imprisonment

20    See, e.g., Franklin E. Zimring & Gordon Hawkins, *Prison Population and Criminal Justice Policy in California* 14 (1992).

21    John F. Pfaff, *The Empirics of Prison Growth: A Critical Review and Path Forward*, 98 J. Crim. L. & Criminology 547 (2008).

22    Zimring & Hawkins, *supra* note 9, at 67–71.

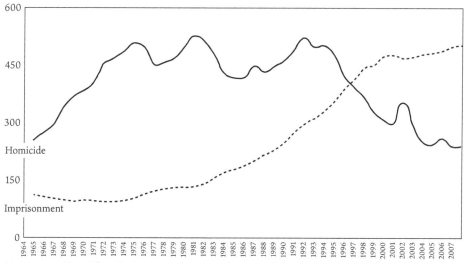

* Imprisonment Figure 1 from Zimring *supra* note 18; Homicide: Figure 1 from ZIMRING, *supra* note 12.

FIGURE 19.5 Homicide (x50) and imprisonment per 100,000 1964–2007[a]

[a]Imprisonment Figure 1 from Zimring *supra* note 18; Homicide: Figure 1 from ZIMRING, *supra* note 12.

would be much larger than any standard economic or policy lags. And the shape of the patterns for homicide and imprisonment are very different for the entire period rather than revealing similarities when lags are introduced. There is a significant relationship between homicide and incarceration trends, but it is negative, (−0.53) over the period 1964–2007. This might be good news for those who suggest that imprisonment reduces crime, but it is bad news for advocates that crime rates drive imprisonment rates.

Figure 19.6 shows trends in robbery and imprisonment to parallel the homicide story.

This time, the overall relationship between robbery and imprisonment is nonexistent (−0.08), consistent with the two trends operating independently of any systematic interaction.

Of course adding time lags and other statistical bells and whistles will produce variation in statistical outcomes. But the central point of these exercises seems secure: the notion that variations in crime in the period after 1964 are driving imprisonment rates, which is clear in the study of interstate variations, is not well supported once attention shifts to the national aggregate. So if that is the appropriate level of analysis (a plausible implication of a normal distribution of growth rates at the state level), it's back to the drawing board.

## Is Volatility a One-Way Street?

In retrospect, the mid-1970s witnessed a transition between relatively stable imprisonment trends to sharp upward variation in incarceration rates. But the description of prison population trends as "volatile" in this period may be inaccurate if that term is intended in its ordinary economic or linguistic sense of changeable or "tending to fluctuate sharply and regularly." The recent history of imprisonment in the United States has established that populations tend to fluctuate sharply and regularly, but only in an upward direction. The "average" increase in incarceration rate per 100,000

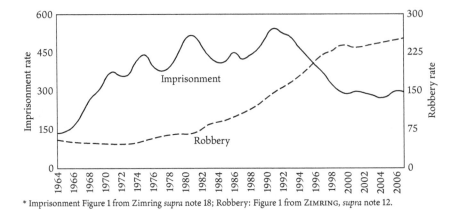

\* Imprisonment Figure 1 from Zimring *supra* note 18; Robbery: Figure 1 from ZIMRING, *supra* note 12.

**FIGURE 19.6** Trends in Robbery Rates and Imprisonment Rates, U.S. 1964–2007[b]
[b]Imprisonment Figure 1 from Zimring *supra* note 18; Robbery: Figure 1 from ZIMRING, *supra* note 12.

population has been about fourfold, a very substantial variation indeed. And there is strong evidence in recent years that growth rates have declined and increases in aggregate population levels are, by recent standards, quite small. Some state systems have declining rates of imprisonment already, and there is reason to believe that stability and decline may touch many systems in the near future.

So declining rates of imprisonment are a likelihood at some point in the American near term. What is not known is the *scale* of decline that might follow the increases of recent history. Are the large increases of recent history indications that the downward variations in incarceration rates might approach the scale of the post-1973 increases? Or are there inertial forces in the politics or governance of imprisonment that can be expected to restrain the downward variation of prison population so that cyclical movements appear non-symmetrical? Illustrations of the contrasting arithmetic of symmetrical versus asymmetrical downward variation are not difficult to construct. The equivalent of a 400% increase in prison population rate is an 80% decrease in rate per 100,000 from the inflated base rate of imprisonment back to break even. Is downward variation of that magnitude either possible or likely in a thirty-year frame of the twenty-first century?

There are no *downward* variations in prison population of that scale in the history of any developed nation on earth, just as there were no precedents for the statistical growth documented in Figure 19.2 until it happened. The number of significant decreases in prison populations in U.S. history is rather small, and the size of recorded declines to date are far less than half the 80% decline that would constitute statistical symmetry with the late twentieth-century increase. California produced a decline in rates of imprisonment in the early 1970s of approximately 30%,[23] and the New York State system, dominated by New York City prisoners, has dropped in the wake of the city's 80% drop in most forms of serious crime.[24] The early California experience lasted just under a decade before it was overtaken by increases in the 1980s.

The extent to which the scale of current imprisonment is reversible is a question not of statistics but of the political economy of imprisonment. There are a variety of institutional and political

---

23    Rosemary Gartner, Anthony Doob & Franklin Zimring, *The Past Is Prologue? Decarceration in California: Then and Now*, Criminology & Pub. Pol'y (forthcoming 2011).

24    Franklin E. Zimring, *The City that Became Safe!, New York and the Future of Crime Control* ch. 8 (forthcoming 2011).

reasons why prison population rates might be stickier on the way down than they proved to be on the way up. Once the physical capacity to imprison has been expanded, there *may* be inertial forces or economies of scale that bias systems to continue to use them. The expanded scale of prison capacity may also reflect changing public preferences for imprisonment and these preferences may endure independent of any real economies in the variable costs of incarceration. And while public preferences and values may not have strong independent influence on rates of imprisonment, this attitudinal software might interact with changes in both crime rates and public fear of crime to create political pressures for penal expansion or limits on contraction.

Of all the modern historical trends in imprisonment, the period after 1994 presents the most impressive evidence of asymmetrical volatility for American imprisonment. This was the era when imprisonment rates in the United States defied gravity, when incarceration rates increased while crime rates decreased. To the extent that the attitudes and political circumstances of the middle and late 1990s hold in the future, the case for volatility as a one-way street is quite strong. But there are two reasons to suspect that the conditions that obtained in the late 1990s will vary. The first issue is that longer exposure to stable or declining crime rates might reduce fear and soften public hostility. There may be time lags of some size before declining crime and violence is transformed into assumptions of social safety. The slowing of growth in incarceration rates seven and eight years after the crime decline started may be a typical lag between statistics and perception in public safety.

There is a second respect in which the 1990s may not be representative of future attitudes toward crime and punishment. The mid-1990s was an era of punitive hostility unparalleled in modern U.S. history and this may not have been closely linked to crime rates. The era of three strikes and truth in sentencing may have been driven by unsustainable levels of fear and hostility rather than a continuing chronic condition. What we know for sure after the mid-1990s is that the software of public fear and concern is more predictive of policy than any trends in crime or drug use. What is not known is the variability of public attitudes in the second and third decade of the twenty-first century. Stay tuned!

## Conclusion

Just as theories of stability of punishment followed sustained periods of little change in prison population, a concern with explaining wide variations in rates of imprisonment grew out of the fourfold expansion of rates of imprisonment in the United States in the generation after 1970. Among the long list of unanswered questions about the determinants of rates of imprisonment is whether the dramatic rise in prison population over the past decades is a new norm for the scale of imprisonment or a precursor to significant declines in the rates of imprisonment in the early decades of a new century.

# Probation, Parole, and Community Corrections

## LAWRENCE F. TRAVIS III AND BRADLEY D. EDWARDS

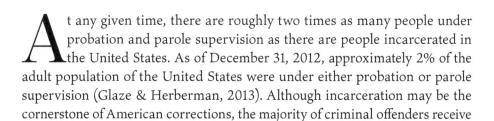

At any given time, there are roughly two times as many people under probation and parole supervision as there are people incarcerated in the United States. As of December 31, 2012, approximately 2% of the adult population of the United States were under either probation or parole supervision (Glaze & Herberman, 2013). Although incarceration may be the cornerstone of American corrections, the majority of criminal offenders receive sentences to probation.

By the end of 1985, the Bureau of Justice Statistics (1987:1) reported that more than 2.9 million persons were under correctional authority, and 74% of all those were under community supervision (probation or parole). By the end of 2012, more than 6.9 million adults were under correctional authority, with more than 4.7 million under probation or parole supervision (Glaze & Herberman, 2013). The majority of persons under community supervision (almost 4 million) were on probation. The combined probation and parole populations account for almost 70% of all those under the custody of correctional agencies. Although the percentage of the correctional population comprised of inmates (in jails and prisons) has increased during the past 25 years, community supervision is still the most common correctional setting.

Probation and parole supervision as currently operated, like the prison, are American inventions. Both involve the conditional release of convicted offenders into the community under supervision. Probationers and parolees experience similar treatment but, as we shall see, there are important differences between the two.

Probation and parole can be considered the "bookends" of imprisonment (see Box 20.1). **Probation** is a sanction generally imposed in lieu of incarceration and, thus, it occurs before imprisonment. **Parole** involves offenders released early

## BOX 20.1  Probation and Parole (2012): The Bookends of Imprisonment

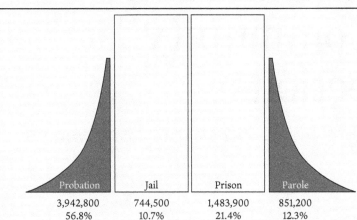

| Probation | Jail | Prison | Parole |
|---|---|---|---|
| 3,942,800 | 744,500 | 1,483,900 | 851,200 |
| 56.8% | 10.7% | 21.4% | 12.3% |

- *Probation* is the sentencing of an offender to community supervision by a probation agency, often as a result of suspending a sentence to confinement. Such supervision normally entails specific rules of conduct while in the community. If the rules are violated, a sentence to confinement may be imposed. Probation is the most widely used correctional disposition in the United States.
- *Incarceration* is the confinement of a convicted criminal in a federal or state prison or a local jail to serve a court-imposed sentence. Confinement is usually in a jail, administered locally, or a prison, operated by the state or federal government. In many states offenders sentenced to 1 year or less are held in a jail; those sentenced to longer terms are committed to a state prison.

Release from prison generally occurs as the result of a decision of a paroling authority, mandatory release, or expiration of sentence.

- *Parole* is the release of a prisoner by the decision of a paroling authority. The offender is placed under the supervision of a parole officer who monitors the offender's compliance with rules of conduct imposed by the paroling authority. Violations of these rules may result in reimprisonment for the balance of the unexpired sentence.
- *Mandatory release* is based on earned "good time" (days earned for good behavior) or other statutory sentence-reduction measures and, though supervision is required after release, does not usually depend on the discretionary decision of a parole board. Supervision rules of conduct, if violated, may result in a return to prison for the time remaining on the sentence.

*Source*: Maruschak and Bonczar (2013)

from incarceration sentences, so it occurs after a period of imprisonment. Therefore, probation and parole flank imprisonment on either side as criminal sanctions.

This chapter examines community supervision in the criminal justice system of the United States. We will describe probation and parole supervision as well as some other forms of community control of offenders. We will explore the history and practice of probation and parole, and we will examine other community-based sanctions and the various populations involved in these sanctions.

# The Origins of Community Supervision

Probation and parole developed in the nineteenth century in the United States, although each had precursors in Western civilization. An examination of the history of community supervision shows how the justice system has changed with the social and intellectual currents in the larger society. Shortly after the creation of the penitentiary, many people came to view incarceration as a less-than-adequate response to all offenders. Probation and parole developed as alternatives to incarceration for select groups of offenders.

Probation evolved from several prior practices in the English courts that allowed judges to grant leniency to offenders and avoid the harsh corporal and capital punishments provided in the common law. Among these were the benefit of clergy, judicial reprieve, and release on recognizance (ROR) (Allen, Eskridge, Latessa, & Vito, 1985:37–40). Each of these practices allowed the sentencing judge to postpone or avoid the execution of sentence.

The **benefit of clergy** was a practice that developed during the medieval period so that members of the clergy were accountable to ecclesiastic (church) courts rather than civil courts. The accused could claim the benefit of clergy to have his or her case moved from the civil courts to the church courts. The test for benefit of clergy came to be one of literacy, in which the court required the accused to read the text of the fifty-first Psalm (see Box 20.2). In due time, illiterate common criminals committed the psalm to memory so that they could pretend to read it and thus avoid the punishments of the king's courts (Clear & Cole, 1986:232).

The fifty-first Psalm, because it allowed many offenders to avoid hanging as the penalty for their crimes, came to be known as the "neck verse." After a period of expansion of the benefit of clergy (from the fourteenth through the eighteenth centuries), the practice was disallowed by statute in 1827. No longer was it possible to escape in this way to the less severe sanctions of the church courts.

**Judicial reprieve** was a common practice in England in the nineteenth century. Under this practice, the offender could apply to the judge for a reprieve, which required that sentencing of an offender be delayed on the condition of good behavior for a specific period. After the allotted time, the offender could ask the king for a pardon. Here, we see the addition of two components of contemporary probation: (1) a set period and (2) the requirement that the offender abide by conditions of good behavior.

**ROR** was a practice (combined with peace bonds) that was a forerunner to bail. While awaiting the arrival of the circuit magistrate, an accused offender obtained release by posting a surety or by having someone vouch for him or her. This practice most directly led to the development of contemporary probation.

## BOX 20.2 Fifty-First Psalm: The Neck Verse

*Have mercy upon me, O God,*
*according to thy loving kindness,*
*According to the multitude of thy tender mercies*
*blot out my transgressions.*

We generally credit John Augustus, a Boston boot maker, with being the father of probation. It was common practice in Massachusetts courts to release offenders on the recognizance of a third party. Augustus began a nearly 20-year career as a voluntary probation officer by posting bail in the Boston Police Court in 1841 for a man accused of drunkenness. Between 1841 and 1858, he supervised nearly 2,000 people. He was so successful that the state of Massachusetts passed legislation authorizing probation as a disposition and provided for the first paid probation officer. Over time, other states emulated the Massachusetts practice. Today, probation is the most common disposition of criminal cases.

Parole also developed in the mid-1800s. By the 1850s, observers of the penitentiary system grew dissatisfied with the effectiveness of incarceration in preventing further criminal behavior by offenders. These critics began to call for changes in incarceration practices that would serve to reform inmates and produce law-abiding citizens. The outcome of this reform movement was parole release and supervision. Parole has two components. The first is discretionary early release from prison. The second component is the period of supervision in the community that follows such a release.

In England and other European countries, several practices were already in place that laid the groundwork for the creation of parole. The term "parole" comes from the French phrase *parole de honeur*, meaning word of honor. Prisoners of war gained release on their "parole" that they would not again take up arms against their captors. This term was later applied to the procedure for allowing prison inmates to return to society prior to the expiration of their prison terms. Essentially, officials expected the prisoners to vow that they would not violate the law, in return for which they were granted release.

Banishment and transportation also have been considered to be precursors to parole, in that these procedures essentially allowed an offender to avoid a more harsh penalty on the condition that the offender not return to the land of the original crime (Barnes & Teeters, 1959). Closer to modern parole practice, however, were release procedures developed by Walter Crofton and Captain Alexander Maconochie. As superintendents of penal facilities, each of these men created a system of inmate discipline that allowed the prisoners to earn early release.

Crofton devised a "ticket of leave" for inmates in the Irish prison system. Prisoners were classified into three stages of treatment, ranging from segregated confinement, through work on public projects (which was increasingly free of supervision), until final release "on license." Successful inmates earned their ticket of leave through hard work and good behavior. When Crofton believed an inmate to be ready for release, he would issue a **ticket of leave**, which authorized the inmate to leave the prison, return home, and report to the local police. There was no supervision of the released inmate.

Alexander Maconochie is often called the father of parole. His system was very similar to that of Crofton. Maconochie operated the British penal colony on Norfolk Island, in the South Pacific. There he classified offenders into three groups and instituted a **mark system**. All inmates began at the penal stage, which involved close supervision while engaging in hard labor with a large group of fellow prisoners. Good behavior and industry earned "marks" for an inmate, and upon acquiring enough marks, the prisoner moved to the next stage. The social stage involved working and living in groups of about seven prisoners, with less supervision than the penal stage. Again, prisoners earned marks leading to promotion to the individual stage, during which the prisoner was allowed a cottage and was given individual work. Prisoners were subject to being moved back to earlier stages for misconduct or laziness. Those in the individual stage who continued to demonstrate good behavior and industry eventually earned a ticket of leave or conditional pardon. Often they were apprenticed to citizens on mainland Australia (Travis, 1985).

The apparent success of these programs was noticed in the United States. In 1870, the American Prison Association in Cincinnati provided the forum for reformers to push for the creation of parole and a system of reformatory discipline in the United States (Lindsey, 1925). With growing support for the early release and reformatory discipline, New York enacted legislation creating a reformatory at Elmira, where first offenders received sentences to terms that would last "until reformation, not to exceed five years." Parole release had been born in the United States.

Simon (1993) has reviewed and assessed the development of parole. He suggested that the practice of third-party recognizance, what he calls "suretyship," was a forerunner to modern parole. **Suretyship** was the practice of a person of good standing in the community taking responsibility for guaranteeing the lawful behavior of another person. When the prison became the dominant form of punishment, Simon suggested, people recognized that not all offenders needed to remain in prison, or at least not for full terms. Parole release and supervision allowed authorities to select worthy offenders and release them from prison. Officials used parole to support discipline, in that well-behaved, industrious inmates who could secure employment (and thus keep busy at socially acceptable activities) received parole. When employment opportunities decreased during the Great Depression, "clinical" parole replaced disciplinary parole. In this revised model, the purpose of parole was to support the treatment and rehabilitation of inmates. In both cases, parole enabled authorities to differentiate between those convicted criminals who could be reformed and those who could not.

We can apply a similar argument to the development of probation supervision, as the functions and definitions of probation have mirrored those of parole. The task of probation evolved from diverting selected offenders from prison through control and discipline in the community, to the provision of treatment and rehabilitative services to offenders who did not need the more intensive treatment of prison.

During the first 6 or 7 decades of its existence, parole faced a number of legal challenges. The practice of discretionary early release from incarceration gained acceptance by the 1940s. In addition, during this era (called the Progressive Era), increasing attention was focused on the role of postrelease supervision of offenders (as well as probation supervision). This led eventually to the current system of parole involving both early release and supervision in the community (Rothman, 1980).

Since the mid-1990s, there has been increased concern about **reentry**, the return of former inmates to life in the community. Throughout the 1990s, as prison populations continued to increase, it became apparent that relatively large numbers of parole violators accounted for a substantial portion of the inmate population (Burke, 2004). In 2012, more than one-quarter of all inmates admitted to state prisons were parole violators (see Figure 20.1).

The twin concerns of assisting released inmates to adjust to law-abiding life in the community and reducing the risk of new

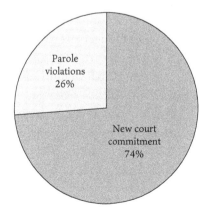

**FIGURE 20-1** Source of new prison admissions.
*Source*: Carson and Golinelli (2013)

crime posed by released offenders led to the development of **reentry courts**, where services for and supervision of parolees are coordinated and monitored in a court environment. These operate much like drug courts in which a judge meets frequently with the offender to monitor progress and, if needed, to change conditions of supervision and release (Lindquist, Hardison, & Lattimore, 2003; Travis, Solomon, & Waul, 2001). In many ways, the contemporary focus on prisoner reentry is similar to the original interest in developing parole (Burke & Tonry, 2006). We might say that we have rediscovered parole in the past decade.

An evaluation of one such program compared offenders enrolled in a specific reentry program with others who either received traditional prerelease services or no reentry programming at all (Wilson, 2007). Of the three groups, those who received no programming had fewer arrests and lower rates of revocation than either the reentry or traditional programming groups. The evaluators and others (Rhine, Mawhorr, & Parks, 2006) suggested that the reentry program was not properly designed and implemented. Correctional personnel seek to learn from their mistakes and improve programs for the future. A more recent evaluation of a different reentry court reported lower rates of rearrests and reconviction for parolees participating in the program (Hamilton, 2010). However, the closer supervision of the program did result in an increased rate of technical violations. It remains unclear how well reentry programs will do in improving parole supervision and outcomes.

## The Organization of Community Supervision: Probation and Parole

Probation and parole, although very similar, differ in how they are organized. Whereas many states charge supervising officers with the responsibility of serving both parolees and probationers, there are other states where the two tasks are administratively separate (Bonczar, 2008). Probation tends to be a county and municipal function. Parole, on the other hand, usually is a state function, even in states where probation officers supervise parolees (U.S. Department of Justice, 1978).

According to the U.S. Department of Justice (1978), parole supervision was exclusively a state function in 44 states. Seven states (the total included the District of Columbia) supplement state-level authority with local systems. Probation supervision is a function of the criminal court, but in most cases, probation officers are employees of the executive branch of the state government. About a quarter of the agencies responsible for the supervision of adult and juvenile probationers are state level, whereas nearly 70% are organized at the county level. The remaining probation agencies are city and municipal organizations. For parole supervision, the numbers are reversed, with more than 90% of agencies charged solely with the supervision of parolees organized at the state level. In places where the same agency supervises both probationers and parolees, more than 90% of the organizations exist at the state level (U.S. Department of Justice, 1978). Thus, for the most part, probation is a local function and parole is a state function.

A survey of parole supervising agencies in 2006 (Bonczar, 2008) revealed that 35 (over two-thirds) of the systems reported combined probation and parole officers, while 17 maintained separate parole supervision staff. Even in states reporting dual roles for officers (probation and parole supervision), often there is a separate local system of probation. In many states, counties can choose to provide probation supervision themselves, or may turn responsibility for the supervision of probationers over to the state.

Probationers are under the jurisdiction of the sentencing court, and held to a set of conditions imposed by the sentencing judge. Probation officers are responsible for carrying out the wishes of the sentencing judge. Parolees, on the other hand, are under the jurisdiction of the state paroling authority, and held to a set of conditions imposed by that authority. Parole officers are responsible for carrying out the wishes of the parole authority, although in most cases parole supervision is independent of the parole release authority (Bonczar, 2008; Rhine, Smith, & Jackson, 1991). In jurisdictions in which the same officers supervise both parole and probation, the officers wear two hats, and their behavior is contingent on the legal status (probationer or parolee) of the client.

Inmates can be released from prison under a variety of terms. Several states allow prisoners to be released from a prison sentence with no parole supervision. These offenders are often said to have "maxed out" their sentence. Those inmates who enter parole supervision most often either receive a discretionary parole or achieve mandatory release. **Mandatory release** occurs at the expiration of a prison term reduced by good behavior, or when a sentencing law requires that inmates completing their prison terms receive supervision in the community for some period of time (Glaze & Bonczar, 2006:8). For the period of their supervision, they are on a conditional release and must obey the rules and conditions of parole or face a return to prison.

**Discretionary release** is granted by a parole board who will typically assess the inmate's perceived likelihood of successfully following the conditions of parole. The use of discretionary parole declined significantly from the 1970s until 2008. In 1977, 69% of inmates released from prison received discretionary parole release (Hughes, Wilson, & Beck, 2001). By 2008, discretionary parole represented fewer than 27% of parolees (Glaze & Bonczar, 2009). In 2012, discretionary release again became the most common type of entry to parole (Maruschak & Bonczar, 2013). Table 20.1 describes the number of offenders entering each type of parole supervision.

In 1984, Congress eliminated parole at the federal level and established a post-confinement monitoring system called **supervised release**. A term of supervised release is imposed at the initial sentencing hearing, requiring the offender to be monitored by a federal probation officer and to abide by certain conditions upon release from prison. Unlike parole, supervised release does not serve as a substitute for imprisonment. If the offender violates the terms of supervised release, he or she can be required to serve the term of supervised release in prison (United States Sentencing Commission, 2010).

Few systematic data exist on the characteristics of probationers and parolees. It is generally safe to say that probationers, for the most part, are offenders who have less extensive criminal records than prisoners. Auerhahn (2007), however, has estimated that the probation population in California is increasingly composed of offenders with prior felony records convicted of violent crimes. If this

| TABLE 20.1   Number of Adults Entering Parole, by Type of Entry, 2012 | |
|---|---|
| Discretionary | 187,003 |
| Mandatory | 128,098 |
| Supervised release | 82,823 |
| Reinstatement[a] | 57,916 |

[a]*Reinstatement includes offenders returned to parole after serving time in prison due to a parole violation.*
*Source*: Maruschak and Bonczar (2013)

is true, then the traditional differences between probationers and parolees may be disappearing. Parolees, on the other hand, having been prisoners themselves, tend to mirror the prison population. In those states where release is discretionary, we might expect parolees to be slightly less dangerous than the general prison population, but this is speculation.

In 2012, more than 2 million adults were sentenced to probation, with an average supervision term of just under 2 years. At the same time, 496,100 persons entered parole supervision from state prisons (Maruschak & Bonczar, 2013). Table 20.2 presents a description of the characteristics of the probation and parole populations in 2012. The probation population contains more females, fewer persons convicted of a violent offense, and fewer ethnic minorities than does the parole population. Given that ethnic minorities and males are more likely to receive prison sentences, it follows that the parole population (comprised of those who had been in prison) would have disproportionately fewer women and whites.

Not only do parole populations generally tend to be composed of offenders with more serious criminal records, but also, largely because of incarceration, parolees tend to have greater needs in the areas of housing, employment, and personal relations than do probationers. One major difference is that parole caseloads tend to be significantly smaller than probation caseloads. Camp and Camp (1996) reported that the average caseload for regular probation in the United States in 1995 was 142 offenders; for parole, the average caseload was 90 offenders. In 2006, the ratio of full-time equivalent officers supervising cases to active parolees was 1:38. However, even though parole caseloads are smaller, the greater needs of the parole population often make them more difficult to supervise than the probation population. Figure 20.2 compares supervision outcomes of probationers and parolees. Of those removed from supervision, nearly 70% of probationers successfully completed their terms, while 58% of parolees did so. Success rates for both probation and parole have increased since 2008 (Maruschak & Bonczar, 2013).

**TABLE 20.2   Characteristics of the Probation and Parole Population, 2012**

| Characteristic | Probation (%) | Parole (%) |
|---|---|---|
| **Sex** | | |
| Male | 76 | 89 |
| Female | 23 | 11 |
| **Race** | | |
| White | 54 | 41 |
| African American | 30 | 40 |
| Hispanic | 13 | 17 |
| **Other** | **2** | **2** |
| Supervision status | | |
| Active | 72 | 82 |
| Inactive | 7 | 5 |
| Absconded | 10 | 6 |
| Out-of-state | 3 | 4 |
| Other | 8 | 3 |

*Source*: Maruschak and Bonczar (2013:18, 21)

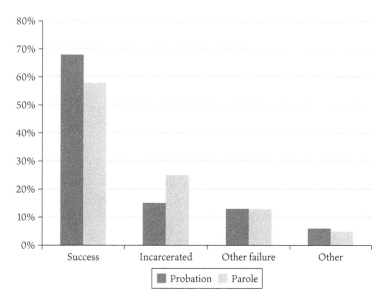

**FIGURE 20.2** Supervision outcomes for adults leaving probation and parole, 2012.
*Source*: Maruschak and Bonczar (2013: 6, 9)

# Other Forms of Community Supervision

Although probation and parole are the major components of community supervision of criminal offenders, other programs play a role in the nonincarceration treatment of convicted offenders. These programs include halfway houses, community service, furlough, work and education, home incarceration, and various diversion programs. Very frequently, courts or parole authorities require participation in these programs as conditions of release under probation or parole. Nonetheless, we will briefly discuss each of these separately.

## Halfway Houses

**Halfway houses** are generally small residential programs based in the community that serve populations of fewer than 30 people (Wilson, 1985). Changes in thinking about the role of the community in the development of socially acceptable behavior spurred the development of halfway houses for both criminal offenders and the mentally ill (Beha, 1975). Although these houses have a long tradition, their application to criminal corrections has experienced tremendous growth in the past three decades (Allen, Carlson, Parks, & Seiter, 1978; Latessa & Travis, 1992).

Halfway houses are so-named because they represent an intermediate step that is halfway between incarceration and community supervision. They are either "halfway-out" houses that deal with parolees and other ex-inmates, or "halfway-in" houses for probationers and others not imprisoned (Keller & Alper, 1970). In either case, treatment is a part of the halfway-house routine.

In addition to providing room and board, halfway houses generally offer counseling services that include group and individual counseling sessions. Some halfway houses restrict their client population to special needs offenders, such as abusers of alcohol and other drugs. Other houses accept a wider range of persons and provide or contract for a wider range of services. Inasmuch as the popularity of halfway houses has increased, relatively little attention has been devoted to their effectiveness. Recent evidence is mixed regarding whether halfway houses reduce recidivism or provide a cost savings to states (Bell et al., 2013; White, Mellow, Englander, & Ruffinengo, 2011). In the past several years, the traditional halfway house name has been changing to "residential reentry center," though the function remains the same.

## Community Service Programs

**Community service orders** are programs in which courts sentence convicted offenders to a number of hours of service to community organizations or governmental agencies (Perrier & Pink, 1985). The work takes place in the community, and the offender is generally at liberty except for the scheduled work hours. The work of the convicted offender is supervised (Umbreit, 1981). See Figure 20.3.

These programs have not been widely used with felons. Langan and Dawson (1993) reported that 4% of felons sentenced in state courts in 1990 were ordered to complete some form of community service. By 2006, that number had changed, with 11% of felons ordered to complete community service as part of their sentence (Rosenmerkel, Durose, & Farole, 2009).

Often community service is symbolically retributive in that the court requires the offender to render some service related to the offense. For example, drunk drivers might be ordered to assist in a hospital emergency room, vandals ordered to clean and repair damaged buildings, and similar reflective penalties may be imposed on other offenders. A variant on community service is the chain gang, in which inmates work on public projects such as cleaning litter from roadsides while chained together in groups. Once discredited as too demeaning, chain gangs have recently resurfaced in some places. Probation officers typically supervise those completing community service sentences. Frequently, community service is a condition of probation (Tonry, 1998).

The Vera Institute of Justice in New York City operated one of the most ambitious community service sentencing programs reported to date (McDonald, 1986). In this program, courts sentenced minor offenders to perform 70 hours of community service work, such as cleaning and maintaining parks and senior citizen centers or restoring buildings for low-income housing. The community service sanction applied to those offenders likely to receive jail terms of 90 days or less and on those likely to receive no sanction because of the pettiness of their offenses. In a 5-year span, nearly 3,500 offenders served community service sentences in three boroughs of New York.

Community service is often a core component of restorative justice programs. The term **restorative justice** refers to efforts to repair the harm to victims and/or communities caused by crime through interventions with the offender. Karp and Drakulich (2004) reported on a statewide program of restorative justice in Vermont that involved those convicted of less serious offenses receiving probation with a condition that they participate in the restorative justice program. Nearly two-thirds of restorative justice cases included community service orders. If restorative justice efforts increase, we can expect an increased reliance on community service in the future.

## Furlough Programs

**Furlough** programs also are relatively recent alternatives to the traditional sanction of incarceration. At base, a furlough program allows an inmate to leave the penal facility for a specified period to perform an identified function. Several prisons and jails operate work and educational furlough programs. Inmates are released, without escort, to participate in educational programs or to report to work. After work or school, they return to the institution.

These programs seek to eliminate some of the more debilitating effects of incarceration, such as the loss of a job or the severance of community ties. Furloughs also help inmates prepare for reentry to the community by gradual exposure to release (Doleschal, 1971). Inmates on these types of furloughs seek work and housing, which they will need on release from the institution.

Furloughs have a relatively long history in American corrections, but their use has changed and grown in recent years. Traditionally, furloughs were available to prison inmates in cases of family emergencies (e.g., to visit seriously ill relatives or to attend funerals). In these traditional furloughs, the inmate and the inmate's family were required to pay all expenses, including the cost of an escorting officer (Fox, 1983:147). In the 1960s, several states began granting furloughs to qualifying inmates for social visits by issuing weekend passes to certain inmates. Today, many states use furlough programs to allow inmates that are near the time of their release on parole to seek employment or arrange for residences. Each year thousands of prison inmates receive furloughs from prison in more than 40 jurisdictions. The federal bureau of prisons grants three types of furloughs. Sixteen-hour furloughs require inmates to return to the institution in the evening, whereas overnight furloughs allow inmates to leave the facility for either 5 or 7 days.

LeClair and Guarino-Ghezzi (1991) studied furlough programs in Massachusetts. They found that prisoners who received furloughs were significantly less likely to commit new offenses after release than those who did not receive furloughs. They suggested that furlough programs serve as a positive reward for good behavior by inmates, and that by going on furlough, inmates may become more committed to adopting a lawful lifestyle. This is, indeed, the theory behind furlough programs. As LeClair and Guarino-Ghezzi suggested, we need to learn more about how furlough programs may work to reduce recidivism.

## Work and Educational Release Programs

In a move related to furloughs, which tend to be brief releases for a specified period, correctional agencies are making use of work or study/educational release. Work or study release refers to the practice of allowing inmates of correctional facilities to leave the institution during the day to attend classes or work at a job. More than 9,000 jail inmates in 1995 were involved in work release programs (Gillard & Beck, 1996), and more than 55,000 prison inmates participated in work or study release programs in that year (Camp & Camp, 1996).

In 2005, 28% of confinement facilities operated work release programs for inmates (Stephan, 2008). More than 5,000 jail inmates were participating in work release programs in 2006 (Minton, 2010).

**Work release** programs allow inmates to secure or maintain employment while serving terms of incarceration. The opportunity for inmates released for work to maintain ties to conventional lifestyles and to their communities is a benefit of work release programs. Such inmates also can help support their families and often must contribute to the cost of their incarceration. This reduces overall correctional costs to the community. Although relatively few inmates participate in such release programs, those who do participate benefit from leaving the correctional facility and by being able to keep jobs or secure an education (Wright & Travis, 1996). See Figure 20.3.

**FIGURE 20.3** Located in Seattle, the Reynolds Work Training Release Facility is Washington State's largest work release facility for males.

Turner and Petersilia (1996) reported an evaluation of work release programming in the state of Washington. They found that almost 40% of inmates participated in work release programs at some point during their term. Most work release participants successfully completed the program, with only 5% committing new crimes. However, they did not find the work release program to reduce later recidivism or correctional costs when compared to what happened with inmates who did not receive a work release placement as is shown in Figure 20.4. In recent years, the use of work release programs has decreased compared to the early 1970s. Turner and Petersilia suggested that the decreased use of work release is a product of increased concerns about public safety and reduced program funding available from the federal government.

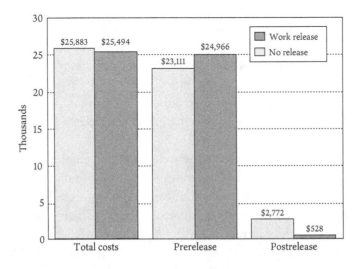

**FIGURE 20.4** Work release costs: Comparison of released and nonreleased offenders.
*Source*: Turner and Petersilia (1996)

## Home Incarceration

As a response to crowded prisons and jails, there has been a resurgence of interest in the practice of house arrest or **home incarceration** (Petersilia, 1986). Offenders sentenced to home incarceration are essentially grounded. They must remain at home except for approved absences, such as attending school, going to work, or keeping medical appointments. While thus incarcerated, the offender is out of society, yet not confined in a jail. The offender retains ties to family and the community, the state faces reduced costs, and the offender generally experiences better conditions of confinement than would exist in a penal facility.

Proponents of home incarceration argue that this practice is more humane and less costly than incarceration (Corbett & Fersch, 1985). These proponents suggest that, for many offenders, home incarceration represents a more satisfactory alternative to incarceration than do the traditional practices of fines or probation. With home incarceration, someone (usually a probation officer) must be responsible for monitoring the offender to ensure that he or she stays home. At midyear 2006, more than 800 jail inmates were on home detention with no other monitoring, and an unknown portion of the nearly 11,000 inmates under electronic monitoring were also on home detention (Sabol, Minton, & Harrison, 2007).

## Diversion

The general rubric of **diversion** incorporates a wide variety of programs that occur at all stages of the justice system. Diversion is included in the discussion of community supervision because its most common formal application is at some point in the court process prior to conviction or sentencing. In most places, the same office provides supervision of both diverted and sentenced offenders: the probation department (McSparron, 1980).

Diversion programs prevent some offenders from passing through the justice system, or minimize the extent of their processing. Supporters hope diverting offenders from the system will enable them to avoid the stigma of a criminal label and other negative effects of justice system processing. Although used for adults in many jurisdictions, diversion programs are more common with juvenile offenders (Latessa, Travis, & Wilson, 1984).

# Being on Paper

We discuss additional types of community sanctions or forms of probation and parole supervision [...]. These include shock probation and parole, electronic monitoring, and day reporting programs. Just as the alternatives discussed above, each of these innovations either represents a form of community supervision or is imposed as a condition of probation or parole. Remember that probation and parole are the core components of community corrections, and that each of these is a form of conditional release from prison. The underlying assumption is that the offender would be in prison or jail if not for his or her participation in community programming.

Community supervision is the punishment of choice for most offenders. The pressures from prison crowding have enhanced the already important role community supervision plays in the justice system. Community supervision is an alternative to imprisonment. We generally hold offenders under community supervision to a higher moral standard than members of the free society, by virtue of the conditions of release. A term probationers and parolees often use to describe their status is to say they are **"on paper."** This refers to the written probation or parole agreements that set out the conditions of release.

## Supervision Conditions

In the final analysis, probation and parole represent an agreement between the offender and the state. In return for the decision not to incarcerate (or for the decision to release from incarceration), the offender agrees to abide by several conditions while at liberty in the community. Violation of any of these conditions can be the basis for revocation of liberty and subsequent incarceration of the offender.

Probation and parole conditions cover a wide variety of behavior and serve a number of purposes (Travis & Latessa, 1984:599). The primary goal of supervision conditions is to prevent future criminality on the part of probationers and parolees. There are two general types of conditions: **standard conditions** that are imposed on everyone under supervision in a jurisdiction, and **special conditions** imposed on individual offenders that relate directly to the offender's status and characteristics (Travis & Stacey, 2010).

Standard conditions of parole and probation vary across jurisdictions. They usually include restrictions on travel and on the freedom to change addresses or jobs, and involve instructions on reporting to the supervising officer. These conditions ensure that the probation or parole officer will be able to monitor the offender. Table 20.3 presents standard conditions of parole in the United States during the past quarter century. Special conditions vary greatly (Jaffe, 1979). They include such things as restrictions on association with particular people, requirements of attending treatment programs, restrictions on the consumption of alcoholic beverages, and restitution orders.

The conditions of probation and parole serve a number of purposes. Some conditions are necessary to ensure that supervision can occur. Thus, offenders may not be allowed to change their jobs or addresses without notifying the supervising officer. They may be required to report to a probation or parole officer on a regular schedule. Offenders who fail to submit to supervision (do not report as directed, change jobs or addresses without notifying their supervising officer, etc.) are called **absconders**, as they absconded (escaped) from supervision. A study of probation absconders (Mayzer, Gray, & Maxwell, 2004) found that these offenders often seem to abscond in the face of probable revocation and they do not appear to differ from probationers who ultimately have their conditional liberty revoked. It seems likely that those who abscond from supervision have violated the conditions of release in other ways as well.

Other supervision conditions impose punishment, such as a requirement that an offender pay restitution, write a punishment lesson, or do community service work. A judge in Painesville, Ohio, sentenced men convicted of soliciting a prostitute to wear a chicken suit and carry a sign that read, "No Chicken Ranch in Painesville." The sign is a reference to a famous Chicken Ranch prostitution house in Nevada (*Cincinnati Enquirer*, 2007). Still other conditions seek to ensure that offenders receive treatment for their problems by requiring participation in educational, psychological, or substance abuse programs.

We also use special conditions to reduce the risk of new criminality. For instance, jurisdictions across the country have placed specialized conditions on the supervision of sex offenders. These conditions often require the sex offender to register on a public database and to live outside of a

**TABLE 20.3  Percentage of American Parole Jurisdictions Imposing Routine Conditions, 1982–2008**

| Standard Condition | 1982 | 1995 | 2008 |
|---|---|---|---|
| Comply with the law | 96 | 90 | 100 |
| Change residence | 92 | 79 | 98 |
| Possess firearm/dangerous weapon | 92 | 90 | 96 |
| Maintain employment/education program | 73 | 81 | 94 |
| Report regularly | 94 | 33 | 87 |
| Permit home/work visits and searches | 42 | 61 | 87 |
| Out-of-state travel | 100 | 88 | 87 |
| Use controlled substances | 63 | 88 | 81 |
| Change employment | 87 | 81 | 79 |
| Pay fees/restitution | NA | 46 | 79 |
| Report arrest/questioning by law enforcement | 50 | 63 | 71 |
| Make first arrival report | 75 | 58 | 63 |
| Submit to medical/drug test | NA | 40 | 63 |
| Undesirable associates/locations | 50 | NA | 60 |
| Alcohol use | 44 | 42 | 54 |
| Obey PO instructions | NA | 23 | 54 |
| Give written/oral information | NA | 55 | NA |
| Waive extradition | 50 | NA | NA |

*Source*: Travis and Stacey (2010)

specified distance of schools, day care centers, parks, and so on. Finally, some conditions do not impose restrictions on behavior, but give the offender notice. This may be the case, for example, when a condition of supervision is that the offender remains on probation or parole until discharged. What this condition does, of course, is tell the offender that supervision does not end until released by the supervising authority.

## Client Perspectives

The experience of being on paper reflects the number and content of conditions as well as the characteristics of the probation or parole officer. A probationer facing conditions that include a curfew, requirements of restitution, restriction on associating with friends, and some period of incarceration will have a qualitatively different experience than will a probationer under less restrictive conditions. Similarly, a parolee whose supervising officer is rule oriented and unsympathetic will experience a different sanction than one whose officer is flexible and empathetic.

The ability to impose special conditions of probation has led to the use of probation to accomplish many correctional goals not necessarily authorized by statute. For example, in a jurisdiction in which there is no law authorizing split sentences, a judge wishing to impose such a sentence can place the offender on probation on condition that he or she serves some time in jail (Talarico & Myers, 1987). In a like fashion, absent a statutory authority to impose restitution, a judge can simply make restitution a condition of probation. Probation and (to a lesser extent) parole are the most flexible of sanctions. This may account, in part, for their popularity among justice system officials.

Criminal justice scholars have asked probationers and parolees for their views on community supervision (Allen, 1985; Gibbs, 1985; Martin, Hanrahan, & Bowers, 2009; Spelman, 1995; Wood & May, 2003). In large part, these offenders prefer probation or parole to any form of incarceration. Many feel fortunate to have an opportunity to prove themselves in the community, but most also identify problems associated with being under supervision.

In some cases, offenders see community supervision as a less desirable sanction than incarceration (Crouch, 1993; Petersilia, 1990; Wood & May, 2003). If the prison or jail term will be short and followed by unsupervised release, but probation or parole supervision will entail close supervision and restrictive conditions, many offenders would rather just "get it over with." They would prefer a short term of incarceration followed by freedom instead of what they expect will be a period of close supervision followed by prison if they are found in violation of conditions. This suggests that, at some level, it is possible to design a community supervision sanction that is as unpleasant as incarceration.

Probationers and parolees most often complain about what they perceive as the pettiness and unfairness of some conditions of release. They also dislike the requirement that they seek approval of their supervising officers for many minor decisions (Williams, May, & Wood, 2008). Wood and May (2003) suggested that African Americans or other minority group members may perceive greater discrimination and unfairness in community supervision than in prison, leading them to conclude that prison is often a less severe sanction than community alternatives. Finally, many are dissatisfied with their officers. Many probationers and parolees believe their officers do not act as advocates for them, and many believe their officers are too intrusive. Offenders also complain about the social distance between themselves and their supervising officer (Helfgott, 1997). In other words, the offenders perceive the officers as having too little in common with them, making it difficult for the officers to appreciate the daily struggles faced by those under community supervision.

As probation and parole have become more intrusive and controlling in recent years, the perceived difference between being on paper and doing time may have decreased. [...] In general, the increase in punitiveness has made community supervision more troublesome to offenders. At the same time, because of crowding, many jurisdictions have shortened incarceration terms. As a result, when offered release on parole for a given period or incarceration for a short period, many offenders choose incarceration. In a sample of Texas prisoners, Crouch (1993:79) found that almost half would choose 1 year in prison instead of 5 years of probation. A study compared probationer and probation officer perceptions of the burden of certain community sanctions relative to imprisonment and found that officers routinely overestimated the severity of sanctions. In general, probationers were much less likely to agree to additional sanctions, such as fines, restitution, and the like to avoid incarceration. Similarly, offenders reported that community service was much less onerous than probation officers thought it to be. The implications of this research are that probation and parole officers may be very limited in their ability to control offender behavior through the threat of sanctions (Flory, May, Minor, & Wood, 2006). If offenders would prefer jail time to intensive supervision, the threat of jail is unlikely to convince them to abide by the conditions of supervision.

## Officer Perspectives

Probation and parole officers lead a "schizophrenic" existence in relation to their jobs. For years, research into the role of the community supervision officer has identified conflicting dimensions of the responsibilities to help but also to control (Clear & Cole, 1986). The officer is expected to befriend and assist his or her clients, as well as to monitor and control them. Most officers think that offender success is primarily a function of rational choice and generally view the offender's complaint of social distance as an excuse (Gunnison & Helfgott, 2011). With reference to parole officers, Studt (1973) identified officer "style" as critical to an understanding of the supervision process. She observed two basic styles: service (emphasis on helping the offender) and surveillance (emphasis on controlling criminal conduct).

Crean (1985:118) reported, "Within a typical work week, a line officer is usually called upon to be an investigator, a biographer, a watchdog, counselor, friend, confidant, reporter, expert witness, and broker of outside services." The line officer is a public employee and responsible to the authority that placed the offender under the officer's supervision. Further, the officer must interact on a regular basis with the offender, the offender's family, law enforcement officials, and representatives of community agencies (Sigler, 1988).

As with most criminal justice jobs, community supervision involves a rather large degree of discretion and responsibility. It also entails a tremendous amount of paperwork. Even though there are psychological, monetary, and social rewards in being a probation or parole officer, there are the concomitant costs of dealing with offenders, danger, and bureaucracy. Nevertheless, probation and parole officers exhibit the characteristics of professionals, and they frequently do not work steady hours. Those who remain at their positions learn to separate work from the other aspects of their lives.

In a study of role conflict among probation officers working in intensive supervision programs, Clear and Latessa (1993) failed to find evidence of effects of different role definitions on individual officers. They compared officers working in one program that was clearly control oriented with those working in another that was clearly treatment oriented. They found that individual officers displayed differences in role definition (seeing themselves as more control or treatment/support oriented), but not in how they approached the jobs. The organizational philosophy of the probation agency appeared to be more important in explaining differences in case treatment than did individual attitudes. Regardless of whether the officer personally prefers control or support as an orientation to the job, the officer is able to perform only in compliance with organizational expectations. As Clear and Latessa noted, a key question that remains is to discover how agencies select officers whose role definitions meet agency philosophy, or how agency philosophy is transmitted to officers and how it influences officer behavior. Fulton, Stichman, Travis, and Latessa (1997) reported that officer role orientation can be changed through training, again suggesting that it is the organizational policy more than the individual officer attitudes that affects a probation or parole officer's style of work.

Probation and (to a lesser extent) parole are correctional interventions that often employ citizen volunteers. Inasmuch as a volunteer started probation, this volunteer involvement is not surprising. Because the primary task of community supervision is to see that offenders can reside safely in the community, there are good reasons for using volunteers. Volunteers can perform many functions for probation and parole officers. The use of volunteers also helps clients by connecting them with law-abiding citizens (Lucas, 1987).

The dual roles of service and surveillance, coupled with heavy caseloads and frequently inadequate community services, often frustrate probation and parole officers and managers. Some areas of inquiry have included burnout and job satisfaction among the ranks of probation and parole officers (Whitehead, 1986). Although the job of community supervision agent has many demoralizing facets, most officers report that the benefits outweigh the drawbacks of the job.

# Offender Rights in Community Supervision

Probation and parole normally are considered privileges and not rights (del Carmen, 1985). Once placed on probation or parole, however, the offender does have a constitutionally protected interest in retaining that status. To date, there have been relatively few U.S. Supreme Court decisions dealing with the acceptability of various conditions of release and supervision practices. State or federal appellate courts have decided most of the existing cases in this area. In 2006, the U.S. Supreme Court decided the case of *Samson v. California*. Samson's parole conditions required him to submit to warrantless searches by police or his parole officer. One such search uncovered criminal evidence resulting in his return to prison. The Court ruled that the search was acceptable because of the parole condition that authorized it.

Essentially, courts have supported all types of probation and parole conditions, as long as those conditions were constitutional, reasonably related to criminality, clearly written, and/or contributed to the rehabilitation of the offender. The decisions of courts vary across jurisdictions, and are indeed case specific. For example, the courts are likely to uphold a prohibition against the consumption of alcoholic beverages in a case in which the offender's criminality stemmed from drunkenness, but void it in a case in which the offender has no history of alcohol abuse.

Probation and parole conditions often serve as an arsenal of leverage for correctional authorities. Because violation of any of the conditions of parole or probation constitutes grounds for revocation and incarceration, the conditions provide the officer with tools for controlling the offender. With regard to revocation, however, the U.S. Supreme Court has set forth due process protections for probationers and parolees.

In 1972, the Court decided the case of *Morrissey v. Brewer*, in which a parolee sought relief after his parole had been revoked. The Court ruled that parolees facing revocation must be granted the following protections: (1) written notice of the claimed violations, (2) disclosure of evidence against the parolee, (3) the opportunity to be heard and to present evidence, (4) a limited right to confront and cross-examine witnesses, (5) a hearing before a neutral body, and (6) a written statement of the decision and evidence on which it was based.

The following year, the Court decided the case of *Gagnon v. Scarpelli* (1973), which dealt with probation revocation. In this case, the Court stated that, at least regarding revocation procedures, there was no substantial difference between probationers and parolees. They granted probationers the same protections as those given to parolees.

Persons under community supervision generally are less restricted and suffer fewer pains than those who are incarcerated. Nonetheless, community supervision is still a punishment for crime, and the status of conviction and being under sentence sets probationers and parolees apart from free citizens. Even with the protections afforded by the *Morrissey* and *Gagnon* decisions, probationers and parolees may have their liberty revoked and may be incarcerated for offenses that would not carry similar penalties for free citizens. In addition, incarceration may follow hearings for which the burden of proof is not as high as the trial standard of proof beyond a reasonable doubt.

Hoffman and Beck (2005) described a pilot program of the U.S. Parole Commission that involved expedited revocation hearings. In many cases, the alleged misbehavior involves violations of the technical conditions of parole and the parolee admits the violation. In these cases, the function of the revocation hearing is to determine the sanction. If the parolee consents, they waive the probable cause hearing and return the parolee to the institution for a dispositional hearing. The researchers concluded that the expedited process was cost-effective and supported by all parties, including defense counsel.

Community supervision serves crime control functions by allowing the state to limit the risk of new crimes being committed through relaxed requirements for revocation (as compared to conviction). Yet, probationers and parolees have protected interests in conditional liberty, and the actions and decisions of probation and parole authorities are constrained by some due process requirements. It is instructive to observe that although a number of states and the federal government have taken steps to eliminate discretionary parole release, most have retained a period of postrelease supervision. Community supervision itself represents a balance between individual interests in avoiding incarceration and community interests in controlling potential criminality.

See Box 20.3 for a table of selected court cases on probation and parole.

Supervision conditions also represent part of the arsenal of the prosecutor. As we discussed earlier, it is common for prosecutors to dismiss new criminal charges when they can proceed to a probation or parole revocation. Kingsnorth, MacIntosh, and Sutherland (2002) studied probation violation processing in eight California counties. They reported that prosecutors frequently seek probation violations rather than file new criminal charges. This is especially true when the new offense is less serious than the one for which the offender was placed on probation.

## BOX 20.3 Selected Cases on Community Supervision

| | |
|---|---|
| *Morrissey v. Brewer* 408 U.S. 471 (1972) | Parolees facing revocation must be granted: written notice of the claimed violations; disclosure of evidence against the parolee; the opportunity to be heard and to present evidence; a limited right to confront and cross-examine witnesses; a hearing before a neutral body; and a written statement of the decision and the evidence on which it was based |
| *Gagnon v. Scarpelli* 411 U.S. 778 (1973) | At least in regard to revocation procedures, there is no substantial difference between probationers and parolees; therefore, probationers are granted the same protections as parolees (for specific protections granted, see *Morrissey v. Brewer*) |
| *Samson v. California* 547 U.S. 843 (2006) | Supreme Court affirmed the decision holding that suspicionless searches of parolees are lawful under California law and reasonable under the Fourth Amendment |

# Community Supervision in the Whole System

[...] We have discussed several areas of overlap between community supervision and other components of the justice system. Pretrial release, diversion from court, prosecutorial charging, incarceration, and the size of the prison population all involve decisions that depend (more or less) directly on the operation of community supervision. For example, if probation and parole were not available as alternatives to incarceration, absent the development of other practices, the prison and jail population would increase threefold. The growth of intermediate sanctions and other changes in community supervision practices show how the criminal justice process is an open system.

The development of intermediate sanctions and their effects on community supervision agencies and practices illustrate the open nature of the criminal justice system. The primary motivation for these new alternatives has been the need to control correctional costs, and the prison population specifically. As the prison population grew, so did community supervision populations. The same forces that produced the increase in prisoners have worked to swell community supervision populations. The war on drugs, for example, brought a large number of offenders into the justice system. Low-level drug offenders are now prime candidates for intermediate sanctions while under community supervision. A common adjustment to truth in sentencing, which requires longer prison terms for violent offenders, has been to divert property and public order offenders from prison to probation or parole.

The prison population crisis has changed the nature of the community supervision population so that there are increased numbers of felons and more serious offenders under probation and parole supervision than historically was the case. The increase in the numbers of offenders provides the impetus for changes in community supervision management, financing, and programs. Because they involve closer supervision and impose more restrictive conditions of release, some of these programs have relatively high rates of supervision failure. Those revoked from intermediate sanction programs often are imprisoned, but now come to prison as community supervision failures.

In these ways, we can see the links between the components of the justice system, and between the justice system and the larger society. A redefinition of the seriousness of drug offenses led to enhanced drug crime enforcement. Increased enforcement changed the size and composition of the correctional population, both those incarcerated and those under community supervision. Seeking ways of managing the larger populations, we have developed intermediate sanctions that have altered traditional community supervision programs. Changes in community supervision, in turn, seem to have put increased pressure on prison populations through increased numbers of supervision failures. [...]

## KEY IDEAS

| | |
|---|---|
| absconders | furlough |
| benefit of clergy | halfway houses |
| community service orders | home incarceration |
| discretionary release | judicial reprieve |
| diversion | mandatory release |

| | |
|---|---|
| mark system | restorative justice |
| "on paper" | special conditions |
| parole | standard conditions |
| probation | supervised release |
| reentry | suretyship |
| reentry courts | ticket of leave |
| release on recognizance (ROR) | work release |

## REVIEW QUESTIONS

1. Distinguish between probation and parole.

2. Briefly trace the origins of community supervision in corrections.

3. Describe the organization of community supervision.

4. Tell what is meant by the term "reentry."

5. Identify five forms of community supervision, excluding traditional probation and parole.

6. Distinguish between standard and special conditions of probation or parole.

7. Describe the role and importance of community supervision in the criminal justice system.

8. Identify the due process rights of probationers and parolees at revocation.

## References

Allen, G. F. (1985). The probationers speak: Analysis of probationer's experiences and attitudes. *Federal Probation, 49*(3), 67–75.

Allen, H. E., Carlson, E. W., Parks, E. C., & Seiter, R. P. (1978). *Halfway houses*. Washington, DC: U.S. Government Printing Office.

Allen, H. E., Eskridge, C. W., Latessa, E. J., & Vito, G. F. (1985). *Probation and parole in America*. Monterey, CA: Brooks/Cole.

Auerhahn, K. (2007). Do you know who your probationers are? Using simulation to estimate the composition of California's felony probation population, 1980–2000. *Justice Quarterly, 24*(1), 28–47.

Barnes, H. E., & Teeters, N. D. (1959). *New horizons in criminology*. Englewood Cliffs, NJ: Prentice Hall.

Beha, J. A. (1975). Halfway houses in adult corrections: The law, practice, and results. *Criminal Law Bulletin, 11*(4), 437–477.

Bell, N., Bucklen, K. B., Nakamura, K., Tomkiel, J., Santore, A., Russell, L., et al. (2013). *Recidivism report, 2013*. Mechanicsburg, PA: Pennsylvania Department of Corrections.

Bonczar, T. (2008). *Characteristics of state parole supervising agencies, 2006*. Washington, DC: Bureau of Justice Statistics.

Bureau of Justice Statistics (1987). *Probation and parole 1985*. Washington, DC: U.S. Department of Justice.

Burke, P. (2004). Parole violations: An important window on offender reentry. *Perspectives, 28*(1), 24–31.

Burke, P., & Tonry, M. (2006). *Successful transition and reentry for safer communities: A call to action for parole*. Silver Spring, MD: Center for Effective Public Policy.

Camp, C., & Camp, G. (1996). *The corrections yearbook 1996*. South Salem, NY: Criminal Justice Institute.

Carson, E. A., & Golinelli, D. (2013). *Prisoners in 2012: Trends in admissions and releases, 1991–2012*. Washington, DC: U.S. Department of Justice.

Clear, T. R., & Cole, G. F. (1986). *American corrections*. Monterey, CA: Brooks/Cole.

Clear, T. R., & Latessa, E. J. (1993). Probation officers' roles in intensive supervision: Surveillance versus treatment. *Justice Quarterly, 10*(3), 441–459.

Corbett, R. P., & Fersch, E. A. I. (1985). Home as prison: The use of house arrest. *Federal Probation, 49*(1), 13–17.

Crean, D. M. (1985). Community corrections: On the line. In L. F. Travis (Ed.), *Probation, parole and community corrections* (pp. 109–124). Prospect Heights, IL: Waveland.

Crouch, B. (1993). *Is incarceration really worse? Analysis of offenders' preferences for prison over probation*. In *Parole and community corrections* (pp. 47–70). Prospect Heights, IL: Waveland.

del Carmen, R. V. (1985). Legal issues and liabilities in community corrections. In L. F. Travis, III (Ed.), *Probation, parole, and community corrections* (pp. 47–70). Prospect Heights, IL: Waveland.

Doleschal, E. (1971). *Graduated release*. Rockville, MD: National Institute of Mental Health.

*Cincinnati Enquirer* (2007). *Sex offenders must wear chicken suit*. Retrieved July 27, 2007, from http://news.enquirer.com.

Flory, C., May, D., Minor, K., & Wood, P. (2006). A comparison of punishment exchange rates between offenders under supervision and their supervising officers. *Journal of Criminal Justice, 34*(1), 39–50.

Fox, V. (1983). *Correctional institutions*. Englewood Cliffs, NJ: Prentice Hall.

Fulton, B., Stichman, A., Travis, L., & Latessa, E. (1997). Moderating probation and parole officer attitudes to achieve desired outcomes. *The Prison Journal, 77*(3), 295–312.

Gibbs, J. J. (1985). Client's views of community corrections. In L. F. Travis (Ed.), *Probation, parole and community corrections* (pp. 97–108). Prospect Heights, IL: Waveland.

Gillard, D., & Beck, A. (1996). *Prison and jail inmates, 1995*. Washington, DC: Bureau of Justice Statistics.

Glaze, L., & Bonczar, T. (2006). *Probation and parole in the United States, 2005*. Washington, DC: Bureau of Justice Statistics.

Glaze, L., & Bonczar, T. (2009). *Probation and parole in the United States, 2008*. Washington, DC: Bureau of Justice Statistics.

Glaze, L., & Herberman, E. (2013). *Correctional populations in the United States, 2012*. Washington, DC: Bureau of Justice Statistics.

Gunnison, E., & Helfgott, J. (2011). Factors that hinder offender reentry success: A view from community corrections officers. *International Journal of Offender Therapy and Comparative Criminology, 55*(2), 287–304.

Hamilton, Z. (2010). *Do reentry courts reduce recidivism? Results from the Harlem parole reentry court*. New York, NY: Center for Court Innovation.

Helfgott, J. (1997). Ex-offender needs versus community opportunity in Seattle, Washington. *Federal Probation, 61*, 12–24.

Hoffman, P., & Beck, A. (2005). Revocation by consent: The United States Parole Commission's expedited revocation procedure. *Journal of Criminal Justice, 33*(5), 451–462.

Hughes, T., Wilson, D., & Beck, A. (2001). *Trends in state parole, 1991–2000.* Washington, DC: Bureau of Justice Statistics.

Jaffe, H. J. (1979). Probation with a flair: A look at some out-of-the-ordinary conditions. *Federal Probation, 43*(1), 25–36.

Karp, D., & Drakulich, K. (2004). Minor crime in a quaint setting: Practices, outcomes, and limits of Vermont reparative probation boards. *Criminology & Public Policy, 3*(4), 655–686.

Keller, O., & Alper, B. (1970). *Halfway houses: Community centered corrections and treatment.* Lexington, MA: D.C. Heath.

Kingsnorth, R., MacIntosh, R., & Sutherland, S. (2002). Criminal charge of probation violation? Prosecutorial discretion and implications for research in criminal court processing. *Criminology, 40*(3), 553–578.

Langan, P., & Dawson, J. (1993). *Felony sentences in state courts, 1990.* Washington, DC: Bureau of Justice Statistics.

Latessa, E. J., & Travis, L. F., III. (1992). Residential community correctional programs. In J. Byrne, A. Lurigio, & J. Petersilia (Eds.), *Smart sentencing: The emergence of intermediate sanctions* (pp. 166–181). Beverly Hills, CA: Sage.

Latessa, E. J., Travis, L. F., III, & Wilson, G. P. (1984). Juvenile diversion: Factors related to decision making and outcome. In S. H. Decker (Ed.), *Juvenile justice policy* (pp. 145–165). Beverly Hills, CA: Sage.

LeClair, D., & Guarino-Ghezzi, S. (1991). Does incapacitation guarantee public safety? Lessons from the Massachusetts furlough and prerelease programs. *Justice Quarterly, 8*(1), 9–36.

Lindquist, C., Hardison, J., & Lattimore, P. (2003). *Reentry courts process evaluation (Phase 1).* Washington, DC: National Institute of Justice.

Lindsey, E. (1925). Historical sketch of the indeterminate sentence and parole system. *Journal of Criminal Law & Criminology, 16*(1925), 9–126.

Lucas, W. (1987). Perceptions of the volunteer role. *Journal of Offender Counseling, Services & Rehabilitation, 12*(1), 141–146.

Martin, J., Hanrahan, K., Bowers, J., Jr. (2009). Offenders' perceptions of house arrest and electronic monitoring. *Journal of Offender Rehabilitation, 48,* 547–570.

Maruschak, L., & Bonczar, T. (2013). *Probation and parole in the United States, 2012.* Washington, DC: Bureau of Justice Statistics.

Mayzer, R., Gray, M., & Maxwell, S. (2004). Probation absconders: A unique risk group? *Journal of Criminal Justice, 32*(2), 137–150.

McDonald, D. (1986). *Punishment without walls: Community service sentences in New York City.* New Brunswick, NJ: Rutgers University Press.

McSparron, J. (1980). Community corrections and diversion: Cost and benefit, subsidy models, and start-up recommendations. *Crime & Delinquency, 26*(2), 226–247.

Minton, T. (2010). *Jail inmates 2009—Statistical tables.* Washington, DC: Bureau of Justice Statistics.

Perrier, D. C., & Pink, F. S. (1985). Community service: All things to all people. *Federal Probation, 49*(2), 32–38.

Petersilia, J. (1986). Exploring the option of house arrest. *Federal Probation, 50*(2), 52–55.

Petersilia, J. (1990). When probation becomes more dreaded than prison. *Federal Probation, 54*(1), 23–27.

Rhine, E., Mawhorr, T., & Parks, E. (2006). Implementation: The bane of effective correctional programs. *Criminology and Public Policy, 5*(2), 347–358.

Rhine, E., Smith, W., & Jackson, R. (1991). *Paroling authorities: Recent history and current practice.* Gaithersburg, MD: American Correctional Association.

Rosenmerkel, S., Durose, M., & Farole, D. (2009). *Felony sentences in state courts, 2006—Statistical tables.* Washington, DC: Bureau of Justice Statistics.

Rothman, D. J. (1980). *Conscience and convenience.* Boston: Little, Brown.

Sabol, W., Minton, T., & Harrison, P. (2007). *Prison and jail inmates at midyear 2006.* Washington, DC: Bureau of Justice Statistics.

Sigler, R. (1988). Role conflict for adult probation and parole officers: Fact or myth? *Journal of Criminal Justice, 16*(2), 121–130.

Simon, J. (1993). *Poor discipline.* Chicago: University of Chicago Press.

Spelman, W. (1995). The severity of intermediate sanctions. *Journal of Research in Crime and Delinquency, 32*(1), 107135.

Stephan, J. (2008). *Census of state and federal correctional facilities, 2005.* Washington, DC: Bureau of Justice Statistics.

Studt, E. (1973). *Surveillance and service in parole.* Washington, DC: U.S. Government Printing Office.

Talarico, S., & Myers, M. (1987). Split sentencing in Georgia: A test of two empirical assumptions. *Justice Quarterly, 4*(4), 611–629.

Tonry, M. (1998). *Sentencing matters.* New York, NY: Oxford University Press.

Travis, L. F., III. (1985). The development of American parole. In H. E. Allen, C. Eskridge, E. J. Latessa, & G. F. Vito (Eds.), *Probation and parole in America* (pp. 19–35). New York: Free Press.

Travis, L. F., III, & Latessa, E. J. (1984). "A summary of parole rules—Thirteen years later": Revisited thirteen years later. *Journal of Criminal Justice, 12*(6), 591–600.

Travis, J., Solomon, A., & Waul, M. (2001). *The dimensions and consequences of prisoner reentry.* Washington, DC: Urban Institute.

Travis, L., & Stacey, J. (2010). A half century of parole rules: Conditions of parole in the United States, 2008. *Journal of Criminal Justice, 38*(4), 606.

Turner, S., & Petersilia, J. (1996). *Work release: Recidivism and corrections costs in Washington State.* Washington, DC: National Institute of Justice.

U.S. Department of Justice (1978). *State and local probation and parole systems.* Washington, DC: U.S. Government Printing Office.

Umbreit, M. S. (1981). Community service sentencing: Jail alternative or added sanction? *Federal Probation, 45*(3), 3–14.

United States Sentencing Commission (2010). *Federal offenders sentenced to supervised release.* Washington, DC. Retrieved from http://www.ussc.gov/Education_and_Training/Annual_National_Training_Seminar/2012/2_Federal_Offenders_Sentenced_to_Supervised_Release.pdf.

White, M., Mellow, J., Englander, K., & Ruffinengo, M. (2011). Halfway back: An alternate to revocation for technical parole violators. *Criminal Justice Policy Review, 22*, 40–66.

Whitehead, J. (1986). Job burnout and job satisfaction among probation managers. *Journal of Criminal Justice, 14*(1), 25–36.

Williams, A., May, D., & Wood, P. (2008). The lesser of two evils? A qualitative study of offenders' preferences for prison compared to alternatives. *Journal of Offender Rehabilitation, 46*(3,4), 71–90.

Wilson, G. P. (1985). Halfway house programs for offenders. In L. F. Travis III, (Ed.), *Probation, parole and community corrections* (pp. 151–164). Prospect Heights, IL: Waveland.

Wilson, J. (2007). Habitation or harm: Project Greenlight and the potential consequences of correctional programming. *National Institute of Justice Journal, 257*, 2–7 (June).

Wood, P., & May, D. (2003). Racial differences in perceptions of the severity of sanctions: A comparison of prison with alternatives. *Justice Quarterly, 20*(3), 605–631.

Wright, J., & Travis, L. (1996). Work release. In M. McShane & F. Williams (Eds.), *The encyclopedia of American prisons* (pp. 510–512). New York: Garland.

## Important Cases

*Gagnon v. Scarpelli*, 411 U.S. 778. (1973).
*Morrissey v. Brewer*, 408 U.S. 471. (1972).
*Samson v. California*, 547 U.S. 843. (2006).